Praise for *Gentleman Revolutionary*

"No full appreciation of the tumultuous founding time of the American republic is complete without the extraordinary, colorful Gouverneur Morris. Richard Brookhiser has a rare gift for deft portraits done with no wasted strokes, and this of the irrepressible Morris is one of this very best."

—David McCullough, bestselling author of *John Adams*

"Brookhiser has crafted a model popular history: tight, lucid, accessible, judicious, and humane. Without a wasted word or a false sentiment, Brookhiser smoothly and insightfully guides readers through two dramatic revolutions. He makes the most of a genial and mercurial protagonist, who could spice his own folly with keen perception."

—*The Washington Post*

"The first question this excellent book provokes is, What has taken so long? . . . There is more good living, more elegant theater, and certainly more documented sexual seduction in Morris's life than in that of any other member of our republic's heroic generation. . . . Brookhiser has once again demonstrated his mastery of the elogy, a portrait in which all that is superfluous is banished, and in which a judicious art has yielded the essence of a life."

—*National Review*

"Brilliantly resurrects one of the most obscure and profoundly interesting [Founders] . . . Mr. Brookhiser, anything but a superficial observer, shows us what to admire in this energetic and compelling man —and a good bit more besides."

—*The Wall Street Journal*

...no one will fail to be charmed by this man of fortitude and achievemen who savored life."

—*Publishers Weekly*

"Acclaimed historian Brookhiser provides an absolutely delightful biography of America's least renowned Founding Father . . . offers another fascinating portrait of a man at the crossroads of American history."

—*Booklist*

"Richard Brookhiser's biographies of the Founders are not only lively, informative, and politically astute—they are pleasingly brief. . . .[A] rich, readable, and insightful biography."

—*Washington Times*

"With his peerless flair of breathing dramatic life into events of bygone ages, Brookhiser paints a remarkable picture of Morris and his times."

—*Human Events*

"An indulgent look at one of the men who played a secondary role in the creation of the United States. Morris's frank enjoyment of life's pleasure gives this biography its charm."

—*Los Angeles Times*

Gentleman Revolutionary

· GOUVERNEUR MORRIS ·

THE RAKE

WHO WROTE

THE CONSTITUTION

RICHARD BROOKHISER

FREE PRESS

NEW YORK TORONTO LONDON SYDNEY

THIS BOOK IS DEDICATED TO

KENNETH WALD

*f*P

Free Press
A Division of Simon & Schuster, Inc.
1230 Avenue of the Americas
New York, NY 10020

First Free Press trade paperback edition 2004

FREE PRESS and colophon are trademarks
of Simon & Schuster, Inc.

For information about special discounts for bulk purchases,
please contact Simon & Schuster Special Sales:
1-800-456-6798 or business@simonandschuster.com

Designed by Chris Welch
Manufactured in the United States of America

1   3   5   7   9   10   8   6   4   2

Library of Congress Cataloging-in-Publication Data is available

ISBN 0-7432-2379-9
0-7432-5602-6 (Pbk)

Acknowledgments

I would like to thank the staffs of the Library of Congress, the New York Public Library, the Special Collections of Rutgers University, and the Alderman Library at the University of Virginia, for their help with unpublished documents. Mary Ellen Jones of the St. Lawrence County Historical Association, and Russ Sprague gave me valuable information about Gouverneur, New York. The Reverend Martha Rollins Overall, priest of St. Ann's Church of Morrisania, kindly showed me the church Gouverneur Morris II built and the graves of his parents.

Linda Bridges, Alan Pell Crawford, Charles Kesler, Susan Shapiro and David Zincavage gave useful assistance. I am especially grateful to Forrest and Ellen McDonald. *City Journal* and its editor, Myron Magnet, let me write a piece about my great New Yorker. My wife, Jeanne Safer, let me have a wonderful line about the skins of the eighteenth-century poor.

I would like to thank my editor, Bruce Nichols, and my agent, Michael Carlisle.

Contents

Part 3 The Brink of Revolution

A Note on Money and Spelling

I have tried to provide islands of modern value in the rush of currency that flowed through Morris's life as a private businessman and a public financier. In his youth the American colonies kept their accounts in pounds, with 20 shillings to the pound and 12 pence to the shilling. (The pound sterling of England was worth almost twice as much as any of the colonial pounds.) But the most common colonial coin was the Spanish dollar, which was worth 4 shillings 6 pence sterling, or about 8 colonial shillings. The pre-revolutionary French livre (equal to 20 sous) was worth about 9 pence sterling. Morris lived through several periods of inflation, at home and abroad.

English was spelled and punctuated differently in Morris's lifetime. Eighteenth-century capitalizing survives in the Constitution: "We the People of the United States, in Order to form a more perfect Union . . ." My compromise between readability and period flavor has been to modernize most of the punctuation, and to leave most of the spelling in its original form.

Introduction

A BIOGRAPHER can feel a moment's hesitation when it comes to introducing his subject, for every traditional means has its drawbacks. If the hero appears *in medias res*, in the midst of some great action, the reader may feel manipulated, even coerced: his attention is being claimed before it has been earned. If the story of a life begins where the life does, in a cradle, then the reader might experience a sense of delay: he wished to read about great men, not infants. For the biographer of Gouverneur Morris, it is perhaps best to let him be introduced by a woman.

In 1795, Harriet de Damas, a French countess, wrote a portrait of a tall, handsome American who had become a fixture of Parisian society.[1] Gouverneur Morris had come to France in 1789, age thirty-seven, as a businessman; three years later, he was appointed the American minister to that country. Mr. Morris had a French first name (his mother's maiden name), which Americans insisted on pronouncing "Gov-er-*neer*"; he had learned French as a child, and wrote it well enough to produce papers on French politics, or little poems for his friends.[2] Mme de Damas called his spoken French "always correct and vigorous," though other Frenchwomen teased him for his mistakes. Mr. Morris cut a figure for many reasons: his impressive bearing (the French sculptor Jean-Antoine Houdon used him as a body double for a statue of George Washington); his wit; his severely elegant clothes and carriage, so different from French silks and colors; and what was severe in a different way, his wooden left leg. When he arrived at a party, the servants watched him; the guests watched him; he watched himself, mindful of the impression he made.

"Superficial observers," wrote Mme de Damas, ". . . might be acquainted with Mr. Morris for years, without discovering his most eminent qualities. Such observers must be told what to admire." The Frenchwoman confronts a difficulty with her portrait head-on: she had known Mr. Morris for only a small part of his life, since his first thirty-seven years had been spent in America. But she plunged ahead confidently.

The superficial observers of his early life "regard Mr. Morris as a profound politician," and indeed he had been involved in politics, often of the most eventful kind. When he was twenty-three years old the American Revolution began, and he watched it pull society and family asunder (one of his elder half brothers signed the Declaration of Independence; another half brother was a general in the British army). He left American towns a step ahead of marauding British armies, and when Morris visited his mother, who supported the crown throughout the war, he had to get passes from both sides to cross their lines. He eventually followed his patriot half brother into the Continental Congress, where he helped accomplish great things, but also engaged in endless petty wrangling. ("We had many scoundrels" in Congress, he would remember as an older man.)[3]

When he was still a young one, age thirty-five, Mr. Morris drafted the Constitution of the United States. The proceedings of the Constitutional Convention were secret, to allow the delegates maximum freedom to speak their minds, so Mr. Morris's role on the Committee of Style was not generally known. But in later years he admitted to a correspondent that "that instrument was written by the fingers which write this letter."[4] Years after Morris's death, an elderly James Madison told an inquiring historian that "the *finish* given to the style and arrangement of the Constitution fairly belongs to the pen of Mr. Morris."[5] James Madison, the careful and learned theorist, is commonly called the Father of the Constitution, because he kept the most complete set of notes of the debates, and made cogent arguments for ratification after the debates were done (he wrote one third of the

Federalist Papers). But Gouverneur Morris, who put the document into its final form and who wrote the Preamble from scratch, also deserves a share of the paternity. The founders were voluminous writers, and much of their writing is very good, but few of them had the combination of lightness and force that generates a great style. Jefferson had it; Franklin had it; Thomas Paine, the passionate and ungainly English immigrant, had it. The only other one of their number who hit that note consistently was Morris. "A better choice" for a draftsman "could not have been made," Madison concluded.[6]

Mme de Damas and her French friends certainly knew about Mr. Morris's political activity: it was one facet of his social cachet, a point of interest like his wardrobe and his leg. A more striking feature of their friend was his manner. Mme de Damas called him "the most amiable" of men. "His imagination inclines to pleasantry, and being abundantly gifted with what the English call *humor,* united to what the French name *esprit,* it is impossible not to be delighted. . . ." Humor and *esprit:* Mr. Morris delighted in the incongruities and follies of life, including his own, and his comments—quick, shapely, and bold—communicated that delight to others. Women found him especially pleasing, perhaps because he took special pains to please them. "Govr Morris kept us in a continual smile," was how one young lady put it.[7] His women friends did more than smile. At the cardtable of the sexes, his wit and looks always trumped his disability, and the one-legged American left a trail of lovers on two continents.

Mr. Morris's good company went beyond good times. When the French Revolution, more stressful than the American, began to suck his glittering friends into poverty, exile, and danger, he gave many of them refuge, and saved several of their lives. Mme de Damas was not one of his lovers, but he did save her life.

But more important than Mr. Morris's career or his behavior was his nature. "Nothing really worthy of him," wrote Mme de Damas, "will be said by any one, who does not ascend to the source of all that is great and excellent in his character." That, she decided, was "a belief that God can will nothing but what is good." This gave him confidence, charity, and hope. "Ever at peace with himself . . . seldom ruffled in his temper, not suffering men or events to have a mastery over his spirit, he is habitually serene, alike ready to engage in the most abstruse inquiries, or to join in the trifles of social amusement." Gouverneur Morris took his life as it came. "He conceives it to be following the order of Providence to enjoy all its gifts. 'To enjoy is to obey.' And upon the same principle he submits, with a modest fortitude, and sincere resignation, to the ills inflicted by the same hand." Living among tottering thrones and shaky republics, Mr. Morris showed the gift of poise.

Gouverneur Morris belonged to that band of brothers that we now call the founding fathers. Some were his friends: he knew and worshipped George Washington for almost twenty years; he knew and squabbled with Paine for almost as long; he was at Alexander Hamilton's deathbed. Some of them were enemies: he thought James Madison was a fool and a drunkard. He knew them all, and was one of their number. The founding fathers-to-be were guided by the pursuit of greatness. They measured themselves by their service to the country they were making. Mr. Morris was moved by the same tidal pull of public good. "This is the seed time of glory," he wrote in one of his sweetest phrases.[8] The second half of his life, after Mme de Damas finished her portrait, had two great public occasions in store for him. He was one of those New Yorkers who pushed early and hard for what became the Erie Canal, a project that made the paper structure of national union economically vital. At the same time, and paradoxically, he was one of those northerners who decided, during the War of 1812, that the nation should be broken up, and the Constitution scrapped. Other Americans would come to the same conclusion, from abolitionists calling the Constitution a deal with the devil to southerners arguing that it gave them a right to secede. But Morris's abandonment of the document he had written is more astonishing than later repudiations.

Yet Mr. Morris, alone among the founding fathers, thought that his private life was as important as his public life. Being a gentleman mattered as much to him as being a great man. When public life was not going well, he could go home—not to bide his time before his next opportunity, or to enjoy the retirement on a pedestal of a Cincinnatus, but because he enjoyed farming, reading, eating, fishing, making money, and making love as much as founding a state. "A characteristic trait, which I must not forget," wrote Mme de Damas, "is his faculty and habit of applying his mind to a single object, of suddenly collecting the whole force of his attention upon one point." That point might be a stumbling economy, or an imperfect constitution; it might also be the parade of domestic life. "He is fond of his ease, does his best to procure it, and enjoys it as much as possible. He loves good cheer, good wine, good company." Mr. Morris's ability to switch from public to private life—his inability ever to banish his private frame of reference, even in the midst of public business—did limit his effectiveness as a public man. He lacked the persistence of the other founders. He could focus on one political idea, but soon he might be focusing on another. One delegate to the Constitutional Convention called him "fickle and inconstant," a charge that rang down the years.[9] But this limitation brought benefits. In an era when American politics was as poisonous as it would ever be, he was remarkably free from rancor. Though a war would finally drive him to it, once the war ended, rancor receded. Even James Madison could not long disturb his peace of mind.

Mr. Morris had many reasons to be happy. He was born to privilege, he worked hard to make himself rich, and he was successful in politics, business, and love: after all his affairs, he married a devoted and intelligent woman (accused, it is true, of being a double murderess, though the accuser, her brother-in-law, was commonly supposed to be somewhat insane). But Mr. Morris also saw many things that could have made him gloomy, bitter, perplexed. He witnessed two revolutions, up close and on the ground, one more turbulent than we remember, the other as turbulent as any has ever been. He fled a town that was about to be burned to the ground, and he saw a corpse that had just been torn apart by a mob. His own body was not only missing a leg, but most of the flesh of one arm. Pessimists and misanthropes have been made of less.

In 1936, as Europe slid to war, William Butler Yeats wrote that there is a gaiety in art, even tragic art, that transfigures the dread of life. Gouverneur Morris was no artist, unless living is an art. He carried his gaiety within himself. It was, we might say, constitutional.

GAIETY TRANSFIGURING ALL THAT DREAD,

—W. B. Yeats, "Lapis Lazuli"

CHAPTER ONE

Past and Youth

SINCE GOUVERNEUR Morris bore his mother's maiden name, and since pleasing, pursuing, and avoiding commitments to women would occupy much of his attention as an adult, it would be interesting to know more about Sarah Gouverneur Morris, the first woman in his life. As it is, the little we do know about her life story and her background provides several clues to what she must have been like.

The Gouverneurs were a family of Huguenots, or French Protestants, who had been driven by religious strife in their homeland to Holland in the 1590s; from there, in 1663, they went to the Dutch colony of New Amsterdam. Sarah Gouverneur, who belonged to the third generation of the family in the New World, retained enough of a French identity to send her only son briefly to a French school. But her own mother, Sarah Staats, sprang from the Dutch who had founded the colony of New Amsterdam and who had been running it for forty years when the Gouverneurs arrived.

The Gouverneurs and the Staatses thus represented something that existed nowhere else in the Thirteen Colonies—an old world of European settlement that preceded the arrival of Englishmen. Since New Amsterdam was a commercial venture based on the getting and spending of the fur trade, she had neither the time nor the desire to cultivate spokesmen; her first literary champion, Washington Irving, only appeared many years after the old world had vanished. Irving's histories and stories about Rip Van Winkle, the headless horseman, and St. Nicholas, the patron saint of Christmas, embroidered every factual detail that he did not invent out of whole cloth; but with the insight of art, he captured important facets of a lost psychology. The people of New Amsterdam were private, stubborn, and conservative. Their women were powerful figures in the household, enjoying rights of property ownership and inheritance that were denied their English sisters (in "Rip Van Winkle," Irving makes a joke out of female independence: poor Rip is hen-pecked). The men and women of New Amsterdam, finally, were losers: England had conquered them in 1664, renaming the city and the colony New York, and English customs and language steadily displaced all rivals as time wore on. Sarah's Dutch grandfather, Dr. Samuel Staats, had briefly moved back to Holland rather than "make himself an Englishman."[1]

In 1689, twenty-four years before Sarah was born, the old world had its last hurrah in New York: Jacob Leisler, a German merchant, led a confused rebellion against the English governor that was supported by most of the city's old families, including the Gouverneurs and the Staatses. After almost two years, Leisler was besieged by troops from England, convicted of treason, and drawn and quartered. Power returned to its new channels, and assimilation proceeded apace—which made the descendants of the old world all the more private and stubborn. Sarah Gouverneur Morris would show such traits over the course of her long life.

Her son's paternal ancestors, the Morrises, were by contrast winners in the lottery of the British Empire. To the brashness that typically attends success, they added a quirky extroversion of their own. The Morrises were a family of originals.

The first Morrises to settle in North America were a pair of Welsh brothers, Lewis and Richard. They fought on Cromwell's side in the English Civil War; after taking one royalist stronghold, they adopted as their family crest a burning castle, with the motto *Tandem vincitur* (Finally conquered). After the Restoration, they moved to Barbados, an English Caribbean colony that was filled with Civil War veterans and refugees. From there they moved in the 1670s to New York: a logical next step, since the new English colony had become a hub for processing the sugar the plantations grew, and for shipping staples to the planters. In 1671, Richard Morris had a son, whom he named Lewis. When Richard died four years later, the elder Lewis, who had no children of his own, became his nephew's guardian.

The Morris family did very well in New York. They bought 500 acres (later expanded to 1,900) from a Dutch farmer named Jonas Bronck, lying ten miles north of the city, stretching east from the Harlem River to Long Island Sound. Centuries later Broncks' land would give its name to the Bronx; the Morrises named their new estate "Morrisania." The elder Lewis Morris also bought 3,500 acres in New Jersey. Altogether he had a grist mill, a sawmill, an iron mine, a sloop, and forty-one slaves.

He and his nephew did not at first get along. The elder Lewis hired a Quaker tutor, Hugh Copperthwaite, whom the younger disliked. One day the boy hid himself in a tree beneath which Copperthwaite was used to pray. As the Quaker was addressing the Lord, young Lewis called his name. "Here am I, Lord," said Copperthwaite, "what wouldst Thou with me?" "Go," the voice answered, "preach my gospel to the Mohawks, thou true and faithful servant."[2] The tutor was preparing to leave on his mission when the trick was exposed, and Lewis's guardian exploded. The boy ran away to Jamaica, supporting himself as a scrivener, or copier of documents, until he finally came home, reconciled with his uncle, and settled down. When the elder Lewis died in 1691, the younger inherited all his bustling property.

The new owner of Morrisania directed his considerable energies into politics. The politics of New York, after Leisler's rebellion, was defined by alliances of prominent families competing with each other for office, and for the favor of governors appointed in London. In 1697, Morrisania was designated a manor—a quasi-feudal status enjoyed by the estates of a dozen other wealthy New Yorkers (Rensselaerwyck, the manor of the Van Renssalaer family, covered 1,100 square miles). In the early eighteenth century the lord of the new manor began holding office—first in the colonial Assembly, the elective branch of the legislature, then as Chief Justice of the Supreme Court. In the latter role he became involved in one of the most famous political trials of the colonial period.

In 1732, the new governor of New York, William Cosby, a professional placeholder who looked on his offices as opportunities for enrichment, brought a suit for what he claimed were arrears in his salary,
and asked the Supreme Court of the colony to erect a special court to
hear his case. When Judge Morris wrote a caustic opinion rejecting
the maneuver, Cosby removed him from the bench. This was a declaration of political warfare. Morris and his allies hired John Peter
Zenger, a poor German printer, to edit a new newspaper in New York,
the *Weekly Journal,* to compete with the established, pro-Cosby paper,
the *Gazette,* and to act as their mouthpiece. The *Weekly Journal* published English political tracts and abusive poems, and called Cosby
and his supporters "monkeys" and "spaniels." Cosby complained of
Morris's "open and implacable malice,"[3] and had Zenger arrested for
seditious libel. Under the common law of seditious libel, any publication that, in the view of a judge, held the government up to contempt
was illegal. The only function of a jury in a seditious libel trial was to
decide whether the accused had actually printed the offensive material. The situation was not a happy one for defendants. The Morris
party, however, brought in Alexander Hamilton, an eloquent lawyer
from Philadelphia (no relation to the future Treasury secretary), who
urged the jurors to vote their consciences. "It is not the cause of a poor
printer, nor of New York alone, which you are trying. No! . . . It is the
cause of liberty."[4] Zenger won his freedom, and Hamilton was given a
5 1/2-ounce gold box and a party at the Black Horse Tavern. In the
next Assembly elections, "the sick, the lame and the blind were all carried to vote" and the Morrisites swept the Assembly.[5]

The Zenger verdict set no legal precedent, since it was sheer jury
nullification. Judge Morris did not intend to lead a popular party; tart,
opinionated, and tactless, he was "not fitted to gain popularity,"[6] and
when London, to get him out of New York, offered him the governor-
ship of New Jersey, he happily accepted, and ran the province with a
firm hand. Morris lacked the principles of a later generation, but he
had a principle of his own; that he and his interests were not to be tri-
fled with.

He lived hard, in the eighteenth-century manner. When he went on a lobbying trip to London, his wife told their younger son, who went along, "Don't let your father sit up late and drink too much wine."[7] The son failed in this task. The older man read as hard as he drank, accumulating a library of over two thousand books—vast by American standards. His fancy stimulating the fancy of others, he became a magnet for tall tales, some of them possibly true. He was supposed to have designed and built a sloop on his New Jersey property, ten miles inland, but because he never considered how to bring it to the water, it rotted where it lay. His will offers verifiable proof of singularity. If any man was "inclined to say anything" at his funeral, wrote Morris, "he may, if my executors think fit." But Morris wished for no mourning. "When the Divine Providence calls me hence, I die when I should die, and no relation of mine ought to mourn when I do so."[8]

LEWIS MORRIS, governor and former judge, died in 1746, leaving his properties, his library, and two sons: yet another Lewis, and Robert Hunter. Their father trained them to argue as boys, encouraging them "to dispute with one another for his diversion" after dinner.[9] Both sons held public office, and both approached public life in a contentious spirit. When Robert Hunter Morris became deputy governor of Pennsylvania, he was advised, by Benjamin Franklin, a leader in the colonial Assembly, that he would have a "very comfortable" time, if only he avoided disputes. "My dear friend," Morris replied, ". . . you know I love disputing. It is one of my great pleasures."[10] Yet Robert Hunter Morris had the art of carrying on political wrangles without personal acrimony. Franklin remembered that even when their official exchanges were "indecently abusive," Morris "was so good natured a man that . . . we often dined together."[11] Robert Hunter Morris left four children, all illegitimate, and died of a heart attack while dancing with a clergyman's wife at a village ball.

Robert's elder brother, Lewis, also followed what had become the family profession of politics. This Lewis Morris, like his father, served in the New York Assembly, and later became Judge of the Court of Admiralty, with jurisdiction over New York, New Jersey, and Connecticut (New York City, the centerpiece of his domain, had become, thanks to its West Indies traffic, one of the largest ports in the Thirteen Colonies). But in him the family traits of feistiness and oddity took a darker turn. "Instead of a hat," he "used to wear upon his head a Loon's skin . . . with all its feathers on."[12] It seems that Judge Morris wore this costume both in society and in court. Since loons are famed for their crazy laughing calls, the judge's cap must have been all the more striking. This is stranger than building a boat in the woods or siring a family out of wedlock. A landlocked boat bothers nobody, and illegitimacy was not uncommon in the eighteenth century. A loon-skin hat proclaims that the wearer is unique, and that his fellows are beneath his consideration. It is a declaration of independence, and insouciance.

The third Lewis Morris married Katryntje (or Tryntje) Staats, daughter of Samuel Staats, the New Amsterdam doctor who had not wanted to become an Englishman. By her he had a daughter, Mary, and three sons—a fourth Lewis, Staats Long, and Richard. Mrs. Morris died in 1731, and Lewis remained a widower for fifteen years. But in 1746, after his father died and he became lord of the manor of Morrisania, he married Sarah Gouverneur, who was fifteen years his junior, and his first wife's niece.

In an age of high mortality, people frequently had second and third spouses, and men frequently took younger ones; in a subworld as small as the descendants of New Amsterdam, the entanglements of intermarriage were almost unavoidable. However unremarkable Lewis's second marriage was for that time and place, his children resented it, fearing particularly the appearance of a half brother who would divide their inheritance. Lewis and Sarah's first two children were girls—Isabella, born in 1748, and Sarah, born in 1749. But on January 31, 1752, at 1:30 in the morning, came a son, who was christened Gouverneur. The parents had two more girls—Euphemia, born in 1754, and Catherine, born in 1757—then stopped reproducing.

Lewis Morris died in 1762, when Gouverneur was ten. His will was a cri de coeur, expressing troubled feelings about his family and himself. He highlighted the dissension that his second marriage had caused by trying to allay it. "[I]t is my desire that all my children use their best endeavors to cultivate a good understanding with each other [and] that they be dutiful to" Sarah.[13] He expressed his displeasure with the education he had given his three older sons. Lewis, Staats Long, and Richard had all been sent to Yale College, which had been founded in neighboring Connecticut at the beginning of the century. But in 1746, the eventful year in which their father inherited Morrisania and took a second wife, he pulled all of them from school. In his will, he condemned Connecticut, declaring that "low craft and cunning" were so "interwoven" in the character of its people "that all their art cannot disguise it from the world, though many of them under the sanctified garb of religion"—Yale was a Congregationalist college— "have endeavored to impose themselves on the world for honest men."[14] Evidently he believed that someone at Yale had cheated him somehow, not a feeling unknown to the parents of college students. But how many proclaim it in their wills?

He saw great promise in his son Gouverneur. This was a perception that was widely held. One New Yorker who knew all the Morrises wrote that Gouverneur "has more knowledge (though still a youth) than all his three other brothers put together"[15]—this, even though the sons of the first marriage were all successful men: Lewis was third lord of the manor, Staats Long an officer in the British army, and Richard a rising lawyer. But Lewis Morris found the family spark only in his last son, and he was determined that it be nurtured. "It is my desire," he directed, "that my son Gouverneur Morris have the best education that is to be had in Europe or America."[16]

In his own life, Lewis Morris saw only failure. "My actions have been so inconsiderable in the world that the most durable monument will but perpetuate my folly. . . . My desire is that nothing be mentioned about me, not so much as a line in a newspaper to tell the world I am dead. That I have lived to very little purpose my children will remember with concern when they see the small pittance I have left them, for children judge the wisdom, goodness and affections of their parents by the largeness of the bequests coming to them. But what I have left them is honestly acquired, which gives me a satisfaction that ill got thousands cannot bestow."[17] Even as the loon-skin hat outdid the family eccentricities, so this bitter cup of despair, hostility, and pride exceeded the whimsical language of Morris's father's will. The clause is absurd as well, for the "small pittance" he complained of was still, even shorn of the New Jersey acres, which had gone to Robert Hunter Morris, a fine estate. Lewis Morris died focused on his failures, convinced that the world would ignore his virtues, and placing all his hopes in a ten-year-old boy.

Lewis divided his estate among his heirs. Morrisania was split in two by a south-running brook; the western portion, 500 acres, and the title of lord of the manor, went to the eldest son, Lewis. Sarah Gouverneur Morris was given a life interest in the 1,400 acres to the east: the land and its income were hers to enjoy, though she could not sell it. At her death, it would pass to Staats Long, at which time he would give Richard and Gouverneur £2,000 apiece (perhaps $90,000 in modern money); the daughters would get £600 each (about $27,000). In the division of personal property, Gouverneur got a slave, and his father's shaving box, seal ring, and a pair of gold buttons that his father had worn daily.

Gouverneur Morris's inheritance thus presented him with a variety of options. If he took after his mother and her family, he might show a stubborn independence. If he took after the Morrises, he would be intelligent, flamboyant, and unusual (depression was also a possibility). His Morris heritage certainly accustomed him to politics: when he was a young man, a cousin would write him that if he failed to "dabbl[e]" in it, he would "impeach . . . [his] mother's continency."[18] He was also accustomed to politics at the highest level; Morrises had made the governor of one colony miserable, and had governed two others. Many of the men who would lead the American Revolution were steeped in politics (Samuel Adams, Benjamin Franklin); others were politically active rich men (George Washington, John Hancock). Morris was one of the few to spring from the governing elite. He would also know, if he were wise, that his place in this elite was not guaranteed. Quite apart from the fluctuations in the fortunes of powerful New York families, he was only the last sprig of the Morrises, a fourth son. His monetary inheritance, though tidy, would be long delayed, and he could claim no portion of Morrisania. If he wished to play a part like those his father, uncle, and grandfather had played in the world, he would have to use his opportunities to make his way.

Gouverneur Morris grew up in the manor house, which stood on the eastern half of the estate on a hill overlooking Long Island Sound. As an adult, he would write of the "brilliance in our atmosphere";[19] in a letter to a European friend, he called the climate of Morrisania *riant* [laughing]."[20] The rivers provided the easiest pathways to New York, or to nearby towns; from Morrisania to the Jersey shore of New York Harbor was a leisurely three-hour sail (an unleisurely one-hour drive today). The manor house had nine rooms and two stories, with a balcony over a porch. The parlor, where Judge Morris sometimes heard Admiralty cases, was done in black walnut and mahogany.

Young Morris did not spend as much time there as he would have liked, for his education took him away from home when he was still a boy ("I have been somehow or other hurried through the different scenes of childhood," he would write when he was twenty).[21] He was sent to a school in New Rochelle, New York, a town ten miles out on the Sound. New Rochelle had been settled by Huguenot refugees in 1688, and Gouverneur's school was run by a Swiss Huguenot minister, who taught his pupils French and the "useful sciences."[22] In 1761, when he was nine years old, he was sent to an institution of continental reputation: the Academy of Philadelphia, founded ten years earlier by Benjamin Franklin. The Academy was housed in a structure that had been built to hold the overflow crowds from the preaching of George Whitefield, the barnstorming evangelist. Morris came with the recommendations of a child of the elite: his sponsor at the school was Thomas Lawrence, a trustee, and former mayor of Philadelphia, who also happened to be the husband of his half sister Mary. The purpose of the Academy was college preparation, and after three years there, in 1764, Morris escaped the snares of Yale, Connecticut, and Congregationalism by entering King's College, an Anglican institution, in New York. The college, which had been founded in 1754, stood on the northern verge of town, overlooking the Hudson River.

Both the Academy and King's were founded to incarnate the latest in eighteenth-century educational ideals; the learning they imparted was to be practical, comprehensive, and freed from the domination of Greek and Latin. Franklin wanted a curriculum grounded on English, history, and natural science, while the first president of King's hoped his students would learn about surveying, husbandry, meteors, and stones.[23] But by the time Morris arrived at each school, the curriculum had shifted back to the standard channels of the classics. Morris would have been a freak among his peers if he had not learned his Caesar and Cicero, his Homer and Xenophon. Perhaps the merrily stoical Horace helped shape his worldview.[24] The exposure to Greek and Latin, on top of his youthful French, surely developed his skill with languages. All his life he would amuse his friends by dashing off tripping little poems; when he acquired French and German friends, he would amuse them with poems in their own tongues. His other skill, which shone in his student days, was mathematics; his first biographer wrote that he used to "amuse himself with rapid calculations in his mind."[25] For the rest, Morris and his classmates tormented the teachers who could not command their respect, throwing books at the head of the Latin master at the Academy, and slandering the morals of the mathematics and natural sciences professor at King's.

*I*N AUGUST 1766, when Morris was fourteen, his hurry through the scenes of childhood was rudely interrupted. While he was home from King's, he accidentally upset a kettle of boiling water on his right arm and side. "You have doubtless heard," wrote one family friend to another, "of the melancholy accident that befell Master Gouverneur last Sunday. I set up with him last night. He rested much better than he had done before . . . though his arm seemed too free from pain for so great a wound, which you know is the first symptom of a mortification."[26] Another friend who had been with him when the accident occurred remembered that he "had borne the torture with a fortitude that would have done honor to an Indian brave."[27] So severe was the burn that his nerves had probably been damaged; years later, William Pierce, a fellow delegate to the Constitutional Convention, would describe Morris's right arm as having "all the flesh taken off."[28] If the wound had become gangrenous, as the family friend feared, then the arm would have had to be amputated. But eight days after that worried letter, the same correspondent added, as a postscript to another note, that "Gouverneur is like to do well." [29]

As an adult, Morris was a man of imposing physical stature, standing over six feet tall. He was also active. He had rambled through the fields and woods of Morrisania as a boy; as a man, he paddled through the swamps of upstate New York and shot the rapids of the St. Lawrence. Here, at the threshold of his manhood, was a disfigurement. Did it keep him out of the army? One half brother was already a British officer, and his other two would serve as generals in the American militia. His nephews, the sons of Lewis Morris, also served in the American army and navy. Gouverneur Morris himself responded imaginatively to things military all his life, drawing up plans of campaign for wars on two continents, and employing military images in his workaday prose (George Washington, the greatest American commander of the age, hardly ever used them). Yet Morris never wore a uniform, nor fought in battle. Neither, of course, did many other civilians, well launched in their careers. Did Morris, given his wound and his proclivities, feel a lack?

Morris's injury did not diminish his attractiveness to women. He rarely paid for sex; "I like only the yielding kiss," he wrote, "and that from lips I love." [30] His lovers were intelligent, appealing, and enthusiastic. Darkness and the elaborate outfits of the eighteenth century could conceal much. What did his women friends think of his arm? Surely they felt it. Did he allow them to see it?

These questions are unanswerable, for Morris matched the fortitude of an Indian brave with a brave's silence. In his case, silence was supported by his own particular equanimity. All his life he would face bad things—and he faced an unusual number—with buoyancy and even-heartedness; this was the first instance.

Gouverneur took more than a year off from King's College to recuperate, but his mind was so quick that once he returned he made up for lost time and graduated with his class in 1768. He gave the commencement address, on the theme of "Wit and Beauty." The sixteen-year-old made an interesting variation on the social contract theories of Hugo Grotius and Samuel Pufendorf, the political philosophers of natural law that students at King's read. "Philosophers who find themselves already living in society say that mankind first entered into it from a sense of their mutual wants." But Morris was skeptical of this calculating rationalism; ". . . the passions of barbarians must have had too great an influence on their understandings" for them "to commence this arduous task." Before men could live together, their passions had to be tamed by another passion—the lure of beauty. "Reason unassisted by Beauty would never have smoothed away" man's primordial "ferocity."[31] Without reading too much into a youthful performance, we can credit Morris with having experienced something ferocious, and with finding the means within his temperament to smooth it.

Part 1

The American Revolution

CHAPTER TWO

War Comes

AFTER GRADUATING from King's, Gouverneur followed his father, grandfather, and half brother Richard in becoming a lawyer, apprenticing himself as a clerk to William Smith, Jr., who lived at the southern end of Broadway in New York City.

The city then clung to the southern tip of Manhattan island. At the tip of the tip stood a large fort, Fort St. George, containing the governor's house. The built-up waterfront lay along the East River where, behind a comb of piers and slips, the houses extended for more than a mile. On the North (or Hudson) River side of the island, the city still showed gaps and green spaces. A 1771 census counted a population of 21,835, less than the population of present-day Poughkeepsie; one sixth of them were slaves. Beyond the city limits lay a pleasant landscape, sometimes rolling, sometimes steeply hilly, of woods, farms, and salt marshes.

Dutch ways still persisted in Brooklyn, Flatbush, and other villages of Long Island; on Manhattan, the northbound Post Road passed the estates of the Stuyvesants, descendants of the last Dutch governor. But the merchants, artisans, sailors, and soldiers of New York were English, by birth or assimilation; all their quarrels (and there were many) were internecine. Peter Van Schaak, a friend of Morris's from King's College who also clerked for Smith, would say, when he had acquired experience of English life, that the manners of New York were those of a provincial English town.

Like any other aspiring lawyer of his day, Morris spent the years of his clerkship drudging in the thickets of English common law, which seemed all but pathless. Smith prepared a study guide for his clerks, but it barely organized the confusion. "[H]ow many hours have I hunted," wrote Van Schaak, "how many books have I turned up for what three minutes' explanation from any tolerable lawyer would have made evident to me!"[1] In October 1771, at the age of nineteen, Morris was sworn in as a lawyer, after which his new colleagues drank his health at Fraunces Tavern.

Morris's mind, versatile and quick, which handled numbers and words with equal ease, took to the law as well, and he made a good start in his profession. His manner must have strengthened his arguments: his voice was strong and rich, and the same man who found him smarter than his siblings also called him "witty, genteel, polite, [and] sensible."[2] On occasion he earned fees of £200 and £300 ($9,000 and $13,500); his mother and his half brother Lewis, the manor lord, gave him their business. He was invited to join the Moot, a lawyers' club which took its name from a legal debating society at London's Inns of Court, and which brought together all the ornaments of the small world of the New York bar. His mentor, Smith, and his half brother Richard (who had succeeded their father as Judge of Admiralty Court) were members. So were several representatives of the large, rich, and politically prominent Livingston family. The family motto was *Si je puis* (If I can), and Livingstons had been doing all they could for themselves in New York since the 1670s, when the first of them to settle in the New World had married a Van Renssalaer.

Robert R. Livingston (the R. stood for a second "Robert," to distinguish him from other Robert Livingstons in different branches of the family) became Gouverneur Morris's lifelong friend. He had grown up at Clermont, a Hudson Valley estate that, even though it was not a manor, was far grander than Morrisania. Tall and easygoing, Robert had intelligence, talents, and energy enough to impress the world, without overshadowing his main claim on its attention, which was that he was a Livingston. Besides Gouverneur Morris and Livingston, the junior members of the Moot included Peter Van Schaak, a sweet-natured young man from Kinderhook whom William Smith called "the first genius of all the young fellows,"[3] and John Jay, Robert Livingston's law partner. Jay, a native New Yorker, was the son of a rich merchant who was one of the owners of the public bowling green opposite the fort. When Jay was six, his father noted that "Johnny is of a very grave disposition and takes to learning exceedingly well."[4] All his life he would be proud, serious, and brilliant. Outside the Moot, Morris, Livingston, Jay, Van Schaak, and other young men also formed a Social Club, spending their Saturday nights at Fraunces Tavern, which served the public, then as now, at the corner of Broad and Pearl streets.

As soon as Morris had a foothold in this New York world, he thought of leaving it. All his life he would be accused of fickleness. Perhaps the hurry of his childhood set the pattern of changeability. In his youth he shuttled from Morrisania to New Rochelle to Philadelphia to New York. Now he proposed to spend a year in London, and two months after his twentieth birthday, he wrote William Smith a letter, both charming and revealing, asking his advice.

"The advantages I expect" from a year abroad, he wrote, "are shortly these. I hope to form some acquaintances, that may hereafter be of service to me; to model myself after some persons who cut a figure in the profession of the law; to form my manners and address after the example of the truly polite; to rub off in the gay circle a few of those many barbarisms which characterize a provincial education; and to curb that vain self sufficiency which arises from comparing ourselves with companions who are inferior to us." Morris's breezy explanation of the source of his vanity suggests that he would have trouble curbing it.

"There are many dangers," he admits, "which it is alleged attend a young man thrown from under his parents' wings upon the gay stage of pleasure and dissipation, where a wanton circle of delusive joys courts his acquaintance, and an endless variety of objects prevents satiety and removes disgust." This warning against the snares of London life sounds more like an advertisement: *dangers* and *delusive* hardly balance *pleasure, joys,* and *endless variety.* Morris then confesses that he has "naturally a taste for pleasure," but argues that his good taste will steer him away from "low pleasures." He concludes with a plea cast as an assertion: "I still have some time left before I tread the great stage of life."[5]

Smith wrote his protégé a good-humored but serious reply, based on family history. "Remember your uncle Robin [Robert Hunter Morris]. He saw England thrice. No man had better advantages, either from nature or education. He began with a figure of 30,000 pounds [over a million dollars]. He did not leave 5000 pounds. I know others that never saw the east side of the great lake, who had no other friends than their own heads and their own hands, to whom your uncle was in bonds. What! *Virtus post nummos?* [a line from Horace—Virtue after money] . . . Spare your indignation. I too detest the ignorant miser. But both virtue and ambition abhor poverty, or they are mad."[6] Morris should stay home, with his nose to the grindstone.

Morris took this good advice, perhaps because, mindful of his circumstances as Smith was, he already believed it. He would spend most of the next two decades working, until he had made for himself the fortune that his father and his uncle had enjoyed.

But he did not postpone his pursuit of pleasure, even if he postponed his travel plans. Older men were not the only people who found him witty and genteel. Morris befriended the daughters of William Livingston, a politician, member of the Moot, and cousin of Robert, who moved his base of operations in 1770 across the harbor to Elizabethtown, New Jersey. Everyone loved the lovely Livingston girls. Morris wrote a vignette of seventeen-year-old Sally Livingston holding court: one admirer sitting "sidelong on his chair with melancholic and despondent phiz prolongated unto the seventh button of his waistcoat . . . another with his elbows fastened to his short ribs . . . in the midst of all this sits Miss with seeming unconsciousness of the whole. . . . The rosy fingers of pleasure paint her cheeks."[7] John Jay was the lucky suitor who won her. Alexander Hamilton, a poor but promising West Indian sent by island patrons to King's College in 1773, courted Kitty Livingston, writing to her about the "roseate bowers of Cupid" and the "complex, intricate and enigmatical" nature of woman.[8] Morris had discovered Kitty first. He sent her poems: "Ease at length my troubled breast/ Sweet tormentor now be kind." He told her "how uncomfortable" his "hopeless passion" was.[9] When she did not reciprocate, he admitted that "I am (as you know) constitutionally one of the happiest of men." Gouverneur's cousin, Robert Morris, son of his improvident uncle, rallied him on his taste for "youth, beauty, claret wine and company." [10] This was gentle enough teasing, but if there was also a note of envy of Gouverneur's capacity for enjoyment, it would not be the last to come his way. Gouverneur's final attitude toward his lost Miss Livingston was gracious. "A heart like yours deserves to be happy, and depend upon it, it will be so." [11]

One distraction Morris did not yet allow himself was politics. The politics of the city and the colony revolved, as it had for decades, around the rivalries of powerful families, and old allies and enemies of the Morrises still set the agenda. When Governor Cosby had removed Gouverneur's grandfather Lewis from the Supreme Court bench, the man he replaced him with was James DeLancey, the son of a Huguenot merchant. Thirty-five years later, the DeLanceys still ran one faction. Their opponents were led by Gouverneur's acquaintances, the Livingstons and William Smith, Jr. These two elite parties had divergent interests: the DeLanceys represented merchants, and the Anglican Church (they had supported the creation of the Anglican King's College). Smith and the Livingstons spoke for the great landowners, and for other Protestants (hence their nickname, the Presbyterian Party). Since the Stamp Act of 1765—London's failed attempt to raise money from its North American colonies by taxing legal documents—New York had also a party of radical Liberty Boys, sailors, artisans, and nouveaux merchants, who set themselves up as champions of colonial rights and who threw their weight to whichever of the established factions most courted them. Each group advanced its cause by the traditional means of New York politics—parades, newspapers, slander, and fists. "We have by far the best part of the bruisers on our side," said one of the Livingston faction during a rough Assembly election. [12] This rowdy and comfortable system was part of Morris's legacy, an item in his inheritance like eccentricity or his father's shaving bowl; for that reason, perhaps, he could take it for granted. "Politics I dislike, and only look on with pity," he wrote in January 1774, "exclaiming with Hamlet, 'What's Hecuba to him, or he to Hecuba?'" [13]

Only four months later, the world of New York politics was repolarized. A tea tax, as hateful as the Stamp Act, had provoked the Liberty Boys of Boston to dump a shipment in the harbor. As punishment, in April 1774 Britain closed the port of Boston, and sent a military governor at the head of four regiments to rule. When word reached New York early in May, meetings were held to elect a committee of protest and response. Morris attended one of them, at Fraunces Tavern, and looked on with interest.

"I stood in the balcony," Morris wrote a friend, "and on my right hand were ranged all the people of property, with some few poor dependants, and on the other all the tradesmen . . . who thought it worth their while to leave daily labor for the good of the country." These were the familiar parties in New York politics: Livingstonites and De-Lancey men (people of property), Liberty Boys (tradesmen). But their old system was cracking up. "The mob begin to think and to reason. Poor reptiles! It is with them a vernal morning, they are struggling to cast off their winter's slough [or skin], they bask in the sunshine, and ere noon they will bite, depend upon it. The gentry begin to fear this." So did Morris. "I see, and I see it with fear and trembling, that if the disputes with Britain continue, we shall be under the worst of all possible dominions"—that of "a riotous mob."[14]

Morris wrote with the sharp conservatism of the young, if they are conservative at all. In the eighteenth century, "mob" (short for *mobile vulgus,* the fickle crowd) was a new word, meaning both an unruly crowd, in the modern sense, and the common people as a whole. A riotous mob, to Morris's mind, was simply a calamity, deserving neither respect nor efforts to understand its motives. A peaceful mob— the ordinary populace in its daily life—could never govern, since it was always manipulated by its betters, or at least by those who were more cunning. In the same letter, Morris switched metaphors from reptiles to sheep. "The bellwethers"—belled male sheep that lead a flock— "jingled merrily, and roared out liberty, and property, and religion, and a multitude of cant terms, which everyone thought he understood, and was egregiously mistaken. For you must know the shepherds kept the dictionary of the day, and like the mysteries of the ancient mythology, it was not for profane eyes or ears . . . the simple flock put them-

selves entirely under the protection of these most excellent shepherds."[15] Morris at age twenty-two was not a democrat, nor would he
ever become one.

But Morris did believe in rights. He believed in his own rights, because he was an aristocrat, whose family had wielded power for seventy years; and because he was consistent and fair-minded, he believed
in extending his own rights to others. His grandfather Lewis Morris
had used John Peter Zenger as a journalistic bruiser, and Zenger's trial
as a piece of political theater. But Gouverneur Morris viewed the
Zenger case innocently, as a defense of a free press; in one of those
beautiful phrases that he regularly produced, he called Zenger's ac-
quittal "the morning star" of "liberty" in America.[16]

In the present situation, Morris wrote, political necessity seemed to
call for a compromise: the colonies should tax themselves and provide
for their own defense, while England, the imperial center, should regulate trade. Its greed would be tempered by prudence. Will England
try to "draw all the profits of our trade into her coffers[?] All that she
can undoubtedly. But unless a reasonable compensation for his trouble
be left to the merchant here, she destroys the trade, and then she will
not profit from it."[17]

The May meetings in New York City elected a Committee of Fifty-
One, which included Jay and Van Schaak, and which encouraged the
formation of similar committees elsewhere in New York. In September, in response to a call from Massachusetts, committees throughout
the colonies sent delegations to Philadelphia to discuss their grievances. Jay went as a delegate from New York, William Livingston as a
delegate from New Jersey. The Continental Congress agreed to an
embargo on trade with the mother country, to be enforced by a Continental Association, and narrowly defeated a proposal to reform the
empire by establishing an American house of Parliament.

The firebrands in Philadelphia, for embargo and against compromise, had come from Massachusetts and Virginia. Massachusetts was
suffering, and its history of religious dissent made all but employees of
the crown susceptible to radical arguments. The gentry of Virginia,
who were as grand as any Hudson Valley landowner, instead of fearing

the common people like Morris, identified themselves with them; they could afford to do so, since the "reptiles" in their colony were black slaves, who would never slough off their skins. The New York delegates had supported both the aggressive embargo and the failed political compromise—a seemingly moderate position that disguised sharp political divisions at home. Most of the farmers in lower New York were deeply suspicious of the embargo, as an attempt by local merchants to gouge them. Samuel Seabury, an Anglican clergyman in Westchester County, played on their fears in a pamphlet attacking the Continental Association as a "venomous brood of scorpions." He was answered by a young member of the emerging patriotic party, Alexander Hamilton, the immigrant at King's College. "The sacred rights of mankind . . . are written, as with a sunbeam, in the whole volume of human nature, by the hand of the Divinity itself. . . ."[18] But the patriots, strongest in New York City, were themselves divided between those who thought that their sacred rights could be secured by reform and those (still only a handful) who wanted more drastic measures.

Before it adjourned in October 1774, the Continental Congress had called for another session to meet in Philadelphia the following May. The new meeting was preceded by a bloody crisis. British troops, searching the countryside around Boston for illegal stores of weapons, had fired on local militia at Lexington and Concord. The news reached New York at the end of April 1775. "It is impossible to describe the state of the town," wrote Morris's mentor, William Smith, Jr. ". . . Tales of all kinds invented, believed, denied, discredited. . . . The taverns filled with publicans at night. Little business done in the day. . . ."[19]

The divisions in New York ran through Morris's family. Lewis the manor lord sided with the patriots. Richard resigned his judgeship rather than continue to serve under the British, though he would not yet actively join the patriotic side. Staats Long, who had moved to England and married the Duchess of Gordon, was by this time the colonel of a regiment in the British army; when hostilities broke out, he offered to resign, but the War Office assigned him to garrison Minorca in the Mediterranean, so that he would not be forced to fight on his native soil.

Two of Morris's Gouverneur uncles, both West Indies merchants, sent cannon to the patriots from their storehouse on Curacao. But Sarah Gouverneur Morris was loyal to the king, and remained so throughout the war. Of Morris's married sisters, Euphemia had a loyalist father-in-law; Catherine and Isabella had loyalist husbands. Isaac Wilkins, Isabella's husband, had a run-in with Lewis Morris, his patriot brother-in-law. Wilkins sat for Westchester County in the New York Assembly, where he and other loyalists blocked the sending of any delegates to the Second Continental Congress. The cause of protest and reform was thus left to committees that were outside the law. When a meeting was called in April at the courthouse in White Plains to select delegates for a "Provincial Congress," Wilkins and a handful of loyalists, including Samuel Seabury, marched in from the pub where they had been caucusing to protest the "disorderly proceedings" and sang a chorus of "God Save the King." Wilkins would pay for this gallant demonstration; patriotic marauders, called "cowboys," would drive him out of his house, and force Isabella to live at Morrisania with her mother. Once the loyalists had left the meeting in White Plains, Lewis Morris and the patriots who remained elected a slate of delegates to the Provincial Congress, including Gouverneur Morris. He had cast his lot with his half-brother and the most clamorous traditions of his forefathers, and against his mother and his sisters.

New York's first Provincial Congress met at City Hall, on Wall Street at the head of Broad Street, in May 1775. The twenty-three-year-old Morris impressed the older delegates. One called him a "fine young fellow," who "cuts a figure."[20] Another said that he understood knotty issues "as it were by intuition."[21] The Provincial Congress nominated delegates to the Second Continental Congress (Jay, Robert R. Livingston, and Lewis Morris were among those picked); it also took on itself the responsibility of governing New York. Troops had to be raised; money had to be issued; loyalists had to be dealt with. There were also the British, who still occupied Fort St. George at the tip of Manhattan.

One irksome loyalist was James Rivington, a printer with a shop on Hanover Square. Rivington published a newspaper, the *New York*

Gazetteer, and a good deal of loyalist propaganda, though he had also printed Alexander Hamilton's replies to Samuel Seabury. In May a patriot mob threatened him, after which he signed a loyalty oath to the patriot cause.

Morris urged that the "unfortunate printer" be treated charitably. "Magnanimity," he wrote one patriot, "will dictate . . . the true line of conduct." "Not one month ago," he reminded another, patriotism "was branded with infamy. Now each person strives to show the excess of his zeal by the madness of his actions." He ended this letter with a credo: "I plead the cause of humanity to a gentleman." Gentlemen should settle public affairs, and they should settle them humanely.[22]

Roman Catholics were as unpopular in New York as reckless printers. Catholics had been falsely accused of fomenting a slave revolt in the 1740s, and they were still the only sect forbidden to have clergymen or a place of worship in the city. More recently, Britain's policy of supporting Catholicism in its Canadian dominions had alarmed Protestants throughout the Thirteen Colonies, and the Provincial Congress condemned the "establishment of Popery along the interior confines of the old Protestant Colonies." Morris did not share his colleagues' fear. "That foolish religious business," he wrote of the no-Popery declaration, ". . . would do as well in a high Dutch Bible as the place it now stands in."[23] Religious polemics belonged in the pulpit not the legislature.

Morris's humanity struck some patriots as craven. In June 1775, the British pulled their last troops in New York City—one hundred men of the Royal Irish Regiment—out of the fort, intending to place them aboard the *Asia,* a 64-gun warship moored in the harbor. The Provincial Congress had agreed to let the soldiers go peacefully, but a party of Liberty Boys stopped them at Broad Street and seized five wagons of weapons. Morris, who happened to be passing by, tried to prevent the seizure. "To be opposed by Mr. Morris staggered me," wrote one patriot.[24] Staggered or not, the patriots kept the arms, though the Provincial Congress, at Morris's urging, eventually returned them to the enemy.

New York was in a revolution, but the goals and the battlelines were not yet clear. The patriots had set up parallel institutions: they were waging economic warfare on England, and preparing to wage actual warfare. But independence had not yet been declared; George III was still their sovereign, and a gilded statue of him stood on the bowling green. (The more prudent patriots also didn't want the city bombarded and burned by the *Asia*'s guns.) Morris felt he was in the midst of an "unnatural quarrel between the Parent and the Child," and still hoped there might be a reconciliation. But he knew that if hope failed, there must be "an appeal to the God of Battles."[25]

This deity did not smile on him. In the fall of 1775 New York sent an army to invade Canada, hoping to deprive the British of a potential base. Morris was not pleased by the quality of it—"for the most part the soldiers from this town [are] not the cream of the earth but the scum."[26] In November, the Provincial Congress, plagued by bad attendance—the population of the city itself was plummeting as loyalists fled—called for new elections. Morris was not returned; the new Westchester delegation included four officers. When the Canadian invasion ended bravely but disastrously in a blizzard under the walls of Quebec, New York prepared for the British counterstroke. In February 1776, Morris applied to be the colonel of a newly raised regiment. This was the only time he would volunteer for military service, and he was not accepted. The position went instead to a militiaman who was a shoemaker in private life, and Morris refused to serve as lieutenant colonel under him. The letter he sent his half brother Lewis is a combination of pique, self-knowledge, and regret: ". . . a herd of mechanicks are preferred before the best families in the colony . . . my little abilities [are] more adapted to the deliberations of the cabinet than the glorious labours of the field."[27]

Morris was reelected to the Provincial Congress—New York's third—in May 1776. He arrived late for his duties, having had to console his sister Catherine, whose husband had been jailed for loyalism. Late though he was, Morris got one of the most fortunate assignments of his life: he was named to a secret committee to deal with George Washington.

Washington had been named commander in chief of the Conti-

nental Army the previous June, and sent to besiege the British in
Boston. Thanks to his artillery dispositions, the British had evacuated
Boston in March 1776. They were sure to strike again, however, and
New York was a likely target. Washington and eight thousand men
had arrived to defend the city in April.

Unlike most Americans, Gouverneur Morris would not have been
impressed merely by Washington's height: they were the same size.
Morris had a far better education—Washington's consisted of some
tutoring and some country schooling—and a quicker tongue and pen.
The Morrises were a more impressive family; several Washingtons, including George, had served in the Virginia House of Burgesses, but
none of them had been appointed to the Governor's Council, the true
mark of the elite in Virginia; none of them had been governors. But
Washington was the one man in his life that Morris never failed to respect. Washington was twenty years older than Morris—just close
enough for the outer edges of friendship, well within the normal range
of paternity (Morris's own father had been fifty-four years older than
his youngest son, almost a grandfather). When Morris met him, the
commander in chief was forty-four—an incarnation of principle,
firmness, and manly power.

What did Washington see in Morris? The most famous story about
the two of them also involves Alexander Hamilton, who would enter
their lives later. According to the story, Hamilton bet Morris a dinner
that he would not go up to Washington, slap him on the back, and say,
"My dear general, how happy I am to see you look so well." [28] Morris
slapped the General and won his bet, but reported that the look of re-
proof he got was the worst moment in his life. The founding father re-
buked two founding youths. There are problems with this story: when
it first appears, it is already in two versions, occurring at different
times. There is also a third story of Morris slapping another officer,
Baron von Steuben. The protean story took hold because people
thought that Morris, proud and pert, might do such a thing. Maybe
Morris never did. But surely one of the reasons Washington enjoyed
the younger man's company (in addition to his devotion) is that Morris had these relaxed and confident qualities.

One of Morris's assignments in June 1776 was to hear evidence of a plot on Washington's life. New York loyalists, expecting a British attack, were supposed to have planned an uprising. Thomas Hickey, a member of Washington's military bodyguard, was to have killed him with a poisoned dish of peas. Hickey was hanged in a field near the Bowery, before a huge crowd. The exposure of the plot was a signal for a general roundup. One loyalist wrote that his fellows "were pursued like wolves and bears, from swamp to swamp, from one hill to another . . . numbers were taken, some were wounded, and a few murdered." [29] Other suspected loyalists were listed for further investigation.

Morris, who sat on a committee of inquiry with John Jay, found that one of the suspects whose name came before him was his half brother Richard. Richard Morris pledged to support the Provincial Congress, and thereby became patriotic enough. Yet another suspect was William Smith, Jr.

Late in June, Morris signed a summons to his mentor, directing him to appear before the committee and show "why you should be considered as a friend to the American cause." Smith's reply was addressed to "Gouverneur Morris, one of the Committee & formerly a clerk in my office." He explained that while he was a friend to American "rights and liberties," he considered "the two countries"—America and Britain—to be linked "under a great covenant." Morris wrote back, appealing to Smith's desire for future "offices and honors"; appealing to his idealism (a "sweet consciousness of integrity . . . warms the bosom of that man who risks all for the benefit of mankind"); appealing most of all to the fact that "the ties between Britain & America are haggled away by the sword of war." [30] Morris's mentor was not persuaded. He stayed loyal to the crown, eventually becoming Chief Justice of Quebec.

Time and experience had pushed Morris over the line of independence. "It already exists in everything but in name," he told the Provincial Congress in an oration of which only fragments survive. "Coining money, raising armies, regulating commerce, peace, war, all these things you are not only adepts in, but masters of . . . I see no reason why Congress is not full as good a word as . . . Parliament, and it is a mighty easy matter to please people, when a single word will effect it."[31] This was the voice of Morris the realist. But his imagination had also been stirred.

> By means of that great gulph which rolls its waves between Europe and America . . . by the productions of our soil, which the Almighty has filled with every necessary to make us a great maritime people, by the extent of our coasts and those great rivers which serve at once to open a communication with our interior country, and teach us the arts of navigation . . . finally by the unconquerable spirit of freemen, deeply interested in the preservation of a government which secures to them the blessings of liberty and exalts the dignity of mankind; by all these I expect a full and lasting defense against any and every part of the earth.[32]

Many patriots spoke in this exalted strain; Washington habitually referred to America as a "rising empire." But Morris had distinguished himself in his young career as witty, cynical, and hardheaded. He was all these things; yet there were also romantic chords in his nature which vibrated powerfully when struck.

Washington and the Americans were not masters of war yet. On July 9, the Declaration of Independence, passed by the Continental Congress in Philadelphia, was read in New York. (Robert R. Livingston had been on the drafting committee, though he had done none of the work.) Three days later, General Sir William Howe and Admiral Lord Richard Howe sailed through the Narrows between Staten and Long Island and into the inner harbor with hundreds of ships and 32,000 men. Washington's forces by this time had risen to 19,000 men, but they were almost all raw militia; the Howe brothers' troops were British and Hessian professionals. The battles of the Duke of Marlborough and Louis XIV in Europe, where troops could be more easily provisioned, had involved masses of men three or four times as large; but Britain had never assembled a sea-land operation as great. The Provincial Congress had already adjourned, and reconvened (as the Fourth Provincial Congress) in White Plains. In late August, the British began to drive the Americans from the New York area like deer. One quarter of the captured city burned, in a fire set by accident or patriotic arson; grateful loyalists were happy to return even to the ruins.

The Fourth Provincial Congress fled yet again, to the Dutch Reformed Church in the village of Fishkill, fifty miles north of the city on the eastern side of the Hudson. For three months, from early September to early December, Morris was truant, staying with his sister Euphemia and her husband in northern New Jersey. "A series of accidents too trifling for recital have prevented me the pleasure of attending," was the only explanation he offered his colleagues.[33] They were not pleased. Robert R. Livingston wrote that Morris was enjoying "his jest and his ease while his friends are struggling with every difficulty and danger...."[34] In truth, the Provincial Congress was not struggling too hard; absenteeism deprived it of quorums more often than not. Considering the troubles that had befallen his family, Morris may have felt entitled to spend some time with them.

Morris resumed his duties in Fishkill early in December 1776; shortly thereafter he learned that his sister Catherine had died at Morrisania. Now it was his family that felt abandoned. He wrote his mother, who was behind enemy lines—she thought them friendly lines—a letter gravely balancing private and public.

"There is one comforter, who weighs our minutes, and numbers out our days. It is He, who has inflicted upon us the weight of public and private calamities, and He best knows when to remove the burthen. I am sorry it is not in my power to see you at present. I know it is your wish that I were removed from public affairs.... But I know it is the duty of every good citizen or man to preserve that post, in which by a superior order he is placed." The distinction between *good citizen* and *(good) man*, so lightly made, deserves comment. Morris believed that each had a duty to serve, but in distinguishing between them, however passingly, he refused to let all of the obligations of manhood be swallowed by those of citizenship.

"What may be the event of the present war, it is not in man to determine. Great revolutions of empire are seldom achieved without much human calamity; but the worst which can happen [to a patriot] is to fall on the last bleak mountain of America, and he who dies there, in defence of the injured rights of mankind, is happier than his conqueror, more beloved by mankind, more applauded by his own heart." The imperial vision of his oration in the Provincial Congress had become a desolate image of failure; even so, it was lit by his ideals.

"My love to my sisters, to Wilkins, whose integrity I love and respect [this, of his loyalist brother-in-law] . . . and such others as deserve it. The number is not great." Wit returned in the end.[35]

CHAPTER THREE

The Young Men's Constitution

FTER HIS DEFEATS in New York in the summer and fall of 1776, George Washington stabilized the patriot cause with winter victories in New Jersey. But the British controlled the mouth of the Hudson, and Westchester County was a lawless no-man's-land. The Provincial Congress decided in February 1777 to move twenty-five miles further north, and across the river, to Kingston. The town of Kingston sat on a bluff, with the blue Kaatskil Mountains in the background, in the remote, still-Dutch heartland of upper New York. The legislators met in a stone building that was already one hundred years old, with a prison in the basement. It stank so that Morris asked if lawmakers could smoke, to drive out the "disagreeable effluvia."[1]

The Fourth Provincial Congress had been empowered by the voters of New York to act as a Convention for writing and ratifying a state constitution, though a lack of quorums had prevented it from accomplishing anything as yet. In Kingston, John Jay was asked to prepare a draft, which he presented to the body in March, and Morris was to acquire his first experience of constitution making.

Many of the prime movers in the Convention were young men: Jay was thirty-one; Robert R. Livingston, returned from the Continental Congress, was thirty; Morris was only twenty-five. But they were intelligent and, for all their youth, politically experienced; the stress of war had given them confidence. As friends, King's graduates, and veterans of the Moot, Jay, Livingston, and Morris had been associated for years; they disagreed with the freedom of old colleagues. They complained to and about each other because they were so used to each other. Jay and Livingston clucked so over Morris's absences because they counted on his contributions.

By venturing a revolution, Americans had swept their institutions aside and were in a position to start afresh—to consult first principles, as the eighteenth century put it. In fact, the example of the British system, and the authority of its most fashionable commentators, predisposed them to a tripartite structure of a governor, a two-house legislature, and a judiciary (Pennsylvania would experiment with a one-house legislature and no governor). But the work of any constitution was in the details.

Morris's relatives had been powerful colonial governors (they fought to limit only the power of governors they disliked), and Morris favored a strong executive. He proposed that the governor be able to veto legislation, and appoint state officials, but his colleagues were more cautious. Robert R. Livingston successfully argued that the veto rest with a Council of Revision, consisting of the governor, the members of the Supreme Court, and the chancellor, or chief judge of the court of equity. A similar dispute arose over the power of appointment: after a day of debating the appointment power, Jay and Morris met with Livingston in his room and agreed to a Council of Appointment, made up of four state senators, with the governor acting only as a tie-breaker. The first compromise enmeshed the governor with the judiciary, and the second bound him to the legislature. The members of the Convention had all the Morrises' bad memories of bad governors, without their experience of being good ones.

Morris fought unsuccessfully to keep voice-voting, instead of the secret ballot proposed by Jay. He succeeded with a proposal to require voters in assembly elections to own property worth £20, or $780. Morris wanted voters to declare a public choice, with all the pressures that entailed, and he wanted them to be men of some means, able to withstand pressure. His distrust of the reptiles had not diminished since 1774.

Neither had his support for rights. Morris fought a series of battles with Jay over the political status of Roman Catholics. Both men had Huguenot ancestors, but Jay's had been driven out of France more recently. His grandfather had fled a wave of Catholic oppression just ninety years ago, which was ninety years after the Gouverneurs moved to Holland; his ancestry was not a family linguistic tradition, but a living wound. In the *Federalist Papers*, Jay would boast that Americans were a "united people . . . professing one religion," by which he meant Protestantism, not Christianity.[2] In Kingston, he vowed "to erect a wall of brass around the country for the exclusion of Catholics."[3] His draft constitution granted "the free exercise of religious profession and worship . . . to all mankind." But on the floor of the Convention, he moved that Catholics be forbidden to own land or vote until they swore before the state Supreme Court that "no pope, priest, or foreign authority on earth" could absolve them of allegiance to the laws. This motion failed.

The next day, Jay offered a milder one, providing that liberty of conscience "shall not be construed to encourage licentiousness, nor be used in such a manner as to disturb or endanger the safety of the state." This passed; who could be in favor of endangering the safety of the state? Morris, however, offered and carried a small but significant amendment: that liberty of conscience not be construed so "as to excuse *acts* of licentiousness or justify *practices* inconsistent with the peace or safety of the state" (italics added).[4] Jay's motion could have been used to prosecute beliefs; Morris wished to be guarded only against bad actions.

Morris had no sympathy with Catholicism. His religious feelings, though earnest, were thoroughly deist: his God was all-powerful, beneficent, and otherwise unknowable. When Morris met large numbers of Catholics in Europe, he found the clergy corrupt—"The Cardinal is very devout," he wrote of one cleric. "He was once the lover of Madame's sister"[5]—the laymen superstitious and stupid, and their beliefs "absurd," "degrading to the Omnipotent, if indeed it were possible for men to honor or dishonor Him."[6] But he would let Catholics worship in New York as they wished. "It was always my opinion," he wrote Peter Van Schaak the following year, "that matters of conscience and faith, whether political or religious, are as much out of the province, as they are beyond the ken of human legislatures."[7]

Another contest of rights in Kingston joined Morris and Jay. Morris moved that the new constitution should urge "future legislatures" to abolish slavery, "so that in future ages, every human being who breathes the air of this state, shall enjoy the privileges of a freeman. ... [T]he rights of human nature and the principles of our holy religion loudly call upon us to dispense the blessings of freedom to all mankind."[8] Slaves had worked at Morrisania for generations. New York was doubly bound to slavery: it had one of the largest slave populations of any northern state, and its colonial economy rested on a symbiotic relationship with the sugar islands of the Caribbean—the rich of New York City refined the sugar that West Indies slaves harvested, while the small farmers in the rural counties used their own slaves to grow produce for the sugar islands. Morris and Jay wanted to wean New York from this pernicious dependence, but New York was not ready to be weaned. Morris's motion failed, by a vote of thirty-one to five. Other northern states, notably Massachusetts and Pennsylvania, less attached to trade with the islands, soon abolished slavery; New York would not begin to follow them until 1799. Morris and Jay, themselves children of slave owners, were indignant. Until America accepted gradual abolition, Jay wrote, "her prayers to heaven for liberty will be impious."[9]

The first constitution Morris had a hand in writing was ratified on April 21. No one was entirely happy with it, but everyone knew that no one ever is. Jay, who had been called from Kingston by news of the death of his mother, wrote Morris and Livingston that, though "the birth" was "premature," since he didn't approve of the Spartan practice of destroying defective infants, "I shall nevertheless do all in my power to nurse and keep it alive."[10] "That there are faults in it is not to be wondered at," wrote Morris, "for it is the work of men perhaps not the best qualified for such undertakings." Morris, who did not commonly criticize himself, must have had his fellow delegates in mind. "God grant that it may work well for we must live under it."[11]

The three friends from the Moot had done well, pending the fortune of war; the case of another friend, Peter Van Schaak, was different. The political divisions that had sundered Morris's family split Van

Schaak's mind, and were ruining his life. The young lawyer was as shy as he was intelligent. "I never knew a man possessed of his acquirements," wrote one friend, "so modest and unassuming." [12] He had joined the first committees of protest, after the closing of the port of Boston in 1774. But he continued to hope that "some middle way should be found out," and he dreaded civil war—the condition toward which New York was drifting—as "the epitome of human wretchedness." [13] When patriot committees asked him to swear allegiance to the new government, he showed the stubbornness that the shy often have, and refused.

Van Schaek's private life was as battered as his public life. Six of his children died between 1771 and 1775, two of them within two days of each other. In 1776, he lost the sight in his right eye (in search of a middle way he had been reading too much Grotius, Pufendorf, and Locke). Caught in a wretched present, his thoughts turned to the past. "Those happy scenes of our clubs, our moots, our Broadway evenings," he wrote Jay, "fill me with pleasing melancholy reflections." [14] In 1778, Van Schaak's wife died of consumption, and he was banished as a loyalist to England. He took as his motto a line from the *Aeneid*, Virgil's epic of exile, *Susperanda fortuna ferendo* (We master fortune by accepting it). [15]

Morris wrote his old friend as soon as he heard that he was leaving America. "I am particularly afflicted, that you should be now obliged to relinquish your country, for opinions which are unfavorable to her rights." Morris considered the conduct of his fellow revolutionaries. "The infancy of the state must apologize for the defects of its legislature ... Adversity is the great school of moderation. If any of my countrymen are come thence unlearned, I will not blame, though I cannot commend." When they had suffered as much as Van Schaak—or, considering his withered arm, Morris—they might be less rigorous.

In public life, Morris went on, "it shall be my object to narrow as much as possible the circle of private wo." He called up the millennial vision of Revelation 21:4: "I would to God, that every tear could be wiped from every eye." But this was the world: " ... so long as there are men, so long it will and must happen that they will minister to the miseries of each other." He tactfully shared a hope with his suffering friend. "It is a delightful object in history, to see order, and peace, and happiness result from confusion, and war, and distress. It is a pleasing hope in life." And he concluded: "It is your misfortune to be one out of the many who have suffered. In your philosophy, in yourself, in the consciousness of acting as you think right, you are to seek consolation...." [16]

Fighting men often honor the courage of their enemies. In his letter to Van Schaak, Morris did something that may be harder: without abandoning or apologizing for his own principles, he consoled, and admired, a man whose principles were different.

In May 1777, the lawmakers in Kingston chose Morris to be one of New York's delegates to the Continental Congress in Philadelphia. But Morris was too busy to attend, for that summer the war came to the heart of New York.

The inner web of North American lakes and rivers had been noticed by white men as early as Samuel Champlain in the seventeenth century. The Hudson River, Lake George, and Lake Champlain formed an almost complete waterway between New York and Montreal, that looked especially seductive on a map. In the early eighteenth century, French and British armies fought terrific battles over obscure forest outposts that controlled key heights and portages. In these wars of empire France hoped to move south from Canada and split the enemy in two. After the Americans revolted, Britain, which by then owned Canada, hoped to do the same thing. A three-pronged operation was planned for the summer of 1777. Major General John Burgoyne was to march south from Canada, at the head of eight thousand British, Hessians, loyalists, and Indians. Lieutenant Colonel Barrimore St. Leger was to swing from the west, via Lake Ontario, the Oswego River, and the Mohawk Valley. General Sir William Howe was to push north from New York City. If all went well—and none doubted that it would—they would converge on Albany, the old Dutch upcountry hub, destroying the rebellion in New York and splitting New England from the middle states and the South. In the event, General Howe decided that more was to be gained by taking Philadelphia. But he left behind him in New York his second in command,

General Sir Henry Clinton, with seven thousand men and instructions to assist Burgoyne "if circumstances warranted."[17]

The plan had much to recommend it. The Mohawk Valley was sown with loyalist Indians, the fruit of years of cultivation by Sir William Johnson, an Irish adventurer who had an Indian mistress and a country gentleman's house smack in the middle of the wilderness. Burgoyne began well. Setting out from Canada in mid-June 1777, he sailed down Lake Champlain and captured Fort Ticonderoga, the northern key to Lake George, by the bold but simple expedient of hauling artillery to a mountaintop that the Americans wrongly thought was inaccessible. With the fort, the Gibraltar of North America, in his hands, Burgoyne's confidence soared. "None but stupid mortals can dislike a lively camp, good weather, good claret, good musick, and the enemy near," wrote one of his aides. "A little fusillade during dinner does not discompose the nerves of even our ladies."[18] Burgoyne expected to enjoy Christmas dinner in Albany.

Political power in Kingston had passed to an interim group, the Council of Safety, meant to bridge the gap between the Fourth Provincial Congress and the officeholders to be elected under the new Constitution. The Council now sent Morris to Fort Edward, on the southern end of Lake George, to investigate the fall of Fort Ticonderoga. "Having no powers," Morris wrote the Council, "I shall do what I think best."[19]

The American commander at Fort Edward was General Philip Schuyler, a hardheaded Dutch landowner whose estate lay near the village of Saratoga, twenty-five miles north of Albany. As a young man he had fought in several frontier battles against the French. Morris found that he had less than five thousand men, almost half of them militia, and only two old iron field-pieces, and that most of his officers, as Morris wrote the Council of Safety, were not "worth a crown."[20] Morris sized up the situation and proposed radical but hopeful measures. "Break up all the settlements upon our northern frontier . . . drive off the cattle, secure or destroy the forage." The gaps between the lakes and the Hudson River looked small on paper, but the terrain in them was wet, wooded, and steep. "If we lay it down as a maxim, never to contend for ground but in the last necessity, to leave nothing but a wilderness to the enemy, their progress must be impeded by obstacles which it is not in human nature to surmount."[21] This was the strategy that Washington, observing from afar, had hit upon: Burgoyne's success, he wrote Schuyler, "will precipitate his ruin."[22] It was the strategy that Schuyler was in fact following, ordering his men to fell trees, dam streams, and do everything possible to slow Burgoyne's advance.

The Council of Safety, however, wanted information that could prevent the public (and perhaps themselves) from panicking. To civilian eyes, the fall of Fort Ticonderoga was a disaster, and Burgoyne an irresistible force. "We could wish," wrote Jay, "that your letters might contain paragraphs for the public . . . the people suspect the worst because we say nothing." Morris replied sharply that he had not known he was to "write the news," whereupon the Council called him home.[23]

The Council had found Morris's letter "disrespectful and unsatisfactory,"[24] but when Morris returned to Kingston at the end of July, he made a report that was vivid and alarming. Whatever Schuyler's strategic possibilities, he was outnumbered by nearly two to one. The loyalist-leaning counties of upstate New York could not send him more militia, while half of the militia he had were New Englanders, who disliked him for a disciplinarian and yearned to serve at home. The only source of reinforcements was the main American army under George Washington, and though a rumor on the Livingston family grapevine described Morris as "hopeless,"[25] the Council sent him and Jay to ask for help.

The commander in chief was marching to Philadelphia, which Howe evidently planned to attack, having sailed from New York with 160 ships and 18,000 men. Washington told the New Yorkers he had no men to spare. They rode on to Philadelphia, where they warned Congress that "the poor remains" of their state "must inevitably fall into the hand of the enemy."[26] Congress directed Washington to send five hundred riflemen to New York, and Morris and Jay returned to Kingston in late August.

Congress had made Schuyler the scapegoat for the fall of Fort

Ticonderoga, and replaced him with General Horatio Gates, a British army veteran with New England friends. Morris was "exceedingly distressed" at the New Yorker's removal, but hoped that the reinforcements would enable Gates "to act with éclat, if he has spirit and understanding sufficient for that purpose."[27] Better than spirit or understanding, Gates had the luck of good timing, for now the British began to suffer reverses, and as Morris, Schuyler, and Washington had predicted, the difficult terrain and their exposed situation made their reverses fatal. St. Leger had already turned back after bloody fighting in the west, and a reconnaissance party of Burgoyne's Hessians and loyalists had been whipped on the Vermont border. Burgoyne himself was moving south through the wilderness at a rate of one mile per day; he had to build forty bridges to cross the aquatic obstacles in his path. Militia flowed in to Gates as the tide turned, and on September 19 and October 6 he and Burgoyne fought two sharp battles near Saratoga.

One hundred fifty miles away, in occupied New York, Sir Henry Clinton finally decided, on October 5, to push north. In three days he cleared all the American positions between him and Albany, and wrote Burgoyne that help was on the way. The message never arrived—the bearer was captured, he swallowed it, and the Americans administered an emetic to retrieve it—but it would have done no good in any case, for Burgoyne's casualties were so heavy and his supplies so low that he had decided to limp back to Canada in retreat.

The government of New York sat in Kingston, like a spider in the center of a web of events, though without a spider's power. Jay had "gone to fetch his wife," Morris wrote Schuyler jauntily. Livingston was "solacing himself with his wife, his farm, and his imagination. Our Senate is doing I know not what. In Assembly we wrangle long to little purpose. . . . I tremble for the consequences, but I smile, and shall continue to do so, if possible."[28] Morris's temperament was tested when it became clear that the British heading up the Hudson from New York were burning patriot dwellings for spite as they went. On October 13, Kingston was evacuated. "The alarm in the town," Morris wrote Livingston, "exhibited more of the drolerie than the pathos of distress. The good dominie [a Dutch Reformed clergyman] and his yefrow [wife] . . . blowing between resolution and pallid fear load about half a ton upon my wagon and then eight of them, children included, were dragged only slowly. Before they went, Willy squealed, Sally bawled, Adam played tricks, and the yefrow [cried] like Hecuba at the taking of Troy." [29]

The lawmakers, driven from New York to White Plains to Fishkill to Kingston, moved once more, to the tiny village of Marble Town. After they left, the marauding British reduced Kingston to "a rubbish of ashes." [30] They were too late to save Burgoyne, however, who, on October 16, too weakened even to retreat further, surrendered to Gates. Morris had balked at supplying the Council of Safety with mere news, but he did not mind sending it to one of the lovely Livingston girls, now married, and to a loyalist no less, but still his correspondent.

> *With politics and nonsense*
> *I've lost my rhyming talents long since . . .*
> *In such a case I needs must choose*
> *(A Hobson's choice) to write the news.*
> *Know then, the great Burgoyne's surrounded,*
> *His arms magnanimously grounded.* [31]

The fighting along the Montreal–New York corridor was temporarily over, with the British in Canada and New York City, and the rebels holding the crucial center. The action would now mainly be elsewhere. Finally New York could spare Morris as a delegate to the Continental Congress. In October 1777 he left for Philadelphia, not to return to his home state, except for visits, for twenty-one years.

CHAPTER FOUR

Running a War

WHILE GENERAL BURGOYNE had been fighting and failing in upstate New York, General Howe, who should have been supporting him, had sailed into Chesapeake Bay, landed his army on the Maryland shore, and attacked Philadelphia from the south. Congress fled before him, in a confusion of "horses galloping, women running, children crying [and] delegates flying,"[1] and settled finally in the town of York, almost ninety miles to the west, across the Susquehanna River. After a visit with the Ogdens in New Jersey, Morris arrived at his new post on January 20, 1778.

The emergency seat of the national government was scarcely bigger than Kingston. Delegates complained of their setting: "Believe me," wrote one, "it is the most inhospitable scandalous place I ever was in."[2] Morris complained of the delegates: "Stuffed in a corner of America and brooding over their situation, they have become utter disagreeables."[3] Many of the glittering members of the early days of the Continental Congress had left, drawn to state politics, or other assignments: Patrick Henry and Thomas Jefferson, the greatest tongue and the greatest pen of the Revolution, had gone home to Virginia; Benjamin Franklin and John Adams, the international celebrity and the hardheaded Yankee firebrand, were serving as diplomats in Europe; George Washington was serving in the army. The loss of tone, together with the country's grim prospects, and the fact that states voted as units, not congressmen as individuals, encouraged absenteeism. There were seldom as many as twenty delegates on the floor at any time, and they fit easily into their meeting place, the courthouse on the town square.

Morris, going on twenty-six, was one of the youngest members of Congress. His enemies would hold that against him: one called him "the Tall Boy."[4] They would also come to resent his self-assurance: "for brass," wrote another, he was "equal to any I am acquainted with."[5] Morris's reputation for a lightness of pivot had accompanied him to Pennsylvania. Among his fellow New Yorkers, he bore the family reputation for impulsiveness and oddity, and his new peers took up the theme. Henry Laurens of South Carolina found Morris "guardless and incautious";[6] Robert Morris of Pennsylvania (no relation) expected him to be "immensely useful if he pursues his objects steadily (for I have been told his only blemish is being a little too whimsical)."[7] Morris himself pleaded guilty to being hopeful: "[I am] by nature a little sanguine and never look upon the dark side of objects unnecessarily."[8]

On his first day in York, Morris was given an assignment that would require him to study a very dark object indeed; he was put on a committee to visit Washington at his winter encampment, and to report on the condition of the army. Washington and his troops had lost Philadelphia to Howe in two autumn battles, but they had not fought badly, particularly in the second engagement at Germantown, a near-run thing, in which the American attack failed in part because the battlefield had been shrouded in fog. After their worthy losses, the army had marched into winter quarters in the rolling countryside of Valley Forge, eighteen miles northwest of Philadelphia, in December. Here their condition was grim, not from ice and snow, for the winter of 1778 was mild enough, but from disease, and lack of supplies and pay. Thanks to resignation and illness, the army had no general officer in charge of food or equipment. What they had instead, according to a doctor in the Connecticut line, was "fatigue—nasty clothes—nasty cookery . . . There comes a bowl of beef soup—full of burnt leaves and dirt, sickish enough to make a Hector spew."[9] The army suffered less from British mauling than from American disorganization and incompetence. When Morris and his fellow committee members arrived at Valley Forge, they were shocked by what Washington told them, and by what they saw. "Our troops," Morris wrote Jay, *"Heu miseros!*

[Alas for the wretches!] The skeleton of an army presents itself to our eyes in a naked, starving condition, out of health, out of spirits."[10]

Morris threw himself into the work of reviving this dejected force. The orderly, mathematical side of his mind rose to the challenge of re-organization and supply. The army needed structural changes—larger cavalry regiments, a corps of engineers—while the states, which were ultimately responsible for supplying it, required precise summaries of its needs. Morris drew up elaborate charts and tables for both purposes; his facts and figures, by making plain how badly off the army was, were polemical as well as practical. Valley Forge also stirred his passions. He "loved" the army, he wrote, "from acquaintance with some individuals and for the sufferings which as a body they had bravely and patiently endured."[11] Bravest and most patient in Morris's eyes was Washington; the bond they had formed in New York was strengthened by the work they did together at Valley Forge, and burnished by the letters they exchanged after Morris returned to Congress. "I was in your debt," Morris began one, meaning he owed Washington a letter. "But, believe me, my heart owes nothing."[12]

At Valley Forge, Morris met the marquis de Lafayette. Lafayette, whose father had died in battle when he was two, had been raised in the mountainous Auvergne in central France. When he made his debut at the court of Versailles—a ritual initiation required of all noblemen—he struck his peers as uncouth and naive: he could not dance, and he loved his wife (a rich heiress to whom he had been married at age fourteen). The American Revolution gave him a reason for being. In the spring of 1777, as a nineteen-year-old captain of the musketeers, he outfitted a ship, the *Victoire,* at his own expense and sailed to the United States. He was going, he wrote his wife, "to offer my services to the most interesting of Republics, bringing to the service only my candor and goodwill without ambition or ulterior motive."[13] The marquis partly deceived himself, for he was consumed with ambition. But he was also candid and good-willed.

He had arrived at Washington's headquarters in August, a bad time for foreign volunteers. Eager to recruit professionals to the cause, America's agent in Europe had been freely offering commissions in

the American army, and a swarm of officers, both idealists and soldiers
of fortune, had crossed the Atlantic to take up their promised ranks.
American officers who had been fighting for two years resented the
newcomers; many of the Europeans disdained the skills of the rustics
they were coming to help. Wearied by the hard feelings that had been
stirred up, Washington did not know what to expect when yet another
European appeared before him. "We are rather embarrassed," he told
the young marquis, "to show ourselves to an officer who has just left
the army of France." Lafayette gave the perfect response: "I am here,
sir, to learn and not to teach."[14] The fatherless young man and the
childless commander in chief became a devoted pair. Their mutual admiration, so far from shutting Morris out, helped draw him and
Lafayette together when they met in January 1778. From the height of
his years, Morris declared that he was "deeply surprised at the mature
judgment and solid understanding of this young man."[15]

Morris returned to York on April 15, and took up another cause
dear to the army's interest—the payment of officers. When the Continental Congress appointed Washington commander in chief, he had
stipulated that he would serve without pay; only his expenses should
be covered. But this example of Roman virtue, however appropriate to
the Father of his Country, could not serve for his officers. Since pay
was erratic, and the paper money in which it occasionally came verged
on worthless, officers needed the hope of future reward. Washington
wanted them to have pensions of half-pay for life. "I do most religiously believe the salvation of the cause depends on it," he wrote
Congress; "and, without it, your officers will moulder to nothing, or be
composed of low and illiterate men, void of capacity for this or any
other business."[16] Many in Congress, however, were leery of committing their states to a peacetime obligation, particularly for the benefit
of an army; was not the standing army the traditional tool of despots?

After weeks of wrangling, the enemies of half-pay offered to support it so long as the measure was referred to the states for approval.
This shirked responsibility, and would surely doom the proposal. The
poisoned compromise split the state delegations evenly, with Pennsylvania "in a mighty flimsy situation," as Morris wrote Washington, who

was following events from Valley Forge.[17] The two delegates from Pennsylvania who were in York were themselves split on the issue; Robert Morris, who supported half-pay, was at his country house in Manheim, twenty-five miles away. "Think one moment, and come the next," Gouverneur Morris urged him.[18] Robert Morris came, and the motion to submit half-pay to the states was defeated, with Pennsylvania's opposition, in the middle of May. Congress then passed a genuine compromise of half-pay for seven years. This was only a stopgap, but it was something.

While Morris was in York, he wrote a letter to his mother. In it, he speaks of having written often and receiving no replies; perhaps other letters went astray in crossing enemy lines. But it is the second of two long wartime letters to her that survive. Sarah Morris was not happy. She was over seventy years old; her family was split; her loyalist in-laws had suffered, and the soldiers of the king she obeyed were filching the books and cutting the trees of her estate. Her son tried to console her. "There is enough of sorrow in this world, without looking into futurity for it. Hope the best. If it happens, well; if not, it will then be time enough to be afflicted, and at any rate the intermediate space will be well filled."[19] He offered to comfort her in person. "[T]he early possession of power [has] taught me how little it deserves to be prized. Whenever the present storm subsides, I shall rush with eagerness into the bosom of private life." But, like Augustine praying to be pure, Morris did not wish for private life yet. Another maternal figure claimed him: " . . . while [the storm] continues, and while my country calls . . . I hold it my indispensable duty to give myself to her."[20] He wrote more bluntly and more beautifully to Robert R. Livingston. "This is the seed time of glory as of freedom."[21] Morris had moved in less than four years from local to state to national politics. York might be as grim a place as Kingston, and both were much less grand than New York, but the destinies of a nation were being decided in York, and in Valley Forge. Everyone touched by the liberal enlightenment professed to disdain power; Morris truly meant it. But he quickened to the presence of glory, in suffering soldiers or in great comrades.

Morris showed his spirit in York, yet he also showed his high spir-

its, which ignited two quarrels with long fuses. On his way to Valley
Forge in January, he and another congressman had stayed at an inn in
Lancaster. There they had become judges in a dispute between a
British convoy that was supplying, with Washington's permission,
enemy prisoners in American custody, and the laws of Pennsylvania.
The British, who had stopped at the same inn, were settling their bill;
because they carried hard currency, the innkeeper offered them a siz-
able discount. An American officer who was escorting them then insisted they should pay at the official local exchange rate, and the
British, unwilling to be gouged, appealed to the two congressmen who
happened to be handy. Morris, never shy, pronounced that the British,
so long as they were proceeding under military safe-conduct, were
subject to the law of nations, not to the laws of Pennsylvania. For good
measure, he wrote a lecturing letter to the Pennsylvania state government. When he arrived in Valley Forge, Joseph Reed, a Pennsylvania
congressman, warned him that he "would not do it if it was to do
again."[22]

In March, Morris became involved in a clash of personalities.
Jonathan Sergeant, Attorney General of Pennsylvania, had brought a
complaint against the deputy quartermaster general of the army, one
Robert Hooper, Jr., for using army wagons for private business.
Hooper, who was a big man, hunted out Sergeant, who was a small
one, and thrashed him, then wrote a letter to Morris declaring that, "as
he had horsewhipped the Attorney General, he proposed to go
through" the entire state government.[23] Morris thought the letter was
rich, and showed it to his friends at Valley Forge, from Washington on
down. Reed, offended for his state, wanted the letter as evidence
against Hooper; but Morris, who had been happy to share it, now refused to surrender it, on the grounds that it was a private communication. Morris was arguably right about the inn bill, and guilty in the
Hooper affair of nothing more than a good time (he later helped to
prosecute Hooper, who was indeed guilty of misusing public property). But he had managed in a matter of months twice to offend the
government of the state in which Congress sat. "You know, he is like
the elephant in war," one New York delegate wrote Robert R. Liv-

ingston, ". . . more destructive to his friends than to his antagonists."[24] He would hear of both offenses again.

In the middle of June 1778, Morris made yet another move—this one, unlike all his previous movements as a legislator, not in flight from an advancing enemy but in the wake of a retreating one. The British decided to consolidate their forces, and evacuated Philadelphia for New York.

The city was bruised by its nine months' occupation. The State House, where the Declaration of Independence was signed, had been used as a hospital, and stank from the garbage and corpses that the British had dumped in a pit outside. British officers had lifted books and a portrait from Benjamin Franklin's library. The citywide bill for property damage and theft amounted to £187,000 (over $6 million today). The underfed inhabitants had a meager look. Robert Morris the Pennsylvania congressman predicted, however, that "they will fatten fast."[25] His confidence was based on the city's fundamental centrality and wealth. Boston was slipping, and New York was still growing. Philadelphia, with a population of 38,000, was clearly the largest and richest city on the continent. It is "to the United States," wrote Robert Morris, "what the heart is to the human body in circulating the blood."[26] Foreigners could be condescending about Philadelphian sophistication. One Frenchman wrote that the ladies "although very well shaped . . . lack grace and make very bad curtsies." Worse, "they pride themselves on a scrupulous fidelity towards their husbands."[27] But American visitors were agog. "To be placed on an elegant sofa alongside one of them, when they are displaying both the artillery of their tongues and eyes," wrote one colonel, was "almost too much for a healthy, vigorous young soldier to bear. . . ."[28]

Morris made a ferocious suggestion to Washington that he fine the city £100,000 for collaborating with the enemy. "Your idea," Washington wrote back gravely, ". . . widely differs from mine."[29] Not for the last time, Morris's quick, sharp mind outran his mild temper. He was more tolerant of principled pacifists. He reported to Robert Livingston that the Moravian Brethren, a German pacifist sect, were being harassed by local patriots. Although they were "averse to bearing arms and taking baths," they were "good husbandmen and mechan-icks."[30] Could New York find some way to woo them? Morris thought no better of the Brethren's practices than he did of the beliefs of Catholics, but he was willing to let them, and the state, profit by their labor.

Morris and Congress returned to Philadelphia at the beginning of summer. The "minutia are infinite," he wrote, and the heat "pestifer-ous."[31] The rank eastern seaboard was responsible for the heat; the minutia proliferated along with congressional committees. Every item of official business, from the long-running responsibilities of govern-ment to the most fleeting problems, was handled by a committee, and the labor of the committees fell on their chairmen. "You must not imagine," Morris wrote years later, "that the members of these com-mittees took any charge or burden of the affairs. Necessity, preserving the democratical forms, assumed the monarchical substance of busi-ness. The chairman received and answered all letters and other appli-cations, took every step which he deemed essential, prepared reports, gave orders . . . and merely took the members of a committee into a chamber, and for the form's sake made the needful communications, and received their approbation. . . ."[32] Morris was one of these movers and shakers. "I have no exercise," he complained in one letter, "unless to walk . . . fifty yards to Congress and to return."[33]

His first significant action beyond the blizzard of daily business was to join his fellow New Yorkers in signing the second new constitution of his acquaintance, the Articles of Confederation. Congress had been considering a form of government for two years. John Dickinson of Pennsylvania had drawn up a draft in July 1776, a week after the Dec-laration of Independence, but "every inch" of it had been haggled over.[34] By November 1777, one delegate wrote, "the child Congress has been big with" was "at last brought forth," though he feared it would "be thought a little deformed."[35] The Articles declared a "firm league of friendship"[36] among the thirteen states, and gave Congress power over foreign policy and warmaking (there was no executive, or national judiciary). Other powers of government, such as raising rev-enue, depended on the approval of the states. State delegations voted as units; nine states had to approve a law, all thirteen would have to approve a change in the Articles themselves. The new government was more than an ad hoc wartime alliance (the Union was declared to be "perpetual"), but not much.[37] By the end of July 1778, ten states had signed the Articles.

Morris also took up two great issues of long-range importance. Sometime in mid-1778, perhaps as early as his return from Valley Forge, he prepared an oration on financial and political reform, not for delivery—neither the journal of Congress nor the letters of the delegates mention it—but to organize his thoughts. The problems of the army that Morris had been grappling with were symptoms of larger problems—feeble credit and feeble government—and he outlined an ambitious plan to address them. The United States needed a foreign loan—but how to raise it? One potential asset the government could call on was land. Many states had colonial-era claims to land beyond the Alleghanies. Morris wanted these assigned to Congress, which could carve a new state for veterans out of them, and pledge the remainder as collateral. Meanwhile, Congress needed permanent sources of revenue. Morris suggested postal charges, a tariff, and a head tax of one dollar per person. Congress had to establish its preeminence by ending state currencies, and demonstrate confidence in its own currency by lifting price controls and publishing a record of its debts.

Morris, fresh from signing the Articles of Confederation, also sketched political reforms of the system he had just approved. "Every gentleman acquainted with our public affairs," he wrote, must know "that a body such as the Congress is inadequate to the purposes of execution." The business of managing financial and military affairs should be removed from congressional committees and given to boards of expert commissioners. Over them there should be a national executive—"either a Committee of three or a single officer such as [a] Chief of the States"—who would superintend their doings, and present their reports to Congress.[38] The grandson and nephew of governors envisioned one for the United States.

By August 1778, Morris began offering his ideas to Congress. In a report on the Board of Treasury, he proposed three permanent offi-

cials: a treasurer, a comptroller, and an auditor. Congress agreed, provided they were reconfirmed annually. The following month Morris
presented a report on money and finance, in which he offered his other
proposals (except for a national executive, which even he sensed was
too radical to be considered). The reforms he was offering were radical
enough. Morris asked the same body that had balked at paying officers' pensions to assume a host of other duties and powers. Congress
printed only sixty copies of his report, and enjoined the printer and the
delegates "not to communicate [it] or any part of it, without leave of
the house."[39] After a month of secret debate, Elbridge Gerry, a delegate from Massachusetts, was asked to revise Morris's handiwork. He
threw out the head tax, the tariff, and the plan for western lands, and
focused on calling in old, depreciated congressional money, hoping
thereby to bolster the value of newer issues. But "every adept in fi-
nanciering," as one congressman put it,[40] went to work on Gerry's report, and in the end, Congress failed even to do that.

Other Americans besides Morris were grappling with the country's
financial problems. One was Philip Schuyler, the New York general
and grandee, who, when he became a congressman the following year,
complained that not one of his colleagues was "adequate to the important business of finance."[41] Another was Alexander Hamilton, now a
colonel on Washington's staff, shortly to be Schuyler's son-in-law, who
was scribbling economic data and ideas in his army pay book. But their
time was not yet. If Congress was a potential national government,
then it would have to get a handle on its financial and structural problems; if it spoke only for an alliance of semiautonomous states, then it
could keep scraping along.

Morris spent more time on issues of foreign policy, which were unavoidable, and which, for the first time during the war, seemed
promising. Since the beginning of the Revolution, the United States
hoped that the enemies of its enemy might become its friends. France,
which had fought Britain four times in the last hundred years, watched
the rebellion with interest, while officially maintaining its neutrality
(Lafayette had left the country and his regiment without permission).
But after Washington's two game battles outside Philadelphia, and

Gates's great victory at Saratoga, Versailles was willing to commit it-self. Rumors of the Franco-American treaty, which had been signed in Paris in early February, reached York in April. If they were true, Morris wrote Jay in one of his winged phrases, then "a spark hath fallen upon the train which is to fire the world." [42]

Britain knew of the treaty before America did. Howe's return to New York was a strategic retrenchment, in preparation for a world war. London also hoped to stifle the Franco-American alliance by offering the rebels generous terms. Parliament surrendered the right to tax the colonies, and sent a three-man peace commission to America, headed by the Earl of Carlisle, a thirty-year-old socialite. Over the spring, summer, and fall, the twenty-six-year-old Morris wrote several official responses to the commission, and a number of essays in the Pennsylvania newspapers, signed "An American," which took a stern view of its offers.

"[T]he principles of your opponents are republican, some indeed aristocratic; the greater part democratic," he lectured, "but all [are] opposed to Kings." He exhorted these opponents to a final effort. "Arise then! To your tents! And gird you for the battle! It is time to turn the headlong current of vengeance upon the head of the destroyer." Britain could be attacked by American agents and raiding parties. "A small sum of money would wrap [London] in flames . . . and the dreaded scalping-knife itself may, in the hands of our riflemen, spread horror through the . . . island." In peace, the United States would rise to greatness. "The portals of the temple we have raised to freedom, shall be thrown wide, as an asylum to mankind. America shall receive to her bosom and comfort and cheer the oppressed, the miserable and the poor of every nation and of every clime." [43]

John Jay wrote, of one of these performances, that it was "strikingly marked with Morris." [44] This was true, and not entirely to his credit. The style that could be so swift and sure in private letters had a tendency to climb on stilts for public performances. Too often, Morris's polemics are high-flying—the temple of freedom—or bombastic—the summons to the tents. Only occasionally does a phrase like "comfort and cheer the oppressed . . . of every clime" express both his

imperial vision and his best personal qualities. His bluster about scalp-
ing knives showed the bloodthirstiness of a civilian (it is impossible to
imagine Washington, who had seen men scalped, writing such stuff).
The analysis of American political opinion showed where Morris
himself stood: the people are included, but republicans and aristocrats
lead the way. Despite his stylistic peculiarities, Morris was the best
Congress then had. "I have drawn and expect to draw," he wrote Livingston in August, "almost if not all the publications of Congress of
any importance."[45]

While Morris flayed the Carlisle commission, he helped plan Con-
gress's official reception of France's first minister, Conrad-Alexandre
Gérard, who arrived in Philadelphia in the flagship of a French fleet in
July. Gérard was received at the cleaned and aerated State House on
August 6, after which Congress and guest repaired to the City Tavern
for twenty-one toasts and a dinner costing $1,424 ($18,000 today).

The benefits of a French alliance were obvious—supplies, money,
troops, and diverting Britain's energy to other theaters. France could
also engage the sympathy of Spain, whose monarch, Charles III, belonged to the same family (the House of Bourbon) as His Most Christian Majesty, Louis XVI. But neither country would help the United
States out of the goodness of its heart. What were their war aims? Did
they match America's? Spain had lost Florida to Britain in the last
round of European conflict; she wanted it back. Spain had gained
Louisiana, the heart of the continent, from France, and intended to
keep it; the arrival of American settlers at Natchez, on the east bank of
the Mississippi, alarmed her. France had lost Canada to Britain. In the
early days of the Franco-American alliance, France proposed a joint
invasion, with an American force attacking Montreal from the south
while a French expedition sailed down the St. Lawrence to besiege
Quebec. Washington vetoed the plan, in a secret letter to Congress,
out of fear that it would succeed all too well: Canada was "attached to
[France] by all the ties of blood, habits, manners, religion and former
connexion of government. I fear this would be too great a temptation,
to be resisted by any power actuated by the common maxims of na-

tional policy."[46] But that still left much else for the new allies to settle among themselves.

Morris discussed America's goals in a private conversation with Gérard in October, and wrote a draft of American war aims for Congress in February 1779. His minimum demands were that an independent United States should stretch from Maine to Georgia on the Atlantic coast, and west to the Mississippi. But beyond these borders he left important American desires unsettled. Frontiersmen depended on navigating the Mississippi, whose spigot, New Orleans, belonged to Spain, while New Englanders counted on fishing the Grand Banks off Newfoundland, the richest waters of the North Atlantic. But Morris let both demands be conditional on trade-offs: to sail the Mississippi, the United States would have to help Spain conquer Florida; to fish the Grand Banks, it would have to waive claims to Nova Scotia. Morris wanted a relatively contained country, which was just what France and Spain wanted. Don Juan de Miralles, who pretended to be a shipwrecked slavetrader but was in fact Spain's unofficial agent in Philadelphia, called Morris "one of the most enlightened voters in Congress and very attached to the cause of the alliance. . . ."[47]

Morris's francophilia was not a legacy of his French heritage (Gérard thought he was Dutch). He wanted the United States to stay compact for its own good. Years later, he admitted that he had been "alarmed" over the vastness of the "Western wilderness, and expressed the wish that some other nation might people it, and by the pressure of foreign force, restrain our domestic feuds."[48] At the time, Gérard wrote home that Morris feared to extend the country westward, lest the frontier be encouraged to stand on its own. "[T]he poverty and vigor of the north were the best safeguards of the republic."[49] Morris's pro-French policy was wrong: the United States would get more out of the alliance by standing up for itself. But his fears of internal animosity were not groundless, as his career would show.

Morris's February 1779 draft of war aims inflamed New England, which tied up Congress for six months debating the status of the fisheries. In the end, Congress decided that while fishing the Grand

Banks was of "the utmost importance," it would not make the right to do so a diplomatic "ultimatum," when the time came to negotiate a peace treaty.[50]

In 1778 and 1779, foreign policy became entangled, as it often does, in domestic squabbles. The bitterest plunged Morris and Congress into a fight between Silas Deane, a diplomat, and Thomas Paine, secretary for the foreign relations committee.

Deane was a Connecticut lawyer who had been a delegate to the First and Second Continental Congresses. He was a man of "plausible readiness and volubility,"[51] as John Adams put it, and Congress sent him to France in 1776 to open undercover negotiations for supplies, even though he did not speak the language. The French government told him to deal with the baron de Beaumarchais, a watchmaker, spy, and playwright who was writing *The Marriage of Figaro* at the time. Beaumarchais ran a dummy company, Rodrigue Hortalez & Company, capitalized by France and Spain, which began funneling muskets and gunpowder to America. Deane stayed in Paris until 1778, when he returned to Philadelphia in the same fleet that brought Gérard.

If Deane expected congratulations for a job well done, he was disappointed. He had won the enmity of Arthur Lee, another American agent in Paris, who happened to be the brother of a congressman. Worse, he and Beaumarchais had drawn commissions on sales of supplies that, Lee charged, were meant to be gifts. As soon as Deane appeared, Congress began to investigate him behind closed doors.

Morris was one of his defenders. Deane, Morris wrote John Jay, "has rendered most essential services." Commissions were an inescapable feature of military procurement in the eighteenth century, and they often shaded into graft. But "many persons" in Congress "are very liberal of illiberality. . . . The storm increases, and I think some of the tall trees must be torn up by the roots."[52]

Deane went public with a self-defense in December 1778. This provoked a public attack at the end of the month by Thomas Paine. Paine's journey through life had been even stranger than Deane's. Born in the bleak and puritanical east of England, Paine had made corsets, cruised on a privateer, preached Methodism, and collected taxes. In 1774, he came to Philadelphia, at age thirty-seven, where he took up a new profession, journalism, and discovered that he was a genius. Paine's pamphlet *Common Sense* (1775), urging the colonies to declare their independence, found 150,000 purchasers in a population of less than 3 million—the equivalent today of a sale of 14 million. *The American Crisis*, a pamphlet written in the grim winter of 1776, achieved immortality:

> These are the times that try men's souls: the summer soldier and the sunshine patriot will, in this crisis, shrink from the service of his country; but he that stands it NOW, deserves the love and thanks of man and woman. Tyranny, like hell, is not easily conquered; yet we have this consolation with us, that the harder the conflict, the more glorious the triumph. What we obtain too cheap, we esteem too lightly:—'Tis dearness only that gives every thing its value. Heaven knows how to set a proper price upon its goods; and it would be strange indeed, if so celestial an article as FREEDOM should not be highly rated.[53]

This was as strong and singing as Morris and Thomas Jefferson at their best, or as Patrick Henry at his most eloquent. The closest parallel to this passage is the speech that Shakespeare gave Henry V on the eve of the Battle of Agincourt—"We few, we happy few, we band of brothers"—except that *The American Crisis* was not written by a playwright two centuries after the fact, but by a journalist on deadline, to be read to cold, desperate soldiers, many of whom would shortly be dead indeed.

Paine had the gifts of a great journalist, and the flaws of a mediocre one. He was slovenly, conceited, and feckless. He quarreled with everyone (though he did not easily hold grudges). He gave all the profits of *The American Crisis* to buy mittens for soldiers, then spent the rest of his life scrambling for pensions and appointments. At the time of his attack on Deane, he was serving as the secretary of the Committee on Foreign Relations.

Writing under his pen name "Common Sense," Paine declared that the French supplies on which Deane had taken commissions were in fact gifts, and he added that he had documents in his office "in handwriting which Mr. Deane is well acquainted with" (i.e., Deane's own) to prove it.[54] Paine had raised the ante: he had publicly revealed that France had helped the United States on the sly, and by offering to produce documents held by the Committee on Foreign Relations, he put the authority of the government behind the revelation. Great powers did many things on the sly, but they wished to keep their doings hidden. Gérard demanded that Congress repudiate Paine.

The quarrel had spiraled beyond the question of Deane's crookedness, to the trustworthiness of the United States as an ally. In the ensuing debate, Morris handled Paine roughly. "And what would be the idea of a gentleman in Europe of this Mr. Paine?" he asked Congress. "Would he not suppose him to be a man of the most affluent fortune, born in this country of a respectable family, with wide and great connexions, and endued with the nicest sense of honor? . . . But, alas, what would he think, should he accidentally be informed, that this, our Secretary of Foreign Affairs, was a mere adventurer *from England,* without fortune, without family or connexions, ignorant even of grammar? . . . And if assured of the fact, and if possessed of common sense"—here Morris mocked Paine's pen name—"would he not think that we were devoid of it?"[55] Morris's efforts to have Paine fired failed, but Paine resigned under his own power.

Historians sometimes treat the fight over Deane as the seed time of American political parties, the conservative revolutionaries defending Deane, the radical ones attacking him.[56] "It gave me great pain," Morris himself said during the debates, "to hear . . . the word *party* made use of. This is a word that can do no good, but which may produce much evil."[57] But the tendencies had been there all along, evident in the different rates at which Americans approached revolutionary action. Morris had seen the tendencies in New York, when he had argued with the Liberty Boys over the British retiring with their armaments, or over the fate of James Rivington, the loyalist printer.

Morris and Paine would have many more dealings, not all of them (surprisingly enough, after that bad start) hostile. This fight had

scarcely died down when Morris was drawn into the whirlpool of
Pennsylvania politics. The state constitution had established a one-
house legislature and a weak executive, in the hope of giving the people a pure and direct voice; Morris called it an "unwieldy mass, badly
jointed."[58] Conservatives, such as Robert Morris and James Wilson, a
young Scottish-born lawyer, wanted a system more like those of other
states, with checks and balances. "Constitutionalists" and "Republicans," as they called themselves, feuded with each other. Meanwhile,
inflation impoverished laborers, who accused the Philadelphia rich of
being gougers and loyalists. The year 1779 was marked with riots, cul-
minating in a battle in front of James Wilson's house that left five men
dead. The Deane/Paine fight had been a culmination of earlier quarrels, but because of the state's size and centrality, the emerging party
system in Pennsylvania would anticipate American politics for the
next twenty years.

Morris tried to keep out of local broils, yet his flamboyant personality made him an attractive target. Joseph Reed, the Pennsylvania congressman he had met at Valley Forge, now in the state government,
raked up his behavior at the inn at Lancaster, and his refusal to surrender the letter of Robert Hooper, the bullying deputy quartermaster, as
symbols of congressional arrogance. Morris managed to soothe Reed
privately ("[I cannot] appear on the public stage against every one who
shall amuse himself with defamation").[59] But while he was protecting
this flank, he became vulnerable on another: his efforts, as chairman of
the Commissary Committee, to supply the French navy with flour, led
local radicals to accuse him of draining off the state's supply. Morris's
enemies, finally, accused him of keeping company with loyalists. If
that meant writing his family, he was clearly guilty.

What ended Morris's congressional career, however, was not fights
in the nation's capital but his own position on a fight at home. For
decades, the colonies of New York and New Hampshire had wrangled
over the mountainous land between Lake Champlain and the Connecticut River. In time, the inhabitants asserted their own claim to it,
calling it Vermont. One of the first victories of the Revolution had
come when Ethan Allen and a party of Green Mountain Boys sur-

prised the sleeping enemy garrison at Fort Ticonderoga. But Allen and his followers were as hostile to the domination of their neighbors as they were to that of Britain. New York State, spurred by rich land speculators, urged Congress to ratify its claim to Vermont. Morris dutifully made the case, but in private he was doubtful. "Vermont is yet Vermont," he wrote Jay, "and I think no wise man will pretend to say when it will cease to be so . . . [T]here are in it some ardent spirits"—the Green Mountain Boys—"whose termigant quality has been too little attended to. Strange that men, in the very act of revolting [i.e., New Yorkers and Congress] should so little consider the temper of revolters [the Green Mountain Boys]. But this is eternally the case."[60]

Morris opposed mobs when they bullied others, but he was reluctant to resist a claim to independence in dubious circumstances. This realism did not endear him to the New York legislature, which met in Poughkeepsie in October 1779 to reelect the state's congressional delegation. Morris was replaced by a politician with the sturdy Huguenot name of Ezra L'Hommedieu.

The arcs of Morris's careers in New York and in Congress reversed each other. At home, he had passed from petty squabbles to writing a constitution. In York and Philadelphia, he had passed from saving a gallant army to petty squabbles. For the moment, he was content to leave public life alone. He was, he wrote Robert Livingston, "no longer that wretched creature, a statesman."[61] Retired at twenty-seven, he settled in Philadelphia, intending to make money and to enjoy himself.

CHAPTER FIVE

Pain and Love

ORRIS HAD BEEN dismissed by his constituents.
John Jay had been sent to Madrid as America's minister to Spain, whence he wrote, in early 1780, a letter
full of solicitude for his friend. "Where is Morris?" he asked New
York's governor George Clinton (no relation to Sir Henry). "Keep him
up. It is a pity that one so capable of serving his country should be unemployed, but there are men who fear and envy his talents and take
ungenerous advantage of his foibles."[1] But Morris was keeping himself up, giving rein to both his talents and his foibles.

Philadelphia lawyers were already proverbial for their skill; Morris's
grandfather had engaged one to defend John Peter Zenger. Now Morris was one. He had taken cases while he was a congressman, arguing
that his salary alone did not cover his expenses or allow him to put
anything by. One case had involved a disputed Pennsylvania election—yet another reason why the local politicians disliked him. Now
he could litigate without the burden of congressional work. Then, as
now, clients were attracted to a counsel with congressional expertise.
Morris also took on Admiralty cases, a family specialty. "[I work] with
a view to eat and drink," he wrote, "without burthening society."[2]

Morris allowed himself the distraction of a social life. In addition to
the parties, dinners, and balls that Philadelphia threw in such profusion, Morris could pay attention to his women friends.

When Morris was a young man, he had courted Kitty Livingston,
and in 1772, when he was twenty, he had told his mentor, William
Smith, in the letter in which he sought advice on whether to visit En-

gland, that he had "naturally a taste for pleasure."[3] In that same year, his cousin, Robert Hunter Morris, wrote him in the following vein: "What in the devil's name is the matter with you? What mistress has jilted you? What whore poxed you?"[4] Talk like his cousin's is the cheap and universal coin of male bragging. It is impossible to tell, from this alone, whether Morris was a profligate or a virgin.

But as he moved through his twenties, the evidence accumulated that he was not the latter. Morris's exchanges of letters with his friends Livingston and Jay, and their letters to each other, assume that Morris is a ladies' man. In February 1778, after Morris arrived in York, he wrote Livingston that there were "no fine women" there.[5] That fall, from Philadelphia, Morris wrote him again: "You say that I have my *Soulagements* [consolations] and I thank you for your wish. I have experienced much pain during my short life," he added, a little tartly, "from being thought to be happier than I was."[6] In the spring of 1779, Jay the Huguenot, in a letter to Livingston, was quite blunt: "Gouverneur is daily employed in making oblations to Venus."[7] That summer, in a letter to Livingston, Morris protested once more, perhaps too much. He was at army headquarters in Middlebrook, in north-central New Jersey, "a dirty village," he pointed out, "where no society can be maintained. . . . The Graces abhor an abode where there is not one Venus to entertain them."[8] There is some teasing in this correspondence, and perhaps, on the part of both the grandee Livingston and the dour Jay, some envy. But the common assumption of all three men is that Morris requires female companionship, and that, given a decent opportunity, he can secure it.

A drawing done of Morris at about this time—the earliest of him that survives—suggests his inclinations, even as it helps explain his success. It is a profile by a Swiss artist, Pierre Eugène du Simitière. It shows a young man with a slightly receding hairline, a sloping forehead, and a large, long nose. He is not classically handsome, but the eye and the mouth redeem all. The eye is large and deepset, and the lashes are very long. The lips are full, especially the lower one. Together, they make an expression that is both lively and dreamy. Morris looks like a man to whom someone is talking, but who is thinking his own thoughts, probably pleasant ones. Women of the twenty-first century who see the picture say they would like to meet the subject.

1780 DISCLOSED the name of a woman Morris loved. She was connected with one of the great catastrophes of his life.

Early in May, Morris planned a visit to the country with Colonel and Mrs. George Plater, a Maryland congressman and his wife. Either in mounting his phaeton, a light, four-wheeled carriage drawn by a pair of horses, or in driving it through the streets, Morris was thrown, and caught his left leg in the spokes of a wheel. The ankle was dislocated and several bones broken. The physicians who attended him (his own was out of town) advised that the leg be amputated. "[W]ith that firmness of mind that accompanies him on all occasions," wrote one acquaintance, he consented "instantly."⁹ Perhaps he was too quick. When Morris's doctor returned to Philadelphia, he offered his opinion that the leg could have been saved.

Morris bore the loss, and the possibility that it was unnecessary, "with becoming fortitude," as Robert Livingston put it.¹⁰ Stories began to crystallize around the disaster. One friend, hoping to buck Morris up, drew the silver lining of losing a leg in such bright colors that Morris supposedly told him, "I am almost tempted to part with the other."¹¹ This sounds like the punch line of a story, very likely told by Morris on himself. The leg was also woven into sexual jokes. When John Jay, off in Madrid, heard about the accident in the fall, he wrote Robert Morris that he wished his friend "had lost *something* else."¹² Later, Jay wrote Gouverneur Morris himself, "I have learned that a certain married woman after much use of your legs had occasioned your losing one." All Morris said in answer to this was that the account was "facetious. Let it pass. The leg is gone, and there is an end of the matter."¹³

But perhaps Morris himself took up Jay's theme. Eleven years later, on another continent, a traveling Englishman, Henry Temple, Viscount Palmerston (father of the prime minister), recorded in his diary that he breakfasted in Paris with "Mr. Morris . . . an American, a gentlemanlike sensible man," who lost a leg "in consequence of jumping from a window in an affair of gallantry." [14] This was the only time Morris and Palmerston met. How had the Englishman learned this version of the story? Almost certainly from his French acquaintances. But who told them? Gossiping Americans, like Jay; or possibly Morris himself, fashioning another punch line. In later years Morris did link his leg with "something else." After flirting with one Frenchwoman, he wondered, in his dairy, if she would consider making an "experiment" with a "native of a New World who has left one of his legs behind him." [15]

In Philadelphia, in 1780, Morris took several months to recover. He spent them in the Philadelphia home of the Platers. George Plater III was a quiet, conventional Maryland planter, active in local politics; two years in the Continental Congress, from 1778 to 1780, were his only service out of state. His wife, Elizabeth Rousby Plater, was delighted to be in the nation's capital—or so it seemed to one French visitor. "Should any stern philosopher be disposed to censor French manners I would not advise him to do so in the presence of Mrs. P***.... [H]er taste is as delicate as her health; an enthusiast to excess for all French fashions, she is only waiting for the end of this little revolution to effect a still greater one in the manners of her country." [16] Colonel Plater was then forty-six years old; his wife was twenty-nine, a year older than Morris.

When Morris almost lost his arm as a boy, he would have been cared for by his mother, helped perhaps by the sisters of whom he was so fond. Now he was recovering in the home of this ardent, sensitive woman. Morris needed her attentions. For the second time in his life he had been maimed. In letters, or in front of visitors, he might armor himself in pleasantries; but his amputation, unlike his burned arm, was a wound he would be unable to conceal. Elizabeth Plater's sympathetic attention must have assured him that the world of women would remain open to him.

The Platers returned to Maryland after the colonel's time in Congress ended; Morris and Mrs. Plater corresponded. His attentions to her seem to have become excessive. In a letter to him of 1782, she speaks of his "sentiments" being what she "would wish them to be," [17] which suggests that they may have been otherwise. Morris's friends knew of his attachment. In a 1783 letter to Morris, Robert Livingston mentioned a rumor about Colonel Plater, asking him if "your friend P——" was "really dead," or if he had "revived in pity to you? [The rumor was false; Plater would go on to be governor of Maryland.] He must certainly know that his death by lessening the sin would lessen your pleasure in loving" Mrs. P——.[18] Morris's friends were not a delicate lot, but Livingston's crack about the nature of Morris's love was a shrewd hit. Morris was grateful for womanly kindness; doubly grateful for the kindness of married women. The love of women pleased and flattered him, as it does every man. But after 1780, whenever a married woman loved him, she proved thereby that he was better than some other man, even a man who was physically whole. Elizabeth Plater was the first in a series of proofs.

In May 1790, almost ten years to the day after his accident, Morris heard another tale of death, this time a true one. He was having dinner in London with an English couple, Mr. and Mrs. Beckford, the latter of whom, in a previous marriage, had lived in Annapolis, Maryland. As Morris was leaving, his hostess told him that Elizabeth Plater had died. "I get away as soon as possible," he wrote in his diary, "that I may not discover emotions which I cannot conceal. Poor Eliza! My lovely friend; thou art then at peace and I shall behold thee no more. Never. Never. Never."[19] This is what Lear says when he holds dead Cordelia in his arms. Morris never wrote like this, or admitted to emotions that he could not conceal. Only Elizabeth Plater had stirred this in him.

Morris had himself fitted with an oaken peg, and though he would later experiment with false legs of copper and cork, he stuck with wood for the rest of his life. Except for an occasional slip in the mud or on stairs, or a tingling in his stump, he was not slowed down, physically or socially. He walked, danced, rode, climbed church steeples, and shot river rapids on his peg. It added to his chic—the fancier the surroundings, the greater the chic. "[D]omestics know not what to make of me, a thing which frequently happens at my first approach, because the simplicity of my dress and equipage, my wooden leg and tone of republican equality, seem totally misplaced at [a] levee. . ."[20] Misplaced maybe, but so cool. The line of the peg would have made Morris, a tall man, seem even taller, especially since he carried himself well. "Few men ever equaled his commanding bearing," wrote a doctor who knew him late in life. "[H]is superb physical organization enlisted attention."[21] He made the most of what he had, and what he had, even minus a leg, was impressive.

Once, Morris recalled his wound with a twinge. Peeling off his stocking one night after dinner in Vienna, he found that he had been wearing it inside out. "I remember to have heard, when young, that this portended good luck, and I remember also that, having gone out one morning early I broke my shin before I got back, and in taking down the stocking to look at it found it was wrong side outward. I bear the mark of that misfortune to this hour, a memento not to believe in such sayings."[22]

By the fall of 1780, Morris could report to Livingston that he had returned "to the beau monde." There followed the obligatory jest: "little then have the beau monde to rejoice," for they were acquiring "a wooden member."[23] Morris poor-mouthed himself, for they were acquiring a source of life. The same Frenchman who had noticed Mrs. Plater found Morris "a young man full of wit and vivacity."[24] Another Frenchman, the marquis de Barbé-Marbois, a diplomat, described Morris in action at a picnic in Chester, in the countryside outside Philadelphia. "We laughed, we drank champagne . . . in a word, this party was like all those of its kind, and I should not speak of it to you but for a little incident which amused me. . . . Governor [sic] Morris, whom the champagne had apparently made pretty drunk, got into a little sulky," a two-wheeled, one-man carriage. But "Mrs. Bingham, a young and pretty woman, took it into her head to get in with him." Anne Willing had been sixteen years old in 1780, when she married William Bingham, twenty-eight. Mr. Bingham had made a fortune in the Caribbean; Mrs. Bingham was as determined as Mrs. Plater to be a social success, and as a lively, rich young Philadelphian was even better placed to do so. "You must know," the marquis went on, "that Govérnér [sic] Morris had once lost a leg in driving a gig, and that that fact was not calculated to reassure Mr. Bingham." There were other facts about Morris that were not calculated to reassure Mr. Bingham. Too drunk to follow them himself, he "begged the fastest of the group to run after his wife and to tell her to get down out of the carriage. . . . The messenger succeeded in stopping the sulky in which Mrs. Bingham was, and he requested her to get out. She refused. 'Madam, it is your husband's command.' . . . Mrs. Bingham called and waved good-bye, whipped up the horse, and continued the journey. . . ."[25]

The marquis de Barbé-Marbois must have liked what he saw of American women, for he married one. The June wedding was cele-brated by three days of dinners, at which Morris shone again. Peggy Chew, one of the bridesmaids, wrote a girlfriend that "Govr. Morris kept us in a continual smile (I dare not say laughter for all the world [outright laughing was considered indecorous behavior in young ladies, almost as bad as riding off in a sulky] but you may admit it in the back room)." Morris would bring many smiles to dinners, car-riages, and back rooms.

CHAPTER SIX

Convulsion Deferred

W HEN MORRIS was in Congress, he had concerned himself with what the United States and France hoped to get out of their war. Before they could get anything, though, they had to win, and for years nothing went well. In 1779, a French fleet and an American army tried to drive the British from Newport, Rhode Island, and failed. The following year saw Arnold's treason, and the enemy's sudden conquest of everything south of Virginia. Congress, powerless to do much else, reorganized itself by establishing extracongressional offices for War, Foreign Relations, and Finance.

Morris made notes to himself, in his retirement, describing the ideal occupants of such posts. The minister of foreign affairs should be a man of solid "circumstances and connexions"—no more Deanes on the take. This was a description of Morris's friend, Robert Livingston, who got the job, though Morris also injected a good deal of himself in the portrait: "a genius quick, lively, penetrating"; a temper "festive, insinuating"; able to "write on all occasions with clearness and perspicuity."[1] The ideal minister of finances was easier to draw: "a regular bred merchant," who was also "practically acquainted with our political affairs."[2] That described only one man in America, and he was Morris's, and everyone's choice for the job: Robert Morris.

Robert Morris had come to America in 1747, at the age of thirteen, from Liverpool, and was apprenticed to a small Philadelphia merchant house run by the Willing family. By 1775, he was the senior partner, and the firm was doing business in London, Lisbon, Madrid, and the

West Indies. Like Gouverneur Morris, he came around to the cause of independence by deliberate stages; when he did, he expressed his convictions in a businessman's phrase: "I am content to run all hazards."[3] After the war began, he replaced his English business with French, and branched out into tobacco, indigo, privateering, and speculation. A large, friendly, fat man, he believed in living well for its own sake, and as a form of self-advertisement; his claret was "of a quality rarely to be met with in America" and his Philadelphia mansion a "temple . . . erected to hospitality."[4] From 1775 to 1778, he served in the Continental Congress, where he specialized in finance and procurement. His business and the nation's were often commingled—to his profit, his enemies alleged. The commingling also benefited the nation: on the eve of the Battle of Trenton, a desperate Washington asked Morris for funds. Morris, out of his own pocket, sent $50,000 (paper) for the troops, and a bag of gold for spies.

Gouverneur and Robert Morris were well suited to be partners. Thinkers who pride themselves on their realism often admire successful businessmen; men of business appreciate industry and intelligence, especially when they are sweetened by good humor and made unthreatening by youth. Their relationship was captured, in a joint portrait, by the Philadelphia artist Charles Willson Peale. Robert Morris stands beside a table, to the right and slightly in front of his partner, as befits his seniority and his wealth. His eyes, which look directly at the viewer, are bright and shrewd; his ample waistcoat conveys solidity. Gouverneur Morris, who sits beside him, is leaning slightly, at an angle of one o'clock. He looks out into the space beyond the right edge of the painting, and smiles. The bottom of his cravat lies carelessly over his waistcoat (Robert Morris's is smoothly tucked down). Gouverneur Morris is the confident, possibly wayward assistant; Robert Morris is the rock. In later years, Gouverneur would prove to be superior in judgment and dependability, as Robert fell by the wayside; but now they made a potent team, with Robert in the lead. When Robert Morris took office as superintendent of finance in May 1781, Gouverneur accepted his offer to be his assistant with a prediction that Robert would save America's finances. "[C]onsequently, malice will blacken

and envy traduce you. I will freely share in this bitter portion of eminence."[5]

The grim state of American finances in 1781 had been years in the
making. A modern economic historian, Clarence Ver Steeg, has laid out
the facts.[6] The United States had raised $1.6 million in foreign loans and
$4 million by requisitions, the feeble substitute for taxation. (Congress
had no power to tax the states; it could only make requisitions on them,
which they paid as they were able, or willing.) Domestic loans—bonds
and IOUs—had raised $20 million; $37 million—almost three fifths of
the whole—had been raised by bills of credit, or paper money. The
United States had financed a war with printing presses, and inflation
was the inevitable result. In March 1780, Congress tried to yank the
reins by issuing new bills of credit, each dollar of which was worth forty
old dollars. But the new dollars, unbacked by any resources, began to inflate away in turn. Since most Americans were farmers, who could
tighten their belts and provide for themselves, they did not suffer as
badly as these figures might suggest. But the credit of Congress was exhausted, and with it, its ability to wage war. Looking at the red ink, even
America's French allies hesitated to offer further loans.

"If you see the doctor," Gouverneur Morris wrote his new boss
gratefully, "tell him that fatiguing from four in the morning till eight in
the evening, and sleeping only from eleven till three agrees with me
much better than all the prescriptions in . . . the world."[7] The Morrises
had much work to do. Their first step was to found a national bank.
"Money is of too subtle and spiritual a nature," Gouverneur Morris
wrote, "to be caught by the rude hand of the law."[8] Efforts to create it
out of thin air, by printing it, or to fix its value, by price controls, would
backfire. The Morrises proposed a Bank of North America, capitalized at $400,000 ($5.2 million today), to encourage economic activity.
The bank would issue its own notes, which would then become a us-
able currency. Congress approved the plan in May, and a timely loan of
a quarter of a million dollars of French silver in the fall helped make up
the capital. When the Bank opened, it employed every means to win
investor confidence. Bank employees paraded containers full of silver
coins from the vaults to the cashiers to show how well funded the

Bank was. At the same time, Robert Morris set himself up as a bank, signing notes issued by the Office of Finance in $20, $50, and $80 denominations. Robert Morris's name carried such clout that the "Morris notes" circulated as cash. Finally, in the manner of all desperate enterprises, the Finance Office shifted its debts among its creditors like peas in a shell game. William Graham Sumner, the nineteenth-century economist and a great admirer of Robert Morris's, called it "the most vulgar kind of bill-kiting."[9] There were "many contrivances to rescue our finances from ruin," Gouverneur Morris admitted years later.[10]

As the summer of 1781 ended, the Morrises heard a rumor, and received a distress call. A French fleet was sailing to American waters, for a joint operation (the target was evidently Virginia, where the British army in the south was now fighting), but if Washington's troops did not get a month's pay, they would quit. The Morrises learned that the approaching French fleet had currency aboard; could they borrow it? The French navy needed the approval of the French army; the relevant official was in Maryland. The Morrises rode south to find him (Gouverneur would act as translator, since Robert knew no French), but on their way they were caught by a messenger who told them that the fleet had landed, and the loan was approved. The Morrises turned north, to go back to Philadelphia, and found the road blocked by French troops marching in the opposite direction, to Yorktown.

Seven weeks later, word reached Philadelphia of Cornwallis's surrender. On November 3, the Morrises joined the French minister at a *Te Deum* to celebrate the victory. As they left, they saw the British colors being paraded to Independence Hall. The occasion was "solemn and awful," as the official diary of the Finance Office (probably written by Gouverneur) put it. In unusual words for a Treasury document, the diarist offered a prayer to "thee, Oh Lord God, who hath vouchsafed to rescue from slavery and from death these thy servants."[11]

The war in North America was almost certainly over (fighting continued in the West Indies). But until a peace treaty was negotiated, the United States would need to keep its army in the field, watching the

British, who still occupied New York. Thanks to hard work, luck, and sleight of hand, the Morrises had financed the Yorktown campaign. But now the larder was truly bare.

The Morrises tried new contrivances. They angled for a loan from Spain; John Jay warned them that Madrid had "little money, less wisdom" and "no credit."[12] They hoped that the war would drag on—not on American soil, but in the Caribbean, where France and Spain were seeking spoils and might pay for American help. In December 1781, they began holding Monday night meetings with Livingston; Benjamin Lincoln, the minister of war; George Washington, the commander in chief; and Charles Thomson, the secretary of Congress, for the purpose of "consulting and concerting measures to promote the . . . public good."[13] This informal "cabinet" sought to give the government some executive cohesion, but it was also interested in lobbying for political and financial reform. For this purpose, Robert Morris turned to Gouverneur Morris's old target, Thomas Paine, who was as broke as the government and eager to be of help. Paine met with both Morrises; Gouverneur, he wrote, "hopped round upon one leg."[14] For $800 a year (about $10,000 today), Paine agreed to write articles "informing the people and rousing them into action."[15] His stipend was kept secret, for, as Gouverneur Morris delicately put it, "a salary publickly and avowedly given . . . would injure the effect of Mr. Paine's publications."[16]

One project that consumed much of Morris's time and ingenuity, though it had little effect, was his plan for a new currency. America's was chaotic. English tokens and Spanish and Portuguese coins all circulated, and each state had different rates of exchange. When he sat down to address this problem, he made two preliminary decisions: the United States should have a decimal system; and its basic unit should be of small value, to convert all the competing currencies into each other without remainders. The basic unit he picked—1/4 of a grain of silver (1/1,750 of an ounce)—was so tiny, however, that values expressed in it seemed huge. The Spanish dollar or piece of eight, the most common coin in the New World, was worth 1,440 of Morris's "quarters." Morris's mathematical skill had led him astray; in the pursuit of precision, his system had become too complex. A few years later, Congress adopted a different decimal system, proposed by Thomas Jefferson, dividing the American dollar (roughly equal to the Spanish one) into 100 cents. Americans would use fractions of dollars and small Spanish coins for decades, as they tried to assign the proper value to items in Jefferson's simpler but cruder scheme. An eighth of a dollar was a bit, which survives in the phrase "two bits"; a sixteenth of a dollar was a picayune, which survives in the name of the *New Orleans Times-Picayune*. But the rough and ready system finally took hold.[17]

In July 1782, the Finance Office issued a report, written by Gouverneur Morris, that was far more important. The Morrises proposed that the United States go to the market once again, with a new issue of loan certificates for investors. These bonds would pay 6 percent interest. They would be backed, not by requisitions on the states or by foreign loans, but by revenues (some of them adopted from Gouverneur Morris's reports to Congress in 1778): a 5 percent tariff on imports; a land tax of one dollar per 100 acres; a head tax of one dollar; and an excise tax of 12 1/2 cents (one bit) per gallon of liquor.

"With money," Morris wrote Jay, "we can do every thing."[18] Some of what he wanted to do was obvious: pay the army; pay the interest on the national debt; establish the credit of the United States. Every responsible person shared these goals. But Morris also envisioned a goal that few shared: a national government, based on the finance system. Congress's "ministers," he wrote, "have the arduous task before them, to govern without power, nay, more, to obtain the power necessary to govern."[19] A funded debt, with taxes and tax collectors, would create that power.

High hopes gave way to desperation, however, as 1782 wound down. Though Morris's report was approved by a congressional committee, Congress as a whole would not enact it. First Rhode Island, then Virginia vetoed the proposal for a 5 percent tariff (such a radical change to the Articles of Confederation required the unanimous approval of all thirteen states). The most Congress would do was ask the states for $1.2 million, to scrape by with interest payments. Jay reported to Congress that all they could expect from Spain was "delay,

chicane and slight."[20] "[O]nly . . . a continuance of the war," Morris
wrote, would "convince the people of the necessity of obedience to
common counsels for general purposes."[21] But France had lost a major
naval battle in the West Indies, and Britain wanted to settle. Clearly,
the war was drawing to a close.

At the end of the year Washington's army went into winter quarters
at Newburgh, New York, fifty miles up the Hudson from New York
City. Now a new fear began to possess the officers—that when peace
arrived, they would be sent home without pay, and only the flimsiest of
IOUs. On December 29, a delegation of three officers, including
Colonel Matthias Ogden, one of Morris's New Jersey in-laws, appeared in Philadelphia to make their case to Congress. The army's un-
happiness filled the Morrises with hope. If the army joined the call for
reform, something might be done.

"The army have swords in their hands," Morris wrote Jay on New
Year's Day, 1783. "You know enough of the history of mankind to
know much more than I have said, and possibly much more than they
themselves yet think of." In other words, if the army were rebuffed, it
could march; if it was not "yet" considering such an option, helpful
friends might suggest it. ". . . I am glad to see things in their present
train. Depend on it, good will arise from the situation to which we are
hastening. And this you may rely on, that my efforts will not be wanting . . . [A]lthough I think it probable, that much of convulsion will
ensue, yet it must terminate in giving to government that power, without which government is but a name."[22]

The army did not see it that way. In February, Morris wrote to
Henry Knox, Washington's artillery commander, at Newburgh, and to
Nathanael Greene, who was commanding the army of the south in
South Carolina. "[A]fter a peace," he wrote Knox, Congress "will see
you starve rather than pay you a six-penny tax."[23] "[W]ith the due exception of miracles," he wrote Greene, "there is no probability that the
states" would ever pay the army, "unless the army be united and determined in the pursuit of it."[24] Knox asked the obvious question: if "the
present constitution is so defective, why do not you great men call the
people together and tell them so?"[25] The military man was telling the

politician: Don't ask the army to do your work for you. Greene gave the obvious warning: "When soldiers advance without authority, who can halt them?"[26]

In early March, the political problem came to the attention of another officer, General Horatio Gates, once the hero of Saratoga, but now disgraced by defeat in the South. The young officers on his staff at Newburgh, where he was posted, saw an opportunity to help both their chief and the army, and they circulated an anonymous call to action. "If this, then, be your treatment while the swords you wear are necessary for the defense of America, what have you to expect from peace . . . [w]hen those very swords . . . shall be taken from your sides?"[27] It is now agreed that the author of the Newburgh appeal was Major John Armstrong, Jr., an aide of Gates's, though Morris had been so associated with stirring the army up that he was long suspected. It took all the authority, the dramatic presence, and the melancholy humanity of George Washington—for it was in Newburgh at a meeting of the sullen officers that, as he read them an appeal to do their duty, he paused and said, "Gentlemen, you will permit me to put on my spectacles, for I have not only grown gray but almost blind in the service of my country"[28]—to turn the army aside from its course.

Morris's actions in the early months of 1783 were folly that (no thanks to him) only just fell short of disaster, and his January 1 letter to Jay is among the worst things he ever wrote. How could such an admirer of George Washington have behaved so unlike him? Surely his civilian's ignorance is implicated in his airy talk of convulsion and swords, though there were also veterans of the battlefield who were willing to play with these materials. Another explanation—it cannot be an excuse—is that Morris's work, from 4:00 A.M. to 8:00 P.M. at the Finance Office, was not only fatiguing but mentally narrowing. For a year and a half he had been studying public life through the prism of America's financial problems. These were crippling, and potentially fatal. But solving them would require a better grasp of military and political affairs than either Gouverneur or Robert Morris, for all their knowledge of the world, showed. There is something, finally, in Morris's conduct in the run-up to Newburgh that is not unlike his proposal to base the currency on a quarter grain of silver. He could fall in love with his ideas, and he could carry them too far. This was a vice of his fertile mind, his social station, and his family background: the lords of Morrisania, who built boats in the woods and wore loon-skin caps, were not always the best models for a statesman.

In justice to the plotters, they did not continue to scheme and murmur. They had not intended to establish a military dictatorship, they had only chosen one of the worst possible ways to reform a republic. Also to their credit is the fact that they were right about Congress. Congress agreed to replace all previous pension plans with an offer of five years' full pay, but since the national government had no dependable source of revenue, the pledge was a sham.

In justice to Morris, when only a few months had passed, he showed a mellow hopefulness. "True it is," he wrote John Jay, who was then in Paris, "that the general government wants energy, and equally true it is, that this want will eventually be supplied. A national spirit is the natural result of national existence. . . . [T]his generation will die away and give place to a race of Americans."[29] Morris always wrote well; he had turned from poisonous phrases back to wise and generous ones.

$\mathcal{I}$N JUNE 1783, Morris saw Morrisania and his mother for the first time in seven years. Sarah Morris was ailing; his sister Isabella and her husband, Isaac Wilkins, were preparing, along with many other loyalists, to move to Nova Scotia. The estate, which was still behind British lines, was in a sad condition. British soldiers had taken cattle and cleared timber, and a loyalist regiment commanded by Colonel Oliver DeLancey (hereditary rival of the Morrises) had camped on the property for two years. Morris added up the damage and presented a bill to Sir Guy Carleton, the British commander in New York, for £8,000 (about $300,000 today). Carleton approved the charges, and it was sent to General Staats Long Morris in England to collect. (He ultimately got £1,341, or about $50,000.) Happily, the British had not touched the wine. "[W]e drank your health in Cape wine," Morris wrote the superintendent of finance, "which has stood on a shelf in this house twenty years to my knowledge, and how much longer I know not."[30]

As peace approached, he resumed contact with his long-suffering friend Peter Van Schaak. The cautious and thorough Van Schaak had been living in exile in Britain, where he had profited from the virtues of his vices. This moderate man who could not believe that British policies, however arbitrary or damaging, were the result of willful indifference or a design to oppress, had—by attending debates in Parliament and following arguments in the press—become convinced that Britain and its leaders were indeed willful and oppressive. His thoughts turned to his home. Morris welcomed him back: "My own heart, worn by the succession of objects which have invaded it, looks back with more than female fondness towards the connections of earlier days."[31] Van Schaak returned to New York in 1785. After so many harrowing years, he resumed his practice as a lawyer, remarried and had a second family, and, like the restored Job, lived out the rest of a long life in peace.

Morris's heart may have been stirred by memories, and by the sight of his old home. But the sorry condition of the estate, and the even worse condition of New York City—haggard, partly burned, its population shaken by the alternating flight and influx of patriots and loyalists as the fortunes of war shifted—determined him to stay in Philadelphia. He needed to make money, and that was the city where it could be made.

Morris gave up his job in the Finance Office, and went to work for Robert Morris as a private junior partner. Gouverneur Morris began to play the great American sport of land speculation, buying 2,800 acres in Pennsylvania, and, with Robert Morris's help, a slice of a 100,000-acre tract in upstate New York. When Robert Morris contracted with the French government to supply it with Virginia tobacco, Gouverneur Morris went to Virginia as his lawyer to untangle the legal problems (a "tedious disagreeable business").[32] Robert Morris bought him a share in a partnership with the merchant William Constable, son of an Irish surgeon in the British army, who had been educated in Dublin and Schenectady, New York; spent most of the war doing business in British-occupied cities; then discovered patriotism just in time to escape reprisal for having been a loyalist. Some of Morris's new business contacts would fail, and some had been scoundrels; they were all trying to figure out how to make money in the post-revolutionary world, and Morris would wheel and deal alongside them for years.

He did not abandon all interest in politics. In 1785 the Constitutionalists, the radical party in Pennsylvania politics, launched an attack on the Bank of North America, drawing on rural resentment of Philadelphia, and populist resentment of rich men, though many rich men, who wished to set up a second bank, aided in the assault. Those old enemies, Morris and Paine, leaped to the Bank's defense, each employing his characteristic tone of voice. Paine's pieces in the newspapers were clear and intense polemics, propelled by simple, striking images. "The proceedings on this business are a stain to the national reputation of the state. They exhibit a train of little and envious thinking, a scene of passion, of arbitrary principles and unconstitutional conduct. . . . As blood, tho' taken from the arm, is nevertheless taken from the whole body, so the attempt to destroy the bank [would] distress the farmer as well as the merchant."[33] Morris delivered a 10,000-word oration before the Philadelphia Assembly, which managed to make economics amusing:

> A grievous complaint is made of the want of money, and yet as grievous a complaint of the only means to obtain any. We have it not at home, and we must not receive it from abroad [that is, by encouraging foreign investors]. Do these gentlemen believe it will rain money now, as it did manna of old? And because they have the same perverseness with the children of Israel, do they expect the same miracles? To experience a want of public credit is, they say, terrible; but to destroy the only means of supporting public credit is, they say, desirable.[34]

The fight over the Bank sputtered on for several years.

In January 1786, Sarah Morris died, age seventy-two. The war had been a strain on her estate and her family, and the much older breach between herself and her stepchildren had never entirely closed. Two months before her death, Richard Morris sued her over her management of the estate. But she had held on to her home and her opinions through everything.

The heir of Sarah's portion of Morrisania was her husband's second oldest son, Staats Long Morris. But he was firmly ensconced in England, a lieutenant general in the British army and a member of Parliament. He would come back to America to dispose of his affairs, but he had no intention of transplanting himself. Richard Morris was interested in money, not land. Lewis Morris, the manor lord, had already inherited his portion of the estate, and was content with it. That left Gouverneur. After long delays, occasioned by Staats's slow progress—he did not arrive in New York until September—and by Richard's stubbornness in maintaining his suit, the Morrises finally came to terms in April 1787. Gouverneur bought the estate from Staats and paid off Staats's obligations, as heir, to Richard and the daughters. These transactions cost him £10,000 ($390,000 today). He could pay a quarter of that out of his own inheritance from his mother. But the remainder had been loaned him by William Constable and his new Philadelphia associates. Morris was not lord of a manor, but he had 1,400 acres, with river views. To keep it, and to keep himself in Cape wine, he would have to continue working at his many ventures.

CHAPTER SEVEN

Secure the Blessings

A BIT OF PUBLIC business lay on Morris's schedule, however. Without asking for it, he had been elected a delegate to the Constitutional Convention.

The Pennsylvania Assembly had chosen him for the state's delegation while he was out of town, celebrating the New Year in Trenton, New Jersey. Morris had been living in Pennsylvania for not quite nine years, and some complained that he had "no stake in their hedge."[1] The criticism of his rootlessness rang false, since Pennsylvania had a tradition of being kind to outlanders; of the original seven-man delegation, four besides Morris were from somewhere else: England (Robert Morris), Scotland (James Wilson), Ireland (Thomas Fitzsimons), and Connecticut (Jared Ingersoll). In the spring, the Assembly added an eighth delegate, the greatest of all transplants, Benjamin Franklin of Boston.

Morris had to know that large political forces were afoot. George Washington was calling for interstate cooperation on canal building, to develop the trans-Appalachian west; Henry Knox had been sounding the alarm over Shays's Rebellion, an uprising of hard-pressed farmers in western Massachusetts; Alexander Hamilton had drafted the call for a Constitutional Convention at a 1786 meeting in Annapolis. But Morris had not involved himself in any of these projects or controversies. He had made his best effort for reform in the Finance Office; the denouement of Newburgh represented a rejection of his efforts. But now he was called upon to try again. "The appointment was the most unexpected thing that ever happened to me," he wrote Knox. "Had the object been any other than it is I would have declined."[2]

Pennsylvania, the host state, chose a large and distinguished delegation. Franklin was a world celebrity; Robert Morris was the money man
of the continent; James Wilson had established a reputation as a political thinker. William Pierce, a delegate from Georgia who wrote vivid
and generally accurate sketches of all his colleagues (he commonly mis-
reported their ages), wrote this panegyric: "Government seems to have
been [Wilson's] peculiar study, all the political institutions of the world
he knows in detail, and can trace the causes and effects of every revolution from the earliest stages of the Grecian commonwealth down to the
present time."[3] The only delegation that matched Pennsylvania's in lus-
ter and depth was the seven-man team from Virginia, led by the young
governor, Edmund Randolph; two senior theorists, George Mason and
Thomas Jefferson's teacher, George Wythe; and one young and even
more brilliant theorist, James Madison. Madison, a year older than
Morris, was small, sober, and driven; at first blush he could seem prig-
gish. He sped through the college of New Jersey at Princeton in two
years, then suffered a nervous collapse, and he lost his first race for the
Virginia House of Burgesses when he would not treat the voters to
drinks. In a committee setting, however, his energy, his thoroughness,
and his immense learning made him a compelling force. After hours,
he revealed a taste for off-color stories. Greatest of the Virginians was
the greatest man in America, George Washington. In the Convention
as a whole there were eight signers of the Declaration of Independence,
including Robert Morris, Franklin, Wilson, and Wythe. Some famous
Americans, notably Samuel Adams and Patrick Henry, stayed home,
while others were otherwise occupied (John Adams was minister to
Great Britain, and Jefferson was minister to France). But the Convention had many ornaments, much solidity, and only a few ciphers.

Judged by his record alone, Morris ranked with the solid rather than
the glittering. At thirty-five, he was among the younger delegates, al-
though he was not, as he had been at Kingston, one of the youngest.
The junior member in Philadelphia was twenty-seven-year-old
Jonathan Dayton of New Jersey (twenty-nine-year-old Charles
Pinckney of South Carolina told everyone that he was twenty-four).
Morris had been selected because the resurgent Republican Party in

Pennsylvania appreciated his talents; even so, he had won only a bare majority of votes in the state Assembly (Franklin and Robert Morris had been elected unanimously). If Gouverneur Morris was to shine in Philadelphia, it would have to be through a special display of his talents on the spot.

Happily, one of his talents was public speaking. Morris was both an orator and an arguer; he could paint a glowing picture, or jab a rival in the gut. These gifts, augmented by his stature and his intelligence, made him a formidable force. William Pierce's portrait of him repeats what had by now become the traditional criticism—"he is fickle and inconstant, never pursuing one train of thinking, nor ever regular"—but wraps it in high, if somewhat alarmed, praise. "He winds through all the mazes of rhetoric, and throws around him such a glare that he charms, captivates, and leads away the senses of all who hear him. With an infinite stretch of fancy he brings to view things when he is engaged in deep argumentation that render all the labor of reasoning easy and pleasing." A good teacher, or a serpent in the garden? Pierce didn't seem to be quite sure. "No man," he concluded, "has more wit, nor can any one engage the attention more than Mr. Morris."[4] James Madison, who took the most complete notes of any delegate, and who posted himself in front of the presiding officer's chair the better to listen, wrote more soberly that "the correctness of [Morris's] language and the distinctness of his enunciation were particularly favorable to a reporter."[5]

The states had answered the call for a Convention, out of the same sense of urgency that had dogged Morris when he went to work for the Finance Office in 1781, or when he took his seat in Congress in 1778: the urgency arising from the United States's failure to cope with its debts. Urgency had become almost routine. The war had been won on loans and luck; a mutiny had been averted with an IOU; but still the government had no dependable source of revenue. Many of the state governments were as badly off: the farmers of Massachusetts had been driven to rebellion by property taxes levied to pay the state's crushing debt. On the bourses of Antwerp and Amsterdam, the money men of Europe traded American securities at a third to a quarter of their face value. The Thirteen Colonies were the first in the world to win independence, but the United States, despite its resources and the industry of some its citizens, was in a fair way to becoming the first Third World nation. The Convention offered itself as a last chance for reform. "[T]he fate of America," as Morris later put it, "was suspended by a hair."[6]

Morris got off to a false start. The Convention, which had been called to meet in mid-May, had a quorum by May 25. Franklin planned to nominate Washington to chair the proceedings, maintaining the symbiosis of their celebrity, but rain kept the eighty-one-year-old man at home, and Robert Morris made the motion in his place, which passed unanimously. Six days later, Gouverneur Morris left town. Business drew him away from the nation's business. A new estate manager at Morrisania required instructions, and one of William Constable's agents had arrived in New York from Europe with the news that their partner Robert Morris's bills were being protested (in effect, his checks were bouncing). America might be hanging by a hair, but Gouverneur Morris spent all of June tending to these matters. Morris was not the only absentee. Delegates came late, left early, or went away for weeks at a time, to nurse illnesses, tend their personal affairs (Pierce, who called Morris inconstant, himself left at the end of June in an effort to stave off bankruptcy), or register their disapproval of the goings-on. Alexander Hamilton of New York stayed away for two months because he despaired of real change; Robert Yates and John Lansing, Jr., the other delegates from New York, left for good in July because they believed the changes that had been approved were too drastic. Morris was back in his seat by July 2, however, ready for work.

He returned at a moment of drama, for the Convention, as Roger Sherman of Connecticut said, was "at a full stop."[7] The issue in its path was the ongoing power and influence of the states. Nearly all of the delegates wanted a government with greater powers, independent of the states, which over the years had withheld requisitions and vetoed the most modest taxes. But how was a stronger national government to be chosen? How would the states be represented in it? Wilson and Madison, the most aggressive minds of Pennsylvania and Virginia, wanted a Congress based on proportional representation, which would shrink the voice of the small states almost to nothing (Virginia and Pennsylvania, the largest, were nine times as populous as Delaware, the smallest). The small states pushed back, insisting that at least one house of Congress be organized as Congress was under the Articles of Confederation, with all states voting as equal units. Two days before Morris returned, Gunning Bedford, Jr., of Delaware, a young, angry fat man—"a bold and nervous speaker," wrote Pierce, "warm and impetuous in his temper"[8]—warned that if the large states changed the principle of representation, "the small ones will find some foreign ally of more honor and good faith." Bedford's threat, delivered on a Saturday, must have been the talk of the delegates all the following week; but Morris, who had tangled with everyone from his dearest friends to Thomas Paine, was not intimidated. "This country must be united," he observed on Thursday, July 5. "If persuasion does not unite it, the sword will."[9] Four of the next five speakers grappled with Morris's sword, either trying to draw it or to twist it deeper.

This sally displayed a quality of Morris's that the delegates would become accustomed to over the next two and a half months: his ability to provoke, and his delight in doing so, whenever anyone showed an arrogance equal to his own. At the end of August, the Convention examined another sore spot, the slave trade. The Carolinas and Georgia, where mortality was higher than it was along the Chesapeake, depended on the traffic to refresh their slave labor force. Most of the delegates, though, northerners and southerners alike, were too humane to proclaim what they permitting, and so the relevant clause then on the floor was wrapped in cotton wool: the "importation of such persons as the several states . . . shall think proper to admit, shall not be prohibited."[10] Morris offered an amendment: the "importation of slaves into North Carolina, South Carolina, and Georgia shall not be prohibited. . . ." This little change, he said, "would be most fair and would avoid the ambiguity. . . . He wished it to be known also that this part of the Constitution was a compliance with those states." With offensive tact, he added that if his language "should be objected to . . . he should not urge it."[11] After two piqued southerners and two anxious northerners shushed him, Morris withdrew his motion.

The Convention tolerated such a man because he was as amusing as he was annoying. He may never have slapped Washington on the back, but he was not afraid to poke fun at Franklin. During a discussion of term limits for the executive, the sage, in a pious mood, declared that "[I]n free governments the rulers are the servants, and the people their superiors.... For the former therefore to return among the latter was not to *degrade* but to *promote* them." To which Morris only remarked that "he had no doubt our executive" would be modest enough "to decline the promotion." [12] On another occasion, Elbridge Gerry of Massachusetts, earnest and crotchety, warned against letting the vice president preside over the Senate. "The close intimacy that must subsist between the president and vice-president makes it absolutely improper." "The vice president then will be the first heir apparent that ever loved his father," said Morris. [13]

These were sly hits at republican cant, and human nature. Sometimes he indulged in broad comedy. Early in August, Morris proposed that foreign-born Americans be citizens for fourteen years before they could serve in the Senate. A lively argument followed, with Wilson, the Scot, opposing such a long residency requirement, while Pierce Butler of South Carolina, an Irishman, supported it. Morris spoke up again, in the name, he said, of "prudence. It is said that some tribes of Indians carried their hospitality so far as to offer to strangers their wives and daughters. Was this a proper model for us? He would admit [immigrants] to his house, he would invite them to his table, [he] would provide for them comfortable lodgings; but would not carry complaisance so far as to bed them with his wife." [14] The delegates' accounts of the Constitutional Convention are interesting, but they are not light reading; most of what lightness there is comes from Morris.

Madison, the careful reporter, occasionally checked his notes of long and controversial speeches with their speakers. One such effort was a "very extravagant" speech of Morris's, probably one of his tangles with Bedford over representation. "It displayed," wrote Madison, "his usual fondness for saying things and advancing doctrines that no one else would.... [W]hen the thing *stared him in the face* (this was Mr. Morris's exact expression) ... he laughed and said, 'Yes, it is all right.'" [15]

Morris spoke 173 times at the Convention, more often than any other member, despite the fact that he missed all of June. Wilson, who spoke 168 times, and Madison, who spoke 161, placed and showed, even though they attended every session. What things, peculiar to himself, did Morris say?

Morris was a passionate nationalist. He had come "as a representative of America";[16] to "form a compact for the good of America."[17] "Among the many provisions which had been urged, he had seen none for supporting the dignity and splendor of the American empire."[18] There were other nationalists at the Convention: Madison; Wilson; Hamilton, when he chose to speak; Washington, though he hardly spoke at all. None were as rhapsodic as Morris. He attacked every centrifugal or sectional force, assailing the states—"What if all the charters and constitutions of the states were thrown into the fire, and all their demagogues into the ocean? What would it be to the happiness of America?";[19] assailing entire regions—the west could not furnish "enlightened" lawmakers, for "the busy haunts of men, not the remote wilderness, were the proper school of political talents";[20] if "the southern gentlemen" persisted in angling for power, "let us at once take a friendly leave of each other."[21] Morris's attacks on the west and the South goaded the sober Madison into saying that he "determined the human character by the points of the compass."[22]

Morris spoke out against democracy in every branch of government. This was not an unusual position at the Convention: "The evils we experience flow from the excess of democracy," Elbridge Gerry said roundly during the Convention's first week.[23] But Morris added a twist of his own. A broad franchise across the board would empower the rich, who would control poor or fickle voters. "[T]he people never act from reason alone. The rich will take advantage of their passions and make these the instrument for oppressing them."[24] "Give the votes to people who have no property, and they will sell them to the rich who will be able to buy them."[25] Morris had had these concerns since 1774, when he smiled at the bellwethers leading the sheep at Fraunces Tavern; such concerns were a hereditary privilege of the Morrises, who had done their share of herding over the years. Morris's solution was to segregate rich and poor each in their own branch of Congress, so that their pride would encourage mutual distrust. "[O]ne interest must be opposed to another interest. Vices . . . must be turned against each other."[26]

Morris attacked slavery more strongly than he had at Kingston. His great philippic came in the course of a discussion of how slaves should be counted in the rule of representation. By August, it was clear that one house of Congress would be apportioned on the basis of population; Delaware would have the fewest representatives, Virginia and Pennsylvania the most. This would also be true of the Electoral College, when that strange system was finally rigged. In both bodies, the southern states wanted slaves to be counted equally with freemen; this would boost the power of their masters, without conferring any benefit upon the slaves, since of course slaves could not vote. Some northerners—notably Rufus King of Massachusetts—asked why slaves should be counted at all? On August 8, Morris rose to ask the same question. Slavery, he began, "was the curse of heaven on the states where it prevailed. . . . Travel through the whole continent, and you behold the prospect continually varying with the appearance and disappearance of slavery. The moment you leave the [New England] states and enter New York, the effects of the institution become visible; passing through [New Jersey] and entering Pennsylvania, every criterion of superior improvement witnesses the change. Proceed southwardly, and every step you take through the great region of slaves presents a desert increasing with the increasing proportion of these wretched beings." But he was just warming up. "Upon what principle is it that the slaves shall be computed in the representation? Are they men? Then make them citizens and let them vote. Are they property? Why then is no other property included? The houses in [Philadelphia] are worth more than all the wretched slaves which cover the rice swamps of South Carolina." Finally, a masterly sentence, long, dense, and relentless. "The admission of slaves into the representation when fairly explained comes to this: that the inhabitant of Georgia and South Carolina who goes to the coast of Africa and, in defiance of the most sacred laws of humanity, tears away his fellow creatures from their dearest connections and damns them to the most cruel bondages, shall have more votes in a government instituted for the protection of the rights of mankind than the citizen of Pennsylvania or New Jersey who views with a laudable horror so nefarious a practice."[27]

The picture of trans-Atlantic woe and hypocrisy that follows the colon is folded like a Chinese screen. At either end stand Americans. Moving inward, the laws of humanity are defied, and the protection of rights is mocked. At the center, a monstrous irony: the act of enslavement is rewarded by votes. In Morris's sentence, the laudable horror of the Pennsylvanian accomplishes nothing. Neither did his speech. Roger Sherman of Connecticut spoke for the majority: "the admission of the Negroes into the ratio of representation" was not "liable to such insuperable objections."[28] The Convention compromised, counting each slave as three fifths of a person.

The nature of the executive was one of the trickiest questions the Convention addressed, not settled until the home stretch. No one knew how long his term should be, how many he should have, or how he should be picked. Franklin favored a plural executive, a committee of three; Gerry feared the executive would be picked by the Society of the Cincinnati, the veterans' group of Revolutionary War officers. Brooding over the entire discussion was the silent presence of Washington, who had in effect been the nation's executive as commander in chief, and had set a very high bar (too high?) for trustworthiness. Morris was a leading spokesman for the executive, repelling assaults on him, and seeking to extend his powers. "We are acting a very strange part," he complained in August. "We first form a strong man to protect us, and at the same time wish to tie his hands behind him."[29] Morris spoke up for his grandfather, his uncle, and the only man he idolized.

Morris's success as an advocate was mixed. His analysis of rich and poor voters was an interesting opinion merely, thrown out for the edification of the delegates, then put aside; he lost on slavery. Nationalism would be an open question for the rest of his life, and beyond. The office of the president that finally emerged was to his liking, but that had more to do with the tidal pull of Washington than anything he said. Morris didn't get everything he wanted, but then no one did. Hamilton had wanted a president for life; Madison thought the national government should be able to veto state laws; George Mason wanted it to be able to pass sumptuary laws, regulating foreign luxuries and conspicuous consumption. Morris took his defeats with better grace than many. For all his sharp words and strong opinions, he was disinclined to sulk. "[T]o the brilliancy of his genius," wrote Madison when he was an old man, "he added what is too rare . . . a readiness to aid in making the best of measures in which he had been overruled." [30]

Morris was an indefatigable speaker, but his greatest service was done as a writer. On July 26, the Convention adjourned for ten days so that all the resolutions that had been so far approved could be offered to a Committee of Detail, for presentation as a draft. In the interval, Washington and Morris went to Valley Forge to fish for trout; Washington looked at the ruined outworks where his men had suffered so. On August 6, the Committee of Detail presented its handiwork, which was followed by five weeks of further discussion.

On September 8, the Convention selected a five-man committee to "revise the stile" and "arrange the articles" of the Constitution. [31] The chairman was Dr. William Samuel Johnson of Connecticut, a sixty-year-old lawyer and classicist who had just been named president of King's College, now christened Columbia. But the energy on the committee would come from its younger members: Rufus King, Madison, Hamilton, and Morris. As with the committee assigned to write the Declaration of Independence eleven years earlier, here was a surfeit of talents. In 1776, John Adams wrote voluminously and Benjamin Franklin wrote well, but the assignment had gone to Thomas Jefferson. Madison, Hamilton, or King would have done a fine job, but they gave the task to Morris. Perhaps his blazing performance over the last two months, like a jockey making his move at the far turn, decided them. His draft was done in four days.

Unlike Jefferson in 1776, Morris was not writing out of his head. He was bound by the resolutions of the Convention. Yet time and again, he shaped and smoothed; and though he was a lawyer, he avoided as much as he could the legalistic repetitions that his profession loves. The effect of his changes is to make for clarity, simplicity, and speed.

Consider a passage from Article VI, based on Article VIII of the draft of the Committee of Detail (one of Morris's improvements was to compress the draft's twenty-three articles into seven). The Committee of Detail said:

> The Acts of the Legislature of the United States made in pursuance of this Constitution, and all treaties made under the authority of the United States shall be the supreme law of the several States, and of their citizens and inhabitants; and the judges in the several States shall be bound thereby in their decisions; any thing in the Constitutions or laws of the several States to the contrary notwithstanding.[32]

Morris made it this:

> This constitution, and the laws of the United States which shall be made in pursuance thereof; and all treaties made, or which shall be made, under the authority of the United States, shall be the supreme law of the land; and the judges in every state shall be bound thereby, any thing in the constitution of any state to the contrary notwithstanding.[33]

Morris's rewrite is not poetry, but it is cleaner. Three clanking "the several States" become "the land," "every state," and "any state." "[T]he acts of the Legislature" become "the laws." Two bits of lint are removed: "and of their citizens and inhabitants" (who else do laws apply to?); "in their decisions" (how else are judges bound?). One seeming bit of lint is added: "or which shall be made," but it actually makes an important point. Morris wanted the states to be bound both by future treaties and by those already in force. Even so, he managed to chip eight words out of a passage that was only seventy words long to start with.

Or consider how Morris cleaned up the prohibition on state armies and navies. The analogous passage in the Articles of Confederation (the old and the new Constitution agreed on this point) had been a lazy bumble:

> No state shall engage in any war without the consent of the united states in congress assembled, unless such state be actually invaded

by enemies, or shall have received certain advice of a resolution being formed by some nation of Indians to invade such state, and the danger is so imminent as not to admit of a delay, till the united states in congress assembled can be consulted: nor shall any state grant commissions to any ships or vessels of war . . . unless such state be infested by pirates, in which case vessels of war may be fitted out for that occasion, and kept so long as the danger shall continue, or until the united states in congress assembled shall determine otherwise.[34]

The Indians and pirates impart an unexpected flavor of a boys' book, but as constitution writing, this simply fails.

Article XIII in the draft of the Committee of Detail had cleaned things up to this:

No State, without the consent of the Legislature of the United States, shall . . . keep troops or ships of war in time of peace . . . nor engage in any war, unless it shall be actually invaded by enemies, or the danger of invasion be so imminent, as not to admit of a delay, until the Legislature of the United States can be consulted.[35]

Morris, in Article I Section 10, wrote this:

No State shall, without the consent of Congress . . . keep Troops, or Ships of War in time of Peace . . . or engage in War, unless actually invaded, or in such imminent Danger as will not admit of delay.[36]

He cuts sixty-one words down to thirty-six, making danger more imminent by describing it more rapidly. Morris the stylist would not admit the delay of inelegant verbiage.

Sometimes Morris saved time by showing instead of explaining. Article II of the draft of the Committee of Detail declared that "The Government shall consist of supreme legislative, executive; and judicial powers."[37] Morris eliminated this entirely, and simply began his first three articles by announcing that "all legislative powers," "the executive power," and "the judicial power" shall be vested in a Congress, a president, and the courts.[38]

Madison described Morris's trimming and polishing best. "The finish given to the style and arrangement of the Constitution fairly belongs to [his] pen ... A better choice could not have been made, as the performance of the task proved."[39]

Did the careful scribe try to smuggle in an argument for nationalism? Eleven years later, Albert Gallatin, a Pennsylvania congressman who had not been at the Convention, claimed on the floor of the House that Morris had played with the punctuation of Article I Section 8. The section begins:

The Congress shall have Power To lay and collect Taxes, Duties, Imposts and Excises, to pay the Debts and provide for the common Defence and general Welfare of the United States ... [40]

Clearly, everything after "Excises" explains what the taxes, duties, imposts, and excises are for. But, said Gallatin, Morris had put a semicolon after "Excises," which made providing for the common defense and the general welfare "distinct power[s]" of Congress. Roger Sherman of Connecticut, however, had spotted the "trick," and a comma was substituted, thereby ratcheting the powers of Congress back to their proper level.[41] At the time the charge was made, Sherman was dead, and Morris was out of the country, Morris was not above sleight of hand, but he made his convictions explicit elsewhere.

The Preamble was the one part of the Constitution that Morris wrote from scratch, and here he showed creativity, and condensed thought. The version of the Committee of Detail was as plain as paint. "We the people of the States of New Hampshire, Massachusetts" and so on through all the states to Georgia, "do ordain, declare, and establish the following Constitution for the Government of Ourselves and our Posterity."[42] This was a roll call, and an announcement. But what the ends of government might be, the Committee of Detail refused to say. The proposed constitutions offered by delegates at various times during the Convention had been more forthcoming. Madison had come to Philadelphia with a plan in his pocket, which defined the "objects . . . of Confederation" as "common defence, security of liberty, and general welfare"—phrases borrowed from the Articles of Confederation.[43] Charles Pinckney's plan quaintly defined the purposes of government as the "common Benefit" of the states, and "their Defense and Security against all Designs and Leagues that may be injurious to their Interests and against all Force and Attacks offered to or made upon them or any of them."[44] Robert Patterson of New Jersey looked to "the exigencies of Government" and "the preservation of the Union."[45]

Morris wrote a grave little essay, as quiet as it is comprehensive.

> We, the people of the United States, in order to form a more perfect union, to establish justice, insure domestic tranquility, provide for the common defence, promote the general welfare, and secure the blessings of liberty to ourselves and our posterity, do ordain and establish this Constitution for the United States of America.[46]

The last of Morris's six goals are Madison's three, rearranged so that "liberty," now prized for its "blessings," opens out to the future. Two inconspicuous rhymes—*insure/secure* and *tranquility/liberty/posterity*—and one strong alliteration—*provide/promote*—bind the paragraph together. In the final version, someone—the printer?—made a tiny improvement, canceling the second, redundant "to."

Morris's Preamble names "the people," rather than the thirteen states, as the source of legitimacy and power. This, not any sly semicolon, was his last statement of nationalism. Later historians dispute whether he intended anything so meaningful: Morris's version, they say, was a verbal maneuver to finesse the fact that some states—Rhode Island had sent no delegates to Philadelphia—might stay out of the Union for years. At the time, critics of the Constitution were not so indifferent. Patrick Henry, who had refused to attend the Convention, identified "that poor little thing—the expression, 'We the *people;* instead of the *states,*'" as a momentous shift.[47]

Truly, it was momentous. Washington had united Americans in war and now—as the hands-down favorite for the new country's first executive—in peace. The delegates to the Constitutional Convention had created a federal government that was far more finished and practical than its predecessor. Yet many Americans still held their states to be semiautonomous. It would be no accident that southern secession in 1861 would proceed under the slogan of "states' rights." When Gouverneur Morris changed "We the people of the states" into "We the people," he created a phrase that would ring throughout American history, defining every American as part of a single whole. Those three words may be his greatest legacy.

As an old man, Madison warned against expending "so much constructive ingenuity"[48] on the phrases of the Preamble. The meat of the Constitution, he believed, was its careful machinery of provisions. The same objections might apply to the self-evident truths in the opening of the Declaration of Independence. The business of that document is the indictment of George III, and the assertion of sovereignty. Strictly speaking, Jefferson's little thoughts about man, nature, and God are superfluous. Anyone interested in such topics can read Locke, or ponder the Bible. Yet Jefferson in 1776 thought it was important to consider first principles, as did Morris eleven years later, and their colleagues, on both occasions, agreed.

After a few adjustments, the document was approved by all the state delegations in attendance on September 15, though Edmund Randolph, George Mason, and Elbridge Gerry announced that they would not sign it. To win them over, Morris thought of a trick, attested in Madison's notes, which Franklin agreed to propose to the delegates on the 17th, their last session: surely everyone could sign "in witness" to the fact that the vote of the states had been unanimous?[49] The trick didn't work, and the Constitution went out into the world with the signatures of thirty-nine framers, minus the holdouts. Morris's occupies the lower left-hand corner of the page.

In later years, Morris's attitude toward the Convention and his handiwork was appreciative without being worshipful. "In adopting a republican form of government," he would write in 1803, "I not only took it as a man does his wife, for better, for worse, but what few men do with their wives, I took it knowing all its bad qualities."[50] One of republican government's flaws was impermanence. The framers, he wrote in 1811, knew they were working with "crumbling materials. History, the parent of political science, had told them that it was almost as vain to expect permanency from democracy as to construct a palace on the surface of the sea. But it would have been foolish to fold their arms and sink into despondence because they could neither form nor establish the best of all possible systems. . . . As in war so in politics, much must be left to chance."[51]

The fight to ratify the Constitution had easy victories and sharp struggles, and it took nine months, until eleven states had ratified, including all the largest ones. Morris took no part in it. Alexander Hamilton asked him if he would contribute to a propaganda campaign that Hamilton had conceived, a series of essays for the New York newspapers, to be signed "Publius." Morris declined. William Duer, another friend of Hamilton's, offered his services, but Hamilton declined to accept them. Hamilton ended up working with Madison and John Jay; the *Federalist Papers* they wrote are clear, earnest, and intelligent, often ringing, but they have made their way without Morris's sparkle. In 1788, Morris went once more to Virginia, to attend to Robert Morris's tobacco business. He visited Washington at Mount Vernon, met local grandees like the Randolphs (Jefferson's cousins), and attended the state ratifying Convention in June. He sent Hamilton keen but lighthearted reports of the debates. "Be of good chear. My religion steps in where my understanding falters and I feel faith as I lose confidence. Things will yet go right, but when and how I dare not predicate. So much for this dull subject."[52]

Morris had disengaged himself once more from public affairs. Having been chosen, against to his will, to make an effort for which he then gave his all, he went back to his private business.

Part 2

The French Revolution

CHAPTER EIGHT

Death and Love

ROBERT MORRIS, Gouverneur's mentor and senior partner, was stretched thin. In the language of modern business, he was highly exposed, juggling a number of ventures, whose prospects of success ranged from decent to dubious. Like many other businessmen in his situation, then and since, he tried to cover himself by pursuing yet more ventures.

As with almost every American of means, he had invested in land. Land speculation was the glimmering El Dorado of the founding period, the way to get rich quick. As early as 1775, he had bought a plantation on the Mississippi River hopefully called the Orange Grove Estate, even though not one orange seed had yet been planted there. Now he was loaded with hundreds of thousands of barren, promising acres along the St. Lawrence and Genesee rivers in upstate New York. If the United States needed a capital, perhaps Trenton, New Jersey, would be a likely site, and a good bet; as a senator in the newly created Congress, he could lobby for his hunch. In 1785, the French government had agreed to pay him 1 million livres ($1.5 million today) in return for supplying France with all its tobacco for three years; shipments from Virginia and Maryland had not come fast enough, however, so he was in arrears. The Penn family, the former proprietors of the colony of Pennsylvania, hoped that the British government would reimburse them for their lost feudal rights. Perhaps they would sell their claim at a discount. Most audaciously of all, Robert Morris hoped to buy the United States's $34 million debt (almost $450 million today) to France at 50 cents on the dollar. With that block of IOUs in hand, he would become at one stroke a major force in European banking.

All these plans and pipe dreams suggested the desirability of sending an intelligent and trustworthy associate to France. The French government, French speculators in American land (as eager as the natives), and Robert Morris's potential French partners on the American debt deal were best dealt with directly. In December 1788, Gouverneur Morris sailed from Philadelphia, arriving in France forty days later. Rival teams of speculators, who had their own designs on America's debt to France, treated him as an enemy agent, which indeed he was. "[B]e on your guard against G. Morris," wrote one to a partner.[1] He carried with him a cargo of solid value: letters of introduction from George Washington. Most such letters, he had written Washington, were "a kind of paper money," but the General's, he knew, would be good as gold.[2] In return, Washington wanted his younger friend to buy him a watch, not "trifling" or "finical," but large and flat, with "a *plain handsome* key."[3]

Gouverneur Morris needed to work and prosper in order to complete his purchase of Morrisania; Europe would offer him an even greater field than Philadelphia. But Morris was going for more than money. His trip would fulfill a fifteen-year-old desire to see the big world, to rub off his barbarisms among the "truly polite." When he had expressed that hope in his youthful letter to William Smith, he had thought of spending time in London, as his grandfather and his uncle had done. London, at just under 1 million souls, was an order of magnitude larger than any American city—a new world compared to New York and Philadelphia, to say nothing of York or Kingston. Paris, at 600,000 almost equally great and bustling, would be a shade more strange.

In the night memory of America lurked the image of France as a bogeyman. Throughout the colonial period, France had been the champion of the Pope and the patron of Indian marauders. Washington had fought Frenchmen on the frontier in his twenties; John Jay's grandfather had fled France as a refugee. Brave Wolfe's death before the walls of Quebec was still a subject for popular song. France represented sin as well as danger. The Frenchmen who visited America during the Revolution and noticed with amusement the fidelity of American wives, were noticed in their turn, for the rubes were as observant as the sophisticates. The twin prospect of threat and laxity could provoke the watchfulness of upright Americans or titillate the curiosity of adventurous ones. The experience of the Revolution, without quite obliterating these American reactions, had overlaid them with gratitude. After the Constitution had taken effect, the U.S. Senate hung a portrait of America's benefactor Louis XVI on its walls; George Washington displayed a similar portrait at Mount Vernon.

Every American emotion, positive and negative, was augmented by France's size, wealth, and power. At 26 million souls, France was six times as populous as the United States. Britain, with a population of only 15 million (one third of it in Ireland), might have a better navy, a larger colonial empire, and a more modern financial system. But travelers who had no national axes to grind routinely spoke of France as the greatest nation of Europe. If they criticized its shortcomings, it was in the course of marveling that such a nation could not do better. Indeed, though she was hemmed by enemies, France had fought her neighbors, sometimes single-handed, for more than a century, and while she had failed to impose her hegemony on the continent, neither had she ever been decisively beaten.

Three great Americans had spent time in France during the Revolution and its aftermath, and their reactions covered the gamut of American attitudes. Benjamin Franklin had joined Silas Deane in Paris at the end of 1776 and stayed, through the signing of the Treaty of Paris, until 1785. He had a high old time. The septuagenarian played the French like a pianoforte, and they delighted to be played by him. "The Spaniards," he wrote an American friend, "are by common opinion supposed to be cruel, the English proud, the Scotch violent, the Dutch avaricious, etc., but I think the French have no national vice ascribed to them."[4] Some ascribed a vice to them, however, and accused Franklin of sharing it. In another letter Franklin defended himself. "Somebody, it seems, gave it out that I loved ladies; and then everybody presented me their ladies (or the ladies presented themselves) to be embraced; that is, have their necks kissed. For as to the kissing of lips or cheeks it is not the mode here; the first is reckoned rude, and the other may rub off the paint. The French ladies have, however, a thousand other ways of rendering themselves agreeable, by their various attentions and civilities and their sensible conversation."[5]

John Adams, who joined Franklin as a diplomat in 1778, and lived in Paris on and off until 1785, had a more mixed reaction. His second night on French soil, a Frenchwoman, punning on his surname, asked him, as a descendant of Adam, "how the first couple found out the art of lying together?" "To me," Adams wrote, "whose acquaintance with women had been confined to America, where the manners of the ladies were universally characterized at that time by modesty, delicacy and dignity, this question was surprizing and shocking." He improvised some tale about magnetic attraction, then added, "[t]his is a decent story in comparison with many which I heard . . . concerning married ladies of fashion and reputation."[6] At the same time, he could not help being thrilled by the country. He called it "one great garden,"[7] filled with "[e]very thing that can sooth, charm and bewitch."[8] Art improved nature. "The richness, the magnificence, and splendor is beyond all description. This magnificence is not confined to public buildings . . . but extends to private houses, to furniture, equipage, dress and especially to entertainments." He worried that it had come at a cost—"the more elegance, the less virtue"—and he worried further that "even my own dear country" would yearn "to be elegant, soft and luxurious."[9] A part of him certainly heard the siren call.

Thomas Jefferson, who took Franklin's place as American minister to France in 1785, was the most censorious. His teenage daughter Patsy could write artlessly about all the beautiful "winders [of] died glass . . . that form all kinds of figures."[10] But her father knew what evil had reared the windows. Though France was blessed by "the finest soil upon earth" and "the finest climate under heaven," it was "loaded with misery, by kings, nobles, and priests, and by them alone."[11] It foreshadowed the hereafter, "where we are to see God and his angels in splendor, and crowds of the damned trampled under their feet." French morals were as bad as the French social system. "Conjugal love having no existence among them, domestic happiness, of which that is the basis, is utterly unknown." Jefferson's harsh reaction was based on the circumstances of his visit as well as ideological disposition. The late 1780s, his time in France, was a period of bad harvests and unusual rural suffering. One of his most affecting letters, a meditation on the unequal distribution of property addressed to James Madison, was prompted by an encounter with a wretched woman day laborer outside Fontainebleau, the site of the royal hunting lodge. Jefferson allowed that the French were temperate—"I have never yet seen a man drunk"—and musical—"[I]t is the only thing which from my heart I envy them, and which, in spite of all the authority of the Decalogue, I do covet."[12]

All three Americans agreed on one point: the disposition of the French to please. The French national character had not calcified into mere arrogance. Perhaps the French could afford to be other things besides arrogant, because they still had so much to be arrogant about. A wistful Franklin wrote, after he returned to Philadelphia, that he still dreamed of Paris, and of "the sweet society of a people . . . who, above all the nations of the world, have in the greatest perfection, the art of making themselves beloved by strangers."[13] Parisians "are the happiest people in the world, I believe," wrote John Adams, "and have the best disposition to make others so."[14] "[S]tern and hauty republican as I am, I cannot help loving these people, for their earnest desire and assiduity to please."[15] Even the begrudging Jefferson admitted that "a man might pass a life" in Paris "without encountering a single rudeness."[16]

Morris's quirky temperament would react upon all these social phenomena during the almost six years he lived in France (perhaps the one sentiment he did not feel, at least initially, was fear of French might, although that would change as France did). One of his first acts upon arriving on this great theater of civilization, power, and temptation was to buy a blank journal, bound in apple-green vellum, in which, on March 1, 1789, he began to keep a diary. He kept it faithfully, writing as much as five hundred words per day. By 1792, the pressure of events began to shorten his entries, and at the beginning of the following year, danger made him stop writing altogether. In the fall of 1794, when he prepared to leave France, he began writing again, which he continued to do for the rest of his life, though seldom with the thoroughness of his first Paris days. When an adult takes up the diarizing habit it can indicate some psychological turning point or need. Morris knew, early on, that Paris was a special place; he wished to observe it, to observe himself, and to observe himself in the reactions of others.

Some of Morris's early associates in Paris were fellow Americans. He overlapped eight months with Jefferson, who would leave in September 1789 to become the United States's first secretary of state. The two American aristocrats were alike in their palates. Jefferson, Morris noted, served a good dinner and "excellent" wines[17] (when Jefferson sailed for home, he took 288 bottles with him). They found, however, that they disagreed in their political views. The Virginian hoped that France might abolish the social distinctions whose oppressive effects he deplored. "How far such views may be right respecting mankind in general," Morris wrote in his diary, "is I think extremely problematical. But with respect to this nation I am sure it is wrong and cannot eventuate well."[18] They also differed in the freedom of their conversation; Morris's risqué expressions, a common friend recorded years later, made Jefferson "blush . . . to the temples."[19]

In late November 1789 appeared the adopted American, Thomas Paine. Paine had designed a single-arch iron suspension bridge, and since 1787 he had spent his time going back and forth between France and his native Britain hoping to build a prototype. Despite their recent collaboration in defense of the Bank of North America, Paine and Morris remained an odd couple. Paine was garrulous, earnest, and sometimes broke. Morris was fluent, witty, and provident. "Paine calls upon me," Morris wrote after one visit, "and talks a great deal upon subjects of little moment."[20] On another occasion, Morris loaned Paine some money, "telling him at the same time that he is a troublesome fellow."[21] Yet he also acknowledged that Paine's writing could be "splendid" and "novel."[22] The two acquaintances would hobble along, until their relations became very much worse.

Morris also saw again the Franco-American hero, the marquis de Lafayette. Lafayette's years in America had given him the most glorious career it was possible for a youth of his disposition to imagine. He had fought for a noble cause, and won the love of a nation. George Washington sent him admiring and heart-sore letters after the marquis returned to France; the state of Virginia presented a bust of him to the city of Paris; the island of Nantucket sent him a 500-pound cheese. Lafayette cherished the love he had earned overseas, and never let the French forget it. When his first two children were born, he named the boy George Washington and the girl Virginia. At his Paris household, his family spoke English, and his messenger was dressed as an American Indian. The young nobleman looked for new idealistic causes to serve. He proposed to settle liberated slaves at Cayenne in French Guiana (which caused Washington to praise "the benevolence of [his] heart");[23] he served in the Assembly of Notables, a 1787 meeting of the princes, dukes, marshals, and other lords of the realm, to discuss reform of the French tax system. The one flaw in him that his American friends began to notice as he entered his thirties was his love of the applause he had received. He would never consciously do a dishonorable thing to win more, but he had not learned the republican art of schooling his ambition. Jefferson thought that Lafayette had a "canine appetite for popularity and fame,"[24] while the marquis made Morris reflect that there were two kinds of ambition, "the one born of pride, the other of vanity, and his partakes most of the latter."[25]

The world of the international upper class that Morris now inhabited could be quite small. At one Paris dinner he saw John Paul Jones, the American naval hero, meet a Scottish nobleman whose seaside castle Jones had raided during the Revolution. After the raid Jones had sent back the family silver, and the young lord now thanked him for his "polite attention."[26] On a business trip to Amsterdam, Morris met General Baron Friedrich von Riedesel, the Hessian commander who had fought at Saratoga while Morris was fleeing to Marble Town; together, they criticized the tactics of General Burgoyne. During a jaunt to London, Morris did a favor for two cosmopolitan ladies. Mrs. Angelica Church, the American wife of an English businessman, had commissioned an allegorical design for the ceiling of a garden folly from Mrs. Maria Cosway, an Italian-born artist. Morris wrote an accompanying verse:

> *Here Friendship adorn'd by the Graces we see*
> *Maria, design'd by thy Art.*
> *Yet the Emblem was sure not invented by thee*
> *But found in Angelica's Heart.*[27]

The three had more in common than their interest in ornamental architecture, for Mrs. Church (the former Angelica Schuyler) was in love with her brother-in-law, Alexander Hamilton, while Mrs. Cosway had captivated another founding father in Paris, the widower Thomas Jefferson. Morris paid no gallant attentions to either woman.

Morris, who took rooms on the right bank in the rue de Richelieu, not far from the Louvre, typically spent his mornings meeting bankers and government officials, and writing his business correspondence, which sometimes included lengthy reports in French. If there were more still to be done, he would write late at night, however long he had stayed out and however much he would add to his diary. In the middle of the day he would make calls, and occasionally sightsee (he had pedestrian artistic tastes, admiring paintings for their subjects rather than their quality). Beginning in the early evening, he would socialize with his French friends.

He had come to France in time to see the sunset of the *salon*. These periodic teas and suppers, presided over by fashionable and intellectual ladies, where everything from love to philosophy might be discussed, so long as it was done cleverly, had begun to lose their aura of excitement and power. "You know, Madame," one politician told an arbitress, "the reign of women is over." "Yes, monsieur," she answered, "but not that of the impertinent."[28] Yet as late as 1789, duchesses of discourse still tried to maintain their sway over society. Mme de Necker, whose Swiss banker husband was a genius at self-promotion, and perhaps at finance, ruled one court of talk. The *salon* of her daughter, the twenty-two-year-old Germaine de Staël, already formidable as the author of a tract on Rousseau, shone with equal glory (Morris called Mme de Staël's gatherings "the upper region of wits and graces").[29] The household in which Morris came to spend the most time was that of the comte and Mme de Flahaut.

Alexandre-Sébastien de Flahaut de la Billarderie was a sixty-three-year-old veteran whose job, as Keeper of the King's Gardens, brought him a small salary, no work—assistants did it all—and two apartments in the Louvre. (Although the royal art collection was housed there, most of the palace was still residential.) His wife, Adelaide, was twenty-eight. The two had been married for ten years. She had already begun her first novel, *Adèle de Senanges,* a tale of romantic love that was clearly wish-fulfillment (Adèle is the short form of Adelaide). A later critic would call it "a pastel so pale as to be almost colorless."[30] "One only finds [her novels]," an even later critic would write, "in the backs of provincial bookcases, or the libraries of old chateaus . . . bound with pink or red leather . . . illustrated with old-fashioned engravings of young people in lace shirt fronts, tragically pledging eternal love in the moonlight. . . ."[31]

Her writing is safe from critics now, for it is no longer read at all. But when she first published her novels, they were widely admired— Pierre Bezuhov read her in St. Petersburg—and there would come a time in her life when they kept body and soul together. Mme de Staël, who did not like Mme de Flahaut, depicted her in one of her own novels as "flatter[ing] the vanity" of those around her "with great skill," while "screening from them what passed in her heart."[32] Another acquaintance, who was more charitable, told her that she knew how to keep her emotional balance. "Your good nature would be the death of more misfortunes than destiny could send your way."[33] Mme Vigée-Lebrun, the French portrait painter, testified that her large brown eyes were "the liveliest in the world."[34] When Morris first met her at a dinner at Versailles late in March, he found her "a pleasing woman. If I might judge from appearances, not a sworn enemy to intrigue."[35]

Her lover, and a frequent guest at her *salon,* was Charles-Maurice de Talleyrand-Périgord, bishop of Autun. Two years younger than Morris, the clergyman came from an ancient aristocratic family. In the ninth century, a count of Périgord quarreled with Hugh Capet, founder of the French royal family. "Who made thee count?" Capet asked. "Who made thee king?" the count shot back.[36] Over the next eight centuries, the family had distinguished itself by high-handedness and rapacity. Charles-Maurice added supple intelligence to the mix. He needed all his wiles to succeed in life, for when he was only months old he suffered a disastrous accident, falling from a chest of drawers on which his nurse had laid him, thus crippling his right foot. The shoe he was obliged to wear as an adult was round like the pad of an elephant; a metal rod ran up the inner side of his leg, to a leathern band which was wound below his knee. Since this disfigurement made a career in the military impossible, his family directed him to the Church, of whose doctrines he believed not a word, although he maintained the forms. He became Mme de Flahaut's lover, and her son Auguste-Charles-Joseph de Flahaut, born in 1785, was generally supposed to be his, rather than her husband's. After a busy and successful career as an ecclesiastical administrator, he was consecrated bishop in March 1789. Morris met him at the Flahauts' in April, though he did not take note of him until two months later, when he described him in his diary as "sly, cool, cunning and ambitious. . . . I know not why conclusions so disadvantageous to him are formed in my mind, but so it is. . . ."[37]

There was nothing like the cut and thrust of Parisian talk in the English-speaking world. Next to the conversation of eighteenth-century France, the poetry of Alexander Pope looks lush and elaborate, the quips of Samuel Johnson like lucky hits with a blunderbuss. For all his early education in the French language and his use of it in business correspondence, Morris frequently felt at sea, especially at first. His French women friends would gently mock his pronunciation. But in time he became adept at the higher badinage. "*Il me dit des méchancetés* (He's telling me naughty things)," one lady exclaimed over supper. "*Ah! Il est bien capable* (He's certainly capable of it)," a friend replied.[38] He could produce his own epigrams: "*[Il y a] deux espèces d'hommes. Les uns sont faits pour être pères de famille et les autres pour leur faire des enfants.*"—There are two kinds of men, one made to head families, the other to give them children.[39]

When the talk turned to politics, it could be learned as well as sup-ple, for the French had read Locke as well as their own *philosophes,* but the third generation of political Morrises was less impressed with their erudition: ". . . none know how to govern, but those who have been used to it," he told one dinner companion, "and such men have rarely either time or inclination to write about it." Political books, therefore, "contain mere utopian ideas." [40] Significantly, he made this observation to another American in Paris; he wouldn't have wasted it on a French-man.

The dank underside of French talk was gossip, which flowed like a drainpipe under the bright surface. At various times Morris heard that Louis XVI tortured cats; that one nobleman was the incestuous off-spring of Louis XV and his own daughter; that another nobleman lived with *his* own daughter. Such stories found a printed echo in *li-belles,* pornographic satires published abroad and nominally illegal, but widely available. In a society where bishops took mistresses (not parading the fact, but certainly not denying it), some of these tales may even have been true. The French did not care whether they were true or not. Everyone was vile, and nothing had consequences. In one of his first letters to Washington from Paris, Morris observed that "when a man of high rank . . . laughs today at what he seriously asserted yester-day, it is considered as in the natural order of things." [41]

Both the virtues and the vices of the French circles in which Morris moved flourished in idleness. The French kings of the seventeenth and early eighteenth centuries had sought to curb a fractious aristocracy by making it spin around the sun of themselves. The nobles had retained many privileges and some responsibilities (chiefly military) but there was not sufficient outlet for their energies. When they could not talk, flirt, or gossip, they played. One day, Morris visited an estate in the country. After breakfast (which was served at noon), the party went to mass. In the gallery of the chapel, where the quality—including a bishop, an abbé, and a duchess—worshipped, "we are amused," Morris told his diary, "by a number of little tricks played . . . with a candle, which is put into the pockets of different gentlemen, the bishop among the rest, and lighted while they are otherwise engaged . . . to the

great merriment of the spectators. Immoderate laughter in consequence . . . This scene must be very edifying to the domestics who are
opposite to us, and the villagers who worship below."[42] Morris hardly
ever darkened a church door, but he knew better than to play games
when he did.

Morris had arrived in Paris at what seemed to be a hopeful political
moment. France was an absolute monarchy in which all power radiated from the sovereign. But at the urging of Jacques Necker, the Swiss
financier, Louis XVI had called a meeting of the Estates-General, an
assembly of representatives of the clergy, the nobility, and the commons, the traditional orders of the realm, which had not met since
1614. The reason the king revived this old forum was money. France's
foreign policy, particularly its support of the American Revolution,
had bankrupted the state. The government could not raise money because the nobility were exempted from paying many taxes. The 1787
Assembly of Notables, in which Lafayette served, had been unable to
propose workable reforms, so the king and Necker were turning to the
nation in an effort to engineer consensus. Superficially, France's situation resembled the United States's at the opening of the Constitutional Convention—war debt; a political system that blocked any
revenue stream; a call for change.

Morris attended the inaugural procession of the Estates at Versailles, the royal palace outside Paris, on May 4, 1789. The day was so
bright that he got a sunburn, and he spent a good part of the ceremony
talking about Robert Morris's tobacco contract with another spectator. But he observed the elaborate ritual. The clergy wore robes of
black, white, gray or red. The nobles (among whom was Lafayette,
representing the Auvergne) wore black, with golden waistcoats and
sashes. The Third Estate, the commoners, were dressed in black. The
king wore a beaver hat with white plumes and a diamond pin. Morris
noticed that "[n]either the King nor Queen appear too well pleased."[43]
Louis XVI was cheered enthusiastically; his queen, Marie Antoinette,
was barely cheered at all.

Louis, mild, benevolent and young for his age at thirty-five, had, by
summoning the Estates, given himself the image of a liberal, patriotic

king. Marie Antoinette, two years younger, was popularly supposed, not without reason, to be against change and devoted to the interests of Austria (she was by birth a Hapsburg). Morris noticed the disparity in their receptions, and pitied the queen's humiliation. ". . . I see only the woman, and it seems unmanly to break a woman with unkindness."[44] The next day, when the session was formally opened, an old commoner in the Third Estate who came in farmer's clothes, instead of the prescribed black, received "a long and loud plaudit."[45] In a letter to America describing this mixture of imposing ceremony and unstable sentiments, Morris detected "the pang of greatness going off."[46]

Once convened, the Estates fell to quarreling over representation. The Third Estate, which was as numerous as the nobles and the clergy put together, wanted voting by head, rather than by Estate, which would boost its relative strength. The dispute consumed the attention of the *salons*. "[T]he conversation degenerates into politics," Morris complained one evening in May.[47] "States General chit chat," he complained again as the month ended.[48] As June wore on, the Third Estate began meeting separately, called itself the National Assembly, and accepted sympathetic clergy and noblemen as members.

The struggle between the Estates seemed to recall Morris's own experiences: the New York Provincial Congress replacing the colonial Assembly, then writing a state constitution; large and small states fighting in Philadelphia. Morris did not see the resemblance. The American state governments had grown out of colonial political experience, then worked together for twelve years before the Constitutional Convention. America did not take its institutions from a drawing board. The French, he wrote early in July, "want an American constitution . . . without reflecting that they have not American citizens to support" it.[49]

Louis XVI had been willing to inaugurate a reform movement that he could control, but when the Third Estate recreated itself as a national legislature with constitutional ambitions, he balked. He no longer had a free hand, however, for when in the second week of July he dismissed Necker, planning to replace him with a group of yesmen, the streets of Paris erupted. Morris went out in a carriage to see the commotion with Mme de Flahaut, and a hunchbacked abbé ("one of her favorites . . . far from an Adonis . . . it must therefore be a moral attachment").[50] They saw a troop of cavalry pelted with stones at the Place Louis Quinze (now the Place de la Concorde). The court at Versailles—a two-hour carriage ride away from Paris—assumed that the disturbances were minor. But on July 14, the fortress of the Bastille in the heart of the city was stormed by a mob, its commanding officer killed, and its prisoners and gunpowder liberated. "I presume," Morris wrote in his diary, "that this day's transactions will induce a conviction that all is not perfectly quiet."[51]

Morris observed these developments with a light heart—he found the abbé's fear during the riot "diverting"[52]—and indeed life went on: he wrote light verse for Mme de Flahaut, he wrangled over the tobacco contract. Yet only a week after the fall of the Bastille, he saw a different face of the mob. He had eaten dinner—in his diary, he noted the price—then waited for his carriage under the arcade of the Palais-Royal, a building next to the Louvre that housed clubs, shops, and cafés. "In this period the head and body of M. de Foulon"—a politician—"are introduced in triumph. The head on a pike, the body dragged naked on the earth. Afterwards this horrible exhibition is carried through the different streets."

Foulon was guilty of two offenses: he had been willing to help the king replace Necker (he would have been the number two man in charge of foreign affairs in the new ministry); and he was accused of keeping bread out of Paris, to starve it into submission. The first offense was real; the second was an urban legend—the reason there was so little bread in Paris was that hail, drought, and ice had impeded growing and milling for a year. After Morris saw the "horrible exhibition," it was shown to Foulon's son-in-law, who was himself "cut to pieces, the populace carrying about the mangled fragments with a savage joy. Gracious God what a People!"[53]

Morris had made his share of rash suggestions in his life as a revolutionary politician—fining the city of Philadelphia; egging on the Newburgh conspirators. But when confronted with instances of summary justice, he had always been sympathetic to its victims, from the

*M*orris at twenty-seven—the young heartbreaker.
[The Emmet Collection, Miriam and Ira D. Wallach Division of Art, Prints and Photographs, The New York Public Library, Astor, Lenox and Tilden Foundations.]

His daily companion after his accident in 1780.

[Collection of The New-York Historical Society, accession number 1954.148.]

Houdon's statue of Morris's hero, George Washington, for which Morris was the body model.

[Library of Virginia.]

Two Morrises: mercurial, relaxed Gouverneur; solid, steady Robert.

[Courtesy of the Pennsylvania Academy of the Fine Arts, Philadelphia.
Bequest of Richard Ashhurst.]

The manor house of Morrisania in the early
twentieth century, a few years before it was torn down.

[Courtesy of the Bronx County Historical Society.]

Morris's summer house in Gouverneur, New York, which still stands.

[Photograph by Emily E. Johnstown. Courtesy of the Gouverneur Museum.]

Morris in 1789—an American in Paris.

[Published as a frontispiece in Anne C. Morris, ed., *Diary and Letters of Gouverneur Morris* (New York, 1888).]

The Constitution, Morris's handiwork.

[U.S. National Archives.]

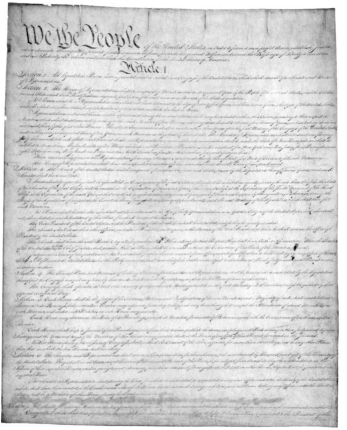

Thomas Paine. "A troublesome fellow."

The Marquis de Lafayette. "He will be
unable to hold the helm."

Talleyrand. "Sly, cool, cunning and ambitious."

[From a print in the Bibliothèque Nationale.]

Adélaide de Flahaut. "Not a sworn enemy to intrigue."

[From a print in the Bibliothèque Nationale.]

Morris at fifty-eight,
married at last.

[Pastel by James Sharples, Courtesy
Frick Art Reference Library.]

Mrs. Gouverneur Morris. "If
the world were to live with
my wife, I should certainly
have consulted its taste."

[Pastel by James Sharples, Collection of Angus J. Menzies.]

The streets of New York—Morris's legacy to the city.

Morris's last resting place—St. Ann's, the South Bronx.

printer Rivington to his Tory in-laws to his friend Peter Van Schaak. In all the evacuations and arsons of the American Revolution, he had never seen anything like this. He had called "the mob" "poor reptiles," but when he had sarcastically predicted that they would soon "bite," he had meant that they would wield political power. Now here was a mob on the move, carrying its trophy. He had already decided that the French had no political experience; was this what they had instead?

During his time in Paris, Morris associated with the rich and well-born—people of his own class, and higher—so his accounts of violence can leave the impression, dear to revolutionary polemic, that only they suffered. But the mob could turn on commoners , too. Some months after the murder of Foulon, Morris learned of a baker who was beheaded and "carried in triumph through the streets. . . . His wife is said to have died with horror when they presented her husband's head stuck on a pole." Morris wrote of this with real wrath. "Providence" would not "leave such abominations unpunished. Paris is perhaps as wicked a spot as exists . . . yet this is the city which has stepped forward in the sacred cause of Liberty." [54]

Morris dined with Jefferson several evenings during the most turbulent July days; the Virginian had been advising Lafayette on a French bill of rights. In his letters, Jefferson described the summary executions but did not dwell on the gore or the tumult. To Paine, then in Britain, he praised the "coolness" of the National Assembly, [55] and to John Jay, he emphasized the virtue of the rioters. "There was a severity of honesty observed, of which no example has been known. Bags of money offered on various occasions through fear or guilt, have been uniformly refused. . . ." [56] Jefferson was hopeful. Many Frenchmen were grimly pleased. When Antoine Barnave, a leader of the Third Estate, was asked what he thought of the deaths of Foulon and his son-in-law, he answered with a question of his own: "What, then, is their blood so pure?" [57]

Less than a week after his encounter with Foulon's dismembered corpse, Morris made love for the first time to Adèle de Flahaut. Recording the event in his diary, he was unusually laconic, slipping behind the mask of three dots. Mme de Flahaut was to help him write a document. "We sit down with the best disposition imaginable but instead of a translation . . ."[58]

Morris had been plucking at the web of Parisian sexuality for months. He picked up a prostitute once in the Palais-Royal, when he was drunk, a deed he evidently considered a lapse, for it made him feel "the object of my own contempt and aversion."[59] Generally, he confined his attentions to the women of his own sphere. He noted pretty arms and eyes, and the willingness with which they were displayed; he conversed with his lady friends as they put on their dresses over their shifts, and as they bathed (such situations arose frequently between French acquaintances, and were not considered unseemly, or particularly erotic). He swatted up worldly conversation. Mme de Staël's husband, a Swedish diplomat, told him that Frenchwomen are "greater whores with their hearts and minds than with their persons."[60]

He and Mme de Flahaut had been actively interested in each other since early spring. After running into him in the gardens of the Tuileries, she invited him to view the statues in the Louvre. The day was not a success. The weather was rainy, and the courtyard muddy. Mousieur le comte came along, and retired with his wife after the sightseeing was done. Morris slipped getting into a carriage, called on another countess whose repartee left him tongue-tied, then scolded his waiter at dinner. "[He] must I think despise me for pretending to talk angrily before I can talk French."[61]

Both he and Adèle persisted, however. By late June, she asked him about his reputation as a ladies' man, which had followed him across the ocean. He first denied it, then, heedless of the contradiction, assured her that "I never lost my respect for those who consented to make me happy. . . . This idea," he added to himself in his diary, "will I know dwell on her mind, because the combination of tenderness and respect with ardency and vigor go far towards the female idea of perfection in a lover."[62]

After the fall of the Bastille, Morris made an explicit proposition: he told Adèle that he could not be "only a friend." He added that he did not mean to inspire a passion in her, that he did not want to feel a passion himself, and that he was timid. "[A] very strange conversa-

tion," he admitted, but he counted on the mixture of brass and diffi-
dence, hot and cold, to capture her interest. ". . . I am much mistaken if
it does not make an impression."[63] Three days later, she countered with
a complication of her own, confessing a "marriage of the heart,"[64]
without identifying her heart-husband [i.e., Talleyrand]. Morris knew
anyway (no wonder he had drawn disadvantageous conclusions about
the bishop). Five days later, in the early evening, between dinner with
Jefferson and his daughters and a call on Lafayette, Morris was left
alone with Adèle at her apartment in the Louvre, and did not complete his translation. "[V]ery sleepy," he wrote toward the end of that
day's diary entry.[65]

As it began, so the affair continued. Morris's emotional reserve,
Mme de Flahaut's devotion to other men (not including her husband),
endless games of cat-and-mouse, intense and stolen bouts of lovemaking (Howard Swiggett, the first biographer to do the counting, concluded that the lovers never spent a whole night together) were the
materials of their attraction. There was also love—braided, as the years
passed, with the thickening rope of death.

CHAPTER NINE

Liberals in Power

THE POLITICAL EFFECT of July's violence was that the king recalled Necker, and put Lafayette at the head of the National Guard, a popular Parisian militia which had arisen to guard the National Assembly. Three months later, a crowd of Parisian women marched out to Versailles and demanded that the royal family come to the city, where they could be watched. There followed a long period of calm in which the new legislature and the newly limited monarch tested their relations with each other.

One of the busier legislators was Talleyrand. Morris attended an autumn session of the National Assembly, sitting behind Mme de Flahaut, and watched the bishop. He was not impressed with what he saw: "... there is a great deal of noisy debate on various subjects, if indeed such controversy can be dignified with the name of debate."[1] Talleyrand made his mark, not by speechifying, but by proposing a plan to nationalize the property of the Catholic Church, worth about 3 billion livres (or $9 billion today). The bishop argued that church property was not owned by individual churchmen, but served a social purpose—"enabl[ing] the clergy to carry out its functions"[2]—that justified the superintendence of the government. The windfall of confiscation would also help the Treasury balance its books.

The man of the hour was Lafayette. The hero of one revolution was once again leading troops in another. This time, however, he enjoyed a lonely eminence, for he was not under the guidance of a greater hero, nor was it clear what loyalty the National Guardsmen he commanded owed him. At a dinner *chez* Jefferson in mid-September—the last one Morris would attend before Jefferson left for home—Morris asked Lafayette if his troops would obey him. Lafayette answered that, although they would not do guard duty in the rain, they would follow him into action. "[H]e will have an opportunity," Morris thought to himself, "of making the experiment."[3] The marquis, who had a dramatic temperament, made skillful use of symbols, inventing a tricolor cockade for the National Guard, with the red and blue colors of the coat of arms of Paris flanking the white of the House of Bourbon, the royal family; this became—and still is—the national color scheme. But he operated in a vacuum of authority, traditional institutions having crumbled and new ones not yet taken hold. The moment he faced a situation not amenable to his charisma, he might be lost. "He means ill to no one," wrote Morris in his diary, but "[i]f the sea runs high, he will be unable to hold the helm."[4]

Morris distilled his impressions in letters to the man both he and Lafayette adored, who since April had been president of the United States. Morris had been acting as Washington's personal shopper, buying not only the watch he had requested but ornaments for the presidential table (Morris's tastes ran to items that were solid and relatively inexpensive). He had also served as Washington's body model, posing for a statue by the French sculptor Jean-Antoine Houdon. Now he was Washington's eyes and ears. His judgments were not kind. Louis XVI he called "a small beer character," who "at the slightest shew of opposition . . . gives up every thing, and every person."[5] Necker was "afloat upon the wide ocean of incidents"; his proposals were "feeble and ineptious."[6] "The new order of things," he concluded, "cannot endure. . . . The present set [of leaders] must wear out in the course of the year."[7]

He backed his judgments with anecdotes. One concerned an evening at Mme de Staël's, when the duc de Clermont-Tonnerre rehearsed an oration he intended to give in the National Assembly. The duke (whose second surname meant "thunderclap") spoke on crime and punishment, an important topic in a country where the old regime had had the power to imprison people indefinitely. The duke argued that criminals should not only be freed at the end of stated terms, but freed from all social stigma as well, which struck Morris as utopian. The speech, Morris wrote, "was very fine, very sentimental, very pathetic, and the style har-

monious." It was greeted with "[s]houts of applause and full approbation. When this was pretty well over I told [the duke] that his speech
was extremely eloquent, but that his principles were not very good. Universal surprise. A very few remarks changed the face of things. The position was universally condemned, and he left the room."[8]

Morris was showing off for Washington—see how I herd this room-
ful of Frenchmen—but he was also making a serious point. Too many in
the French political elite spoke for effect; if the effect misfired, they were
too ready to change their minds. Americans called Morris fickle and inconstant, but Morris felt surrounded by people more fickle than he. The
penchant of the French for oratory was analogous to their fondness for
theory and for gossip. Neither words, nor ideas, nor rumors were
grounded in experience, and they could change in the blink of an eye.

Morris's counsel to his French friends was a mixture of the solid and
the inflammatory. The National Assembly expected the sale of national land, including church property, to float an issue of paper livres,
called *assignats*. Morris, the veteran of too many American financial
schemes, thought the revenues would not come in at the rate the
French expected, and the *assignats* would therefore degenerate into
unbacked paper. He was right. Four hundred million livres-*assignats*
were issued in December 1789. Six years and many issues later, 100
livres-*assignats* were worth only 1.4 livres in hard money.

Morris's other bit of advice, repeatedly offered to Lafayette, was
that he should wage war against Austria and Britain by invading Flanders (the present-day Belgium) and Holland. Austria owned Flanders,
and Britain would not tolerate a French power play so near its shores.
Morris thought such an invasion would be winnable, and the old
Francophile in him wanted to see a French victory. Besides, he explained, "[y]ou want something to turn men's attention from their present discontents."[9] Morris, blithely throwing armies about the map of
Europe, could never foresee the true costs of war. His advice, however,
had the merit of realism, for the nations of Europe were looking for
easy targets—Britain had its eyes on Spain; Prussia, Russia, and Austria had theirs on Poland—and even France, given its troubles, might
be another victim. Better for it to strike first.

One of the channels for his advice was Mme de Flahaut, who was still, despite her connection with him, Talleyrand's mistress. Morris and Adèle mingled their lovemaking with politics. At one midday tryst at the Louvre, Adèle said she hoped to exert a moderating influence on Marie Antoinette through the queen's physician, who was one of the regulars at the Flahaut *salon*. Morris thought that Adèle might well have a good effect. Since the queen was "weak, proud, but not ill-tempered . . . a superior mind would take that ascendancy which the feeble always submit to. . . ." "I would give her a man every night," Adèle answered pertly, "and a mass every morning." The two lovers also drew up a new ministry, in case Necker should fall. They naturally put Talleyrand in the financier's place as chief minister of the realm. *"Enfin, mon ami,"* Adele said, *"vous et moi nous gouvernerons la France"* (Then, my friend, you and I will govern France). "[T]he kingdom," wrote Morris in his diary that night, "is actually in much worse hands."[10]

They had each other whenever they could, wherever they were. In their intoxication they made love in her apartment at the Louvre; in his carriage; and in the visitors' waiting room of a convent in Chaillot where Adèle's old governess lived as a nun. Morris did not record their encounters in graphic detail, unlimbering instead the full battery of eighteenth-century euphemisms, reinforced with his own odd humor. They performed "the rites";[11] he conferred "the joy"; they did "the needful."[12] They "sacrificed to the Cyprian Queen [Venus]";[13] they "perform[ed] the first commandment given to Adam, [i.e., be fruitful and multiply] or at least we use the means."[14] Over and over, Morris boasted, like a teenager (or at least, like a teenager who knows Latin), that he was *suaviter in modo, fortiter in re*—gentle in manner, resolute in the deed.[15]

Adèle sought to impress Morris with her fidelity, promising to be true to him rather than Talleyrand. He sought to impress her with his independence. "I . . . insist that she shall pursue only the dictates of her own inclination and understanding. . . . She is hurt at my reasonableness."[16] Adèle nevertheless managed to make her rational American promise to give her a golden ring. "So I find I have a wife upon my hands indeed."[17] When she was not trying to overcome his coolness with ardor, she flirted with William Short, Jefferson's former secretary.

Morris, for his part, flirted with other Frenchwomen, including the wife of one of his French bankers, and Mme de Staël.

Their erotic solar system included two fixed planets. The lesser was her husband, who appears as the traditional cuckold of French and Italian comedy, Morris praising the excellent partridges he brought home, and on which Morris supped, Adèle hoping he might become the French minister to the United States (thus allowing her, as she explained, to follow Morris there). The greater planet was Talleyrand, who knew well what was going on, but chose to ignore Adèle's behavior while he pursued his own affairs, until January 1790, when he reproached her with betrayal. In a panic, she told Morris she must write him and try to patch things up. She gave "many reasons" for doing so, none of which Morris felt were sensible. "[H]owever I agree for one she does not give": "it is necessary to her peace" of mind.[18]

Notes of tenderness do come through the din of passion and calculation. One afternoon, after tea, Morris visited Adèle and found her suffering from an old ailment: an *accoucheur,* or male midwife, had injured her during the delivery of her child, "since which she has suffered much by pain in the side. . . ." Morris's intimate and unhappy experiences with doctors always made him treat illness with seriousness and compassion. He gave Adèle medical advice but did not "attempt to caress her"[19]—a considerate omission. Another time, after he had set her down at the Louvre and driven off to call on Lafayette, he realized with regret that he had "need . . . of her conversation."[20] Even in the cool and self-regarding pages of his diary, Adèle comes off as an intelligent and lively companion—not, indeed, unlike him.

*I*N FEBRUARY 1790, Morris left Paris and Mme de Flahaut for an extended stay in London. Robert Morris's affairs, it was becoming clear, were shaking at their foundations. Robert Morris's fundamental problem was that he was operating in two divergent markets: he had plunged in land, and he hoped to plunge in government paper, or debt. But as the American government got its finances in order, land became a less attractive investment by comparison, while the value of the government paper he hoped to buy kept going up. As a U.S. senator,

Robert Morris's principles and his interest tugged in opposite directions. By supporting a strong and solvent federal government, he indirectly undermined his own prospects as a land speculator. More and more often, the richest man in America found that his bills were being protested in European cities.

Gouverneur Morris, meanwhile, was doing better than his patron. He got good tips from home. Alexander Hamilton, the new Treasury secretary, was a discreet man, but insiders tried to divine his intentions. After dining with Hamilton, Robert Morris's old associate, William Constable, wrote Gouverneur Morris breathlessly that the debts of the individual states would "undoubtedly" be paid by the federal government.[21] Constable guessed right. Meanwhile Gouverneur Morris's land investments, along the Genesee and St. Lawrence rivers in upstate New York, were more compact than his friend's unwieldy ventures.

Gouverneur Morris's main reason for going to Britain, however, was that he had an assignment from George Washington. The president wanted him to sound out British intentions on issues left over from the Revolutionary War. Britain had promised to vacate frontier forts on American soil, from upstate New York to Detroit, which controlled the fur trade, and to compensate American slave owners for liberated slaves. Neither of these things had been done. Britain had also neglected to send a minister to its former colonies, or to propose a new treaty regulating commercial relations with them. The former was a mark of disrespect; the latter left important economic interests in limbo. Washington directed Morris to use his "abilities, address and delicacy."[22]

Morris, with his restless mind and uninhibited tongue, was not an obvious choice for a diplomat. But Washington had clearly been impressed with his sprightly letters on French affairs. (If he had known of the bellicose advice Morris had been giving Lafayette, he might have thought better of the assignment.) The success of Morris's mission was foreshadowed on the day of his first call on the foreign secretary, the Duke of Leeds. Before being shown into the duke's office, Morris noticed, on the table of a meeting room, where it had evidently been a topic for discussion, a map of Poland. The neighbors of that unhappy country were carving it up, and Britain was watching what they did.

This was a more pressing matter at the moment than American commerce or forts in Detroit. When Britain's thoughts turned to the New World, it was only to wonder if the United States would allow a British army to march from Canada across American territory to attack Spanish possessions (the answer to that was an emphatic no). Morris was not the first, nor would he be the last, American diplomat in London to find that the United States was low on the list of British concerns. "These men," Morris wrote Washington after much fruitless talk, "do not yet know America. Perhaps America does not yet know itself. . . . We are yet but in the seeding time of national prosperity. . . ."[23]

For the rest, Morris visited with his half brother the general. He learned of the death of Mrs. Plater and wrote his little rhyme for Angelica Church and Maria Cosway. He saw quite a bit of Thomas Paine, who had appeared in Paris the previous autumn promoting his design for a bridge, and who was now doing the same in London. Morris and Paine consulted with Edmund Burke, the great liberal politician, about how best to help American sailors who had been impressed into the British navy, and Morris heard Burke perform in Parliament. "His speech contained [enough] matter to make a fine one, and to mar the best."[24]

Morris returned to Paris in November. In his nine months abroad, titles of nobility had been abolished, and Necker had resigned, unsuccessful and unlamented, though there had been no dramatic shifts of course. There was greater change *chez* Flahaut, for Morris found that Viscount Henry Wycombe, a twenty-five-year-old British nobleman, was Adèle's newest lover. The young man's father, a liberal British peer, had sent him to France to learn manners, and he had evidently done well. Morris called at the Louvre his first night back in Paris and found Lord Wycombe *"un peu enniché"* (somewhat settled in).[25] The next day, Mme de Flahaut would not receive her American friend.

Morris and Adèle began a new bout of emotional warfare. There were recriminations and ruptures, seductions and distractions. Morris imagined he had seen Adèle for the last time, and congratulated himself on getting out of a "sentimental scrape."[26] Then he vowed to "recover my empire over her,"[27] which he did by employing *fortiter in re.*

She offered not to see Lord Wycombe, but Morris refused her offer. Morris in turn distressed her by flirting with Lady Sutherland, the wife of the British minister to France, and with the marquise de Nadaillac, whom he described as "virtuous and coquette and romantic . . . [w]hat fine materials for seduction!"[28] One December evening, the comings and goings at the Louvre were so dense that he found himself with Adèle, Lord Wycombe, and Talleyrand (M. le comte was out). "She has just now much the advantage of me," Morris noted like a scorekeeper at a tennis match.[29]

Adèle de Flahaut was an ardent woman, and not prudent with her emotions. But she had good reason to seek out so many well-connected men. Her husband, now sixty-four, was a bad politician, a flamboyant reactionary royalist. Whichever way France went, it was not likely to go his. The salary for his no-show job had been cut by one third, and he had been publicly criticized as a parasite by a member of the National Assembly. Adèle was seeking security for herself and her son; she was willing to try the renegade bishop, the one-legged American, or the young *milord*.

Gouverneur Morris was true to his original intentions. He wanted intellectual and physical intimacy. He prized Adèle's mind as well as her touch. But he had no interest in marriage, or any definite relationship. His father had been a distant and depressed figure. He did not covet a union like Colonel Plater's, or Mr. Bingham's, or the comte de Flahaut's. Ultimately he valued his freedom more than Adèle's happiness. One weary afternoon at the Louvre, when Adèle was sick and heartsick both, she told him, *"Si jamais je vous ai fait de la peine, vous me l'avez bien rendu"*—If ever I hurt you, you have surely paid me back.[30]

In November 1790, France received an unexpected blow from across the English Channel. Edmund Burke published *Reflections on the Revolution in France*. The long pamphlet was a shock, as much for who said it as for what it said. Burke had not only helped American seamen; in a long career of liberalism, he had supported the American Revolution, Irish Catholics oppressed by their Protestant landlords, and Bengalis robbed by the East India Company. Now, however, he assailed the course of events in France. Burke saw the abolition of titles, the populist imagery invoked by Lafayette, and the enforced move of the king and queen to Paris as dangerous alterations of the social fabric. In "this new conquering empire of light and reason . . . [a]ll the decent drapery of life is to be rudely torn off. All the superadded ideas, furnished from the wardrobe of a moral imagination . . . to cover the defects of our naked shivering nature, and to raise it to dignity in our own estimation, are to be exploded. . . ." A nation stripped of custom and ritual, Burke warned, could maintain order only by calculation and force. "In the groves" of the Revolution "at the end of every vist[a], you see nothing but the gallows."[31]

Three months later, Burke was answered by Thomas Paine's *The Rights of Man.* Paine set his plain speech, by turns biting and matter-of-fact, against Burke's operatic eloquence. He scoffed at Burke's talk of drapery and wardrobes: "He pities the plumage, but forgets the dying bird."[32] The French Revolution had ended real injustices. "The older [governments] are, the less correspondence can they have with the present state of things. Time, and change of circumstances and opinions, have the same progressive effect in rendering modes of government obsolete, as they have upon customs and manners."[33] Burke's vision of the gallows struck Paine as delirious. "Whom has the National Assembly brought to the scaffold? None."[34] (This was literally true, since the mob was not the National Assembly, though Paine ought to have reflected what influence the former might have on the latter.) *Reflections on the Revolution in France* was an instant bestseller; *The Rights of Man* was an even greater one.

Morris read *The Rights of Man* in early April; Paine, who had come back to Paris, was telling him proudly how popular his pamphlet was. Morris found "good things" in both Burke and Paine.[35] Unlike Burke, he had no illusions about the old order. One night at Mme de Nadaillac's, he met the abbé Maury, a leader of the right wing in the National Assembly, and some "proud aristocrats" who were his supporters. They struck him as rotten and petty. Maury "looks like a downright ecclesiastical scoundrel, and the rest . . . have the word *Valet* written on their foreheads in large characters. Maury is formed to govern such men and such men are formed to obey him or anyone else."[36] But unlike

Paine, he had no faith in the apostles of the new order. "There is not a man among them fitted for the great tasks in which they are engaged," he wrote Washington, "and greater tasks are perhaps impending."[37]

Greater tasks or greater trials. On April 18, the Monday before Easter, the king and queen left the Tuileries Palace in Paris to spend Holy Week in the suburb of Saint-Cloud, halfway to Versailles. Louis was suffering from religious guilt. In addition to nationalizing church land, the government over which he presided had nationalized the Roman Catholic Church by requiring its priests to swear an oath of loyalty to the new regime. The Pope had condemned this requirement and those who obeyed it. Talleyrand, who had sworn the oath, had been excommunicated. Louis, torn between his office and his conscience, wished to celebrate Easter away from public scrutiny. His carriage was stopped at the palace gate, however, by an angry crowd, which was soon joined by the National Guard. For almost two hours, Lafayette vainly commanded his own soldiers to move aside; one Guardsman called the immobilized king a pig.[38] In the end, the carriage and its occupants stayed home. "[V]ery much of a riot at the Tuileries," wrote Morris in his diary. "I am a long time in expectation of a battle, but am at length told that the King submits."[39] Lafayette, humiliated, resigned; but then, Morris noted caustically, "found afterwards various reasons for not doing it. This is like him."[40]

The conclusion Louis XVI drew from the Tuileries riot was that he was a prisoner rather than a head of state, and he resolved to escape in earnest. In June, Morris was back in London, negotiating with the Penn family to buy their compensation. There, at the end of the month, he heard that the king and queen had fled Paris in disguise. Their goal was the Flanders border, two hundred miles to the northeast, where they could be free from their revolutionary overlords, and perhaps be helped by Marie Antoinette's royal Austrian relatives. "This," Morris realized, "will produce some considerable consequences. If they get off safe a war is inevitable." How could France live in peace with a rival power that was assisting its runaway king? But "if they are retaken it will probably suspend for some time all monarchical government in France."[41] How could the nation trust a sovereign who didn't trust it?

Just short of their goal, Louis and Marie Antoinette were stopped and recognized in the Argonne woods town of Varennes. Six thousand armed peasants and National Guardsmen escorted them back home.

When Morris himself returned to Paris at the beginning of July, he found Paine "inflated to the eyes and big with a litter of revolutions." Paine and the marquis de Condorcet, a mathematician friend of Jefferson's, had founded a republican club, calling for Louis to be deposed. Marie Antoinette's physician told Morris that the thirty-six-year-old queen's hair had turned gray from her ordeal. Morris called her husband a "miserable creature," [42] who would remain in place only because there was no alternative.

The flight to Varennes destroyed the mystique of royalty. The greatness Morris had felt going off at the opening of the Estates-General two years earlier vanished utterly in the stealthy escape and the enforced return. It also ended Lafayette's effectiveness. He had wished to keep the king safe, and to keep him wedded to the Revolution—to force him, in effect, to be a royal Washington. Clearly, he had failed. Before the king had been retrieved, Lafayette was threatened by a prim young lawyer in the legislature, Maximilien de Robespierre: "You, M. Lafayette, will answer to the Assembly on the fate of the King with your head." [43] When Morris called at Lafayette's his second night back, the general was out, and his wife was "half wild." [44] The liberal nobility who had begun the Revolution, and the erratically liberal king who had occasionally supported it, were spent forces.

Louis XVI and Lafayette nevertheless hung on in their posts for another year, while France was preoccupied with inflation, constitutional tinkering, and, at long last, the Austrian war that Morris had recommended. In this strange twilight period when the king had been stripped of power and respect, Morris chose to help him. The American republican, whose comments on Louis's political skills had been as cruel as they were funny, now became an informal adviser. Perhaps Morris was moved by Louis's distress, as he had been by the suffering of American troops at Valley Forge. Perhaps, disdaining all sides, he felt obliged to prop up the weakest, lest its equally unworthy enemies prevail.

For whatever reason, Morris wrote Louis helpful letters, and the draft of an address to be given to the National Assembly. He even learned, in November, that someone had suggested he become France's minister of foreign affairs ("I laugh at this," he commented in his diary).[45] His correspondence with Louis XVI sparkled with the wit he lavished on Washington. He advised the king not to bribe legislators, because they were not "worth corrupting." He suggested that Louis give bread to the poor as a grand gesture, observing that the French "seldom concern themselves with the good, but rhapsodize over the beautiful."[46] His proposed speech would have made Louis sound like Morris at the Constitutional Convention. Of the Declaration of the Rights of Man, Louis was supposed to say that since "such pronouncements hav[e] so far produced only metaphysical discussions, a King need not comment on them, as his functions demand a knowledge of Man as he is, rather than as he ought to be."[47] Louis never gave this speech.

Morris even drew up a constitution for France. His third effort at constitution writing was a very Anglo-American document. The king was the executive, with control over foreign policy, the military, the colonies, and commerce. He also had the power to veto laws and appoint administrators, down to the level of mayors. The legislature was to consist of a Senate, appointed to life terms by the king, and a National Assembly, elected for staggered eight-year terms by married men twenty-five or older. Only the National Assembly could propose taxes. Judges were also to be appointed by the king, but there was to be trial by jury. Apart from the fact that the executive was hereditary, Morris's framework was not unlike the most conservative ideas bruited in Philadelphia in 1787. True to his strictures on the Declaration of the Rights of Man, his Preamble (which he called "Principles") wasted no time enumerating human rights. Instead, he declared that "the position of a state, its climate, the extent of its territory and the habits and manners of its citizens, have an influence in determining the proper form of government."[48] Two revolutions in two countries had made Morris a comparative anthropologist: as men varied from place to place, so did their duties, rights, and opportunities. The one universal exception he recognized was religious liberty: "religion is the relation between God and man; therefore it is not within the reach of human authority."[49]

There was an obvious contradiction between Morris's view of the world and his handiwork: if men differed so, how could an American advise Frenchmen? While Morris was writing his constitution in December 1791, he was visited by a man, whose name he did not record in his diary, who had undertaken a similar project. His caller had sent "a constitution for America to Gen. Washington. He says that he has made such objects his study for above 50 years. That he knows America perfectly well though he has never seen it, and is convinced that the American Constitution is good for nothing. I get rid of him as soon as I can but yet"—here was the Morris touch—"I cannot help being struck with the similitude of a Frenchman who makes constitutions for America and an American who performs the same good office to France. Self love tells me that there is a great difference . . . but self love is a dangerous counsellor."[50]

He drew close, in sentiment at least, to the queen. Here the source of his attraction is easy to understand: he had written in 1789 that it was unmanly to break a woman with unkindness, and now the unkindnesses were coming thick and fast. One December afternoon he attended the Comédie Française, sitting in the balcony, and saw the queen in a seat below his. One of her attendants pointed out Morris to her, and their eyes met. "My air, if I can know it myself, was that of calm benevolence with a little sensibility."[51] In a crowded room and a hostile world, he wanted to show her support.

Here Morris's emotional and erotic life intersected with public events. Through the varied tapestry of his relations with women—the *méchancetés*, the Cyprian rites, the medical advice, the valued conversations—there ran a thread of affection. Morris liked women and he listened to them; that was why he was successful with so many of them, however warily he juggled his successes. But in the new France, love had a political resonance. Versailles had long been dominated by royal mistresses (only Louis XVI's uncharacteristic fidelity broke the pattern). More recently, the *salons* of the enlightened had taken their cue from bright liberal hostesses. As the Revolution approached and progressed, however, the omnipresence of women came to seem part and parcel of a decadent system. Rousseau, that strange intellectual scout, had set the critical tone in his *Letter to D'Alembert* decades earlier. "Follow the hints of Nature, consult the good of society, and we will find that the two sexes must meet occasionally, but live apart."[52] Now his prophetic discomfort with the power of women was widely shared. If virtue was manly, then vice was effeminate.

The most conspicuous victim of political misogyny was Marie Antoinette, who had been the subject of a flood of political pornography since the early 1780s, in which the kindest epithet bestowed on her was *l'Autrichienne*, the feminine form of Austrian, but also playing on *chienne* (bitch). She was depicted as a masturbating bisexual nymphomaniac, surrounded by lustful officers and lesbian aristocrats with whom she coupled insatiably. A 1790 print showed an awkward Lafayette kneeling before her and fondling her crotch; the primary butt was not him, but her boundless lust.[53] Adèle de Flahaut's suggestion that the queen be given a man each night was a mild echo of this filth.

Adèle herself with her cuckold husband and her international cast of lovers was closer to the image of an old regime whore than Marie Antoinette, but she was not very close. For the image was a fantasy—a projection of all the traits that the new masculine mood rejected. The elite was also reaping all the tales that their own libelous tongues had told; when gossip was popularized and politicized, it became lethal.

Without consulting any French pornography, Burke had intuited some of this in his *Reflections*. In the new "scheme of things," he had written, "a queen is but a woman; a woman is but an animal; and an animal not of the highest order."[54] But Burke was a royalist, who valued queens more than ordinary women. Morris respected the queen because she was a woman. At the end of the year he asked one of Marie Antoinette's friends if he might have a lock of her hair.

At the beginning of February 1792, he heard news from the United States which yanked him away from his constitutional daydreams and France's fantasy life: President Washington had appointed him minister to France.

CHAPTER TEN

Radicals in Power

WASHINGTON APPOINTED Morris, relying on their long friendship and on Morris's firsthand knowledge of the country. But when the nomination went to the Senate, there was a sharp debate.

Some of the senators had all the old objections. Roger Sherman of Connecticut, who knew Morris from the Continental Congress and the Constitutional Convention, credited him with a "sprightly mind" and a "ready apprehension," but warned that he was "an irreligious and profane man. . . . I am against such characters."[1] Sherman did not know about Mme de Flahaut, Mme de Staël, Mme de Nadaillac, and his other French friends, but he would have known of Morris's Philadelphia socializing.

Equally important, the French Revolution had become an issue in the emerging American party system. Distance had not dimmed Secretary of State Thomas Jefferson's hopes for the Revolution, and by a happy coincidence, the American politicians who were most skeptical of its success were those who disagreed with him on other matters, or who stood in the way of his ambition. By praising the French Revolution, Jefferson and his friends could attack them. Jefferson had already used what we should now call a blurb that he wrote for the Philadelphia edition of Paine's *Rights of Man* to pick a fight with Vice President John Adams (Jefferson hailed Paine's work as a corrective to "political heresies which have sprung up among us," meaning the opinions of John Adams).[2] When Paine learned in London of Morris's nomination, he wrote Jefferson that the appointment was "most unfortunate."[3] Jefferson didn't need to be told; he thought Morris had been poisoning the president's mind against the Revolution with his ironic letters.[4] During the debate in the Senate, Jefferson's ally James Monroe of Virginia attacked Morris as a "monarchy man ... not suitable to be employed by this country, nor in France."[5] After more than two weeks of discussion, Morris was confirmed by a vote of 16 to 11.

The president sent a monitory letter to his successful nominee. Washington touched lightly on the political complexion of the vote —Morris would need no assistance divining that. He did feel it necessary, however, to read his no-longer-so-young friend a lecture (Washington was now almost sixty, Morris had just turned forty):

[Y]ou were charged ... with levity and imprudence of conversation and conduct. It was urged that your habits of expression indicated a hauteur disgusting to those, who happen to differ from you in sentiment. ... [T]he promptitude, with which your lively and brilliant imagination is displayed, allows too little time for deliberation and correction; and is the primary cause of those sallies, which too often offend, and of that ridicule of characters, which begets enmity not easy to be forgotten, but which might easily be avoided, if it was under the control of more caution and prudence.[6]

Morris vowed to put away childish things. "*I now promise you,*" he wrote back, "that circumspection of conduct which has hitherto I acknowledge formed no part of my character."[7] Morris took a new house, on the rue de la Planche, on the left bank of the Seine, across the river from the Louvre and the Tuileries.

After the inevitable delays, the new minister was presented to the king and queen at the beginning of June 1792. It was the first time, despite all his observation and advice, that he had met the royal family face to face. The foreign minister had given Morris permission to forgo the traditional dress sword, since it would have hung unflatteringly alongside his wooden leg. The queen showed him her son, age seven, and remarked that he was not yet very big. "I hope, Madame," Morris replied, "he will be large and truly great."[8] He would be dead in three years.

Paine was back in France, driven there after having brought out a second part of *The Rights of Man* that was a frank call to world revolution. "[T]hough the vegetable sleep will continue longer on some trees and plants than on others, and though some of them may not *blossom* for two or three years, all will be in leaf in the summer, except those which are *rotten*."[9] He told Morris that he was "cock sure of bringing about a revolution in Great Britain."[10] Instead, the British government moved to prosecute him, and he fled their hostile attentions, never to return to his native country again.

On the surface, Morris honored the promise he had made to Washington to be circumspect. At his first meeting with the foreign minister, he admitted that, as a "private individual," he had offered constitutional suggestions to French politicians; but now that he was a "public man," it was his "duty not to meddle with their affairs."[11] His earliest letters to the secretary of state were models of vivid reporting. "The best picture I can give of the French nation is that of cattle before a thunderstorm. . . . [W]e stand on a vast volcano, we feel it tremble and we hear it roar but how and when and where it will burst and who may be destroyed by its eruptions it is beyond the ken of mortal foresight to discover."[12]

Below the surface of his official duties, however, Morris was laboring to save Louis XVI from destruction. In June, there was a second popular irruption into the Tuileries; Prussia, which had come into the war on Austria's side, now took up the king's safety as a cause and issued a threatening manifesto, which drove the radicals to desperation. Morris and Louis's advisers together plotted to bribe enough soldiers to guarantee another escape, or at least some safety in the event of another confrontation. The king gave Morris 1 million depreciated livres of his own money for safekeeping. Like a good banker, Morris informed him of the risks. His own house "did not strike him as any safer than the palace of the Tuileries," but "if his Majesty could find no other person to take charge of it he would consent . . . and put it to the use he would be good enough to indicate."[13] The only extenuation a diplomat might plead for such conduct is that Louis XVI was still nominally head of the state to which Morris was accredited, and could justly take steps to protect himself. Still, the American minister was meddling in French affairs.

The feared attack came on August 10. Across the river that morning, Morris heard "[t]he cannon begin, and musketry mingled with them announce a warm day."[14] The royal family was bundled to the National Assembly, and rebellious soldiers and citizens fought with loyalist troops, killing six hundred of them, and burning their stripped and mutilated corpses on bonfires. The weather was oppressively hot; the leaves were already falling, and later that week Morris noted that some perch, which were alive at six in the morning, were spoiled by midday. "So rapid a state of putrefaction I never yet saw."[15]

This was the second French Revolution. The king would be formally deposed in a matter of weeks; Morris gave the bulk of Louis's funds to a co-conspirator, and sent the rest of them to England. The National Assembly itself was a dead letter, to be replaced by a National Convention, which was supposed to begin work on yet another constitution (no one would be consulting Morris this time), though the power in the state had passed to the militias of Parisian neighborhoods (or *sections*) and the political clubs that rallied them.

As a diplomat, Morris lived in a bubble of immunity. But accidents always happen, especially in revolutions. His fellow diplomats, who asked for their passports as they were recalled by their governments, experienced delays and other forms of petty harassment. In a letter, Morris felt constrained to remind a colleague that "observations respecting the legality of a government should not be committed to post offices subject to its inspection."[16] Meanwhile, the French elite with which he had been wont to socialize was in hiding, or under arrest, or being executed. A guillotine went up outside the Tuileries at the end of August. "Another man is beheaded this evening for *Crime de lezé Nation*" (crimes against the state), Morris noted in his diary. "He published a newspaper against the Jacobins [a radical political club]. This is severe at least."[17] Foreign armies pushed in from the frontiers—a bombardment at Verdun over a hundred miles away was heard in the city—spurring the radicals to murder their enemies summarily in the city's prisons. There were times when the tension in the diplomatic community became extreme. "I laugh a little too much at the distresses of the Baron Grand Cour," Morris wrote one night, "and Lord Gower gets a little too much in a passion with Lord Stair." [18]

When he needed his nerves, they did not fail him. On the night of August 29, militia of the local *section* came to Morris's door. "[A] number of persons enter, upon an order to examine my house for arms said to be hidden in it. I tell them that they shall not examine—that there are no arms and that they must seize the informer [responsible for the false report] that I may bring him to punishment. I am obliged to be very peremptory and at length get rid of them." The next morning, their superior, the *Commissaire de Section*, called on Morris and made his government's apologies. Morris remarked that he "behaved very well." [19]

It was well that Morris's bluff had worked, for, though he was not hiding arms in his house, he was hiding aristocrats. Mme de Flahaut and her son had sought shelter there on August 10; the comte de Flahaut was hiding in another place, though he had visited them several times. Yet another refugee appeared at Morris's door shortly after the militia left. No one marked for death, however, could long trust his life to a Parisian bolt hole. Shortly thereafter, Adèle paid a morning call on the assistant secretary of the Commune of the Tenth of August, the new revolutionary regime of the city. Besides the zealots, both virtuous and bloodthirsty, that the Revolution had thrown up, were the scoundrels, taking advantage of their positions. Many governments consist of little else, but times of turmoil give scoundrels unusual power. Mme de Flahaut asked the assistant secretary, who was in his dressing gown having his hair done, for passports for herself and her husband. He refused, and withdrew to an inner room to complete his toilet. He had left a stack of passports on his desk, however, and she reached for them. Through the glass of his inner door, he saw her, and strolled back out to say that they were of course useless without his signature. She left with a signed passport, which she returned the next day, and blanks on which she forged his signature. Perhaps she had bribed him, with money or herself; perhaps the tableau of her need and his power had given him gratification enough. Adèle and her son crossed the Channel at the end of September; Morris would not see her again for three years.[20]

Talleyrand was able to make a less harried exit, with a passport that was his reward for writing the new government's justification for deposing the king. He shortly found himself in the English countryside, in Surrey, in a circle of exiles enjoying the hospitality of Mme de Staël. Fanny Burney, the unmarried English novelist, who came to know the exotic refugees, was charmed with them, not least with Talleyrand. "His powers of entertainment are astonishing, both in information and raillery."[21] But all was not well in Surrey. Fanny's father, Dr. Burney, learned from a friend that Mme de Staël was having an affair with one of her guests. "I do not wish our Fanny to have the smallest connection with such an adulterous demoniac. . . ."[22] Fanny leaped to Mme de Staël's defense. It was, she wrote her father, "a gross calumny . . . she loves him even tenderly, but so openly, so simply, so unaffectedly and with such utter freedom from all coquetry. . . ."[23] They were, of course, having an affair.

After the degradation of his king, Lafayette concluded that the Revolution had betrayed itself, and at the end of August he rode away from his army with a party of officers, hoping to reach Holland. The Austrians captured him, however, and imprisoned him as a dangerous revolutionary. "[M]y cell," he wrote, "is three paces broad and five and a half long. . . . The wall next to the ditch is dripping with moisture. . . . I am often afflicted with fever; I have no exercise, and little sleep. . . ."[24] "Thus," Morris wrote Jefferson, "his circle is completed. He . . . is crushed by the wheel he put in motion. He lasted longer than I expected."[25] Morris directed the Dutch bankers who handled the United States's transactions to advance 10,000 livres on the credit of the nation for Lafayette's personal expenses in prison, and to tell the Austrians that America would hear with "great concern" if their hero "should be in want."[26] Some months later, he would loan Mme de Lafayette 100,000 livres of his own money.

Morris stayed at his post. He represented the United States, but to whom did he represent it? One government had collapsed, and its interim replacements might fall to revolutionary rivals, or invading enemies. The most pressing problem before him was monetary: the United States owed a payment of 6 million livres on its debt to France, and Morris had to decide whether it should be paid, and to whom. William Short, who was now minister to Holland, and thus responsible for dealing directly with the money men of Amsterdam, doubted that a debt contracted with Louis XVI could be collected by the men who had overthrown him. If "a bond given to A.," he wrote Morris, has been "robbed by B. . . . could you, knowing that, pay the money to B. and consider yourself honestly discharged from A.?"[27] Morris told Short to pay the money on schedule to the government *du jour*. He urged it from expedience. "[L]et who will be king or minister, those who bring money will be well received."[28] He also urged it as a matter of right. "The corner stone of our own Constitution is the right of the people to establish such governments as they think proper."[29] If the French wished to have a bad government, or many governments in succession, that was their affair. The American minister would meddle to save lives, but he would honor his country's obligations.

He would not, however, enter into new obligations, particularly if they carried a whiff of corruption. One way that the United States had agreed to pay down its debt was to give $800,000 to French agents in America, who needed it to buy supplies for the French colony of Santo Domingo—today Haiti and the Dominican Republic. (Sugar islands made huge profits, but they required high maintenance, since they produced few staples locally.) This was a particularly attractive arrangement for the United States, since the French would be spending their money in America. As France crashed, Morris was now approached by three officials—M. Monge, minister of the Marine, M. Le Brun, minister of foreign affairs, and M. Clavière, minister of public contributions—who wanted him to authorize payment of the $800,000 directly in France. M. Le Brun was both urgent and insulting, reminding the American minister that "[your] independence is our work . . . we do not say this to stir your gratitude but to excite your goodwill."[30] Morris put the ministers off, saying he could not act on his own responsibility. In fact, he divined their true motive: greed. If the $800,000 were paid in Europe, they could take nicks from it in the form of commissions, and other graft. If it were paid in the United States, the opportunity would be lost to them. Beautiful women in distress were not the only targets of revolutionary rascals.

In the whirl of events, Morris's distance from his capital, at a time when a trans-Atlantic crossing typically took a month or two, and could take much longer, was a source of perplexity to him. Morris wrote President Washington and gave him two options. "I need not tell you, Sir, how agreeable [it] would be to me . . . to have positive instructions." On the other hand, "[t]he United States may wish to temporize and see how things are like to end, and in such case, leav[e] me at large with the right reserved to avow or disavow me according to circumstances. . . ."[31] Morris was willing, if necessary, to be made a scapegoat; but the risk would be sweetened by the freedom, which he always relished, of acting on his own.

On September 20, French artillerymen turned back a charge of Prussian grenadiers at the Argonnes town of Valmy; an army of revolutionaries had stopped the premier professional soldiers of Europe. The poet Goethe, who had come on the campaign as a flunky of the Duke of Saxe-Weimar, told the beaten Germans that "from this place and this time forth commences a new era in world history and you can all say that you were present at its birth."[32] Through the fog of the war, Morris heard conflicting and inaccurate reports of what was happening at the front. Before him, in Paris, the new National Convention met and declared the end of the monarchy, and the inauguration of a new calendar—Year One of the Republic. One of the delegates was Thomas Paine. On the grounds that he had "sapped the foundations of tyranny, and prepared the road to liberty,"[33] Paine was given French citizenship, and elected as a member from Pas-de-Calais. He accepted the honors, even though he knew little French. But he knew enough to understand the cries of *"Vive Thomas Paine"*[34] that greeted him when he took his seat.

Pressed by cares, and anxious not to leave compromising records in case the militia revisited his house, Morris shrank his diary entries to brief notes of the weather and public events. More details are preserved in his letters. "Some days ago a man applied to the convention for damages done to his quarry. . . . The damage done to him was by the number of dead bodies thrown into his pit and which choked it up so that he could not get men to work at it."[35] Early in January 1793, he abandoned his diary altogether.

The National Convention was in the midst of trying Louis Capet, as he was now called, having been stripped of his title. The mild and indecisive young man was charged with a long list of crimes, from killing his own subjects to plotting against the Revolution he had sworn to uphold. There was much truth to the latter accusation. But had he not been sufficiently punished for this by losing his throne? Many of the delegates thought so, among them Paine. In a speech read for him by a translator, he urged France, "the first of European nations to abolish royalty," to be "the first to abolish the punishment of death."[36] Perhaps the former monarch could be rehabilitated by being exiled to the republican atmosphere of the United States. After the Convention voted—narrowly—for execution, Paine pleaded to delay the sentence. Jean-Paul Marat, a radical journalist, screamed that Paine's translator must be mistaken. Louis was beheaded on January 21, on a morning of winter fog.

In his report to Jefferson, Morris wrote of the "solemnity" of the occasion—"I have seen grief such as for the untimely death of a beloved parent"[37]—though other observers were struck by the indifference, or even lightheartedness of the populace. Morris had sent Jefferson a more balanced epitaph for Louis XVI back in August, when the throne first fell. "The King . . . has an uncommon firmness in suffering [but] not the talents for action."[38]

The former Keeper of the King's Gardens was arrested shortly thereafter. One of the passports that Mme de Flahaut secured had been for her husband, who had not yet used it, instead lying low in the Channel port of Boulogne. There he was seized, then managed to escape by bribing his jailers. The authorities still had one way to control him, however: his honor. They arrested his lawyer as an accomplice to his escape, and the old man, even more gallant at the end of his life than he had formerly been comical, turned himself in, took full responsibility, and was executed.[39]

Throughout the spring of 1793 Morris was subject to searches and arrests. After one incident, he was obliged to complain to his friend Le Brun. "I beg, Sir, that you will have the goodness to secure me against similar accidents, troublesome in themselves, and scandalous from their publicity." [40]

To avoid difficulties, he bought twenty acres and a house in the village of Seine-Port, twenty-seven miles down the river from Paris, and spent as much time there as possible. "My little territory," he wrote, had "a pretty little garden and some green trees, and more grass than my neighbors. . . . The river is about the size of the Schuylkill at Tweed's ford, but deeper. . . . My prospect is rural and extensive." In one direction he could see "the ruins of baths which once belonged to the fair Gabrielle, favorite mistress to Henry the Fourth." In the other stood "the magnificent pavilion built by Bouret," a financier. "He expended on that building and its gardens about half a million sterling, and after squandering" two million more, "he put himself to death because he had nothing to live on. . . . [T]he objects just mentioned are well calculated to show the vanity of human pursuits and possessions. My time is spent in reading and writing. . . ." [41]

Much of his official correspondence was devoted to helping American ship captains whose vessels had been captured by French privateers for the offense of carrying British goods. (France had declared war on Britain in February.) The efforts of the two belligerent superpowers to harass and control American shipping would be a cause of complaint for the next twenty years. Morris also provoked the French government by continuing to shelter aristocrats. He let the comtesse de Damas stay at Seine-Port, then refused to let her be arrested there. As Le Brun wrote a colleague, the deed "shows only too well Morris's natural disposition to cover with the mantle of impunity persons suspected of aristocracy." [42] Morris denied the charge. "It never entered my mind . . . to interfere with the carrying out of the law of France. My opposition was founded only on the circumstance of an arrest in my house; I explained in a very clear manner to your commissaries that I would have given up the person if I had been asked, instead of [being shown] an order to *take* her." [43] As proof of his goodwill, he offered to bring the "citizenness" into Paris himself. The countess survived this imbroglio; in the caprice of despotism, sometimes a spirited delaying action was enough to spare a life.

When he could, Morris enjoyed himself. At one dinner in Paris, Morris's host offered his guests two bottles of Greek wine, then as now, cheap stuff. But by mistake, the second bottle actually contained Tokay, or fine Hungarian dessert wine—"some of the best," wrote Morris, "I ever tasted. I drink the greater part of it, praising always his Greek wine, till his brother-in-law, astonished at my choice, tastes it and all is discovered."[44] Morris bought, for a few sous a bottle, some Tokay sealed with the Hapsburg double eagle, which had found its way to a Paris grocery store. It had been part of the empress Maria Theresa's wedding present to her daughter, Marie Antoinette.

The widow Capet was tried in October 1793. Like Louis, she was accused of some things that she had actually done, such as corresponding with her Austrian relatives on the eve of the war. The prosecutors focused their energy, however, on her fantasy crimes, most notably the charge that she and her sister had molested her son. The "fucking tart," as one editor called her,[45] was guillotined on October 16. Despite royalist fantasies that he had somehow escaped, the son would die in prison, of tuberculosis, in 1795.

Paine gave no speeches in defense of the former queen's life, for by this time he himself was falling victim to the shifts of revolutionary politics. Morris described him in one letter as "besotted from morning till night," and added, "he would be punished if he were not despised."[46] Despised or not, punishment was coming. Paine had allied himself with a faction of the National Convention called the Girondins, named after the Gironde, a region of France from which several of them came. In the last days of the monarchy, they had been radicals, pushing for a republic. Once in power, they advocated a policy of world revolution. Paine agreed with both views, though his primary link to the faction was that many of the Girondins spoke English. As the situation of the country worsened, however—with depreciating currency, an ever-widening coalition of foreign enemies, and rebellions in several provinces—another faction, the Jacobins (who took their name from the former convent which was their meeting place), came to the fore. They were not more ruthless than the Girondins, but they were more focused, and they were better politicians. The leading Girondins were purged from the Convention in the summer, and executed along with Marie Antoinette in the fall. Achieving immortality through honesty, the Convention declared that "Terror is the order of the day." Parliamentary immunity protected Paine for a while, but he was arrested on Christmas morning.

"Thomas Paine is in prison," Morris wrote Jefferson in January 1794, "where he amuses himself by publishing a pamphlet against Jesus Christ."[47] Morris was referring to Part I of *The Age of Reason,* an attack on organized religions, particularly Christianity, which the former Methodist preacher had first published in French. The book does all that humor and literalism can do to undermine Christian dogma. "[I]t appears that Thomas [the disciple] did not believe the resurrection; and, as they say, would not believe, without having ocular and manual demonstration himself. *So neither will I;* and the reason is equally as good for me and for every other person, as for Thomas."[48] Paine was not an atheist but a deist. In substance, his beliefs were not far from Morris's, though his aggressive polemics were worlds away. After talking with one superstitious old Catholic, Morris wrote that he would be unlikely, at his age, to find a better faith. "[T]herefore it is best to leave him in possession of his present property."[49] Meanwhile, Paine petitioned for release as an American citizen. The French responded that, by serving in the Convention, he had forfeited that status. "[I]f he is quiet in prison," Morris told Jefferson, "he may have the good luck to be forgotten. Whereas, should he be brought much into notice, the long suspended axe might fall on him."[50] Paine never forgave Morris for his tactical inattention; it marked the end of their long and curious relationship.

Morris's own fate was being decided by the interplay of French and American politics. In April 1793, before the Girondins fell, they had dispatched as their minister to the United States Edmond-Charles Edouard Genet, a charming and enthusiastic thirty-year-old. Morris, who dined with him before he left, thought he had "the manner and look of an upstart."[51] Genet's missions were to ask for a speedier repayment of the American debt; to arm French privateers in American ports; to encourage private invasions of Spanish Louisiana from American soil; and generally to promote fraternal comradeship between the two republics. Jefferson, the secretary of state, was not opposed to any of this; he gave one of Genet's agents an introduction to the governor of Kentucky. American partisanship had grown sharper since his own passage of words with Vice President Adams in 1791. Jefferson's supporters, who called themselves Republicans, and a party led by Treasury Secretary Alexander Hamilton, who called themselves Federalists, disputed a range of issues from finance to foreign policy to constitutional interpretation. The Republicans held banquets in Citizen Genet's honor, seeing him as a celebrity foreign well-wisher. "It is beyond the power of figures or words to express the hugs and kisses [they] lavished on him," wrote a Federalist journalist. ". . . very few parts, if any, of the Citizen's body, escaped a salute."[52]

Very soon, however, it became apparent that Genet's welcome had gone to his head. He openly challenged the Washington administration to be friendlier with France, and he fancied he could appeal to the people over the president's head. Jefferson had his own doubts about Washington's instincts, but he knew that crossing the Father of his Country in public was madness. Genet "will sink the republican interest if [we] do not abandon him," Jefferson wrote Monroe.[53] By August the Washington administration, Federalists and Republicans alike, asked France to recall its bumptious minister.

By then the Jacobins were happy to purge Girondin diplomats. They found Genet guilty of "giddiness" and "vanity,"[54] and of needlessly offending a friendly nation, and they summoned him home, undoubtedly to be executed. (Genet prudently stayed put, and married the daughter of Governor George Clinton of New York.) The United States's request to recall Genet, however, gave France the opportunity to request the recall of Morris. The Jacobins could thus get rid of two obnoxious men in one swoop.

Morris knew that the French government had asked for his recall, but months passed before the machinery of the American government

produced a replacement. It turned out to be the earnest Virginia Francophile, James Monroe, who arrived in Paris in August 1794. French
parties meanwhile had come and gone "like the shadows of a magic
lantern," as Morris put it.[55] Robespierre and the Jacobins had ruled,
and in their turn been guillotined. Morris, relieved to be free from the
"torment of attention" to business,[56] shut up his houses in Paris and
Seine-Port and left France in mid-October for Switzerland. By the
end of the month, he was dining on the shores of Lake Geneva with
Jacques Necker, the man who had summoned the Estates-General to
deal with the French debt, and with Mme de Staël, who had come
home from Surrey.

WHILE MORRIS was still at his post, he had gotten a letter from
N. J. Hugon de Basseville, who was secretary of the French ambas-
sador to the court of Naples, and who, in an earlier incarnation, had
tutored Robert Morris's children. "I do not ask you, sir," wrote Basseville, "if you have not more than once regretted the tranquil banks of
the Delaware; it is enough for a philosopher to have seen a revolution
in his own country." Then, he asked, "why has ours not resembled
yours in every way?"[57]

Why should the two revolutions have resembled each other in any
way, given the different circumstances of the two countries? Yet the
closeness in time, the appearance of key actors in both, and the similarity of some ideals, led many to expect a similarity of outcomes. Even
the skeptical Morris thought he was competent to give his French
friends advice; he certainly believed he was competent enough to
meddle. So Basseville's question was a good one.

As a man who had helped write two constitutions, Morris thought
that France's revolutionary constitutions had been undone by the
overwhelming power of a one-house legislature, which was itself "at
the mercy of such men as could influence the mob."[58] The legislature
bullied and finally overthrew the king, and the political clubs and their
riotous supporters bullied the legislature. This view accurately described the course of the Revolution during the time he was in France.
The forces that should have checked the runaway legislatures were in-

competent to their task. We know Morris's low opinion of the king; he had an equally low opinion of his supporters, who busied themselves with "little paltry intrigue[s] unworthy of anything above the rank of footmen and chambermaids."[59]

But these were only political problems. The constitution maker did not think constitutions by themselves could make or unmake a nation's happiness. Morris believed that France's problems were more fundamental.

Partly they were a matter of national temperament. "The French will all tell you," Morris wrote an American colleague early in his stay, "that their countrymen have *des têtes exaltés*" (inflamed imaginations). "A Frenchman loves his King as he loves his mistress—to madness—because he thinks it great and noble to be mad. He then abandons both the one and the other most ignobly because he cannot bear the continued action of the sentiment he has persuaded himself to feel."[60] This erotic simile confuses as much as it explains: was Talleyrand madly in love with Adèle de Flahaut? Was Morris calm? The sudden shift from worship to execration does describe the course of Louis XVI from the opening of the Estates-General, when he was cheered, to the return from Varennes, when he was doomed. But bolder leaders had managed to command the passionate devotion of the French for years at a stretch; another such was in the offing as Morris wrote.

A problem easier to be analyzed was education. The French, Morris believed, were not properly trained to live in freedom. This was true of both the leaders and the led. It was an opinion he formed early, and held stubbornly. "[A] nation not yet fitted by education and habit for the enjoyment of freedom," he wrote John Jay two weeks before the Bastille fell, " . . . will greatly overshoot their mark."[61] "[S]upposing that they should even adopt a good [constitution]," he wrote Washington, a year after he left France, " . . . they will not be easy under it, for they never appeared to me to have the needful education . . . for free government."[62]

But how was a lack of that magnitude to be made up? In the constitution he wrote for France, Morris included an article (Article VII) on "Education and Worship." He proposed that 30 percent of the

Catholic Church's tithes be devoted to public education, and that one tenth of that be reserved for a National Academy.[63] Morris's interest in education was typically American; Washington wanted the United States to have a national university, and he and Jefferson hoped to lure the faculty of the University of Geneva to staff it.

It was too late, however, for such measures to help France—or Europe. Morris would spend the next four years touring a war-torn continent.

CHAPTER ELEVEN

Europe at War

"I FLOAT, DEAR lady, like all light substances on the stream of time, too indolent to row, too ignorant to steer. . . ."[1] So Morris wrote, as he journeyed, to one of his friends from his Paris days. In a life of light letters, this was only one more, even as, in a life of ever-changing residences, he was only extending the series.

But Morris had a special reason for being in motion at this time of his life. The pressures of the last five years—of what he had done and seen—required release. At the end of December 1794, he wrote Washington a summary of his experiences in Paris, as balanced and somber as an inscription on a tomb. "I saw misery and affliction every day and all around me without power to mitigate or means to relieve, and I felt myself degraded by communications I was forced into with the worst of mankind. . . ."[2] A man who valued his ability to bring relief, both to himself for his own injuries and to his friends in their grief, had been impotent; a man who did not suffer fools had been obliged to treat with fools, thieves, and murderers. Morris had feasted on horrors, and though in the Europe of the 1790s they could not be put out of mind, he could put some distance between himself and them.

The twin engines of his travels were love and politics. After leaving Switzerland in November, he went north, and arrived in Hamburg early the next month. Hamburg lies on the right bank of the Elbe, fifty miles inland from the North Sea. It had ben an independent commercial city since the Middle Ages, and a major port for American goods since independence. This was reason enough for Morris to visit there, but in March 1795, Hamburg acquired another attraction.

After escaping from France, Adèle de Flahaut had lived in London, evidently supported by her old friend Lord Wycombe. Talleyrand was a frequent visitor, though indigence did not make her attractive in his eyes. If the letters of his that survive can be trusted (they may not be authentic), he seems to have behaved rather coldly toward the mother of his son. She worked at her novels, too poor to hire a copyist—"I was a real writing machine," she remembered years later.[3] When writing did not bring in enough money—and when did it?—she made women's bonnets. In time, she left London for the continent. Morris arranged for her lodgings in the Hamburg suburb of Altona.

In the second week of April he picked her a violet "on the south side of a steep hill," the first of the season.[4] He gave it to her, with a little poem.

> *Reçois les prémices que je viens de cueillir;*
> *Depuis longtemps tu sais qu'elles te sont consacrées—*
> *Mes travaux et mes soins, mes jeux et mon loisir,*
> *Les fleurs du printemps et les fruits de l'été.*

> *Voilà l'hiver qui vient, et d'un pas de géant,*
> *Où le jour est si triste et la nuit est si bonne;*
> *Jouissons au plus vite, jouissons, chère enfant,*
> *Car déjà je me sens au milieu de l'automne.*[5]

> *Take the first fruits I have just picked;*
> *You know that they are all for you—*
> *My work and my cares, my jests and my leisure,*
> *The flowers of spring and the fruits of summer.*

> *See winter come, with a giant's step,*
> *When the day is so sad and the night is so good;*
> *Then let us celebrate, my dear child,*
> *Because already I'm in the midst of fall.*

Morris's original is much better than this translation, for it rhymes and almost scans. Although his verses are never quite good enough to be good, they are charming. The wonder is that they are not awful.

Adèle no doubt appreciated the flower; what did she think of the poem? The theme is an ancient one: nature speeds through its cycles, from birth to death and back, but our lives do not come round again. Our night ends all, so seize the day. But what poetic convention allowed Morris to say that his work and his jests had been all for her (literally, consecrated to her)? They had done much for, and to, each other, but he had always withheld the pledges she had sought. After the execution of her husband, she was free to take another. But Morris had assured her, when he was thirty-seven, that he would not marry her. Now that he was forty-three, though he was feeling intimations of mortality, he was still not ready to commit himself.

Twice that spring, Adèle was "taken with a bleeding from the breast"[6]—a possible sign of a tumor, and reason for her to provide her son with stepfather, in case he should lose his mother.

In June 1795, Morris left Adèle and Hamburg for England. While he was living in Paris, he had taken an extended trip of nine months there; now that he had no fixed abode, he would take twelve. Love and verse occupied his thoughts. In a poem written for his sister-in-law, the wife of General Morris, he asked himself the question, could he still be attractive at a dance? Nature's answer was no; but the author chose to ignore it. "In nature's spite, / To Cupid I devote the night." When he rewrote the poem in French on a rainy day, it ended more anxiously. *Je puis aimer toujours, mais comment puis-je plaire?*—I can always love, but how can I please?[7]

Most of Morris's time, however, was taken with politics. He was presented to George III, and had one of those bland conversations, punctuated with interjections—"Oh, aye," "Ah, what!"—that everyone who met the monarch had.[8] He met a figure of the American future, the twenty-eight-year-old John Quincy Adams, son of Vice President John Adams; Morris found him "tinctured with suspicion"[9]—a judgment that would ring down the decades. He met William Pitt, the prime minister and son of a prime minister. Given his family, Morris moved comfortably in a world where elections had not quite untangled themselves from hereditary succession.

He renewed an acquaintance, made on a previous visit, with William, Lord Grenville, Pitt's cousin and foreign minister. He and Grenville consulted about European affairs, and Morris promised, when he resumed his travels on the continent, to write Grenville reports of the state of opinion in the courts of central Europe. Morris was not a mere medium of news, but freely offered his suggestions. The main problem, from Grenville's point of view, was that Prussia, wearied with fruitless exertions, had dropped out of the anti-French coalition. To woo it back, and thereby reestablish the European balance of power, Morris proposed a grand territorial swap, like a game of musical chairs. The heart of the deal was that Prussia would acquire Hanover, in north-central Germany, the homeland of the British royal family, while Britain would pick up Flanders. Holland and Austria would be compensated in various ways, and Morris even offered rewards for France—in one version, the territory of Alsace on her eastern border, in another, her former Caribbean and Indian colonies, now British prizes of war. Morris's reason for giving France overseas possessions showed his perverse intelligence—the more she had to lose, the more fearful she would be.[10]

When Morris finally returned to America, his political enemies would accuse him of having been on Grenville's payroll. This was absurd; he didn't need the money. The pleasure of hearing himself talk and reading himself write was compensation enough. Five years earlier, Morris had given similarly ambitious advice to Lafayette. Now that France had changed, he was offering his advice to the other side. At all times, Morris enjoyed playing with maps.

One thing he saw in the British Isles made him think of home. On a trip to Scotland, he inspected a newly opened canal, that bisected the country at the bottleneck between the Firth of Forth on the North Sea coast and the Clyde River, on the west. He admired the locks, the stonework, and the vessels using it. "When I see this," he wrote in his diary, "my mind opens to a view for the interior of America which hitherto I had rather conjectured than seen."[11]

In May 1796, he heard news of Adèle from a French émigré in London. Her health had not turned for the worse, but their intimacy had, for Adèle was said to be engaged to the Portuguese minister to Denmark (the Danish border was then a few miles north of Hamburg). Morris left for Hamburg in June. He did not question his old lover about her plans immediately upon his arrival, but one night, when he had taken her for a drive in his carriage after dinner, she told him along the way (*"chemin faisant"*) "whereabouts she is with her Portuguese lover." [12] Jose Maria de Souza-Botelho Mourao e Vasconcellos was thirty-seven, seven years younger than Morris, two years older than Mme de Flahaut. He had read *Adèle de Senanges*, her first novel, and conceived a desire to meet its author. Morris's diary says no more about him, or Adèle's connection to him, at this point. In their games of cat-and-mouse, there had been both scenes and silences. The laconic diary could be a facade, masking a frank conversation; it could be the true record of things unsaid. Morris left Hamburg at the beginning of July.

Over the next eight months, he visited the major cities of central Europe, and several of the lesser ones. He was by now an accomplished traveler, who had learned that "the art of living consists . . . in some considerable degree in knowing how to be cheated." [13] His account of life on the road in the Holy Roman Empire glitters with the comedy of discomfort—bores, vermin, astonishing food—which English travel writers would raise to the level of art. At one dinner, he was exposed to a "Saxon delicacy"—candied beetles. "These animals resemble in some respects what in America they call the locust, but are not so large, and have, besides, the hard cover of a bug to their wings, which cover is a bright brick-colored brown. How it should enter into people's head to eat them, unless driven to it by famine, one could hardly conceive, and the making them into sweetmeats is utterly inconceivable." [14]

Both the petty states and the major powers belonged to a dying world. Berlin, the capital of Prussia, was "a great unpeopled town," a stage set. "The immense appearances, I think, want solidity." All that remained of the power amassed by Frederick the Great was the brutal manners of realpolitik; negotiating with Prussians was easy, Morris explained to Grenville, "for it is not necessary to clothe propositions in honest and decent forms."[15]

Vienna made him rediscover his American priggishness. "A great number of women of the town are here," he wrote of midnight mass three days before Christmas. "The principal object of a great part of the congregation" was making assignations. " . . . I own that this mode of employing an edifice dedicated to sacred purposes does not accord with my feeling."[16] New Year's Day made him more thoughtful. The Prince Esterhazy, captain of the Hungarian guard, came to court in a scarlet uniform embroidered with pearls—"four hundred and seventy large pearls and many thousands of inferior size." Esterhazy was "the richest subject in Europe." Yet he lived in such a style that his estate was mortgaged to creditors, who paid him an allowance, which he regularly exceeded. "Here is the history of the feudal system in its decline. . . . [T]he government rejoices at the consequent humiliation of a haughty nobility, without considering . . . the power which is to spring up in its stead."[17] Once the nobles fell, would the local Neckers and their successors be any better?

The sinking star of feudalism still shed light. General Moszyn'ski, a Polish nobleman in Vienna, wore epaulettes set with huge diamonds. "But a finer thing than his jewels . . . was the conduct of his servant, who, when his master was made prisoner during the late troubles in that miserable country, possessed himself of his valuables and whispered to him, 'If you escape, you will find me at Leipsic [Leipzig].'"[18] The master escaped, and the servant was true to his trust.

The old order could not survive without leaders as competent as its servants were loyal. The revolutionary who was pushing old rulers over like ninepins as Morris moved about Europe was Napoleon Bonaparte, a Corsican artillerist who had survived the Jacobins who first advanced him in the French army, and who was now leading an invasion of northern Italy, toppling Austrian satraps and native regimes alike. Morris followed his progress from afar, through the usual scrim of gossip, bias, and misinformation. Time and again, wise heads told Morris that Napoleon was really a coward, and that he owed his victories to luck or the incompetence of his opponents. Morris, catching the bug, would opine that "he will probably now meet the usual fate of French armies east of the Alps"—that is, he would be defeated.[19] Yet somehow, the parvenu and his troops always managed to win. If it was luck, it was a long run of it.

He consoled himself for what had, or hadn't, been said in Hamburg. In Berlin he met again with one of his consolations from Paris, Mme de Nadaillac. There was a baron who was in love with her and wished to marry her, and the king of Prussia wanted her to be his mistress. "It would be ridiculous" for her, Morris admitted, "to succumb now to a *voyageur* who treats everything lightly, and yet such a thing might happen.... [T]he struggle between her reasonings and her wishes gives no small interest."[20] In Dresden, Morris met a Mme Crayen, who put up no struggle. The king of Saxony was besotted with her, but she loved the American stranger. They "worship[ped] on the Cyprian altar," and "brighten[ed] the chain together" (one brightens a chain by rubbing it). The "lively sense" of their lovemaking convinced her, Morris wrote boastfully, that she had become pregnant.[21] Balked with Adèle, Morris wanted lovers who were no trouble, either because they were unavailable or available without strings.

In the spring of 1797 he returned to Hamburg. There he saw Adèle, and her supposed fiancé, Souza. Souza, who had just returned from a diplomatic trip to Berlin, told Morris that the Prussians considered him a "great democrat."[22] Morris would puzzle any European—too liberal for monarchists, too conservative for revolutionaries, too skeptical for both. In Hamburg, Morris also ran across a figure from Adèle's past, Lord Wycombe, who only now realized that Adèle had once hoped to marry him. "[H]e seems to be very angry at it, though, in fact, he has nothing to complain of. He seemed a proper subject to work upon, and therefore she exerted herself to get hold of him."[23] To distract himself, Morris carried on with his landlord's two daughters (the younger, he wrote in an image that slides creepily from metaphor back into reality, "begins to feel the gentle hint from nature's tongue").[24]

Adèle evidently feared that she was losing her hold on Souza, because in the summer she applied to the French consular agent in Hamburg for a passport to return home. After the fall of Robespierre, Frenchmen of unapproved political opinions faced less risk of being guillotined. But since France still forbade the return of aristocratic émigrés, Adèle had to present documents showing that she had lived in Paris from 1792 to 1795. These were, of course, forgeries, but the diplomat approved them; corruption was as useful in getting into France as in getting out. She returned to Paris, and left Morris's life forever, in October 1797. Souza married her after all, in 1802—"in order," he told her, "that you would make me laugh."[25] Her son became one of Napoleon's generals. Fanny Burney, who had married one of the Frenchmen marooned in Surrey, found herself "charmed and delighted" when she at last met Mme de Souza.[26]

Morris hardly mentioned Adèle in his diary during his months in Hamburg, never revealingly. This was the long, cool diminuendo of a hot and cold affair—of long absences and furious, furtive lovemaking, of planning governments and hiding from mobs, of sickness, jealousy, and intelligent conversation. Can a man want so much without wanting more? Morris had been happy to woo Mme de Flahaut, but only in competition with Talleyrand, Wycombe, and her husband. His success in a scrum of lovers may have assured him, as Mrs. Plater had after his injury, that he was a whole man; it may have recalled being a brilliant youngest son among hulking older half brothers. But he would not have her alone. Perhaps something about his father's depression and his mother's stubbornness had made the idea of marriage unattractive, or perhaps his father's age during his boyhood had made it seem a state for late-middle-aged men. Only time and circumstances would change his mind.

A far greater star of the morning of the Revolution than the former Mme de Flahaut passed through Hamburg in the fall of 1797. Lafayette had been held in several prisons, ending finally in the Austrian fortress of Olmutz (now Olomuc, in the Czech Republic). After years of stern treatment, in which he wasted away and lost much of his hair, his wife and daughters were allowed to share his imprisonment. Mme de Staël wrote Morris a letter, by turns imperious and flattering, asking him to procure their freedom. "You have influence; [no one is] so stupid as not to consult a man like you."[27] As he had in the case of Paine, Morris doubted the efficacy of a direct demand upon the jailers. "[M]en do not easily allow they have done wrong . . . the most urgent solicitations would perhaps be fruitless; for it would be difficult to comply with them, without admitting the injustice in question."[28] Nevertheless, he applied to the Austrian imperial chancellor. Mercy, he argued, would require no explanations and no excuses. "[S]ince no one has had any right to know why his Majesty, the Emperor, determined to detain [Lafayette] as a prisoner, so no one can assume that of demanding why his kindness has set him at liberty." It would also please an even greater ruler. "Think, also, that forgiveness granted to others is the only unobjectionable title, of which we can avail ourselves before the King of Kings."[29] The emperor himself received a private appeal from George Washington, in the last year of his last term as president. What finally freed Lafayette was not appeals to forgiveness, but French arms. Napoleon and his subordinates, after driving the Austrians from northern Italy and pursuing their armies within sight of Vienna, accepted their demands for peace. One of Napoleon's stipulations was that Lafayette be released. The political position the aging hero represented, of idealistic constitutional monarchy, was so impotent that the French government no longer condemned him. They did not, however, want him in France, so the two nations agreed to set him and his family free in Hamburg. Morris advised him not to speak of the injustices he had suffered: so many had suffered far worse.

Talleyrand had a better recovery from his reverses. Exile had taken him from the English countryside to the woods of the United States, where he made some money in American real estate, and was astonished to see Alexander Hamilton, now retired from the Treasury, working at night in his New York law office (why had he not used his opportunities to make better provision for his future?). Talleyrand was permitted to return to France in the summer of 1796, thanks to the influence of Mme de Staël, and only a year later he became foreign minister, also thanks to her influence, even though no one else liked him ("to enter a government in which nobody wants you," said one admiring observer, "is no mean trick").[30] Now that he was back in power, after experiencing its transience, he would not make Hamilton's mistake. *"Il faut y faire une fortune immense, une immense fortune"* (I have to make an immense fortune, a really immense fortune).[31]

Paine had been freed from prison a month after Morris left France. He attacked George Washington in print for not having demanded his release, and made plans, as Morris had done for Lafayette, for a French invasion of England. He put his hopes on the young General Bonaparte and, in the words of another displaced revolutionary, the Irishman Wolfe Tone, drank "like a fish."[32] Years later, still drinking, he would return to America, his reputation blasted by his criticisms of Washington and Christ, and die in New York, in Greenwich Village. Morris never saw him again.

Morris spent his last year in Europe touring little German cities, then returning to an Adèle-less Hamburg to prepare his journey home. His activities had become somewhat boring, perhaps even to him. But one deserves mention. From the moment he had left France, he had helped French acquaintances in distress. He loaned them money on the most generous terms: "If fortune smile upon you, you will return the money. If not, allow me to treasure the consoling thought that I have alleviated your troubles for a short period."[33] He gave it, without even the pretense of a loan: "The enclosed letter will supply you with what you want. Do not speak of obligations."[34] He gave, what was equally valuable, good counsel. "Try to make everyone understand how necessary it is to forgive, and to forget the past, thinking only of the future."[35] As a geopolitician, he was reckless; as a guide to living, he could be acute.

Morris took inspiration from many of the émigrés he saw. When he first came to Dresden, he found the streets filled with them, fleeing eastward, allowed to stay only three days. (Years later, Adèle remembered posted warnings in German towns against Jews, vagabonds, and émigrés.) "Unhappy people!" wrote Morris. "Yet they are employed in seeing everything curious which they can get at; are serene, even gay. So great a calamity could never light on shoulders which could bear it so well." The weight of suffering, he realized, "is not diminished by the graceful manner of supporting it." Grace, however, spared the sufferers the additional burdens of "spleen and ill-humor."[36]

But whom else did this describe? Who else was habitually serene, even gay? This was the face that Morris had been wearing, and recommending to friends and family members for years. Morris's gaiety came partly from religious belief, for though he honored neither the Sabbath nor the marriage vow, he "hope[d] in the kindness of that Being who is to all his creatures an indulgent father."[37] On the surface of it, this is a paradoxical hope, since divine indulgence is not what émigrés and other sufferers experience. But suffering itself had its lessons. "Do not say, madame," Morris wrote the comtesse d'Albani, one of the many miscellaneous almost-celebrities he had met (she was the widow of "Charles III," pretender to the throne of England), "that life is a sad thing. Without reverses it would soon become insipid, and we find that the happiest mortals are those who have been taught, through some sad experience, the value of this world's goods."[38] In a treatise of moral philosophy, such advice could be enraging. Coming from a man with a stump and a fleshless arm, who so clearly enjoyed this world's goods, it was consoling, even inspiring.

Morris sailed from Hamburg at the beginning of October 1798. Two months later, the ship he was on approached Long Island in the teeth of a nor'wester, and he had one of those encounters that come to self-assured men. "This morning at two o'clock the captain comes to ask my advice whether we should stand in for Rhode Island, or stand off. I tell him I will not pretend to advise, he must act according to his own judgment, but I will give him my opinion on any state of facts which he may represent."[39] The much-blown traveler landed in Newport and, after more storms and other travails, arrived in New York at the end of the month. On the last Sunday of the year Morris attended divine worship at Trinity Church at the head of Wall Street.

Part 3

Brink of Revolution

CHAPTER TWELVE

American Passions

ONE OF THE New Yorkers who greeted Morris on his return was Alexander Hamilton, recently promoted to major general and second in command of the United States army. Hamilton wanted his old friend to take a role in the national government—"His talents are wanted," he wrote Rufus King; "men like him do not super-abound"—but Morris told him that he intended to lead a private life.[1]

Morrisania wanted his attention. The best fertilizer, as the proverb says, is a master's footsteps, and his estate had not felt his for over a decade. The roof leaked, so he decided to rebuild the house. He spared no expense, embarking on a course of improvements that would cost him $50,000 to $60,000, or well over half a million today. He entertained generously, if imperiously. "When he spoke," wrote a frequent guest, "he expected the listening ear. On a certain occasion . . . perceiving the attentions of his hearers beginning to flag, he suddenly ejaculated, 'I shall address the tea pot' and he accordingly closed his argument with that silent representative."[2] His determination to live in the style to which he had become accustomed could make his countrymen gape. "[U]pon entering the inn," wrote a traveler who crossed his path, "I found Gouverneur Morris with two French valets, a French traveling companion and his hair buckled up in about a hundred papillottes [paper curlers]. His wooden leg, papillottes, French attendants and French conversation made his host . . . stare most prodigiously and gave me some idea how the natives looked when poor Cook made his entrée at the friendly isles."[3]

He took on a complex civil suit, *Le Guen* v. *Gouverneur & Kemble*, involving a shipment of East Indian cotton and indigo that had passed through the hands of half a dozen middlemen, one of whom (Isaac Gouverneur) was Morris's uncle. The climactic hearing in Albany lasted seven days and involved eight lawyers, including Hamilton, who was on the opposing side, representing Lewis Le Guen. Morris, wrote one of the lawyers, "at times astonished us with bursts of sublime eloquence—at other times he was flat and uninteresting." Hamilton, "wound up with passion," sometimes went too far. "Hamilton," Morris noted in his diary, "is desirous of being witty, but goes beyond the bounds and is open to a severe dressing."[4]

Outside the courtroom, Hamilton wanted Morris to reenter public life because American politics seemed to be in the gravest state since the ratification of the Constitution, perhaps since the end of the Revolution. Federalists and Republicans had been feuding throughout the second term of George Washington. Morris had urged his idol to stand for office a third time ("[I]t is not given to every man to bend the bow of Ulysses"),[5] but Washington, tired of the political broils, and intent on teaching a last lesson about transferring power in a republic, had stepped down, to be succeeded, in the election of 1796, by his vice president, John Adams. The feuding continued as before. Washington, after trying to maintain a balance between the parties, had steadily found himself drawn to the side of the Federalists. Adams, the target of Jefferson's blurb for *The Rights of Man*, was also commonly reckoned among them. The Republicans were led by Jefferson, now, by a quirk of the Electoral College, vice president, and by James Madison, once the friend and adviser of Hamilton and Washington, now their enemy.

One of the leading Federalists in New York and nationally was Alexander Hamilton. Morris had known him since the Revolution. They had shared several experiences—going to King's College, serving in the Continental Congress—though never at the same time (Hamilton was five years younger). Both men had a self-consciously "realistic" turn of thought, which Morris expressed in the flourishes of his tongue and pen, Hamilton through the relentless thrust of his arguments. Their refusal to be satisfied with airy ideals or soothing phrases was based, in part, on the hard things each had seen in his life. But, as their experiences differed, so did their temperaments. Morris's early injuries were brutal and obdurate, never to be repaired, only graciously lived with. The injuries Hamilton experienced in the West Indies were more insidious. His parents had fastened on him the burden of illegitimacy, and his father had compounded it by abandoning his lover and their children when Alexander was nine years old. His mother's death when he was eleven completed the tale of a bleak and shamed youth. His subsequent rise in the world was meteoric: by the time he was twenty, he was a colonel on Washington's staff; by the time he was thirty-two, he was Treasury secretary. Hard work, it seemed, could fix his and the world's problems. So although Hamilton was witty enough, he, unlike Morris, lacked a true sense of humor: he had too much to do.

The two political parties disputed everything from foreign policy to Hamilton's visionary intention of molding America into a flourishing industrial power (the Republicans equated luxury with corruption, and cherished an agrarian ideal). As sundering as their disagreements was the manner in which they expressed them. Tempers ran as high as differences ran deep. Early in 1798, Representative Matthew Lyon, a Republican from Vermont, spat in the face of Representative Roger Griswold, a Federalist from Connecticut, who in return clubbed him with a hickory cane, all this in the cloakroom and on the floor of the House. The newspapers, as vicious as they were lively, whipped the frenzy up. On another occasion Hamilton, accused by a Republican journalist of secret dealing in government securities when he was Treasury secretary, had felt compelled to reply that the money he had paid his supposed agent had in fact been blackmail, extorted because he had been sleeping with the recipient's wife.

What brought politics to a fever pitch in the second half of the Adams administration was a new strain in America's relations with France, to which the Genet episode had been a mere prelude. The villain of the piece was Morris's old friend Talleyrand. Early in his term Adams had sent three special envoys to Paris to protest French harassment of American shipping. The envoys expected to deal directly with the minister of exterior relations. But, after one fifteen-minute interview with Talleyrand in October 1797, he put them off, while mysterious intermediaries appeared in his stead, suggesting that the United States must pay money—"a great deal of money"—to France and to themselves personally before negotiations could even begin.[6] It was the old story of Le Brun and the debt repayments all over again. Talleyrand and his minions were not trying to affront the United States; they were playing by the rules of diplomacy and public service as they understood them. But the American envoys were shocked, and when they reported the French shakedown to Congress in the spring of 1798, America was outraged. The Federalists, profiting from popular wrath, passed laws against suspicious aliens and Republican journalists, and expanded the army against a French attack, bringing Washington out of retirement to command and making Hamilton his right hand.

Morris arrived in New York just as the war fever had peaked. French setbacks in Ireland and Egypt had caused Talleyrand to moderate his tone; some Americans (including President Adams) began to balk at the cost of a military establishment. If the prospects of a war were fading, however, political warfare raged unabated. The Republicans accused the administration of plotting a military dictatorship, as the first step to a monarchy. The Federalists viewed their enemies as Jacobins; Hamilton, with bellicose jauntiness, explained that the political stakes included "true liberty, property, order, religion and of course *heads*."[7]

Morris, who would soon be drawn back into politics, would not take part in its bitterness, at least not yet. His time in Europe helped him keep an even keel. Sitting on the rim of a world war, Americans borrowed its ideological terminology for their own disputes. Morris, who had been in the vortex, could not be so facile. Federalists and Republicans might speak of each other as Jacobins and monarchists, ready to make use of guillotines and putsches. But Morris had lost acquaintances to the guillotine, and watched royalists plot vain coups.

He also knew an earlier world of politics. Morris had seen the first stirrings of ideological party strife during his years in Pennsylvania, when the Constitutionalists and the Republicans had fought over the state government and the Bank of North America. (The Pennsylvania Republicans, who had supported a bank and a strong executive, were now Federalists, while the Constitutionalists, suspicious of both, had become Republicans.) But he had sprung out of the older world of colonial New York politics, in which parties formed around rival families, and friendships were also family affairs. One survival of that system was his intimacy with Robert R. Livingston. Local accidents determined Livingston's course: Hamilton, who had worked with the Livingstons to secure New York's ratification of the Constitution, had imprudently boosted Rufus King, newly moved to the state, for a Senate seat that the Livingstons considered theirs. One did not cross a New York grandee without suffering the consequences, and when Jefferson and Madison reached out to the Livingstons as allies, they responded. Morris, for his part, devoted to Washington and detesting the French Revolution, made himself a Federalist once he returned home. Yet Morris and Livingston had been friends since their twenties. The two men maintained their old cordiality.

Morris paid his respects to another old friend, now in disgrace. Robert Morris had been imprisoned for debt before Gouverneur had returned from Europe. The rare claret, the temple erected to hospitality, and all his holdings would not pay a twentieth of his obligations. Gouverneur visited Robert and his wife in their prison in Philadelphia in the fall of 1799. His sketch of his ruined patron is a mixture of clarity and pity. Robert Morris had "behaved very ill," dragging creditors into the depths with him. His wife now "put . . . on an air of firmness which she cannot support, and was wrong to assume." Their visitor kept up a "lively strain of conversation" to distract them from their woes. When the debtors were finally freed, he would do more than that, giving Robert Morris an annuity that would allow the sexagenarian to keep a roof over his head.[8]

At the end of the year, Morris had the duty of delivering Washington's eulogy. He had written Washington in mid-December, urging him to stand as the Federalist candidate for president in 1800 in place

of John Adams (Washington was always first in the heart of Morris).
Washington never read the letter. He had gone riding in a snowstorm
at Mount Vernon, got soaked, and died of an inflamed throat. The
city fathers of New York asked Morris to deliver an oration at St.
Paul's Chapel, where Washington had gone to worship after his first
inauguration, ten and a half years ago. Morris did not consider the
speech a great success—"Pronounced my oration badly," he noted in
his diary—for eulogy was not naturally his vein. He was always more
comfortable as an advocate, when he could employ the sallies for
which Washington had once gravely chided him.[9]

The death of Washington removed more than a national icon. The
nation lost a symbol of seriousness, and the last psychic brake on unre-
strained partisanship. Politics would enter a long period of irresponsi-
bility, punctuated by ugliness.

In the spring of 1800 one of New York's senators resigned his seat,
and the state legislature (which then elected senators) picked Morris
to fill out the remaining three years of his term. The last time Morris
had sat in Congress, almost twenty years ago, the states voted as units,
attendance was spotty, and the accommodations, in York at least, were
quite grim. Now senators and representatives voted as individuals, and
there were three additional states—Vermont, Kentucky, and Tennessee: the emerging frontier, against which Morris had warned at the
Constitutional Convention. Accommodations in the new city of
Washington, to which the government moved at the end of 1800, were
still grim, however. The city was little more than a few public buildings, a few boardinghouses, and swamp; Morris had lived as well in the
roadside bugholes of central Europe. In a letter to one of his European
friends, the Princess of Thurn and Taxis, Morris described his new
abode: "We want nothing here but houses, cellars, kitchens, well informed men, amiable women, and other little trifles of the kind. . . . If,
then, you are desirous of coming to live in Washington, in order to
confirm you in so fine a project, I hasten to assure you, that fieldstone
is very abundant here . . . that there is no want of sites for magnificent
hotels; that contemplated canals can bring a vast commerce to this
place; that the wealth, which is its natural consequence, must attract

the fine arts hither; in short, that it is the very best city in the world for a *future* residence." [10]

Morris was a loyal Federalist in most things. He supported Federalist press restrictions for, although he was proud of his family's role in the Zenger case, he disapproved of journalists who told lies or revealed official confidences, as Paine had done when he worked for the foreign affairs committee. Republicans also supported such restrictions, only wishing them to be enforced by the states, not the federal government (especially when it was controlled by Federalists). But Morris saw that the Federalists were in political trouble. The taxes levied to support a war that had not happened were onerous. "The truth is," he wrote Rufus King, now minister to Britain, "that a direct tax, unpopular everywhere, is really unwise in America, because property here is not productive." The Republicans "have had just cause to complain of the manner in which money is raised, and [since] our expenditure is far from economical . . . no applause is to be expected on that score." [11]

Like many parties in difficult straits, the Federalists fought among themselves. President Adams hoped to repair his fortunes by sending new envoys to France, and by dismantling the army. Hamilton thought that both moves were rash, and that Adams was literally mad. Morris, more charitably, called the president *"unbiegsam"* (unbending). [12] The Republicans, meanwhile, moved with disciplined unity toward their goal, and in the election of 1800 the vote of the Electoral College gave Vice President Jefferson and his running mate Aaron Burr a victory.

The Electoral College was one of the more unusual improvisations of the Constitution Convention. According to the original plan, each elector voted for two men, and the top two vote-getters became president and vice president. In the elections of 1789 and 1792, every elector cast one vote for the Father of his Country. The only suspense concerned who should finish second, which John Adams managed twice to do, though he trailed far behind Washington. In the election of 1796, however, both Adams and Jefferson had finished ahead of their respective running mates, which led to the anomaly of the victorious president having his defeated rival as vice president. Now another anomaly occurred. The Republicans had been determined to let no Federalist slip in between their candidates—with the result that Jefferson and Burr tied.

Burr, who would turn forty-five in early February, had made his career as a lawyer and politician in New York, but Morris's long sojourns in Philadelphia and Europe had deprived him of all but the most recent acquaintance with him. Burr was the son of the Reverend Aaron Burr, president of Princeton, and the grandson of the Reverend Jonathan Edwards, the great preacher and philosopher. Credulous observers made of these religious antecedents an aristocratic pedigree that impressed Burr's contemporaries and gave Burr his imposing self-assurance.[13] New Englanders probably were impressed by Burr's family history, though it is doubtful that Morris or the Livingstons, to say nothing of the Randolphs and the Pinckneys, cared much about a pair of dead Congregationalist divines. As for Burr, he was confident because of his qualities—intelligence and charm—and his achievements—a brave war record and the love of beautiful women.

One attainment Burr lacked was any definite political program or philosophy, and this now gave many of the defeated Federalists hope. The tie in the Electoral College was to be broken by the House of Representatives. States would vote as units, and everyone's quick count showed that the Republicans controlled eight state delegations, and the Federalists six, with two split. If Federalists in the House supported Burr, the deadlock would continue. If Burr could then coax some well-placed Republican congressmen to his side, Jefferson might be supplanted by a possibly better man.

Adèle de Flahaut had disliked Jefferson, calling him *"faux et emporté"* (false and hotheaded).[14] Ordinary Federalist politicians detested him; "they consider Mr. Jefferson," Morris wrote, "as infected with all the cold blooded vices."[15] (How did the hot head of the Frenchwoman's Jefferson run with the cold blood of the Federalists' Jefferson? By expressing sweeping sentiments with the detachment of an intellectual.) But Morris had always gotten along with him well enough. When Jefferson surrendered his main duty as vice president, presiding over the Senate, Morris would write the Senate's valedictory tribute, praising his "intelligence, attention and impartiality."[16] Burr he judged to be an unknown quantity, on whom it was pointless to build hopes.[17] In any case, the Republicans had wanted Jefferson, and they were the majority. "Since it was evidently the intention of our fellow citizens to make Mr. Jefferson their President," Morris wrote Hamilton from Washington in mid-December, "it seems proper to fulfill that intention."[18]

Hamilton believed that Burr was a completely known quantity. From mid-December on through the month of January 1801, he sent a stream of letters from New York to Morris and other Federalists denouncing Burr as a bankrupt, a Bonaparte, and a political corsair. Hamilton claimed not to hate Burr; the two men socialized occasionally, and, in the small legal world of New York, they also appeared in the same courtroom (they had both been lawyers for Lewis Le Guen). But he hated the idea of Burr holding high office. Burr, he wrote Morris, is "daring enough to attempt every thing, wicked enough to scruple nothing."[19]

Neither Hamilton's onslaught nor Morris's doubts had any effect on the Federalists in Washington. "They appear to be moved by passion only," Morris wrote Hamilton early in January. "You, who are temperate, *in drinking*"—a jest at Hamilton's sex scandal—"have never perhaps noticed the awkward situation of a man, who continues sober after the company are drunk."[20]

Those few Federalists who did not want to intrigue with Burr hoped to get assurances from Jefferson. In the middle of February, after the House had begun balloting—the deadlock there would hold for thirty-five ballots—Jefferson ran into Morris outside the Senate chamber (the Capitol was as yet barely begun; Congress met in the passage that now connects the Rotunda to the Senate). Years later, when asked what they had said, Morris politely refused to reveal it. "[I]t was . . . that sort of conversation where, among gentlemen, there is so much confidence implied, that it would be indelicate to cite facts. . . ."[21] Jefferson's memory of the encounter was that Morris told him he could end Federalist resistance by pledging to keep the funding of the public debt, to keep up the navy, and to keep lesser Federalist officeholders in their posts. Jefferson remembered making no promises. Other Federalists approached Jefferson's allies with the same proposals, and some believed they got satisfaction, though Jefferson always insisted that he had commissioned no one to bargain for him. Then as now, Washington insiders claimed to know more than they in fact did, while Jefferson, who was not quite *faux,* as Mme de Flahaut thought, was nevertheless capable of not always hearing what he himself said. However it was, enough Federalist die-hards abstained on the thirty-sixth ballot to give Jefferson ten states and victory.

In the interval between the Federalist collapse and Jefferson's inauguration, Morris answered a letter from Robert Livingston. Livingston had missed standing in Burr's shoes, for when the Republicans were looking for a New Yorker to run with Jefferson, he had briefly been considered. Perhaps to assuage his disappointment, Livingston had written that if Morris had been Jefferson's running mate (a neater trick than Talleyrand coming back into office), the House would have made him president. Morris gracefully waved the hyperbolic compliment aside, then turned to recent events. "The election by the House of Representatives will doubtless have excited heats, and animosities, at a distance. Here the most perfect good humour prevailed, from beginning to end." With the writer, perhaps; of whom else was he thinking? He had known all along, he claimed, that the pro-Burr Federalists "would be disappointed, and, therefore, [I] looked on with perfect composure. Indeed, my dear friend, this farce of life contains nothing, which should put us out of humour." [22]

The election of 1800 had been the United States's first peaceful transition, not from man to man, as had happened in 1796 when Adams succeeded Washington, but from party to party. It had, however, been a closer call than Morris let on: the Republican governors of Pennsylvania and Virginia had thought of dubious outcomes in which they would be obliged to call up their militias. Nor had the peaceful result allayed ill feeling. Most Federalists felt the rage of losers. President Jefferson intended that they should continue to feel it, for though his inaugural address, delivered on March 4 ("too long by half," Morris wrote in his diary),[23] contained a generous sentence—"We are all republicans, we are all federalists"[24]— he wrote privately that he would "sink federalism into an abyss from which there shall be no resurrection."[25]

Morris escaped the general mood not only because of his natural cheerfulness but because of an almost casual insight into the function of partisanship. Political parties were not mentioned in the Constitution, because they were thought to be bad things. Madison, in his *Federalist* essays, called them "factions"; Washington, in his Farewell Address, had warned against them. The framers (including Madison and Washington) had almost immediately set two parties up, but they could not acknowledge what they had done. More precisely, none of them could acknowledge the legitimacy of the party that was not his. Federalists thought their opponents were undermining the state; Republicans thought their opponents were perverting it. The difference between Jefferson's inaugural address and his private thoughts was not an instance of hypocrisy. His public statement was truly generous, but it dealt in generalities: all Americans, he was saying, supported the principles of freedom and constitutionalism. He expected Federalist Party members of goodwill, however, to join his party, which understood the proper balance of these principles. Parties as such would then wither away.

In an 1800 letter to Rufus King, months before the crisis in the House, Morris virtually stumbled upon a more profound understanding of the role of opposition. "*Nil desperandum de Republica* [Don't despair of the Republic] is a sound principle. Let the chair of office be filled by whomsoever it may, opposition will act as an outward conscience, and prevent the abuse of power."[26] Morris's observation is politically prescient: it brings parties into the checks and balances of the Constitution. It is psychologically acute as well, for the phrase "outward conscience" is large with implication. Parties will generate a morality of partisanship, keeping each other honest. Morris's thought was more important than anything he had said at the Constitutional Convention, and a worthy appendix to everything that had been said there. Not being of a systematic turn of mind, he never elaborated it; perhaps he never fully appreciated it. In the poisonous atmosphere of the next fourteen years, no one, including even himself, would act on it consistently.

In their meeting outside the Senate chamber, Morris had not asked Jefferson to maintain the integrity of the judicial branch, which was just as well, since it was one of the new president's goals to pare the judiciary back. From Jefferson's point of view, he was simply restoring the status quo. On the eve of his inauguration, in February 1801, the lame duck Congress had passed a Judiciary Bill adding seven district and sixteen circuit judges. The Republicans thought these last-minute appointments were pure Federalist patronage ("an hospital for decayed politicians," said John Randolph, a young Republican congressman from Virginia).[27] Morris himself admitted in a letter to Livingston that this was one motivation: "That the leaders of the federal party may use this opportunity to provide for friends and adherents is, I think, probable, and if they were my enemies I should not condemn them for it. . . . They are about to experience a heavy gale of adverse wind. Can they be blamed for casting many anchors to hold their ship through the storm?"[28] But Morris had backed the Judiciary Bill because it brought impartial justice "near to men's doors. . . . Depend on it that, in some parts of this Union, *justice* cannot readily be obtained in the State courts." Morris's grandfather had been removed from his judgeship by a local oligarch, and Morris believed an expanded federal judiciary would diminish the power of contemporary local bullies.

When the new Republican majorities in Congress proposed a bill to disband the new federal courts, Morris became alarmed. The Constitution (Article III Section 1) stated that "Judges, both of the supreme and inferior courts, shall hold their offices during good Behavior. . . ." This provision had been adopted to give judges independence; wasn't abolishing their jobs a way of controlling them? Morris, speaking in the Senate, characterized the Republican proposal thus: "[Y]ou shall not take the man from the office, but you may take the office from the man; you shall not throw him overboard, but you may sink his boat under him; you shall not put him to death, but you may take away his life."[29] If the judiciary had no independence, then the legislature was unchecked, and the French Revolution had shown where that could lead (perhaps the politics of Europe offered a useful parallel after all). "[S]ee . . . what has happened in your own times," he told the Senate. By 1790, "the only question" in France "was, who will become the despot." [30]

Morris's rhetoric did not prevent him from going to tea at the White House, where he found Jefferson "very civil, but with evident marks" of discomfort—not surprisingly, since Morris had just accused his party of wishing to become despots. The wife of Secretary of State James Madison, the plump and beautiful Dolley, struck him as having "good dispositions"—she was friendly, perhaps flirtatious—which he attributed to "the shriveled condition" of her husband. [31] When a new Judiciary Bill repealing the old one passed in March 1802, Morris wrote Livingston that "[w]e have here as yet nothing of importance except destroying the Constitution." [32] Morris took his defeat lightly, because that was his temper, but the seeds of disaffection had been planted.

The New York legislature failed to reelect Morris to a full term at the end of 1802, so that he struck his last blow for Federalism as a lame duck. Talleyrand helped give him his opportunity. The Frenchman was now working for Napoleon Bonaparte, the First Consul, and their foreign policy was simple: peace in Europe, expansion in North America. The object of France's desire was Louisiana, the inner watershed of the continent that France had given to Spain in the middle of the eighteenth century. In 1800, Bonaparte and Talleyrand forced Spain to sign a secret treaty giving it back. Spain was a feeble, and therefore a good neighbor to the United States, but the prospect of Napoleonic France occupying the mouth and the west bank of the Mississippi was something else entirely. In preparation for the French takeover, the Spanish officials still running the colony from New Orleans denied Americans the right to navigate the river. Hoping to pick up western votes, congressional Federalists urged Jefferson to respond aggressively. "No nation," Morris told the Senate, "has a right to give another a dangerous neighbor without her consent." [33] He made a prediction. "There must be [war] either with France or England." If the United States fought France (plus Louisiana), the western states would be ruined; if it fought England, the eastern states would be. "[L]et the war be with whichsoever of those nations it may, one half of the United States must be peculiarly injured."[34]

He also made what was, along with his encouragement of the Newburgh near-mutiny, the worst argument of his public life. France would encourage slave revolts from Louisiana, "stimulat[ing] with a prospect of freedom the miserable men who now toil without hope." But slaves must believe "that it is impossible for them to become free. Men in their unhappy condition must be impelled by fear and discouraged by despair. Yes. The impulsion of fear must be strengthened by the hand of despair."[35] How had the man who had railed against the three-fifths rule and the slave trade, and their corrupting effect on republican institutions, come to this point? Morris was ever prey to the speaker's vice of following the flow of his own words. The repetition of his argument, after the "Yes," shows him in the act (the speech was taken down by shorthand). But Morris's willingness to offer the argument in the first place sprang from a related vice of his—saying unpleasant truths in the most offensive way possible. He had not wanted to give slaveholders an inflated stake in the government, but they had won it. Very well—he would make them appeals suited to their natures. Whatever his reasons, it was a wicked argument, and if he had come to the point of saying such things, it was just as well that he was leaving public life.

This period marked the sour end of his relations with Lafayette. The hero's wife wrote him a letter stating that she would repay the 100,000 livres Morris had loaned her in 1793 with 53,000 livres, citing a new French law that established conversion rates for debts contracted during the revolutionary inflation. She was hiding behind the law, and Lafayette was hiding behind her. Morris let the matter drop. "I only wish them a clear conscience," he wrote. "Unhappily, that they will not have, and will ever bear me, in consequence, a sincere hated. The ungrateful man never thinks of his benefactor without a pang, and how should one not detest the object that causes such suffering and lowers one in one's own eyes?"[36]

His Senate years saw his fiftieth birthday approach and pass, and he occasionally felt his age. He called his dancing at one dinner party hobbling, and wrote that only the smallness of the party excused "the ridiculousness of this attempt."[37] But he found yet another lady friend, Sarah Wentworth Morton, a Boston poetess whom he met when he was visiting Philadelphia (the City of Brotherly love had always been kind to him). Her verses had earned her the titles the "American Sappho" and the "American Mrs. Montagu." Lady Mary Wortley Montagu was not on the level of Sappho, and Mrs. Morton was not on the level of either. But the new country was proud of her efforts. Gilbert Stuart painted three portraits of her, including one teasing composition in which a bust of George Washington (one of her subjects) looks on solemnly while the lady slips a bracelet on her lovely wrist.[38]

Mrs. Morton also had her share of troubles, for her husband, Perez Morton, a successful lawyer and orator, had had an affair, seven years after their marriage, with her younger sister, Frances, who then killed herself after bearing his child. This lurid episode was discussed in the Boston newspapers, and in a novel, *The Power of Sympathy,* written by William Brown, one of the Mortons' neighbors. "Oh, why did Willy do such a thing?" Sarah's mother asked Brown's mother. "The names are fictitious," Mrs. Brown replied.[39] The considerate Mr. Brown had changed "Morton" to "Martin."

An intelligent woman with an unsatisfactory husband was, as ever, an attractive combination. Morris made his approaches; Mrs. Morton claimed she was "indisposed." Morris knew that was *"en règle"* (part of the game).[40] The game progressed, and Morris dined with both Mortons in Boston in the summer of 1803. "[M]onsieur," he wrote, "was cordial, all things considered."[41]

The problem of Louisiana was solved by Robert Livingston, whom Jefferson had made minister to France. Napoleon abruptly decided that Europe offered a better field for his energies, and Talleyrand told the startled American that the heart of the continent was for sale. After some dickering, the deal was done for $15 million. Most Federalists, who had wanted to use Louisiana as a stick with which to beat

Jefferson, were unhappy when he bought it. But Morris was proud of his friend's success, and he did not quibble at the cost. "A few millions more or less . . . really seems unworthy of notice."⁴²

No politician ever retired with more satisfaction or fewer regrets than Morris. He thought the Constitution was tottering, or already fallen, but he refused to be alarmed. "I have made up my mind to float along as gently as I may."⁴³ His equanimity rested, in part, on his limitations. He lacked the lifelong follow-through of a Washington; if his advice went unheeded, his pride was touched, and he shrugged off the problem along with the affront. If the founding of the state had rested on him, or men like him, it would not have happened. But devotion to public life is not an unmixed blessing. Many politicians are persistent troublemakers, especially if their pride is wedded to their ambition.

A week after the Fourth of July, 1804, one of Morris's nephews came to Morrisania to tell him that Alexander Hamilton had been killed that morning in a duel, by the vice president of the United States. Aaron Burr had not been unaware of the harsh things Hamilton had said of him during the endgame of the election of 1800; Hamilton had repeated them all again that spring when Burr, hoping to provide for himself after his vice-presidential term ended, ran for governor of New York, and went down to defeat. At last, Burr had had enough. The gentlemen began a correspondence, and met for an interview at Weehawken, across the Hudson from Manhattan.

The duel was not simply a personal feud, however. Burr and his Federalist admirers had been in contact throughout Jefferson's first term. But the Federalists were by now even more desperate than they had been after the election of 1800. Peace and prosperity, capped by the coup of the Louisiana Purchase, guaranteed Jefferson's reelection. A band of Federalist die-hards in New England plotted a secession of the North, and thought they had Burr's support. Hamilton, hearing of their schemes, was appalled.

The next day, July 12, Morris went down to the city and learned that Hamilton was still alive, in a house on Greenwich Street, where he had been taken after being shot (Burr was unharmed). "Go there," Morris wrote in his diary, in clipped rhythms recalling his days in

France. "When I arrive he is speechless. The scene is too powerful for me, so that I am obliged to walk in the garden to take breath. After having composed myself, I return and sit by his side till he expires." When the doctors opened the body, they found that Burr's bullet had snapped a rib, pierced the liver, and lodged in the spine. "A most melancholy scene—his wife almost frantic with grief, his children in tears, every person present deeply afflicted, the whole city agitated, every countenance dejected. . . . I am wholly unmanned by this day's spectacle."

Morris was asked to give the eulogy, and the next day he talked it over with one of Hamilton's legal colleagues. They ran over the difficult points of Hamilton's life: his illegitimate birth; his character flaws ("indiscreet, vain, and opinionated"—Morris might have recognized them); his unpopular opinions. There was the irony of Hamilton's death: "He was in principle opposed to dueling, but he had fallen in a duel. I cannot thoroughly excuse him without criminating Colonel Burr, which would be wrong. . . ." Wrong for two reasons: because in dueling, Burr had only been following the gentleman's code; and because Morris did not want to encourage the incensed mourners to riot. On top of everything else, there was no time to memorize anything lengthy. "The corpse is already putrid, and the funeral procession must take place to-morrow morning."

The next morning, the funeral procession began two hours late. It ended at Trinity Church, where Morris spoke in the open air, inaudible to nine tenths of the crowd. "Get through the difficulties tolerably well; am of necessity short. . . . I find that what I have said does not answer the general expectation. This I knew would be the case; it must ever happen to him whose duty it is to allay the sentiment which he is expected to arouse. How easy would it have been to make them, for a moment, absolutely mad!"[44]

The duel blasted both Burr's future and the secession plot. But the underlying political wounds were not cauterized. It would be easy to make Americans, for years, absolutely mad.

CHAPTER THIRTEEN

Work and Love

I N HIS RETIREMENT from public life, Morris wrote Mme
de Staël, urging her to visit America. "As soon as you arrive,
you will come to Morrisania, partake what our dairy af-
fords, and refresh yourself. [You may] gather peaches, take walks,
make verses, romances; in a word . . . do whatever you please. When
my hermitage shall have lost its attractions, you shall establish yourself
in the city, where, by the aid of a good cook, you will contrive to live
very well. Here, as elsewhere, people amuse themselves with discussions, *bon mots*, slandering their neighbors and the like. Life is everywhere much the same in the long run."[1] So he tempted her with the
pastoral ideal of urban sophisticates, old as Horace and Virgil: the
country retreat, never sundered from the place in town.

Morris spent much of the first decade of the new century, however,
traveling through true country—the wilderness of western and northern New York. He gratified his love of boating, and inspected his land
investments along the Genesee and St. Lawrence rivers. Where the
Oswegatchie River, a tributary of the St. Lawrence, flows over a rock
formation called the Natural Dam, he built himself a summer house,
with two-foot-thick stone walls, that still stands. There he sampled "a
most delicious syrup made from the maple tree," and the "finest fishing
for trout that I ever yet saw."[2] But he was also exploring a matter of
public business and national benefit—the possibility of a western canal.

Throughout Morris's youth, most New Yorkers lived on Long Island, and in New York City and the Hudson Valley; a few brave souls
had ventured down the Mohawk River. The great barrier to westward

movement was the Iroquois Confederacy, six well-organized and ag-gressive native tribes that had historically good relations with the crown. The Revolutionary War removed this difficulty, since most of the Iroquois sided with the British, whose defeat left them subdued or exiled. While Morris was in France, some developers had begun to open up the new landscape. William Cooper, a self-made land speculator from New Jersey, founded Cooperstown in central New York, and, thanks to its success, served in Congress, sent his sons to Yale and Princeton, and hosted Talleyrand at his rural estate. But travel to western New York was onerous, as it was to every place in the United States beyond the Alleghanies. Enough settlers had made it over the mountains to westernmost Virginia and North Car-olina that two new states, Kentucky and Tennessee, had been created for them. But their easiest contact with the outside world was not back through their home states, but down the Mississippi, and through New Orleans.

Tempted by the possible gains and undaunted by the actual difficul-ties, Americans dreamed of canals. One visitor to Mount Vernon, be-tween the war and the writing of the Constitution, recalled that canals and interior navigation were George Washington's "constant and fa-vorite theme. . . . Hearing little else for two days from the persuasive tongue of this great man, I confess completely infected me with the canal mania."[3] Not all of Washington's acquaintance were infected. James Madison explained the great man's mania by saying that "a mind like his, capable of great views . . . cannot bear a vacancy."[4] In New York, Cadwallader Colden, a colonial official who was a contemporary of Morris's father and grandfather, had beaten Washington to the idea by fifty years. As early as 1724, he pointed out that there were two pos-sible routes across New York into the interior: one taking the Mohawk west to Oneida Lake, then curving northwest by the Oswego River to Lake Ontario; another continuing directly west to Lake Erie. The most natural path to the coast from western New York was down the St. Lawrence River. But in 1724, when Colden wrote, the St. Law-rence was controlled by France, the enemy, and therefore to be avoided. After the American Revolution, when the St. Lawrence was controlled by Britain, the former enemy, New Yorkers would seek to avoid it for the same reason.

Morris had the canal mania during the Revolutionary War. When the Council of Safety sent him, in 1777, from Kingston to Fort Edward to consult with General Philip Schuyler, he had held forth on the subject. In the words of one of the officers who was present, "Mr. Morris, whose temperament admitted of no alliance with despondency . . . frequently amused us by descanting with great energy on what he termed the 'rising glories of the Western World.' One evening in particular . . . he announced, in language to which I cannot do justice, that at no very distant day the waters of the great western inland seas [i.e., the Great Lakes] would, by the aid of man, break through their barriers and mingle with those of the Hudson."[5] This memory was recorded half a century after the fact, when public figures and their friends were vying for the parentage of a good idea, but the story is not inherently unlikely—"descanting with great energy" certainly sounds like Morris, and the hope was by no means unique to him.

During his European sojourn, Morris had seen canals at work. The low country of Flanders, through which he passed on visits to Antwerp and Amsterdam, was one elaborate web of artificially improved rivers, and the canal bisecting Scotland particularly impressed him. Soon after he returned home, he visited western New York. In July 1800, after the Senate adjourned, he went up the Hudson, and through Lake George and Lake Champlain, to Montreal (the old invasion route, now traveled in peace); then up the St. Lawrence to Lake Ontario, and so westward, to the mouth of the Genesee River, and finally to Niagara Falls and Lake Erie. There he stopped, and returned the way he had come. In his descriptions of what he had seen, he summoned all the language of the romantic sublime.

"There is a brilliance in our atmosphere," he wrote one of his business friends in Hamburg,

which you can have no idea of, except by going to Italy, or else viewing one of Claude Lorraine's best landscapes, and persuading yourself, that the light there exhibited is a just, though faint copy of

nature. . . . Still less can I pretend to convey to you the sentiment excited by a view of [Lake Ontario]. It is to all purposes of human vision an ocean; the same majestic motion too in its billows. . . . After
one day's repose at Niagara, we went to view the Falls. To form a
faint idea of the cataract, imagine that you saw the Firth of Forth
rush wrathfully down a steep descent, leap foaming over a perpen-
dicular rock one hundred and seventy-five feet high, then flow away
in the semblance of milk, from a vast basin of emerald.

Most enthusiastically of all, he looked at the future—a future pop-
ulated by men. He described his passage, above the Falls up the Niagara River, to Lake Erie.

[I]n turning a point . . . I saw riding at anchor nine vessels, the least
of them above a hundred tons. Can you bring your imagination to
realize the scene? Does it not seem like magic? Yet this magic is but
the early effort of victorious industry. Hundreds of large ships will,
in no distant period, bound on the billows of these inland seas. At
this point commences a navigation of more than a thousand miles
[through the chain of the Great Lakes, to Lake Superior]. Shall I
lead your astonishment up to the verge of incredulity? I will. Know
then, that one tenth of the expense borne by Britain in the last campaign [in Europe] would enable ships to sail from London through
Hudson's river into Lake Erie. As yet, my friend, we only crawl
along the outer edge of our country. The interior excels the part we
inhabit in soil, in climate, in everything. The proudest empire in
Europe is but a bauble, compared to what America *will* be, *must* be,
in the course of two centuries; perhaps of one![6]

Morris was ever contemptuous of the politics of frontiersmen, but
here he foresaw the frontier transformed into civilization. His rhetoric
in this letter is the sublime of progress.

Morris enjoyed traveling through upstate New York for one other
reason: the pleasure of physical activity. In a trip in the fall of 1803, his
voyage down the Oswego River was "dangerous and exciting. . . . [T]he

sea ran so high as to greatly alarm my ship's company." One passenger, he noted happily, "was frightened even to roaring, and, when he got on shore, declared he would rather return home on foot than go again on board of the boat with me."[7] When the party reached Lake Ontario, a storm was blowing, the pilot was laid low by fever, and Morris had to do what the timid captain had begged him to do in the nor'wester off Long Island, and set the course himself. "[W]ith no other resource than my recollection of a former voyage, and, having fixed what I believe to be the spot, we luckily enter the harbor we were making for through a very high surf and by a rocky point, which we narrowly escape."[8] In 1887, when the American Statesman, a series of biographies published by Houghton Mifflin, made the bizarre assignment of Gouverneur Morris to the young Theodore Roosevelt, the only commonality (besides old New York roots) between the caustic wit and the eager, earnest politician was their shared delight in exercise and the outdoors. Morris the cripple and Roosevelt the asthmatic each had a heavy investment in their own strength and recklessness.

Morris was not the only New Yorker considering improvements to navigation. As he traveled through upstate, his friend Robert Livingston, back on the Hudson, was pushing an invention that, in the long run, would be even more significant than a western canal. For Livingston was the backer of Robert Fulton, a painter turned inventor whom Livingston had met in Europe, and in August 1807 they launched a boat powered by a Watt steam engine. The Steam-boat, as New Yorkers proudly and simply called it—it was the only one in the world—plied the Hudson from New York to Albany. In November, Morris dined with a Mr. Walton, of Ballston, a town north of Schenectady, who told him "that, by means of the steam-boat, he can leave his own house on Monday morning and dine with me on Tuesday, do some business in New York on Wednesday morning, and be again at home of Thursday evening," for a four-day round trip, including work and pleasure.[9] At a time when a stage coach from New York to Albany took three days, and a sailboat anywhere from three days to two weeks, depending on the winds, this was revolutionary.

The Lewis and Clark Expedition, which left St. Louis in 1804 and returned two years later after exploring the Missouri and Columbia rivers, was the great adventure of the federal government during the Jefferson administration. It was not a journey of discovery, since French trappers had been traveling most of Lewis and Clark's route for a century and a half (the husband of Sacajawea, their Shoshone guide, was named Toussaint Charbonneau). But their journey was bold, colorful, and patriotic all at once, and stirred the national imagination. The real steps toward national growth, however, were being taken by old aristocrats in upstate New York, exploiting the tamer landscape of their home state. Lewis and Clark traversed the wilderness, much of which remains wilderness today. If a canal to Lake Erie could be dug, however, the heart of the continent would blossom.

Jefferson himself was mindful of the economic opportunities closer to home. In December 1806, his annual message to Congress touched on roads and canals. Republican thrift had built up a surplus in the Treasury, and Jefferson proposed spending it on internal improvements, if a constitutional amendment allowing such appropriations should be passed. (He did not think the "general welfare" clause of the Preamble gave sufficient sanction.) "By these operations," Jefferson wrote, "new channels of communication will be opened between the states . . . and their union [will] be cemented by new and indissoluble ties." [10] In 1808, his Treasury secretary, Albert Gallatin ("an intelligent fellow," Morris would conclude when he met him, [11] not knowing, or forgetting, that Gallatin had once accused him of being a trickster), sent a report to Congress proposing a $20 million program—$280 million today—of road and canal building, cutting across capes and bypassing waterfalls from Maine to Georgia, and from the coast to the Mississippi. New Yorkers hoped that some of this federal largesse might help build their canal.

IN THE MIDST of these gathering projects, Morris gathered one of his own. He hired a housekeeper who would become much more. The servants at Morrisania were a motley lot: "wild Irish, some French who have fled Napoleon's conscription—a few cutthroat English, a portion of Americans who disdain subordination—also a small number of

Germans."[12] Housekeepers "of low birth and education" could not maintain order among them; only a "reduced gentlewoman"—that is, a lady of Morris's class who was in need of work—could command their respect.[13] In October 1808, he drove down to New York to engage the services of such a gentlewoman, Miss Anne Cary Randolph.

Mr. Morris and Miss Randolph had met twice before, in the 1780s, when he had been in Virginia managing Robert Morris's tobacco contract. Nancy Randolph, as she was called, was the daughter of Colonel Thomas Mann Randolph, master of Tuckahoe, a plantation on the James River west of Richmond that Morris visited. In his letters from Tuckahoe, Morris described the colonel—"a gentleman possessing one of the best fortunes in this country"—and his wife—"an amiable woman . . . not in much good health"[14]—but made no mention of their daughter Nancy—not surprisingly, since she was only a girl (thirteen years old in 1788, the time of his second visit). When he met her again in New York, she was living in a boardinghouse, run by an "old Mrs. Pollock,"[15] on Greenwich Street. Her twenty years' descent, from Tuckahoe to urban indigence, had been as rough as it was steep, and the first stage of it had been a matter of public notoriety.

The Randolphs were a first family of Virginia, as eminent as they were numerous. If they produced no suns like Washington or Jefferson, they supplied many a bright star. Peyton Randolph was the last Speaker of the colonial House of Burgesses, and a delegate to the First Continental Congress. "Under temptations and difficulties," Jefferson once wrote, "I would ask myself what would . . . Peyton Randolph do in this situation?"[16] Edmund Randolph was a delegate to the Constitutional Convention, and Jefferson's successor as secretary of state. Jefferson's mother was a Randolph, as was one of his sons-in-law: two somewhat unusual marriages, since Randolphs preferred to marry their own Randolph cousins, whenever they could. In 1789, such a marriage occurred when Nancy's older sister Judith married her first cousin Richard Randolph. The newlyweds settled at a plantation on the Appomattox River named Bizarre (many Virginia plantations had poetic, even hifalutin, names: one near Bizarre was called Horsdumonde). Nancy soon came to live with them.

Richard Randolph had two younger brothers—Theodorick and John. Of the three, John was the most talented, soon to show a vein of eloquence and invective as bitter as it was brilliant. He was also the oddest—his voice never broke, and he never shaved. "[F]rom my earliest recollection," he once said, "I have remarked in myself . . . a delicacy or effeminacy of complexion that but for the spice of the devil in my temper would have consigned me to the distaff or the needle."[17] In a portrait by Gilbert Stuart, he looks like a strange, flaxen-haired boy. All three brothers were generous, passionate, and undisciplined—a common constellation of traits among Virginia aristocrats. They were also all smitten with Nancy. Nancy Randolph first sat for a painter years later, and the work he produced is not very good, but it does show an impish smile, bright eyes, and an inviting bosom, which must have been even more attractive in her late teens. Theodorick and John each asked her to marry him; Richard, who was in no position to do so, asked her never to marry anyone. She became engaged to Theodorick, whose good luck, however, did not hold, for he died of tuberculosis in February 1792.

The internal affairs of the Randolph family came to general notice that fall. Richard, Judith, Nancy, and John were visiting relatives in September, when Nancy was taken ill; her hosts heard screams in the middle of the night. Rumor soon supplied the explanation: Nancy had been pregnant, and had given birth; slaves had found a dead white baby on a pile of shingles; the father was Richard, who had killed the infant by exposing it. "To refute the calumnies," Richard published an open letter in the *Virginia Gazette and Advertizer* in April 1793, announcing that he would appear at the next session of the county court, where his accusers, he demanded, should "stand forth and exert themselves" to convict him of a crime.[18] He seems to have thought he could bluff the gossips into silence. Instead, when he appeared at court he was arrested.

Richard Randolph had to hire lawyers, and the lawyers he hired were the greatest defense team that has ever appeared in an American court: Patrick Henry and John Marshall. They conceded nothing, not even that a child had been born, or that Nancy had been pregnant. The seasoned Henry examined the witnesses. He demolished one woman who testified that she had seen Nancy, naked and round-bellied, through a crack in her door. "Madam, which eye did you peep with?" Henry asked, then turned to the audience and declared, "Great God, deliver us from eavesdroppers!"[19] The young Marshall, a Richmond lawyer, argued the case to the jury, carefully examining every damning detail and showing that it had an innocent explanation (Richard and Nancy were publicly affectionate; but if they had had a guilty connection, would they not have feigned indifference?). Judith testified to the innocence of her husband and sister. The slaves who had found the dead child were forbidden, by Virginia law, to testify against white men in a felony matter. The jury barely deliberated, acquitting Richard Randolph of all charges.

Nancy Randolph, therefore, was also innocent of incest and murder. But her life had nevertheless been blighted at the age of eighteen. Henry and Marshall, in contesting the assertion that any child had been born, also introduced testimony implying that, if one had, the father was Theodorick. Yet even if Nancy had been impregnated by her dying fiancé, rather than by her brother-in-law, she was hardly marriageable. If no man would have her, she would have to live the remainder of her life as a family dependant.

Further clouds gathered round Bizarre. Richard died in 1796, of a sudden fever, leaving Judith and two young sons, the elder of them a deaf-mute. The responsibility of running the plantation fell to John— no light thing, since tobacco prices were in a long, steady decline. Nancy's widowed sister and her brother-in-law could not have been pleasant company, for Nancy or for each other. Judith admitted that hers was a "gloomy disposition."[20] For a time, John could direct his spice of the devil to politics. Elected to the House of Representatives in 1798 when he was only twenty-five, he became, after his cousin Jefferson reached the White House, chairman of the Ways and Means Committee. Representative Randolph was an extreme, and extremely quotable, Republican: the issue of the Hamilton-Burr duel pleased him—"It reminded me of a sinking fox pressed by a vigorous old hound"—and he judged Morris's eulogy, which he read in the newspapers, "wretched."²¹ In 1805, however, he bungled an important political task, impeaching but failing to win the conviction of Justice Samuel Chase, the most aggressive Federalist on the Supreme Court.

In the straitened circumstances of Bizarre, Nancy Randolph was a small but real burden to her sister and her brother-in-law. She was an emotional burden as well, for she was the only one of the Randolphs at Bizarre who seemed determined to live, relishing her rare opportunities to visit, and craving news from the "Beau Monde."²² In the spring of 1805, smarting from political failure, John asked Nancy to leave.

Over the next three and a half years, she drifted north. How she managed to live is unclear, though it is clear that she lived badly. In a letter to John from Newport, Rhode Island, she asked for $50 (he did not send it). How Morris learned of her situation is also unclear. In August 1808, in upstate New York, he met a "Mr. Bell from Virginia," with whom he conversed "pleasantly"; perhaps he recounted something.²³ After meeting Miss Randolph at old Mrs. Pollock's, Morris went back upstate, where he spent the winter. Was he already hoping for more than a housekeeper? Unfortunately his diary at this period tells more about his travels than his personal relationships. Morris was observant, and an intelligent, unhappy woman would have attracted his notice. He was available, having left Mrs. Morton to her poetry and her husband years before. While he was in Schenectady, he had a sobering experience, an illness so alarming that he made a will. The ailment passed, though when he was in Albany, he experienced a symbolic death, the temperature falling so low that the ink froze in his pen. The first event, if not the second, must have reminded him of the passing years. It was twenty years since he had met Adèle de Flahaut, twelve since she had passed out of his life.

He returned to Morrisania in February of the new year, and wrote Nancy a series of letters. He wished her to begin her new employment. "Pride may exclaim 'Miss Randolph cannot descend to the rank of a servant under whatever name, or however elevated and distinguished.' Pride is such a wrangling disputant that I will not argue with him."²⁴ He also set the stage of their personal relationship. "I once heard, but have no distinct recollection, of events which brought distress into your family. Dwell not on them now. If ever we happen to be alone you shall tell your tale of sorrow when the tear from your cheek may fall in my bosom."[25] This was an offer of friendship. But did he expect Miss Randolph to fall into his bosom along with her tears? He was fifty-seven years old and rich; she was thirty-four years old and poor. Did he intend her for a kept woman? "[A]las! Time in taking away the ardor has not wholly quelled the rashness of youth. I can only answer that I will love you as little as I can."[26] He added that no illicit connection with his housekeepers had ever existed, or been suspected—". . . certainly I have never approached . . . them with anything like desire."[27] Morris was laying out the terms of their intercourse: he was taken with Miss Randolph, and intended to pursue her, but he promised to pursue her honorably.

He also gave her, what he gave so well, words of encouragement. He spoke of virtue, "which I do not use in the tea-table sense that calls a woman virtuous though she have the malice of a dozen devils . . . but to express a pure heart, a chastened spirit, fortitude, benevolence, charity." This was indirect praise, singling out qualities he saw in her, whatever Virginia gossips had said sixteen years ago. He concluded with his life-long credo: "The incidents of pleasure and pain are scattered more equally than is generally imagined. The cards are dealt with fairness. What remains is patiently to play the game, and then to sleep."[28]

Morris was attracted to Nancy Randolph, as he had been to other women, by the combination of spunk and suffering, which allowed him to be both a fellow struggler and a benefactor. His previous serious lovers had suffered from bad marriages, for which he had offered himself as recompense. Nancy Randolph had, in some ways, suffered more than they had; if he offered himself to her now, he would find no marriage barring a possible union. In April 1809, he wrote in his diary that he brought "Miss Randolph of Virginia" home to Morrisania.[29]

Morris made one effort to check if there were any other bar to their happiness. Nancy had surely told him her version of the events of September 1792, and he surely believed it. But early in December 1809 he wrote Richard Randolph's surviving lawyer. Patrick Henry had gone before the highest Judge; John Marshall was now Chief Justice of the

Supreme Court. Morris presented his situation as a party matter: " . . . connected [as I am] with so many worthy men as fill the Federal ranks," Republicans would naturally seek to "affix a stigma" on Morris, or "on any one of us, however inconsiderable he may be personally considered. Now it is from consideration for friends I esteem . . . that I [write]." [30] Why so many considerations? Was it verbal wordplay, or nervousness as he neared his goal? What "reputation," Morris asked, had Miss Randolph left in Virginia? The Chief Justice answered judiciously. Virginians had disagreed about the case, but the circumstances were "ambiguous," and Judith Randolph, "who was most injured by the fact if true," had let Nancy live under her roof for twelve years. [31]

Morris now made haste. On Christmas Day, he entertained a party of friends and in-laws at Morrisania. One of them was Isaac Wilkins, his old Tory brother-in-law who had returned from his exile in Nova Scotia to be an Episcopal clergyman. "Many of the family whom I expected," the host wrote in his diary that night, "are detained by the weather. I marry this day Anne Cary Randolph—no small surprize to my guests." [32]

The new couple had their portraits painted, in the following year, by a traveling English artist, James Sharples. Sharples's portrait of Mrs. Morris made her look like the cat that ate the canary. Like all previous portraitists, Sharples failed to capture her mercurial husband. What he did get, in the subject's penetrating gaze, was his intelligence and sarcasm. Mr. Morris seems to know what the viewer is thinking, and he does not care one whit.

The marriage was an unpleasant surprise to Morris's nephews and nieces, who had expected one day to divide the estate of the aging bachelor. One of them, Mrs. Gertrude Meredith of Philadelphia, was bold enough to express her chagrin in a letter to him. Morris's reply was sweetly lethal. "[I]f the world were to live with my wife, I should certainly have consulted its taste; but as that happens not to be the case, I thought I might, without offending others, endeavor to suit myself. . . ." [33] Morris had consulted the Supreme Court, but no lesser tribunal.

CHAPTER FOURTEEN

War Comes Again

GOUVERNEUR MORRIS'S political quiescence during this long period of canal-planning and wife-taking sprang from a cheery pessimism. He thought the affairs of the nation were in the hands of incompetent men with bad principles, and this made him easy of mind and light of heart. The political bitterness that brought death to Alexander Hamilton had festered for years. Vice President Burr was indicted for murder in New York and New Jersey, though he was not prosecuted, since no jury of gentlemen would convict a duelist. In 1807, Burr was tried for treason, on account of his plottings in the Louisiana Territory, which were so deep and indefinite that historians still have not explained them; he was acquitted. Napoleon's turn from the New World to the Old plunged Europe into war, and finally economic war. Each belligerent great power—France by the Berlin Decrees, Britain by the Orders in Council—sought to prevent neutrals from trading with its enemy. America's response was to make it a crime for Americans to trade with anyone, driving the commercial states of the Northeast to despair.

Through all these crises the Republican Party maintained itself in office, led by its great Virginians, whom Morris disdained without exception. He thought Jefferson an amiable and otherworldly theorist; his opinion of the "shriveled" James Madison, who succeeded Jefferson as president in the election of 1808, was lower, and would sink lower still. For James Monroe, who had replaced him as minister to France, and who now seemed to be the next Virginian in line for the White House, he felt nothing but contempt. When Jefferson favored

Monroe with an appointment, Morris, recalling Matthew 21:42, wrote that Jefferson had showed his Christian spirit, for he "has taken special care that a stone which the builders rejected should become the first of the corner."[1]

Morris believed that when the policies of Virginia Republicanism had been crowned by unignorable failure, then the people would reject them. "[N]ations, like individuals, are not to be reasoned out of vice, much less out of folly, but learn wisdom and virtue in the school of affliction.... [R]ascals are more likely to repent at the gallows and whippingpost, than at the gaming table and dramshop."[2] Until the instructive crisis came, he would keep his thoughts to himself, and a small circle of relatives and friends. "I consider it a vain task to preach to unbelievers."[3] He woke from these pleasant hopes of doom only when national politics became entangled with the progress of New York's canal.

New York's official canal-planning began in a spirit of bipartisan cooperation. In March 1810, the state legislature appointed a seven-man commission to report on the feasibility and cost of such a project. All factions in the state were represented, the leading Republican commissioner being the mayor of New York City, DeWitt Clinton. The forty-one-year-old Clinton had already been in politics for twenty-two years. His mentor was his uncle, George Clinton, who had been governor of the state for so long that he had earned the title "The Old Incumbent," and was now serving the second of two terms as vice president. Tall, intelligent, and imperious, DeWitt Clinton had lofty ambitions for his city and state, both economically and intellectually. He studied Indian languages and archeology, and helped found local learned and artistic societies. Morris was skeptical of these latter endeavors. When one of his dinner companions excused his late arrival by saying that he had been detained at a meeting to found a Philosophical Society, Morris asked where would they find the philosophers?[4] But the aging Federalist and the rising Republican saw eye-to-eye on the issue of economic development. The legislature named Morris chairman of the Canal Commission, in recognition of his eminence and his enthusiasm.

In the summer of 1810 the commissioners set out across the state to examine possible routes. Most of them traveled to Oswego by water, and they had a miserable time. DeWitt Clinton's journal echoes Morris's accounts of central Europe a decade earlier. Clinton complained of "drunken people in the adjacent room . . . crickets in the hearth . . . rats in the walls . . . dogs under the beds . . . the whizzing of mosquitoes about our heads, and the flying of bats about the room."[5] Morris, the more experienced traveler, went by carriage to Niagara Falls, taking his bride with him, in an early version of the classic honeymoon trip (a second carriage carried his French cook). The commissioners rendezvoused at Lewiston on the Niagara River. Morris's diary implied that there were disagreements among the commissioners—he worried whether the "most correct" opinions would prevail[6]—but they were soon composed, and never aired. The commissioners thought of themselves, and presented themselves to the public, as a phalanx of the state's elite, united in a common purpose.

On their way back east, the Morrises added religion to business by visiting a community of Shakers on the Massachusetts border. This sect had been founded in the eighteenth century by Mother Ann Lee, an Englishwoman who claimed to be the female Christ, and who taught communism, trance dancing, and celibacy. The couple heard a sermon that urged them "to abandon worldly pursuits, pleasures, and enjoyments, and, more especially, the conjugal pleasures. . . ." Morris found this last an "unnatural (and therefore impious) doctrine."[7]

The following year Morris presented the commission's findings to the legislature in a report that was polemical and poetic by turns. He argued for a route going all the way to Lake Erie, scorning the shortcut to Lake Ontario. "[A]rticles for exportation, once afloat on Lake Ontario, will, generally speaking, go to Montreal, unless our British neighbors are blind to their own interest, a charge which ought not lightly to be made against a commercial nation."[8] He pointed out the dangers of feeding a canal with water drawn from rivers, which are subject to floods and droughts. "[I]n the spring, the careful husbandman and miller will open every ditch and sluice to get rid of that water which, though at other times a kind friend and faithful servant, is then a dangerous enemy and imperious master." [9] Happily, New York could feed its canal from its numerous lakes. Morris introduced into the report a hobbyhorse of his: the notion that the entire canal could be an inclined plane, slanting gently down from Lake Erie to the Hudson. This was a daydream, ignoring the need for locks and aqueducts to surmount local changes in elevation, and once professional surveyors so concluded, Morris would drop the notion. He made another prediction, however, which must have struck observers as no less fantastic, but which turned out to be reasonably correct. "There is no part of the civilized world in which an object of such great magnitude can be compassed at so small an expense." [10] Morris thought the canal could be dug for $4 million (over $50 million today). Who would pay? A private company, Morris argued, could not raise the money. "Few of our fellow citizens have more money than they want. . . . But the public can readily, at a fair interest, command any reasonable sum." The borrower should be the federal government, since more states than New York— including states not yet created—would profit. "[T]hose who participate in the benefit, should contribute to the expense. . . . The wisdom, as well as the justice of the national legislature, will, no doubt, lead to the exercise on their part of prudent munificence." [11]

That DeWitt Clinton would sign such a document showed how far his family, and the Republican Party, at least in New York, had come. DeWitt's uncle George had opposed the Constitution; once it was ratified, he became the strictest of constructionists. In February 1811, as vice president, he broke a tie vote in the Senate on rechartering the Bank of the United States; the elder Clinton voted no, on the grounds that chartering a bank was not a power expressly granted to the federal government. Now his nephew was willing to use federal money to dig a canal.

The next step was to present the plan to Congress, but Morris sandwiched into his duties as canal commissioner the writing of another report, this time on the street plan of New York City. The small town in which he had studied law and taken his first steps in politics had grown to a population of 96,000, and pushed north to Houston Street, two miles beyond Manhattan's wedge-shaped tip. New York City might lack philosophers, but it had energy, and it was in the process of passing Philadelphia to become the nation's largest city. In 1807, the state had appointed Morris to a three-man commission to plan for the city's growth beyond Houston Street. Now their report, unsigned but marked with his prose rhythms, forsook the gnarled streets of the old Anglo-Dutch town for a vast grid of 12 parallel avenues running eight miles up the length of the island and 155 streets at right angles to them. Hills, streams, and marshes would be overlaid; old roads and paths that meandered across the grid would be abandoned. (The only significant survival was the slanting former Indian trail of Broadway, and the commissioners had wanted to abolish even that.)

The plan was an implicit critique of the baroque star patterns that the designers of Washington, D.C., had envisioned for the streets of the nation's capital. The city of capitalism would be based on economy, not Italianate affectation. "Straight-sided and right-angled houses," wrote Morris, "are the most cheap to build, and the most convenient to live in." [12] So the planners envisioned nearly two thousand rectangular city blocks, each divided into rectangular lots. Morris's two plans, for the canal and the streets, shared a determination to cut through natural obstacles for human use. They had another link: if the canal to Lake Erie were dug, then the produce of the heartland would flow to the world through New York City, making additional streets all the more necessary.

In December 1811, Morris and Clinton went to Washington at the behest of their state to lobby. They called at "the palace"—the White House—and met with congressmen (a "mess of democrats; a pleasant society enough, though not select"). [13] The appeal they presented to President Madison, though probably written by Morris, reflected the self-assurance of both men. "We do not assign reasons in . . . support [of a canal], because they will not escape your penetration; neither do we solicit your patronage, because we rely on your patriotism." [14] Though Madison told the New Yorkers he was an "enthusiast" for canals, he was "embarrassed" by constitutional "scruples" about paying directly for New York's. [15] Gallatin, the Treasury secretary, found a compromise solution: a land grant of 4.5 million acres in northern In-

diana, whose revenues would fund the project. Shortly after the New
Year, Madison submitted an omnibus canal bill to Congress including
Gallatin's suggestion, and praising the New York canal for its "honor-
able spirit of enterprise."[16]

Yet the bill died in committee. In a report to the state legislature in
the spring of 1812, Morris and Clinton urged New York to go it alone,
"making a manly and dignified appeal to her own power."[17] The rebuff
still stung, however, and the lobbyists assigned a reason, "operating
with baneful effect, though seldom and cautiously expressed. The
population and resources of the state of New York furnish no pleasant
reflections to men, whose minds are imbued with state jealousy."[18] At
the Constitutional Convention the delegates in apportioning representation had put New York in fourth place for population, behind
Virginia, Massachusetts, and Pennsylvania, and tied with Maryland.
In the 1810 census, New York had become the largest state in the
Union. In the First Congress, New York had had only six representatives; in the Twelfth, it had twenty-seven. A canal would add wealth to
numbers.

Morris and Clinton refrained from saying what the political consequences of New York's growth might be. The Republican Party's success at the national level had been based on an alliance of Virginians
and New Yorkers, attempted in every election since 1800 with a vice-
presidential candidate from New York (Aaron Burr in 1800; George
Clinton in 1804 and 1808). But Virginia had always been the senior
partner. Now in 1812 DeWitt Clinton was considering the top spot
for himself. At home, Clinton was happy to work with Federalists; nationally, he was willing to pick a fight with fellow Republicans. President Madison might overlook Clinton's ambitions in the name of the
spirit of enterprise, but other politicians were more gimlet-eyed.

There was yet another reason for the failure of the canal bill, however—the approach of war. Britain and France both had adopted a
bullying attitude to the remote neutral nation, but Britain, thanks to
its navy, had more opportunities to bully. First Jefferson, then Madison had tried every means of resistance that was pacific, or purely defensive, and Morris had mocked them for it. They believed, he said, "in

defence of territory by reduction of armies, and in vindication of rights by appointments of ambassadors";[19] they wanted to repel the British navy "with a mosquito fleet of gun-boats."[20] With the failure of every alternative, Madison felt driven toward war. A new generation of his party, meanwhile, was eagerly demanding it. In 1811, a crop of fire-eating southerners and westerners had entered Congress, among them John C. Calhoun of South Carolina, age twenty-nine, and Henry Clay of Kentucky, age thirty-four (Madison, by contrast, had turned sixty in 1811). These were the frontiersmen whom Morris had always feared, but who only now attained real power; Clay was elected Speaker during his first term in the House. A typical warhawk, Calhoun spoke fervently about "the laws of self-preservation" and "the shield of honor";[21] he also thought Canada could be overrun in only four weeks. The lone Republican voice opposing the firebrands belonged to the increasingly alienated John Randolph. "There is a fatality, Sir, attending plenitude of power. Soon or late, some mania seizes upon its possessors; they fall from the dizzy height, through the giddiness of their own heads."[22]

Morris saw the wheels of war in motion when he was in Washington lobbying. One day he stayed in his room, "los[ing] thereby the opportunity of hearing Mr. Randolph make a much admired speech"—one of his desperate anti-war philippics.[23] A week into the new year, "a thumping majority" passed a bill to raise a 25,000-man army.[24] In this state of things there was no time for canals.

In the spring of 1812 Vice President George Clinton died at the age of seventy-two. Once again, Morris was asked to deliver a eulogy. In May, DeWitt Clinton visited him at Morrisania, to talk about his late uncle, and current politics. Morris's advice to him was momentous, coming from the author of the Constitution. "[I]n the degenerate state to which democracy never fails to reduce a nation, it is almost impossible for a good man to govern, even could he get into power, or for a bad man to govern well." Morris's solution was to call for a Convention of northern states to "consider the state of the nation," and propose repeal of the three-fifths rule. "[T]he southern states must then either submit to what is just or break up the Union." DeWitt Clinton, he believed, "acknowledge[d] the force of these observations," though he could hardly proclaim them as a political platform.[25] Two weeks later, Morris eulogized the Late Incumbent; always his severest critic, he felt his speech was badly delivered and "better received than such speaking deserved."[26]

Morris's politics from mid-1812 on defined a contradiction. The canal he had been working for would be an agent of consolidation, uniting vast tracts of the country economically, just as the Constitution, which he had written twenty-five years earlier, had united it politically. Yet now the economic nationalist was proposing constitutional changes in the form of demands, and welcoming disunion if the demands were rejected. As late as 1811, he had been content with the serene cynicism of the past decade. "As in war so in politics, much must be left to chance; or, in other words, to combinations of which we are ignorant."[27] In private life, the cynic traveled, made money, and enjoyed himself. "I . . . enjoy from my window the exhilarating view of approaching spring," he wrote early in 1812 after turning sixty. "Oh, my friend, had we also a renewed spring of life. . . ."[28] What changed his mind only months later?

All his life Morris believed that men acted only under the threat of disaster. If times were peaceful, it was useless to reason with them. But when disaster struck, then men must act. The impending disaster now was war with Britain, compounded by loss of opportunity. Morris had urged Lafayette to go to war two decades earlier, but France was a great nation. The United States, with no army, scarcely any navy, and no national bank, was preparing to take on the greatest power on earth. In doing so, it would ignore Morris's canal. Faced with such folly, Morris was ready to act again. In June 1812, Congress declared war on Great Britain. (Ironically, London had just repealed its obnoxious Orders in Council, but word of the deed reached Washington too late for second thoughts.) "I believe, sir," wrote Morris in a letter at the end of the month, "that men of honor and worth must prepare for scenes more serious than electioneering."[29]

All the talk of conquering Canada was quickly shown up as empty rant. In Detroit, an American army surrendered ignominiously to a smaller British force. On the Niagara River, another American army, commanded by Stephen Van Rensselaer, the lord of the manor of Rensselaerwyck and a member of the Canal Commission, failed in an attack on Queenston on the Canadian side when the New York militia would not leave the state. The only ally the United States had in its warmaking was distant France, but on October 19 Emperor Napoleon evacuated Moscow, to begin his long, disastrous retreat. Morris, studying his maps, had predicted that Napoleon would evacuate on October 20; "the varlet was off a day sooner than I supposed."[30] For once, his low opinion of Bonaparte proved to be correct.

In the election of 1812 Morris helped throw Federalist support to DeWitt Clinton, who tried to unseat Madison by being all things to all men, telling Federalists that he opposed the war and Republicans that he would prosecute it more vigorously. He carried the usual Federalist bastions (New England, Maryland, Delaware) as well as New York, but Pennsylvania held firm for Madison, and gave him his margin of victory. Morris had foreseen that, too: "Pennsylvania . . . may be led to cover with her broad shield the slave-holding states: which, so protected, may for a dozen or fifteen years exercise the privilege of strangling commerce, whipping Negroes, and bawling about the inborn inalienable rights of man."[31]

But electioneering, as he had said, was not his real concern. He thought the war was wicked, that paying for it was equally so, and that Federalists who supported the war shared in its wickedness. Latecoming successes in 1813, such as the recapture of Detroit, or naval victories at sea and on the Great Lakes, did nothing to change his attitude. The war was wicked because, despite all the talk of the rights of neutral nations to trade and sail the seas, it was in fact "a war of conquest,"[32] which "complete[d] the guilt of those by whom this country has so long been misgoverned."[33] Paying for the war was wicked because "the debt . . . is void, being founded in moral wrong. . . ."[34] As for any "federalist, whose vote may in any wise support this war," he would be guilty of "treason" to his party, and his country. But he would be guilty of worse; his deed "would be an act of impiety as well as treachery."[35]

Morris's passionate polemics were occasionally brightened by profound insights. The danger of having an independent mind is going off half-cocked; the benefit is seeing what others miss. In the divisions of the War of 1812 he saw a great sectional split. "Time . . . seems about to disclose the awful secret that commerce and domestic slavery are mortal foes; and, bound together, one must destroy the other. I cannot blame Southern gentlemen for striving to put down commerce, because commerce, if it survives, will, I think, put them down. . . ."[36] He was ahead of time by half a century, but he was truly ahead of it. He also indulged in gossip almost at the level of his old French friends. "I supposed him," he wrote of President Madison in early 1813, "to be out of his senses, and have since been told that he never goes sober to bed. Whether intoxicated by opium or wine was not said. . . ."[37]

Morris's specific wartime suggestions went far beyond the election advice he had offered DeWitt Clinton. At his blackest, he hoped for a revolt of New England. "I hear some of the brethren exclaim, 'O Lord! O Lord! why, this is civil war!' Unquestionably it is civil war. And what of it?" If New York would not join in, then he hoped New England would invade it, and take it out of the Union by force. "[T]he prick of the Yankee bayonet will make you skip like squirrels."[38] At the very least, the Constitution that he had written had to be overhauled. "The present form," he admitted, "was good, but has been so much perverted that it can hardly be restored to what it was. If, therefore . . . good citizens mean that posterity should inherit freedom"—the goal of the Preamble—"they] must persuade [them]selves not merely to permit, but to effect a change."[39] Even though he might be tearing up his life's greatest achievement, Morris believed he was being true to his life's course. "It seems to me I was once a member of Congress during a revolutionary war. . . . We once had hearts—hearts that beat high with the love of liberty."[40] His heart was beating again.

He did all that "a gouty, one-legged old man"[41] could do, speaking at public anti-war meetings in New York and White Plains in the summer and fall of 1812, and expressing his opinions thereafter in a stream of letters, not just to the usual friends and family but to officeholders: Timothy Pickering, the Federalist senator from Massachusetts, who agreed with him; and his friend Rufus King, Federalist senator from New York, who would not go so far as to welcome Yankee bayonets in their state.

In the midst of war and disaffection, Morris became a father. On February 9, 1813, Gouverneur Morris II was born. Nancy was thirty-eight; Morris had just turned sixty-one. Children cannot literally renew the spring of life, and liveliness, which they can renew, in Morris's case needed no refreshing. But he loved the strange, late addition to his existence. In the fall of 1813, on a trip upstate, he wrote a letter to Nancy, in rhyme:

> *Kiss for me, my love, our charming boy.*
> *I long to taste again the joy*
> *Of pressing to his father's breast*
> *The son and mother. Be they blest*
> *With all which bounteous Heaven can grant;*
> *And if among us one must want*
> *Of bliss, be mine the scanty lot.*
> *Your happiness, may no dark spot*
> *Of gloomy woe or piercing pain*
> *Or melancholy ever stain.*[42]

In a lifetime of loving letters, this was one of the few that he had written to people who were happy. His relatives were not happy to see the wealthy old man reproduce; one of them, punning on the Russian marshal who had beaten Napoleon, nicknamed the child "Cutusoff."[43]

That same fall, Napoleon made what seemed to be his last stand at Leipzig, and lost. In 1791, on the same night that Louis XVI had made his doomed flight to Varennes, his younger brother, the comte de Provence, was able to escape to Flanders. Now the survivor was restored to the throne of France as Louis XVIII. In April 1814, Morris delivered an oration in New York celebrating the return of the Bourbons and "the Deliverance of Europe from the Yoke of Military Despotism." This speech he allowed himself to call "tolerably well written" and "in part, well delivered."[44]

Eager to conclude a war that one side considered a sideshow and the other considered a curse, Britain and America had sent peace commissioners to the Belgian city of Ghent. Yet while they wrangled, the war still dragged on. When the British tried to invade northern New York by the old route of Lake Champlain, they were decisively beaten at Plattsburg. When they tried to move up Chesapeake Bay, they chased Madison and the government from Washington, burned the White House and the Capitol, and were only stopped outside Baltimore. Former President Jefferson wrote his protégé a letter of consolation: "Had General Washington himself been now at the head of our affairs, the same event would probably have happened."[45] Happily for the Virginians, Morris never saw this communication, and thus was unable to comment on it.

CHAPTER FIFTEEN

Revolution Deferred

IN 1814, THE MORRISES resumed contact with Nancy's estranged family. The Randolphs were in a bad way. John had been turned out of Congress by a son-in-law of Thomas Jefferson who had moved to his district expressly to still his flamboyant anti-war voice; the defeated politician brooded and read Byron. In the spring of 1813, the plantation house at Bizarre had burned down, and Judith had to move into a house in a nearby town across the street from a tavern. Judith's elder son, St. George Randolph, was not only a deaf-mute; his awareness, growing with his natural urges, that there could never be a woman in his life had driven him insane. The family's hopes focused on the younger son, Tudor, who was a student at Harvard. But there, he showed signs of tuberculosis, the same disease that had killed his uncle Theodorick.

Nancy had not seen her sister Judith since she had left Virginia. She had seen her cousin John only once, in December 1811, when she had accompanied Morris on his canal-lobbying trip to Washington. Then Morris had urged Randolph to call on Nancy—not, it seems, from any hope of effecting a reconciliation between the two of them, but to ensure that a decent civility be shown her, and him. Randolph had complied. In the summer of 1814, Morris made a more expansive gesture, suggesting that Tudor come to Morrisania for a visit, and that his mother and uncle see him there. They would find "good air, milk, vegetables, and fruit . . . a comfortable house, an affectionate sister, and a good friend."[1] Tudor arrived at Morrisania in August, looking so ill he was put to bed; when he had a hemorrhage, the Randolphs were asked to come as soon as possible.

Judith and John arrived in late October. At first all went well. The Bizarre Randolphs greeted their successful transplanted kinswoman with seeming warmth. John, as the man of the family, following the protocol of the day, formally gave his sister-in-law and his nephew permission to stay at Morrisania for as long as they wished. A mishap occurred after John left for a boardinghouse in New York City; his carriage hit a pile of stones and overturned, and he was badly shaken. Everyone at Morrisania came down to New York to visit the other ailing Randolph.

On All Hallow's Eve, John sent Nancy a letter, care of her husband. John began by announcing that the eyes of man and God were upon her; then he got down to specifics. Mrs. Morris had "impos[ed] upon the generous man to whose arms you have brought pollution." Nancy was in fact a double murderess, having killed not only her own child, found on the shingle pile in 1792 ("your hands ... deprived of life that of which you were delivered"), but also Richard Randolph. This new charge he justified by his own suspicions—"My brother died *suddenly*"—and by those of Tudor, who "imparted to me the morning I left Morrisania his misgivings that you had been the perpetrator of that act." He added other charges, lesser only by comparison, such as that she had had an "Othello" (a slave lover) at Bizarre, and that she had lived as a *"drab"* (a prostitute) after leaving it. Now "[c]hance has again thrown you under my eye. What do I see? A vampire that, after sucking the best blood of my race, has flitted off to the North, and struck her harpy fangs into an infirm old man." Randolph forecast her future deeds from her past. She might carry on "lewd amours" behind her husband's back, or kill him and their son, even as she had killed Richard and her child. "If he be not both blind and deaf, he must sooner or later unmask you unless *he too die of cramps* in his *stomach*. You understand me. ... Repent before it is too late."[2]

One key to the virulence of this letter is its similarity with John Randolph's day-to-day rhetoric. There may be no understated way to tell a man that his wife is a killer, and that he may be her next victim, but if there were, Randolph was not the man to choose it. His speeches in Congress were furnished from the same wardrobe of tropes—*pollution, Othello, vampire, harpy*—that he used in this letter. "Sir, [the question of slavery] is not a *dry rot,* which you can cover with the carpet until the house tumbles about your ears; you might as well try to hide a *volcano* in full *eruption;* it cannot be hid; it is a *cancer* in your face" (italics added).[3] He spoke that way because he thought that way. All his life his language was vivid, his temper aggressive, and his imagination morbid.

Another ingredient that went into writing the letter may have been opium. Morris might scribble down rumors of Madison's opium use. Randolph had been using the drug since 1810, when a horse crushed the toes of his right foot. On his way to Morrisania, he had fallen down a flight of stairs at an inn, hurting an ankle and a shoulder; then he had his carriage accident. A weak body, bad luck, and bad medicine were unhappy companions for a bitter mind.

John claimed a solid source of information in Morris's own family—David B. Ogden, a nephew, and Martin Wilkins, a great-nephew. These two relatives had visited Randolph when he was recuperating in his New York boardinghouse. Their motives for resenting Nancy were obvious: it was Wilkins who had made the joke about "Cutusoff." Ogden could ill afford to be cut off. A local politician and a land speculator, who was prominent enough to be painted by John Trumbull (his face is dark, fleshy, and intelligent—not unlike Morris's, except for the lack of sparkle), Ogden was in several kinds of debt to his uncle. In a memo to himself, John Randolph wrote that Ogden told him that Gouverneur II was the son of a servant, not of Gouverneur. John might not be considered a reliable note-taker, but Ogden witnessed the memo.

In all his accusations, John did not say who he thought had been the father of the child Nancy had borne in 1792. He scoffed at the idea that it could have been Theodorick—"long before his death . . . he was reduced to a mere skeleton"[4]—and he said that Richard would have "perish[ed] on the same gibbet by your side" if the prosecution had been more aggressive. But he held Richard guilty only of disposing of the body, to protect his sister-in-law. No doubt he believed that a woman who would copulate with slaves and paying customers would have had no dearth of lovers.

Nancy fell ill after getting John's letter, then fought back. She wrote warning letters to Wilkins and Ogden, then produced, in January of the new year, a forty-page answer to John, which she copied and mailed to interested parties in Virginia. She asked the obvious questions about his "filthy accusations":[5] if she was "a negro's concubine," why had he let his nephew Tudor stay with her? If she was "a common prostitute" and "the murderess of her own child and of your brother," why had he politely greeted her when he arrived at Morrisania? She reminded him that he had once courted her, though thanks to his "stormy passions," "mean selfishness," and "wretched appearance," he had failed. She admitted that she had given birth in 1792, but insisted that the baby was stillborn, and that the father was Theodorick. "I was betrothed to him, and considered him as my husband in the presence of . . . God." John's tales of prostitution were all lies, though "if suffering could have driven me to vice, there was no want of suffering."

She defended her husband, for whom John professed concern. "I loved my husband before he made me his wife. I love him still more now that he has made me the mother of one of the finest boys I ever saw; now that his kindness soothes the anguish which I cannot but feel from your unmanly attack." She finished with a Shakespearean reference. "I trust you are by this time convinced that you have clumsily performed the part of 'honest Iago.'" Nancy was like her cousin in one thing: Randolphs did not pull punches.

There may have been moments during this deadly catfight when Morris wondered what sort of family he had married into. His preferred manner, where his own interests were at stake, ran to *suaviter in modo*. To Wilkins and Ogden he wrote bland letters expressing the assurance that of course they would defend the reputation of his wife. When Judith Randolph wrote from Virginia, protesting that she had had nothing to do with John's, or Tudor's, performance, Morris replied that he would "vindicate your honor."[6] To a friend in Virginia, he wrote that he would not sue John, since that would only spread his libels. His "communications gave me no concern, for Mrs. Morris had apprised me of the only fact in his possession, before she came to my house, so that her candor had blunted the point of his arrow." That only fact would have been the stillborn child. He offered his own thoughts on Nancy's accusers: they "hate her because she is happy."[7]

John Randolph hated Morris for the same reason. He and Morris were not utterly unalike. They opposed the war; they were aristocrats; they were unusual. But there the resemblance ended. Morris was rich, a father, and happily married to the last of his many lovers. Randolph was financially pressed, single, childless, and sexless. Morris, who had a peg leg, enjoyed himself. Randolph, who had crushed toes, took opium. A gloomy mind could not miss the contrast.

FAMILY BUSINESS did not distract Morris from public business. In October 1814, the Massachusetts legislature had called for a Convention of delegates from the New England states, to consider the state of the nation and their region. On December 15, the delegates met in the State House in Hartford, Connecticut, a building as light as it is dignified, under the gaze of a Gilbert Stuart portrait of George Washington. With a few late additions, the Convention had twenty-six delegates from three states (Massachusetts, Connecticut, Rhode Island), two counties in New Hampshire, and one county in Vermont. They were thus following, in truncated form, the campaign advice Morris had given DeWitt Clinton two years earlier. In a letter written just before Christmas, Morris praised the Convention in the language of the Magi as "a star in the East . . . the day-spring of freedom and glory. The madmen and traitors assembled at Hartford will, I believe, if not too tame and timid, be hailed hereafter as the patriots and sages of their day and generation."[8]

The Hartford Convention met in secret for three weeks, opening each session with a prayer. (During one of their deadlocks the delegates to the Constitutional Convention had rejected Benjamin Franklin's suggestion that they pray because they did not want to give the appearance of desperation, and because they had no funds to pay a clergyman.) Almost half of the delegates had served in Congress or in high state office; the rest were local figures—state legislators, probate court judges. They are better known to history by their relatives: Connecticut sent a nephew of Morris's old colleague, Roger Sherman; Massachusetts sent the father of Henry Wadsworth Longfellow. The leaders had a reputation as moderates: George Cabot, the presiding officer, said his purpose was to keep "hot-heads from getting into mischief,"⁹ while Harrison Gray Otis, who worked on all the important committees, was called "a hare trembling at every breeze."¹⁰

The recommendations the Hartford men offered on January 5, 1815, were cloaked in moderation. They proposed seven amendments to the Constitution. Three were immediate reactions to the war: no declarations of war except by a two-thirds vote in both houses of Congress; no interdiction of trade with any country except by the same margin; and no general embargos lasting more than sixty days. Three amendments were partisan assaults on the Republicans: no new states admitted without a two-thirds vote in both houses of Congress (thus raising the bar for future Kentuckys and Tennessees); no foreign-born federal officeholders (a slap at such Republicans as the Irish Matthew Lyon and the Swiss Albert Gallatin); a one-term limit on the presidency, and no consecutive presidents from the same state (to break the seemingly endless chain of two-term Virginians). Only one amendment addressed an issue that had been discussed in Philadelphia in 1787: the Hartford men opposed the three-fifths rule.

More controversially, the convention asked that states be allowed to divert taxes collected for the federal government to their own defense. The convention complained of a federal policy that left the New England seacoast undefended (Britain occupied half of Maine), while the state militias were conscripted to fight battles on the Canadian frontier. But letting states defend themselves was a first step toward letting them conduct their own foreign relations. Most radical was the coda of the Hartford Convention: a call for a second convention in Boston in June if these proposals were rejected. That convention "must act as such urgent circumstances may then require."¹¹ This was the threat that converted suggestions into demands. The mutinous officers at Newburgh had said nothing balder.

The Hartford men were playing for time. They wanted to see what, if anything, the peace commissioners had agreed upon at Ghent. The British were known to have made exorbitant demands, insisting on an independent nation for their Indian allies in the American Northwest. The northwest border, which the Louisiana Purchase had pushed to the Rockies, would then be rolled back to Ohio. "The British ministers," Morris wrote sarcastically when he read this demand, have discovered "that our copper-colored brothers are human beings. . . . Take care, my good friend, that they do not make a similar discovery respecting our ebony-colored brethren."[12] The Hartford men also awaited news from the South. A British expedition had landed in Louisiana in December with the evident intention of taking New Orleans. If the federal government could not defend the mouth of the Mississippi, New England hard-liners expected the west to join them in disaffection. "If the British succeed," wrote Senator Timothy Pickering in January "—and if they have tolerable leaders I see no reason to doubt of their success—I shall consider the Union as severed."[13]

The Gouverneur Morris of 1787 would have scoffed at most of the Hartford Convention's proposals. In Philadelphia he wanted the president to take the lead in foreign policy, seeing him as "the general guardian of the national interests."[14] Though embargos had not been a topic of much discussion, he had strongly supported other commercial regulations—export taxes, laws favoring American shipping—and it could be assumed that, having no principled objection to lesser measures, he would back stronger ones in more desperate circumstances. The man who had labored for the suffering army at Valley Forge certainly would not have favored giving military power to the states. His speech on the Indians who let guests sleep with their wives had been meant to mock the idea of immigrants easily becoming senators, but he had argued for nothing more exclusive than a fourteen-year citizenship requirement. He had opposed term limits in all cases, as leading to instability. "A change of men is ever followed by a change of measures. . . . Rehoboam will not imitate Solomon."[15] The only points on which the young Morris agreed with the Hartford men were suspicion of new states, and detestation of the three-fifths rule.

When Morris read what the Hartford men had done, he was in fact contemptuous. "They have fallen short," he wrote Rufus King, " . . . and will be laughed at by many."[16] "Such humble language," he wrote another correspondent, had "a squeaking sound." But he understood, and approved of, the threat. If their "modest propositions are rejected," New England would resort to "cannon law."[17]

Why had Morris given up so? The last national issue before the war that had engaged his attention had been the Judiciary Act of 1802, which scaled back the federal courts. Morris often said that he considered the Constitution "dead" from that date.[18] This diagnosis reflected his inattention. The federal judiciary had been pared down, but John Randolph's 1805 attack on the Supreme Court had failed. Chief Justice John Marshall had not begun his long counterattack, but he was known to be no friend to Republican measures. It was not the alleged death of the Constitution caused by the Judiciary Act, but the War of 1812 that drove Morris to desperation.

In our minds the War of 1812 has taken its place in the string of American wars, more inglorious than others perhaps, but also shorter. To Morris and his contemporaries, it was the second war the United States had fought. The Revolution had been a desperate defense of our rights. The War of 1812 was a defense of the right to sail and trade, but it was also an attempt to seize Canada. The Revolution had been led by George Washington. The War of 1812 was being misled by the unmilitary James Madison, and by generals most of whom were as incompetent as he.

Morris saw the War of 1812 as a war of Virginia against the North, specifically New York. "The question to be settled between the Northern and Southern states, reduced to its simple elements, is merely this: Shall the citizens of New York be the slaves or masters of Virginia?"[19] This too was mistaken, as far as Virginia was concerned. Virginia, in the person of Madison, had been dragged into war by the Clays and Calhouns in his party, whom Virginia, in the person of John Randolph, had vainly resisted. But it was true that New York's interest had been neglected to satisfy the greed of other sections of the country.

New York's paramount interest was its canal. The canal would turn upstate hamlets into towns and cities, and New York City, with its grid, into a world city indeed. The canal would reach beyond New York to the Great Lakes, supplying settlers and drawing out their produce in ships of over 100 tons. This was the vision Morris had seen while sailing, shooting rapids, and tending to his properties. Who needed Canada, with such a prospect? But Morris's vision had been set aside for a predator's dream, the quick pounce on a sure thing—only, the sure thing had slipped away in three years of bumbling conflict.

Was this reason enough to break up the nation? A rash man would say so, and the war and the rejection of his canal had made Morris a rash man. "Generally speaking," he had written in the spring of 1814, "wisdom gives moderate counsels, but there are cases in which moderation is dangerous, and even ruinous."[20] Morris's extremism is striking, coming from the draftsman of the Constitution: the southerners who would fulfill his sectional prophecies by taking their states out of the Union could not speak with such perverse authority.

But Morris's willingness to scrap his handiwork also has an intellectual advantage over later critics of the Constitution, as it has over the men of the Hartford Convention in their moderate guise. Both the critics to come and the Hartford men labored to maintain the fiction of legality. John C. Calhoun, his days as a young nationalist past, would argue in the 1830s that states had a right to nullify the operation of federal laws that were oppressive to them. His intellectual heirs of the Confederacy would argue in the 1860s that, the Union being a compact of states, they had a right to secede when a man as obnoxious as Abraham Lincoln was elected president. In the interval until their threat should be called in, the men of Hartford claimed to be "interpos[ing]" the "authority" of their states against "deliberate, dangerous, and palpable infractions of the constitution. . . ."[21] This is tugging the Constitution, like a tablecloth, over disunion as well as union. It is asking permission to leave in a huff; it is pretending that political debate can be conducted by threats. Morris had no patience for such evasions. Having written the Preamble to the Constitution, he knew how it ended: "to . . . promote the general welfare, and secure the blessings of liberty to ourselves and our posterity. . . ." If, as he believed, the federal government was manifestly and deliberately failing to do that, then the Constitution was dead, and that is why as many northern states as possible should leave. Leaving was not constitutional, for the Constitution had failed. "[T]he union, being the means of preserving freedom, should be prized as such," Morris had written Harrison Gray Otis in 1813, "but . . . the end should not be sacrificed to the means."[22] Morris might misjudge circumstances. But his moral position is clear.

In February 1815, commissioners from New England made their way to Washington, bearing the results of the Hartford Convention. They were overtaken by other messengers. First came the news from New Orleans: British generals who had beaten Napoleon's troops in Europe had been crushed by frontier Indian fighters. Then came the terms of the Treaty of Ghent, which were surprisingly good: not worth a war (nothing was said of the rights of sailors), but the British had agreed to abandon both their Indian allies and the coast of Maine. If the double news did not exactly mean victory, it meant something equally overwhelming: relief. Accompanied by the sound of ringing church bells, the New England commissioners went quickly and quietly home. Thus ended, wrote Morris, a war "rashly declared, prodigally maintained, weakly conducted, and meanly concluded."[23]

CHAPTER SIXTEEN

Acceptance

THE TREATY OF GHENT had closed the book on almost a quarter century of revolutionary and Napoleonic world war. The book flew open again in the spring of 1815 when Napoleon escaped the island of Elba to which his vanquishers had confined him and rallied the French army. Morris was not alarmed. "Bonaparte," he wrote, "will be quelled, and his associate conspirators brought to condign punishment."[1] One of those conspirators was Charles de Flahaut, Adèle's son, now thirty years old. General Flahaut, as handsome as his mother and with as many lovers, was at the emperor's side at Waterloo, and fled thence to England. No note of this echo of the past reached Morris through the clangor of events. He made his final judgment of the French at the end of the year. "That tract of country always produced a turbulent race. Caesar or Tacitus, I forget which, characterized them as 'too proud to obey, too ferocious to be free.' A firm hand is needful to govern them. Their ruler must flatter their vanity, and punish severely the slightest attempt to diminish his authority. . . . [L]ike a vicious horse with a cart," France "may kick and plunge, but the whip and the spur well applied will tame her."[2] The observer of two revolutions had no general theory to cover both cases. Americans in distress could assert their natural rights, but Frenchmen were too volatile to be allowed the privilege.

With the return of peace, New Yorkers turned their thoughts back to a canal. Morris once again advised New York to go it alone, suggesting that the Canal Commission be empowered to issue $5 million in bonds, backed by the state. As each stretch of the canal was completed, it should be opened to navigation, and the tolls used for upkeep and interest on the debt. He was as confident as he had been before the war that the "natural effect" of the work would be to "make New York mistress of the union."[3] Washington was not as alarmed as it had been by this prospect, for the war seemed to have purged it of regional jealousies. In Congress, Calhoun introduced a canal bill, intended to combat every "low, sordid, selfish and sectional spirit."[4] Madison, however, had not been purged of his scruples; his last act as president was to veto the bill as "contrary to the established and consistent rules" of constitutional interpretation.[5] New York went ahead anyway, without the federal government's help, and on July 4, 1817, DeWitt Clinton, now governor, presided over a groundbreaking at Rome, a village a hundred miles northwest of Albany whose name reflected the state's hopes.

Morris did not see the ceremony. But he did not need progress on his cherished canal to sweeten his political temper. In the postwar world, he executed one more political reversal, as dramatic as any of his earlier ones, and became an advocate of stoicism and acceptance. Having written the Constitution after one war, and abandoned it during the next, he embraced it again in peace.

Not that he approved all the policies coming out of Washington. His correspondence chiefly concerned finance, "a matter which," as he wrote Rufus King, "from the course of my life, I ought to know something about, if I be not a very stupid fellow."[6] After letting the Bank of the United States lapse, Congress wished to charter another. In 1781, Morris had helped found the Bank of North America when the country was in desperate need of credit, but now he thought the proposed national bank would be inflationary, and he opposed it. "The first bank in this country was planned by your humble servant," but "what was medicine then would be poison now."[7] It was proposed to pay off the war debt with a land tax, and many Federalists supported this move as a matter of fiscal responsibility. Morris opposed this, too. Direct taxes, he lectured Rufus King, are "ungracious and tormenting, and when pushed are no longer taxation but confiscation."[8] He saved his choicest words for protective tariffs, which raised prices and artificially stimulated manufacturing. Why, he asked, should "those who till the soil . . . be laid under heavy contribution to support the scum of England and Ireland who come out to live in ease and idleness as mechanics[?] We already have . . . poor children who can be pent up, to march backward and forward with a spinning jenny, till they are old enough to become drunkards and prostitutes."⁹

But all these measures were follies of peacetime, and Morris was now once more at peace with America. His mood found expression in his advice to his party. Burned by the bad timing of the Hartford Convention, the Federalists turned to one of their more moderate voices, Rufus King, as their presidential candidate in 1816. King, the transplant from Massachusetts, had been living at his farm in Jamaica, in the county of Queens, for years. He was by now a downstate rural grandee, like Morris. In the spring of 1816, Morris wrote him a jocular letter of congratulation. "I . . . am pleased to learn, that you stand a candidate for the government. The office, could it be restored to what we made it by the Constitution, is of great dignity." But now, like a warship with its upper deck removed (cut down "from a seventy-four to a razee"), "it is not worth your acceptance. I feel, therefore, and applaud your selfdenial. . . ."¹⁰ Since King had absolutely no chance of winning—he would carry only three out of nineteen states against the next Virginian president, James Monroe—it was gracious of his friend to mock the office for which he contended.

Morris's real strategy for the election of 1816, politeness aside, was revealed in a letter some months later to a Federalist Committee of Correspondence in Philadelphia. The Committees of Correspondence before the Revolutionary War had been designed to stir up revolutionary sentiment; much of Morris's correspondence during the War of 1812 had had the same purpose. The Federalist Committee of Correspondence of 1816, however, was an ordinary campaign organization, designed to view with alarm and point with pride. Morris told them to spare their efforts.

"[T]he best course you can pursue is to leave . . . the whole ground" to the enemy. "If you come forward, Democrats"—still a term of abuse, especially among Federalists, but soon to become the legitimate name of Jefferson's heirs—"will stifle their feelings to support their party, not so much because they love it, as because they hate you. If you leave them to themselves, they will split and abuse each other."

This was Morris speaking in the voice of Machiavelli, counseling non-resistance as a political ploy. Then he shifted to a different tone. "But, gentlemen, let us forget party, and think of our country. That country embraces both parties. We must endeavor, therefore, to save and benefit both." He recurred to a pet theory of his—that there was no point preaching in time of peace, since men would only listen at the approach of a crisis. "[W]hen it arrives, the people will look out for men of sense, experience, and integrity." Now he gave the argument a twist that, if it was not new for him—he had always had friends and associates across party lines, from DeWitt Clinton to Robert R. Livingston to Peter Van Schaak—was certainly fresh after the rancor of the last four years. "Such men may, I trust, be found in both parties; and, if our country be delivered, what does it signify whether those who operate her salvation wear a federal or a democratic cloak?"[11]

Morris was not the only Federalist who was willing to let the old feuds alone. Worn out by strife, defeat, and their own mistakes, so many supporters of the minority party decided to work with the triumphant Republicans that the postwar period came to be known as the era of good feelings, and Rufus King's hapless race for the White House was the last presidential effort any Federalist would make. Morris's attitude, however, was notable coming from one who had been so bitter. His advice now contradicted his insight after Jefferson's election that political losers could serve as the outward conscience of the winners. But he correctly estimated the Federalists' ability to play that, or any other role. When he was courting Nancy Randolph, he had told her that the cards of life were fairly dealt, and that our lot was to play them, then sleep. As with men, so with political parties. It was time for Federalism to fold its hand.

He ended the letter with a self-portrait, and a credo. "Perhaps the expression of these sentiments may be imprudent; but, when it appears proper to speak truth, I know not concealment." That was certainly true of him, whether he spoke truth or (as he sometimes did) folly. "It has been the unvarying principle of my life, that the interest of our country must be preferred to every other interest."[12] He had defined the country's interest very erratically on occasion, but he had always sought it.

In his poison pen letter to Nancy, John Randolph had called Morris an "infirm old man." His constitution was naturally stronger than Randolph's, and his wits had always been steadier. But infirmities had begun to dog him, and in 1816, when he turned sixty-four, he had reached the age at which his own father died. Morris's chronic ailment was gout, the inflammation of the joints caused by deposits from the kidneys. James Gillray, the great turn-of-the-century English caricaturist, did a famous cartoon of gout as a demon biting a bare foot. Gout was a disease associated with high living, and the upper classes who could afford to indulge themselves. Morris was a likely candidate on both counts. Gout had "paid . . . its first call" on him when he was living in France.[13]

In the summer of 1816, Morris described himself, in a letter to a companion of his Hamburg days, as "only peep[ing] out occasionally from the threshold of my hermitage." The letter is an envoi, a counterpart, on the personal plane, of his advice to the Philadelphia Federalists. "I lead," he wrote, "a quiet and, more than most of my fellow-mortals, a happy life." Praise of his wife led him to thoughts about marriage. "The woman to whom I am married has much genius, has been well educated, and possesses, with an affectionate temper, industry and a love of order. That I did not marry earlier is not to be attributed to any dislike for that connection. On the contrary it has long been my fixed creed that as love is the only fountain of felicity, so it is in wedded love that the waters are most pure." This was a challengeable statement, especially by anyone who had met the writer in Europe, where his only experience of wedded love had been loving the wives of other men. Morris was evidently aware of the difficulty, for he immediately addressed it. "To solve the problem of my fate it was required to discover a woman . . . who could love an old man." This begs several questions: why should his amorous fate have been a problem? Why could it only be solved when he was old? Still, he had found such a woman, and he had loved her for more than seven years, despite an extraordinary effort to destroy their happiness.

He turned to their son. "The sentiments of a father respecting an only child render his opinions so liable to suspicion that prudence should withhold them even from a friend. I will only say, therefore, that some who would have been more content had he never seen the light"—the Ogdens, the Wilkinses, and the Merediths—"acknowledge him to be beautiful and promising."

He closed with himself. "You may, then, opening your mind's eye, behold your friend as he descends, with tottering steps, the bottom of life's hill. . . ." From the time of his carriage accident, any instance of tottering had been a bitter humiliation, a failure of hard-won self-control and élan; but now gout and the years forced it on him. "[L]ooking back, I can, with some little self-complacency, reflect that I have not lived in vain. . . ."

This boast demands examination. However base and foolish the statesmanship of the War of 1812 had been, the statesmanship of the Revolution and the Founding had been glorious. Morris belonged to a generation of leaders who were proud of what they had done, and intensely anxious that their deeds be remembered. In that context and in that company, could he say that he had not lived in vain?

He was no philosopher. His thoughts occurred in bursts, in letters and speeches, and he wrote no coherent account of them. But that was true of most of his peers. His enemy Madison and his friend Hamilton had, with some help from John Jay, written *The Federalist,* a treatise that still repays study. Wise as it is, it is an occasional performance, and each author squirreled important insights (sometimes changing his opinions) in other documents. Washington, Jefferson, and the other founders wrote in the same scattershot fashion. The only one to assemble anything like a *Summa* was Paine, in *The Rights of Man* and *The Age of Reason*—but Paine had been only erratically useful to his two adopted homelands.

What Morris thought, here and there, and never quite swept together, was that God, all-powerful and virtually unknowable, rules the world, and directs events as He sees fit. Liberty is a blessed state, although some nations, by virtue of their temperaments, cannot safely enjoy as much liberty as others. Even the citizens of the freest do not pay much attention to reason, unless a crisis drives them to it. Experienced governors, who ought to be in office at all times, might then be called upon. In good times or bad, men should enjoy the rights to work, write, and worship (this was the only sense in which Morris would have thought that all men are created equal). If this collection of principles is not consistently inspiring, it is free from cant, as good as the principles of most of Morris's peers, and better than those of most of his French friends.

Good principles make a man admirable; a good style makes him arresting. Morris's sparkling prose still shines after two centuries. Reading it, we hear a voice—so vivid, we imagine the speaker has just left the room, and so delightful that we want him to come back. The moral source of his style is confidence: he knows who he is, and that he is right; he knows, from long experience, that he will please most of his auditors; and he does not care about those he does not please.

Morris performed two special services as a public man. As Jefferson immortalized the Continental Congress's view of first principles, so Morris had applied his finish to the Constitutional Convention's view of fundamental law. Morris did not leave his country on paper: he worked to plan a canal that should make it bloom. A handful of other men might have buffed the Constitution almost as smoothly, but he was the one who did it; a handful of New Yorkers pushed for the Erie Canal—he was one of the most eloquent and energetic. For the rest, he gave many hours of intelligent and industrious labor as a New Yorker, a financier, and a diplomat. This more than compensates for his bad ideas and outrageous advice.

He performed one more service that became known only after his death. His diary bore witness to another Revolution and Founding that did not go so well. Many other writers have told France's story, but his record—published in extracts in the nineteenth century, and fully only on the eve of World War II—is indelible.

Yet there is another sense in which he had not lived in vain. Morris was an important founding father, but he was something else, useful in a different way to his friends and acquaintances. He was a gentleman. In his case, that is a moral even more than a social term. Born to riches and power, he had also learned to live well. Nature gave him a buoyant and appreciative temperament, but he had fostered those qualities, despite severe trials. His conduct, from his teens on, is marked by courage, courtesy, and warmth—by affection for his friends, sympathy for the afflicted, and disdain for bullies. His example is still useful. The founding fathers can show us how to live as citizens. Morris can show us how to enjoy life's blessings and bear its hurts with humanity and good spirits. "At sixty-four," he concluded his letter, "there is little to desire and less to apprehend. Let me add that, however grave the form and substance of this letter, the lapse of so many years have not impaired the gayety of your friend. Could you gratify him with your company and conversation, you would find in him still the gayety of inexperience and the frolic of youth." [14]

His gout became crippling in the fall. His diary entries ceased early in October, with the first frost, and he made a new will at the end of the month. David Ogden and Martin Wilkins were not mentioned. Another nephew got a bequest, and yet another was told that if the principal heir, Gouverneur Morris II, should die young, he might inherit the estate, so long as he assumed the Morris name and arms. He gave his wife a life interest in his property, plus an annuity of $2,600 a year ($32,500 today). If she married again, her annuity would be increased to $3,200, "to defray the increased expenditure, which may attend that condition." [15]

"Sixty-four years ago," he said as death approached, "it pleased the Almighty to call me into existence—here, on this spot, in this very room; and now shall I complain that he is pleased to call me hence?" [16] The end was painful. He suffered a blockage of his urinary tract, and he tried to clear the obstruction with whalebone, no doubt from one of his wife's corsets. But he had known pain before. On his last day, November 6, he quoted poetry—not his own, but Gray's *Elegy Written in a Country Churchyard*:

> For who, to dumb Forgetfulness a prey,
>   This pleasing, anxious being e'er resigned,
>   Left the warm precincts of the cheerful day,
>   Nor cast one longing lingering look behind? [17]

Postscript

M ORRIS DIED leaving one project, and a few old colleagues, behind him.

The Erie Canal, begun by Governor DeWitt Clinton on July 4, 1817, was finished in 1825, two years ahead of schedule. Clinton, still governor, poured a ceremonial bucket of Lake Erie water into the Atlantic at Sandy Hook, off New York Harbor. The volume of commerce that the canal was soon carrying fulfilled the most sanguine hopes of its projectors. At night, wrote one observer, the "flickering head lamps" of the boats making their way across the heart of New York shone like "swarms of fireflies."[1] The produce of a continent went out past Sandy Hook to Europe and the world, enriching New York all the more. Whatever their political opinions, Morris and his fellow patricians had made a confident bet on their country and their city, which was paid back manyfold.

Deploring the illiberality of both Bonaparte and the restored House of Bourbon, the marquis de Lafayette was a marginal figure in French politics for many years. In 1824, at the age of sixty-seven, he returned to the country he had served more successfully than his own for a triumphal visit. When he saw Houdon's statue of Washington (which had used Morris for the body model), he said it was the very image of his hero. Six years later, in 1830, there was a second French Revolution, and the tricolor flew again, though this time much less blood flowed. Lafayette, who took an active part, saw the reestablishment, at the end of a long life, of a constitutional monarchy, the ideal of his youth. Talleyrand came out of retirement, at the end of an even longer life, to help the new regime over several international rough spots. In his last days he was reconciled to the Catholic Church. While receiving extreme unction, he told the attending priest, "Do not forget I am a bishop."[2]

In the United States, the remnants of Morris's generation gave way to a new cohort of leaders. In 1820, one of the last founders to hold office, Rufus King, argued passionately against allowing slavery in the new state of Missouri. So a survivor of the Philadelphia Convention looked ahead to the issues that would produce the Civil War. John Randolph did his best to make civil war inevitable, by linking the cause of states' rights to the institution of slavery; his passionate polemics made a convert of the young nationalist John C. Calhoun. Contrary to the end, Randolph freed all of his own slaves in his will. Released from the burden of leadership, James Madison spent a quiet retirement. In 1831 the historian Jared Sparks asked him for his views of the man who had written the Constitution that Madison had done so much to prepare and expound. Madison could scarcely have been unaware of Morris's low opinion of him as an officeholder, though happily he had been spared knowledge of the details. The estimate he gave Sparks was as generous as it was just.

Morris also left a ghost story. One night, so the story went, when Nancy was staying at his north country summer house, two horsemen banged on the front door, demanding a treasure that her husband had taken while he was in France. At this, Morris stepped from a portrait on the wall and waved the riders away. After they fled, he led Nancy to the hidden treasure. The story captures this truth: if Morris in death could have faced down ruffians and been generous to his wife, he would certainly have done so. At the end of the twentieth century, the people living in his old summer house still reported mysterious bangings on the front door.[3]

The real treasure Morris had hoped to leave his wife and son was diminished by a very real ruffian, his nephew David Ogden. Morris had endorsed one of Ogden's mortgages, which left his estate liable for a load of debt—more than $100,000, according to Nancy. She was reduced to the severest economies. She forewent her annuity. She sued to recover debts that her husband had not bothered about. She sued to remove an executor of the estate who had mismanaged some land sales. She was sued by her lawyer, a son of Alexander Hamilton, for legal bills that she considered exorbitant. She rented out the farms of Morrisania, and fretted when her tenant's cows broke into her corn. The struggle was unremitting, but by the time Gouverneur II reached his majority, she was finally able to pass on to him his father's estate, free and clear.

She had read her husband's diaries, with aching eyes, at night after her son was in bed. Some passages, evidently sexual, have been crossed out, possibly by her, though considering what remains the censor had a light hand. We will never know what she censored from her own past. She had claimed, in her correspondence with John Randolph, that Theodorick was the father of her child, and that the baby was stillborn. Yet Richard Randolph, her brother-in-law, had loved her, and many desperate men and women have killed newborns. What we can say is that the inferences John drew from her alleged crimes were false. She loved her husband and son. More galling to John, she had endured. She died age sixty-two in May 1837.

Gouverneur Morris II had the long Morris nose and his father's commanding stature (so much for David Ogden's tales about his paternity). Like his father, he was interested in transportation, serving as president of railroad companies, the next stage of development after canals. As the tracks of the Harlem line pushed up through his patrimony, he profitably sold off swathes of it. In 1841, he gathered the remains of his parents and of earlier Morrises and buried them at St. Ann's, an Episcopal church he had built in honor of his mother. A year later, once again following his father, he married a Virginian, Patsey Jefferson Cary, one of Nancy Randolph's nieces. The last bottle of Marie Antoinette's imperial Tokay was drunk in Morris's house in 1848.

New York City grew beyond Gouverneur Morris's imagining, filling his grid, the rest of Manhattan, and four surrounding counties. What was once Morrisania now lies in the South Bronx. The Number 6 train stops at 138th Street and Brook Avenue, laid over the south-running brook that once divided the estate in two. 138th Street is a commercial strip, poor but bustling, dotted with fast-food restaurants and cheap clothing and furniture stores. Depending on the closest holiday, the fire escapes of the tenement housing above the storefronts are hung with Puerto Rican, Haitian, or Mexican flags. A few blocks east and north stands St. Ann's Church (the little blue and white metal sign that Episcopalians hang in front of their houses of worship also identifies it as *Iglesia de Santa Ana*)—all that remains in the Bronx, aside from a few place names, of the Morrises.

The building is capacious but plain, reflecting a simple era of Episcopal worship. All the eccentric Morrises of the seventeenth and eighteenth centuries are listed on a tablet on the rear wall of the sanctuary. Set in the floor, beneath an iron grate, is a stone that was inscribed first by Morris's widow, then by his son. Nancy wrote:

> *Conjugal affection*
> *Consecrates this spot where*
> *the Best of men was laid*
> *untill a vault could be erected*
> *to receive*
> *his precious remains*

Gouverneur II added, more conventionally, a tribute to

> *the wife and mother*
> *in memory of whom*
> *this church*
> *was erected*
> *to the God she loved*
> *by filial veneration*

In the yard outside, the state of New York erected a stone tablet with a list of Gouverneur Morris's accomplishments, which can be read from the sidewalk, if anyone wished to. At the end of a short, leaf-strewn path, his vault lies half-sunken in a slope of the yard; beside it stands an elm tree, spared from blight by remoteness from its fellows, whose crown spreads like a huge umbrella.

New York has been attacked again, as it was when Morris was a member of the Provincial Congress. He knew his share of destruction, sometimes firsthand, sometimes at one remove, from evacuating Kingston to reentering Philadelphia; from the Prussian artillery within earshot of Paris to Napoleon rampaging across Europe. If he thought his country's warmaking was wickedly at fault, he would not hesitate to counsel revolution. If he thought it was in the right, he would do his work wherever duty placed him, whether in small towns or among rioting foreign mobs.

No one now knows that. Morris's grave is on no city tour; it is mentioned in only the most comprehensive reference works. The people on 138th Street are of a different culture and class, while the wealthy and educated have forgotten him even more completely than they have his great contemporaries (Hamilton at least is buried in Trinity Churchyard, at the head of Wall Street). Yet of all the founding fathers, he would be the least distressed by their ignorance. Despite many trials, he savored life. He did it by following the formula he offered one of his correspondents: "To try to do good, to avoid evil, a little severity for one's self, a little indulgence for others—this is the means to obtain some good result out of our poor existence. To love one's friends, to be beloved by them—this is the means to brighten it."[4] He had enjoyed his life. Let the passersby enjoy theirs.

Notes

Morris has been fortunate in his biographers and editors. Jared Sparks was given access to Morris's papers by his widow, and his three-volume work—*The Life of Gouverneur Morris, with Selections from his Correspondence and Miscellaneous Papers*—contains generous selections from his letters, diaries, essays, and speeches. Anne Cary Morris, a granddaughter, offers, in her two-volume *The Diary and Letters of Gouverneur Morris*, a narrative scaffold with a somewhat different selection of Morris's writing. Both were edited for the sake of prudery and conciseness. Beatrix Cary Davenport's two-volume work, *A Diary of the French Revolution by Gouverneur Morris*, offers—uncut—the diary that Morris began in Paris on March 1, 1789, and continued until January 5, 1793, when he wrote that "[t]he situation of things is such that to continue this journal would compromise many people" unless his entries became so brief as to be "insipid and useless. I prefer therefore the more simple measure of putting an end to it" (Davenport II, p. 598). Davenport includes numerous letters that fill out the record.

The biographies by Daniel Walther (1932; trans. 1934), Howard Swiggett (1952), Max M. Mintz (1970), and Mary-Jo Kline (1978) are listed in the Bibliography, and gratefully cited in these Notes. In 1887, the twenty-eight-year-old Theodore Roosevelt was commissioned to do a biography of Gouverneur Morris, but found that the Morris family "won't let me see the old gentleman's papers at any price. I am in rather a quandary"—Edmund Morris, *The Rise of Theodore Roosevelt* (New York: Random House, 1979), p. 379. Roosevelt made good use of public documents and his own talents, but I have not relied on his book (which was published in 1888).

Much of Morris's story is in French. I have translated the conversation and poetry that appear in Sparks, Anne Cary Morris, and Davenport, but have mostly relied on their translations of his letters, the speech he wrote for Louis XVI, and his proposed French constitution. The American impressions of the prince de Broglie, the marquis de Chastellux, and the marquis de Barbé-Marbois, as well as standard modern works on the period—Furet and Richet's *The*

French Revolution, Orieux's *Talleyrand*—have been published in English. I had to translate the biographer of Mme de Souza, and was rash enough to translate Rousseau.

I have used the following collections of unpublished papers:

The Papers of Gouverneur Morris: Library of Congress

The Papers of John W. Francis: New York Public Library

The Papers of Robert Morris (Gouverneur's cousin, not the financier): Rutgers University

The Cabell Family Papers: Alderman Library, University of Virginia

All unattributed references to diaries or letters are from the Papers of Gouverneur Morris: Library of Congress.

INTRODUCTION

1. Mme de Damas's letter is in Sparks I, pp. 506–12.

2. Swiggett, p. 331, quoting Abigail Adams—a useful source, since she was an intelligent phonetic speller. Today the residents of the upstate New York town of Gouverneur, founded on land Morris owned late in life, pronounce the name "Gov-ah-*noar.*" Interestingly, Frenchmen of Morris's acquaintance did not consider him French; the prince de Broglie, who met him in America, called him "Governor" (Balch, p. 234); so did the marquis de Chastellux (Chase, p. 167). The upshot of all this would seem to be that the accent is on the last syllable and that the vowels are not Frenchified.

3. Swiggett, p. 42.

4. Morris II, p. 574.

5. Sparks I, p. 284.

6. Ibid., p. 285.

7. Read, p. 202.

8. Mintz, p. 94.

9. Farrand III, p. 92.

CHAPTER ONE

1. Burrows and Wallace, p. 98.

2. This, and other information on the first Morrises, is found in the *New York Post,* "Famous New York Families: The Morrises," May 11, 1901. The quotation marks around dialogue reported two centuries after it was spoken are obviously a narrative convention for relaying a family tradition. But there is no reason, apart from a killjoy spirit, for doubting that tradition.

3. Alexander, p. 9.

4. Burrows and Wallace, p. 155.

5. Ibid.

6. Alexander, p. 5.

7. McAnear, p. 165.

8. Sparks I, p. 5.

9. Franklin, p. 1432.

10. Ibid.

11. Ibid., pp. 1432–33.

12. Jones, p. 140.

13. Mintz, p. 14.

14. Ibid., p. 15.

15. Jones, p. 140.

16. Mintz, p. 15.

17. Ibid., pp. 13–14.

18. Kline, p. 5.

19. Morris II, p. 389.

20. Swiggett, p. 353.

21. Sparks I, p. 17.

22. Mintz, p. 9.

23. Ibid., p. 18.

24. Morris "delighted in Horace"—"Recollections of Gouverneur Morris," John W. Francis Papers.

25. Sparks I, p. 6.

26. Jonathan Landon to Robert Morris, August 27, 1766, Robert Morris Papers.

27. Delafield, p. 75.

28. Farrand III, p. 92.

29. Jonathan Landon to Robert Morris, September 4, 1766, Robert Morris Papers.

30. Davenport I, p. 354.

31. Mintz, p. 31.

Chapter Two

1. Mintz, p. 27.

2. Jones, p. 140.

3. Mintz, p. 26.

4. The standard biography of Robert R. Livingston is Dangerfield. For young John Jay, see Pellew, p. 7.

5. Sparks I, p. 17.

6. Ibid., p. 19.

7. Swiggett, pp. 18–19.

8. Miller, p. 63.

9. Mintz, pp. 40–41.

10. Kline, p. 27.

11. Ibid., p. 26.

12. Kammen, p. 360.

13. Sparks I, pp. 20–21.

14. Ibid., p. 25.

15. Ibid., pp. 23–24.

16. John. W. Francis Papers.

17. Sparks I, p. 26.

18. Burrows and Wallace, p. 224.

19. Kline, pp. 37–38.

20. Mintz, p. 48.

21. Sparks I, p. 40.

22. Mintz, pp. 51–52; Swiggett, p. 27.

23. Kline, p. 43.

24. Mintz, p. 53.

25. Swiggett, p. 26.

26. Mintz, p. 57.

27. Ibid., p. 00.

28. Farrand III, p. 85. Mintz (pp. 169–70) gives the dubious provenance of all three stories; one we owe to former president Martin Van Buren, who heard it from a judge, who heard it from a senator, who heard it from Alexander Hamilton. Swiggett (p. viii) presents a bluff argument for disbelieving them; on the other hand, an academic historian told me that he loved the Washington/Morris/Hamilton version because it was so characteristic of all three men.

29. Bobrick, p. 211.

30. Mintz, pp. 63–65. For the long, tangled career of William Smith, Jr., see Schechter, *passim.*

31. Sparks I, pp. 99–100.

32. Ibid., p. 103.

33. Mintz, p. 70.

34. Ibid., p. 69.

35. Sparks I, pp. 119–20.

Chapter Three

1. Mintz, p. 74.

2. *The Federalist Papers,* p. 38.

3. Mintz, p. 75.

4. Sparks I, p. 125; Kline, p. 78.

5. Davenport I, p. 265.

6. Davenport II, p. 8.

7. Van Schaak, p. 131.

8. Mintz, p. 76.

9. Kline, p. 79.

10. Sparks I, p. 127.

11. Mintz, p. 77.

12. Van Schaak, p. 440.
13. Ibid., pp. 55, 62.
14. Ibid., p. 100.
15. Ibid., p. 129.
16. Ibid., pp. 130–32.
17. Bobrick, p. 271.
18. Ibid., p. 273.
19. Kline, p. 83.
20. Mintz, p. 80.
21. Kline, p. 84.
22. Bobrick, p. 254.
23. Kline, p. 82.
24. Ibid.
25. Mintz, p. 83.
26. Ibid., p. 84.
27. Sparks I, p. 141.
28. Ibid., p. 145.
29. Mintz, p. 85.
30. Pratt, p. 110.
31. Mintz, p. 86.

Chapter Four

1. Weigley, p. 133.
2. Mintz, p. 88.
3. Kline, p. 106.
4. Swiggett, p. 73.
5. Mintz, p. 126.
6. Swiggett, p. 47.
7. Mintz, p. 89.
8. Kline, p. 170.
9. Flexner, *Revolution*, p. 261.
10. Sparks I, p. 154.
11. Mintz, p. 101.
12. Sparks I, p. 174.
13. Schama, p. 27. Schama is rather contemptuous of Lafayette, and anyone who follows his later career through Morris's eyes will not think well of him. Against this must be set Lafayette's glorious career in America, and George Washington's high opinion of him.
14. Bobrick, p. 295.
15. Mintz, p. 92.
16. Sparks I, p. 151.
17. Mintz, p. 100.

18. Ibid.
19. Sparks I, p. 159.
20. Ibid., p. 158.
21. Mintz, p. 94.
22. Ibid., p. 91.
23. Ibid., pp. 95–96.
24. Kline, p. 102.
25. Weigley, p. 142.
26. Ibid., p. 134.
27. Balch, p. 234.
28. Weigley, p. 152.
29. Swiggett, p. 55.
30. Ibid., p. 43; Kline, p. 160.
31. Mintz, pp. 113–14.
32. Sparks I, p. 217.
33. Ibid., p. 113.
34. Jensen, p. 251.
35. Ibid., pp. 252–53.
36. Rossiter, p. 351.
37. Ibid., p. 358.
38. Kline, pp. 113–14.
39. Ibid., p. 120.
40. Ibid., p. 122.
41. Miller, p. 52.
42. Mintz, p. 102.
43. Ibid., pp. 111, 103, 112–13.
44. Sparks I, p. 184.
45. Mintz, p. 113.
46. Washington, p. 328.
47. Kline, p. 143.
48. Morris II, p. 551.
49. Sparks I, p. 192.
50. Kline, p. 144.
51. Bobrick, p. 194.
52. Sparks I, p. 198.
53. Paine, p. 91.
54. Keane, p. 176.
55. Sparks I, p. 202.
56. See Mintz, p. 119.
57. Sparks I, p. 200.
58. Kline, p. 157.
59. Ibid., p. 148.

60. Sparks I, p. 212.
61. Kline, p. 168.

CHAPTER FIVE

1. Swiggett, p. 78.
2. Kline, p. 172.
3. Sparks I, p. 17.
4. Kline, p. 26.
5. Ibid., p. 107.
6. Swiggett, p. 59.
7. Ibid., p. 66.
8. Ibid., p. 72.
9. Sparks I, p. 223.
10. Mintz, p. 140.
11. Sparks I, p. 224.
12. Kline, p. 176.
13. Mintz, p. 141.
14. Davenport II, p. 247.
15. Davenport I, p. 234.
16. Chastellux, p. 135.
17. Kline, p. 178.
18. Ibid., p. 177.
19. Davenport I, p. 504.
20. Davenport II, p. 64.
21. John W. Francis Papers.
22. Morris II, p. 216.
23. Chastellux, p. 131.
24. Chase, p. 167.
25. Read, p. 202.

CHAPTER SIX

1. Sparks I, p. 230.
2. Ibid., p. 229.
3. Ver Steeg, p. 6.
4. Ibid., p. 37.
5. Mintz, p. 145.
6. See Ver Steeg, pp. 43ff.
7. Mintz, p. 148.
8. Sparks I, p. 220.
9. Kline, p. 202.
10. Morris II, p. 599.
11. Kline, p. 206.

12. Ibid., p. 223.
13. Ibid., p. 216.
14. Keane, p. 217.
15. Ibid., p. 218.
16. Ibid.
17. See McKusker, pp. 80–88. The New York Stock Exchange listed prices in eighths of dollars (bits) until April 2001. See also Koch and Peden, pp. 54–56.
18. Kline, p. 220.
19. Sparks I, p. 239.
20. Kline, p. 249.
21. Ibid., pp. 250–51.
22. Sparks I, p. 249.
23. Mintz, p. 160.
24. Sparks I, p. 251.
25. Mintz, p. 160.
26. Sparks I, p. 251.
27. Flexner, *Revolution*, p. 504.
28. Ibid., p. 507.
29. Sparks I, p. 266.
30. Ibid., p. 264.
31. Van Schaak, p. 372.
32. Kline, p. 299.
33. Paine, pp. 361–62.
34. Sparks III, p. 451.

Chapter Seven

1. Kline, p. 305.
2. Mintz, p. 177.
3. Farrand III, pp. 89–90.
4. Ibid., p. 92.
5. Madison, p. 23.
6. Farrand III, p. 391.
7. Madison, p. 225.
8. Farrand III, p. 92.
9. Madison, pp. 232–33.
10. Ibid., p. 496.
11. Ibid., p. 504.
12. Ibid., pp. 353–54.
13. Ibid., p. 564.
14. Ibid., p. 401.
15. Farrand III, p. 534; Madison, p. 23.
16. Madison, p. 232.

17. Ibid., p. 268.
18. Ibid., p. 246.
19. Ibid., p. 247.
20. Ibid., p. 261.
21. Ibid., p. 275.
22. Ibid., p. 262.
23. Ibid., p. 40.
24. Ibid., p. 227.
25. Ibid., p. 384.
26. Ibid., p. 225.
27. Ibid., p. 392.
28. Ibid., p. 393.
29. Ibid., pp. 450–51.
30. Sparks I, p. 286.
31. Madison, pp. 574–75.
32. Rossiter, p. 379.
33. Ibid., p. 397.
34. Ibid., pp. 353–54.
35. Ibid., p. 383.
36. Ibid., p. 391.
37. Ibid., p. 374.
38. Ibid., pp. 386, 392, 394.
39. Sparks I, p. 284.
40. Rossiter, p. 389.
41. Farrand III, p. 379.
42. Rossiter, p. 374.
43. Ibid., pp. 361, 351. The Articles of Confederation explicitly guaranteed the defense, liberties, and general welfare of the states; Madison's plan implicitly accepted that intention.
44. Farrand II, p. 134.
45. Rossiter, p. 367.
46. Madison, p. 582.
47. Simon, p. 23.
48. Farrand IV, p. 84.
49. Madison, p. 619.
50. Morris II, p. 436.
51. Ibid., p. 527.
52. Syrett V, p. 7.

CHAPTER EIGHT

1. Davis, p. 168.
2. Davenport I, p. xxxiii.

3. Ibid., pp. xxxiii–xxxiv
4. Van Doren, p. 609.
5. Ibid., pp. 639–40.
6. Butterfield, p. 207.
7. Ibid., p. 216.
8. Ibid., p. 222.
9. Ibid., p. 210.
10. Brodie, p. 235.
11. Koch and Peden, p. 395.
12. Ibid., pp. 382–83.
13. Van Doren, p. 760.
14. Butterfield, p. 238.
15. Ibid., p. 310.
16. Koch and Peden, p. 383.
17. Davenport I, p. 36.
18. Ibid., p. 113.
19. Ingersoll, p. 453.
20. Davenport I, p. 516.
21. Ibid., p. 570.
22. Ibid., p. 358.
23. Washington, p. 597.
24. Malone, *Rights,* p. 45.
25. Davenport I, p. 156.
26. Davenport II, p. 166.
27. Davenport I, p. 530.
28. Maricourt, p. 67.
29. Davenport I, p. 286.
30. Orieux, p. 55.
31. Maricourt, p. 167.
32. Ibid.
33. Orieux, p. 55.
34. Maricourt, p. 60.
35. Davenport I, p. 17.
36. Orieux, p. 4.
37. Davenport I, p. 108.
38. Davenport II, p. 302.
39. Ibid., p. 148.
40. Ibid., p. 54.
41. Davenport I, p. 61.
42. Ibid., pp. 111–12.
43. Ibid., p. 66.
44. Ibid., p. 67.

45. Ibid., p. 68.
46. Ibid.
47. Ibid., p. 85.
48. Ibid., p. 98.
49. Ibid., p. 136.
50. Ibid., p. 142.
51. Ibid., p. 148.
52. Ibid., p. 144.
53. Ibid., pp. 158–59.
54. Ibid., pp. 255–56.
55. Koch and Peden, p. 478.
56. Ibid., p. 487.
57. Schama, p. 406.
58. Davenport I, p. 164.
59. Ibid., p. 44.
60. Ibid., p. 292.
61. Ibid., p. 29.
62. Ibid., p. 119.
63. Ibid., p. 157.
64. Ibid., p. 160.
65. Ibid., p. 164.

Chapter Nine

1. Davenport I, p. 232.
2. Furet and Richet, p. 126.
3. Davenport I, p. 221.
4. Ibid., p. 223.
5. Ibid., pp. 383–84.
6. Ibid., p. 385.
7. Ibid., p. 387.
8. Ibid., p. 328.
9. Ibid., p. 507.
10. Ibid., p. 235.
11. Ibid., p. 226.
12. Ibid., p. 407.
13. Davenport II, p. 62.
14. Davenport I, p. 293.
15. Ibid., p. 318.
16. Ibid., p. 243.
17. Ibid., p. 245.
18. Ibid., p. 413.
19. Ibid., pp. 260–61.

20. Ibid., p. 237.
21. Ferguson, p. 271.
22. Davenport I, p. 464.
23. Ibid., p. 604.
24. Ibid., p. 493.
25. Davenport II, p. 48.
26. Ibid., p. 55.
27. Ibid., p. 64.
28. Ibid., pp. 119, 123.
29. Ibid., p. 80.
30. Ibid., p. 158.
31. Burke, pp. 92–93.
32. Paine, p. 448.
33. Ibid., p. 539.
34. Ibid., p. 453.
35. Davenport II, p. 156.
36. Ibid., p. 138.
37. Ibid., p. 77.
38. Schama, p. 549.
39. Davenport II, p. 164.
40. Ibid., p. 166.
41. Ibid., p. 207.
42. Ibid., pp. 212–13.
43. Schama, p. 555.
44. Davenport II, p. 211.
45. Ibid., p. 300.
46. Ibid., pp. 266–68.
47. Ibid., p. 250.
48. Sparks III, p. 482.
49. Ibid., p. 483.
50. Davenport II, pp. 322–23.
51. Ibid., p. 318.
52. Rousseau, p. 195.
53. Schama, p. 205.
54. Burke, p. 93.

Chapter Ten

1. Swiggett, p. 225.
2. O'Brien, p. 103.
3. Swiggett, p. 226.
4. O'Brien, p. 130.
5. Swiggett, p. 225.

6. Washington, pp. 799–800.
7. Davenport II, p. 403.
8. Ibid., p. 436.
9. Paine, p. 657.
10. Davenport II, p. 368.
11. Ibid., p. 429.
12. Ibid., pp. 444, 449.
13. Ibid., p. 477.
14. Ibid., p. 490.
15. Ibid.
16. Ibid., p. 512.
17. Ibid., p. 517.
18. Ibid.
19. Ibid., pp. 518–19.
20. Maricourt, pp. 150–51.
21. Hemlow and Douglas II, p. 14.
22. Ibid., p. 25.
23. Ibid., p. 22. The Burneys "had wandered out of the sedate drawingrooms of *Sense and Sensibility* and were in danger of losing themselves in the elegantly disordered alcoves of *Les Liaisons Dangereuses*"—Cooper, p. 64.
24. Sparks I, pp. 407–8.
25. Davenport II, p. 531.
26. Ibid., p. 561.
27. Ibid., p. 509.
28. Ibid., p. 507.
29. Ibid., p. 515.
30. Ibid., p. 527.
31. Ibid., p. 566.
32. Schama, p. 640.
33. Keane, p. 349.
34. Ibid., p. 351.
35. Davenport II, p. 597.
36. Paine, p. 388.
37. Davenport II, p. 602.
38. Ibid., p. 492.
39. Maricourt, pp. 159–63.
40. Sparks II, p. 312.
41. Morris II, pp. 43–44.
42. Walther, p. 240.
43. Ibid., p. 242.
44. Davenport II, p. 586.
45. Schama, p. 800.

46. Morris II, p. 48.
47. Sparks II, p. 393.
48. Paine, pp. 670–71.
49. Davenport II, p. 11.
50. Sparks II, p. 393.
51. Davenport II, p. 595.
52. Cobbett, p. 104.
53. Elkins and McKitrick, p. 363.
54. Ibid., p. 369.
55. Morris II, p. 37.
56. Ibid., p. 70.
57. Davenport II, p. 579.
58. Ibid., p. 570.
59. Ibid., p. 571.
60. Davenport I, p. 567.
61. Ibid., p. 129.
62. Morris II, p. 116.
63. Sparks III, p. 489.

Chapter Eleven

1. Morris II, p. 296.
2. Swiggett, p. 293.
3. Maricourt, p. 175.
4. Morris II, p. 81.
5. Ibid., p. 82.
6. Swiggett, p. 297.
7. Morris II, pp. 109–10.
8. Ibid., pp. 134–35.
9. Ibid., p. 138.
10. Ibid., pp. 156, 184.
11. Ibid., p. 129.
12. Diary, June 27, 1796.
13. Morris II, p. 75.
14. Ibid., p. 248.
15. Ibid., pp. 174, 190.
16. Ibid., p. 244.
17. Ibid., pp. 248–49.
18. Ibid., pp. 249–50.
19. Ibid., p. 227.
20. Ibid., pp. 180, 183.
21. Swiggett, p. 320.
22. Morris II, p. 295.

23. Ibid., pp. 295–96.

24. Swiggett, p. 322.

25. Ibid., p. 359.

26. Ibid.

27. Sparks I, p. 440.

28. Ibid., p. 441.

29. Ibid., p. 446.

30. Elkins and MicKitrick, p. 567.

31. Ibid., p. 871, though Cooper (p. 86) argues that this famous story is false.

32. Keane, p. 437.

33. Morris II, p. 85.

34. Ibid., p. 103.

35. Ibid., p. 105.

36. Ibid., pp. 202–3.

37. Ibid., p. 203.

38. Ibid., p. 23.

39. Diary, December 1, 1798.

Chapter Twelve

1. Syrett XXII, p. 192.

2. John W. Francis Papers.

3. Swiggett, p. 365.

4. Goebel II, pp. 88, 86, 83.

5. Sparks III, p. 82.

6. Elkins and McKitrick, p. 572.

7. Syrett XVIII, p. 329.

8. Morris II, p. 378.

9. Ibid., p. 380.

10. Sparks III, p. 130.

11. Ibid., p. 128.

12. Morris II, p. 396.

13. "Aaron Burr had 100,000 votes from the single circumstance of his descent from President Burr and President Edwards"—John Adams to Thomas Jefferson, November 15, 1813, Cappon, p. 399.

14. Davenport I, p. 256.

15. Morris II, p. 401.

16. Malone, *Ordeal,* p. 458.

17. See Morris II, p. 397.

18. Sparks III, p. 132.

19. Syrett XXV, p. 272.

20. Sparks III, p. 134.

21. Ibid., p. 256.

22. Ibid., p. 154.

23. Morris II, p. 405.

24. For discussions of this famous phrase, see Elkins and McKitrick, p. 753, and Joseph J. Ellis, p. 182.

25. Elkins and McKitrick, p. 754.

26. Sparks III, p. 128.

27. Adams, *Randolph*, p. 58.

28. Morris II, p. 405.

29. Sparks III, p. 371.

30. Ibid., p. 375.

31. Morris II, p. 417.

32. Ibid., p. 422.

33. Sparks III, p. 409.

34. Ibid., p. 415.

35. Ibid., pp. 417, 414.

36. Morris II, p. 412. George Morgan presents a balanced discussion of this quarrel, pp. 394–96.

37. Morris II, p. 388.

38. Flexner, *Agony*, pp. 311–12.

39. Milton Ellis, p. 362.

40. Swiggett, p. 362.

41. Ibid., p. 363.

42. Sparks III, p. 203.

43. Morris II, p. 453.

44. Ibid., pp. 456–58.

Chapter Thirteen

1. Sparks III, p. 243.

2. Diary, August 14, 1808; September 1, 1808. For the history of Morris's upstate house, see Rossie et al., pp. 12–13.

3. Watson, p. 246.

4. Flexner, *New*, p. 82.

5. Sparks I, p. 497.

6. Sparks III, pp. 142–44.

7. Morris II, pp. 439–40.

8. Ibid., p. 440.

9. Ibid., p. 507.

10. Malone, *Second*, p. 555.

11. Morris II, p. 536.

12. Crawford, p. 201.

13. A[nne] C[ary] Morris to Joseph C. Cabell, October 14, 1831, Cabell

Family Papers; Gouverneur Morris to Anne Cary Randolph, March [n.d.] 1809.

14. Swiggett, p. 137.

15. Anne Cary Morris to Josesh C. Cabell, October 14, 1831.

16. Koch and Peden, p. 590.

17. Crawford, pp. 116–17.

18. Ibid., pp. 77–78.

19. Ibid., p. 92.

20. Ibid., p. 145.

21. Adams, *Randolph*, pp. 83–84.

22. Crawford, p. 148.

23. Diary, September 17, 1808. Swiggett (pp. 395–96) has another theory.

24. Gouverneur Morris to Anne Cary Randolph, March [n.d.] 1809. In courting Nancy as an employee, and something more, Morris wrote her three letters in March 1809, whose arguments I have, in arranging thematically, taken out of sequence: March 3, 9, and a letter whose first page has been removed from the letterbook (March n.d.).

25. Gouverneur Morris to Anne Cary Randolph, March 3, 1809.

26. Gouverneur Morris to Anne Cary Randolph, March 9, 1809.

27. Gouverneur Morris to Anne Cary Randolph, March n.d. 1809.

28. Gouverneur Morris to Anne Cary Randolph, March 3, 1809.

29. Swiggett, p. 399.

30. Gouverneur Morris to John Marshall, December 2, 1809.

31. Crawford, p. 197.

32. Diary, December 25, 1809.

33. Swiggett, p. 403.

Chapter Fourteen

1. Morris II, p. 431.

2. Sparks III, p. 216; Morris II, p. 472.

3. Sparks III, p. 251.

4. John W. Francis Papers.

5. Cornog, p. 111.

6. Morris II, p. 520.

7. Ibid., p. 521.

8. *Journal of the Senate*, p. 66.

9. Ibid., p. 69.

10. Ibid., p. 73.

11. Ibid., p. 75.

12. Burrows and Wallace, p. 421.

13. Morris II, p. 536.

14. *Public Documents*, p. 59.

15. Ibid., p. 60.
16. Ibid., p. 64.
17. Ibid., p. 63.
18. Ibid., p. 61.
19. Morris II, p. 431.
20. Ibid., p. 509.
21. Adams, *Madison*, p. 394.
22. Adams, *Randolph*, p. 206.
23. Morris II, p. 535.
24. Ibid., p. 536.
25. Ibid., p. 541.
26. Ibid.
27. Ibid., p. 527.
28. Ibid., p. 537.
29. Ibid., p. 543.
30. Ibid., p. 548.
31. Ibid., p. 543.
32. Ibid., p. 573.
33. Ibid., p. 543.
34. Ibid., p. 551.
35. Ibid., p. 549.
36. Ibid., p. 552.
37. Ibid., p. 548.
38. Ibid., p. 559.
39. Ibid., p. 566.
40. Ibid., p. 564.
41. Ibid., p. 566.
42. Swiggett, p. 418.
43. Ibid., p. 417.
44. Morris II, p. 565.
45. Adams, *Madison*, p. 1071.

Chapter Fifteen

1. Crawford, p. 227.
2. Ibid., pp. 234–40.
3. Adams, *Randolph*, p. 184.
4. Crawford, pp. 235–36.
5. Ibid., pp. 245–53.
6. Swiggett, p. 435.
7. Ibid., p. 426.
8. Morris II, p. 575.
9. Adams, *Madison*, p. 1111.

10. Ibid., p. 1113.
11. Ibid., p. 1115.
12. Morris II, p. 568.
13. Adams, *Madison*, p. 1117.
14. Madison, p. 567.
15. Ibid., p. 349.
16. Morris II, p. 578.
17. Ibid., p. 579.
18. Ibid., p. 578.
19. Ibid., p. 557.
20. Sparks III, p. 304.
21. Dwight, p. 361.
22. Sparks III, p. 290.
23. Morris II, p. 588.

CHAPTER SIXTEEN

1. Sparks III, p. 340.
2. Ibid., p. 341.
3. Ibid., p. 347.
4. Adams, *Madison*, p. 1283.
5. Ibid., p. 1285.
6. Morris II, p. 594.
7. Ibid., p. 599.
8. Ibid., p. 594.
9. Ibid., p. 598.
10. Sparks III, p. 355.
11. Ibid., p. 361.
12. Ibid.
13. Morris II, p. 499.
14. Ibid., pp. 600–601.
15. Swiggett, p. 441.
16. Morris II, p. 602.
17. Ibid.

POSTSCRIPT

1. Gordon, p. 56.
2. Cooper, p. 374.
3. Swiggett, p. 447; *Gouverneur (N.Y.) Tribune Press,* "Historic Morris 'Mansion' on the Mend," March 4, 1992.
4. Morris II, p. 43.

Bibliography

Adams, Henry. *History of the United States During the Administrations of James Madison.* New York: Library of America, 1986.

———. *John Randolph.* Armonk, NY: M. E. Sharpe, 1996.

Alexander, James. *A Brief Narrative of the Case and Trial of John Peter Zenger,* ed. Stanley Nider Katz. Cambridge: Harvard University Press, 1963.

Balch, F. W., trans., "Narrative of the Prince de Broglie," *Magazine of American History,* I (April 1877).

Chastellux, marquis de. *Travels in North America,* trans. Howard C. Rice, Jr. Chapel Hill: University of North Carolina Press, 1963.

Cobbett, William. *Peter Porcupine in America,* ed. David Wilson. Ithaca, NY: Cornell University Press, 1994.

Cooper, Duff. *Talleyrand.* New York: Grove Press, 1997.

Cornog, Evan. *The Birth of Empire.* New York: Oxford University Press, 1998.

Crawford, Alan Pell. *Unwise Passions.* New York: Simon & Schuster, 2000.

Dangerfield, George. *Chancellor Robert R. Livingston of New York.* New York: Harcourt Brace, 1960.

Davenport, Beatrix Cary. *A Diary of the French Revolution by Gouverneur Morris,* 2 vols. Boston: Houghton Mifflin, 1939.

Davis, Joseph S. *Essays in the Earlier History of American Corporations.* Cambridge: Harvard University Press, 1917.

Delafield, Julia. *Biographies of Francis Lewis and Morgan Lewis.* New York: A. D. F. Randolph & Co. 1877.

Dwight, Theodore. *History of the Hartford Convention.* Freeport, NY: Books for Libraries Press, 1970.

Elkins, Stanley, and Eric McKitrick. *The Age of Federalism.* New York: Oxford University Press, 1993.

Ellis, Joseph J. *American Sphinx.* New York: Alfred A. Knopf, 1997.

Ellis, Milton. "The Author of the First American Novel," *American Literature,* 4 (January 1933).

Farrand, Max, ed. *The Records of the Federal Convention.* New Haven: Yale University Press, 1937.

Ferguson, E. James. *The Power of the Purse.* Chapel Hill: University of North Carolina Press, 1961.

Flexner, James Thomas. *George Washington in the American Revolution.* Boston: Little, Brown, 1968.

———. *George Washington and the New Nation.* Boston: Little, Brown, 1970.

———. *George Washington: Anguish and Farewell.* Boston: Little, Brown, 1972.

Franklin, Benjamin. *Writings.* New York: Library of America, 1987.

Furet, François, and Denis Richet. *The French Revolution,* trans. Stephen Hardman. New York: The Macmillan Company, 1970.

Goebel, Julius, Jr., ed. *The Law Practice of Alexander Hamilton.* New York: Columbia University Press, 1964–81.

Gordon, John Steele. *The Great Game.* New York: Scribner, 1999.

Hamilton, Alexander, James Madison, and John Jay. *The Federalist Papers.* New York: New American Library, 1961.

Hemlow, Joyce, and Althea Douglas, eds. *Fanny Burney: Journals and Letters.* Oxford: Oxford University Press, 1972.

Ingersoll, Charles J. *Recollections, Historical, Political, Biographical and Social.* Philadelphia: J. B. Lippincott & Co., 1861.

Jensen, Merrill. *The Articles of Confederation.* Madison: University of Wisconsin Press, 1959.

Jones, Thomas. *History of New York During the Revolutionary War.* New York: New-York Historical Society, 1879.

Journal of the Senate of the State of New-York. Albany: S. Southwick, 1811.

Kammen, Michael. *Colonial New York—A History.* New York: Charles Scribner's Sons, 1975.

Keane, John. *Tom Paine.* Boston: Little, Brown, 1995.

Kline, Mary-Jo. *Gouverneur Morris and the New Nation 1775–1788.* New York: Arno Press, 1978.

Knox, Katharine McCook. *The Sharples: Their Portraits of George Washington and His Contemporaries.* New Haven: Yale University Press, 1930.

Koch, Adrienne, and William Peden. *The Life and Selected Writings of Thomas Jefferson.* New York: Modern Library, 1944.

Madison, James. *Debates in the Federal Convention of 1787,* ed. James McClellan and M. E. Bradford. Richmond, VA: James River Press, 1989.

Malone, Dumas. *Jefferson and the Rights of Man.* Boston: Little, Brown, 1951.

———. *Jefferson and the Ordeal of Liberty.* Boston: Little, Brown, 1962.

———. *Jefferson the President: Second Term 1805–1809.* Boston: Little, Brown, 1974.

McAnear, Beverly. "An American in London," *Pennsylvania Magazine of History and Biography,* 63 (April 1940).

McKusker, John J. *How Much Is That in Real Money?* Worcester, MA: American Antiquarian Society, 2001.

Maricourt, baron André de. *Madame de Souza et Sa Famille.* Paris: Emile-Paul, 1907.

Miller, John C. *Alexander Hamilton: Portrait in Paradox.* New York: Harper & Brothers, 1959.

Mintz, Max M. *Gouverneur Morris and the American Revolution.* Norman, OK: University of Oklahoma Press, 1970.

Morgan, George. *The True Lafayette.* Philadelphia: J. B. Lippincott Co., 1919.

Morris, Anne Cary. *The Diary and Letters of Gouverneur Morris,* 2 vols. New York: Charles Scribner's Sons, 1888.

O'Brien, Conor Cruise. *The Long Affair* . Chicago: University of Chicago Press, 1996.

Orieux, Jean. *Talleyrand,* trans. Patricia Wolf. New York: Alfred A. Knopf, 1974.

Paine, Thomas. *Collected Writings.* New York: Library of America, 1995.

Pellew, George. *John Jay.* New York: AMS Press, 1972.

Pratt, George W. *An Account of the British Expedition Above the Highlands of the Hudson River. . . .* , N.p.: Ulster County Historical Society, 1977.

Public Documents Relating to the New-York Canals . . . New York: William A. Mercury, 1821.

Read, Elizabeth. "The Chews of Pennsylvania," *Magazine of American History,* 4 (March 1880).

Rossie, Fowler, Edwards, DeKalb, and Hammond. *Centennial Souvenir History of Gouverneur.* Watertown, NY: Hungerford-Holbrook Co.; 1905.

Rossiter, Clinton. *1787 The Grand Convention.* New York: The Macmillan Company, 1966.

Rousseau, Jean Jacques. *Lettre à D'Alembert.* Paris: Garnier-Flammarion, 1967.

Schama, Simon. *Citizens.* New York: Alfred A. Knopf, 1989.

Schechter, Barnet. *The Battle for New York.* New York: Walker & Company, 2002.

Simon, James F. *What Kind of Nation: Thomas Jefferson, John Marshall, and the Epic Struggle to Create a United States.* New York: Simon & Schuster, 2002.

Sparks, Jared. *The Life of Gouverneur Morris, with Selections from his Correspondence and Miscellaneous Papers,* 3 vols. Boston: Gray & Bowen, 1832.

Swiggett, Howard. *The Extraordinary Mr. Morris.* Garden City, NY: Doubleday & Company, 1952.

Syrett, Harold C., et al., eds. *The Papers of Alexander Hamilton* 26, XXX vols. New York: Columbia University Press, 1961–87.

Van Doren, Carl. *Benjamin Franklin.* New York: Viking Press, 1938.

Van Schaak, Henry C. *The Life of Peter Van Schaak.* New York: Appleton & Company, 1842.

Ver Steeg, Clarence L. *Robert Morris, Revolutionary Financier.* Philadelphia: University of Pennsylvania Press, 1954.

Walther, Daniel. *Gouverneur Morris Witness of Two Revolutions,* trans. Elinore Denniston. New York: Literary Digest Books, 1934.

Washington, George. *Writings.* New York: Library of America, 1977.

Watson, Elkanah. *Men and Times of the Revolution; or, Memoirs of Elkanah Watson.* New York: Dana & Company, 1856.

Weigley, Russell F., et al., eds. *Philadelphia: A 300-Year History.* New York: W. W. Norton & Company, 1982.

Index

ABOUT THE AUTHOR

Richard Brookhiser is the author of *America's First Dynasty: The Adamses, 1735–1918* (2003); *Alexander Hamilton, American* (1999); *Founding Father: Rediscovering George Washington* (1996); and *The Way of the WASP* (1991), all published by The Free Press. He is a Senior Editor at *The National Review* and a *New York Observer* columnist. He contributes to such publications as *American Heritage* and *The New York Times*, and he lives in New York City.

Exploring GenderSpeak

Personal Effectiveness
in Gender Communication

SECOND EDITION

Diana K. Ivy

Texas A&M University–Corpus Christi

Phil Backlund

Central Washington University

Boston   Burr Ridge, IL   Dubuque, IA   Madison, WI
New York   San Francisco   St. Louis
Bangkok   Bogotá   Caracas   Lisbon   London   Madrid   Mexico City
Milan   New Delhi   Seoul   Singapore   Sydney   Taipei   Toronto

McGraw-Hill Higher Education

*A Division of The **McGraw-Hill** Companies*

EXPLORING GENDERSPEAK:
Personal Effectiveness in Gender Communication

This book is printed on acid-free paper.

1 2 3 4 5 6 7 8 9 0 DOC/DOC 9 0 9 8 7 6 5 4 3 2 1 0 9

ISBN 0-07-290392-9

Vice president/Editor-in-chief: *Thalia Dorwick*
Editorial director: *Phillip A. Butcher*
Sponsoring editor: *Marjorie Byers*
Editorial assistant: *Suzanne Driscoll*
Marketing manager: *Kelly M. May*
Project manager: *Christine Parker*
Production supervisor: *Rose Hepburn*
Director of design MHHE: *Keith J. McPherson*
Photo research coordinator: *Sharon Miller*
Photo researcher: *Elyse Rieder*
Compositor: *Shepherd Incorporated*
Typeface: *10/12 Palatino*
Printer: *R. R. Donnelley & Sons Company*

Cover image provided by: *FPG International LLC,*
Autumn Leaves in Pool of Water © Montes De Oca, Art 1998

PHOTO CREDITS

1–1: Copyright 1999. PhotoDisc, Inc. All rights reserved.
2–1: Roger Dollarhide/Monkmeyer
3–1: Copyright 1999. PhotoDisc, Inc. All rights reserved.
4–1: Copyright 1999. PhotoDisc, Inc. All rights reserved.
4.1: Courtesy Outdoor Advertising Association of Americas, Inc.
5–1: Arvind Garg/Photo Researchers
6–1: Comstock
7–1: Sven Martson
8–1: Copyright 1999. PhotoDisc, Inc. All rights reserved.
9–1: Copyright 1999. PhotoDisc, Inc. All rights reserved.
10–1: Jim Pickerall/Stock Boston.
11–1: Copyright 1999 Photo Disc, Inc. All Rights Reserved.
E–1: Corbil

Library of Congress Cataloging–in-Publication Data
Ivy, Diana K.
    Exploring GenderSpeak: personal effectiveness in gender communication /Diana K. Ivy, Phil Backlund.—2nd ed.
        p.   cm.
    Includes bibliogrpahical references and index.
    ISBN 0-07-290392-9 pbk.)
    1. Communication—Sex differences.   I. Backlund, Phil.
II. Title.
P96.S48I96   2000
305.3—dc21   99-27151

http://www.mhhe.com

About the Authors

DIANA K. IVY received her undergraduate degree in speech communication and theatre from Texas Wesleyan University in her hometown of Fort Worth, Texas. After serving Wesleyan for four years as Assistant Director of Admissions, Ivy pursued graduate education in the Department of Communication at the University of Oklahoma. Concentrating on instructional and interpersonal communication there, she received her M.A. in 1984 and her Ph.D. in 1987. Ivy's first faculty position was in the Department of Speech Communication at Southwest Texas State University, where she received the Professor of the Year Award from the Nontraditional Student Organization and the departmental Outstanding Teacher Award. She then served four years as Basic Course Director in the Department of Communication at North Carolina State University. Currently, Ivy is an Associate Professor of Communication Arts and Director of the Women's Center for Education and Service at Texas A&M University-Corpus Christi.

PHILIP M. BACKLUND received his undergraduate degree in business administration and a master's degree in speech communication from Humboldt State University (California). His first academic position took him to the University of Alaska in Fairbanks as an assistant professor. After spending two years in that interesting environment, he and his family moved to Denver, Colorado where he pursued his Ph.D. in speech communication at the University of Denver. During his graduate program, he taught full and part time for Arapahoe Community College. After receiving his Ph.D., he and his growing family moved to Utica, New York where he taught at Utica College. After two years in New York, he and his family returned to the west to Central Washington University where he is currently a professor of speech communication and Associate Dean of the College of Arts and Humanities. The students of Central Washington University have twice honored Phil with the Associated Students Distinguished Professor of the Year Award. Phil enjoys family activities, basketball, and windsurfing.

To Important Women
Hazel, Carol, and Karen
DKI

To Judy, Shane, Ryan, Matt
Kari, Emily, and Madison
PB

Contents

Part Three
LET'S TALK: INITIATING AND DEVELOPING RELATIONSHIPS

Preface

"The only constant is change." That piece of wisdom became more real than ever for us as we worked on the second edition of this text. Many things have changed since we first wrote about this subject, but we realize that the way women and men are communicated about in society, as well as how they communicate with each other, will continue to evolve. What hasn't changed since the first edition is the fascination with this topic.

Through our use of this text in gender communication classes and from the feedback of colleagues who use it as well, we have become more firmly committed to the receiver orientation to communication and personal effectiveness approach, as outlined in Chapter 1. We have seen students struggle with this approach to communication, because many of them are used to thinking about improving communication skills from a sender perspective. They have been taught that a communicator's goal is to be as clear and understandable as possible with others. But less often have they been taught that they are responsible for the effect or impact of their communication on others. Understanding that aspect and learning to adapt one's communication to others form the basis of the receiver orientation that we embrace in the text and in our teaching. Once students understand this perspective, ponder it, and then attempt to use it in their interactions with others, most come to see its value and the potential for receiver-oriented communication to transform (or at least enhance) their relationships. So we have retained this undergirding principle in the second edition of *Exploring GenderSpeak: Personal Effectiveness in Gender Communication*.

The text also goes beyond a description of how men and women are communicatively alike and how they are different. We encourage students to consider the myriad of influences—from physiology to culture to media—that affect their communication with women and men. Most important, as students explore this information, they are challenged to learn about themselves in ways that may expand their individual conceptions of what it is to be a man or a woman. As students explore attitudes and stereotypes, gender-role identity and self-esteem, and communication in relationships, they may come to see that differences between the sexes are not so great as some might suggest.

Another element we have retained in the second edition relates to our grounded or application-oriented approach. Over the years we have found that students find value in the concrete, the applicable, the reality based. If your students are like ours, they are cognizant of the fact that they need a theoretical, research-driven background on a given topic. But what they really seek is a translation of that information into a recognizable, useful form. Another way of saying this is that, in the area of gender communication especially, students continually seek empowerment. They seek ways they can use what they learn to more effectively establish and improve their relationships with others. Some textbooks merely report research results without offering possible interpretations of the findings or applications of the information. The result of this practice is that the reader or the instructor must act as an interpreter, making sense of research findings that are often contradictory and providing avenues for practical application to daily life. One of the things we continue to do in *Gender-Speak* is to depict realistic events in the lives of students, offer explanations for those events via cutting-edge research, and then provide a range of communicative options students may employ for enhanced personal effectiveness in their interactions and relationships.

We also continue our efforts to speak to college students using language and examples they find provocative. Students have demonstrated to us that they are much more likely to embrace this content and allow it to challenge their relational lives because the language is accessible, current, and engaging. The text has been written primarily for college undergraduates enrolled in courses focusing on the effects of gender on the communication process. Such courses may be represented in university curricula as upper-division courses, while at community colleges, for example, they may be more introductory in nature. *GenderSpeak* is appropriate for both these levels. While some prior exposure to basic concepts and theories of interpersonal communication will serve the reader well, this exposure is not requisite to an understanding of the content of this text.

Organization of the Second Edition

Our own and others' use of the text led to a few organizational changes for the second edition of *GenderSpeak*. We retained the general four-part structure, but altered the order in which some chapters appear, condensed some information and combined chapters, and provided new chapters. The second edition is organized into eleven chapters and an epilogue, within four major sections. Part One, "Communication, Gender, and Effectiveness" contains an overview of the communication process, including our emphasis on the receiver of communication, a discussion of key terminology, and a description of the various components within the personal effectiveness approach.

Part Two, "Influences on Our Choices," encourages readers to explore the many influences that shape their identities, attitudes, expectations, and communication as women and men. This section is based on an assumption that students must first understand what is influencing them—in terms of choices they make about themselves and about communication—before they can work to improve their communication skills and their relationships. Specific topics of discussion include the nature versus nurture argument, the development of gender identity and self-esteem, and the influence of mediated communication on sex and gender.

"Lets Talk: Initiating and Developing Relationships" is the title of Part Three, which continues to be one of the most unique aspects of the text. This section focuses on the role of gender communication in the initiation, development, maintenance, and sometimes termination of personal relationships.

Once the building blocks of gender communication and relationship development are conveyed, students proceed into the final section of the text. In Part Four, "The Contexts for Our Relationships: Personal Effectiveness in Action," five chapters explore ways in which gender communication affects and is affected by the following contexts or life-situations: friendships (same-sex versus cross-sex), intimate or romantic relationships, marital relationships, the workplace, and educational settings. A chapter within this section also investigates the downside of human relationships—power abuses in the forms of sexual harassment, sexual assault, and partner violence.

Specific, major organizational changes for the second edition include:

- A new Chapter 3 examines the development of gender identity and self-esteem, as affected by such forces as cultural interpretations of femininity and masculinity and agents of socialization, such as families, peers, and schools. This chapter follows Chapter 2's exploration of biological and social influences on sex and gender.
- Chapters 3 and 5 from the first edition both dealt with language—the former from the perspective of how language is used to describe or talk *about* the sexes and the latter regarding the use of language in communication *between* the sexes. For the second edition we streamlined this material and combined these chapters. We then moved this new Chapter 5 out of Part Two, which focuses on influences on communication; it is now the first chapter in Part Three on relationship initiation and development.
- The two interpersonal communication and relationship development chapters from the first edition have also been streamlined and condensed into one chapter.
- The friendship chapter (Chapter 7) is still the first chapter in Part Four, "The Contexts for Our Relationships." Information on marital relationships no longer constitutes its own chapter, but is now contained in Chapter 8, "Beyond Friendship: Gender Communication in Love, Sex, and Marriage." The information on family communication and the influence of family life on gender, previously contained in the marital relationships chapter, now forms a substantial section within Chapter 3 on gender-role identity development. The contextual chapters on workplace and education appear as Chapters 10 and 11.

- Chapter 9, "Power Abuses in Human Relationships" is another new addition to this edition of the text. Our goals were to provide a more concentrated coverage of the topic of sexual harassment than in the first edition and to add important information on sexual assault and partner violence. The theme of power is explored throughout our discussion of the three areas of abuse.
- A final organizational element is the addition of an Epilogue entitled, "The Impacts of Social Movements on Gender Communication: You Must Know Where You've Been to Know Where You're Going." For many of you this chapter will serve as a prologue rather than an epilogue, because you will choose to assign it to students first as a means of providing historical context for the remainder of the text. No matter when you introduce this material in your course, it will help your students recognize major social trends that affect our understanding of gender communication today.

What's New in the Chapters?

- Chapter 1 contains an expanded discussion of current and historical types of feminisms, such as third-wave feminism, as well as the view that "feminism is dead," often termed the "postfeminist" perspective.
- In Chapter 2, we include a discussion of the rise in popularity of women's sports, in terms of how men's and women's aggression is viewed differently in American culture.
- The media chapter now includes an expanded discussion of men's depictions in advertising and the potential effects of male objectification and commodification. Updated research appears on women's and men's television roles, as well as the effect of such depictions on real relationships.
- Another significant change to the media chapter is the inclusion of a section on pornography and its effects on identity, self-esteem, and relationships. We first explore varying definitions for key terms; then we examine different points of view on the issue, primarily described as Anti-Pornography and Anti-Censorship perspectives.
- The newly revised relationship chapter includes a section that explores the world of cyber-relationships. Specific topics of emphasis include the control that technology gives the individual over communicating an identity to others, ways that on-line users establish virtual relationships, and how they translate those virtual relationships into real ones.
- Chapter 7 includes a new section on issues in cross-sex friendships, along with a historical perspective of men's friendships that illustrates how much they have changed over past decades.
- Chapter 8 now offers a more streamlined, updated discussion of gender communication in intimate relationships, including marriage. New sections focus on the role of communication in sexual situations and on the development of communication patterns in marital relationships.

- Chapter 10 on workplace communication contains an updated discussion of the controversy over Affirmative Action and its effects on women's and men's career advancement. We also provide research on ways professionals attempt to balance or juggle career, home, and family. Updates on sexual harassment, particularly pertaining to changes in laws that affect our professional lives, will help students better understand this complex topic.
- The education chapter provides recent findings of AAUW surveys, in terms of how girls are improving their achievement and self-esteem in schools. Updates on educational sexual harassment and legal developments, especially as pertain to peer harassment, are also included.

Pedagogical Features

Each chapter contains seven pedagogical features to serve as aids for instructors and students alike. A new *Case Study* introduces each chapter, with the exception of Chapter 9. In this chapter on power abuses, case studies are embedded for each of the three main topics. In some instances, case studies represent actual events that occurred or emerged from discussion in the gender communication classrooms of the authors. The case study device is used not only to gain attention from readers as they delve into a new topic, but to orient or alert the reader to the nature of the discussion that lies in the next pages.

A *Hot Topics* section follows the case study or opening information, as a means of helping students get a sense of the scope of the chapter. These bulleted phrases can serve as topical outlines of chapter content, which students can check against *Key Terms* sections at the end of each chapter in preparation for exams or to simply check their understanding of chapter content.

A new feature, the *Recap Box*, contains a list of important terms from the previous section of reading. These boxes appear intermittently within each chapter as a reminder to students of important concepts they will want to retain.

Quotes throughout the chapters provide fascinating (and sometimes appalling) insights related to concepts discussed on the page. These "pearls of wisdom" come from film and television personalities, athletes, political figures, musicians, and historical figures.

We retained the series of *Discussion Starters* which follows the *Key Terms* listing for each chapter. Instructors may use these questions as a means of generating class discussion over chapter content, as actual assignments, or as thought provokers for students to consider on their own time.

Finally, complete *References* to research cited within the text appear at the end of each chapter. Students may find these references useful as they prepare assignments and/or conduct their own research projects. Instructors may use the references to gather additional material for their own research or to supplement instruction.

Acknowledgments

This project has certainly been a team effort; thus there are many people to acknowledge and thank. The authors wish to thank the many folks we've been privileged to work with at McGraw-Hill, including our sponsoring editor, Marjorie Byers, editorial assistant Sue Driscoll, project manager Christine Parker, photography researcher Sharon Miller, and designer Keith McPherson. We also wish to thank our original editor on this project, Hilary Jackson, because without her enthusiasm, support, advice, and vision, this book would never have seen the light of day, nor the prospect of going into a second edition.

We are grateful to our colleagues in the field of communication whose advice and encouragement throughout the review process for this text were invaluable. Reviewers who helped shape the second edition include:

Diana Carlin, University of Kansas; Karla Kay Jensen, Texas Tech University; Linda Krug, University of Minnesota, Duluth; and Jamey A. Piland, Trinity College, Washington, DC. First edition reviewers to thank include: Elizabeth Altman, University of Southern California; Janis Andersen, San Diego State University; Cynthia Begnal, Pennsylvania State University (whose enthusiasm continually encouraged us); Cynthia Berryman-Fink, University of Cincinnati; Dan Cavanaugh, Southwest Texas State University; Judith Dallinger, Western Illinois University (whose detailed reviewing over the course of the project contributed greatly to the outcome); Pamela Dunkin, Southern Oregon State University; Karen Foss, Humboldt State University; Meredith Moore, Washburn University; Anthony Mulac, University of California, Santa Barbara; Robert Smith, University of Tennessee, Martin; Helen Sterk, Marquette University; and Julia Wood, University of North Carolina, Chapel Hill.

Thanks also go to our colleagues in the Departments of Communication at Texas A&M University-Corpus Christi and Central Washington University, for their unwavering support and for being kind to us when we told them yet another book-revision story. We are particularly indebted to Nada Frazier Cano, graduate of Texas A&M University-Corpus Christi, for her brilliant work on the Epilogue and for her proofreading and editing skills on all of the chapters. And a very special thanks goes to our dear friend and support system extraordinaire, Steven Beebe, Southwest Texas State University, for his advice, empathy, good humor, and encouragement of fellow authors.

No project for the benefit of college students has probably ever succeeded without the help of college students. We have many to thank at both A&M-Corpus Christi and Central Washington for being sources of inspiration for the creation and revision of this textbook. Students of gender communication deserve our thanks for providing the motivation to write this text and the "fuel" for a good deal of its content.

Finally, we thank our families and friends for their listening ears, thought-provoking questions, lively arguments, and persistent belief in this book and its authors.

Diana K. Ivy
Phil Backlund

PART ONE

COMMUNICATION, GENDER, AND EFFECTIVENESS

GENDER JARGON AND EFFECTIVE COMMUNICATION

Learning to Talk the Talk

Hot Topics

- What gender communication is and why you are studying it
- How such terms as sex, gender, gender-role identity, sexual orientation, heterosexism, and homophobia have distinct meanings
- What feminism, patriarchy, and sexism mean today
- How uncertainty affects gender communication and motivates us in relationships
- How to communicate from a receiver orientation
- What it means to be personally effective in communication with women and men
- How values are associated with gender communication that leads to successful and satisfying relationships

WHAT IS GENDER COMMUNICATION?

You can hardly get onto the Internet, open a magazine or newspaper, or turn on the television these days without coming across a discussion of "problems that plague the sexes." Lots of people are talking about societal issues dividing women and men, whether they involve situations of professional communication between coworkers of both sexes, confusion over interpersonal signals, competing messages of homemaker versus careerism, or verbal exchanges that result in violence. One thing is for certain: Communication between women and men is a popular topic of conversation, study, and research—more now than ever, it seems. But is this popular topic all there is to the term *gender communication*? What all is encompassed by the term? Just what *is* this topic you're going to read about and study?

First you need to understand that we're putting the words *gender* and *communication* together to form a modern label for an ancient phenomenon. Gender communication is a unique, fascinating subset of a larger phenomenon known as communication. From our perspective, not all communication is gender communication.

Here's a simple way to understand this perspective of gender communication: **Gender communication is communication *about* and *between* men and women.** The front part of the statement—the "about" aspect—involves how the sexes are discussed, referred to, or depicted, both verbally and nonverbally. The back part of the definition—the "between" aspect—is the interpersonal dimension of gender communication, and it's a bit harder to understand.

We believe that communication becomes *gendered* when sex or gender overtly begins to influence your choices—choices of what you say and how you relate to others. For example, two students could be talking about a project for class. The students could be both male, both female, or of opposite sexes. The sex composition of the communicators doesn't matter in a judgment of whether gender communication is going on or not. Thus far, the conversation about the class project doesn't necessarily involve gender communication. But what happens if the conversation topic shifts to a discussion of political issues especially relevant to women, or who the interactants are dating, or opinions regarding parenting responsibilities? For these topics, the awareness of one's own sex, the other person's sex, or both may come into play; thus gender communication is occurring. Notice that we said "may come into play," because the topic doesn't always dictate whether or not gender communication is occurring.

Take another example: You may be talking with someone about the weather or some local current event. The topic isn't related to sex or gender, but as the conversation progresses you find that you are becoming attracted to the other person. You become acutely aware of your own and the other person's sex. *Now* we would say that gender communication is happening. For a situation that doesn't involve attraction, what if you merely become aware, during a conversation, that you are presenting sort of a "female view" of something and are seeking a "male view," or vice versa? That sounds like playing into stereotypes, but in some situations you may become aware that your own slant on something is overtly affected by your sex or gender. See the difference between these two examples and the first example of classmates discussing a project? When sex or gender becomes an overt factor in your communication, when you become conscious of your own or another person's sex or gender, then gender communication is operating.

However, some scholars believe that gender is an all-encompassing designation, that it is so pervasive a characteristic of a person that communication cannot escape the effects of gender. In this view, all communication is gendered (Spender, 1985; Thorne, Kramarae, & Henley, 1983; Wilson Schaef, 1981). These viewpoints—our more restricted approach to gender communication and the more pervasive perspective—aren't necessarily contradictory, meaning that you can study gender communication and operate from both perspectives. In other words, the information in this text can be applicable whether one views gender communication as a specific form of communication, or whether one believes that all communication is gendered. Essentially, there is no "right" conceptualization of the relationship between gender and communication; it's too complicated a topic to merely suggest a right or wrong approach.

WHY STUDY GENDER COMMUNICATION?

Gender communication is *provocative, popularized, pervasive, problematic,* and *unpredictable*—which makes it fascinating to study.

Provocative. Gender communication is *provocative* because we're all interested in how we're perceived, how we communicate with other human beings, and how others respond to us. We're all especially interested in communication with members of the other sex for several reasons—the most obvious being that we cannot experience the other sex firsthand. Also, we're interested in the possible rewards that may result from effective gender communication.

Popularized. Have you read those popular books that claim the sexes are from different planets or different cultures? As we've said, gender communication is a hot topic in our culture, evidenced by the many books, TV shows, Internet newsgroups, films, and songs devoted to the topic. But it's important to separate the popularized material from the scientific or research-based information about gender and communication. They both have their place, and we draw from each in this textbook. Since you're more likely to be aware of the popularized treatments of gender, we offer a balance by reviewing research findings that provide meaningful insights into sex, gender, and communication.

Pervasive. Gender communication is *pervasive,* meaning that interaction with women and men occurs every day, every hour. The sheer number of contacts we have with members of the other sex heightens interest in the effects of sex and gender on the communication process. When those contacts affect us in profound ways, such as in social or work relationships, the importance of these relationships and the pervasiveness of our interactions with significant people further necessitate improved understanding of gender communication.

Problematic. Saying that gender communication is *problematic* doesn't mean that all gender communication centers around problems, but that it is complicated. Communication itself is complex; it's not a simple process that can be accomplished just because we're human beings who learned language at some early age or because we've been talking all our lives. When you add sex and gender (like other forms of human diversity) into the communication process, you expand the complexity because now there is more than one way of looking at or talking about something.

Unpredictable. Gender communication is *unpredictable* in that societal norms, rules, and roles have changed dramatically and seem to change more every day. For example, often our students talk about their difficulties with seemingly simple rituals, such as dating etiquette. Female students reveal their own inconsistency, in that they want a guy to treat them to a night out, but they also like offering to pay for themselves. Male students complain, "If I open the car door for my date, she'll think that I don't respect her as a competent, 'liberated' woman who can take care of herself. But if I don't open the car door, she'll think that I was raised by wolves and have no manners at all." In these situations and countless others, lessons learned while growing up come into conflict with changes in society, leaving confusion as to what is appropriate behavior.

If you have reason to believe that communication between men and women is so confusing that maybe it isn't worth it to try to improve, or that you'll just stumble along until the right person automatically understands what you say, think, and feel, we have a better suggestion: Hang in there with this course you're taking and this book you've been assigned to read. We not only summarize research-based and popularized information in this text, but also provide practical suggestions about how to apply the knowledge to your life's experiences. Your textbook authors and your instructor want you to not only *know* the current information on gender communication, but also to be able to *use* the information to enhance your communication skills and enrich your relationships. The first thing to know is the lingo.

GENDER JARGON

Many gender-related terms are assigned different meanings, primarily by the media. Your own experience also may give you meanings that differ from textbook terminology. So to reduce the potential for confusion, we offer you here some common gender communication terms and their most commonly used meanings. Becoming more skilled in your communication with men and women begins with the use of current, sensitive, accurate language.

Is It Sex or Is It Gender?

You've probably already heard the terms *sex* and *gender* used interchangeably. For the sake of clarity, we use them in this text with exclusive meanings, even though some people think the terms are interchangeable. For our purposes, the term *sex* means the biological/physiological characteristics that make us female or male. At some points in this text we use the term *sex* to refer to sexual activity between men and women, but it will be clear to you whether the term is meant as a categorization of persons or an activity.

The term used most often in this text (even in the title) is *gender*. Most narrowly, gender refers to psychological and emotional characteristics of individuals. You may understand these characteristics to be masculine, feminine, or androgynous (a combination of both feminine and masculine traits). But gender encompasses more than this. Defined broadly, the term *gender* includes personality traits, but it also involves psychological makeup; attitudes, beliefs, and values; sexual orientation; and gender-role identity (defined below).

> *I can't stand people that can't stand one of the sexes. We've only got two. Why would you dislike one of them?*
>
> *—Drew Barrymore, actor*

Gender is constructed, meaning that one's femaleness or maleness is more extensive than the fact of being born anatomically female or male. What is *attached* or *related* to that anatomy is taught to you through our culture, virtually from the time you are born. In their book on gender and society, Thorne, Kramarae, and Henley (1983) explain, "gender is not a unitary, or 'natural' fact, but takes shape in concrete, historically changing social relationships" (p. 16). Culture, with its evolving customs, rules, and expectations for behavior, has the power to affect your perception of gender. For example, if you were raised in the Middle East, your views regarding the status and role of women in society will be quite different than if you were raised in the United States. Perhaps you grew up with strict rules for appropriate male-female behavior, such as "men ask women out on dates; women do not call men for dates." When you encounter members of other cultures (or your own culture, for that matter) who do not adhere to clearly drawn gender lines or who operate from rules different than your own, then the notable difference may reinforce your original conception of gender or cause it to change.

When studying communication about and between women and men, it is helpful to use the term *sex* as a biological determination and *gender* as something that is culturally constructed. Thus, you'll see references in this text to the "opposite or other sex," meaning a comparison between female and male. If you understand the notion of gender as a broad-based, multifaceted concept, then you understand why there is no such thing as an "opposite gender."

Viewing gender as culturally constructed allows one to change or reconstruct gender. This is a powerful idea. For example, the way you see the gender of "male/masculine" or "female/feminine" is not the way you *have* to see it. You can learn to see it differently and more broadly if you discover new information. This is discussed more thoroughly in Chapter 2, but for now consider these examples: What if a guy discovers that "being a man" doesn't mean that he has to be strong and emotionally nonexpressive? He might decide that he's tired of always being the strong one, that he'd rather express his emotions and get some help instead. A woman might realize that her abilities in climbing the ladder of professional success are stronger than her nurturing instincts, so she chooses a career over motherhood as her primary life's work.

Might these discoveries alter one's vision of gender? Possibly, but these people don't merely replace one stereotypical trait with another; they expand their options and find new ways of seeing themselves in relation to others. That's one of the goals of this text—to give you different ways of seeing things, including gender.

Here's one more example to clarify the notion of gender-as-constructed. While genetic research makes choosing the sex of one's child more of a reality every day, most of us still will have no control over the sex of our children. However, we have much to do with the development or construction of the child's gender. What's the first question most people ask when they hear the news that a baby has been born? Generally, the first reaction is, "Is it a boy or a girl?" "Pink or blue?" Imagine if you asked a new mother, "Is it a boy or a girl?" and the answer was, "Yes." (That's not the usual response, so you might conclude that the new mother must still be suffering the effects of childbirth!) But once we find out the biological sex of the child, different sets of expectations, attitudes, and treatments—what can be termed stereotypical gender "baggage"—are called up in our brains and enacted. Thus, friends present the proud parents with a baseball mitt for a male baby and a doll for a female baby. People talk to girl babies quite differently than to boy babies. If gender were not societally induced or constructed, we would not feel the need to align the sex of a child with a particular object or color, or to alter our style of communication.

One of the more provocative illustrations of these ideas comes from the story "X: A Fabulous Child's Story" written by Lois Gould (1972). Gould offers a fictional account of a child named X whose parents participated in an experimental study by not revealing to anyone the biological sex of the child. The story progresses from infancy through childhood, as X plays with other children, goes to school and deals with sex-specific bathrooms, and is pronounced mentally healthy by a psychiatrist. What is most fascinating in this story is people's reactions to X. Adults and children alike in the story had extreme difficulty in coping with not knowing the child's sex. It was as if they didn't know how to behave without sex-based information to guide them. Students who read this story also reveal discomfort in not knowing the sex of the child.

Biological sex suggests several things about how women and men communicate and are communicated with, but biology isn't destiny, and that's the powerful potential of studying gender communication. A person's sex isn't easily changed, but a person's conception of gender is far more open to change and development.

Gender-Role Identity and Sexual Orientation

In this text, we use the term *gender-role identity* as a subset of gender to refer to the way you view yourself, how you see yourself relative to stereotypically feminine or masculine traits. Your self-esteem may be connected, in part, to your gender-role identity, meaning that sometimes people's self-esteem is affected when they measure themselves against some ideal or stereotype of what a woman or man is supposed to be.

Associated with this "measure" of masculinity or femininity is your general perception of appropriate roles for women and men in the society of which you are a member. The term *gender-role identity* thus encompasses not only your vision of self, but your vision of the roles or functions for human beings within a given culture. While your gender-role identity is affected by your sex and your gender, it is within your control to change this identity. But what about a remaining element within the broad-based view of gender—an element over which you have no control?

> *A lot of my peer group think I'm an eccentric bisexual, like I may even have an ammonia-filled tentacle or something somewhere on my body. That's okay.*
>
> Robert Downey, Jr., actor

To use the term *sexual preference* to designate a person as heterosexual, homosexual, or bisexual is to use outdated terminology. The word *preference* implies that a person *chooses* his or her sexuality, that a person can make a conscious decision about sexuality. The prevailing view today is that one's *sexual orientation*, that is, to whom one is sexually attracted or with whom one has sexual relations, is a characteristic of a person, not a person's choice (Majors, 1994). Many members of the gay and lesbian community in this country and abroad contend that they were born gay, not shaped into homosexuality by life's experiences or societal factors. Whatever your view of the choice/no-choice distinction, being inclusive, sensitive, and contemporary in language usage requires referring to a person's sexuality as an orientation, not a preference.

Discriminatory attitudes and behavior that communicate the belief that heterosexuality is superior to homosexuality or bisexuality are termed *heterosexist* (Griffin, 1998). Often this form of discrimination manifests itself by omission, rather than by commission—meaning it's not what you say, it's the assumption you communicate by what you leave out or don't say. To illustrate what we mean here, have you ever heard an instructor use a real or hypothetical example involving homosexuals to illustrate or clarify a principle or concept in a class? Even today in a world that is more enlightened about different forms of sexuality, when instructors casually provide an example depicting dating behaviors of a homosexual couple, for instance, the reactions of students across the room may be such that the example can't continue. Students often seem so taken aback by such a reference as "John and Bob out on a first date" that the lesson, the point of the example, becomes lost. Has this happened at your institution? When one of your textbook authors tries to use homosexual examples in gender and interpersonal communication courses, the giggles across the room, the strange looks that pass between students, and the chatter that invariably ensues obstruct the point of the example. Thus an instructor's choice to primarily, if not exclusively, use examples of heterosexual interaction to clarify information about human communication, as well as students' protestations at merely raising an example involving homosexual individuals, may represent heterosexism of omission. Instances of more obvious, concrete discrimination against anything not heterosexual represents heterosexism of commission.

Some measure of confusion surrounds the term *homophobia*. To date, we have found three usages of this term: (1) Homophobia can refer to a general fear of persons who are homosexual in sexual orientation. (2) The term may also describe the fear of being labeled a homosexual. (3) Within homosexual communities, homophobia may be used to mean behavior or attitudes that indicate a self-hatred or severe loss of self-esteem. In these cases, the homosexual individual, out of anger or hatred for her or his orientation, acts or thinks in ways that inflict that anger onto the self. As is the case with all gender-related terminology, choosing to use current, clear communication will help minimize the opportunity for misunderstanding in a diverse culture.

Feminism: The New "F-Word"

When you first saw the term *feminism* in the title of this section, what thoughts or images came to mind? Did you react with, "Oh no, not this stuff again!"? Did you think of the women's liberation movement of the 1960s and 1970s? Did the unfortunate term *femi-Nazi*, made popular by Rush Limbaugh in the early 1990s, come to mind? It's very illuminating to find out what people, especially college students, think about feminism these days.

We first heard the term *feminist* referred to as the new "F-word" by a communication colleague, although you may have seen or heard this reference in recent years (DeFrancisco, 1992). When students in gender communication classes are asked, "Do you believe that women and men should receive equal opportunities and treatment in all facets of life?" they reply with a confident, hearty affirmative. When asked, "Are you a feminist?" the response is much more convoluted, with the most prevalent response being, "Well, no, I wouldn't call myself a feminist." Research suggests that although people may believe in equality, many do not consider themselves feminists and do not want to be called this F-word (Bellafante, 1998; hooks, Vaid, Steinem, & Wolf, 1993).

Why has the image of feminism deteriorated or become distorted, such that what people report readily coming to mind are visions of angry, radical, bra-burning, man-hating, humorless, masculine women storming out of the headquarters of the National Organization for Women (NOW) to try to gain superiority over men? These negative connotations in large part come from selective images the media transmit to the mass audience. For example, did you know that there are no documented accounts of actual bra-burning episodes among "women's libbers" in the late 1960s? Only one incident was remotely connected—a protest of the 1968 Miss America pageant in which protesters threw their bras into a trash can! Yet the bra-burning image of feminists made headlines (Wallis, 1989).

In the most basic sense, a feminist is a person—male or female—who believes in equality, especially sex and gender equality. Well-known feminist author Susan Faludi (1991) suggests that "Feminism's agenda is basic: It asks that women not be forced to 'choose' between public justice and private happiness. It asks that women be free to define themselves—instead of having their identity defined for them, time and again, by their culture and their men" (p. xxiii).

In a more specific sense, feminism involves a reaction to power imposed by a male-dominated system or *patriarchy* (derived from a Greek word meaning "of the fathers"; hooks et al., 1993). Noted gender researcher Dale Spender (1985) describes patriarchy as a self-perpetuating society "based on the belief that the male is the superior sex" (p. 1). Often patriarchal practices or attitudes are referred to as *sexist*, typically pertaining to discriminatory treatment of women. But the term *sexism* simply means the denigration of one sex and the exaltation of the other, or, stated another way, valuing one sex over the other.

> *I'm a feminist who wears makeup and still keeps high heels in her closet. I'm a feminist who enjoys intimate sexual relationships with men. I'm a feminist who believes that our "f" word means a willingness to grapple with the issues of race and class and disability, age and sexual difference, both within and outside our movement.*
>
> *Marcia Ann Gillespie,*
> *editor, Ms. magazine*

Thus, sexism does not refer exclusively to devaluing women, just as racism does not refer exclusively to the denigration of one specific race in preference for another. Given this definition of sexism, there can be no such thing as "reverse sexism," even though some have used this term in specific reference to the discriminatory treatment of men.

Perhaps you believe that our society is not male dominated or that patriarchy or sexism is okay because "that's just the way it is." Maybe you feel that no opportunities have been denied either sex or that neither sex has endured particular suffering during your lifetime. But stop and think for a moment, not only on a personal level, but on a global one. Which sex is still the most underrepresented among decision makers, such as political leaders and judges, and among highly paid corporate executives? Which sex still holds more of the most low-paying jobs and earns 71 cents to the other's dollar of wages? (1997, U.S. Bureau of Labor Statistics) Conversely, which parent is most often denied child custody in divorce proceedings, simply because of that parent's sex? Perhaps you haven't yet seen any overt instances of sex discrimination in your personal life. But what about missed opportunities—those jobs, benefits and rewards, or relationships that did not come your way merely because someone held a limited view of which sex is best suited for a certain circumstance?

Today many women have adopted feminist ideals and taken advantage of some of the breakthroughs that feminists fought to obtain, such as being able to combine a career with marriage and childrearing. In an article in *Ms.*, marking the magazine's 25th anniversary, one young feminist writes:

> Generally, young women are no more ungrateful for the radical improvements in our quality of life than any other crop of brassy feminist upstarts in history. In fact, I think we are more attuned to our privileged place in the world as a result of the women's studies, ethnic and cultural studies, and comprehensive history classes many of us took in college. Most of us know. . . that at some point in history, someone we strongly identify with was burned, detained, gassed, lynched, whipped, relocated, imprisoned, exploited, and/or maligned in service to the status quo, and that this is still happening all over the globe in new and improved ways. It tends to make a person cranky at least, enraged and empowered to do something about it at best. There are [those of us] who want nothing more than a chance to be part of the history and legacy, to infuse our own spirits into the body and soul of this movement. (Higginbotham, 1997, pp. 99–101)

There are many "feminisms"—meaning different interpretations or approaches to achieving the goal of sexual equality. Some view this as a splintering or disintegration of feminism rather than a representation of a movement or ideology that has diversity at its core, both historically and in contemporary times. It's inaccurate to refer to *"the* feminists," as so many TV and radio news and talk show personalities did in their coverage of the 1998 Paula Jones lawsuit against President Bill Clinton and the ensuing White House sex scandal, as some chose to call it. Asking such a question as "Where are *the* feminists in all this presidential legal turmoil?" assumes that all feminists should appear, en masse, or speak up (with completely united voices) about the situation (Gillespie, 1998). When feminists differ in their particular "brand" of feminism or in their political or social views, it doesn't signal the demise of a movement. It's interesting, for example, that people don't fret over the demise of such organizations as political parties when their members disagree on key issues such as abortion, taxation, and health care reform.

Some newer-to-the-movement or younger feminists call themselves Third Wave feminists (Heywood & Drake, 1997), while critics contend that feminism is dead or "stolen" (Hoff Sommers, 1994) and that we have moved into a "postfeminist" existence (Denfeld, 1995; Roiphe, 1993). A provocative cover for a 1998 issue of *Time* magazine presented four pictures of women's heads: black and white photos of Susan B. Anthony, Betty Friedan, and Gloria Steinem, followed by a color photo of the TV character Ally McBeal with the caption, "Is Feminism

Dead?" The corresponding story presented a fairly negative picture of current "Duh Feminism," stating, "If feminism of the `60s and `70s was steeped in research and obsessed with social change, feminism today is wed to the culture of celebrity and self-obsession" (Bellafante, 1998, p. 57). While Third Wave feminism and postfeminism are still being defined, they have rejuvenated discussions about the nature of feminism and its place in modern society (Faludi, 1995). Gloria Steinem (1997) believes that "Thanks to feminist parents as well as to women's studies and a popular culture that occasionally pays tribute to a feminist workview, this new generation has a better idea of the complexity involved in making lasting change" (p. 83).

Today, individuals have many options when it comes to gender communication and behavior. This relatively recent development stems from changing roles, a wider, more tolerant view of what is considered appropriate behavior, and increased opportunities for both men and women. Many of the changes in societal expectations, opportunities, and relational patterns

> *The issues of feminism are alive and as vital today as they were years ago. It is the stereotype of the militant, hairy-legged, bra-burning feminist that is outdated. I look forward to a time when women are judged by their characters and ideologies, not their hairstyles and hemlines.*
>
> Suzanne Vega,
> singer/songwriter

resulted (and continue to result) from the work of feminists and their supporters. If you don't already have a viewpoint toward feminism or established conceptualizations of the terms we've discussed in this section, this course you're taking and text you're reading may lead you to some interesting thinking along these lines. Now that you have mastered some of the basic gender-related lingo, let's move on to how those terms are put to use in the communication process.

RECAP

gender communication, sex, gender, gender-role identity, sexual orientation, heterosexism, homophobia, feminism, patriarchy, sexism, postfeminism, Third Wave feminism

COMMUNICATION: A COMPLEX HUMAN PROCESS

Communication is a word that you hear frequently, especially since technology has become so sophisticated that we can easily and quickly interact around the world. As the channels for communicating have expanded, so have the meanings of the term *communication.* In fact, two communication theorists back in the 1970s isolated 126 definitions of communication (Dance & Larson, 1976). For our purposes, here's a fairly basic perspective of communication.

Human communication isn't static; it's an ongoing and dynamic process of sending and receiving messages for the purpose of sharing meaning. To accomplish this purpose, people use both *verbal* and *nonverbal* communication (including body movement, physical appearance, facial expression, touch, tone of voice, etc.). Communication flows back and forth simultaneously, both verbally and nonverbally, between *sender* and *receiver* (DeVito, 1998; Wood, 1998).

In the comic strip below, depicting a conversation between Nancy and Sluggo, Nancy can be labeled the *sender* and Sluggo the *receiver.* Nancy initiates a conversation by asking Sluggo a question. Sluggo receives the message and responds verbally and nonverbally. Note Nancy's confused nonverbal reaction in the second frame. The conversation continues, as messages are exchanged between sender and receiver. The point of the cartoon is that even though messages have been transmitted between sender and receiver, effective communication may not be the end result. Two additional components related to this basic perspective of communication warrant brief explanation: *uncertainty reduction* and the *receiver orientation to communication.*

Reducing Uncertainty about Others

In the introductory paragraphs of this chapter, unpredictability was listed as one of the reasons to study gender communication. Let's explore this a bit further. Humans like to be able to form expectations and to predict how others will behave. These expectations and predictions are comforting; thus,

NANCY reprinted by permission of United Feature Syndicate, Inc.

they are powerful motivators in human interaction. Based on their past and ever-expanding experiences, people strive to anticipate a situation, predict how certain behaviors will lead to certain reactions from others, act accordingly, and reap positive rewards from the situation. Berger and his colleagues have contributed a significant amount of research about this process of *uncertainty reduction.* According to these researchers, when people cannot form adequate expectations and are unable to predict what will happen in situations, they experience uncertainty (Berger & Bradac, 1982; Berger & Calabrese, 1975). One reaction to this discomfort is to communicate to gain information and reduce uncertainty.

Can you imagine how the notion of uncertainty reduction applies to communication between women and men? Can you see it operating in your own communication? As we said earlier, communication between the sexes has changed dramatically and is still changing. The factors contributing to the changes are contributing to uncertainty, too. The world has become a smaller place—with almost instant access to other people and other cultures we have more of a global community now. The likelihood is increasing that you will become friends in college with someone from a vastly different culture than your own and that you will travel abroad or use technology to communicate with people worldwide. As advanced technology, greater mobility, and easier access have resulted in greater diversity within our own culture, the complexity of communication has compounded. These factors significantly increase our uncertainty about how to communicate effectively.

Consider this example of a male-female encounter: Mary sees Paul across the room at a party and is attracted to him. From watching him at a distance, she thinks that he may have come to the party alone, but she feels uncertain. She doesn't know Paul and doesn't know if he's dating someone steadily, or even married for that matter! Mary's uncertainty is high, but not high enough to keep her from finding out some information about Paul. She learns from Peter, the party host, that Paul is single, but Peter doesn't know if Paul came with a date or not. So, Mary's uncertainty is somewhat reduced, leading her to try a more direct method. She strikes up a conversation with Paul, showing that she finds him interesting, and learns that he came to the party alone. While her uncertainty about Paul hasn't completely disappeared, it has been significantly reduced via communication. Now this Peter, Paul, and Mary example may not fit your experience, but do you get the general idea about how uncertainty reduction works in human communication?

Reducing uncertainty and increasing predictability about communication with others are perplexing tasks. Sex roles in our society have shifted dramatically. For example, today men and women alike are taking longer to marry than in past generations. More women are entering the workforce and more men are actively involving themselves in childrearing, such that even the very basic roles of breadwinner, homemaker, childcare-giver, and the like have changed. As these roles evolve and the rules governing people's behavior fall by the societal wayside, you may experience high uncertainty,

> *Sometimes I wonder if men and women really suit each other. Perhaps they should live next door and just visit now and then.*
>
> *Katharine Hepburn, actor*

low predictability, and resulting confusion, possibly even disillusionment. This often generates a "take your best guess" mentality. If your best guess fails, you are once again reminded of the unpredictable nature of gender communication. One goal of this text is to help you reduce uncertainty and to increase predictability both for yourself and for your relationships.

Becoming Receiver Oriented in Your Communication

While both roles of sender and receiver in the communication process are important, we believe the receiver's interpretation of the sender's message makes the difference between shared meaning and misunderstanding. Thus, this approach is termed the *receiver orientation to communication.* What the sender *intends* to convey is important, but it is less important than what the receiver *thinks is being conveyed,* or how the receiver interprets the message. You may clearly understand your intentions in what you say, but a listener may take your message in a different way than you originally intended. The result of not taking a receiver-orientation can sound like this: "What do you MEAN, I'm late in calling you?! I said I'd call you AROUND five o'clock. Six-thirty IS around five o'clock!" In an instance like this, obviously the sender intended something different than the receiver's interpretation. Taking a receiver-orientation—stopping to think about how your message will be understood by a listener *before* you say it—can greatly enhance your skill as a communicator.

When one is misunderstood, a typical response is to think that the receiver is at fault for not understanding the message. This reaction becomes particularly relevant to gender communication when you consider how often women report that they do not understand men because they do not react like women. And men get frustrated with women when they do not communicate or interpret communication like men. Here's our proposition to you:

> If people would spend more time figuring out how a listener will best hear, accept, understand, and retain a message and less time figuring out how they want to say something to please themselves, then their communication with others would vastly improve.

This sounds like the "golden rule of communication," doesn't it? Have you considered this receiver orientation to communication before? Do you currently communicate from this perspective, even though you didn't know what to call it? Think of it this way: If you talk, but no one is there to listen or receive what you say, has communication occurred? Some will say yes; at the very least the sender has communicated with the self. But others will argue that without a listener, communication does not occur, making the receiver the most necessary link for the communication process to work. Again, this is part of the receiver orientation to communication.

If communication breaks down (as it seems to regularly), whose fault is it? Rarely is it completely the sender's fault for breakdowns. Sometimes the best forethought, insight, experience, and skill applied to a situation still lead to misunderstanding on the part of a receiver. But, in a receiver-oriented view of communication, the sender is responsible for communicating in a manner that will be most easily understood by the receiver; the receiver's responsibility is to attempt to understand the intent of the sender.

Say, for instance, Bonnie sees Clyde outside of class and wants to start up a conversation with him. She says, "Hey, Clyde, that was pretty funny in class today when the professor called on you just as you were about to nod off to sleep!" Clyde, feeling self-conscious and embarrassed, replies angrily, "Oh, so everybody got a big laugh out of that, huh?" You can see that this conversation is not going the way Bonnie intended; she just meant to lightly tease Clyde to get a conversation going. Clyde took Bonnie's statement as criticism, as though she were making fun of him. Obviously, in this situation, the message intended and sent did not equal the message received. Who would you say is most responsible for the miscommunication in this situation?

From a receiver orientation to communication, we could say that the sender, in this case Bonnie, should have used more caution in her message to Clyde. If she'd thought about the effect her humorous line could have on Clyde, she might have considered a different approach, one that wouldn't appear to Clyde as though she was poking fun at his expense. Perhaps she could have merely made a general funny comment about class, rather than one that involved Clyde personally. Now, if you are saying to yourself, "That Clyde must be one touchy character; he really overreacted and missed the boat," then you are adopting a sender orientation to communication. Again, you are emphasizing what was *said* rather than how it was *taken*. Let's consider a more serious example, one involving gender communication that has more dire consequences than Bonnie and Clyde's misunderstanding.

Before a board meeting at a local corporation, a few executives are milling about, drinking coffee and talking about the upcoming meeting. Maria says good morning to a coworker, Jerry, as he comes up to her on her way to the boardroom. He says, as he puts his arm around her waist, "You know, you are a breath of fresh air in this joint, because I sure like a little perfume and soft skin next to me in the morning. Makes the workday go a lot easier, don't you think? Why don't you sit by me at this meeting?" Maria is so taken aback that she cannot respond, except to extract herself from Jerry's grasp, collect her wits, and get ready for the board meeting. Maria views Jerry's comments as a form of sexual harassment—unprofessional and inappropriate communication in the workplace. That may or may not be how Jerry intended it. Perhaps he communicates to female coworkers in a sexualized manner on purpose to belittle them or assert male prowess. Or perhaps he believes that he was simply complimenting Maria, trying to make her feel more comfortable before the meeting started or merely offering some harmless teasing to break the tension of the morning.

While we recognize that this sexual harassment example is rather dramatic, and maybe you reacted strongly to it, we offer it here for a reason. Instances of sexual harassment constitute prime illustrations of what we mean by taking a receiver orientation to communication. Whether or not a sender of a message intends to be harassing is not the main issue; what matters more is how the target or receiver of the message interprets it. The topic of sexual harassment is dealt with more fully in subsequent chapters. Just realize for now that in most situations, instead of defending your intentions when you communicate poorly or inappropriately, you can learn lessons for the next time. Considering in advance how a receiver will interpret your message will go a long way toward improving your skills as a communicator. This is an especially critical stance to assume for gender communication because of its increased complexity. It's advisable in every situation, as illustrated in these examples, to focus on the receiver of your message *before, during,* and *after* you communicate. Given how gender complicates the process, as depicted in the harassment example, it's even more advisable to consider the receiver's point of view as most important.

You will see the receiver orientation to communication reiterated throughout this text, so comprehending this perspective is a key to understanding the remaining chapters. But we want you to recognize that the receiver orientation is only one perspective within the communication discipline; there are several other ways to view the process, including the traditional sender-based approach. However, we are firmly committed to the belief that a receiver orientation is the most fruitful approach, especially when the communication process is complicated by the effects of gender. This orientation, together with a focus on uncertainty reduction, form the basis of our approach to enhancing your gender communication skills—the *personal effectiveness approach.*

RECAP

---

verbal and nonverbal communication, sender, receiver, uncertainty reduction, receiver orientation to communication

THE PERSONAL EFFECTIVENESS APPROACH TO GENDER COMMUNICATION

Have you ever had difficulty communicating with someone of the other sex? Sure, everyone has. Ever wished that you were better at it? What does "better" mean? We continually conduct surveys at our universities to better understand students' concerns about gender communication. Here are a few of our male students' questions and concerns:

"In a conversation with a woman, when a problem's solved, why does the woman still want to continue the conversation?"

"My wife says that men don't listen. I think that women listen too much."

"In a serious situation, would women rather that guys get emotional and get everyone else upset, or not show emotion and risk getting someone else upset later?"

From female respondents to our surveys, we receive questions like these:

"When guys say, 'I'll call you,' what do they really mean?"

"Why is it that men find it so difficult to say what they mean if emotional aspects are involved? Is it that they are afraid of what other men will say? Or is it because they feel they will be viewed as less of a man?"

"Guys usually want sex from women. So, after a woman goes to bed with a man, why does he talk as though he no longer respects her?"

There is no lack of advice from the popular press or personal opinions on gender communication problems. Through our classroom experience and research, we have developed our own point of view—the *personal effectiveness approach.* Getting "better" in your gender communication depends on becoming a more personally effective communicator.

Each of us will have many different relationships in our lives. Each relationship consists of three things: the self, the other person, and the situation. Which of these three things do you have the most direct control over? Clearly, it is yourself. You can exert some control over the situation, and now and then you can influence another person. But with some self-awareness, learning, and skill, you can be proactive and improve your ability to control your own communication behavior.

You already control your own communication behavior to some degree. However, you may not do it as well as you would like. Did you ever find yourself saying or doing something (especially with someone of the other sex!) and thinking, "Where did *that* come from?" Occasionally, we all feel that we aren't in control of things around us, that we merely react to people and circumstances. But, at other times, we do plan something and it does work. So you already do have some control and you already know some things about communication and gender. You've experienced some level of success, but you've also had some failures. Becoming more personally effective involves developing greater control over your own communication behavior and a greater ability to influence the development and success of relationships.

We believe that adhering to the principles of the personal effectiveness approach can help you improve your success in relating to others. Personal effectiveness begins with knowledge and a perception of yourself and your own tendencies, extends to your knowledge of the "rules" of society, and includes your knowledge of the communication process. It also involves judgments that other people make about you. Let's examine these components one at a time.

Personal Effectiveness: Your Own Perception

At various times, you may have looked at how some people communicate and thought "They are good at this; I wish I was that good." Then you probably looked at others and thought "They need some help." No one can be effective *all* of the time, but each of us can be effective *more* of the time. The following four elements work together to help you be more effective more of the time.

1. *Repertoire.* You have been communicating for a number of years and have developed patterns of communication that feel natural to you. Within these patterns are communication behaviors that you frequently use. Some work most of the time, some don't, and sometimes you may not know which to use. But few of us want to be the kind of person who always communicates or responds a certain way—like a "default mode"—no matter who we're dealing with or what situation we're in. That's taking a comfortable pattern or behavior too far for most of us, and it can quickly land us in a communicative and relational rut. One of the goals of personal effectiveness is to expand the range of behaviors or repertoire at your disposal. You want an enlarged communicative "bag of tricks" from which to choose when you confront various communication situations so that you're not locked into some predictable pattern. The expanded repertoire is especially helpful in those uncomfortable situations that involve members of the other sex. The rest of this text offers many ways to expand your repertoire, with special emphasis on how this expansion process can enhance your gender communication and your relationships.
2. *Selection.* Once you have expanded your repertoire, you need to know which behavior to choose. In subsequent chapters, we talk about selecting the most appropriate behavior for various circumstances. For now, just realize that the selection depends on an analysis of your goals, the other person's goals, and the situation. Decisions are also based on what you might value. At the end of this chapter, we outline some values that can be applied to selecting your communication behaviors for female-male relationships in particular.

3. *Skill.* To be personally effective, you also need the skill to perform a be- havior so that another person accepts it and responds positively. We spend a good deal of time in this text discussing this skills element of per- sonal effectiveness, as it applies to various situations you may encounter. We also encourage you to observe others, to ask questions of your in- structor and classmates to find out how they deal with certain situations, and then to develop and practice your communication skills to enhance your view of yourself and your relationships.

4. *Evaluation.* This element involves your ability to judge your own suc- cess. You need to be able to assess if your efforts have been effective in the way that you wanted them to be and to use this information to adapt your behavior the next time. If you don't evaluate, you won't know what to change; you might continue to make the same mistake over and over.

These four elements are central to your perception of your personal effec- tiveness. You will be more successful in gender communication if you:

1. Develop a wider range of communication behaviors from which to choose.
2. Know how to analyze a situation and select the most appropriate behav- iors from your repertoire.
3. Perform those behaviors with skill.
4. Carefully evaluate the result.

As we said at the beginning of this section, personal effectiveness only be- gins with a perception of self. It also includes the views that others may have of you as an individual. The next section describes personal effectiveness as a social judgment.

Personal Effectiveness: Others' Perceptions

People interact with each other and make judgments about effectiveness all the time. If you think about it for a minute, you've probably been involved in conversations with people and then walked away thinking, "So much for *that*" or "What a head case." For another example, say you ask a person, "What time is it?" and he or she responds "Tuesday." You're likely to call into ques- tion that person's effectiveness. On the other hand, if the conversation goes smoothly you are likely to judge her or him as "pretty good at this." The point here is that only part of a judgment of effectiveness comes from the viewpoint of the communicator; the remainder rests with the person who receives the communication.

This means that one fundamental aspect of becoming more personally effective is to increase the number of times you are positively regarded or evaluated by people who communicate with you. Let's say that you have ob- served someone else interacting in an effective way with a member of the other sex, and you wish to emulate this behavior. For example, one of your buddies is especially skilled in first conversations—the exchange that occurs when people first meet. You'd like to get better at this kind of communication, so you add your friend's behavior to your "bag of tricks" (*repertoire*) and try it out in a subsequent encounter (*selection*). In a way you are practicing new communication *skills* on others. This is something that happens all the time; many of us notice how others behave, then adopt and adjust their behavior to fit our own style and try it out on others. The last step is to *evaluate* the results of this experiment. When you do this, it is wise to go further than just your own reactions or judgments of effectiveness; you will want to seek honest feedback from others—including, at times, the person or persons directly involved in the encounter. You may want other friends to observe you and give you feedback as to the appropriateness and effectiveness of your communication, or you may just tell someone later about the encounter and ask what that person thinks. You may even want to ask, at the moment or at some later point, what the receiver of your communication thinks or thought about your behavior. It doesn't hurt to get a simple "perception check" on how one is coming across. That may sound crazy to you—too forced or like too much trouble for something that ought to be simple. But this is exactly how most of us go about developing any skill. If you want a better golf swing, a better pasta dish, or a better research paper, it's likely that you go through this process, with the final step being to use both self-evaluation and evaluation by others to help you improve for the future. The process of developing personally effective communication skills works much the same way.

Here's an example of a student who had his own perception of some imperfections in his behavior, but who also sought his instructor's help in working through the process of becoming more personally effective. Put yourself in the student's situation and see if it sounds familiar. Dennis was concerned about his inability to talk to women.

TEACHER: How do you feel during a conversation?
DENNIS: Bad; I just feel really awkward.
T: When does this happen?
D: Every time I talk to a woman.
T: Well, I saw you talking with Marci yesterday. You looked like you were doing fine.
D: I guess I was, but Marci is a friend. I don't have any trouble talking to her.
T: So it's not all women, right?
D: Yeah, I guess I just have trouble talking to women I'm interested in dating.
T: Let's go back to what happens. Can you describe what happens to make you feel awkward?
D: Well, there are these long pauses, and I get so nervous. Other guys don't get that nervous when they talk to women.
T: Okay, anything else?

D: Because I'm so nervous, I can't look at her; I just stare at the floor. And sometimes I can't finish the sentences I start.

T: Dennis, I think we're getting somewhere. We started with the general problem of your inability to talk to women and have narrowed it down to some specific behaviors, such as eye contact, pauses, and sentences. Here's what I'd like you to do: Work on those three things as goals. Next time you talk to a woman you're interested in, work to maintain eye contact about half the time, have some questions or comments ready so that pauses last no longer than a few seconds, and try to finish every sentence you start.

We are glad to report that Dennis is now happily married with three kids (just kidding). The moral of this story is that to become more personally effective, you need to be able to take a realistic look at your own behavior, and you should not be afraid to solicit honest feedback from others. Doing so will enable you to assess your communication strengths and weaknesses and then pinpoint the kind of behaviors you want to change.

Our point in presenting the personal effectiveness approach to gender communication to you is that you are likely to change while taking this course and reading this text. We don't suggest that you merely learn to "figure people out" only to get more of what you want. We *do* suggest that you develop yourself, that you change your behaviors for the better. If you want to be more personally effective, you may need to communicate differently than you do now. Ideally, you will feel more empowered by what you learn from this text and the course you're taking. The goal is to become more effective, to increase your repertoire of communication behaviors, and to know when and how to use those behaviors. You will want to further develop your ability to analyze what is going on and to communicate in a way that is beneficial for you and those you encounter. As a result, you'll find your communication with both men and women more satisfying.

VALUES TO GUIDE YOUR CHOICES

How do you make wise choices in gender communication? Not making wise choices has probably gotten a lot of us into trouble. An assessment of your personal values, with regards for human beings and relationships, can be useful. To close this chapter, we did just that: We developed a list of values

---

RECAP

personal effectiveness, repertoire, selection, skill, evaluation relevant to gender communication and offer them as useful guides for you as you enhance your communication ability and personal effectiveness.

Value 1: Equality of Power

Some relationships function successfully with an uneven distribution of power (e.g., parent-child, mentor-protégé, employer-employee), although abuses of the power imbalance exist within these relationships as well as within other types. However, when an imbalance of power isn't necessarily societally induced or an appropriate expectation for a relationship, as in marriage, dating and romantic relationships, work relationships, or friendships, an ideal and a goal to work toward is an even distribution of power or control. Empowerment—power *to* rather than power *over*—involves a shared approach to power or control that capitalizes on the strengths of each relational partner (Bate & Bowker, 1997; Thorne, Kramarae, & Henley, 1983). There are dozens of examples of imbalanced control in a relationship. Nagged spouses are ridiculed; abusive relationships in which one partner completely dominates the other are cruel realities. We believe that individuals should work to achieve and maintain a balance of influence, control, or power in their relationships. In later chapters we talk more specifically about how that can be accomplished.

> *One of the things about equality is not just that you be treated equally to a man, but that you treat yourself equally to the way you treat a man.*
>
> *Marlo Thomas, actor*

Value 2: Talking about It Makes It Better

We profoundly believe in the power of communication to help solve the problems we face. Take a stereotypic view of male-female communication for a moment. The stereotypic male doesn't express his feelings, while the stereotypic female is passive and submissive. Neither approach is particularly effective (let alone accurate). We have all heard of the trend for children who have difficulty expressing anger and frustration to wind up using physical violence as a means of solving problems. Let's face it, this can be a fairly typical male reaction. Think of the last time you saw two guys start to fight and then one says to the other, "Say, we're having an interpersonal conflict; let's sit down and talk this out." It just doesn't happen that way too often, does it? Our point is that talking it over is absolutely critical to effectiveness in relationships. The willingness and ability to sit down and talk about the topic at hand, the relationship, each other's feelings, and possible solutions to problems are critical to personal effectiveness.

Value 3: Confirmation and Acceptance

Research suggests that a basic dimension within every communication situation is the feeling of acceptance or rejection (Beebe, Beebe, & Redmond, 1998; Cissna, Garvin, & Kennedy, 1990; Sieburg, 1969). When we talk with someone, we can go away saying, "That person accepted me and what I had to say." Or we could say that our point of view was rejected. The communication of acceptance is a very important part of establishing satisfying relationships, since relationships don't progress if someone feels rejected. For now, simply recognize the value of a basic communicated acceptance of another person as fundamental to effective female-male relationships.

Value 4: Freedom of Choice

When we talk about becoming more personally effective and developing the ability to direct the course of a relationship, we include the possibility that you will influence or persuade someone else. With that possibility comes more responsibility. A value we hold central to this process is the freedom of the other person to choose his or her own line of action. If someone walks up to you with a gun and says, "Your money or your life," that person is severely restricting your freedom of choice. People often manipulate the emotions of their partners to get what they want, which restricts the partner's freedom to choose. We hope that you value the right of each person in a relationship to choose her or his own response to attempts at persuasion. This means you'll need to be able to say to someone, "I tried to persuade you, but you made your own choice and I respect that." This isn't easy to do, but it's critical to long-term success in relationships. While the information in this text will help you become more persuasive in male-female relationships, you should also use these persuasive skills in a manner that respects the other person's freedom of choice.

Value 5: Treating Another Person as an Individual

Stereotyping is hard to avoid. Can you imagine starting from scratch with every person you meet, meaning that you can't use past experiences to clue you as to what to expect? Consider for a minute how you expect college professors to do certain things when they walk into a classroom. You expect salespersons to behave in certain ways when you enter a store. You may have some stereotypical views of people from other cultures. In some ways, stereotypes help to reduce our uncertainty and increase our ability to predict what will happen. But sometimes those stereotypes seriously limit the range of possibilities. For example, what if you applied an inaccurate stereotype to a person from another culture, only to discover that you misjudged the person and possibly lost out on a unique friendship? In your experience, what negative consequences have you encountered when you have treated someone as a stereotype?

Get even more specific: In your relationships, should you stereotype women and men based on their sex? We suggest not—not just because there are so many differences between people, but because no one likes to be treated as a stereotype. A man doesn't like to be told that he is just another unfeeling, inexpressive male. No woman likes to be told that "all women are too emotional." No one likes to be told that "You are just like everyone else." In the first place, we are all different and that difference needs to be recognized and celebrated. Second, actions based on stereotypes do nothing to advance a relationship. And third, stereotypes can negatively affect someone's self-esteem. When possible, treat people as individuals, not categories.

Value 6: Being Open-Minded and Willing to Change

Have you ever talked with persons who are completely closed minded? It's frustrating, and frequently we have a reaction like, "Oh, what's the use? They'll never change their minds anyway, so there's no point in even talking." That's not a desirable reaction in effective communication. A basic dimension of personal effectiveness is the belief on the part of other people that we are open to change. In a relationship, the more each person believes that the other person can be influenced, the more they are both likely to communicate. So we believe that it is important to be open to persuasion. We don't suggest that you believe everything people tell you or do everything people ask of you, but if there is sufficient cause, it's okay to change your mind. Open-mindedness and the ability to change are positive values for all relationships.

CONCLUSION

In this opening chapter, we offered a definition of gender communication and described it as provocative, popularized, pervasive, problematic, and unpredictable. We also explained key terms so that you would more fully understand the gender jargon used in the remainder of this textbook. We explored the communication process from a receiver orientation and introduced the personal effectiveness approach to gender communication. As we stated, one goal of this text is to help you develop greater personal effectiveness so that you understand more of what is happening when women and men communicate. At the same time, we want you to understand your own communication behavior more fully so that you can predict the potential impact of your communication behaviors on other people. If you can do that, you will be better at selecting the best option from your repertoire of communication behaviors. Finally, we want to develop your ability to explain why things worked out the way they did, because knowing why is the first step in changing things. Information enables people to understand what is happening, to explain why it is happening, and to predict what will happen in the future.

Key Terms

gender communication	feminism	repertoire
sex	patriarchy	selection
gender	sexism	skill
gender-role identity	postfeminism	evaluation
sexual orientation	Third Wave feminism	values
sexual preference	uncertainty reduction	confirmation
heterosexism	receiver orientation	stereotyping
homophobia	personal effectiveness	

Discussion Starters

1. Think about how the *roles* and *rules* have changed for men and women in our society. What kinds of *roles* did your parents model for you when you were growing up? What kinds of attitudes have you developed about appropriate roles for women and men in our society? What are some of the *rules* for behavior that operated during your parents' or grandparents' generation? Do these rules seem outdated to you today? Are there some rules that are unchangeable?

2. What comes to mind when you hear the phrase *Women's Liberation Movement*? What comes to mind when you hear the term *feminism*? Do you consider yourself a *feminist*? a *postfeminist*? a *Third Wave feminist*? Why or why not?

3. Now that you have a clearer understanding of what sexism is, think of something you consider to be really sexist. It could be a policy or practice, or something that you saw, read, or heard. What was your reaction to this sexist stimulus at the time? What is your reaction now? If your reactions are different, why are they different?

4. Recall a situation in which your interpretation of a message (as the receiver) did not match a person's intentions (as the sender). It could be something simple such as a miscommunication over the time or place where you were supposed to meet someone, or it could be something more serious, such as misunderstanding an instructor's explanation of an upcoming assignment. Analyze that situation: Was it a same-sex or mixed-sex conversation? What do you think the sender of the message intended to communicate? How did you, as the receiver, interpret the message? What was said (or done, nonverbally) during the conversation that was the primary cause of misunderstanding? How was the situation resolved? Using a receiver orientation to communication, what could the *sender* in the conversation have done to make the situation better? How could you, as the *receiver*, have reduced the potential for misunderstanding?

5. Consider the communication behavior repertoire or "bag of tricks" explained in this chapter. Then think about communication situations (especially with members of the other sex) that give you the most trouble. What communication behaviors could you add to your repertoire that would improve your future success in these kinds of situations?

6. Think of two very different relationships that you have currently with members of each sex. Now imagine how those two people see you. What makes having a relationship with you important to each of them? How do they view your communication ability? Are their views different? Do you think that sex or gender has an impact on these persons' views of your communication ability? If so, why so?

7. How are your values reflected in your communication? Consider the six values presented in this chapter. Which of these values are already consistent with yours? Which ones represent new ideas for you? Are there values that you would add to our list?

References

BATE, B., & BOWKER, J. (1997). *Communication and the sexes* (2nd ed.). Prospect Heights, IL: Waveland.

BEEBE, S. A., BEEBE, S. J., & REDMOND, M. V. (1998). *Interpersonal communication: Relating to others.* (2nd edition) Boston: Allyn & Bacon.

BELLAFANTE, G. (1998, June 29). Feminism: It's all about me! *Time,* 54–62.

BERGER, C. R., & BRADAC, J. J. (1982). *Language and social knowledge: Uncertainty in interpersonal relationships.* London: Edward Arnold.

BERGER, C. R., & CALABRESE, R. J. (1975). Some explorations in initial interaction and beyond: Toward a developmental theory of interpersonal communication. *Human Communication Research, 1,* 99–112.

CISSNA, K. N., GARVIN, B. J., & KENNEDY, C. W. (1990). Reliability in coding social interaction: A study of confirmation. *Communication Reports, 3,* 58–69.

DANCE, F. E. X., & LARSON, C. E. (1976). *The functions of human communication.* New York: Holt, Rinehart, & Winston.

DEFRANCISCO, V. (1992, March). *Position statement: How can feminist scholars create a feminist future in the academic environment?* Paper presented at the Tenth Annual Conference on Research in Gender and Communication, Roanoke, VA.

DENFELD, R. (1995). *The new Victorians: A young woman's challenge to the old feminist order.* New York: Warner.

DEVITO, J. A. (1998). *The interpersonal communication book* (8th ed.). New York: Longman.

FALUDI, S. (1991). *Backlash: The undeclared war against American women.* New York: Crown.

FALUDI, S. (1995, March–April). "I'm not a feminist but I play one on TV." *Ms.,* 31–39.

GILLESPIE, M. A. (1998, May–June). The backlash boogie. *Ms.,* 1.

GOULD, L. (1972, December). X: A fabulous child's story. *Ms.,* 105–106.

GRIFFIN, G. (1998). Understanding heterosexism—the subtle continuum of homophobia. *Women & Language, 21,* 33–39.

HEYWOOD, L., & DRAKE, J. (Eds.). (1997). *Third Wave agenda: Being feminist, doing feminism.* Minneapolis: University of Minnesota Press.

HIGGINBOTHAM, A. (1997, September–October). Shall we dance? *Ms.,* 99–101.

HOFF SOMMERS, C. (1994). *Who stole feminism? How women have betrayed women.* New York: Simon & Schuster.

hooks, b., VAID, U., STEINEM, G., & WOLF, N. (1993, September–October). Let's get real about feminism: The backlash, the myths, the movement. *Ms.,* 34–43.

MAJORS, R. E. (1994). Discovering gay culture in America. In L. A. Samovar & R. E. Porter (Eds.), *Intercultural communication: A reader* (4th ed.) (pp. 148–154). Belmont, CA: Wadsworth.

ROIPHE, K. (1993). *The morning after: Sex, fear, and feminism on campus.* Boston: Little Brown.

SIEBURG, E. (1969). *Dysfunctional communication and interpersonal responsiveness in small groups.* Unpublished doctoral dissertation, University of Denver, Denver, CO.

SPENDER, D. (1985). *Man made language* (2nd ed.). London: Routledge & Kegan Paul.

STEINEM, G. (1997, September–October). Revving up for the next 25 years. *Ms.*, 82–84.

THORNE, B., KRAMARAE, C., & HENLEY, N. (1983). Language, gender, and society: Opening a second decade of research. In B. Thorne, C. Kramarae, & N. Henley (Eds.), *Language, gender, and society* (pp. 7–24). Rowley, MA: Newbury.

U.S. BUREAU OF LABOR STATISTICS. (1997). As reported in: How are we doing? (1997, September–October). *Ms.*, 22–27.

WALLIS, C. (1989, December 4). Onward, women! *Time*, 80–89.

WILSON SCHAEF, A. (1981). *Women's reality: An emerging female system in the white male society.* Minneapolis: Winston.

WOOD, J. T. (1998). *Communication mosaics: A new introduction to the field of communication.* Belmont, CA: Wadsworth.

PART TWO

INFLUENCES ON
OUR CHOICES

CHAPTER TWO

BIOLOGICAL AND SOCIAL INFLUENCES ON GENDER

Nature and Nurture Revisited

CASE STUDY: ANYTHING SOUND FAMILIAR?

"I don't think women belong in combat, because they're simply not as strong as men. I'm not sexist or anything, but I just don't want to see women on the front lines getting blown up. What if we had a situation where women soldiers were taken prisoner or something?"

"That DID happen—it happened in the Gulf War. A couple of women were shot down over Iraqi territory, held hostage, then released. And we didn't hear anything about them caving or giving away secrets to the enemy or anything. So why is it harder for you to think of female than male POWs?"

"I guess it's going to happen sooner or later—probably in my lifetime—that a woman will become president of the United States. But it's just hard to think about or imagine; how will she deal with all the aggressive male congressmen trying to get her to see things their way? How will she respond to partisan criticism?"

"Will she react more emotionally to things than male presidents, especially if she's PMSing? For example, would a female president find it more difficult than a male president to order a bombing that might wipe out civilians as well as the target?"

"Not only that, what if she's more aggressive than we're used to in a woman, meaning what if she's more comfortable in a loud debate than at a photo op where she's supposed to be kissing babies? What will the country think about that? And if we have a hard time with this, what does that say about us as a society, as a nation?"

"I think we need to start off with a female vice president, just so we can get used to the idea before a woman gets elected to the top office."

"I don't think men and women should compete against each other in sports, simply because male athletes are generally stronger, bigger, and faster.

It just wouldn't be fair competition. In the long run, it could be deflating or demotivating for the women. And they could get really hurt."

"But I know some women who could kick just about any guy's butt in just about any sport. What about them? Should they be kept out of the top sports and the big money, just because of their sex?"

"If it's so hard to imagine co-ed sports like football or boxing, why not start out with less confrontational sports, like golf, tennis, swimming, or even bowling? Start integrating those by having girls and boys play against each other (and with each other, as teammates) in tennis matches, golf tournaments, and swim meets. Sports will never be integrated if we don't start off when we're young—in the schools."

The conversational examples above are actual exchanges that have occurred over recent years in your textbook authors' classes. We need not label, by sex, the authors of the comments, because the opinions expressed are held by women and men alike who take our courses. Do you detect any "leaps" on the part of the interactants, meaning that they started with a biological property and then either relied upon or rejected a social interpretation of that biology to develop an opinion? For example, we still hear quite often the exchange about a female president making decisions when she's menstruating. The stereotypical leap from this monthly biological process to brain functioning has not gone away.

Some people believe that because biological differences between women and men are natural and uniquely human, they are something to be appreciated, not downplayed or resented. These biological properties "make the world go 'round," so why be concerned about them? Others believe that biological sex differences are fairly insignificant; the real issue is the social interpretation of those differences. Sometimes the interpretation is that the sexes are more biologically alike than different. But at other times, society uses biological differences as a disguise or excuse for perpetuating a power differential between the sexes.

Of the many internal and external factors that influence communication with members of the opposite sex, biological and social factors have a profound, if sometimes subconscious, psychological effect on your identity and your gender communication. When you read the information about biological and social influences that follows, think about the following things: (1) the extent to which your biological sex (being male or female) is a part of your identity; (2) how you have been shaped by social interpretations of biology, as well as other influences, such as family relationships, friendships, education, and experiences; (3) your psychological response to these first two things, in terms of how you have formed your identity; and (4) how you communicate that identity to others.

Hot Topics

- How social interpretations of biological sex differences can lead to communication based on stereotypes
- Social interpretations of such anatomical sex differences as sexual organs, reproductive functions, and judgments of physical strength

- Social interpretations of hormonal differences related to nurturance, aggression, and cycles
- Research on sex differences in brain functioning and cognitive ability
- How social influences affect the development of gender-role identity
- How androgyny, masculinity, and femininity relate to gender-role identity
- Gender-role transcendence and the expanded communication repertoire

STEREOTYPING: HE-MEN AND SHE-WOMEN?

Have you ever been talked to or treated a certain way, merely because of your sex? Can you recall a situation when someone sized you up because you were a woman or a man, and then talked to you based on a stereotype of what your sex was supposed to be?

Here are some common examples. People assume that because men tend to have more muscle mass than women, all men can lift all kinds of heavy things. They often get called on to help people move, help rearrange bulky furniture, or lift heavy boxes and objects. Many men have strained their backs or, worse, developed hernias and detached retinas from all of the lifting they are "supposed" to be able to do. Why assume that a guy always has the strength or, for that matter, *wants* to do physical labor?

And for the women, have you ever taken your car to a service center for repairs and been treated by the mechanic as though you don't speak English? (Yes, men are treated this way too, but there seems to be some expectation that men can understand car maintenance better than women.) People who don't know you may assume a lot about you, simply because of your sex. And we all know of more serious examples of sexual stereotyping and discriminatory treatment than these.

In Chapter 1 we discussed uncertainty reduction as a motivation to communicate. When people are uncertain and don't know you as an individual, they communicate with you based on extremely limited information—your sex and other physical attributes that can be perceived with the basic senses. In the absence of more extensive information, people tend to rely on socially learned stereotypes because they provide some basis for how to proceed. But if someone always stops there—relying on a stereotype without exploring what makes you a unique person—you probably won't like that kind of treatment.

For example, take a physical property of the sexes, such as most men's higher level of muscle mass (which many use as a biological measurement of strength), and attach to that an expectation that men shouldn't cry or express their emotions (a social interpretation of strength). Apply this same thinking to women, and you have the notion that since they tend to have less muscle mass than men, women will be much more susceptible to physical threats, such as in a POW situation (a conclusion we alluded to in the opening conversational examples). Can you begin to see how conceptions of biological sex differences become intertwined with social influences embedded within one's culture? What kind of communication results from such thinking? Granted, this is fairly complex, but if you grasp these ideas, then you find yourself at the center of the nature-nurture dialogue.

As you proceed through this chapter, you may ask, why focus on sex *differences*, as opposed to *similarities*? One answer simply relates to human nature: While people don't intend to widen any kind of gender gap, it seems that they are quite interested in learning how their sex differs from the opposite one. We are curious as to what makes us unique and individual, so it doesn't seem as captivating to talk only about similarities between women and men. A second, more important reason is this: Exposing sex and gender differences so that people see them for what they really are increases understanding and cooperation between men and women, rather than adding to the mystery or suspicion that may tend to divide us. If you know that someone is different from you but don't know why or don't care to find out what those differences are all about, then you have separated yourself from that person. But if you recognize a difference and communicate your understanding and acceptance of that difference, then you can get along better and celebrate the individuality—yours and the other person's.

BIOLOGICAL SEX AND SOCIAL INTERPRETATIONS

Biological differences between men and women continue to be hot topics these days. Studies of brain functioning, hormonal effects, or anatomical abnormalities can be found in magazines, newspapers, and on television talk shows. The headline on the cover of an issue of *Time* magazine reads, "Why Are Men and Women Different?" followed by "It isn't just upbringing. New studies show they are born that way." In the cover picture, a little boy is flexing his upper arm muscles for a little girl, whose facial expression indicates either admiration or complete boredom, depending on your point of view.

While this chapter will inform you about biological sex differences, those differences are neither our central focus nor critical to our approach to gender communication. We won't suggest that one sex is physically superior to the other. Indeed, we don't want to make too much out of biological differences because we've seen that they sometimes become a cop-out. It's easy to chalk up a discussion of gender by citing biological differences and leave it at that, without exploring more deeply the ramifications or consequences of those differences. It's easy to say "Men and women are just naturally different, so stop trying to understand it or fight it. Just let nature take its course." This type of comment implies that somehow biology gives us permission to behave in a certain way—even if that way is discriminatory. For many of us who study gender communication, this is not a workable stance. So while we want to explore the biology, we are most interested in how communication is affected by the social translations of that biology.

"Innies" and "Outies":
Anatomical Differences
and Social Interpretations

Three divergent anatomical properties of men and women are examined in this section: differences in sexual organs, reproductive functions, and physical strength. Some of the biological findings described here may be quite familiar to you; some may surprise you. But we challenge you to think about the social interpretations of the biology in ways that you might not have thought of before now. Think also about how those interpretations are reflected in communication between women and men.

Sexual Organs

Since your first class in human biology, you have known that the combination of XX chromosomes creates a female fetus and the XY combination

The male is by nature superior, and the female inferior; the one rules, and the other is ruled. The lower sort are by nature slaves, and it is better for them as for all inferior that they should be under the rule of a master.

Aristotle, Greek Philosopher

creates a male, in the majority of instances. (There are some exceptions, but we'll leave that for others to explain.) Early on, human embryos develop both male and female sex organs, but the presence of the extra X or the Y chromosome causes the secretion of hormones and the differentiation of sex organs. The fetus starts to form internal female or external male genitalia at around three or four months into development (Devor, 1989; Unger & Crawford, 1996).

Think for a moment about the consequences of that simple differentiation of genitalia. Consider the interesting parallel between the sexes' genitalia and their roles in society. For centuries the male penis has been viewed as a symbol of virility—an external, outward sign of men's strength and their ability to assert themselves in the world. The externality of men's sexual organs has been interpreted socially to identify men as the actors, doers, leaders, and decision makers in many aspects of life, such as in relationships, work, and politics. In contrast, the internal genitalia of women is paralleled with the more passive, submissive profiles that women have traditionally assumed—profiles endorsed by men, and often, society in general. The social interpretations of women's sexual organs identify them as reactors, receivers, followers, and beneficiaries of men's decisions.

Maybe you have never considered these parallels before; maybe your reaction to these ideas is: "The world has changed; these depictions of women and men are past history, so why draw the parallel to sexuality?" If that's what you're thinking, then congratulate yourself. We agree that, for many people, these profiles no longer apply and thus the biological parallel doesn't apply either. But at times you may be painfully reminded that within many institutions in society—business, education, political arenas—more than mere echoes of this "historical" view of women and men still exist.

You should never say anything to a woman that even remotely suggests you think she's pregnant unless you can see an actual baby emerging from her at that moment.

Dave Barry,
columnist & author

Reproductive Functions

While the sexual organs represent the more obvious anatomical sex differences, perhaps the most profound difference rests in the sexes' reproductive functions. Researchers Bermant and Davidson (1974) define biological sex as "separateness: a division of reproductive labor into specialized cells, organs, and organisms. The sexes of a species are the classes of reproductively incomplete individuals" (p. 9). We know that it takes both eggs and sperm to rectify this "incompleteness," so this is not the differentiating reproductive function to which we refer. What makes the sexes so different in this regard is the woman's capacity to carry a developing fetus for nine months, give birth, and nurse an infant. These tasks have long been protected, even to the extent that turn-of-the-century medical information warned women against too much thinking or exercise so as not to divert blood away from their reproductive systems (McLoughlin, Shryer, Goode, & McAuliffe, 1988). The reproductive capabilities of men and women have more profound social translations than any other.

To better explain that last statement, allow us to re-create for your a segment of a rather lively discussion that occurred at a gathering of some friends. We were talking about biological sex differences when one of the men commented that sex differences exist in their current form because of centuries of hunter-gatherer cultures. These are societies in which the men combed the land, hunted the food, and protected their families from danger, while the women had the birthing and child-rearing duties and developed tools to gather and carry the food (Brown, 1980; Coward, 1983). This separation of labor formed the basis of a social structure that worked very well; thus it continued into modern times, in the opinion of our friend at the party. But more important than a mere anthropological lesson, the point in this explanation of sex differences is that because of simple biology, whole societal structures were set in place. Did you ever think that so much might rest on the capacity to reproduce? This is a prime example of what we mean by biological factors contributing to a wide range of social norms and expectations.

Granted, our friend had a valid point; in historic times and in some cultures today, women's roles are defined by their biology. Men's roles in these cultures seem balanced with women's roles of child maintenance. (We say "in some cultures" because renowned anthropologist Margaret Mead has documented cultures in which the sex roles are reversed and are not based on reproductive capabilities.) We understand the argument that because women have birthing and nursing capabilities they are more innately nurturing and, thus, are the more likely candidates to hold primary childcare roles within families and society. We also understand that men, because of their biological makeup, are not physically bound to infants, so they are the more likely candidates to provide economic sustenance for the family. You can understand this explanation for the origin of the wife as homemaker, husband as breadwinner dichotomy.

But did you ever stop to consider how arbitrary the decision might have been—the decision for women to be the baby-birthers? Whether you believe that the decision was made by a divine entity or occurred as just a fluke of evolution is not the focus of our discussion here. However you believe it occurred, what if the decision had been made in the reverse? Have you ever thought about what kind of world we'd be living in if the conception, pregnancy, birthing, and nursing tasks were biological capabilities of men? Would men still be seen as actors, doers, and decision makers, and women as reactors, receivers, and decision followers? Would the power structure that accompanies going out into the world and making a living versus staying at home with children be reversed as well? How would communication between men and women be affected?

Medical knowledge and technology have progressed to the point that women, in particular, can benefit from alternatives to their own biology— alternatives that continue to change our social structure. Although still able to carry and give birth to babies, women now have several methods of preventing conception. In fact, some contend that the development and accessibility of the birth control pill contributed more than other events or discoveries in altering male-female dynamics in recent U.S. history (Hain, 1997). In addition, if women do become pregnant, they do not necessarily have to be the biologically designated, primary childcare-givers once the baby is born. Many women choose to return to work (or have to work because of economic constraints) or pursue other endeavors. These choices affect how the sexes view each other, as well as how they communicate. So, since modern families are beginning to make nontraditional decisions regarding child-rearing, are we witnessing the breakdown of the hunter-gatherer approach to family life?

> *I have a brain and a uterus, and I use both.*
>
> *Patricia Schroeder, former Congresswoman*

Reprinted with special permission of King Features Syndicate.

What would be the social reaction if the father of a newborn baby chose to take time off from his job or even quit to be the primary childcare-giver? A colleague of ours recently resigned his faculty position at a university to be the primary caregiver for his children while his wife continued her successful career as an attorney (Cavanaugh, 1997). In the late 1980s, this was such a rare occurrence that it was the subject of an ABC *Nightline* television program. The main guest on the program was describing how the law firm where he worked negotiated a "paternity leave" for him, so that his wife could resume her career and he could take care of their new baby. How did people react to his decision? One guest on *Nightline* applauded the family's decision and the "revolutionary" option created by the law firm, encouraging other businesses and institutions to initiate similar policies. However, most of the program's guests were not so optimistic. While they didn't discredit the spirit of the paternity leave, they felt that in reality it would prove to be an unwise decision. They anticipated that the man's colleagues would ridicule and devalue his decision, that eventually he would be viewed as anything but a "team player" like other lawyers in the firm, and that his career would suffer dramatically.

But in the 1990s, men as primary caregivers has become more commonplace. Articles citing the experiences of stay-at-home dads and Mr. Moms, as well as publications with helpful advice for fathers (e.g., *At-Home Dad, Dad-to-Dad, Full-Time Dads*) are more prevalent now than a decade ago (Steinberg, 1995; White, 1998). From a social perspective, the reactions to stay-at-home dads are most interesting. They report varied responses from women and a good deal of expected razzing from men. One dad reported that it was very tough at first because of people kidding him about being Mr. Mom, relatives placing bets on when he'd go back to work, and the rebuffs he got from mothers at the playground (Steinberg, 1995).

What are the social backlashes for women who don't follow the more traditional path of motherhood? Have you heard criticism leveled at women who choose not to have children, or who return to their careers while their babies are still quite young? Often these women are ridiculed for "rocking the biological boat" and for being "selfish." If a man chose not to father any children or not to become the primary caregiver for a newborn because it would disrupt his career goals, do you think that he would receive as much criticism as women who make the same choices? In sum, even though it isn't as unusual to see women returning to work after giving birth and men choosing to be primary childcare-givers, statistics indicate that this profile of family is still much more the aberration than the norm. Census Bureau figures report that only 16 percent of preschoolers have working moms and at-home dads (Steinberg, 1995). But although the hunter-gatherer model still prevails in modern American culture, things are changing—albeit slowly.

Physical Strength

When the subject of biological sex differences is introduced, students are quick to comment about issues surrounding physical strength and endurance. Heightened by ongoing events in the Persian Gulf and other places in the world involving American troops, such topics as biological attributes of male and female soldiers, differing fitness standards, and women in front-line combat generate provocative discussions (Diamond, 1997; Hamilton, 1997; Schafer, 1998). A common theme in these discussions is the debate over whether women, because their bodies are higher in fat and lower in muscle in comparison to men's, are adequately equipped with the strength and endurance necessary for combat or sustained military action. Some contend that if women are able to endure childbirth, they ought to be able to handle combat. What do some experts say about muscle versus fat composition, strength, and sex differences?

According to research, across adult age groups, men's body fat tends to average around 10 percent less than women's (Bailey & Bishop, 1989; Dolnick, 1991). Scientists attribute this discrepant fat level of the sexes primarily to the female body's purpose of protecting a fetus. Besides men's higher concentrations of muscle, four other factors give men more natural strength than women: (1) a greater oxygen-carrying capacity; (2) a lower resting heart rate; (3) higher blood pressure; and (4) more efficient methods of recovering from physical exertion (Stockard & Johnson, 1980). Because of these characteristics, men have long been thought of as the stronger sex, women the weaker sex. But let's take a closer look at determinations of strength.

Strength is defined in *Webster's* dictionary as force, invulnerability, or the capacity for exertion and endurance. If you examine strength from a vulnerability or endurance angle,

> There's nothing wrong with the ladies. God bless them; let them play. But what they're doing is eliminating much of the available time when young players can get on the course.
>
> *Jack Nicklaus, golfer*

then the sex-typed strength argument breaks down a bit. Research documents the following differences between males and females:

1. Male fetuses experience many more developmental difficulties and birth defects, average an hour longer to deliver, and have a higher death rate than female fetuses.
2. For the top 15 leading causes of death in the United States, men have higher death rates than women.
3. Women outlive men by seven to eight years.
4. Men do not tend to see themselves as ill or susceptible to disease or injury, when they actually are more susceptible.
5. Men generally drive more recklessly than women, accounting for three out of every four traffic fatalities.
6. In some sports requiring extreme levels of endurance (such as ultra-marathons and dogsled racing), women are catching up to and surpassing men (Cahow, 1997; Dolnick, 1991; Jacklin, 1989; McLoughlin, et al., 1988).

Another aspect of the vulnerability angle relates to the sexual organs. In ordinary circumstances, men's external sexual organs are more readily injured than women's. (Several athletic clothing and equipment manufacturers have made their fortunes off of this very fact.) This is not to say that women cannot be injured, but that the female sex organs' internal location make them less accessible to injury than men's. Thus, if strength equates to invulnerability, the stereotype of men being the stronger sex doesn't quite work, as these examples show.

Could it be that the notion of male strength has more to do with social interpretations than biological fact? The answer to that question is no, if you equate strength with higher muscle mass, and yes, if you equate it with vulnerability. Most often a determination of strength depends on the individual, not the sex. We've all seen some women who were stronger (in terms of muscle strength) than some men and vice versa. But it's quite fascinating when you realize how many social expectations and stereotypes are steeped in the basic biology.

As an example of a social interpretation of the "strength" issue, how many men reading this text can recall being told, "Boys are supposed to be strong; boys don't cry"? Can you remember a time when you or a male friend didn't *feel* very strong, but were reminded to hide that feeling, so as to appear strong to everyone else? Sometimes instances like this occur amidst crisis or trauma, when men may be expected to be the "strong ones" so everyone else can fall apart. If you've ever been in a hospital waiting room when a man has showed his emotions about a sick loved one, did you notice other people's reactions or do you recall your own? Many times people are so completely stunned by a male emotional display, they don't know how to react.

What about situations that aren't related to crisis or trauma, such as more commonplace instances of disappointment, depression, or a bad case of the blues? Many men are so programmed to be strong, to mask or at least downplay what they are feeling, that they react emotionally only when they are alone, if they react outwardly at all. Because of this pressure to stay strong, sometimes they release the emotion through physical exertion or in destructive ways. Men explain that, while women say that they want men to be more emotional, to demonstrate their feelings rather than internalize them, when these men have let their emotions show, the women "freak." This is not to say that all women react negatively to male emotion or that women always show their emotions. Some women were taught just like men to "buck up" and rein in their emotions. But the pressure to be "strong" just isn't the same for women in most cases. Why do we tend to equate strength and weakness with an honest demonstration of human emotion?

Biological designations can have profound, far-reaching social implications that can seriously influence your communication with others. A more personally effective way to communicate with men and women is free from the limitations of biological stereotypes.

Social Interpretations of "Raging" Hormones

According to Jacklin (1989), hormonal differences "are among the most common biological causes given for behavioral sex-related differences" (p. 129). However, as hormonal studies are becoming more frequent and are utilizing more sophisticated methods, they are producing inconsistent results. We still do not know exactly the effects of hormones on human behavior. Some of the complexity results from not knowing where the genetics end and environment begins. Most problematic of all are some researchers' conclusions about their results—conclusions that translate into social interpretations that then dictate "appropriate" sex roles and behavior (Bleier, 1984).

You may already be aware that the three main groups of hormones (androgens, estrogens, and progestrogens) are contained within all humans, just at varying levels. For simplicity sake, we have chosen here to explore those hormones most associated with masculinity (androgens, more specifically, testosterone) and femininity (estrogens). We've pared some complex information down to three key elements: hormonal effects on nurturance, aggression, and cycles. These functions are the most distinctive for the sexes and have the most significant social interpretations.

Nurturance

Stereotypically, nurturance is associated with women's mothering roles, but it is defined as the "giving of aid and comfort to others" (Maccoby & Jacklin, 1974, pp. 214–215). Research by Anke Ehrhardt has determined a relationship between female hormones and the inclination to nurture. Ehrhardt and colleagues (1980; 1984) examined young girls who had been prenatally "masculinized" by receiving large doses of androgens (male hormones) from drugs prescribed for their mothers. Subjects rarely fantasized or daydreamed about marriage and pregnancy, nor did they show much interest in caring for small children. They more often gave career a higher priority than marriage in discussions of future plans, generally liked to play and associate with boys more than girls, and were more likely to exhibit high levels of physical energy. These studies and other evidence have led researchers to link hormones and nurturance.

But many researchers argue that the ability to nurture goes beyond biology. Stockard and Johnson (1980) caution that "hormonal influence helps prompt the appearance of and interest in nurturing behavior, but social situations and interactions also exert an influence, making it possible for males as well as females to nurture" (p. 137). Such experiences as participation in childbirth, early contact between parents and infants, and even whether one has had experience with younger siblings may affect one's ability to nurture. Given this information, why does society tend to readily associate femininity with the ability to nurture and comfort, as though men were incapable of doing so? Granted, the association between motherhood and nurturance is deeply ingrained in our culture; thus, it is a reasonable connection. But does it have to be the only connection?

If a man finds that he has a stronger or equally strong nurturing tendency as his wife or partner, should his masculinity be threatened? Think about why, until only recently, mothers were almost always awarded custody of children in divorce proceedings, regardless of which parent was actually the better nurturer. Conversely, if a woman isn't particularly fond of children and isn't at all interested in motherhood, does this mean that she has a hormonal deficit, or that she is somehow less feminine than women who want to bear children? It's easy to see how hormonal functioning can lead to labels and stereotypes for the sexes—labels that affect our opportunities and influence our choices in communicating.

Aggression

Hyde (1986), a noted gender psychologist, states that "gender differences in aggression are generally considered to be a reliable phenomenon" (p. 51). Sex role researchers Stockard and Johnson (1980) assert that in all known societies, men behave more aggressively than women. These researchers admit that this aggressive behavior may be learned, but they provide evidence to indicate that hormones influence aggressive behavior. However, another gender psychologist, Marie Richmond-Abbott (1992) believes that "it is difficult to characterize aggression as a sex difference because even defining aggression presents a problem" (p. 52). Aggression can be displayed verbally or physically, but it is not always clear whether a certain behavior

> *When women are depressed, they either eat or go shopping. Men invade another country.*
>
> *Elaine Boosler, comedian*

is aggressive, assertive, coercive, energetic, persuasive, dominant, competitive, violent, and so on. Despite definitional problems, aggressiveness is often discussed as a male characteristic related to androgens, while passivity relates to the female system's lack of androgens.

Stockard and Johnson (1980) reviewed investigations of boys and girls who received high dosages of androgens (male hormones) before birth. In these studies, both male and female subjects had higher energy levels (than control group subjects) and preferred boys' games, toys, sports, and activities. Female subjects exhibited "tomboy" characteristics and behaviors and were more likely to start family fights than control group female subjects. Internationally noted sex-role scholars Maccoby and Jacklin (1980) reported that male aggression related to hormonal functioning was a conclusive, demonstrable sex difference. However, gender researcher Anne Fausto-Sterling (1985) discovered that approximately half of the most recent studies attempting to link male aggression and testosterone levels produced results that contradicted studies reviewed by Maccoby and Jacklin. So, studies continue in attempts to better understand the relationship between hormonal levels and resulting aggressive behavior. Why do we still tend to associate masculinity with aggressive behavior, femininity with passive behavior? Could it again be the case that judgments about aggression and the sexes have more to do with social influences than biological fact?

A few examples will help us try to answer those questions. First, think again about the messages that lots of little boys receive—messages from their mothers and fathers, siblings, peers, the media, and other sources. In addition to those messages about strength that we discussed in an earlier section, boys are warned not to "act like a sissy" and are chastised for anything resembling feminine behavior. One of the worst insults one can level at a boy or a man is to call him a girl or a woman. You see fathers, uncles, and older brothers teaching young boys to stick up for themselves, to develop aggressive attitudes by playing contact sports, and to rough-and-tumble with the best of them. Granted, things are changing and not all parents raise their male children in this manner, but the male-as-aggressor stereotype is still around for some reason.

As another example, some men are verbally aggressive in their jobs. Perhaps they have been in situations where going along or hanging back didn't get them very far, so they come to believe that verbal aggression can enhance success on the job. Aggressive behavior might take the form of emphatic sales pitches, interruptions of subordinates, or fevered attempts to persuade colleagues. Quite often this aggressive behavior in men on the job is expected, tolerated, and rewarded. As a result of positive reinforcement, we might say that these displays of aggression are due to social factors rather than "raging hormones."

We're not certain that men are particularly proud of the legacy of aggression; in fact, many of them are working hard to turn this legacy around. Many men are of the opinion that the expectation to be strong and aggressive constitutes a burden they'd rather not carry. They have begun to resent the

Girls had it better from the beginning. Boys can run around fighting wars for made-up reasons with toy guns going kksshh-kksshh and arguing about who was dead, while girls play in the house with their dolls, creating complex family groups and solving problems through negotiation and role-playing. Which gender is better equipped, on the whole, to live an adult life, would you guess?

Garrison Keillor, author & radio personality/storyteller

implication that being a "real man" means being aggressive, competitive, emotionally aloof or detached, and in control all the time. They have begun to seek alternatives to aggressive behavior.

Now consider the sexual flip-side of aggression. What happens when girls carry tomboyish behaviors into adulthood? How do most people react when women exhibit aggressive behavior? Unfortunately, many people react negatively, as though a woman who expresses this stereotypically masculine trait is experiencing hormonal imbalance or behaving inappropriately. Occasionally, off-base, derogatory insinuations about sexual orientation are made. Some men are threatened or put off by aggressive women, because they don't welcome another context for competition. Some women are put off by unexpected, aggressive behavior in women too.

Here's an example: As more and more women enter the workforce and begin to achieve higher ranks, they realize that in some situations passive communication that doesn't rock the boat isn't the best professional strategy. When women demonstrate their expanded repertoire of communication behaviors in professional encounters, how do people react? Have people's reactions to female aggressive behavior changed with the times? If a female manager were to argue aggressively with her coworkers or boss, interrupt the verbal contributions of colleagues, or aggressively strive to achieve a promotion, think about whether she would be viewed through the same lens as a man behaving similarly. In most cases we believe not, but it is more likely today than in times past that female aggressive behavior will be accepted, which reflects how society's expectations of appropriate behavior for women and men are evolving.

As a final example for this section, think about one more context involving socially acceptable aggression: the sporting arena. Acting out aggression on the football field, in the hockey rink, or boxing ring is encouraged, expected, and rewarded in men. But, as more women's sports gain notoriety and respectability, how do people view female athletic aggression? This is an area that is changing as we speak. Female athletes competing in traditionally male sports are gaining popularity and acceptability in society every day (Phillips, 1997). A few examples include Olympic gold medal–winning U.S. women's teams in ice hockey, basketball, softball, and soccer; the establishment of a professional women's basketball league (the WNBA); the introduction of female referees into the NBA; and the increasing popularity of women's professional boxing, due to the efforts of athletes like Christy Martin (Fried, 1997; Hoffer, 1997; Howard, 1997; Lasswell, 1996; Salter, 1997; Starr & Rosenberg, 1997). Most people encourage female verbal and physical aggression in the sporting context, as long as that aggression isn't aimed at male competitors. Maybe you think that statement is harsh, but can you think of any sports that allow direct, physical competition between women and men? Apart from the occasional anomaly—such as the famous 1973 "Battle of the Sexes" tennis match between Billy Jean King and Bobby Riggs, a female Indy 500 race car driver back in the 1980s, a female place kicker who had a short-lived stint in college football, and a female pitcher with a mean fast ball who burned up minor league baseball in the summer of 1998—few women are given the opportunity to compete against men in either professional or collegiate ranks. No contact sports on these levels, such as football, basketball, soccer, rugby, wrestling, or hockey, place the sexes in direct competition with each other. Neither do many noncontact sports, with the exception of mixed doubles matches in tennis, some endurance races (often called ultramarathons), and dogsledding.

Perhaps the rise in popularity of women's sports will affect people's stereotypical notions about aggression. As stereotypical notions become outdated, people try to find new ways to communicate. For example, if you alter your expectation that "men don't cry" (if you ever held that expectation), then your communication with a man who is expressing his emotions will likely change to reflect your broader set of sex-role expectations. If you believe that aggression doesn't "look right" on women, witnessing a woman's basketball game or boxing match might change your mind. If your communication evolves along with changes in your views of and expectations for the sexes, then you are probably becoming more personally effective.

Cycles

When we think of biological cycles, we typically associate them with women's biology in general and with premenstrual syndrome (PMS) in particular. Three decades ago, the medical profession largely chalked up women's menstrual discomfort (e.g., irritability, headaches, cramps, bloating, and mood swings) to hypochondria. In Ramey's (1976) groundbreaking research on PMS, 60 percent of subjects reported experiencing menstrual discomfort. When enough research documented women's reports of menstrual problems over time, the medical

You can't accept one individual's [opinion], particularly if it's a female...but when they get a period, it's really difficult for them to function as normal human beings.

Jerry Lewis, actor

community researched the malady, reversed their position, and declared PMS a disease (Richmond-Abbott, 1992). Some scholars believe that labeling PMS a disease has added credibility to the condition, but it has also reinforced an old stereotype. Dramatic accounts of outlandish, over emotional, even violent behavior, as well as exaggerated images of women unable to meet their responsibilities, have been attributed to PMS. There's even a T-shirt sporting the message, "I Have PMS and ESP. That Makes Me A Bitch Who Knows It All." In their book on women's psychology, Unger and Crawford (1996) state: "The view that their reproductive cycle makes women vulnerable to psychological problems helps to limit women, to define them as dangerous and deviant, and to exclude them from a role in society equal to that of men" (p. 566). So, at the same time that diagnosing the condition legitimizes women's complaints and brings folklore into reality, it can give society more impetus to question women's abilities. Just how does that happen?

One example highlighted by events in the Persian Gulf is women's ability to participate with men in life-threatening combat, a topic that we mentioned earlier in discussing the physical strength of the sexes. Some of the arguments about the effects of women's cycles on mental functioning relegate women to background or support positions in times of conflict. Accusations are made that because women's bodies cycle and their hormones "rage," they cannot be trusted to pilot F-16s, to withhold information if captured, or to make decisions as to when weapons should be fired. Please realize that it is not our intent here to attempt to convince you that women should be allowed in combat. The point is that social interpretations of women's cyclical biology negate or call into question women's ability in many contexts.

The most commonly cited warning about this issue is, "Would you want the hand of a woman with PMS on the button to detonate a nuclear bomb?" (Kleiman, 1992, p. 2E). This question implies that women are such victims of their own biology that they could not possibly be relied upon in critical situations. What is most interesting here is that the same argument could be made about men's levels of testosterone and resulting aggressive behavior. Do men's hormonal functioning and bent toward aggression better equip them to "put the hand on the button"? If that statement seems comical to you, it's likely because that kind of argument is hardly ever made. While society is quick to link female hormonal functioning with debilitation, the same cannot be said for men.

But what about the notion of a male biological cycle? The male cycle is more than a mere notion, according to research. Tracking back a bit, researchers in the mid-1970s began to investigate male hormonal functioning as evidence of a male cycle. Ramey (1976) found that men displayed regular variations in emotions over each 24-hour period within a six-week time frame. Ramey also detected a 30-day cycle for men's hormonal functioning. During these cycles, men's physical strength, emotionality, and intellectual functioning were affected. More recently, Doreen Kimura's (1987) internationally noted research identified a tentative link between seasons of the year and men's cognitive functioning. According to Kimura, when testosterone levels are lower in the spring, men's mathematical and analytic skills are enhanced. These abilities decrease in the fall when testosterone levels are higher. The popular press has picked up on this research, having fun comparing women's monthly periods to what they call men's seasonal "commas" (Kleiman, 1992, p. 1E). This research is in such a tentative stage that caution must be taken in citing the findings as fact. But let's pretend for a moment.

What if, a few years from now, evidence overwhelmingly documents the existence of a male cycle? What would be the social reaction to such news? Do you think that jobs, opportunities, responsibilities, and social roles would change to reflect this biological "instability" in men? Could this alter communication between women and men in some way? We don't know the answers to these questions, but if this scenario becomes reality, it is likely that the social interpretations of the biology will be far more interesting than the biology itself.

Mind over Matter: Are Men's and Women's Brains Really Different?

Current information regarding sex differences and brain functioning have caused more than mild controversy. Brain functions are extremely complex, tied into hormonal functioning, and related to cognitive abilities. This is not meant to be an introductory physiology lesson, so we review only the primary research findings, emphasizing their social interpretations.

Brain Functioning

Some researchers report sex differences in brain size, glucose metabolism counts, and cerebral blood flow (Gur, et al., 1982; Gur, et al., 1995; Halpern, 1986). But others conclude that studies in this area actually show minimal differences (indicating that the sexes' brains are actually more similar than different) and are primarily used to engender divisiveness (Bleier, 1984; Gibbons, 1991; Tavris, 1992). Highly respected gender researcher Celeste Condit contends that a good deal of research on sex differences and the brain is biased in its assumptions and faulty in its methods, constituting a form of "bad science" (Condit, 1996, p. 87).

Man is more courageous, pugnacious, and energetic than woman, and has a more inventive genius. His brain is absolutely larger, but whether or not proportionately to his larger body, has not, I believe, been fully ascertained.

Charles Darwin, evolutionist

Research has shown that the brain has two hemispheres that house various human capabilities. The left hemisphere is primarily responsible for the production of language, while the right hemisphere manages spatial ability. Studies have attempted to find a relationship between hemisphere dominance and sex, hypothesizing that hormones cause women's and men's brains to develop differently. It has long been thought that men perform better on tests of spatial skills while women excel on tests of verbal ability, as a result of this hormonal and brain functioning (Kimura, 1987). Since most of the social interpretations of the information on brain functioning relate to cognitive abilities, let's explore this area before considering interpretations.

Cognitive Abilities

Almost anything one reads about sex differences in cognitive ability begins with a review of psychologists Benbow and Stanley's (1980) report of years of research on math abilities in gifted girls and boys. A consistent pattern emerged over two decades of conducting this research: Boys outscored girls on the math portions of the SAT. This finding led to the conclusion that male dominance in math was related to hemispheric specialization in the brain, that is, that the right hemisphere was more fully developed in men than in women. Recent research supports the notion that differing cognitive abilities are related to the use of various areas of the brain (Gorski, as in Thornton, 1992; Gur, as in Bowden, 1995).

However, social scientists on the nurture side of the nature-nurture argument have other explanations for sex differences in cognitive functioning, insisting that sex roles affect the picture. They suggest that since boys are expected to excel in math, they are encouraged and coached by parents and teachers. Taking more advanced math courses in school and participating in athletics improves boys' math and spatial abilities as well, while mothers' attitudes and anxiety about the difficulty of math inhibits girls' achievement (Eccles, 1989; Linn & Petersen, 1986).

Concerning verbal ability, the general opinion for decades was that females outperformed males in such capacities as language acquisition, vocabulary, spelling, writing, and verbal expressiveness. But, again, research has produced findings to the contrary. Researchers now believe that, if there once was a gap in verbal abilities and math and spatial abilities between the sexes due to brain differences and hormonal functioning, this gap has all but disappeared (Hall, 1987; Holden, 1991; Hyde & Linn, 1988; Unger & Crawford, 1996). If the human brain hasn't changed, then what explains the sexes performing more similarly in specific areas than in times past?

One explanation relates to changing times and changing parents. Perhaps more parents have backed off the old stereotypes, believing now that female and male children can do anything, given encouragement, support, and education (Shapiro, 1990). Another explanation regards teaching. If teachers demonstrate sex bias in their instruction, such as coaching boys in math while sending messages to girls that say "you probably won't be good at this," these biases have ways of becoming eventualities. Teachers who refrain from sex-biased behaviors are helping students to maximize their potential, regardless of expectations for their sex (Ehrenreich, 1992). In sum, societal shifts are affecting students' visions of what they can accomplish, and the gender gap in cognitive ability is narrowing.

That's a hopeful trend in that it will affect the way we think about the sexes' abilities. Maybe the stereotype that "women talk too much"—a myth that most people don't connect with biologically superior verbal ability—will die a well-deserved death. Maybe the image of the "strong, silent type" of man will deservedly fade away, too. Maybe male-dominated fields related to math and spatial skills, such as engineering, science, and technology, will open up even further to women. Maybe men will feel more comfortable in fields traditionally filled with women, such as teaching or other helping professions that rely heavily on verbal abilities. These are a lot of maybes, but the thought that things are changing, stereotypes are fading, and past expectations are loosening should give you a feeling of relief and a sense of freedom. Does this information make you feel that way? If it doesn't, if the changes feel threatening, what might be some causes for your concern? It's interesting to ponder how we can be influenced by biological sex differences, but also how we can choose to interpret the biology and communicate with others as a result.

RECAP

stereotypes, biological differences, social interpretations, sexual organs, reproductive functions, physical strength, hormones, nurturance, aggression, cycles/mood shifts, brain functioning, cognitive abilities

SOCIAL INFLUENCES ON PSYCHOLOGICAL GENDER

In the first major section of this chapter we talked about biological *sex* differences; note here that we have switched focus to psychological variables or *gender-role identity*. In quick review, recall from Chapter 1 that the term *sex* is generally used to refer to maleness and femaleness based on biology, while *gender* is a much broader psychological and cultural construct. Gender is culturally based and socially constructed out of psychological characteristics related to androgyny, femininity, and masculinity. Gender also contains such things as attitudes and beliefs, sexual orientation, and perceptions of appropriate roles for women and men in society. First, let's focus on one property of the larger concept of gender, gender-role identity.

Who ARE You, Psychologically Speaking?

The process of developing gender-role identity involves acquiring information about social norms and roles for men and women (a social function), then adjusting one's view of self, one's role in society, and one's behavior in response to those norms (a psychological function). Some prefer to call this "socialization," defined by sociologists Davidson and Gordon (1979) as the "process by which people learn attitudes, motivations, and behaviors commonly considered appropriate to their social positions" (p. 9). However, socialization recurs throughout the life cycle and includes gender role development as only one facet. For example, a person can experience socialization upon moving to another state or country, changing jobs, or encountering new relationships. For our purposes in this discussion, focusing on gender-role identity within the larger framework of socialization helps us understand how we come to develop our sense of self, our own vision of appropriate roles and behavior for women and men, and our patterns in gender communication.

Theories of Gender-Role Identity Development

A few theories have been generated to explain the phenomenon of gender-role identity development. We summarize some of the more prominent ones, then explore the connection between gender-role identity and gender communication.

Social Learning Theories

Social psychologists Mischel (1966) and Bandura (1971) are noted for their research on social learning theory as an explanation for human development. This theory suggests that children learn gender-related behavior from their social contacts, primarily their parents and peers. Through a process known as identification, children model the thoughts, emotions, and actions of others. This role modeling has a powerful effect on how children see themselves, how they form gender-role identities.

A related practice involves a sort of trial-and-error method in which children learn what behaviors are expected of each sex. Some behaviors in little girls and boys are rewarded by parents, teachers, peers, and other agents of socialization; the same behaviors enacted by the opposite sex are punished. As children continue to receive positive and negative responses to their behaviors, they generalize to other situations and come to develop sex identities as girls or boys (Peach, 1998).

One problem with this theory is the suggestion that children develop according to sex-role stereotypes, which is considered by some theorists to be a limited or confining view of human development. For example, what if a little girl rejects stereotypical girlish behavior, because she likes the status or acceptance she sees little boys receiving? When she wants to model their behavior in order to gain that status, it may not work for her the same way it does for boys. She might be labeled a tomboy, perhaps gaining her some acceptance, but also occasional ridicule. If she patterns her behavior after same-sex models, it is possible that she will not receive the respect, power, and status that she wants. If a little boy is surrounded predominantly by models of the opposite sex, like his mother and most of his preschool and elementary school teachers, what happens if he closely models their behavior? He may be chastised, ostracized, and labeled effeminate or a "sissy." These examples illustrate what some consider to be a weakness in the theory—its emphasis on sex-role stereotypes as guides for behavior and identity development.

However, we know that our sense of identity is affected by how we imitated or learned from our parents. Think about who you modeled your behavior after; was it your mom or your dad, or some of both? Did you pattern more after a same-sex parent or an opposite-sex parent? Maybe an important model for you was a sibling, a grandparent, or other significant person when you were growing up. Maybe you didn't grow up with two parents. As our own culture continues to diversify, the numbers of single-parent families are growing. If you've experienced this last kind of family profile, what effect do you think the focus on one parent had on your view of sex roles?

An example illustrates this idea of modeling your behavior after that of your parents. This story has been around awhile, but it's a good one. A woman describes how she always followed in her mother's footsteps, especially in the kitchen. It seems that she recalled her mother always cutting one end off a ham before putting it in a pan to bake. That was the way her mother did it, so that was the proper way to bake a ham. She prepared hams this way in her own home and taught her daughter to do so as well. One holiday when the three women (we'll call them the grandmother, the mother, and the daughter) were gathered in the kitchen preparing the holiday meal, the grandmother saw the granddaughter religiously cut off one end of the ham before putting it in a pan to bake. The granddaughter thought nothing of it; that's just the way you cooked a ham. The grandmother burst out laughing, finally realizing what the granddaughter was doing. The granddaughter responded to the laughter by insisting that her mother had taught her that this was how you baked a ham. Wasn't it "grandma's way"? When the grandmother explained that the only reason she lopped off one end of the ham was because back then she didn't own a pan big enough for a large ham, these women laughed at themselves for years of misguided tradition.

Sometimes we don't realize that we've taken on the traits, mannerisms, or communication behaviors of a role model until someone points that out to us. Has anyone ever told you that you sound like or talk like one of your parents? This realization can be a point of pride. It can also be quite maddening—no matter how much you love your family—to discover that you mirror them in many ways. But that doesn't mean that you don't form your own sense of individuality and your own ideas about the roles of men and women, especially since social roles have changed so much over time. We aren't just mirrored images of our parents; we can make choices about who we are and who we want to be.

But we are definitely affected or socialized by the gender roles that were enacted in our families. Because of the influence parents have on children's understanding of gender, many modern parents are trying a nongendered approach. They are giving children gender-neutral toys, games, and books in efforts to avoid the more traditional items that often perpetuate stereotypes (like Barbie, GI Joe, and traditional fairy tales). We address the effects of family influence, the role that friendships play in gender identity development, and teachers as role models in subsequent chapters. But for now, think about those people and experiences that had the most influence on you. Who or what is most connected to your gender-role identity today?

Cognitive Development Theory

One of the more prominent gender-role identity theories results primarily from the work of Lawrence Kohlberg. According to Kohlberg (1966), as children's minds mature, they gain an understanding of gender roles and self-identity without external reinforcement (in contrast to the suggestions of social learning theory). This theory essentially suggests that children socialize themselves into feminine or masculine identities via progress through four stages of mental ability. In stage one, very young children are beginning to recognize sex distinctions, but they cannot attach a sex identity to a person. They are likely to say such things as "Daddy is a girl." In stage two, children learn their own sexual identity, as well as how to correctly attach sex-identifying labels to others (Ruble, Balaban, & Cooper, 1981). They understand that their own maleness or femaleness is unchangeable. In stage three, children learn that there are sex-role "ground rules," or guidelines for sex-typed appropriate behavior, that stem from one's culture. Children become motivated to behave in accordance with those rules, persuading others to conform, too. For example, girls want to wear ruffly, "girly" clothing, while boys are appalled at the thought of playing with dolls. At this point, children begin to value and imitate those behaviors associated with their own sex, more so than opposite-sex behaviors.

This progress continues into stage four, when children separate their identities from those of their primary caregivers (typically their mothers). For boys, the importance of their fathers' identity and behavior is compounded. But because female children cannot separate themselves from the mother's female identity, they remain at stage three, unlike their male counterparts who progress through all four stages. In essence, a girl's development is stunted because her sex identity is the same as her mother's. Can you anticipate any problems with this theory? One of the major criticisms of this theory surrounds its use of a male model of development that is then generalized to all humans. The model suggests that girls' development is somehow less complete or advanced than boys'.

Gilligan's Approach to Gender-Identity Development

Carol Gilligan (1982) challenged human development theorists in her ground-breaking book *In a Different Voice: Psychological Theory and Women's Development.* Gilligan's approach expands previous views of human development to account for both female and male paths to gender identity. In a nutshell (which does not do justice to this theory), the core of identity development rests within the mother-child relationship. The female child connects and finds gender identity with the mother, but the male child must find identity by separating himself from this female caregiver. Thus, unlike male development which stresses separation and independence, female identity revolves around interconnectedness and relationship. As communication researchers Wood and Lenze (1991) explain, "This results in a critical distinction in the fundamental basis of identity learned by the genders. For men, the development of personal identity precedes intimacy with others, while for females, intimacy with others, especially within the formative relationship with the mother, is fused with development of personal identity: the two are interwoven processes" (p. 5). Gilligan's theory offers insight into how men and women function. But Gilligan's critics claim that the theory focuses too heavily on female development, that it implies an advantage for females who can identify with a same-sex caregiver, while merely drawing occasional comparisons to how the process works for males. How, then, does one make sense of all these theories? Does a "best" theory of gender-role identity exist?

While the theories described above significantly contribute to our understanding, they tend to dichotomize, focusing heavily on maleness and femaleness. From our point of view, this focus depletes the broader concept of gender; it relegates it to an "either-or" discussion of sex. Another problem is that each theory tends to focus primarily on childhood development or how children discover gender and corresponding social expectations. What we believe to be more interesting for our discussion of gender communication is a model that begins with how we experience gender as children, but shifts to how we progress or transcend that experience later in life. A theory of transcendence would offer real insight into how adults negotiate and renegotiate their gender-role identities, over time and given experiences and education.

The theory that we believe best serves our purpose in this text is termed *gender-role transcendence.* Besides being contemporary and interesting, this theory is empowering. It gives us real hope in terms of understanding one another, improving our gender communication and our relationships with one another, and lessening the divisiveness that accompanies the female-male dichotomy.

Gender-Role Transcendence and Androgyny

Several researchers have developed, expanded, and refined a theory of gender-role identity development called *gender-role transcendence.* However, our discussion begins with the notable contributions of sex-role psychologists Joseph Pleck and Sandra Bem, in a comparison of traditional sex-role identity development theory and gender-role transcendence.

In traditional views of development, the term sex role is defined as "the psychological traits and the social responsibilities that individuals have and feel are appropriate for them because they are male or female" (Pleck, 1977, p. 182). The emphasis here is on the two designations—masculine and feminine. Masculinity involves instrumental or task-oriented competence, and includes such traits as assertiveness, self-expansion, self-protection, and a general orientation of self *against* the world. Femininity is viewed as expressive or relationship-oriented competence, with corresponding traits that include nurturance and concern for others, emphasis on relationships and the expression of feelings, and a general orientation of self *within* the world (Eccles, 1987; Parsons & Bales, 1955).

Critics of traditional views of gender-role development believe that the prevailing theories perpetuate the male-female dichotomy and limit individuals' options, in terms of variations of identities. Gender-role transcendence theory responds to this criticism. Within transcendence theory, Pleck (1975) envisions a three-stage sequence of gender-identity development. The first two stages resemble Kohlberg's (1966) cognitive development model. However, stage three represents the departure point of this theory from the more traditional ones. Stage three occurs when individuals experience difficulty because the rules of behavior no longer seem to make sense or because they begin to suspect that they possess both expressive (feminine) and instrumental (masculine) abilities (Eccles, 1987).

> *I would prefer that individuality would transcend gender. But I've had a baby, and I really believe that the male and female are different. I was a big feminist in my college days, and I used to say it was nurture. But I really think a lot of it's nature, too.*
>
> Liz Phair, *singer/songwriter*

At this point, individuals may "transcend" their understanding of the norms and expectations of gender to develop "psychological androgyny in accordance with their inner needs and temperaments" (Pleck, 1975, p. 172). *Androgyny* is a term made popular by gender scholar Sandra Bem (1974); the term is derived from the Greek *andros* meaning man and *gyne* meaning woman. Persons who transcend traditional role definitions no longer rely on those definitions when determining their own behavior or when assessing the behavior of others. When this occurs, the "individual heads toward a resolution . . ., which in terms of gender-role development involves the integration of one's masculine and feminine selves into self-defined gender-role identity" (Eccles, 1987, p. 232). Communication researcher Harold Barrett (1998) describes the shift in emphasis on biological sex to psychological gender this way: "The emphasis now is less on determination of role by sex—male versus female—and more on awareness of gender plurality in an individual's nature" (p. 83). The notion of "gender plurality" is another way of conceiving of androgyny or gender transcendence.

Like other theories of gender-role identity development, transcendence theory begins with a discussion of child development. However, it emphasizes adolescence as a period when traditional definitions of what is male and female are likely to be challenged for the first time. The theory then tracks into adulthood as changing values, social pressures, and life events (e.g., marriage, new jobs, parenting, retirement) cause adults to reevaluate their gender-role identities. Transcendence, then, may occur in adolescence and adulthood; however, it does not occur in everyone. Some people continue throughout adulthood to adhere to traditional roles and definitions of what is female and male.

The concept of androgyny is more understandable if you envision a continuum with masculinity placed toward one end, femininity toward the other end, and androgyny in the middle. You don't lose masculine traits or behaviors if you become androgynous, or somehow become masculine if you move away from the feminine pole. Androgyny is an intermix of the feminine and the masculine. Some androgynous individuals may have more masculine traits than feminine, and vice versa.

Perhaps diagrams will clarify the idea of androgyny further (see Figure 2–1). The first diagram depicts two bell curves, one labeled masculine and one labeled feminine. If you adopt a traditional view of sex roles, then you fit under one of the two curves in this diagram, depending on your sex. In the second diagram, you see that the bell curves have merged somewhat, such that the overlap in the middle represents androgyny. As individuals continue to challenge traditional sex-typed roles and to experience gender-role transcendence, they widen their identities to include male and female traits and behaviors. Over time, the androgynous identity continues to widen, as depicted in the expanded androgynous area of the third diagram.

While their identity expands, androgynous individuals' *repertoire of communication behavior* also has the capacity to expand. This should sound familiar, since it is fundamental to the personal effectiveness approach to gender communication. In Chapter 1, we explained how effective individuals develop a wider range of communication behaviors from which to choose, know how to analyze

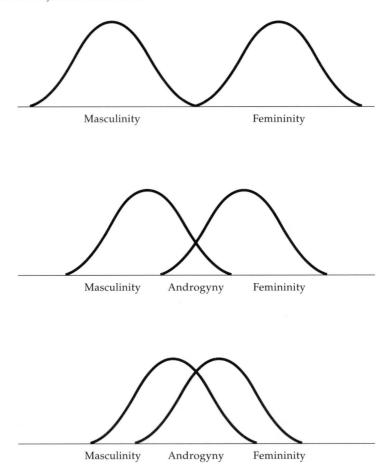

Masculinity   Femininity

Masculinity   Androgyny   Femininity

Masculinity   Androgyny   Femininity

FIGURE 2-1.   Continuum of Gender-Role Transcendence

a situation and select the best behaviors from their repertoire, enact those behaviors, and evaluate the results. Because the process of gender-role transcendence causes an individual to incorporate feminine and masculine traits into a unique blend, that individual is more likely to choose to behave in ways that aren't confined by traditional, stereotypical notions of how men and women are *supposed* to behave. For example, an androgynous male may be more likely than a masculine type of male to talk about and openly express his emotions because he does not buy into the notion that revealing emotions is "unmanly." Androgynous individuals tend to expand their repertoires of behavior; in general, they are adaptive to situations and comfortable with communicative options—options that become extremely helpful in the complicated realm of gender communication (Bem, 1987; Davidson & Gordon, 1979; Eccles; 1987; Greenblatt, Hasenauer, & Friemuth, 1980; Kelly, O'Brien, & Hosford, 1981). Results from a study in which subjects indicated strong identification with both masculine and feminine traits (i.e., androgyny) led researchers to suggest that "androgyny may be a new gender ideal" (House, Dallinger, & Kilgallen, 1998, p. 18).

Another advantage of an androgynous orientation involves how you see and respond to others—an important component of the receiver orientation to communication. To be your most receiver oriented, you need to be able to accept people for what makes them unique. Because androgynous individuals have expanded views of sex roles and corresponding behavior,

If I'm androgynous, I'd say I lean towards macho-androgynous.

John Travolta, actor

they tend to be more generally accepting and less judgmental of others whose behavior deviates from social expectations for the sexes.

What is your reaction to the theory of gender-role transcendence and the concept of androgyny? Some of you may be thinking that the theory reduces the importance of masculinity or femininity, that it waters down unique, important properties of being female or male. If you have these thoughts, you're not alone. The trick is to view androgyny as you would a glass that is half full, rather than half empty. Rather than taking away from the distinctiveness of the sexes, androgyny is a way of recognizing and celebrating qualities of the masculine and the feminine—a way of making these qualities *human*, rather than options for one sex but not the other.

Wouldn't it be great, for instance, for a guy to be able to communicate in a nurturing, caring fashion to women and men alike, without risking rejection or embarrassment for being unmasculine? Wouldn't it be great if women felt more comfortable and less guilty if they discovered they're not really nurturing by nature? Wouldn't it be a relief if the only thing differentiating the sexes was biology, so that other judgments were based on *individual* qualities, not gender?

We've made the case for gender-role transcendence and androgyny, but of course there are some cautions regarding this information. First, while we believe that androgyny and repertoire expansion fit together logically, we don't mean to suggest that the *only* way to expand the communication repertoire is to adopt an androgynous gender-role identity. A person who aligns himself or herself with a traditionally feminine or masculine gender-role identity may still expand the communication repertoire. In many situations, this individual may behave appropriately and be viewed as an effective communicator. So, it's important to keep in mind that, while we contend it is more likely that an androgynous person will develop a greater repertoire than a traditionally sex-typed person, this is a trend, not a hard and fast rule.

The second caution is sort of a reverse of the first. We don't mean to insinuate that *all* androgynous people are *automatically* effective communicators in *all* situations, just because they embody masculine and feminine traits and behaviors. As you are becoming aware, there are neither easy answers nor "quick fixes" in gender communication. We believe that gender-role transcendence broadens your approach and enhances your repertoire and that it is a desirable position from which to communicate with others, but it offers no guarantees.

CONCLUSION

This section of the text is about influences on your choices. Biological influences discussed in this chapter affect your view of self. Social influences, as well as your own attitudes about appropriate roles for others to assume in society, shape your view of self. Out of these biological and social influences, you form a psychological response—your gender-role identity—which is expressed in your communication with others. Developing personal effectiveness in gender communication starts with introspection—with a long, hard look at yourself in terms of your sex and your gender-role identity. As you learn more about the effects of gender on the communication process, your identity may begin to change. Or you may become more comfortable with your current view of self, so that it solidifies. We challenge you to answer the following questions for yourself, either after reading this chapter or this text, or after taking a course in gender communication: What is your current gender-role identity? What aspects of your biology most affect this identity? What social influences most shaped your identity? Are you in the process of changing your gender-role identity? How does your communication (particularly with members of the opposite sex) clue people as to your gender-role identity? How can you become more personally effective in communicating who you are to others?

Key Terms

nature	vulnerability	social learning theory
nurture	hormonal functioning	modeling
biological sex	nurturance	cognitive development
stereotypes	aggression	theory
dichotomy	cycles	gender-role
social interpretations	premenstrual syndrome	transcendence
sexual organs/genitalia	brain functioning	androgyny
reproductive functioning	hemispheres	gender plurality
hunter-gatherer cultures	cognitive ability	communication repertoire
paternity	gender-role identity	personal effectiveness
physical strength	socialization	

Discussion Starters

1. On a sheet of paper, list 10 of the most common adjectives describing women; then list 10 for men. Discuss in class whether these adjectives reflect stereotypes or "real" traits. Have people's stereotypes for the sexes changed? In what ways?
2. Think about the *reproductive capabilities* of women. What if someday science and technology were to progress to the point where men could carry

a fetus and give birth? It sounds crazy now, but what if they could someday? Would they still be "men"? After all, what is the real definition of a man? A woman?

3. How are men able to show their *nurturing* sides in today's society? Are there some ways that are more acceptable or expected than others? What does it take to make a man feel comfortable enough to show his nurturing capabilities?

4. What's the difference between *assertive* and *aggressive* behavior? Are women suspected of acting aggressively, when they think that they are only acting assertively? What does *aggressive* communication sound like? *assertive* communication? *passive* communication?

5. What if more research continued to document the existence of a *male cycle* and the medical community labeled it *TS* for testosterone syndrome? Do you think that the existence of a male hormonal cycle is possible? Thinking specifically, how would a male cycle affect perceptions of women and men in society? How would it affect gender communication?

6. Consider the various theories of *gender-role identity development* that were discussed in this chapter. What are the main strengths of *social learning theory, cognitive development theory,* and *Gilligan's theory?* Their main weaknesses?

7. How does an *androgynous* person's communication differ from that of a *traditionally masculine* or *feminine* person? Are there any immediately detectable differences? Is *androgyny* reflected more in attitude or identity than in communication style?

8. How does knowledge of biological, social, and psychological influences enhance your personal effectiveness in gender communication? Take this question apart: If you understand female and male biological functioning, can that knowledge make you a more effective communicator? If you recognize how social structures are influencing your view of sex roles, as well as your view of yourself within society, can that recognition affect your communication? How is your psychological response to these influences—your *gender-role identity*—related to your communication with others?

References

BAILEY, C., & BISHOP, L. (1989). *The fit-or-fat woman.* Boston: Houghton Mifflin.

BANDURA, A. (1971). Social-learning theory of identificatory processes. In D. A. Goslin (Ed.), *Handbook of socialization theory and research.* Chicago: Rand McNally.

BARRETT, H. (1998). *Maintaining the self in communication.* Incline Village, NV: Alpha & Omega.

BEM, S. L. (1974). The measurement of psychological androgyny. *Journal of Consulting and Clinical Psychology, 42,* 155–162.

BEM, S. L. (1987). Masculinity and femininity exist only in the mind of the perceiver. In J. M. Reinisch, L. A. Rosenblum, & S. A. Sanders, (Eds.), *Masculinity/femininity: Basic perspectives* (pp. 304–311). New York: Oxford University Press.

BENBOW, C. P., & STANLEY, J. C. (1980). Sex differences in mathematical ability: Fact or artifact? *Science, 210,* 1262–1264.

BERMANT, G., & DAVIDSON, J. M. (1974). *Biological bases of sexual behavior.* New York: Harper & Row.

BLEIER, R. (1984). *Science and gender: A critique of biology and its theories on women.* New York: Pergamon.

BOWDEN, M. (1995, January 27). Science offers proof: Men and women do not think alike. *Corpus Christi Caller Times,* p. A4.

BRASH, R. (1965). *How did it begin?* New York: David McKay.

BROWN, J. K. (1980). A note on the division of labor by sex. *American Anthropologist, 72,* 1074.

CAHOW, K. L. (1997, Fall). Survival tactics. *Spohn Quarterly,* 12–16.

CAVANAUGH, D. (1997). Personal communication, November.

CONDIT, C. (1996). How bad science stays that way: Brain sex, demarcation, and the status of truth in the rhetoric of science. *Rhetoric Society Quarterly, 26,* 83–109.

COWARD, R. (1983). *Patriarchal precedents.* London: Routledge & Kegan Paul.

DAVIDSON, L., & GORDON, L. (1979). *The sociology of gender.* Chicago: Rand McNally.

DEVOR, H. (1989). *Gender blending: Confronting the limits of duality.* Bloomington: Indiana University Press.

DIAMOND, J. (1997, February 2). Military closing fitness gender gap. *Corpus Christi Caller Times,* p. A17.

DOLNICK, E. (1991, July-August). Super women. *Health,* 42–48.

ECCLES, J. S. (1987). Adolescence: Gateway to gender-role transcendence. In D. B. Carter (Ed.), *Current conceptions of sex roles and sex typing* (pp. 225–241). New York: Praeger.

ECCLES, J. S. (1989). Bringing young women to math and science. In M. Crawford & M. Gentry (Eds.), *Gender and thought: Psychological perspectives* (pp. 36–58). New York: Springer.

EHRENREICH, B. (1992, January 20). Making sense of la difference. *Time,* 51.

EHRHARDT, A. A. (1984). Gender differences: A biosocial perspective. In T. B. Sonderegger (Ed.), *Psychology and gender* (pp. 37–57). Lincoln: University of Nebraska Press.

EHRHARDT, A. A., & MEYER-BEHLBURG, H. (1980). Prenatal sex hormones and the developing brain: Effects on psycho-sexual differentiation and cognitive functions. *Annual Progress in Child Psychology and Child Development,* 177–191.

FAUSTO-STERLING, A. (1985). *Myths of gender: Biological theories about women and men.* New York: Basic Books.

FRIED, C. (1997, Fall). One on one. *Sports Illustrated's Women Sport,* 70–73.

GIBBONS, A. (1991). The brain as "sexual organ." *Science, 253,* 957–959.

GILLIGAN, C. (1982). *In a different voice: Psychological theory and women's development.* Cambridge, MA: Harvard University Press.

GREENBLATT, L., HASENAUER, J. E., & FRIEMUTH, V. S. (1980). Psychological sex type and androgyny in the study of communication variables: Self-disclosure and communication apprehension. *Human Communication Research, 6,* 117–129.

GUR, R. C., GUR, R. E., OBRIST, W. D., HUNGERBUHLER, J. P., YOUNKIN, D., ROSEN, A. D., SKOLNICK, B. E., & REIVICH, M. (1982). Sex and handedness differences in cerebral blood flow during rest and cognitive activity. *Science, 217,* 659–661.

GUR, R. C., MOZLEY, L. H., MOZLEY, P. D., RESNICK, S. M., KARP, J. S., ALAVI, A., ARNOLD, S. E., & GUR, R. E. (1995). Sex differences in regional cerebral glucose metabolism during a resting state. *Science, 267,* 528–531.

HAIN, P. (1997). Personal communication, October.

HALL, E. (1987, November). All in the family. *Psychology Today,* 54–60.

HALPERN, D. (1986). *Sex differences in cognitive abilities.* Hillside, NJ: Lawrence Erlbaum.

HAMILTON, H. E. (1997, November). *Women's bodies, women's voices: Images of technology in the combat exclusion debate.* Paper presented at the meeting of the National Communication Association, Chicago, IL.

HOFFER, R. (1997, Fall). Pow! *Sports Illllustrated's Women Sport,* 74–81.

HOLDEN, C. (1991). Is the "gender gap" narrowing? *Science, 253,* 959–960.

HOUSE, A., DALLINGER, J. M., & KILGALLEN, D. L. (1998). Androgyny and rhetorical sensitivity: The connection of gender and communicator style. *Communication Reports, 11,* 11–20.

HOWARD, J. (1997, Fall). So good, so fast: How did the U.S. women shoot past the rest of the world in soccer? *Sports Illllustrated's Women Sport,* 68–69.

HYDE, J. S. (1986). Gender differences in aggression. In J. S. Hyde & M. C. Linn (Eds.), *The psychology of gender: Advances through meta-analysis* (pp. 51–66). Baltimore: Johns Hopkins University Press.

HYDE, J. S., & LINN, M. C. (1988). Gender differences in verbal ability: A meta-analysis. *Psychological Bulletin, 104,* 53–69.

JACKLIN, C. N. (1989). Female and male: Issues of gender. *The American Psychologist, 44,* 127–134.

KELLY, J. A., O'BRIEN, G. G., & HOSFORD, R. (1981). Sex roles and social skills in considerations for interpersonal adjustment. *Psychology of Women Quarterly, 5,* 758–766.

KIMURA, D. (1987). Are men's and women's brains really different? *Canadian Psychology, 28,* 133–147.

KLEIMAN, C. (1992, January 23). Males and their raging hormones. *Raleigh News and Observer,* pp. 1E, 2E.

KOHLBERG, L. (1966). A cognitive-developmental analysis of children's sex-role concepts and attitudes. In E. E. Maccoby (Ed.), *The development of sex differences* (pp. 82–173). Stanford, CA: Stanford University Press.

LASSWELL, M. (1996, February 7–13). Women's hockey comes into its own, as Team USA makes its move to win one of the sport's first Olympic medals. *TV Guide,* 18–22.

LINN, M. C., & PETERSEN, A. C. (1986). A meta-analysis of gender differences in spatial ability: Implications for mathematics and science achievement. In J. S. Hyde & M. C. Linn (Eds.), *The psychology of gender: Advances through meta-analysis* (pp. 67–101). Baltimore: Johns Hopkins University Press.

MACCOBY, E. E., & JACKLIN, C. (1974). *The psychology of sex differences.* Stanford, CA: Stanford University Press.

MACCOBY, E. E., & JACKLIN, C. (1980). Sex differences in aggression: A rejoinder and reprise. *Child Development, 5,* 964–980.

MCLOUGHLIN, M., SHRYER, T. L., GOODE, E. E., & MCAULIFFE, K. (1988, August 8). Men vs. women. *U.S. News & World Report,* 50–56.

MISCHEL, W. (1966). A social learning view of sex differences in behavior. In E. E. Maccoby (Ed.), *The development of sex differences* (pp. 56–81). Stanford, CA: Stanford University Press.

PARSONS, T., & BALES, R. (1955). *Family, socialization, and interaction process.* New York: Free Press.

PEACH, L. J. (1998). Women in culture: Introduction. In L. J. Peach (Ed.), *Women in culture: A women's studies anthology* (pp. 1–12). Malden, MA: Blackwell.

PHILLIPS, J. (1997, July-August). A new season for women's sports. *Ms.,* 86–88.

PLECK, J. H. (1975). Masculinity-femininity: Current and alternative paradigms. *Sex Roles, 1,* 161–178.

PLECK, J. H. (1977). The psychology of sex roles: Traditional and new views. In L. A. Cater, A. F. Scott, & W. Martyna (Eds.), *Women and men: Changing roles, relationships, and perceptions* (pp. 181–199). New York: Praeger.

RAMEY, E. (1976). Men's cycles (They have them too you know). In A. Kaplan & J. Bean (Eds.), *Beyond sex-role stereotypes.* Boston: Little Brown.

RICHMOND-ABBOTT, M. (1992). *Masculine and feminine: Gender roles over the life cycle.* New York: McGraw-Hill.

RUBLE, D. N., BALABAN, T., & COOPER, J. (1981). Gender constancy and the effects of sex-typed televised toy commercials. *Child Development, 52,* 667–673.

SALTER, S. (1997, November 3). Women refs will blaze a difficult trail. *Corpus Christi Caller Times,* p. A15.

SCHAFER, S. M. (1998, March 1). Recruits, sergeants differ on coed training. *Corpus Christi Caller Times,* pp. A17, A18.

SHAPIRO, L. (1990, May 28). Guns and dolls. *Newsweek,* 56–65.

STARR, M., & ROSENBERG, D. (1997, March 24). She's breaking the ice. *Newsweek,* 67.

STEINBERG, L. (1995, June 18). Mr. Moms find same rewards, pressures as women. *Corpus Christi Caller Times,* pp. G1, G3.

STOCKARD, J., & JOHNSON, M. (1980). *Sex roles.* Englewood Cliffs, NJ: Prentice-Hall.

TAVRIS, C. (1992). *The mismeasure of woman.* New York: Simon & Schuster.

THORNTON, J. (1992, March). His brain is different. *Self,* 114–116, 164, 166.

UNGER, R., & CRAWFORD, M. (1996). *Women and gender: A feminist psychology* (2nd ed.). New York: McGraw-Hill.

WHITE, D. (1998, July 12). Stay-at-home dad shares sacrifices, rewards of new role. *Corpus Christi Caller Times,* pp. H1, H3.

WOOD, J. T., & LENZE, L. F. (1991). Gender and the development of self: Inclusive pedagogy in interpersonal communication. *Women's Studies in Communication, 14,* 1–23.

CHAPTER THREE

BECOMING A WOMAN, BECOMING A MAN, AND BECOMING A PERSON

The Development of Gender-Role Identity

CASE STUDY

For a boy growing up in the 1950s and 1960s, male gender roles were well defined. Movie and TV role models included John Wayne, Robert Young, Marshall Dillon. Macho images of "we can do it all" ruled. Men didn't cry, never showed their feelings, handled everything, were invulnerable, and dominated women. One young boy, Mark, was small, thin, and felt much less than confident. In high school he was a nerd and his friends were other nerds. College was not much better. He and most of his friends still judged their masculinity against the cultural stereotype and found themselves coming up short.

In the early 1970s, Mark was a graduate student in a department of sociology that had only one female professor (Kathy). A few male professors believed women had no business teaching college because they were not smart enough or capable of mentoring male graduate students. In addition, these men saw women professors as an obvious distraction. After three years of harassment, Kathy left. Mark found this astonishing because Kathy was easily the best teacher in the department and had helped Mark a great deal. This injustice caused Mark to begin to learn about discrimination against women through reading about the developing feminist movement. As Mark learned about changing roles for women, he also learned about masculine models and found out that the stereotyped model was not the only one available. As Mark learned about different roles for men, he changed his former belief that he was somehow deficient because he wasn't macho enough. His self-concept changed and his self-esteem improved.

Mark's situation matched the experience of many women and men of that era. American society had relatively rigid definitions of masculinity and femininity. The women's movement caused a reexamination of gender roles at both the individual and the societal levels, resulting in a broadening of role definitions. For many men and women, this reexamination allowed them to understand and accept themselves more fully even if they didn't match the stereotype. Mark's son Steve, growing up in the 1980s and 1990s, has the advantage of a broader range of role models in the media and in real life. We still have Rambo and Arnold, but we also have Robin Williams and Paul Reiser.

In Chapters 1 and 2, we made a distinction between biological sex and socially constructed gender. Biological sex begins with anatomy and extends to all the potentials and limits that come with that anatomy. Socially constructed gender refers to the significance or meaning related to that anatomy by the culture. Some researchers regard gender roles as a completely social construction used to organize society and shape its individual members (Epstein, 1988). In this view, gender not only shapes a personal identity, but it shapes society as well. As Epstein (1988) states, "gender distinctions are basic to the social order of all societies . . . gender orders society and is ordered by it " (p. 6).

As gender is basic to a person's identity and to society, questions of how gender-role identity develops and how it impacts communication become important to our consideration of personal effectiveness in gender communication. What does it mean to be a woman in this culture? To be a man? How does a person "become" a man or a woman? What does this have to do with gender communication?

Hot Topics

- Gender as a socially constructed concept.
- Changing definitions of masculine and feminine
- Social functions of stereotypes
- Development of self—how society "gets into" the person
- Theories of socialization including gender schema theory
- Impact on gender identity development of family, school, play, toys, clothes, and games
- Gender identity, self-esteem, and change
- Development of self through social relationships
- Conforming to socially approved gender identity and the risks of nonconformity

BECOMING A GIRL OR A BOY: CONSTRUCTING GENDER

The first question out of virtually anyone's mouth after the birth of a baby is, "Is it a girl or a boy?" If those asking the question didn't find out the baby's sex, perhaps they wouldn't know how to treat the baby. Recall "The Story of X," which we referred to in Chapter 1, a short story in which the parents kept the sex of their child hidden until physical development made it obvious. People just didn't know what to do with the child, or how to treat "it." Without knowing the sex of the child, how could "it" be socialized into the right identity? The consternation shown by the people in the story shows how strongly we use gender as an organizing theme for all sorts of communication behavior.

This chapter begins with a consideration of sex and gender, focusing on what each brings to identity development. In describing gender as socially constructed, we point out that different societies construct gender in different ways. If gender roles can be defined differently at the societal level, then it follows that they also can be defined differently at the individual level. Through this chapter, you may gain a greater awareness of how your own gender role has been constructed and what you might do to change your performance of that role if you think it useful.

Biological Sex

Original thoughts on gender and sex held that male-female differences were born with the person. Men became mechanics because men were born with those attributes. Women were caregivers because they were born with those attributes. Obviously, this view of gender role identity did not allow for potential changes or individual differences. Biology does not account for everything, but it does have an impact.

Effects of Biology

After birth, biological sex sets the female and male infant on distinctly different paths. Some psychologists contend that the basic fact that women are caregivers for both male and female infants begins a developmental process that leads daughters to define themselves through a primary identification with the mother and sons through a primary separation from the mother (Chodorow, 1989). Boys' process of separation begins to establish a masculine identity based in independence and distance as central components of the male identity.

Communication researcher Anderson (1998) supports this view and believes that any analysis of sex and gender differences should begin with an analysis of the two basic differences between men and women: mating and childrearing. He describes a biologically based view of mating that maintains a man is biologically predisposed to mate with a range of women in an effort to ensure that his genes will continue. Women, on the other hand, want their children to survive. This means they are selective in their mates, seeking the strongest and the best. This basic biological fact depicts men as the sexual initiator or aggressor and women as selective (to the limits of the right to choose). The second aspect Anderson discusses is childrearing. It only takes a man a few minutes to make his contribution to the birth of a child, but it takes a woman years of care to develop her offspring. This factor helps make the male sex the one that ranges far and wide, gathers the food, and has the adventures. Women stay at home.

However, Anderson (1998) goes on to make the point that biology is not destiny. He cites a number of sources (Archer, 1991; Halpern, 1986; Rosaldo, 1974) to support this point. Halpern (1986) states: "biological determinism allows the possibility that females and males may, by self-determination or some other means, overcome sex-related biological predictions or tendencies" (p. 68). Anderson summarizes the sentiments by stating, "Biological sex differences create biological tendencies—they do not determine individual's behavior . . . a thorough review of the evidence on sex differences reveals that they are a function of culture, biology, and their interaction" (p. 98).

A point accepted almost without question is that each sex *must* have an identity—masculine or feminine, one or the other. Why? Is this the best view? Gould (1988) was one researcher who believed that we should avoid polarization of gender identity and that men and women can exhibit behaviors generally associated with the other sex depending on the situation. Men can be caregivers (and do quite well) when the situation calls for it; women can be strong and assertive when they choose. While this sounds like common sense, when this view was first expressed it marked the first time gender-related behaviors were seen as separate from both biological sex and gender-role identity. Gender-related behaviors are just that—behaviors—and they aren't necessarily part of the individual who is doing the behaving. This view fits well with our idea of personal effectiveness—an individual can "borrow" any behavior he or she chooses, irrespective of the sex with which it is normally associated.

This push and struggle for a gender-role identity affects a child throughout his or her life. Biology is not destiny, and neither is socialization. The different paths biology begins can be altered through maturation, social interaction, and self-talk (Wood, 1994). Changing gender-role identity is one of the central points of this text and will be touched on again later in this chapter.

Biology and Behavior

In North American society, people presume that there are two and only two sexes. All people are one or the other, and no person changes sex without major surgery. This belief links gender so strongly to sex that many see the two classifications as the same. Because gender and sex are so strongly linked, children (and some adults) tend to see them both as containing two distinct, nonoverlapping groups. A boy is a boy and a girl is a girl. As children mature, it sometimes takes direct educational intervention if they are to learn that gender is not necessarily dualistic and that an individual person may have a blend of feminine and masculine characteristics—exactly what we advocate in this text.

The distinction between sex and gender reflects different perspectives or assumptions about the causes of behavior. The use of the term *sex* conveys the assumption that an individual's characteristics are an essential part of her or his personality. Sex differences in communication behavior are part of the nature of men and women, but gender differences originate in the social system rather than within the individual (Unger, 1990). Biological sex forms the basis for a social categorization system known as gender (Keashly, 1994).

Using the term *gender* differences, then, implies that behaviors are a reflection of societal beliefs and expectations. As such, behaviors can be chosen; one does not *have* to behave as society would prescribe.

Clearly, a view of gender differences based in biological sex will not work as a theory of individual gender identity. If gender roles are not based in biological differences or innate tendencies, in what are they based?

Gender as an Organizing Construct for Individuals and Society

Socialization can be defined as the process through which individuals learn their culture, develop their potential, and become functioning members of society (Lindzey, 1997). The primary vehicle for this socialization is communication. Individuals are socialized into a culture that defines which behaviors are considered appropriate. Social institutions such as the family, religion, and education provide training grounds for "how to be." In addition to these broad social institutions, a wide variety of subcultures exist. These range from the general (corporate and recreational) to the very specific (Hell's Angels). Within each of these cultures, gender roles are defined (Lindzey, 1997). Gender permeates not only levels of society, but its systems as well. Our judicial system, military system, religious system, educational system, and to a large extent, our corporate system are gendered in that each system describes how men and women are to behave in the system and sometimes dictates how they will relate to each other (Wood, 1993). Advice is everywhere.

Norms and Stereotypes

In each level of society, social norms guide expectations and actions that can differ according to gender. Considering the various classes you are in, are there different expectations for women and men in any of these classes? Is there, perhaps, an expectation that a man will take the lead in small group discussion? Will women be more passive? In this situation, what would happen if a woman took a strong, assertive lead in the small group? In many situations, choosing another course of action, deviating from the norm, creates social disapproval ("Who does she think *she* is?"). Conformity to the norms becomes a means for social control. How many times have you felt pressure to behave in a stereotypic way as a man or woman?

Social influence is effective, particularly when it encourages continuation of stereotyped portrayal of the sexes. Stereotypes can be useful, but they are often too general, exaggerated, inaccurate, and unfavorable, and they are very difficult to dislodge. Problems occur when a person builds up mental pictures of a sex and then defines all members of the sex according to these images, regardless of individual differences. This process becomes negative when individuals are damaged because they are defined in terms of assumed group characteristics. If a man is stereotyped as strong, then he may be viewed negatively if he expresses weakness or vulnerability. Social pressure makes it difficult to be different from what the culture says one should be.

Even when a person or couple is different than the norm, the difference may be explained in terms of the norm. Sociologist Hochschild (1989) argued that culture designates particular emotions as appropriate for genders and individuals through what he termed "feeling rules." These rules govern how individuals engage in emotional work and how they learn to recognize which feelings are appropriate and which ones need to be repressed. Hochschild (1989) described a couple whose relationship was at odds with the cultural norm in that the woman in the relationship was a highly paid executive. Both husband and wife found her salary embarrassing, kept it a secret from family and friends, and did not discuss it between themselves. His gender identity precluded him from recognizing her financial contribution and her identity precluded her from expecting any type of help from him regarding the homemaking chores. The two individuals appeared to have a nontraditional relationship, but the discrepancy between the society-prescribed norms and the relationship reality led both participants to develop explanatory rationalizations rather than to accept their situation. They used traditional values to rationalize their differences from the norm.

Cultural Differences in the Construction of Gender

One way of understanding the nature of gender as a social construction is to compare the white, middle-class view of gender with other cultures' view of gender. Social conceptions of gender vary widely. For example, Waldron and Mare (1998) analyzed gender as a culturally determined construct in Japan and the United States. They found that culture was a more influential variable than sex on communication style. American women and men were relatively similar in communication styles, and Japanese women and men were also relatively similar to each other in communication styles; but there were large differences between the two cultures. This suggests that culture and biological sex act together in determining the gender communication style of a given person.

The North American dualistic view of gender is not the only way culture is conceived in all societies. Devor (1992) describes aboriginal cultures that have more than two gender categories and that accept the idea that gender may be changed without changes in biological sex. Some North and South American native peoples have legitimate social categories for persons who wish to live according to the gender role of another sex. For these cultures, gender is completely unrelated to sex.

In the United States, researchers have compared different economic levels and racial groups for gender differences. When considering socioeconomic levels as a factor, it appears gender roles are more flexible in middle-class families than in working- and lower-class families (Lackey, 1989; Lips, 1995), though families who move upward socially tend to be more likely to embrace traditional gender roles (Lips, 1993). Race also has an impact. Research indicates that African-Americans hold less stereotyped behavioral expectations according to gender than whites. African-American women are esteemed for their independence and strength, and African-American children are socialized into gender beliefs that are less rigid than those among whites (Binion, 1990; Houston & Wood, 1996; Lips, 1995). African-American men and women are more

---

RECAP

---

biological sex, gender, socialization, social norms, stereotypes, cultural differences

---

androgynous than whites of both sexes (Deleon, 1993). Compared to whites, African-American children are socialized to view gender as less polarized (McAdoo, 1990), though African-American parents tend to express greater concern for their girls to be feminine and their boys masculine (Dugger, 1991).

For Hispanic populations such as Puerto Rican and Mexican-American, the data show stronger support for a more deferentially subordinate female role than in either African-American or white populations. Hispanic societies also place motherhood above all else (Garcia, 1991; Lips, 1995). This role is reinforced by powerful religious socialization that tends to promote subservience to men (Anzaldua, 1995). Studies also show that Hispanic men do not normally exhibit excessive masculinity by the standards of the broader American culture. Economic patterns, cultural values of family, nurturance, and concern for others frequently moderate excessive masculinity (Deleon, 1993).

Most societies use sex and gender as a significant way to understand the world around them. People, objects, and ideas are commonly characterized as inherently male or female (Devor, 1992). Some languages, such as Spanish and French, have sex-linked designations. For example, in Spanish, a table is feminine (*la mesa*) and a floor is masculine (*el piso*). Gender, then, becomes a nearly universally accepted organizing construct. In these languages, gender is a legitimate way to classify objects and people.

DEFINITIONS OF FEMININITY AND MASCULINITY

Communication writers West and Zimmerman (1987) commented that a person does not *have* gender, but *does* gender. Since gender is a social construct based in social interaction, definitions of femininity and masculinity can and do change according to the needs of the society that creates the definition (Deaux & Lafrance, 1998). In the previous section, we made the point that gender is constructed. This section describes some of the ways in which it has been constructed.

A Little History

When American society was organized more closely around agriculture, the differences between masculine and feminine were less distinct (Cancian, 1989). Both women and men assumed responsibility for the family and for economic survival. Since the husband's work was in the same physical location as that of the wife (or very close to it), the two were much more interdependent. This interdependence created, to a degree, a sense of shared and relatively equal responsibility for the family. However, when factories emerged and men began to work in a place outside the home, the concept of separate gender identities expanded greatly. Men's working environment and separateness led to an impersonal, public, do-the-job, and utilitarian attitude. Women remained at home and became more directly associated with the personal, the private, the nurturing, and the emotional (Ryan, 1979). Women also began to be referred to as weak and decorative, inferior, negative, and trivial (Monedas, 1992).

Although agrarian societies were more equal in sharing responsibility, sharing did not translate into social influence for women. Admonitions against women's speech are very old, dating back to biblical times. Communication researchers Borisoff and Merrill (1998) detail societal sanctions against women's participation in public discourse. In fact, many male doctors and educators (in the 19th century there were very few female professionals) believed "that the female brain and internal organs would be injured by sustained intellectual effort" (Borisoff & Merrill, 1998).

As society slowly changed, so did definitions of feminine and masculine. Qualities that had been important to women in agricultural life such as ambition, strength, and decisiveness were slowly deleted from the feminine gender identity. Qualities important to men in agricultural society such as emotionality, nurturance, and interdependence (essential to family life) were likewise removed from the masculine gender identity. As women were confined to the private domain, femininity was redefined as nurturing, relational, and caring for others. As men became more removed from the home, masculinity was redefined to include independence, aggressiveness, self-control, and achievement (Cancian, 1989).

Stereotyped Definitions of Femininity and Masculinity

Stereotypes have been around for a long time and, as we indicated earlier, have lasted well past their usefulness. However, if we are to contemplate changing gender identity, examining the stereotypes is a useful place to begin.

Stereotyped definitions of both sexes were summarized by communication researchers Borisoff and Merrill (1998). The stereotyped woman, they said, is to be soft-spoken (when she speaks at all), self-effacing by reflecting uncertainty and humbleness, compliant through submissiveness, emotional, and subjective. The stereotyped man should be an ineffective listener, emotionally inexpressive, categorical and certain in his language use, and dominating in discussions. Other sources (Brannon 1976; Lindzey, 1997) summarize masculinity as including five points:

1. Allow no sissy stuff (feminine characteristics).
2. Be a big wheel (emphasize money and status).
3. Be a sturdy oak (tough and confident).
4. Give 'em hell (be daring, aggressive, and violent).
5. Be a macho man (emphasize sexual aggression and conquests).

Even within gender role definitions, subtypes have emerged. For example, male subtypes include the athlete, blue-collar worker, businessman, and macho man. For women, subtypes include housewife, career woman, sexy woman, and feminist. Characteristic behaviors depend on which subtype the person falls into (Deaux & Lafrance, 1998).

According to the traditional definition, femininity results in warm and continued relationships with men, a sense of maternity, interest in caring for children, and the capacity to work productively and continuously in female occupations (Devor, 1992). This definition leads to all sorts of prescriptions for female behavior. Warm and continued relations with men and an interest in maternity suggest that women be heterosexual, which in turn requires women to focus on their attractiveness to men. Since power is supposedly a masculine attribute, femininity must be expressed through movement, dress, and speech that communicates weakness, vulnerability, ineffectualness, and availability for service.

In contrast, Pleck (1981) said masculinity in our society is conveyed through one or more of the following:

1. Displaying success or high status in their social group.
2. Exhibiting a manly air of toughness, confidence, and self-reliance.
3. Demonstrating aggression, violence, and daring.
4. Avoiding anything associated with femininity.

This definition requires men to organize themselves and society in a hierarchical manner. Competition is motivated by a goal of individual achievement, and it requires participants to show a degree of emotional insensitivity to the hurt or loss of others. This stereotype leaves little room for relationships.

These societal stereotypes and personal definitions of the self interact in some interesting ways. For example, a person who believes the gender stereotypes about emotional expression is likely to report that his or her own emotions match the stereotype (Grossman & Wood, 1993). Women who believe that the intensity of emotional experience is greater for women than for men reported personally experiencing more intense emotions. In contrast, men who endorse gender stereotypes indicating that men are less emotional report fewer emotional feelings. People who believe the stereotypes tend to live their lives according to the stereotypes.

Changing the Stereotype

The societal conditions that gave rise to the current stereotypic definitions of masculinity and femininity occurred over a hundred years ago, and these conditions have changed a great deal in the past three decades. However, the definitions themselves have not. Riesman (1990) said the "institutionalized roles of husband and wife continue to provide a blueprint for marriage, situating men's work primarily in the public sphere and women's in the private sphere" (p. 51). Femininity remains linked to the home, family, emotional expressiveness, and caring for others. Masculinity continues to focus on the public areas of work and is associated with power, relationally emotional reserve, and productivity (Wood, 1994).

Changing Masculinity

In an article with the interesting title, "Thicker Thighs by Thanksgiving," writer Ann Dobosz (1997) describes the new wave of men's magazines such as *Men's Health, Details, Maxim,* and *Men's Fitness,* which focus on self-improvement and include topics such as diet tips, relationship columns, sex advice, health information, and information on how to do "masculine" better. Men's magazines are catching up to what women's magazines have been doing for years. The danger, as Dobosz points out, is that the focus on "shaving creams, sexual performance, and well-toned abs may create a men's culture as warped and obsessive as women's mass culture" (p. 91). Is that what we want?

Writer Michael Segell (1996) commented on the changing masculine role in his article "The Second Coming of the Alpha Male," which he described as "a guide to blending the best of traditional male behavior with the fresh emotional insight called psychological potency" (p. 13). He argued for the utility of certain traditional aspects of the male role such as fearlessness, the ability to completely hide emotions, the ability to take risks, and the ability to be aggressive. According to Segell, aggression and dominance (male characteristics), not sensitivity and submissiveness (female characteristics) were responsible for superior self-esteem in both men and women. "For men seeking new challenges to prove their adequacy, there is perhaps no greater one than reversing the decline of the role of the father in the family" (p. 17). While women have taught men a great deal in the past two decades, "Men can also show off their inherent talents by sharing them with their wives. Teach them the merits of doing rather than feeling, putting a filter on emotions in the workplace, and developing a problem-solving approach to conflicts. Each sex still has something the other desperately wants" (p. 17).

However, Cooper Thompson, a writer and speaker about changing men's roles, maintains that taken to an extreme, masculinity promotes violence (Thompson, 1992). For example, he found that high school boys use the word *fag* as the most humiliating put-down. If a boy is called a fag, it means that he is perceived as weak or timid—and therefore not masculine enough for his peers. There is enormous pressure for him to fight back, and not being tough at these moments only proves the allegation (Thompson, 1992). This leads boys to what Thompson sees as the two most critical socializing forces in a boy's life:

> Homophobia, the hatred of gay men (who are stereotyped as feminine) or those men believed to be gay, as well as the fear of being perceived as gay; and misogyny, the hatred of women . . . Homophobia is the hatred of feminine qualities in men while misogyny is the hatred of the feminine in women . . . . The United States Marines have a philosophy which conveniently combines homophobia and misogyny in the belief that "When you want to create a group of male killers, you kill 'the women' in them." (p. 79)

The cost of being this masculine is high. Toughness leads to increased chances of stress, physical injury, and early death (Thompson, 1992). The societal cost is also high. Many women encounter male resistance to the expansion of women's roles, men who are not willing to accept women as equals, and in a wide variety of settings, men who are continuously engaged in attempts to dominate.

Thompson (1992) suggests that boys must learn a different pattern. Boys must express a range of emotions and learn nonviolent means of resolving conflicts. They must learn to accept vulnerability, to ask for help, to be gentle and nurturing, and to accept those attitudes and behaviors that have traditionally been labeled as feminine. Clearly, certain qualities such as courage, physical strength, and independence, which have been traditionally associated with masculinity, are positive qualities and should be nurtured in men and developed in women.

Changing the stereotypical masculine role has not been and will not be easy. Both roles are rooted in long-standing cultural patterns. Awareness of options and support for those options are the only two vehicles for making the change possible.

Changing Femininity

The cultural definitions of femininity have a history of negative characteristics. Have these negative views changed? Greene (1997) examined psychological perspectives on the meaning of *feminine* and *femininity* from the early part of this century to the present. She concluded that although times have changed and definitions have moved from negative to a celebration of the feminine, the cultural belief in two distinct genders makes it unlikely that future meanings of femininity will not be influenced by their biological roots. In similar research Lueptow, Garovich, and Lueptow (1995) compared gender stereotypes as measured by ratings of adjectives reflecting masculine or feminine traits across a 17-year period from 1974 to 1991 in over 3600 college students. Contrary to predictions and despite dramatic changes in sex roles and attitudes during this time period, perceptions of gender-typed personality traits not only stayed stable but slightly increased. These are not encouraging results.

However, there is some evidence that perceptions are changing slightly. Jackson, Fleury, and Lewandowski (1996) examined sex differences in definitions of feminism and support for feminism. They found some men supportive of feminism and changes in the traditional stereotype. It is interesting to note that these were men who scored high on stereotypic feminine characteristics. Pennell and Ogilvie (1995) compared the use of gender-related concepts in other- and self-perception with female and male college students. They found that being feminine was evaluated more positively than being masculine in the perception of others. Feminine characteristics were viewed as useful.

These few research results do not prove a trend. Their mixed character mirrors the struggles of society to search out the most meaningful changes to long-standing role definitions. Many of the questions of change need to be answered at the level of the individual. Each of us needs to decide how to be a woman or a man. Each of us can be supportive of others who are attempting positive change.

Gender Identity as Prophecy

Gender identity definitions can be a self-fulfilling prophecy. For example, women who believe that the intensity of emotional experience is greater for women than it is for men report experiencing more intense emotions. Men who endorse gender stereotypes indicating that men are less emotional, report few emotional feelings. Both men and women who accept gender stereotypes are more likely to report stereotypic levels of self-esteem (Deaux & Lafrance, 1998).

Likewise, gender identity is an "other-fulfilling" prophecy. The influence of other people's expectations are well established in social psychology. Belonging to a social group will have a strong influence on one's behavior. If a boy in junior high school belongs to a group that makes sexual jokes about girls, he is likely to make the jokes and laugh at others' jokes to prove he is one of the guys. More pervasively, when people hold different expectations for the performance of women and men, they will be likely to act on these expectations in such a way as to shape the opportunities available to the individual man or woman (Deaux & Lafrance, 1998). This, in turn, influences the man or woman to behave in a particular way.

In sum, most people simply cannot live up to the ideal of masculinity and femininity as commonly defined. The frustration and disillusionment that may set in when the ideal is not reached can have lasting effects on the individual's self-esteem (Bate & Bowker, 1997). Unthinking acceptance of the gender stereotypes can have severe negative effects on the individual. The more one consciously knows about options in defining femininity and masculinity, the easier it is to select a definition that fits one's own personality.

Gender is a relatively complex concept. Originally masculinity and femininity were seen as opposite ends of the same spectrum. Masculine was opposite of feminine, and both were defined to the exclusion of the other. These definitions both shaped the personality of men and women, but more importantly, they shaped the way each sex was treated. If we begin moving away from sex-based gender identity to a more inclusive human-based gender identity, we allow each sex a broader range of acceptable behaviors. Do you think it possible to develop definitions to the point where gender identity is not sex based at all, but more dependent on how each individual defines herself or himself?

RECAP

---

social construct, femininity, masculinity, agrarian society, nurturance, interdependence, aggression, stereotyped definitions, alpha male, homophobia, self-fulfilling prophecy, other-fulfilling prophecy

LEARNING TO BE GIRLS AND BOYS

How do we learn to be boys and girls? We learn first based on how we are treated by people important to us. Gender perceptions act as an organizing factor in how people perceive another person. For example, research on perception of infants clearly shows that adults of both sexes view the same behavior differently depending on whether the infant is labeled a boy or a girl (regardless of the real sex). Infants labeled as boys were reported as showing more pleasure and less fear than those labeled girls. Negative emotions displayed were identified as anger when the observer thought the infant was a boy and as fear when the observer thought the infant was a girl (Condry & Condry, 1976). Masculine and feminine labels make a difference in how an infant is treated. An angry infant is likely to be reprimanded or ignored, whereas a fearful one is likely to be held and soothed (Stewart, Cooper, Stewart, & Friedley, 1996). Research has shown that parents talk with daughters more and that from just after birth until about two years of age, daughters tend to be more responsive, demonstrate more social competence, and have a higher level of social involvement with the mother (Golinkoff & Ames, 1979; Gunnar & Donahue, 1980). Communication scholars Barbara Bate and Judith Bowker (1997) make the interesting point that "In the United States we often have the circumstance of a girl who learned to play sports because 'my dad wanted a boy.' We rarely have the circumstance of a boy who learns to sew because 'my mom wanted a girl'" (p. 19).

Learning continues through the first few years of life. Devor (1992) describes the developmental view of gender in young children from 3 through 8 years old. The interesting aspect of children's understanding of gender is that they believe gender to be changeable. They see gender not as being based on anatomy, but as a role that can be changed much like changing a hair style. As children start to understand themselves as individuals separate from others, they begin to understand that others see them and respond to them as particular people and as a particular gender. Children first learn gender roles based on what sociologists call the "generalized other." This is a generalized view of women and men in their gender roles. As children get older, interaction with certain people or modeling leads them to see some people as "significant others." These individuals begin to shape the individual meanings of gender for the particular child.

Parental perceptions, significant others, and role models all guide parents' behavior toward the child, thus helping form the child's own definition of his or her gender role. These factors shape gender-role development. The theories described below attempt to account for how this shaping occurs.

Theories of Socialization

Learning how one acquires gender roles gives insight into controlling or changing the effects of the process. The theories presented below describe different perspectives on how a person becomes gendered.

Social Learning Theory

Social learning theory considers socialization basically in terms of rewards and punishments. Children gain approval and are rewarded for appropriate behavior and punished for doing something inappropriate. Like other behaviors, gender roles are learned directly through reprimands and rewards, and indirectly through observation and imitation (Bandura, 1986). The logic is simple. Different reinforcement occurs for doing either girl things or boy things. In thinking about the consequences of girl or boy behavior, the child learns to behave so that the label applied to herself or himself is associated with rewards. This becomes the basis for gender identity. A child develops an awareness that the two sexes behave differently and that two gender roles are proper. Parents, teachers, and peers model gender role behavior during these critical primary socialization years, and children imitate. Social learning theory is not interested in biological influences, unconscious motivation, or other internal processes, but views gender socialization in terms of environmental influences.

Boys seem to have more difficulty learning their role than girls. Lynn (1969) tried to account for this difficulty by asserting that male role models in early childhood are scarce and boys must somehow manage to put together a definition of masculinity based on incomplete information. They are often told what they should not do rather than what they should do ("Boys don't cry"). Girls have a somewhat easier time in this regard because of continuous contact with the mother and the ease of using her as a model. Lynn further contended that a lack of exposure to male role models at an early age leads boys to view masculinity in a stereotyped manner. This may help explain why the male model is usually seen as less flexible and why males remain insecure about their gender identity. Social learning theorists claim that there are numerous consequences. Male peer groups encourage the belief that aggression and toughness are virtues, exhibit hostility to both females and homosexuals, and view cross-gender behavior among males more negatively than when it occurs in females. Men's fear of ridicule results in exaggerated antihomosexual and sexist remarks to ensure that others do not get the wrong idea (Lindzey, 1997). Through the social learning process, a boy learns to prefer the masculine role, deciding that it is more desirable and brings more esteem.

Girls do not have it much easier, if at all. Even young children are bombarded with stimuli that suggests that higher worth, prestige, and rewards are accorded to the male. Boys can embrace the gender roles that flow from these messages. Girls on the other hand, are offered gender roles associated with less worth and must model behavior that may be held in low esteem. Some young girls, when given a choice, say they would prefer to be boys (Geis, 1993), though it usually doesn't take too long before many girls come to prefer the female role over the male, perhaps due to the increased flexibility.

The gender role identity of parents can influence the type of behavior rewarded and punished in their children. For example, in a large-scale study of mothers and their children, Jacobs and Eccles (1992) explored the influence of gender-stereotypic beliefs on mothers' perceptions of 11- and 12-year-old children. The results showed that mothers who had more strongly held gender stereotypes believed their daughters had lower math ability and their sons had higher math ability. Similar patterns were found for the mothers' estimates of their children's sports ability—they believed their sons were more athletic than their daughters. These beliefs were further shown to influence the children's own assessment of their abilities, which reflected the biased views of the mothers. These gender stereotypes, mediated by the beliefs mothers held about their own children's ability, affected the degree to which children believe they did or did not have ability in math and in social domains.

Social role can also influence how people learn their gender role, as women's and men's behavior is, to an extent, a function of social role in addition to gender role. Both men and women are more dominant in a social role that calls for dominance (for example, supervisor) than in roles that call for submissiveness (employee). Apparently, people can shift from dominant to submissive behaviors as a function of their current interaction (Deaux & Lafrance, 1998). If behaviors can change to match the situation, different types of rewards and punishments could likely change how people view their gender roles.

Certainly imitation and rewards are important, but social learning theory's drawback is its inconsistency. For example, a girl may be rewarded for a masculine activity, such as excelling at sports, but retain other aspects of her feminine role. The rewards and punishments appear to be related to specific behaviors, not a personality pattern.

Cognitive Development Theory

Cognitive development theory offers another view of the process of gender-role socialization. Simply put, a child's level of understanding of the world varies with the stage of cognitive development. The mind matures through interaction with the environment. Unlike social learning theory, the child takes an active role in structuring her or his world. Kohlberg (1966), who formulated the model, claims that children learn their gender roles according to their level of cognitive development and their degree of comprehension of the world.

In Kohlberg's view, children do not recognize the permanence of their sex until between the ages of five and seven, though by age three children begin to self-identify by sex and accurately apply gender-related labels to themselves. Although they are too young to understand that all people can be so labeled, this is the beginning of gender identity. By age six, a girl knows she is a girl and will remain one. It is at this point that a gender identity can be developed. Also at this point, the child begins to develop a sense of the self, and as gender is a central part of the self, the two become strongly entwined (Lindzey, 1997).

Once children develop a gender identity, they organize most of their behavior around it. It is at this point that children actively seek models that are labeled as girl or boy or male or female. Identification with the same-sex parent begins to occur. As a child understands her or his own gender, she or he will tend to behave in a manner consistent with that label, saying, in effect, "I am a boy; therefore I want to do boy things." Psychologists Martin and Little (1990) found that "once children can accurately label the sexes, they begin to form gender stereotypes and their behavior is influenced by these gender-associated expectations" (p. 1438). The opportunity to do boy things (and to gain approval for them) is rewarding. Social learning theory applies here, but while reinforcements are important, the child essentially wants to perform roles consistent with her or his own self. Gender consistency motivates children to seek out social interactions where they can learn gender appropriate behavior.

However, like social learning theory, cognitive development theory cannot account for the whole of gender-role socialization.

Gender Schema Theory

Gender schema theory states that once the child learns an appropriate cultural definition of gender, this definition becomes the key structure around which all other information is organized (Bem, 1983). A schema is a cognitive structure that helps to interpret the world. Before a schema can be formulated and gender-related information viewed through it, the child must be old enough to accurately identify gender. When a girl learns that cultural prescriptions for femininity include politeness and kindness, she incorporates these traits into her emerging schema and she begins to behave in a polite and kind way. This type of schema provides prescriptions about how to behave and can strongly influence a child's sense of self-esteem. How a child feels about himself or herself as a person becomes tied to adequacy in behaving according to gender schema.

As children develop gender schema, they increasingly use them as key organizing perspectives. Schema related to a child's own sex appear to develop first, and they become more complex and detailed than schema for the other sex. Using his or her own schema, a child takes in new information, plans activities, and chooses roles. The development and subsequent role of gender schema may help us understand why it is so difficult to dislodge gender-stereotypical thinking.

Bem (1983) concluded from her research with adults that people who are the most sex-typed are also those who process new information on the basis of gender differences. In cultures that closely adhere to attitudes emphasizing gender differentiation, gender schemas are likely to be complex and elaborate. More recent work by Bem (1993) on gender socialization provides another perspective for gender schema theory that describes the effect culture has on gender acquisition. According to Bem, every culture contains assumptions about behavior that are part of its social institutions. She maintains that there are three fundamental culturally-shared beliefs regarding males and females:

1. Women and men are totally different and opposite beings.
2. Males are superior to females.
3. Biology produces natural and inevitable gender roles.

> # *RECAP*
>
> ---
>
> generalized other, significant other, socialization, social learning theory, reinforcement, social role, cognitive development theory, gender schema theory, gender polarization

Despite evidence against gender polarization and biological predestination, these beliefs remain. Bem notes that most children accept these beliefs without recognizing that alternatives are possible. As these children grow older, they cannot envision their (or any) society organized differently. As a theory, gender schema provides another view of how we learn our gender roles. Each of the three theories we discussed helps explain the socialization process, though none explains it completely.

Exploring the role of information in this process can be illuminating. If learning is based on information, one might reasonably ask if there is an equal amount of information available about boys and girls. It would appear that there is not. Both girls and boys receive more information from society about boys and men than about girls and women (Lindzey, 1997). Since both boys and girls receive less information about girls and women, boys may not easily develop an ability to talk about female interests, and girls' self-esteem may suffer. Without a balance of information, both sexes may not learn very much about feminine values and attributes. Gender beliefs are usually learned at an age when children do not have the ability to evaluate the information. Thus, they learn the expectations of gender-related behavior and incorporate them into their daily lives, and the behavior comes to feel "natural." While some of this learning can be altered by parents, friends, and the like, these cultural lessons are very enduring and difficult to change later in life when it may be both useful and important to do so.

The Family as a Socializing Agent

The family is by far the most significant agent of socialization. Gender differences in treatment of female and male children begins before birth. For example, parental preferences for one sex over the other is strong. Parents indicate that their first concern is having a healthy baby. Beyond this consideration, most couples prefer male over female children, especially in a first or only child, a finding that has not changed since the 1930s and is true for much of the world (Beal, 1994; Moen, 1991). In 1988, college students were asked the question, "If you could have only one child, which sex would you prefer?" and 80 percent of the male students preferred a male child, while 58 percent of the women surveyed preferred a daughter (Pooler, 1991). Perhaps an informal poll could be taken on this issue in your class.

Strong cultural differences in favoritism exist. Favoring male babies appears to be strongest where gender stratification is a dominant feature as in countries with traditional values, strong religious beliefs, and a low level of technological development. For example, Chinese traditions of vastly preferring sons over daughters continue, as demonstrated in the Chinese proverb, "Raising a daughter is like weeding another man's garden" (Carmondy, 1989). In some countries, this preference results in the underreporting of female births, female infanticide, neglect of female infants, abortion of female fetuses, and a wide range of economic considerations. This has led to sex ratio figures in China, India, and other Asian countries of 100 to 115 boys born to every 100 girls (Lloyd, 1994; Park & Cho, 1995). There is a clear global preference for boys, which can have dire consequences for the well-being of daughters.

> *I dedicate the game to my mother, Ann. She was a fighter like me. They say like mother, like daughter. Well, in this case, it might be like mother, like son.*
>
> David Wells, former New York Yankees' pitcher, after throwing a perfect game.

After the birth of a child, the family maintains the major responsibility for socializing the child during the critical years of life, even when other socializing influences exist. In the family, the child gains a sense of self, learns language, and begins to understand norms of interaction with parents, siblings, and significant others in her or his life. Differential treatment of the sexes starts the day the child is born. Early research on sex-typing of infants by Rubin and his colleagues (1974) found that sex-typing begins on the day of birth. Both parents were found to be likely to describe sons as strong, firm, and alert, while they described daughters as delicate, soft, and awkward, although there were no differences between the boys and girls in weight, length, or health. Later research found parents engaged in more physical, rougher play with sons (Ross & Taylor, 1989), described male babies as big and tough and female babies as cheerful and gentle (Stern & Karraker, 1989), believed that girls need more help than boys (Snow, Jacklin, & Maccoby, 1983), and encouraged closer physical proximity with toddler daughters (Bronstein, 1988). Fathers were found to be significantly more likely than mothers to differentiate between their sons and daughters and to encourage more traditional gender-specific behavior in their sons (Fagot & Leinbach, 1995; Hardesty, Wenk, & Morgan, 1995).

Studies support Block's (1984) belief that boys develop "wings" that permit them to explore realms outside the home while girls develop roots that tend to anchor them. Girls are encouraged to participate in activities that keep them close to their homes and families, while boys are provided more opportunities for play and other activities away from home and independent of adult supervision, a finding that holds in both Western and non-Western cultures (Erwin, 1992). Parents reinforce these stereotypic gender roles in many ways through parenting style. Research by child development specialist Eccles and her colleagues (1990) indicates that parents perceive the competencies of their children in such areas as math, English, and sports in terms of their children's sex, and that these influences are independent of any real difference in the children's competencies. The socialization process appears to encourage gender-appropriate norms leading to separation and independence for males and connection and interdependence for females. Since the communication process plays a dominant role in the family structure, we turn to family communication patterns and their impact on sex and gender.

Family Communication

In the early 1970s, Virginia Satir (1972) wrote a book called *Peoplemaking*. In her introduction to the book, she called the family the "factory" where the person is made. "You, the adults, are the *people makers*" she said (p. 3). We have always appreciated this perspective. Families do create people, not just children. The family structure continues to shape and mold an adult throughout her or his life. As humans, our society is never finished socializing us. Given the centrality of the family to our definitions of ourselves and the power of the family to socialize people, it seems highly appropriate that we examine this context more deeply as it affects gender communication and the development of gender-role identity.

Gender is important as a variable in families for at least two reasons. First, the gender identity of the individuals who begin the family will guide (even govern) a large part of the communication that takes place within the family. Second, the family has the ability to influence the gender identities of the children it raises. The family has the power to reinforce the status quo regarding gender-role identity, or it can use that power to give the people it makes a broader, more complete view of how to be a boy or girl, man or woman. In the sections that follow, we use the concepts of patterns, power, and intimacy to discuss how the family structure can support the development of personally effective people with strong gender identities.

Is it possible to raise children who do not conform to gender identity stereotypes? Clearly it is not easy, if it is even possible. Macintosh (1992) writes about her efforts to raise gender-neutral children, concluding that girls and boys just seem to gravitate toward the stereotyped gender identity. For example, she

> You're fooling yourself if you think you've got new and improved males because you see three or four dudes out there doing diapers and dishes.
>
> *Bill Cosby, actor, comedian, & author*

cites an example where "at a little league game during the summer, fearful that this young daughter might be absorbing the stereotype 'boys play while girls watch,' her parents readily assured her that she too could participate when she was eight years old. 'Oh,' she exclaimed with obvious delight, 'I didn't know they had cheerleaders.'" (p. 18). While one anecdotal story doesn't prove a trend, it does illustrate the issue.

Patterns

The family has long been viewed as a "system" by researchers and writers concerned with family communication. Satir (1988) gives a nice analogy that helps explain the family as a system. Picture the family as a mobile, the kind that hangs over a child's crib, but instead of using animals, picture it with the members of the family. As events (such as leaving for college, getting ill, getting a new job, losing a job) touch one member of the family, the events will affect everyone else. But unlike a mobile, members of a family can create their own change, their own reverberations through the system. This view of communication is generally known as the "pragmatic" approach, so named and described by Watzlawick, Beavin, and Jackson (1967). They argued that any given communication behavior is simply a reaction to particular interactive situations and that understanding one person in a family or one communication act is only possible by understanding the system or pattern in which the act takes place. This view extends to the societal level as well. Communication behaviors, in this view, are not the result of people, but of other communication behaviors. The pragmatic researcher believes that identification of recurrent patterns will effectively explain what is happening within a system such as a family or a society (Trenholm, 1991). The recurrent patterns do not change easily. If the pattern includes a particular stereotype for gender roles, the momentum of the pattern will reinforce the stereotype.

Here's an example of how patterns work in a family. It's 8:30 on a Saturday morning, and six-year-old Matt knocks on his mom and dad's bedroom door, hears a "Come on in," and runs into the room. He's greeted with smiles and hugs. He then snuggles with his mom and dad for a while, they all chat, and then everyone gets up. This brief example speaks volumes about the interaction within the family. Matt knows it is okay to go into the bedroom with permission, and he knows he will most often be warmly welcomed. Physical expressions of affection are apparent, as is talking with mom and dad. We don't know how far-fetched this example sounds to you, but we can assure you that it is real. What kind of child is being made here?

As we talk about making people and patterns, we turn our attention to the role of these patterns in gender-role development. Extensive research exists describing the family's role in the socialization of children. It is not our place here to review all that research, but to point out some of its more significant aspects as it relates to gender communication. As you might guess, families with traditional sex role behaviors tend to develop children who stereotype the sexes (Repetti, 1984). Conversely, extensive interaction between father and child was associated with the development of androgyny in children (Lavine & Lombardo, 1984). Research on patterns of interaction showed differences between parents and differential treatment of children based on the sex of the child. Bellinger and Gleason (1982) and Buerkel-Rothfuss, Covert, Keith, and Nelson (1986) found that parents do not speak the same way to daughters as they do to sons. Golinkoff and Ames (1979) found that both mothers and fathers took more conversational turns with sons than with daughters and had longer conversations with daughters.

Beebe and Masterson (1986) describe the difference between person-centered and position-centered patterns of communication in a family. Position-centered patterns focus on the relative stable position a person holds in the family. Person-centered families place a high value on the individuality of each member. It appears that the person-centered approach encourages androgynous communication and the ability to behave flexibly in a gender role. As Galvin and Brommel (1991) state: "A key point in this process would be that the parents view each child as naturally fitting somewhere within the broad range of gender communication patterns, rather than pressuring the child to fit the parents' own gender ideal" (p. 122).

The traditional family model holds that men are more position centered. This stance has had an impact on the male role in the family. Men have traditionally been less involved in parenting than women. They see fatherhood as conditional, requiring their involvement only if it does not jeopardize their role as breadwinner (Lamb, Pleck, & Levine, 1987). Sociologists Harris and Morgan (1991) describe this perspective in more detail. They argue that

> contemporary American norms encourage paternal involvement but that there is no single model fathers should follow . . . . Fathers are seldom negatively sanctioned if they spend little time with their children because of long work hours or frequent travel (p. 532).

Some people are beginning to notice the impact of fathers' absence on their children. In a strongly worded article, psychologist Chris Bacorn (1992) argues for the increased role of fathers in parenting. He states:

> There are men who spend time with their children, men who are covering for all those absentee fathers . . . fathers who quietly help with homework, baths, laundry and grocery shopping. Fathers who read to their children, drive them to ballet lessons, who cheer at soccer games . . . . These are the real men of America, the ones holding society together . . . . If fathers were to spend more time with their children, it just might have an effect on the future of marriage and divorce. Not only do many boys lack a sense of how a man should behave; many girls don't know either, having little exposure themselves to healthy male-female relationships. With their fathers around, many young women might come to expect more than the myth that a man's chief purpose on earth is to impregnate them and then disappear (p. 13).

A woman should be home with the children, building that home and making sure there's a secure family atmosphere.

Mel Gibson,
actor & director

One of our primary goals in this text is the reduction of sex-stereotyped behavior, communication, and gender roles. Parenting has an impact on each of these. Research has found that both boys and girls develop less traditionally sex-stereotyped attitudes about male and female roles when their fathers are highly involved in child care (Sagi & Sharon, 1984). That is a point worth considering.

Power and Empowering

In the early 1970s, when one of your authors, Phil, had his first son, Phil happened across an article by psychologist Robert White (1965) titled the "Experience of Efficacy in Schizophrenia." In this article, White was pondering the roots of mental illness, specifically forms of schizophrenia. Among other ideas, White came to the conclusion that some aspects of schizophrenia could be traced back to early childhood and early language development. He noted that one symptom of schizophrenia is the patient's belief that her or his efforts do not matter. A schizophrenic believes it doesn't make any difference what he or she does; it won't affect anyone anyway. White was interested in how this belief might have originated. The conclusion he came to was interesting; he found that family communication patterns had a major impact. White concluded that infants need to develop the connection early in life between their own actions and an impact in the outside world. White believed that if an infant cried, something should happen—the infant should be picked up, held, changed, fed, or whatever it took to meet the infant's needs at that time. White believed that the first six months were critical for the infant. This was the time when the infant began to believe that he or she could affect the outside world and mold it to meet needs, and thus the infant could begin to feel a sense of power. White believed that a child could not be spoiled before six months of age; after that, some tempering was in order to avoid creating an overindulged child.

What does all this have to do with power? In Phil's family, it meant a number of things. It meant kids should be able to use language to influence the world around them, that they should see that their efforts to influence through spoken language would have some effect. Who was the most influential part of their world? Phil and his wife Judy. So, from the time Phil and Judy's children could put together a basic sentence, they were allowed to change their parents' minds occasionally. If one of the children gave a sufficiently good reason, Phil and Judy changed their minds and went along with his request. At two years old, the arguments were very simple. At 21 years, the reasoning got pretty elaborate. Has this worked? It seems to have. Phil and Judy have three boys who are highly verbal, effective socially, and solidly self-confident. Now, we're not saying that this one strategy was the sole reason for the way they are turning out, but it helped. Each son knows he will not always get what he wants, but each knows that it is worth the effort to ask. In addition, each son seems to have transferred this ability to situations outside the family. Each knows it is worth the effort to ask the teacher, the principal, the boss, the friend. The effort may not succeed, but each boy knows that if he puts together a well-thought-out point of view, sometimes things will go his way.

We describe this extended example for two reasons. First, it is an example of a consciously developed communication pattern that seems to work. Second, it is an example of one of the values we have described in this text—that of empowerment. A person (in this case, a child) can develop a more positive view of herself or himself through positive reinforcement. As this self-concept develops, the person begins to feel that he or she has a greater control or influence over situations, greater responsibility, and eventually greater power. This is particularly true for female children. If a girl can develop a strong sense of her ability to influence the world around her through communication, she is much more likely to be effective as an adult woman.

Empowering someone else (especially a child) requires that someone give up power. In traditional families, this may be difficult to do, particularly for a man. Galvin and Brommel (1991), in their family communication text, discuss examples of people who attempt to get power through indirect and devious ways. We are sure each of you knows examples of a parent who held power through fear, one who used guilt to get his way, one who played helpless so that the other person would do things for her, or one who intimidated.

Intimacy

Much of the literature on family communication concerns itself with how communication within the family system serves to bring the members together or pull them apart as the family moves through the various phases of its development. An analytical model developed by family scholars Olsen, Sprenkle, and Russell (1979) describes the variables of cohesion, adaptability, and communication as part of this process. As described in Galvin and Brommel (1991), the model attempts to understand family communication through the functions of "1. establishing a pattern of cohesion, or separateness and connectedness, and 2. establishing a pattern of adaptability, or change" (p. 19). Patterns of separateness or connectedness, and rigidity or adaptability have an impact on how children see these two dimensions. A male child in a connected, adaptive family learns to incorporate these characteristics into his gender role much more so than a male child who does not. Female children appear to develop these connections much more easily (Devor, 1992).

Family cohesion is one of those variables where it is possible to have too much of a good thing. Too little cohesion leaves family members feeling alone, disconnected, and alienated. Too much cohesion draws a family so tightly together that it develops an "us against them" mentality and the members' individual growth is restricted. The key is finding the balance between connection and independence. For a family, this is a continual struggle, as the changing events in a family, no matter what type, bring new issues and feelings that pull one way or the other. Two factors apply here to a discussion of cohesion and intimacy—nonverbal communication and self-disclosure.

Nonverbal Communication. The nonverbal communication patterns of a family reveal much about the family structure and the feelings of the members (Hickson & Stacks, 1989) and form a central part of the communication pattern developed by any family. Two aspects of nonverbal communication—time and affection—have a clear impact on the connectedness of the family and on how the children develop gender roles.

One of the parental rallying cries of the 1980s was "quality time" with children. Economic and work pressures of the past two decades had helped push parents out of a great deal of contact with their children. We know of fathers who leave for work before the kids get up and return from work after they have gone to bed in the evening. As fathers move from the traditional model to a more involved role in the family, they do experience a great deal of stress as a result of attempts to schedule working time around couple time and the demands of being a parent (Cooper, Chassin, & Zeiss, 1985). But the pressures and the desire for a career also have had an impact on the amount of time mothers spend with their children and their spouses. The onset of parenthood can put so much pressure on time that time management may be the greatest single challenge young married couples face as they make the transition to parenthood (LaRossa, 1983).

Few things substitute for time spent as a family. When a spouse or parent chooses to spend time with the other spouse or the children, it sends a message about priorities within the family. If a family has a conversation about its own communication patterns, one topic that could be discussed is the type and amount of time spent together. Some families make a point of having dinner together a specified number of evenings a week. Others set aside family evenings. There are many different patterns of time within families, and obviously not everyone will get the amount of time they want. But, as a factor in the cohesiveness of the family, time needs careful consideration.

Another indication of the amount of family cohesion is the degree of physical affection present in the patterns of interaction. A wide range of sources speak to the role touch plays in infant care (Lamb, 1982; Montagu, 1971), and others to the role of touch in relationship bonding (Anderson & Sull, 1985; Jones, 1986; Nguyen, Heslin, & Nguyen, 1976). Touch is clearly a powerful factor in the development of any relationship. Research suggests that fathers and mothers touch children for different reasons. Fathers seem to touch more in play, while mothers touch for caretaking (Lamb, 1977). Some years ago, we came across two letters in advice columns in newspapers. The first talked of a father who had trouble holding his infant son because he said he "couldn't kiss a guy." The other talked of a father who played roughly with his sons to the point that they cried in pain. Both are examples of inappropriate patterns of touch within a family that will likely lead to inappropriate gender roles for the sons. Some men appear to fear physical contact with their sons. Clearly, we do not believe this is an effective pattern for fathers and sons. We know of one father of three sons who has continued an uninterrupted pattern of physical affection (even through the teenage years) with his sons. The pattern appears to have had a positive influence on their development and how they view themselves as males. Given the force of this variable and the clear danger of abuse and violence, it is valuable to examine the pattern of touch within a family. How much physical affection is evident between parents? What are the patterns of touch present between each parent and each child? We suggest that you consider the role of touch and attempt to use it effectively to increase the level of intimacy in the family and to model a broader style of gender-role identity.

Disclosure. Family intimacy is demonstrated through a number of methods, not the least of which is shared understanding and knowledge. The primary means of reflecting understanding and sharing knowledge is through disclosure. Self-disclosure has long been considered a skill for fostering intimate communication within families (Gilbert, 1976; Jourard, 1971). Historical patterns of disclosure also appear to work against increased intimacy with the father. Children of both sexes tend to self-disclose more to their mothers than to their fathers and mothers receive more information than fathers (Pearson, 1989).

We talked earlier about the value of positiveness within the family communication pattern. Obviously, not all disclosure can or should be positive. However, as Gilbert (1976) has pointed out, the impact of negative disclosure has to be weighed carefully. Gilbert described the curvilinear relationship between disclosure and relationship satisfaction. As she described the relationship, feelings of satisfaction increase as disclosure increases up to a point, then increased disclosure may lead to decreased satisfaction. She strongly suggested that working toward ever-increasing levels of disclosure won't always have a positive effect. Care needs to be taken in developing the family pattern for the amount of both positive and negative disclosure.

We suggest that you think carefully about the way nonverbal communication and disclosure are dealt with when you develop your family communication patterns. Both have a tremendous impact on the quality of communication, neither develops easily, and both can be a critical element in helping the children of the family develop effective gender-role identities. Arntson and Turner (1987) analyzed the role of parents in sex-role socialization, and, not surprisingly, they found that parental models were a significant factor in a child's gender identity. Wood (1994) maintains that a child is "talked into" society by the significant people in his or her life. The family is clearly the first and probably the most influential factor in talking the child into society and shaping the development of the child's gender-role identity. However, the family is not the only agent.

RECAP

---

family soicalization, favoritism, peoplemaking, patterns, system, pragmatics, person-centered families, position-centered families, power, empowerment, intimacy, nonverbal communication, disclosure

---

OTHER AGENTS OF SOCIALIZATION

Besides parents, a great many other societal factors influence gender identity. Space doesn't allow a complete review, but we cover some of the major factors below.

Clothes and Toys

After birth, the first things acquired for an infant are clothes and toys. When the sex of a baby is not known, friends and family members try to buy "neutral" gifts to avoid embarrassing themselves or the parents by choosing gifts that are the wrong color or toys that suggest the wrong sex. After the arrival of the child, most parents decorate the room with feminine or masculine decorations. Color-coded and sex-typed clothing of infants is almost universal. One study found that over 90 percent of infants observed in a shopping mall could be readily categorized by sex according to the characteristics of their clothing (Shakin, Shakin, & Sternglanz, 1985). Sex-oriented clothing provides the initial labels to ensure that children are responded to "appropriately."

Along with clothing, toys form a powerful force of socialization. A clothing-toy link is especially true for girls who buy fashions for their dolls. Considering that over 250 million Barbie dolls have been sold in the past 25 years and that over 20 million outfits are bought each year, the seeds for clothing addiction in girls are sown early. Toys for girls encourage domesticity, interpersonal closeness, and social orientation, whereas boys receive not only more categories of toys but toys that are more complex and more expensive and that foster self-reliance and problem solving (Hughes, 1994; Leaper, 1994). Children's advertisements in catalogs and on television reinforce gender typing in toys. Next time you go to the store, note how the aisles are organized and how pictures on the boxes suggest how girls and boys should use the toys. Boys receive more sports equipment, tools, and vehicles. Girls receive dolls, fictional characters, and children's furniture. "Parents and other adults encourage sex-type play by selecting different toys for female and male children, even before the child can express her or his own preference" (Pomerleau, Bolduc, Malcuit, & Cossette, 1990, p. 365). Parental expectations are revealed by the kinds of toys they provide for their children.

Boys' games are usually more complex, competitive, and rule governed, and they allow for a larger number of participants than girls' games. (Ignico & Mead, 1990). Girls games are more ordered, such as hopscotch or jump rope that are played in small groups with a minimum of competitiveness. Boys are generally directed toward power, self-reliance, the use of talk to hold center stage, vying for status, and asserting themselves. Girls are directed toward affiliation, interdependence, shared interaction, cooperativeness, communication as relationship building, and responsiveness toward others. This stereotype that associates competitiveness with masculinity but not femininity is consistently supported by research (King, Miles, & Kniska, 1991; Maltz & Borker, 1982). In the United States, boys and girls hear more negative messages about boys doing girl-style play than girls doing boy-style play. Overall, girls have more freedom of action beyond the sex-defined boundaries, not only in games, but in life as well.

Carol Gilligan (1982), in her analysis of human development, noted that little boys are more likely to argue about rules when playing games. Girls tend to stop the game (and the argument) if it looks like relationships will be threatened. For girls, the relationship is more important than the game. Harrigan (1977) states the distinction strongly: "Girls' games teach meaningless mumbo-jumbo—vague generalities or pre-game mutual agreements about 'what we'll play'—while falsely implying that these blurry self-guides are typical of real world rules" (pp. 49–50).

Peers and School

As children get older, they are gradually introduced into the world outside the family. Parents' gender expectations at home become extended into the child's social world. Parents initiate the first relationships for their children and for the first few years of life, children prefer playing with children of a similar age, sex unspecified. However, as children move into school this preference changes quickly. Activities and games in schools are strongly related to gender roles and are a powerful influence in socialization (Lindzey, 1997). For example, when Jane pressures Dick into playing house, she is usually the mother and he the father. Or she becomes the teacher while he is the pupil. On the other hand, if Dick talks her into a game of catch, he might criticize her awkwardness and lack of skill. What would social learning theory say about the likelihood of Jane's gaining expertise in baseball? These mixed-sex games usually dissolve into conflict and both children wind up feeling worse about the other sex. Obviously this does not happen all the time, but it occurs often enough that each sex tends to want to stick to its own. Mixed-sex play usually only happens when no same-sex person is available to play with.

Schools function as powerful influences in the gender socialization of children. Educational institutions are given the responsibility for ensuring that children are trained in the ways of society, but they do it in a way that perpetuates many stereotypes (Lindzey, 1997). Schools are generally set up for competitive, independent work where initiative is valued, which are

---

RECAP

gender-oriented clothes, toys, and games; peers; schools

---

generally seen as masculine values. Schools and teachers do not treat the two sexes equally, and we explore this more fully in a later chapter on education. One of the most telling points emerged from research by Sadker and Sadker (1994) who asked children of all grade levels, "What would it be like to become a member of the opposite sex?" Both boys and girls preferred their own sex, but girls found the prospect of becoming boys intriguing. They were willing to try it out for a while. Boys, on the other hand, found the prospect intensely disgusting and humiliating. One boy even said, "If I were turned into a girl today I would kill myself." Do schools perpetuate the privileging of one sex over the other?

Socialization theories stress the importance of peer interactions. Sex segregation and the influence of peer groups increase throughout the school years through play, games, and schooling. Sex boundaries are closely watched and enforced by peers (Maccoby, 1994). It's common to hear boys say, "Only sissies play with girls!" The worlds of boys and girls become that much more divided and each sex learns less about the other (Inhoff, Halverson, & Pissigati, 1983). When children do interact, reinforcement from adults and from peers occurs more frequently for contact with same-sex peers than with opposite-sex peers. Boys seem to be particularly strong in their gender-role attitudes (Lindzey, 1997). A major consequence is that "boys and girls will meet in adolescence virtually as strangers, having learned different styles of interaction" (Fagot, 1994, p. 62). The lack of cross-sex interaction impoverishes both sexes and results in restricted gender-role identities. Given the socialization patterns, it is no wonder some people think men and women are from different planets!

GENDER IDENTITY, SELF-ESTEEM DEVELOPMENT, AND CHANGE

Gender and Self-Esteem

Gender identity is closely intertwined with a person's self-esteem. For an individual like Mark, described in this chapter's case study, his perceived inability to live up to the cultural stereotype for masculinity caused a major negative impact his self-esteem. It was only after he changed his view of masculinity that his self-esteem changed for the better. Mark is not alone in connecting self-esteem and gender identity. If we are to develop a healthy self-esteem and effective gender communication, then an exploration of gender's impact on self-esteem is in order.

Definitions

Self-esteem is a difficult concept to define. In summarizing varying definitions, psychologist Chris Mruk (1995) described self-esteem as having at least five dimensions: competence (beliefs about the ability to be effective), worthiness (being valued by others), cognition (beliefs about our character and personality), affect (self-evaluation and the feelings generated), and stability or change. A person develops beliefs about himself or herself over each dimension and these beliefs result in a judgment of the self. This judgment is based on the person's impression of *how* she or he is doing in life versus how the person *thinks* he or she should be doing (Mruk, 1995). What a person thinks she or he should be doing comes, to a large degree, from the culture. The culture supplies gender roles as a highly influential "should."

Psychologists Pope, McHale, and Craighead (1988) view self-esteem this way: ". . . self esteem arises from the discrepancy between the perceived self, or self-concept (an objective view of the self) and the ideal self (what the person values, or wants to be like)" (p. 4). If there isn't much difference between the perceived- and the ideal-self, the person will have a positive self-esteem. Gender researcher Peggy Orenstein (1994) defines self-esteem as being derived from two sources: how a person views her or his performance in areas that are important to him or her, and how a person believes she or he is perceived by significant others. From these definitions, a flavor for the concept of self-esteem can be obtained. A person's self-esteem has a powerful impact on his or her communication.

Learning about the Self

Learning how we are perceived by others is not an easy process. Most people will not tell you directly how they see you, but will do so indirectly through their behavior toward you (Baumeister, 1998). In many cases, this knowledge can only be obtained through indirect processes, explicitly involving other people for comparison. We judge ourselves by comparing ourselves to others. Being tall or short, smart or stupid, fast or slow, are factors only known relative to other people. In fact, (Mead, 1934) maintains that every part of what is known about the self is derived from others. Mead refers to this as "reflected appraisals"—other people's appraisals of a person. These appraisals shape people's understanding of themselves—people's views of themselves are quite similar to how they think others see them.

As part of this process, a person will receive appraisals of how she or he is performing the applicable gender role from both men and women. As our society places a great deal of emphasis on being an acceptable

> *Some of us are becoming the men we wanted to marry.*
>
> Gloria Steinem, author & political activist

woman or man, these appraisals take on special significance. Wood (1994) believes sex does influence self-esteem in predictable directions. Women in this society gravitate toward the acceptance-rejection component of self-esteem, whereas men tend to gravitate toward the competence (success or failure) aspect of self-esteem (Mruk, 1995). For women, this research suggests that self-esteem is tied to acceptance by others. For men, self-esteem is more likely tied to feelings of success. Is this point of view similar to your experience?

Gender and Self-Esteem

Gender does influence self-esteem in numerous ways (Mruk, 1995). An infant has no control over which sex he or she is born as, but, as we noted above, the infant is saddled with all the cultural expectations of that sex even before life occurs. As communication researcher Julia Wood suggests, "to be a human being is to be inescapably, incessantly gendered" (1994, p. 145). Gender brings with it a whole range of categories, values, and expectations that an infant can only respond to passively.

Psychologists Josephs, Markus, and Tafarodi (1991) describe sex differences in self-esteem as based in the different societal roles for each sex:

> For men, evaluating the self positively and feeling good about one's self should derive, in part, from fulfilling the goals ascribed to their gender— being independent, autonomous, separate, and better than others. For women, feeling good about one's self, or believing one's self to be of worth should derive, at least in part, from being sensitive to, attuned to, connected to, and generally interdependent with others. (p. 392)

Sexist aspects of society can prevent or discourage women from pursuing competence, thus making them more dependent on being valued by others for their self-esteem. This can lead to more vulnerability, more dependence on others, and less self-confidence. The flip side for men can be just as negative. Pushing men toward the competence dimension of self-esteem cuts them off from the nurturing aspects, thus increasing the possibility of developing problems such as an unhealthy lifestyle and attempting to be too macho (Mruk, 1995).

The sources from which girls and boys draw their self-esteem also differ. Boys usually identify qualities such as ambition, energy, power, initiative, ability to get things done, and control. Boys tend to talk about their success with sports or with girls. Girls tend to talk about generosity, sensitivity, and consideration and care for others (Block, 1983; Gunnar-Von Gnechten, 1978). These traits, as you can readily see, fit closely with the cultural stereotype for each sex.

Orenstein (1994) analyzed the self-esteem of teenage girls. She cites the American Association of University Women's report *Shortchanging Girls, Shortchanging America,* which researched attitudes toward self, school, family, and friends of 3,000 boys and girls between the ages of 9 and 15. "For a girl, the passage into adolescence is . . . marked by a loss of confidence in herself and her abilities, especially in math and science. It is marked by a scathingly critical attitude toward

Reprinted with special permission of King Features Syndicate.

her body and a blossoming sense of personal inadequacy" (p. xvi). Orenstein concluded that girls emerge from their teenage years with reduced expectations and have less confidence in themselves and their abilities than do boys.

An intriguing aspect of the research reveals that African-American girls retain their overall self-esteem during adolescence more than white or Latina girls. In many ways, Latina girls' self-esteem crisis is the most difficult. Between the ages of 9 and 15, the number of Latina girls who are "happy with the way I am" plunges by 38 percentage points (Orenstein, 1994). Ideally, according to Orenstein, girls should develop in their teenage years a healthy self-esteem with "an appropriate sense of their potential, their competence, and their innate value as individuals. They feel a sense of entitlement: license to take up space in the world, a right to be heard, and to express the full spectrum of human emotion" (p. xix).

While perhaps not having the same negative effect on self-esteem, men's roles have been depicted as stereotypically as women's roles. In these stereotypes, all men were socialized to dominate, control, and subordinate women, and they were uncomfortable in situations that did not adhere to old, established rules. Most teenage boys grew up under these rules and then became uncomfortable with strong women (girls) because they were supposed to be in control and make the moves (Nichols, 1975). Thus boys felt their self-esteem attacked by relationships and situations that did not fit the stereotype. If they weren't in control, they weren't much of a man because they didn't live up to the stereotype.

Sex differences in self-esteem can be analyzed more closely by focusing on six specific aspects of esteem.

1. Power, Influence, and Esteem. *Power* is a term we use a number of times in this text. Regarding self-esteem, psychologist Coopersmith (1967) described power as the ability to manage or direct one's environment. This ability is quite central to a person's self-esteem and self-concept (Stake, 1992). A powerless person generally does not feel confident and generally has a poorer self-concept. Given the fact that women generally have lower levels of power in society, Miller (1986) contends that women must be constantly attuned to and responsive to others, especially to the dominant man who determines their fate. Thus, relationships and interdependence with others will be more central to the self-concept of women.

Power may be a term that leans too far, however, to the masculine side. Some women in self-esteem enhancement groups object to the term because it seems to carry too many negative connotations (as in "power over someone" or "abuse of power"). An alternative word may be *influence* (Mruk, 1995). Having a say over the events in one's life does develop a feeling of competence. While competence has been identified primarily as a factor in self-esteem for men, that may have more to do with societal beliefs than women's disinterest in competence. For each of us, the ability to set and achieve goals is a factor of self-esteem. Conversely, too many failures leads to a sense of incompetence and powerlessness.

2. Acceptance versus Rejection. Acceptance and rejection are opposite expressions of how others react to us (Mruk, 1995), and, as we stated earlier, appear to be more important to women than to men. Differences between the sexes are not only apparent in the relative importance of acceptance and rejection, but also in how they are communicated. Acceptance can be communicated by respect, care, concern, admiration, liking, and so on. Rejection is communicated through being ignored, devalued, used, or even abandoned. Sex differences in the communication of acceptance or rejection are relatively apparent in that men are much less likely to communicate acceptance than women in many situations (Deaux & Lafrance, 1998). Obviously, being valued by others in a positive way can enhance self-esteem and being negatively valued can lessen it. If men have trouble communicating acceptance, many women may feel rejected by men, which in turn has a negative impact on self-esteem.

3. Body Image. Naomi Wolf (1991), in her critique of America's beauty industry, describes the tremendous negative effect of the beauty myth of thinness on self-esteem. She found that many women would rather lose 10 to 15 pounds than achieve any other goal. Millions of three- and four-year-old girls equate fat with badness even before they can read (Heyn, 1989). Cosmetic surgery rates have skyrocketed, all in an effort to meet an almost impossible cultural image of thinness. Stratton (1993) suggests that mannequins serve as models of what women think they should look like, and many strive for that level of thinness. All of this has a strong, negative effect on the self-concept and esteem of women.

4. Comparisons. Comparison to other people also influences your sense of self-esteem. For example, you can gain or lose more self-esteem if your spouse wins a major award than if your former neighbor wins it. If a romantic partner succeeds at something that you are trying to be good at, you may feel jealous or threatened. When the comparison process makes you look bad, the only way to limit the damage is to reduce the closeness. Comparison also has an impact on expectations of other people. Rosenthal and Jacobsen's classic study (1968) showed that teachers' initially false expectations about their students led to changes in the performances of the students that confirmed those expectations. If someone important to you expects you to act in a certain way related to your gender role, you are likely to do so and try to live up to those expectations.

Given the traditionally subordinate role of women and the cultural emphasis on women's physical appearance, comparisons may have a particularly strong impact on the self-esteem of women (Deaux & Lafrance, 1998). For many women and men, the only way to determine success is by comparison with the behaviors of others.

5. Toward the Extremes. Women toward the masculine end of the personality continuum and men toward the feminine end may find themselves in a double bind. The masculine woman who feels depressed, for example, might feel uncomfortable expressing her feelings in a feminine manner, but expressing them in a masculine way may not be recognized as legitimate by others. A feminine man might want to talk about his feelings with someone but feel hesitant to do so because of the societal expectations of how a man should act (Wood, 1994). This type of social pressure subtly causes these men and women to find other men and women like them so as to get reinforcement for their interpretation of gender identity, thus perhaps causing even further isolation.

6. Adequacy. When men feel adequate, you never hear them talk about masculinity. It seems that it is when men feel less than capable that they talk about this thing called manhood (Josephs, Markus, & Tafarodi, 1991). Pleck (1981) stated that men who embraced challenges, sought risks, and channeled their aggression into business, sports, and community affairs worried less about their masculinity. Segell (1996), in writing about the new alpha male, maintained that a focus on becoming a fully developed human, embracing the best of traditional masculinity and acquiring new skills in support and nurturance, would be the best route to feelings of success and positive self-esteem. Women's feelings of inadequacy stem, to a significant degree, from cultural stereotypes surrounding physical appearance (Wolf, 1991) and from role denigrations related to ability. It is interesting to note that increased participation levels of women in sports have contributed to an increase in the self-esteem and confidence of women. It would appear that individuals who meet their conception of their ideal gender-role identity think about gender less than other people.

Change

Earlier in this chapter, we discussed the belief that biology is not destiny. Here we make the point that neither is culture. Any individual's gender-role identity can change if the person has the motivation to do so. Research has shown conclusively that gender identity can change through a variety of means. For example, Risman's (1989) study of men who became primary parents showed that these men became more nurturing, attentive to other's needs, and emotionally expressive than men in general. Other research showed that a man's job affected his personality more than his personality affected his work (Kohn & Schooler, 1982). In similar research related to women, Miller, Schooler, Kohn, and Miller (1979) found that women too were affected by their jobs more than they affected their jobs. Epstein (1982) found that female executives developed senses of personal power, entitlement, and ambition that they had

Somewhere out in this audience may even be someone who will one day follow in my footsteps, and preside over the White House as the President's spouse. I wish him well!

Barbara Bush,
former First Lady

not possessed at the outset of their careers. It seems clear that individuals can alter their gender identity both by changing situations and by self-talk (Wood, 1994). Thus the effects of early socialization can be moderated by a variety of later experiences. Early socialization is not destiny.

When people try to change their gender-role identity or any other aspect of their behavior, interpersonal relationships are an extremely important determinant of success or failure. People who succeeded in changing their role identity reported considerable help and support from other people, much more so than people who failed to change (Heatherton & Nichols, 1994). Since self-esteem and self-concept are integrally linked to communication, both interpersonally and intrapersonally (Chatham-Carpenter & DeFrancisco, 1997), both are built, maintained, and changed by how one chooses to communicate with the self and with others (Markus & Cross, 1990; Vocate, 1994). Thus one strategy for change is to enlist the support of significant others or to develop relationships with people who will support the changes and give feedback on their effectiveness. Given the importance of social roles and environment, self-esteem is most likely to change at points in life where there is substantial change in one's social environment.

We discuss Sandra Bem's (1974) concept of androgyny in a number of places in this text and we agree with her belief that femininity and masculinity are not polar opposites, but arbitrary social constructs. Any given individual can be strongly masculine or strongly feminine, show few (if any) gender-linked personality attributes, or be androgynous, which is a blend of each set of characteristics. The personally effective gender communicator does demonstrate a blend of these characteristics. Women can assert power, engage in highly active endeavors, demonstrate independence, and use male-associated verbal and nonverbal patterns of communication when it meets their goals. Men can be subjective, passive, noncompetitive, dependent, and use female-associated verbal and nonverbal patterns of communication when it meets their goals. Androgynous men can use warm, complementary social behaviors when these responses are helpful, and androgynous women can use effective assertive skills. Both approaches result in greater communicative effectiveness (Kelly, O'Brien, & Hosford, 1981). The key is the willingness to learn the patterns of the other sex and incorporate them into one's repertoire of communication behavior. The key is a willingness to learn and change.

Change may be more difficult for men because men have traditionally undervalued, even denigrated, feminine characteristics. However, it can be to a man's advantage to develop a broader range of communication skills because they may lead to better friendships, more success as a father and husband, and perhaps a more successful professional life. For women, the ability to take on masculine patterns can mean greater success in the workplace, more control over relationships, and a higher level of influence over destiny. For neither sex does this mean the loss of masculinity or femininity, but the expansion of possibilities. This ability to blend in interpersonal situations does enhance personal effectiveness. A long-term factor in the success of these new patterns will be acceptance and support of the new patterns both by friends and society.

CONCLUSION

Learning to be a woman or man is both interesting and problematic. The point in this chapter has been to describe societal conceptions of masculinity and femininity and how these conceptions influence an individual person as she or he develops a gender-role identity. Most of us struggle with how to be a woman or a man, how to act, and how to relate to the other sex. This chapter presents ideas and information that may help with this struggle. Learning to become a more personally effective gender communicator necessitates learning about how your own gender-role identity affects you and your communication. The more you know about that and the alternatives available to you, the more control you can have over your own role. You can also learn to have more effect on the gender role development of other individuals as well. You might serve as a role model for them!

Key Terms

biological sex	alpha male	favoritism
gender	homophobia	peoplemaking
socialization	self-fulfilling prophecy	patterns
social norms	other-fulfilling prophecy	system
stereotypes	generalized other	pragmatics
cultural differences	significant other	person-centered families
social constructs	social learning theory	position-centered families
femininity	reinforcement	power
masculinity	social role	empowerment
agrarian society	cognitive development	intimacy
nurturance	theory	nonverbal
interdependence	gender schema theory	communication
aggression	gender polarization	disclosure
stereotypic definitions	family socialization	

Discussion Starters

1. Who had the greatest influence on your *gender-role identity?* Was he or she a role model for you? What aspects of her or his gender role enactment did you appreciate? Did you know any negative role models? In what way were they negative?

2. Do you think that media (television, movies, videos) portray gender roles accurately? What examples of role models are worth emulating? Talk with your classmates about their perceptions of gender roles in the media. Should the media portray roles accurately or in an idealized form?

3. Are societal definitions of *masculine* and *feminine* changing? If so, how? Are the changes for the better? In what directions do you think they should be changing? How has your definition of the ideal gender role changed in the past few years? Do you think it will change more in future years?

4. How is *self-esteem* tied to gender roles? Can people be positively or negatively affected by how they might be "doing" as a boy or girl? If you know people who do not live up to the socially accepted definition of their sex, how do they deal with that? Are people who do match society's ideal gender role happier than people who don't?

5. In the past 10 years or so, toy manufacturers have attempted to develop gender-neutral toys. For the most part, these toys have not succeeded in the marketplace. Why do you think this is? Should parents try to give their children gender-neutral toys or toys that are typically associated with the other sex? What effects do you think toys have on the development of gender-role identity?

6. "Grrrl" power is a growing phenomena in the late 1990s. What does it mean to you? What do you see as the purpose or goals of "grrrl" power? Should there be a "boy power?" What might that accomplish?

References

ANDERSON, P. A. (1998). Researching sex differences with sex similarities: The evolutionary consequences of reproductive differences. In D. J. Canary & K. Dindia (Eds.), *Sex differences and similarities in communication* (pp. 83–100). Mahwah, NJ: Lawrence Erlbaum.

ANDERSON, P. A., & SULL, K. K. (1985). Out of touch, out of reach: Predispositions as predictors of interpersonal distance. *Western Journal of Speech Communication, 49,* 57–72.

ANZALDUA, G. E. (1995). The strength of my rebellion. In S. Ruth (Ed.), *Issues in feminism: An introduction to women's studies* (pp. 269–273). Mountain View, CA: Mayfield.

ARCHER, J. (1991). Human sociology: Basic concepts and limitations. *Journal of Social Issues, 47,* 11–26.

ARNTSON, P., & TURNER, L. (1987). Sex role socialization: Children's enactments of their parents' behaviors in a regulative and interpersonal context. *Western Journal of Speech Communication, 51,* 304–316.

BACORN, C. N. (1992, December 7). Dear dads: Save your sons. *Newsweek,* 13.

BANDURA, A. (1986) *Social foundations of thought and action: A social cognitive theory.* Englewood Cliffs, NJ: Prentice-Hall.

BATE, B., & BOWKER, J. (1997). *Communication and the sexes* (2nd. ed.). Prospect Heights, IL: Waveland.

BAUMEISTER, R. F. (1998). The self. In D. T. Gilbert, S. T. Fiske, & G. Lindzey (Eds.), *The handbook of social psychology, Vol 1* (4th ed., pp. 680–740). New York: McGraw-Hill.

BEAL, C. R. (1994). *Boys and girls: The development of gender roles.* New York: McGraw-Hill.

BEEBE, S. T., & MASTERSON, J. T. (1986). *Family talk: Interpersonal communication in the family.* New York: Random House.

BELLINGER, D. C., & GLEASON, J. B. (1982). Sex differences in parental directives to young children. *Sex Roles, 8,* 1123–1139.

BEM, S. L. (1974). The measurement of psychological androgyny. *Journal of Consulting and Clinical Psychology, 42,* 155–162.

BEM, S. L. (1983). Gender schema theory and its implications for child development: Raising gender-aschematic children in a gender-schematic society. *Signs, 8,* 598–616.

BEM, S. L. (1993). *The lenses of gender: Transforming the debate on sexual inequality.* New Haven, CT: Yale University Press.

BINION, V. J. (1990). Psychological androgyny: A black female perspective. *Sex Roles, 22,* 487–507.

BLOCK, J. H. (1983). Differential premises arising from differential socialization of the sexes: Some conjectures. *Child Development, 54,* 1335–1354.

BLOCK, J. H. (1984). *Sex role identity and ego development.* San Francisco: Josey-Bass.

BORISOFF, D., & MERRILL, L. (1998). *The power to communicate: Gender differences as barriers* (2nd ed.). Prospect Heights, IL: Waveland.

BRANNON, R. (1976). The male sex-role: Our culture's blueprint for manhood and what it has done for us lately. In D. David & R. Brannon (Eds.), *The 49% majority* (pp. 1–49). Reading, MA: Addison-Wesley.

BRONSTEIN, P. (1988). Father-child interaction: Implications for gender role socialization. In P. Bronstein & C. P. Cowan (Eds.), *Fatherhood today: Men's changing role in the family* (pp. 107–126). New York: John Wiley.

BUERKEL-ROTHFUSS, N. L., COVERT, A. M., KEITH, J., & NELSON, C. (1986). *Early adolescent and parental communication patterns.* Paper presented at the meeting of the Speech Communication Association, Chicago, IL.

CANCIAN, F. (1989). Love and the rise of capitalism. In B. Riesman & P. Schwartz (Eds.), *Gender in intimate relationships* (pp. 12–25). Belmont, CA: Wadsworth.

CARMONDY, D. L. (1989). *Women and world religions.* Englewood Cliffs, NJ: Prentice-Hall.

CHATHAM-CARPENTER, A., & DEFRANCISCO, V. (1997). Pulling yourself up again: Women's choices and strategies for recovering and maintaining self-esteem. *Western Journal of Communication, 61,* 164–187.

CHODOROW, N. (1989). *Feminism and psychoanalytic theory.* New Haven, CT: Yale University Press.

CONDRY, J. & CONDRY, S. (1976). Sex differences: A study of the eye of the beholder. *Child Development, 47,* 812–819.

COOPER, K., CHASSIN, L., & ZEISS, A. (1985). The relation of sex-role self-concept and sex-role attitudes to the marital satisfaction and personal adjustment of dual-worker couples with preschool children. *Sex Roles, 12,* 227–241.

COOPERSMITH, S. (1967). *The antecedents of self-esteem.* San Francisco: Freeman.

DEAUX, K., & LAFRANCE, M. (1998). Gender. In D. T. Gilbert, S. T. Fiske, & G. Lindzey (Eds.), *The handbook of social psychology, Vol 1* (4th ed., pp. 788–828). New York: McGraw-Hill.

DELEON, B. (1993). Sex role identity among college students: A cross-cultural analysis. *Hispanic Journal of Behavioral Sciences, 15,* 476–489.

DEVOR, H. (1992). Becoming members of society: Learning the social meanings of gender. In M. Schaum & C. Flanagan (Eds.), *Gender images: Readings for composition* (pp. 23–33). Boston: Houghton Mifflin.

DOBOSZ, A. M. (1997, November-December). Thicker thighs by Thanksgiving. *Media,* 89–91.

DUGGER, K. (1991). Social location and gender-role attitudes: A comparison of Black and White women. In J. Lorbert & S. A. Farrell (Eds.) *The social construction of Gender.* (pp. 38–59). Newbury Park, CA: Sage.

ECCLES, J. S., JACOBS, J. E., & HAROLD, R. D. (1990). Gender role stereotypes, expectancy effects, and parents' socialization of gender differences. *Journal of Social Issues, 46,* 183–201.

EIDELSON, S., & EPSTEIN, D. (1982). Development of a measure of dysfunctional relationship beliefs. *Journal of Consulting and Clinical Psychology, 50,* 715–720..

EPSTEIN, C. F. (1982, November). *Changing perspectives and opportunities and their impact on careers and aspirations: The case of women lawyers.* Paper presented at the Annual Scientific Meeting of the Gerontological Society of America, Boston, MA.

EPSTEIN, C. F. (1988). *Deceptive distinction: Sex, gender, and the social order.* New Haven, CT: Yale University Press.

ERWIN, P. (1992). *Friendship and peer relations in children.* Chichester, UK: John Wiley.

FAGOT, B. (1994). Peer relations and the development of competence in boys and girls. In C. Leaper (Ed.), *Childhood gender segregation: Causes and consequences* (pp. 53–66). San Francisco: Josey-Bass.

FAGOT, B. & LEINBACH, M. D. (1995). Gender knowledge in egalitarian and traditional families. *Sex Roles, 32,* 523–526.

GALVIN, K. M., & BROMMEL, B. J. (1991). *Family communication: Cohesion and change* (3rd ed.). New York: Harper Collins.

GARCIA, A. M., (1991). The development of chicana feminist discourse. In J. Lorber & S. A. Farrell (Eds.), *The social construction of gender gap* (pp. 269–287). Newbury Park, CA: Sage.

GEIS, F. L. (1993) Self-fulfilling prophecies: A social psychological view of gender. In A. E. Beall & R. J. Sternberg (Eds.) *The psychology of gender* (pp. 9–54). New York: Guilford Press.

GILBERT, S. (1976). Self-disclosure, intimacy, and communication in families. *Family Coordinator, 25,* 221–229.

GILLIGAN, C. (1982). *In a different voice: Psychological theory and women's development.* Cambridge, MA: Harvard University Press.

GOLINKOFF, R., & AMES, G. J. (1979). A comparison of fathers' and mothers' speech with their young children. *Child Development, 50,* 28–32.

GOTTMAN, J., MARKMAN, H., & NOTARIUS, C. (1970). The typology of marital conflict. *Journal of Marriage and the Family, 6,* 192–203.

GOULD, K. H. (1988, September-October). Old wine in new bottles: A feminist perspective on Gilligan's theory. *Social Work,* 411–415.

GREENE, S. (1997). Psychology and the re-evaluation of the feminine. *Irish Journal of Psychology, 18,* 367–385.

GROSSMAN, M., & WOOD, W. (1993). Sex differences in intensity of emotional experience: A social role interpretation. *Journal of Personality and Social Psychology, 65,* 1010–1022.

GUNNAR, M. R., & DONAHUE, M. (1980). Sex differences in social responsiveness between six months and twelve months. *Child Development, 51,* 262–265.

GUNNAR-VON GNECHTEN, M. R. (1978). Changing a frightening toy into a pleasant toy by allowing the infant to control its actions. *Developmental Psychology, 14,* 157–162.

HALPERN, D. F. (1986). *Sex differences in cognitive abilities.* Hillsdale, NJ: Lawrence Erlbaum.

HARDESTY, C., WENK, D., & MORGAN, C. S. (1995). Paternal involvement and the development of gender expectations in sons and daughters. *Youth and Society, 267,* 283–297.

HARRIGAN, B. (1977). *Games mother never taught you.* New York: Rawson.

HARRIS, J. M., & MORGAN, S. P. (1991). Fathers, sons, and daughters: Differential paternal involvement in parenting. *Journal of Marriage and the Family, 53,* 531–544.

HEATHERTON, T. F., & NICHOLS, P. A. (1994). Personal accounts of successful versus failed attempts at life changes. *Personality and Social Psychology Bulletin, 20,* 664–675.

HEYN, D. (1989, July-August). Body hate. *Ms.,* 35–36.

HICKSON, M. I., & STACKS, D. W. (1989). *Nonverbal communication: Studies and applications* (2nd ed.). Dubuque, IA: Wm. C. Brown.

HOCHSCHILD, A. (1989). The economy of gratitude. In D. Franks & E. D. McCarthy (Eds.), *The sociology of emotions: Original essays and research papers* (pp. 95–113). Greenwich, CT: JAI Press.

HOCHSCHILD, A., & MACHUNG, A. (1989). *The second shift: Working parents and the revolution at home.* New York: Viking/Penguin.

HOUSTON, M., & WOOD, J. T. (1996). Difficult dialogues, expanded horizons: Communicating across race and culture. In J. T. Wood (Ed.), *Gendered relationships* (pp. 39–56). Mountain View, CA: Mayfield.

HUGHES, F. P. (1994). *Children, play, and development.* Boston: Allyn & Bacon.

IGNICO, A. A., & MEAD, B. J. (1990). Children's perceptions of the gender-appropriateness of physical activities. *Perceptual and Motor Skills, 71,* 1275–1281.

INHOFF, G. E., HALVERSON, C. F., JR., & PISSIGATI, K. A. L. (1983). The influence of sex-role stereotypes on children's self- and peer-attributions. *Sex Roles, 9,* 1205–1222.

JACKSON, L. A., FLEURY, R. E., & LEWANDOWSKI, D. A. (1996). Feminism: Definitions, support, and correlates of support among female and male college students. *Sex Roles, 34,* 687–693.

JACOBS, J. E., & ECCLES, J. S. (1992). The impact of mother's gender-role stereotypic beliefs on mothers' and children's ability perceptions. *Journal of Personality and Social Psychology, 63,* 932–944.

JONES, S. E. (1986). Sex differences in tactile communication. *Western Journal of Speech Communication, 50,* 227–249.

JOSEPHS, R. A., MARKUS, H. R., & TAFARODI, R. W. (1991). Gender and self-esteem. *Journal of Personality and Social Psychology, 63,* 391–402.

JOURARD, S. M. (1971). *The transparent self.* New York: Van Nostrand Reinhold.

KEASHLY, L. (1994). Gender and conflict: What does psychological research tell us? In A. Taylor & J. B. Miller (Eds.), *Conflict and gender* (pp. 168–190). Cresskill, NJ: Hampton.

KELLY, J. A., O'BRIEN, G. G., & HOSFORD, R. (1981). Sex roles and social skills in considerations for interpersonal adjustment. *Psychology of Women Quarterly, 5,* 758–766.

KIMMEL, M. (1987). *Changing men: New directions in research on men and masculinity.* Newbury Park, CA: Sage.

KING, W. C., JR., MILES, E. W., & KNISKA, J. (1991). Boys will be boys (and girls will be girls): The attribution of gender role stereotypes in a gaming situation. *Sex Roles, 25,* 607–623.

KOHLBERG, L. (1966). A cognitive-development analysis of children's sex role concepts and attitudes. In E. Maccoby (Ed.), *The development of sex differences* (pp. 82–173). Stanford, CA: Stanford University Press.

KOHN, M., & SCHOOLER, C. (1982). Job conditions and personality: A longitudinal assessment of their reciprocal effects. *American Journal of Sociology, 87,* 1257–1286.

KRUEGER, D. L. (1986). Communication strategies and patterns in dual career couples. *Southern Speech Communication Journal, 15,* 164–173.

LACKEY, P. N. (1989). Adults' attitudes about assignments of household chores to male and female children. *Sex Roles, 20,* 271–281.

LAMB, M. E. (1982). Early contact and maternal-infant bonding: One decade later. *Pediatrics, 70,* 763–768.

LAMB, M. E. (1997). The development of mother-infant and father-infant attachments in the second year of life. *Developmental Psychology, 13,* 637–646.

LAMB., M. E., PLECK, J. H., & LEVINE, J. A. (1987). Effects of increased paternal involvement on fathers and mothers. In C. Lewis & M. O'Brien (Eds.), *Researching fatherhood* (pp. 109–125). London: Sage.

LAROSSA, R. (1983). The transition to parenthood and the social reality of time. *Journal of Marriage and the Family, 45,* 579–589.

LAVINE, L. O., & LOMBARDO, J. P. (1984). Self-disclosure: Intimate and nonintimate disclosures to parents and best friends as a function of Bem sex-role category. *Sex Roles, 11,* 735–744.

LEAPER, C. (1994). Exploring the consequences of gender segregation on social relationships. In C. Leaper (Ed.), *Childhood gender segregation: Causes and consequences* (pp. 76–86). San Francisco: Josey-Bass.

LINDZEY, L. L. (1997). *Gender roles: A sociological perspective* (3rd. ed.). Upper Saddle River, NJ: Prentice-Hall.

LIPS, H. M. (1993). *Sex and gender: An introduction.* Mountain View, CA: Mayfield.

LIPS, H. M. (1995). Gender-role socialization: Lessons in femininity. In J. Freeman (Ed.), *Women: A feminist perspective* (5th ed.) (pp. 128–148). Mountain View, CA: Mayfield.

LLOYD, C. (1994). Investing in the next generation: The implications of high fertility at the level of the family. In R. Casses (Ed.), *Population and development: Old debates, new conclusions.* Washington, DC: Overseas Development Council.

LUEPTOW, L. B., GAROVICH, L., & LUEPTOW, M. B. (1995). The persistence of gender stereotypes in the face of changing sex roles: Evidence contrary to the sociocultural model. *Ethology & Sociobiology, 16,* 509–530.

LYNN, D. B. (1969). Curvilinear relation between cognitive functioning and distance of child from parent of the same sex. *Psychological Review, 76.* 236–240.

MACINTOSH, P. (1992). Masculine/feminine. In M. Schaum & C. Flanagan (Eds.), *Gender images: Readings for composition* (pp. 17–22). Boston: Houghton Mifflin.

MACCOBY, E. E.(1994). Commentary: Gender segregation in childhood. In C. Leaper (Ed.), *Childhood gender segregation: Causes and consequences* (pp. 87–97). San Francisco: Josey-Bass.

MALTZ, D. N., & BORKER, R. (1982). A cultural approach to male-female miscommunication. In J. J. Gumpertz (Ed.), *Language and social identity* (pp. 196–216). Cambridge, England: Cambridge University Press.

MARKUS, H., & CROSS, S. (1990). The interpersonal self. In L. A. Pervin (Ed.), *Handbook of personality: Theory and research* (pp. 576–608). New York: Guilford.

MARTIN, C. L., & LITTLE, J. K. (1990). The relation of gender understanding to children's sex-typed preferences and gender stereotypes. *Child Development, 61,* 1427–1439.

McADOO, H. P. (1990). The ethics of research and intervention with ethnic minority parents and their children. In C. B. Fisher & W. Warren (Eds.) *Ethics in applied developmental psychology: Emerging issues in an emerging field* (pp. 273–283). Norwood, NJ: Ablex Publishing.

MEAD, G. H. (1934). *Mind, self and society.* Chicago: University of Chicago Press.

MILLER, J. B. (1986). *Toward a new psychology of women* (2nd. ed.). Boston: Deacon Press.

MILLER, J., SCHOOLER, C., KOHN, M., & MILLER, K. (1979). Women and work: The psychological effects of occupational conditions. *American Journal of Sociology, 85,* 66–94.

MOEN, E. (1991). Sex selective eugenic abortion: Prospects in China and India. *Issues in Reproductive and Genetic Engineering, 4,* 231–249.

MONEDAS, M. (1992). Men communicating with women: Self-esteem and power. In L. A. M. Perry, L. H. Turner, & H. M. Sterk (Eds.), *Constructing and reconstructing gender: The links among communication, language, and gender* (pp. 197–208). Albany: State University of New York Press.

MONTAGU, A. (1971). *Touching: The human significance of the skin.* New York: Perennial Library.

MRUK, C. (1995). *Self-esteem: Research, theory, and practice.* New York: Springer.

NGUYEN, T., HESLIN, R., & NGUYEN, M. L. (1976). The meaning of touch: Sex and marital differences. *Representative Research in Social Psychology, 7,* 13–18.

NICHOLS, J. (1995). *Men's liberation: A new definition of masculinity.* New York: Penguin.

NYE, F. I. (1982). *Family relationships: Rewards and costs.* Beverly Hills, CA: Sage.

OLSEN, D., SPRENKLE, D., & RUSSELL, C. (1979). Circumplex model of marital and family systems: Cohesion and adaptability dimensions, family types, and clinical applications. *Family Process, 18,* 3–23.

ORENSTEIN, P. (1994). *School girls: Young women, self-esteem, and the confidence gap.* New York: Anchor Books.

PARK, C. B., & CHO, N. (1995). Consequences of son preference in a low-fertility society: Imbalance of the sex ratio at birth in Korea. *Population and Development Review, 21,* 59–84.

PEARSON, J. (1989). *Communication in the family.* New York: Harper/Collins.

PENNELL, G. E., & OGILVIE, D. M. (1995). You and me as she and he: The meaning of gender-related concepts in other- and self-perception. *Sex Roles, 33,* 29–57.

PLECK, J. H. (1981). *The myth of masculinity.* Cambridge, MA: MIT Press.

POMERLEAU, A., BOLDUC, D., MALCUIT, G., & COSSETTE, L. (1990). Pink or blue: Gender stereotypes in the first two years of life. *Sex Roles, 22,* 359–376.

POOLER, W. S. (1991). Sex of child preferences among college students. *Sex Roles, 25,* 569–576.

POPE, A., McHALE, S., & CRAIGHEAD, E. (1988). *Self-esteem enhancement with children and adolescents.* New York: Pergamon.

REPETTI, R. L. (1984). Determinants of children's sex-stereotyping: Parental sex-role traits and television viewing. *Personality and Social Psychology Bulletin, 10,* 457–468.

RIESSMAN, C. (1990). *Divorce talk: Women and men make sense of personal relationships.* New Brunswick, NJ: Princeton University Press.

RISMAN, B. J. (1989). Can men mother? Life as a single father. In B. Risman & P. Schwartz (Eds.), *Gender in intimate relationships* (pp. 155–164). Belmont, CA: Wadsworth.

ROSALDO, M. Z. (1974). Women, culture, and society: A rhetorical overview. In M. Z. Rosaldo & L. Lamphere (Eds.), *Women, culture, and society* (pp. 17–42). Stanford, CA: Stanford University Press.

ROSENTHAL, R., & JACOBSEN, L. (1968). *Pygmalion in the classroom.* New York: Holt.

ROSS, H., & TAYLOR, H. (1989). Do boys prefer daddy or his physical style of play? *Sex Roles, 20,* 23–31.

RUBIN, J. Z., PROVENSANO, F., & LURIA, Z. (1974). The eye of the beholder: Parents' views on sex of newborns. *American Journal of Orthopsychiatry, 44,* 312–319.

RYAN, M. (1979). *Womanhood in America: From colonial times to the present* (2nd. ed.). New York: New Viewpoints.

SADKER, M., & SADKER, D. (1994). *Failing at fairness: How America's schools cheat girls.* New York: Charles Schibner's.

SAGI, A., & SHARON, N. (1984). The role of the father in the family: Toward a gender-neutral family policy. *Children & Youth Services Review, 6,* 83–99.

SATIR, V. (1972). *Peoplemaking.* Palo Alto, CA: Science and Behavior Books.

SATIR, V. (1988). *The new peoplemaking.* Mountain View, CA: Science and Behavior Books.

SEGELL, M. (1996, October). The second coming of the alpha male. *Esquire,* 12–17.

SHAKIN, M., SHAKIN D., & STERNGLANZ, S. H. (1985). Infant clothing: Sex labeling for strangers. *Sex Roles, 12,* 955–964.

SHERIF, C. W. (1982). Needed concepts in the study of gender identity. *Psychology of Women Quaterly, 6,* 1982, 375–398.

SNOW, M. E., JACKLIN, C. N., & MACCOBY, E. E. (1983). Sex-of-child differences in father-child interactions at one year of age. *Child Development, 54,* 227–232.

STAKE, J. E. (1992). Gender differences and similarities in self-concept within everyday life contexts. *Psychology of Women Quarterly, 16,* 349–363.

STERN, M., & KARRAKER, K. H.(1989). Sex stereotyping in infants: A review of gender labeling studies. *Sex Roles, 20,* 501–522.

STEWART, L. P., COOPER, P. J., STEWART, A. D., & FRIEDLEY, S. A. (1996). *Communication and gender* (3rd ed.). Scottsdale, AZ: Gorsuch Scarisbrick.

STRATTON, M. (1993, November). *Women in the window: The image of beauty portrayed by store mannequins.* Paper presented at the meeting of the Speech Communication Association, Miami, FL.

THOMPSON, C. (1992). A new vision of masculinity. In M. Schaum & C. Flanagan (Eds.), *Gender images: Readings for composition* (pp. 77–83). Boston: Houghton Mifflin.

TRENHOLM, S. (1991). *Human communication theory* (2nd. ed.). Englewood Cliffs, NJ: Prentice-Hall.

UNGER, R. K. (1990). Imperfect reflections of reality: Psychology constructs gender. In R. T. Hare–Mustin & J. Marecek, J. (Eds.) *Making a difference: Psychology and the construction of gender* (pp. 102–49). New Haven, CT: Yale University Press.

VOCATE, D. R. (Ed.) (1994). *Intrapersonal communication: Different voices, different minds.* Hillsdale, NJ: Lawrence Erlbaum.

WALDRON, V. R., & MARE, L. D. (1998). Gender as a culturally determined construct: Communication styles in Japan and the United States. In D. Canary & K. Dindia (Eds.), *Sex, gender, and communication: Similarities and differences* (pp. 179–202). Mahwah, NJ: Lawrence Erlbaum.

WATZLAWICK, P., BEAVIN, J. B., & JACKSON, D. (1967). *Pragmatics of human communication.* New York: W. W. Norton.

WEST, C., & ZIMMERMAN, D. H. (1987). Doing gender. *Gender & Society, 1,* 125–151.

WHITE, R. (1965). The experience of efficacy in schizophrenia. *Psychiatry, 28,* 199–21.

WOLF, N. (1991). *The beauty myth.* New York: William Morrow.

WOOD, J. T. (1993). Enlarging conceptual boundaries: A critique of research on interpersonal communication. In S. Bowen & N. Wyatt (Eds.), *Transforming visions: Feminist critiques of speech communication* (pp. 19–49). Cresskill, NJ: Hampton.

WOOD, J. T. (1994). Engendered identities: Shaping voice and mind through gender. In D. R. Vocate (Ed.), *Intrapersonal communication: Different voices, different minds* (pp. 145–168). Hillsdale, NJ: Lawrence Erlbaum.

CHAPTER FOUR

PICTURES, PORNO, AND POP
Gender and Mass Media

CASE STUDY: A DAY IN THE LIFE

It's 6:30 AM, the clock radio alarm goes off, and a couple of people on a morning talk-radio show are chatting away. Rey shuts off the alarm, rolls out of bed, and begins his morning routine. Over his usual bowl of cereal, he scans the local newspaper and the *Wall Street Journal,* reading stock indexes with interest and making a mental note to check the stock exchange later in the day. While shaving, he turns on the Weather Channel for a quick check of the local forecast, then switches to CNN for the latest headlines. CNN cuts to a commercial that irritates Rey—one in which a husband looks foolish in front of a young male stock analyst because his wife knows more about a certain kind of mutual fund than he does. Rey thinks to himself, "male-bashing again," switches off CNN, and channel surfs between other cable news sources, MSNBC and Fox News. Before he leaves the house, he checks his VCR and satellite dish setup to make sure the VCR will correctly record the network nightly news (which he tapes every weekday because he doesn't leave work in time to see the broadcast), as well as a few of his favorite television programs. If something comes up at work, he might not get home to catch these shows, so better to tape them than miss them.

On the drive to work, Rey tunes in his car radio and checks back with the talk-radio program. An air personality says, "Well, scandals are nothing new in politics . . ." Rey decides he's heard enough and is more in the mood to listen to a CD. About halfway between his home and the office, Rey puts the CD on pause and uses his cell phone to call ahead to the office and check in with his secretary so he can anticipate what will be happening when he gets there. She says it's pretty quiet, but that a few faxes did come in overnight; they're on his desk for him to read when he gets there. He cues up the CD again and notices he's reached that point in the drive where he passes a bank's digital billboard calculating increases in the national debt.

Rey arrives at the office; his secretary is on the phone so he swings by the central mailboxes and picks up his mail, including more messages and a couple of magazines he subscribes to. When he gets to his desk the light on his phone is blinking, indicating that he has voice mail messages. He takes off his coat, lays the mail on top of the faxes on his desk, and thumbs through the first couple of ads in one of his magazines. Then he picks up the phone and dials in his code to start listening to voice mail messages while, at the same time, punching the start-up key on his computer. The computer screen fires up and a mail icon with the statement, "You've got mail," appears. Once he's gone through the 10 or so voice mail messages and noted on his digital pocket recorder who to call back, he begins to read the interoffice e-mail. Later he'll log onto the Internet to read his other e-mail —the postings to an electronic bulletin board he subscribes to as well as messages from colleagues across the country, the occasional family member, and a buddy who's now working in Australia. Hopefully just before lunch he'll remember to use his Web browser to check the latest stock trends. He'd love to knock off early today to catch the newest Ah-nuld action film, but no doubt something would come up and his secretary would page him. There's nothing so irritating as somebody's beeper going off in a movie theatre. Too much going on, too many things and people to deal with, too little time.

HEY—wasn't technology supposed to SAVE us time? Do you think Rey, who is bombarded by media and surrounded by technological innovations, feels that they keep him informed and save him time or that they impinge on his time? Is Rey running the media or is the media running him? By the way, you probably think that Rey is some hot shot financial guy or corporate hon-cho—he's actually a high school principal, and this is an average day.

How much media and technology do you consume each day? What influence do they have on you? What messages about the sexes are communicated via the media you consume? That's the topic of this chapter.

Hot Topics

- Theories of media effects that show how consumers process mass media
- The impact of stereotypical depictions of women and men in advertisements on attitudes about the sexes
- Gendered messages in prime-time television shows and social issues programming
- Communication about the sexes via daytime soap operas and talk shows
- Gender-bending in film and how men's and women's film roles impact viewers
- The pervasive influence of pornography and the effects of its consumption on women's and men's attitudes and relationships
- Song lyrics and music video portrayals of the sexes

THE POWER OF MEDIATED COMMUNICATION: EFFECTS ON OUR LIVES

Probably no other force influences our daily lives more than media. Parents are hugely important, teachers have significant impact, friends affect us in profound ways—but we have come to believe that, over time, media have the strongest effect on us out of all possible influences. Consider how often you compare real life—work, family, relationships—to how these things are depicted in movies, television, song lyrics, and music videos. It's common to hear someone refer to something on television, such as, "I just don't trust that guy I went out with last night; he reminds me of Richard Fish on *Ally McBeal*," "My wife and I have arguments kind of like that couple on (pick a sitcom, any sitcom)," or "I felt like I was in a Hallmark card commercial." Media are highly influential in how they communicate messages *about* women and men.

Some argue that technology has made it easy for us to escape reality, meaning that media have allowed us to avoid connecting with one another. The claim is that, for many people, movies, television, the Internet, and music take the place of a social life and substitute for a roommate or spouse—a substitute that can be shut out with just the click of a switch. What do you think about that claim? Do various forms of media act as substitutes for something in your life?

A Bombardment of Media

You are literally bombarded with forms of mass communication every day and the effects of this bombardment are dramatic, as research documents (Comstock & Strzyzewski, 1990; Dambrot, Reep, & Bell, 1988; Lindlof, 1987, 1991; Press, 1991a). For example, one study found that over 11,000 magazines are currently published and distributed in the United States; the average American spends about 110 hours per year reading these magazines (Pratkanis & Aronson, 1992). Your modern existence is jammed full of mass communication every sunrise to sunset, but just how are you affected by it?

As a college-educated person, you are probably an above-average critical consumer of mass communication, meaning that you consciously select mediated messages to take in and to filter out. However, a great deal of mediated information is absorbed unconsciously, even by the most critical of consumers. Few of us have time in our busy lives to focus concentrated attention on all the mediated messages we receive in a typical day and make conscious decisions about their effects. This critical thinking process becomes a skill we use less often as we take in more and more mediated information. Just how this absorption affects us has been the subject of a good deal of attention among media researchers.

Theories about the Effects of Media Consumption

In the 1970s, media scholar Gaye Tuchman described how, as mass media grew "exponentially" during the years between World War II and the beginning of the 1980s, "so did study of the media" (1979, p. 528). Several theories have emerged that attempt to explain how media affect consumers.

Hypodermic Needle or Direct Effects Theory

This early theory viewed the mass audience as passively and directly consuming mediated messages. The imagery was that of a hypodermic needle that "injected" mass communication directly into the veins of its noncritical consumers (Vivian, 1999). This theory offered an inadequate, overly simplistic explanation of media effects because it ignored how other factors might influence the process.

Uses and Gratifications Theory

Media expert John Vivian (1999) describes the uses and gratifications approach as a theory that no longer viewed mass audiences as passive sponges, but rather as active "users" of media. Research has focused on how consumers are motivated to use various media and what gains, rewards, or "gratifications" they receive from such consumption (Palmgreen & Rayburn, 1985; Rubin, 1986). Media researchers have employed uses and gratifications theory to better understand such things as the uses people make of television news or commercial advertising (Rayburn, Palmgreen, & Acker, 1984), the pleasure people derive from soap operas (Lemish, 1985; Rubin, 1985), and children's music (Christenson, 1994).

Agenda-Setting Theory

This theory dates back to the work of Robert Park in the 1920s, who proposed that the media do not merely report, reflect, or dramatize what is important in society, media actually guide what we think is important. Vivian (1999) explains "the media create awareness of issues more than they create knowledge or attitudes. The media do not tell people what to think but what to think about" (p. 404). For an example of how this theory applies to gender concerns, consider talk shows. Many consumers of these shows believe that the issues raised constitute critical social, political, and economic concerns. In essence, viewers may be allowing a media outlet to set an agenda for what should be most important to them (Heaton & Wilson, 1995).

Cultivation Theory

This theory suggests that media consumption "'cultivates' in us a distorted perception of the world we live in, making it seem more like television portrays it, than it is in real life" (Bittner, 1989, p. 386). The media blur reality and fantasy, what life is really like and how it appears on television or in movies. Media scholar George Gerbner and various colleagues are among the most prominent researchers to use cultivation theory to better understand the relationships between the social reality of violence and crime to media's depiction of it (Gerbner, Gross, Eleey, Jackson-Beeck, Jeffries-Fox, & Signorielli, 1977; Gerbner, Gross, Morgan, & Signorielli, 1980). Gerbner, who began his investigations of television violence in 1967, contends that a typical American child will see 32,000 on-screen murders before she or he turns 18 (as in Vivian, 1999). To help you understand cultivation theory, just remember this easy example: Think about people who believe that romantic relationships are supposed to happen just like in Hollywood movies, happy endings and all.

Advertising: Selling a Product or Selling Sexism?

Advertising is a huge and pervasive industry. Estimates suggest U.S. advertisers spend over $150 billion *per year*, exposing the average person to about 1,800 advertising messages *each day* (Lazier & Gagnard Kendrick, 1993). Researchers contend that advertising has a powerful effect that goes well beyond the purpose of selling products to consumers. As media researchers Lysonski and Pollay (1990) point out, advertising "creates a pervasive and persuasive communication environment that sells a great deal more than just products. Through the use of imagery, the display of life-styles, and the exercise and reinforcement of values, advertisements are communicators of culturally defined concepts such as success, worth, love, sexuality, popularity, and normalcy" (p. 317). Do you think that gender should be added to that list?

A great deal of research has been conducted on the ways women and men are depicted in print and electronic advertisements, as well as the messages these ads communicate to media consumers. Media researchers Wells, Burnett, and Moriarty (1998) explain that *stereotyping* "involves presenting a group of people in an unvarying pattern that lacks individuality and often reflects popular misconceptions" (p. 49). Let's look at an overview of the various stereotypical portrayals of the sexes, including a few exceptions, and then consider the overall effects on consumers.

Babes in Bras: Female Depiction in Advertising

Programmatic research spanning two decades by marketing professors Alice Courtney and Thomas Whipple (1974, 1980, 1983, 1985) forms the basis for the claim that advertising has a major impact on individuals' views of gender in society.

Homemakers and Sex Objects

From the compiled results of numerous studies, Courtney and Whipple produced the following comprehensive list of female *gender-role stereotypes* in advertising, corroborated by subsequent national and international research (Kang, 1996; Lanis & Covell, 1995; Lin, 1997; Liu, Inoue, Bresnahan, & Nishida, 1998; Milner, 1994; Rakow, 1992):

1. Women in isolation, particularly from other women
2. Women in sleepwear, underwear, and lingerie more than in professional clothing
3. Young girls portrayed as passive and in need of help
4. Women as kitchen and bathroom product representatives
5. Women appearing more than men in ads for personal hygiene products (e.g., deodorants, toothpaste)

6. An abundance of women serving men and boys
7. Medical advertisements depicting male physicians interacting with hysterical, hypochondriacal female patients
8. Women more often depicted in family- and home-oriented roles than in business roles
9. Young housewives shown performing household duties, whereas older men act as product representatives who give advice to housewives
10. Women portrayed as decorative, nonfunctioning entities
11. Fewer depictions of older women than older men
12. Fewer depictions of minority women than minority men
13. Fewer women than men advertising expensive luxury products
14. Few women depicted actively engaged in sports
15. Ads overtly critical of feminist rights and issues

> *A good man doesn't just happen. They have to be created by us women. A guy is a lump, like a doughnut. So first you gotta get rid of all the stuff his mom did to him. And then you gotta get rid of all that macho crap they pick up from beer commercials. And then there's my personal favorite, the male ego.*
>
> *Roseanne, actor & talk show host*

Many manufacturers and advertisers still either ignore how the public feels about sexist ads or find segments of the market that like their ads and buy their products. One study compared magazine advertisements from 1979 to ads from 1991 to determine if depictions of women had been "modernized." The findings are disheartening: Stereotypical female depictions—including portrayals of women as weak, dependent, childish, domestic, irrational, subordinate, mentally feeble, and scantily clad—were actually more prevalent in 1991 ads than in 1979 ads (Kang, 1996). Although more ads now show women in business settings, the use of women as decorative objects—physically attractive but having nothing to do with the product being advertised—is on the rise as well (Lanis & Covell, 1995).

Killing Women Softly

Perhaps some of you are familiar with the work of Jean Kilbourne, particularly her educational films. Kilbourne's first film, entitled *Killing Us Softly*, was released in 1976; her follow-up film, entitled *Still Killing Us Softly*, was released in 1987. Both of these powerful films provide Kilbourne's commentary in tandem with example after example of ads reflecting female stereotypes, many of which Courtney and Whipple unearthed in their research. Kilbourne (1998) asserts that advertising presents women almost exclusively in one of two roles: housewife or sex object. Her examples include women pathologically obsessed with cleanliness and ridding their husbands' shirts of "ring around the collar," and thin, tall, long-legged mannequin-like women with perfect skin and no signs of aging. These portrayals have severe effects on women, as Kilbourne states: "A woman is conditioned to view her face as a mask and her body as an object, as *things* separate from and more important than her real self, constantly in need of alteration, improvement, and disguise. She is made to feel dissatisfied with and ashamed of herself, whether she tries to achieve 'the look' or not. Objectified constantly by others, she learns to objectify herself" (p. 129).

In particular, women of color fare poorly in ads, both in the quantity of depictions and the quality of the roles, according to Gail Baker Woods, author of *Advertising and Marketing to the New Majority* (1995). Woods reports that "Less than 20 percent of all ads with blacks feature black women. When they are seen, black women are often portrayed as 'jive'-talking, sassy 'sisters' or overweight, wise-cracking, church-going women" (p. 28). Hispanic, Asian-American, and Native-American women are less represented in advertisements than African-American women, who are less represented than white women.

One media analyst suggests that "Progress has been made in the 1990s, however there's still a disproportionate amount of gravity-defying breasts and giggly silliness in advertising . . ." (Fawcett, 1993, p. S1). Lazier and Gagnard Kendrick (1993) contend that it is "shocking to see the minuscule 'advancement' made in the imagery of women over a decade and a half." They then explore the question, "How can this stereotypical sexism survive given the incredible changes in women's social status?" (p. 206) They wonder, like we do, why stereotypical images of women still predominate in print and electronic media. Their conclusion is that ads

> "reflect our current culture—one of the traditional balance of power (male). The ads reflect the critical components of culture—its stereotypes, its bigotries, its biases, its dominant values, its tendency toward the status quo, and the on-goingness of the traditional. The ads also reflect the ongoing confusion in our culture (by both men and women) of what women are" (pp. 206–207).

An Exercise in Ad Analysis

Look at the billboard advertisement reproduced in Figure 4.1. Some of you might think there's nothing inherently wrong or sexist about this advertisement. The ad is simply catching the eye of motorists in Dallas, Texas, and effectively selling a product. However, others of you may look at this ad and think, "Not another scantily clad woman selling beer!" Using the following set of questions, analyze this ad; supply your own answers to the questions first, then we'll provide our perspective.

1. Who is the target audience for this product?
2. What's being sold here, beer? Sexuality? Leisure? Status?

FIGURE 4.1.

3. Is there anything unusual in the fact that only a woman appears in this ad, given that men are the predominant beer drinkers in the country?
4. What is your interpretation of the clothing the woman is wearing (or lack thereof)?
5. Do you find anything sexist in her body position, meaning her prone position on the billboard?
6. What is your interpretation of the positioning of the beer bottle underneath the woman's body?
7. What is the meaning of the caption, "Tap into the cold, Dallas"?

Compare your answers with those of your classmates, particularly classmates of the opposite sex. This comparison will demonstrate how subjective a judgment of sexism can be.

Here's our interpretation of this advertisement: Since more men than women drink beer, it's safe to assume that this ad is geared more toward a male target audience rather than a female one. We think it's a sexist ad for many reasons, the main one being that it represents yet another attempt on the part of advertisers to use a woman's sexuality for profit. What's really being sold here is the woman and her sexuality, not beer (Hall & Crum, 1994). If that wasn't the case, then why not show just the beer bottle and the caption? The message to men is, "If you drink this brand of beer, you'll attract a woman who looks like this, who'll dress like this and lay down for you like this." What messages do women get from a huge billboard like this?

That interpretation is reinforced by the vulnerable position of the woman (in only a bathing suit) lying on her back with one arm up which conveys a sexual, submissive message. The fact that she is on top of a cold beer bottle suggests sexual imagery, if you want to go so far as to construe the neck of the beer bottle, intentionally placed underneath and between her legs, as a phallic symbol. Concerning the caption, one wonders if it is the beer that is to be tapped or the woman. Research shows that some men respond to sexual images of women in media with views that support sexual aggression and assault (Lanis & Covell, 1995; MacKay & Covell, 1997).

At this point you may disagree with us or wonder if we don't get out much. We realize that someone isn't likely to pull off a Dallas freeway to critique this billboard. Perhaps the argument could be made that, in isolation, this one ad isn't sexist. But what about the trend for advertisers to display women, typically in revealing attire, draped across the hoods of cars or posed in various suggestive positions with objects such as oversized beer bottles or shiny motorcycles between their legs? What's being communicated when sexist ads appear with such regularity?

Any Relief in Sight?

Some manufacturers have changed their approach to advertising products for female consumers—the operant word in this statement being *some*. Laura Zinn (1991), a *Business Week* writer, describes ads for women's products that show promise, such as Maidenform lingerie ads and Nike's women's athletic wear ads. Past Maidenform ads displayed the "Maidenform Woman," always a young, beautiful, thin woman who turned up in strange places wearing only her bra and panties. In efforts to change with the times, Maidenform launched a series of less sexist ads. One ad in the series depicted a baby chick, a Barbie doll, a tomato, and a fox, with the caption, "A helpful guide for those who still confuse women with various unrelated objects" (Zinn, 1991, p. 90). Since increasing numbers of women are making sports and exercise a significant part of their lives, Nike and Reebok ads in particular have wisely reflected the trend toward less sexist advertising. These companies have made serious, laudable, successful attempts to communicate to female consumers that they understand them and find them important, but they are the exception, not the rule.

A few other companies have made creative attempts to "clean up their advertising acts." Anheuser-Busch, for example, has been hugely successful with its reptile ads. The Swedish Bikini Team has disappeared from one beer company's ads. But when men and women appear together in ads, women still are too often portrayed less than fully clothed and in sexy, flirtatious, and vulnerable ways. We don't see sexism lurking at every turn, but we do worry about the prevalence of sexual images of women being used to sell all kinds of products—especially products geared to men.

Advertising's Effects on Women: Bodies, Sex, and Self-Esteem

Feminist media researchers Goldman, Heath, and Smith (1991) describe the harmful effects of stereotypical, idealized advertising images on female consumers. They contend that "a growing proportion of female viewers have

Whenever J...turn on TV, J am reminded of the millions of women who have stringy hair, large pores, overweight figures, and rough hands.

Warren Beatty,
actor & director

grown antagonistic to the uninterrupted procession of perfect, but unattainable looks that daily confront them. Women don't have to be feminists to feel oppressed by images of perfection and beauty that batter and bruise self-esteem . . ." (p. 335). Lazier and Gagnard Kendrick (1993) express increasing concern about the results of media images of women: "Portrayals of women in advertising are not only potentially debilitating and demeaning, but they are also inaccurate. We do not have a demography of demigoddesses. Women today are considerably more than flawless decorative objects, dependent upon or defined by men" (pp. 200–201).

Several studies across decades have been conducted on our culture's obsession with thinness, as reflected in advertising (Gagnard, 1986; Lee, 1995; Myers & Biocca, 1992; Silverstein, Perdue, Peterson, & Kelly, 1986). We won't go into detail on each, but the results are consistent and overwhelming:

1. Women receive many times more advertising messages about thinness and body shape than men.
2. The volume of these ads in prominent magazines and on television is staggering.
3. The trend toward severe thinness is inescapable in ads, creating an ever-widening gap between the weight of an "average" American woman and the "ideal."
4. Thin female models are perceived to be more attractive than average weight or overweight models in ads.
5. The majority of African-American models, including supermodels Tyra Banks and Naomi Campbell, are slim, although the thinness standard isn't as extreme among black women as for other racial and ethnic groups.
6. The pressure to be thin is not as great for men as for women, as evidenced by the greater number of average weight and overweight male models in ads in comparison to females.
7. Young women's images of their bodies become distorted when they are presented with images of ideal body shape. (Many simply believe that they cannot be "thin enough," and they suffer great self-esteem loss trying to achieve the unreal perfect body presented by the media. One survey found that a large percentage of fourth-grade girls reported being on diets.)

8. The term *heroin chic* was coined late in the 1990s to describe the gaunt, un-healthy look of many top fashion models. Kate Moss is the poster child for this look; she is also one of the top models in the world, admired by count-less numbers of young women.

We've all heard the phrase "sex sells," but women's sex *really* sells, as tel-evision ads prove time and time again. Many women and men alike grow weary of women's bodies and sexuality, and to a lesser extent men's sexuality as well, being used in every possible way to draw a viewer's or reader's at-tention and sell a product—*any* product. One recent example is an ad for a new light bulb created by GE, called "Enrich." A man's voice—deep, rich, and sensual—slowly describes what attracts a man to a woman, all in physi-cal terms, of course. As a thin, young, beautiful model wearing a sexy red dress that bares her shoulders and neckline walks toward the man in the frame, the ad encourages us to buy the new light bulb because the woman looks better for her man "in this light." What will it take to have a situation in which "sex *doesn't* sell?" Do you think it will ever happen?

Mixed Signals Create Confusion

People are confused by images in the media; at times, this confusion has con-sequences for their relationships and communication. Many men wonder if women want to be treated as equals and professionals, as traditional help-mates and caregivers, or as sex kittens because the media readily provide con-tinuous, seemingly acceptable images of each.

One source of confusion is the cover pictures on women's magazines and the contradictory headlines describing the magazine's contents. Extremely thin female models, their breasts squeezed into outfits to create cleavage, ap-pear on the covers of *Cosmopolitan*—opposite headings such as "How to Get Your Boss To Take You Seriously." In ads found in various print sources, the images of women create a paradox that is only compounded by reading the copy accompanying the ad (Jackson, 1991; Sullivan & O'Connor, 1988). For ex-ample, an ad meant to depict a typical day in the life of a professional career woman shows her dressed in a business suit with briefcase in hand, but the copy says she'd really like to be anywhere but at work; she's on the job, but ac-tually thinking of her man.

Probably the best, and most insidious, example of mixed signal advertising has been perpetrated by the makers of Virginia Slims cigarettes, whose ads first emerged during the heyday of the women's liberation movement. The first tele-vision and print ads were done in sepia tones, to look like old-fashioned movie reels or still photographs. In the TV ads, a voice-over described how some women in history got into trouble for being rebellious and smoking. These ads then cut to modern-day images of women, accompanied by the motto (origi-nally sung) "You've come a long way, baby, to get where you got to today!" The point was to illustrate how women's status has improved in American society.

The 1990s versions of these ads could only legally appear in magazines and on billboards because of new laws restricting cigarette advertising. They depicted youthful, attractive women doing fun, active things (as active as you can be with a cigarette in your hand), while further employing the language of liberation. The paradox comes when you compare the visual images to the wording across the ads, such as "Now's your chance to tell the world just how far you've come" and the repeated sentence, just under the name Virginia Slims and next to the cigarette pack, "It's a *woman* thing." This ad campaign has long been criticized by health care officials and feminists alike who resent the fact that a tobacco company continues to ignore women's health issues and packages the product as though it epitomizes liberation, women's rights, and feminism. Is the company trying to convince young women that smoking equals liberation and that it's a "woman's thing" to smoke? What do teenage and adolescent girls think when they see these ads?

Studs in Suits: Male Depiction in Advertising

Just as there are female stereotypes in advertising, male *gender-role stereotypes* appear as well. More research has been conducted on the ways women are depicted in advertisements, but several studies provide interesting revelations about men in ads.

Corporate Success, Great Dad, and Bumbling Idiot

Studies in the 1980s showed that men were typically portrayed as dominant, successful professionals in business settings or engaged in fun activities in settings away from home (Courtney & Whipple, 1983). They were still portrayed this way in the 1990s, but a new trend presented men in decorative, nonfunctional roles that had no relation to the product being sold (Lin, 1997). Male depictions also began to include domestic tasks such as taking care of children, preparing family meals, and doing household chores (Craig, 1992; Kanner, 1990; Richmond-Abbott, 1992). One example is a television ad for a long-distance carrier in which a young man calls his mother while doing laundry, apparently for the first time. He says, "Mom, you said one cupful of detergent, right? Oh, one *capful*." At this point he looks at a sudsy washer and says "Gotta go, Mom."

While some think these ads realistic and humorous, others see them as male-bashing. A Hyundai ad from a few years ago was particularly memorable, if for no other reasons than its blatant role reversal and sexual innuendo—and the fact that it was hugely successful. The ad created twice as much awareness of the company than before. In it, two women critique men who get out of fancy sports cars, saying that one "must be compensating for a shortcoming." When a man arrives in a sensible Hyundai, one woman says to the other, admiringly, "I wonder what he's got under *his* hood." Researcher Philip Patterson (1996) views this ad as an example of what he terms *power babe commercials* in which "women enjoy the upper hand over men" (p. 93). He is critical of two prominent stereotypes of men in advertising, what he calls *Rambo* and *Himbo depictions:* "The image of men in advertising is either that of a 'Rambo,' solo conqueror of all he sees, or a 'Himbo,' a male bimbo" (p. 94). But reporter Bernice Kanner (1990) contends that male-bashing ads are on the way out. Kanner points to changing societal roles, in that as more women choose to work outside the home, domestic duties may be shared between wives and husbands. Kanner warns that "men have become too sophisticated as shoppers for advertisers to risk alienating them" (p. 20).

About two years after our first edition of this text came out, we got a letter from a professor whose class used our book and found an omission in the media chapter. They didn't see a list of male stereotypes that corresponded to the Courtney and Whipple list of depictions of women. So the class created one, and we think it's well worth printing here. According to Lynn Wells' students at Saddleback College in Mission Viejo, California (to whom we're grateful), male depictions in ads include the following:

1. Stud/Cowboy, like the Marlboro Man
2. Jock, who can perform in all sports
3. Handyman, who can fix anything
4. Young and "hip," as in a 7-Up ad
5. Handsome, ladies' man, as in beer commercials
6. Kind and grandfatherly, as in insurance ads
7. Professional, knowledgeable
8. Couch potato man
9. Blue collar worker, sometimes seen as a sex symbol
10. Androgynous, as in Calvin Klein ads
11. Romantic, coffee man
12. Fonzie type, Joe Cool
13. Helpless, as in the "Got Milk" commercials
14. Just a kid, who needs a woman to save him

What advertising types can you add to this list?

Media analyst Jennifer Nicholson, in a 1992 article in *Adbusters,* suggests that the societal roles of men and corresponding depictions in ads reflect a sort of male image schizophrenia. Nicholson explains: "By creating a variety of new male identities, advertisers gain access to a wider collection of pocket-books. Whether the '90s man is actually changing is irrelevant—the point is to convince him that he's part of a market-driven trend" (p. 21). She cites varying depictions of men in television and print ads, including businessmen with babies strapped to their backs, dads preparing sack lunches before their kids go off to school, a "sensitive new age guy (SNAG)" who is "politically correct and even eligible to be called a feminist" (p. 23), men in Jockey underwear and Calvin Klein cologne ads, and scantily clad men working out in Soloflex commercials. The more varied the depictions of men in ads, the more messages are conveyed that there are diverse, nonstereotypical roles for men in society.

Advertising's Effects on Men

Most women prefer not to relate to men as though they were macho stereo-types. But then they wonder if men actually want such treatment, given that macho images of men still pervade many forms of media from magazine ads depicting rugged men in their pick-up trucks to infomercials pushing the lat-est exercise equipment. One study focused on views of magazine ads contain-ing images of men that ranged from traditionally masculine to androgynous (Garst & Bodenhausen, 1997). Male subjects with traditional gender identities did not change their attitudes after viewing nontraditional depictions of men in ads. Men with nontraditional gender identities identified more strongly with androgynous depictions of men in ads, as well as with feminism and nontraditional views.

If you're a male reader, what's your reaction to an ad in which a scantily clad man is depicted as a sex object, as some would argue Calvin Klein, Ver-sace, and other magazine ads do? Look at the new twist to Virginia Slims ads, for example. One depicts two women (one with the ever-present cigarette in hand) looking at each other, smiling a knowing smile, with a caption that reads, "What's the first thing we look for in a guy? A really great . . . um . . . personality." The guy in the ad has his back to them and is dressed in a t-shirt tucked into a tight pair of jeans. Another ad has a woman smoking and look-ing up at a man, laughingly, with this caption underneath, "Just because we laugh at your stories doesn't mean we believe 'em for a second."

Or how about the now-infamous Diet Coke ad from the early 1990s, in which a hunky, sweaty construction worker removes his shirt and downs a Diet Coke to the delight of the women working next door who watched the clocks for their "Diet Coke break"? As one female columnist wrote, "For a lot of us, this ad is sweeter than a thermos full of sugar substitute for a whole lot of reasons. Most obvious: It is so grand to take off the place mats and turn those tables" (Loohauis, 1994, p. 5C). For the guys, do you notice these ads more or in a different way than, for example, Victoria's Secret lingerie ads, which only re-cently began appearing on television? Do these ads make you feel bad about yourself in comparison to some stud women swoon over? Or do you find them refreshing and realistic because women show their "appreciation" of men?

Many scholars believe that men are the next targets for an all-out assault on self-esteem, mainly because the market for assaulting women's self-esteem—which forces them to buy products and services ranging from simple beauty remedies to full-scale plastic surgery—is saturated, profits maxed out. Research on American college students shows that "up to two thirds of young women and one third of young men experience significant dissatisfaction with their body size, shape, condition, or appearance in relation to most advertising cam-paigns" (Raeback-Wagener, Eickenhoff-Schemeck, & Kelly-Vance, 1998, p. 29).

Writer Ann Marie Dobosz explores this trend in an article for *Ms.* (1997). She explains, "There is an element of ad-inspired obsession with buying products and with measuring up to an unobtainable ideal of masculinity. Men's magazines have seen a conspicuous rise in ads for beauty and image products" (p. 91). She points to a significant increase in ads showing half-clothed male bodies, which encourage men to think of themselves as sex objects. Mass communication scholar Carolyn Lin (1997) agrees: "Rather than elevating both genders to more realistic portrayals, it appears that men, too, are getting caricatured in roles as sex symbols. This 'downgrading' of the traditional middle-class male image—from a breadwinner and responsible adult to simply a 'playmate'—is indicative of how advertisers are willing to sexually exploit men to market their products" (p. 247). You may find you have become so sensitized to sexually objectifying ads—of both men and women—that you hardly notice them any more. Since sexually objectifying female ads don't seem to be going away, do you think it's a form of equality to sexually objectify men in ads?

Worries About Young Consumers

It is possible for advertising to affect your self-esteem and gender-role identity, as well as your expectations for and communication with members of the opposite sex. But what about possible effects on people who have not yet developed the ability to critically analyze and selectively retain mediated information? Research continues to explore the impact of ads that accompany children's television programming, in terms of the numbers of male characters and the roles they enact, the lack of positive female portrayals, and the predominant use of male voice-overs in television commercials (see below). As cultivation theory suggests, these factors have the potential to reinforce for children conventional gender-role definitions, meaning that children may come to believe that life is supposed to be like it is portrayed in commercials. Advertising may also influence how children develop their own sex and gender identity and how they come to expect certain behavior from women and men (Kolbe, 1991; Macklin & Kolbe, 1984).

The Voice of Authority in Television Commercials

Voice-overs for ads represent unseen authorities or product experts, who typically greet the viewer, introduce the product or service, and conclude the ad with emphatic praise or a final sales pitch (Marecek, et al., 1978). Of the voice-overs for hundreds of American television commercials analyzed in three studies in the 1970s, researchers reported that more than 93 percent used male voices, while less than 7 percent used female (Culley & Bennett, 1976; Maracek, et al., 1978; O'Donnell & O'Donnell, 1978). In more current research, media analysts Allan and Coltrane (1996) found that women's voice-overs in American television commercials only increased by 2 percent from the 1950s through the 1980s, leading them to conclude that the "male bastion of authoritative voice continues unscathed" (p. 199). One study of television ads broadcast during Super Bowls from 1989 through 1994 produced interesting, if not predictable, results. Media researcher Bonnie Drewniany (1996) indicated that "One would hope to hear an equal number of male and female voice-overs, but the power of the male voice came across

---

RECAP

hypodermic needle theory, direct effects theory, uses and gratifications theory, agenda-setting theory, cultivation theory, stereotyping, female gender-role stereotypes, mixed signal advertising, male gender-role stereotypes, power babe commercials, Rambo and Himbo depictions, voice-overs

---

loud and strong 167 times, while the female voice was heard a mere sixteen times" (p. 89). International studies reveal similar trends: Twice as many male as female voice-overs occur in television commercials in Japan, and four times as many in Taiwan (Liu, Inoue, Bresnahan, & Nishida, 1998).

However, media researcher David Kalish (1988) contends that in the United States "advertisers are slowly becoming more flexible in their choice of voice-over artists" (p. 30). Even in Drewniany's (1996) Super Bowl study, 10 of the 16 spots using female voice-overs aired during the 1993 and 1994 games, which might be an indication of progress on this front. Celebrity women with distinguishable voices, such as Lauren Bacall and Kathleen Turner, have done television commercial voice-overs. But women who do voice-overs have a common vocal characteristic—their voices are low, deep, and husky, sort of a blend of masculine and feminine. Since things are improving *very* slowly in the area of voice-overs, do you think society still perceives masculine-sounding voices as having more credibility, particularly as product or service spokespersons?

LESSONS FROM THE SMALL SCREEN: TELEVISION AND THE SEXES

Ninety-eight percent of American households contain at least one television set; most homes have more than one set (Vivian, 1999). More than two-thirds of American television-viewing households are cable subscribers (Dominick, 1998). Former chair of the Federal Communications Commission Newton Minow (1991) reports that average household television viewing increased from two hours a day in the 1960s to over seven hours a day in the 1990s. When you consider that the latter figure equals about 49 hours of TV watching per week, this activity amounts to more than the average 40-hour work week. Video recording has greatly expanded television's impact by allowing consumers to tape and watch cable and network programming as well as films when convenient. Some experts estimate that more than 85 percent of American homes have VCRs and that many families own as many VCRs as television sets (Dorr & Kunkel, 1990; Krendl, Clark, Dawson, & Troiano, 1993). Once DTV (digital television) becomes available and affordable, that seven hours of viewing per day will increase (Goldberg, 1998). We've all no doubt seen futuristic ads in which someone handles all of life's needs (such as banking, purchasing groceries and clothing, and communicating with others) through the use of a telephone, television, and computer interface. Soon those won't be futuristic ads; they'll reflect reality. Since it's unlikely that exposure to programming will decrease any time soon, it seems reasonable that television's depiction of the sexes will continue to have an impact on the viewing audience.

Television: Mirroring Reality or Creating It?

Television is a rapidly changing industry; it's likely that some of the television shows we refer to in this chapter will be off the air when you read this material. But one thing will remain: a chicken-or-egg argument about whether the media merely reflect what is happening in society or actually create the issues and trends that then become relevant in society. Perhaps it's a bit of both.

On the "media reflect reality" side, one could argue that the economic pressures and changing lifestyles of young professionals in the 1990s are reflected in such sitcoms as *Friends* and *Working*. On the other hand, many media researchers support the "media drive or create culture" view, believing that television actually expands viewers' range of behaviors (Comstock, 1983; Larson, 1989). Probably the best example of this view was the hit series *Seinfeld*, which media scholars believe at once expanded language and created a whole new way of relating to friends, jobs, parents, lovers, and life in general. Yet another school of media thought contends that television programming, for the most part, neither reflects nor creates reality; rather, its exaggerated portrayals and overly dramatized situations are nowhere near the realities of most people's lives. (Maybe *Buffy the Vampire Slayer* is a good example of this perspective?) In this view, television programs and other forms of media serve purely as escapism and entertainment for consumers, as uses and gratifications theory suggests (Rubin, 1986).

The Changing Roles of Men in Prime-Time

To better understand depictions of the sexes in prime-time television programming, media researcher Marvin Moore (1992) conducted an extensive survey of family depictions in American prime-time television programming from 1947 to 1990. Moore analyzed 115 "successful family series," defined as prime-time programs that aired for more than one season (p. 45). Ninety-four percent of these television families were white and two-thirds involved the traditional family profile of a married couple, with or without children.

Moore found that men's roles were "exaggerated, with a large number of male single-parent portrayals and an emphasis on the family roles over work roles" (p. 58). (At the time, the program *Full House* was popular.) Moore points out that while such portrayals reflect positive roles for men, they may also create false images and distortions of reality. Moore might argue today that the male sportscasters (one who is in the throes of divorce) in the sitcom *Sports Night* are more the reality than Peter Berg's Dr. Billy Kronck on *Chicago Hope,* who decided to drastically cut his hours at the hospital so he can stay home and take care of his and Dr. Diane Grad's new baby daughter. (Interestingly enough, this is the plot line the show's creators came up with upon learning that the actor, Peter Berg, wished to more fully pursue a film acting and directing career.)

The Kinder, Gentler Male Character

Are there any depictions of men on television that are breaking new ground? Media scholar Stephen Craig (1992) argues that a feminized or reconstructed male has emerged in prime-time television programming. These male characters are not buffoons or wimps, but likable, masculine men who struggle as they learn about themselves, how to communicate with the women in their lives, and how to be better parents. Several highly successful shows have capitalized on this trend, including *Mad About You, Everybody Loves Raymond, Party of Five* (primarily in the character of Charlie), and *ER. ER* has remained the top- or second-rated show among viewers for several years as its lead characters Dr. Mark Green and Dr. Peter Benton continue to work on their roles as fathers. Dr. Doug Ross (in actor George Clooney's last two years on the show) curtailed his womanizing and returned to his love, nurse Carol Hathaway.

The expanded depictions of male roles are proving popular with male and female viewers alike. However, early responses of male viewers to such characters as Paul Buchman in *Mad About You* were none too positive, revealing a gender gap in TV-watching preferences. The female star of the show, Helen Hunt, tried to offer a reporter a reason for some men's negative reactions to the show: "I could get killed for this, but I've always believed that men struggle to see how they can fit relationships into their lives. For women, it *is* their lives. Why would someone want to be reminded of something they have trouble doing? *Cops* sounds a lot better than spending a half-hour watching a couple navigate their lives" (as in Parish Perkins, 1994, p. 7E). Craig (1992) explains that the changing male characterization is not a consequence of raised gender consciousness, but of the feminization of prime-time—a trend for prime-time programming to reflect the interests of female viewers who have departed daytime viewing to enter the workforce. Craig explains, "The 'enlightened' gender portrayals of prime time are more the result of the economic motivations of the producers, networks, and advertisers to reach (and please) working women rather than any morally-driven social consciousness" (p. 8).

The Non-PC Male Character

Another trend in male depictions in prime-time television is what media scholar Robert Hanke (1998) terms the *mock-macho sitcom*. These shows "address white, middle class, middle-aged men's anxieties about a feminized ideal for manhood they may not want to live up to, as well as changes in work and family that continue to dissolve separate gender spheres . . ." (p. 76). Shows like *Home Improvement* and the now-retired *Coach* mock masculinity in that they simultaneously present "male comic television actors who ridicule their own lack of self-knowledge" and men who are "objects of laughter" (p. 76). In each of these sitcoms the main male character is a devoted husband

and father who is an equal partner with his wife, but who often goofs up and admits he doesn't understand women. This characterization is also termed the *playful patriarch* (Traube, 1992). Tim, "the Tool Man," and Coach Hayden Fox are fairly macho male characters who, through situations and communication with others, often end up the butts of jokes. But, in the end, they learn valuable lessons and become better people.

Hanke (1998) also suggests that, disguised in humor, programs like these may send antifeminist messages to the mass audience. For example, Tim in *Home Improvement* often comes into conflict with wife Jill's views and has arguments with Karen, Jill's "feminist friend." Hanke contends that these exchanges provide "an opportunity for Tim Taylor to rebut feminist arguments and to make nonsense of feminist sense. Insofar as Tim's comic style includes tendentious jokes that make women the targets, these moments offer male viewers the pleasure of seeing the rational norms of feminist criticism subverted" (p. 80). Some politically incorrect characterizations seem to go too far, such as the character of the father in the sitcom, *Jesse,* whose 1998 reincarnation of Archie Bunker makes audiences wince.

Other male characters reflect blended roles, meaning that more shows than in past decades depict multidimensioned, complicated men. The epitome of this trend can be found in *NYPD Blue*'s Detective Andy Sipowicz, played by multiple–Emmy winner Dennis Franz. While Sipowicz has expressed sexist and racist attitudes over the years, frequented prostitutes during his prerecovery days as an alcoholic, and is quick to anger in his often brutal interrogation methods, his character also includes sympathetic dimensions. You'd probably call him a macho guy, but his emotional side, his subtle ways of responding to bittersweet moments endear the character (and the actor) to the viewing audience. He may be one of the most integrated, richly portrayed male characters in television.

The Slower-to-Change Roles of Women in Prime-Time

From *Xena: Warrior Princess, Buffy the Vampire Slayer, Sabrina the Teenage Witch, Ally McBeal's* short skirts, and the *Baywatch* women's cleavage, one might get the strong impression that June Cleaver and Lucy Ricardo are *long gone.* But are these extreme images rather than the average depiction of the female character on prime-time television? Research has found some fascinating, and at times depressing, trends about women and prime-time TV.

Glad to See the '80s Go

Marvin Moore's (1992) analysis of families in 1980s prime-time television was critical of some portrayals of women. He asserted that, while television programs depicted men in nontraditional roles, communicating that men have the freedom to choose different paths for themselves without societal sanctions, women's changing roles in society were largely ignored. Moore found that mothers and wives in family series were rarely identified as having occupations;

they were predominantly home centered and supported by their male counterparts in the shows. The reality was that huge numbers of women entered the workforce during the '80s, to support themselves and subsidize the family income. Moore's primary example was the lead female character in one of the most successful sitcoms of the decade, *The Cosby Show*'s Claire Huxtable. She was a successful lawyer, but rarely referred to her job and was only occasionally depicted in legal settings. Hanke (1998) offers the character of Jill Taylor on *Home Improvement* as an example of a '90s woman who chose to work outside the home, as Jill did in the show's second season, but who was rarely seen at her job and rarely discussed it with her husband.

A subsequent study to Moore's analyzed 10 of the most popular sitcoms in the United States from the 1950 to 1990, focusing on such variables as the depiction of equal sex roles, dominance of certain characters, stability of family relationships, and family satisfaction. The results detected, with some fluctuation across the 40-year span, a general decline in both the quantity and quality of female roles (Olson & Douglas, 1997).

Women Juggling Home and Work

However, in the decade of the '90s, the percentage of family profiles in TV shows that included and actually showed a woman working outside the home increased considerably. Several studies have examined how contemporary women are depicted in prime-time television, with specific regard for the portrayal of tension between a female character's personal life and her work (Atkin, 1991; Faludi, 1991; Japp, 1991; Vande Berg & Streckfuss, 1992). Although professional women are many more times central characters or significant family members in prime-time television programs than in decades past, they are still more likely to emphasize their love lives over their working lives.

Media and gender researcher Phyllis Japp (1991) explored this trend, explaining that the typical emphases for TV's working women are their relationships with men (and, for some, their relationships with their children) and the tension created when they juggle work and these relationships. While this tension constitutes a reality for many contemporary women, the personal and relational elements in television characters' lives receive

> *I went in and said, "If I see one more gratuitous shot of a woman's body, I'm quitting..." I think the show should be emotional story lines, morals, real-life heroes. And that's what we're doing....*
>
> *David Hasselhoff, actor*

more emphasis or "air time" than the professional, career-oriented elements. Current incarnations of this tendency can be found in *Suddenly Susan, Maggie Winters, Jesse,* and *Ally McBeal,* which all have as their original premise rebuilding life after a breakup with a man. In fact, we've never seen lawyers work as little as the ones in *Ally McBeal.* In the office, they are mostly depicted chatting amongst themselves about their latest interpersonal challenge or love affair. They are often seen in court, but rarely if ever are they seen actually preparing for trials. (We grant that this is a comedy, but the focus on the personal over the professional still sends a message.)

Even the 1998 rave sitcom, *Will and Grace,* deemed innovative for the platonic friendship relationship between its two main characters—one gay, one straight—included an early episode in which Grace, clad in wedding dress and veil, was in a crisis over her impending (and canceled) nuptials (Jacobs, 1998). Japp concludes that "Little cultural guidance exists for creating a credible, well-rounded image of a working woman, for such a character is necessarily a composite embodying cultural meanings of 'woman' and 'work,' concepts that have long been on opposite sides in American cultural mythology" (p. 50). Similar sentiments emerge from the work of communication researchers Vande Berg and Streckfuss (1992) who surveyed female characters in prime-time television. They concluded that "television continues to present working women as lacking the competitively achieved occupational hierarchical power and status of male workers" and that female characters are defined through "stereotypically domestic, expressive, and socio-emotional roles" (p. 205).

One such portrayal can be found in the character of Daphne Moon in the hit sitcom *Frasier.* There was no pretense about this character's status; she was introduced to the show as a live-in housekeeper for the pompous Frasier Crane and physical therapist for Frasier's father. There are no lead female characters in this show; the supporting female characters include: (1) Frasier's co-worker Roz, who was pregnant during the 1998 season and now copes with single motherhood, a character whose sexuality is her main feature and who constantly struggles in relationships with men; (2) Lilith, Frasier's ex-wife who occasionally visits Seattle, typically when her latest marriage or romance has ended and she needs a sexual encounter with Frasier to restore her self-esteem; and (3) Maris, the unseen but peculiar and estranged wife of Niles, Frasier's equally status-conscious brother. The sitcom reached a milestone in 1998, being the first show to ever win five straight Emmy Awards for Best Television Comedy Series. Yet the female characterizations in the show won't win any awards for progressivism.

Breakthrough TV Roles for Women, in a Distant Galaxy

Scholars suggest that recent spin-offs of the *Star Trek* series broke new ground for female depiction. While untrue of the original series, most of the women's roles in the more recent shows were high-ranking officers, doctors, security specialists, engineers, and scientists. In fact, the January 1995 cover of *Entertainment Weekly* magazine pictured actress Kate Mulgrew, in full uniform as Captain Kathryn Janeway of the Starship Enterprise in the *Star Trek: Voyager* series, with a caption that read "Boldly Going Where Only Men Have Gone Before." In the interview that accompanied the cover, the actress expressed her view of the female-as-captain innovation in her show: "Women have an emotional accessibility that our culture not only accepts but embraces. We have a tactility, a compassion, a maternity—and all these things can be revealed within the character of a very authoritative person" (as in Kim, 1995, p. 16).

Media analyst Minh Luong (1992) asserts, "*Star Trek: The Next Generation* broke new ground by introducing women as senior commanding officers, as well as casting women in traditionally male-dominated occupational roles" (p. 1). Interestingly enough, this program, with its nontraditional female depiction and "enlightened" treatment of gender issues in occasional episodes, was the number one show on television among 18- to 49-year old male viewers (Svetkey, 1992). However, feminist media scholar Leah Vande Berg (1993) believes that, while roles have expanded for women in the *Star Trek* series, the roles are more "feminized" than "feminist." *Star Trek: The Next Generation*, in particular, Vande Berg claims, went "where primarily male, Anglo, heterosexual men have gone before" (p. 34).

Breakthrough Roles on Planet Earth

Certainly the characters of Roseanne Connor and Murphy Brown can be seen as groundbreakers for women's roles. The lead character in *Roseanne* was a contradiction—a challenge to the social norm of femininity, a struggling, outspoken, blue-collar worker, and a sarcastic, yet devoted wife, mother, and sister (Faludi, 1991; Rowe, 1990). Media author Susan Douglas (1995a) calls the actress Roseanne a "pioneer" who "ripped the veneer of flawlessness off TV motherhood and showed a household in which siblings scream at each other, parents disagree and have sex, and the doting mom yells to her kids, 'Go to your room and live in fear,' adding sardonically in an aside, 'To think I suckled them'" (p. 77). Douglas goes on to point out that *Roseanne* was one of the few prime-time shows with a white cast to get high ratings from black audiences, citing statistics from 1993 in which *Roseanne* was the "only show with a white lead to be among the top 20 shows with both black and white audiences" (p. 77).

The central character in *Murphy Brown* has been studied for many reasons, primarily because she was one of the first strong, independent, career-minded, persistently single female characters (since *The Mary Tyler Moore Show*) who developed over time and seemed to defy stereotypes. At the same time, she was a recovering alcoholic and retained some unattractive, negative dimensions to her persona, like her abrasiveness with people. Bonnie Dow, in her 1996 book, *Prime-Time Feminism*, points out that *Murphy Brown* offered "validation of women's progress embodied in the power of the lead character and in its exploration of the costs of that progress" (p. 137). The show depicted a "progressive portrait of a professional woman," as well as "subtler themes about the lessons of liberation" (p. 137). As Diane English, co-creator of the sitcom, told a reporter, "I had never seen a strong, competent woman on television who also had the courage of her convictions, who wasn't trying to please everyone, who allowed herself to be rude and who didn't edit herself. These are traits you would normally find in a man. I really, basically, wrote Murphy as a man in a skirt" (Clark, 1993, p. 5C).

The character of Murphy Brown defied the corporate, scratching-to-the-top stereotype by becoming pregnant late in the run of the series. She approached single-mom challenges with humor, insecurity, and determination. In the final years of the series, she faced the challenge of breast cancer, treatment, and recovery, reflecting one of women's greatest fears. The show began to lose its audience and its appeal, as always happens, but the character of Murphy Brown will most likely be remembered as a groundbreaking role for women in prime-time television.

An important, if not controversial, breakthrough role came in the form of the character played by Ellen DeGeneres on the prime-time sitcom *Ellen*. Much has been written about this role and this show, as well as the courage of the actress-comedian to come out to the TV-viewing world, both in her personal life and in her on-screen persona. One reporter described it this way: "*Ellen* ended as inauspiciously as it began five seasons ago, just one year after it made history and a few short months after DeGeneres was hailed as *EW*'s [*Entertainment Weekly*] 1997 Entertainer of the Year. On April 30 of last year, 36.2 million viewers watched its lead character, Ellen Morgan, not only come out of the closet but become the first leading gay prime-time character *ever*, and a test case for the nation's tolerance" (Cagle, 1998, p. 28). No matter what your sexual orientation or your views on gay rights, it's hard to disagree that *Ellen* has had a significant impact on the television landscape.

The Fourth Network's Contributions

The Fox Network reliably presents television images that depart from the mainstream, all the while, as some suggest, shaking up the dominant culture. One of the primary departures exists in roles for women. Female characters in Fox's sitcoms aren't afraid to speak their minds, show their sense of humor, and be disrespectful to men if they deserve it. But the biggest differences are that the single women characters aren't desperate for marriage and are allowed to admit that they actually like sex. The sitcom *Living Single* is one such refreshing departure, with its nontraditional portrayals of women and groundbreaking roles for African-American women. As Douglas (1995a) explains,

> "Except for the women on *Living Single*, African American women are rarely the title characters in the land of sitcoms. Black women on sitcoms embody the extremes without getting enough chances to show how they actually manage cultural tensions between the pressure to conform and the desire to preserve their ethnic identity. This may be why Khadijah on *Living Single* is so popular among African American women: she is one of the few female characters to finesse these tensions" (pp. 78–79).

The lead character on Fox's *Ally McBeal*, while not yet considered a groundbreaking role for women, has generated a good deal of interest and research. The plot lines involving court cases are really frames for relational dimensions, which play out in a uniquely postmodern way. As one reporter suggests, "Fans catch echoes of their own lives and relationships on a show that often raises questions about the way women and men get along, platonically and romantically, in today's workplace" (Huang, 1998, pp. 1C–2C).

Implications for Prime-Time Television Watchers

While it's beyond our focus in this book to delve deeply into the effects of television viewing on children, research continues to show that television has a lot of power to shape girls' and boys' visions of themselves and their notions about how men and women behave (Douglas, 1995b). Whether as an adult you tend to relate more to traditional portrayals or to the ground-breaking characterizations of the sexes, one implication is that our communication with relational partners, as well as attitudes about gender roles and behavior in relationships, is influenced, in varying degrees, by sitcoms and television dramas.

For example, many of our traditionally-aged college students reluctantly admit that they watch *Beverly Hills 90210* (jokingly referred to as *Beverly Hills Whine 0210*) and *Melrose Place,* two of Fox's more successful shows. They say that they really hate these shows, but they watch them every week any way. For some, following the antics of Beverly Hills residents from high school through college or a rotating group of California yuppies is definitely escapist activity. For others, it's possible that the interaction and relationships among the characters may affect their expectations or create some impression of how relationships ought to function and men and women ought to communicate.

The Influence of Social Issues Programming

The label *social issues programming* refers to the kind of prime-time informational program that tackles a social or political issue, such as gun control legislation, reproductive rights, or gay marriage. This type of television is nothing new in daytime fare; however, daytime discussions typically occur within an already established format, such as a talk show or local interview program with invited guests or panelists. In the 1990s networks and cable companies were challenged to explore social issues not only through a movie-of-the-week format, but also through extended prime-time evening talk shows, "town hall debates," and informative panel discussions and forums.

The Agenda-Setting Potential of Social Issues Programming

Social issues programming is both similar and different to the news magazine shows such as *Dateline NBC, 20/20, 48 Hours,* and the grandparent of them all, *60 Minutes.* They are similar in that they are nonfictional and usually involve reporters or news people as creators and hosts of the shows. One of the primary aspects common to both formats is the agenda-setting

"IF ELECTED, I PROMISE A RED-HOT SEX SCANDAL."

Reprinted by permission of the artist, Harley L. Schwadron.

function they serve for the mass audience. If a network devotes one of its 8:00–9:00 PM or 9:00–10:00 PM time slots to a town hall debate on political scandal or a forum on juvenile crime, that sends a clear signal to the viewing public that "this topic is *really* important." The primary difference between the two types of programming is the range of topics—news magazines typically cover several topics in one episode whereas social issues programs typically focus in depth on one general issue. Of special interest for our purposes are the programs that have the potential to inform and instruct the viewing public about gender issues.

One Network's Provocative Social Issues Program

One way to better understand social issues programming is to describe a highly provocative program that aired on ABC in the mid-1990s. News anchor Peter Jennings hosted a forum entitled *Men, Sex, and Rape* that featured two panels of experts placed in the middle of a small auditorium—six female experts on one side of the stage, six male experts on the other side. The show's producers even divided the audience seating by sex to further dramatize how women and men tend to hold polarized opinions of the issue of sexual assault and rape. The male line-up included such experts as Warren Farrell, author of the book *Why Men Are the Way They Are*; John Leo, columnist for *Time* and other magazines; and well-known Florida attorney F. Lee Bailey. (Note that this program aired prior to the O. J. Simpson trial, after which F. Lee Bailey became a household word in more households than just those of attorneys. It also aired before the book *Men Are From Mars, Women Are From Venus* hit the best seller list, or else author John Gray would have no doubt made it onto the men's panel.)

The female panel included such experts as Susan Faludi, author of *Backlash: The Undeclared War Against American Women*; Naomi Wolf, author of *The Beauty Myth* and other books that have made her a central voice of third-wave feminism (described in Chapter 1); Catharine MacKinnon, well-known feminist and attorney at the University of Michigan School of Law whose work is renowned both in and out of feminist circles; and Mary Koss, the researcher whose important work on sexual assault and rape we review in Chapter 9.

Here's the gist of the 90-minute program. After Jennings's brief introduction, the program cut to a short video clip of a scantily-clad woman entertaining a room full of men at what looked like a bachelor party. Jennings then asked panelists for their reactions to the tape, followed by their comments about both stranger and acquaintance rape. The discussion included such aspects as how men and women view rape and respond to rape education efforts differently, methods of education and prevention, as well as treatment for victims and rehabilitation efforts for rapists, and legal aspects. Exchanges between panelists occasionally turned to banter, such as when one of the female panelists responded to Warren Farrell's defensive comments about men with something along the lines of, "You just don't get it, do you?" At several key points in the program, Jennings turned to audience members for pre-arranged comments on the subject or for personal stories of sexual assault and rape.

More About Economics Than Conscience

We don't mean to sound cynical or jaded, but it's highly likely that social issues programming continues to air on various networks and cable channels less out of social conscience, with the goal of advancing our culture, and more out of economics. In essence, such shows air because they're cheap. The same goes for news magazine shows; they don't cost much to produce and don't involve big salaries for actors or expensive locations. Here are a few social issues programs of interest to the subject of gender communication:

1. In the fall of 1991, shortly after the Clarence Thomas Senate confirmation hearings, ABC sponsored one of their *Town Hall Debates*. These programs are arranged as open forums, encouraging exchange between invited guests or experts and members of the audience. Ted Koppel usually hosts the programs because they air through the vehicle of ABC's *Nightline*. This particular program featured a few of the (braver) senators from the Senate Judiciary Committee, who engaged in lively interaction with a highly critical audience.
2. In 1992, Linda Ellersby and Harry Hamlin co-hosted a Lifetime cable program about sexual harassment in the workplace. This program aired less than a year after the Clarence Thomas Senate confirmation hearings.

3. Occasionally, different network reporters and news personalities produce and host prime-time shows on gender-related subjects. For example, ABC's John Stossel focused on the subject of physiological differences between the sexes, which involved current medical information on brain functioning in women and men. Other shows have emphasized the communication between marital partners. One in particular followed John Gray (Mr. *Mars/Venus*) as he presented speeches and worked with married couples to improve their relationships.

Are Viewers Getting the Social Message?

Little has been written on the effects of this type of programming; however, two studies have been conducted to determine viewers' reactions to dramatizations of social issues. Mass media researcher Andrea Press (1991b) studied women's reactions to an episode of the 1980s television drama *Cagney and Lacey*. The episode dealt with abortion, reproductive rights, and justice. Specifically, Press found that women's language and views about abortion were affected by the language used and views expressed in the episode. According to Press, "When the moral language adopted by television differs from that of viewers, television viewing influences viewers to adopt its terms" (p. 438). Press's study indicated that television programming could serve an educational function, if only to cause viewers to talk about an issue in a different way.

Communication researchers Wilson, Linz, Donnerstein, and Stipp (1992) examined the effects of viewing a television movie about acquaintance rape on attitudes about rape. Wilson et al. explored "whether exposure to this movie could serve an educational function by decreasing acceptance of rape myths and/or increasing the belief that date rape is a serious social problem" (p. 181). Overall, the results of the study indicated that the film served an educational function for viewers. More specifically, male and female viewers of varying ages (ranging from 18 to around 50) altered their perceptions about the problem of date rape after viewing the television movie. After watching the program, viewers were less likely to place blame on female victims of date rape, more likely to perceive women as being coerced into sexual activity, and more concerned about the seriousness of date rape as a societal problem than before viewing the movie.

What effects do social issues programs have on the American viewing public? Research has yet to fully investigate this type of television programming; however, it appears that social issues programming may accomplish the following things:

1. By utilizing an accessible medium—the home television set—these programs bring social issues into a forum that is likely to catch people's attention.
2. They have the potential to educate the public about social issues of increasing importance.
3. They may provide new ways to think about issues, meaning that viewers may understand an issue in a more in-depth way when a televised source discusses it.
4. They may spark healthy dialogue about an issue after the program has aired.

However, these programs may also present only one side of an issue, one that reflects certain biases of the reporters, the networks or cable companies, or the commercial sponsors. Whether social issues programmers feel a responsibility to provide even-handed treatments of issues; whether these programs actually affect people's attitudes and, more importantly, their behaviors; and exactly to what extent the programs influence women, men, and the communication between them represent provocative research challenges.

Daytime Television: Not Just for Women Any More

Daytime television has its own viewing audience that includes a mix of people—full-time homemakers, teenagers (watching late afternoon programs), people who work part-time, college students (some of whom arrange their class schedules around their favorite soaps), shift workers home during the day, and others who use VCRs to record their favorite programs to watch at their leisure. In this section, we discuss two formats of daytime programming—soap operas and talk shows—with special regard for what these programs may communicate about women and men.

As the Culture Turns

Daytime dramas have been popular with radio and television audiences for many decades, and research on their effects dates back to the 1940s. An estimated 40 million viewers tune in daily to their soaps (Whitmire, 1996). One set of researchers views soap operas as extensions of childhood fairy tales; they suggest, "Dilemmas of identity, emotional anxieties, and other personal conflicts do not all reach resolution at the end of childhood. Thus, once grown up women have left behind the period when they may legitimately listen to fairy tales, other forms of popular culture are needed . . ." (Livingstone & Liebes, 1995, p. 157). A great deal has been written, primarily on the functions soap operas serve in society, predominant roles male and female family members play on soaps, communication between characters, and viewers' perceptions of the parallels between soaps and real life (Freud Loewenstein, 1993; Irwin & Cassata, 1993; Mumford, 1995; Scodari, 1998; White, 1995).

Before we go further in this discussion, let's address a popular misconception—that soap operas are watched exclusively by women. Daytime television programming has been, and still is to a great extent, targeted to the perceived needs and circumstances of women. This is understandable, given that over 67 percent of daytime viewers are women (Papazian, 1990). However, a study of the viewing behaviors of college students revealed that although the soap opera audience was predominantly female, it included a surprising number of faithful, male soap opera viewers (Lemish, 1985). Some of our male students reveal, albeit somewhat reluctantly, that they regularly watch certain soaps.

Gender and media expert Marlene Fine's (1981) research continues to affect subsequent investigations of soap opera viewing. Fine examined the kinds of relationships and interactions that take place within relationships that daytime soap operas regularly portray. She discovered that women were most often portrayed in family settings, men were primarily depicted in professional settings, and men and women were most often portrayed in romantic heterosexual relationships. Fine concluded, "The general picture of soap opera relationships is one in which male-male relationships are professionally defined and female-female relationships are interpersonally defined. Men venture into the realm of intimate relationships almost solely through their encounters with women, and then generally through romantic involvements" (p. 101).

A Dose of Reality

Not only do soap operas affect viewers' perceptions of reality, viewers also may be prone to take cues from various forms of television programming about what to expect from members of the opposite sex as well as how to communicate with them. Fine (1981) determined that over 20 percent of the female-female and the male-female conversations in soap operas concerned romance, while only 3 percent of all male-male conversations focused on romance. Another finding showed that the fantasy world of the soap opera depicts women and men involved in intimate attachments and revealing their most intimate feelings to each another. Fine contends that this does not mirror real life where traditional sex roles separate men and women and where intimate thoughts and feelings quite often are expressed to friends rather than to romantic partners.

Media scholar John Fiske (1987), in his book *Television Culture*, discusses the contradiction between the depiction of male characters in soap operas and reality as follows:

> Women's view of masculinity, as evidenced in soap operas, differs markedly from that produced from the masculine audience. The "good" male in the daytime soaps is caring, nurturing, and verbal. He is prone to making comments like "I don't care about material wealth or professional success, all I care about is us and our relationship." He will talk about feelings and people and rarely express his masculinity in direct action. Of course, he is still decisive, he still has masculine power, but that power is given a "feminine" inflection. (p. 186)

This kind of depiction, Fiske suggests, is offered to please the primarily female audience of the daytime soap opera; thus, the soap opera man could be considered an economically derived creation. The problem then becomes one of separating reality from fantasy. If a woman expects men to behave and communicate like male characters on soaps, it's fairly safe to say that she will likely encounter some disillusion in her life. While the notion that someone would be so foolish as to assume that people will behave like television or movie characters may sound exaggerated or overstated, it's not all that outlandish. Probably more times than we'd like to believe, people compare their experiences and relationships to dramatic versions and become disillusioned when their own lives don't measure up.

Soap opera portrayals also have the potential to affect how people form expectations about sexual behavior. Media scholar Katherine Heintz-Knowles's research shows that "behavior performed by characters who are attractive, powerful, and popular is much more likely to be imitated by viewers" (as in Whitmire, 1996, p. A7). Her survey results revealed that 594 sexual behaviors were shown during a five-week period of soap opera programming, which averages to 6.1 behaviors per hour, compared to 6.4 such behaviors per hour in a similar survey in 1994. Of those sexual scenes, only 58 depicted discussions about contraception or the consequences of sexual activity.

Other studies have found that sexual activity depicted on television has not decreased and that it seems to be a predominant activity for unmarried partners and within extramarital affairs. Even given the rising societal concern about contraception, AIDS, and other sexually transmitted diseases, discussions or actions in the plot lines that show a concern for (or even an awareness of) these issues are almost nonexistent in both daytime and prime-time serials (Sapolsky & Tabarlet, 1991; Schrag, 1990). In attempts to caution or educate the public, a full-page newspaper ad purchased by Planned Parenthood displayed the headline, "They did it 9,000 times on television last year." The ad copy warned against viewing sex from a "Don't worry; be happy" mentality, one that stresses enjoyment without responsibility, pleasure without consequence.

Do you think that soap operas have a responsibility to educate the public or to depict characters acting responsibly on a variety of social issues? Or do you think that the public receives education in other forums, leaving television programming to fulfill an escapist function?

From Phil to Oprah to Jerry

Here are a few good questions for you: What do talk shows communicate to modern women and men? Are these shows examples of how men and women are supposed to talk to each other? (We *really* hope not.) Do these talk shows set an agenda for the viewing public?

Since there are between 20 and 30 nationally syndicated daytime (and a few prime-time) talk shows on the air (some of the more recent ones include *The Rosie O'Donnell Show* and *The Roseanne Show*), the popularity of these shows cannot be denied (Heaton & Wilson, 1995). Talk shows used to be primarily the province of women. Feminist author Naomi Wolf suggests that among the early effects of talk shows, "That daily act of listening, whatever its shortcomings, made for a revolution in what women were willing to ask for; the shows daily conditioned otherwise unheard women into the belief that they were entitled to a voice" (as in Heaton & Wilson, p. 45). These shows, particularly *The Phil Donahue Show* and *The Oprah Winfrey Show*, provided a platform for discussions of women's issues. Even though there are still more female than male viewers, corresponding to higher numbers of women at home during the day, the audience expanded during the decade of the '90s to include greater numbers of men.

The success of the slug-fest known as *The Jerry Springer Show* made this talk show one of the first to be aired as part of a national network's prime-time lineup. But many media scholars (as well as members of the public) are outraged by what they see on shows such as *Springer*. Media critics Heaton and Wilson (1995) assert: "As the number of shows increased and the ratings wars intensified, the manner in which issues are presented has changed. Shows now encourage conflict, name-calling, and fights. Producers set up underhanded tricks and secret revelations. Hosts instruct guests to reveal all. The more dramatic and bizarre the problems the better" (p. 45). The heightened competition and changing nature of the talk show led prominent hosts to retire (as was the case for Phil Donahue), move on to other things (like Geraldo Rivera did), or work to keep the quality of their shows high (as Oprah Winfrey made a decision to do in the late 1990s). Host Jenny Jones faced legal trouble when the events on one show resulted in the subsequent murder of one guest by another.

Gender Determinism and Agenda-Setting

Feminist media critic Roseann Mandziuk (1991) contends that talk shows seriously delimit gender boundaries. The intimate nature of talk programs corresponds with the cultural stereotype that women are supposed to be sensitive, nurturing, and responsive. This intimacy is exemplified by host-guest-audience relationships; the camera close-ups of tearful guests who are commended for their brave, emotional displays while recounting personal narratives on national television; the accessibility phone callers have to some shows; and the occasional personal disclosure or reaction of the host. The format also reinforces women's existence, thus "genderizing" this programming. The spontaneity of discussion limited by interruptive commercial breaks mirrors the realities of women's multitask existence. And the fact that there's never enough time to give full treatment to any issue sends a message, primarily to women, that "conversation is never finished" and that "there is always more to be learned, always another talk show to seek out for information on another day" (Mandziuk, 1991, p. 13).

Mandziuk also suggests that talk shows, particularly those aired during the day, may actually be instructing women what they should worry about; in other words, the programs serve an agenda-setting function. What are the possible ramifications of believing that "being a man trapped inside a woman's body" is one of the most critical issues facing contemporary women? While some topics may be deemed outlandish or trivial, such as a problem with a husband who likes to dress in women's lingerie or a girl who flirts with her sister's boyfriend, other topics may make some women wonder if they're *supposed* to be worried about these issues. A greater problem ensues when the larger, general public "ghettoizes" important issues, such as reproductive rights, sexual harassment, and child care, by labeling them women's issues rather than societal or human issues. As Mandziuk contends, "Precisely because they are talked about in the context of women's programming, issues which demand political solutions become personalized and hence are easily dismissed from being worthy of serious consideration as part of any public policy agenda" (p. 19).

Heaton and Wilson (1995) suggest, "The very same stereotypes that have plagued both women and men for centuries are in full force. Instead of

---

RECAP

feminized or reconstructed male, feminization of prime-time television, mock-macho sitcom, playful patriarch, social issues programming, news magazine shows

---

encouraging changes in sex roles, the shows actually solidify them" (p. 45). The men on these programs are certainly not God's gifts to *woman*kind, as Heaton and Wilson report, "Women viewers are given a constant supply of the worst images of men, all the way from garden-variety liars, cheats, and con artists to rapists and murderers" (p. 45). And the women fare no better: "If there is a man for every offense, there is certainly a woman for every trauma. Most women on talk TV are perpetual victims presented as having so little power that not only do they have to contend with real dangers such as sexual or physical abuse, but they are also overcome by bad hair, big thighs, and beautiful but predatory 'other' women" (pp. 45–46).

Have you ever considered the instructive potential or the agenda-setting function of talk shows? Perhaps you recall talking about particular shows in your college classes or in conversations with friends, dates, or your spouse. Have your perceptions about women and men—their gender-roles and issues—been influenced by one of these talk shows?

LESSONS FROM THE BIG SCREEN: FILM AND THE SEXES

Here's an interesting exercise: Imagine that you had to put together a time capsule, a snapshot of American life that represented your time on this Earth, something that future generations would stumble upon and use to better understand their heritage. No doubt you'd turn to media to help you fill the capsule; no doubt you'd include some movies. The question is: Which movies would you include and why? Going even further, if only three movies would fit in the capsule, which three would you make sure got in? Would you include films from different genres, such as a western, a romance, and a horror movie? Would you include a classic like *Casablanca*, a futuristic film like *Star Wars*, or a movie that depicts your version of typical American life? It's interesting to share responses to this exercise (and it makes for good dinner conversation). But what's most intriguing is people's answers to the question, Why did you pick that movie? Responses tend to reveal people's value systems; people pick certain films so that things they care most about in life can be communicated to future generations. What would your choices say to future generations about your view of the sexes? Would your choices reveal a patriarchal or an egalitarian, feminist value system?

According to film scholar Thomas Doherty (1988), "American motion pictures today are not a mass medium" (p. 1). He contends that the film industry caters to one audience—teenagers. Although Doherty made this statement a decade before the highest grossing movie of all time, *Titanic,* was released, that movie proves his point: The repeat business of teens and preteens put *Titanic* over the top. But when you consider how much wider the market and corresponding audience is for film nowadays via video rentals, pay-per-view services, and cable companies showing first-run movies soon after their initial theatrical releases, then the argument could be made that film is much more of a "mass" medium than it used to be.

Gender-Bending in the Movies

Film has the power to communicate gender roles. It may not be a blatant message about roles women and men play in society or about how we communicate in relationships; the more subtle messages that we see and hear repeatedly are more likely to sink in on some level and affect us. On the most basic level, if a subject is dramatized on the big screen, it's there for a reason; it has to be important, right? The potential effect on children is even greater, as the significant impact of Disney films on kids shows. Research shows time and again how various forms of media, including film, affects children's views of themselves, how male and female characters are supposed to behave, who are the good guys and who the bad guys, and so on (Hoerrner, 1996; Van Evra, 1990).

One phenomenon in film that stirs up a good deal of talk and controversy, not surprisingly, has to do with gender. Before we begin discussing that topic, here are a few questions for you to think about: Have you seen any movies that affected how you interact with members of the opposite sex, at work or in your social or family life? Was there a memorable movie that changed your views about women's and men's roles or that changed one of your relationships? Might it have been *Sleepless in Seattle, Forget Paris, Titanic,* or *You've Got Mail*? (Or were those simply "date flicks"?) Can movies affect you in this way?

One for the Capsule

For your textbook authors, one such memorable, outlook-altering movie was *Tootsie,* a movie that to this day conjures up confused but pleasant thoughts about gender roles. If you haven't seen this movie, rent it, but until then, here's a synopsis of the plot. Dustin Hoffman plays Michael, an actor who desperately wants work, but whose opportunities are limited because of his reputation as being "difficult." When his agent tells Michael that no one will hire him, Michael sets out to prove him wrong by auditioning for a role on a popular soap opera. The twist is that the role is for a woman, so Michael auditions in drag as an actress named Dorothy Michaels. After landing the part, Michael encounters a number of sticky situations because of his hidden identity. The stickiest situation arises when Michael realizes that he's falling for Julie, another actress on the soap, played in the movie by Jessica Lange. As Michael (via Dorothy) becomes good friends with Julie, he is confronted with how to admit the deception and still have a chance with Julie.

One amazing aspect of this movie is how Dustin Hoffman's portrayal of Dorothy, through the character of Michael, becomes real to viewers, so real that when Michael reveals his true identity in one of the final scenes, audiences are sad because they are going to miss Dorothy. Another fascinating aspect of this movie was that it fulfilled a fantasy for many people—walking in the opposite sex's shoes, seeing how they are treated, and getting to know an attractive member of the opposite sex without the hang-ups and pressures that often accompany romantic relationships. It was also intriguing to think about the opportunity of putting one's new-found insight into the opposite sex to work in a relationship. As Michael explained to Julie in the last scene of the movie, "I was a better man with you, as a woman, than I ever was as a man. I've just got to learn to do it without the dress."

The film *Tootsie* frames the rest of our discussion nicely, because it exemplifies the theme of *gender-bending*, a term referring to media depictions in which characters' actions belie or contradict what is expected of their sex. But our use of this term is not limited only to people who have masqueraded in films as members of the opposite sex. The example of *Tootsie* serves to start our thinking, but gender-bending doesn't necessarily mean actors in drag.

Buddies on a Dead-End Road

Thelma & Louise was a groundbreaking gender-bending film on many counts; one film critic termed it "a butt-kicking feminist manifesto" (Schickel, 1991, p. 52). It was an open-road, "buddy" film, but with female instead of male buddies (Glenn, 1992; Kroll, 1991). One of the most laudable effects of this film was that it sparked a great deal of discussion. In fact, it still sparks discussion. Although the film opened in May 1991, people still talk about it and film critics still write about it. One movie authority describes it this way: "*Thelma & Louise* came out swinging, an astounding, mind-blowing revisionist examination of the American Experience, an ode to beauty and freedom, a crash course in feminism, violence, and the loss of the American Dream. It was, above all else, a film that made you *feel*, like it or not" (Hoffman, 1997, p. 69).

Few people came out of theaters saying, "What a cute, fun little movie." Some people were outraged at what they perceived to be an inappropriate level of violence in the film, although only one person gets shot (the rapist). While the film contains violent images, critics maintained it had nowhere near the violence depicted in other films of the day. As one reporter explains:

> *Thelma & Louise*'s filmmakers and stars countered that the real source of the outrage was the fact that the violence was directed at men. [Susan] Sarandon (aka Louise) said that the controversy showed "what a straight, white male world movies occupy. This kind of scrutiny didn't happen with that Schwarzenegger thing [1990's *Total Recall*] where he shoots a woman in the head and says 'Consider that a divorce!'" (Bowers, 1997, p. 74)

Female audiences for this movie had complex emotions. They cheered what they perceived to be "payback," especially in the scene with the trucker and his rig. At the same time, they felt odd to be applauding revenge, as Hoffman (1997) explains: "For some, it allowed an understanding as to why some women remain in abusive relationships and some women snap. For others, it was terrifying to realize that they themselves were applauding violent retribution, at least for the moment, in the dark anonymity of the theater" (p. 69).

Male Caricatures in *Thelma & Louise*

Besides the dominant images and "radical" behaviors of the leads, male characters in *Thelma & Louise* were portrayed in an atypical fashion for the movies. These portrayals led to claims of male-bashing, based on contentions that the male characters were unrealistic and exaggerated, particularly because they were repeatedly vanquished by the two women. One critic from the New York *Daily News* asserted that the movie justified violence, crime, and drunken driving and was "degrading to men, with pathetic stereotypes of testosterone-crazed behavior" (Johnson, as in Schickel, 1991, p. 52).

Film researcher Robert Glenn (1992) suggests that "Feminists have perpetuated a behavioral definition of sexism that has been fictionalized and lampooned for more than a decade in films and television. *Thelma & Louise* effectively reconstructs these identifiable caricatures in order to paint an extremely unflattering portrait of men as insensitive and ignorant savages who treat women as functional objects to be used and manipulated" (p. 12). From this viewpoint, the caricatures or overdrawn images of men in the film were created in efforts to further highlight the victimization of the two female characters.

What messages about women and men did audiences get from this movie? Some people came away thinking that women were winning some kind of war against male oppression, that they were retaliating against unacceptable male behavior in like fashion. This is a gender-bender message taken to an extreme. However, while believing that the movie made a significant statement about relationships between men and women in the '90s, some film critics and feminist scholars contend that *Thelma & Louise* was not a triumphant women's rights movie. They point out that the film depicts the desperation of women in modern times—women who counter the powerlessness they feel with some very isolated, extreme actions, but who, in the long run, are still out of power in a patriarchal system (Klawans, 1991; Leo, 1991; Shapiro, 1991). This theme is epitomized by the ending (which we won't give away for those readers who have yet to see it).

Descendants of *Thelma & Louise*

A few movies have followed in *Thelma & Louise*'s blazing trail, such as *A League of Their Own, Waiting to Exhale, The First Wives Club, Boys On the Side,* and *The Associate.* While none of these depicts such a violent scene as the attempted rape in the first half-hour of *Thelma & Louise,* all contain female leads in tight-knit groups of friends who experience bad choices and disappointing relationships and who are rebuilding their lives.

One movie late in the '90s that probably best fits the gender-bender bill is *GI Jane*. In this movie, actress Demi Moore plays a navy officer who becomes the first woman admitted into the Navy Seal training program, one of the most challenging programs in the military. The character rails against double standards—one set of standards for men and an easier set for women. She realizes she's a token player in a political game, but is determined to set a precedent that women can succeed in such a program and make a valuable contribution in combat situations (Butler, 1997).

Can you think of some gender-bending movies that depict men in non-stereotypical roles? *Kramer vs. Kramer* from the early 1980s could be an example of a gender-bending film. The main male character is a father raising his son after the mother leaves the family. He eventually has to fight for custody of his son upon the mother's return. He even gets fired because of time spent away from his job to care for his young son. It's interesting that this is another Dustin Hoffman movie; again Hoffman's character expands the traditional male role.

Another one of our favorite gender-bending movies is *Mrs. Doubtfire*, first, because we love Robin Williams, and second, because the movie was just great fun. The movie is a gender-bender more because of its portrayal of fatherhood than because Williams dresses as a woman for much of it. Unlike Hoffman's character in *Tootsie*, Williams's character didn't take on a woman's persona for the purpose of gaining some empathy for womankind. *Father's Day*, *The Birdcage*, *Mother*, and *In and Out* are other examples of male gender-bending movies.

Perhaps *Disclosure*, the film based on the Michael Crichton novel, can be considered gender-bending as well because it depicts a high-powered woman sexually harassing a man in a subordinate professional role (Maslin, 1994). Sexual harassment scholar Jill Axelrod (1993), who studies ways that sexual harassment is portrayed in film, suggests that "Men tend to be assigned roles in which they exhibit physical and intellectual power, thus reinforcing the stereotype that men are dominant. Switching roles, thereby depicting the woman in high-status role and the man in the low-status position, alters the sex stereotypes" (p. 111). We have serious difficulties with the film *Disclosure*, mainly because it was one of the first, big-budget, widely released films with A-list stars to focus on sexual harassment. The problem is that it dealt with sexual harassment in a titillating rather than serious way by showing harassment as it occurs in 5 percent of the cases instead of in the 95 percent of cases in which men harass women. It gave the public a false message about sexual harassment and in many ways was a misogynistic (that is, woman-hating) film. Do other films come to mind that you believe expanded men's range of options in similarly dramatic ways as *Thelma & Louise* did for women?

History documents the power of the media to sweep change through a culture. Will other gender-bending movies that are bound to explore these issues further make a significant impact in the 21st century? Who can predict? In any case, gender-bender movies challenge us to think further and deeper, and in ways that may be new to us. They challenge us to take inventory of our attitudes and expectations about women and men. They ask us to reconsider how we communicate with one another and how we derive pleasure out of our relationships.

THE COMMUNICATIVE POWER OF PORNOGRAPHY

We usually don't begin our coverage on a topic with a disclaimer or apology, but this subject is different—*really* different. Pornography is a topic that continues to generate a great deal of research and writing, and there is no way we can do justice to that body of information in a short section within this chapter on media. Many books and articles offer insightful analyses of the pervasiveness of pornography in modern existence, its effects on how women and men are viewed in our culture, and its impact on everyday relationships between men and women. All we offer here is a snapshot—a highly condensed introduction to the topic—just to get you thinking about pornography, perhaps in a way you haven't before. If what we discuss here makes you angry or increases your interest to learn more, then we've done our job. Just realize that we barely skim the surface of the complexities of this aspect of media.

Multiple Definitions of Pornography: The Beginnings of Controversy

A specific, universally agreed-upon legal definition of pornography doesn't exist. In legal contexts, *obscenity* is the term used, but not all pornographic material meets the legal standard of obscenity (deGrazia, 1992; Tedford, 1993). Sometimes the term *erotica* is confused with pornography, although erotica differs in that it pertains to material that portrays sex as an equal activity involving mutual sensual pleasure, not activity involving power or subordination (Steinem, 1983; Unger & Crawford, 1996). Strictly speaking, erotic material isn't pornographic, but material that some deem pornographic may also contain erotica. (We told you this was a complicated topic.) Several scholars have offered descriptions of what the term *pornography* might encompass, even tracing the reference to its linguistic roots. In our view, researchers Neil Malamuth and Victoria Billings (1984) offer one of the clearest explanations of terms:

> Numerous attempts have been made to define pornography and to distinguish it from what some consider its more acceptable form—"erotica." The word pornography comes from the Greek "writings of prostitutes" (*porno* = prostitute and *graphein* = to write). In recent definitions, material has been classified as pornography when the producer's intent is to elicit erotic responses from the consumer, when it sexually arouses the consumer, or when women characters are degraded or demeaned. Pornography has been distinguished from erotica depending upon whether the material portrays unequal or equal power in sexual relations. (pp. 117–118)

Realize that some people would take two elements from the Malamuth and Billings definition—the "intent to elicit erotic responses" and the "sexually arouses the consumer" parts—and call them something other than pornography.

In their minds, material that accomplishes these two purposes falls in the realm of erotica or sexual expression; it moves out of that realm and into pornography when it degrades or demeans people. But that can be a very fine line at times, can't it? If two people watch the same sexual scene in a film, for instance, one may find it sexually arousing while the other thinks the sexual activity is degrading—to the actors, to one sex or the other, or as a whole.

Definitions Born of Political Activism

Catherine MacKinnon and Andrea Dworkin are prominent activists on a variety of feminist fronts, especially in efforts against pornography. Each has written multiple books and articles discussing the serious negative effects of pornographic images on women's lives and American culture in general. MacKinnon (1993) argues, "It is not the ideas in pornography that assault women: men do, men who are made, changed, and impelled by it. Pornography does not leap off the shelf and assault women. It is what it takes to make it and what happens through its use that are the problem" (p. 15). MacKinnon and Dworkin made one of the most tangible contributions to the antipornography effort to date by trying to get a civil rights bill, in the form of an antipornography ordinance, passed in Minnesota in the 1980s. The definition of pornography in this bill was written from the standpoint of women's victimization, which is understandable given the very small numbers of men who are victimized in pornography. MacKinnon and Dworkin's definition is as follows:

> *Coming to terms with women as real people and not as fantasies is part of growing up.*
>
> Sting, singer/songwriter & actor

> "Pornography" means the graphic sexually explicit subordination of women through pictures and/or words, including by electronic or other data retrieval systems, that also includes one of more of the following: (1) Women are presented dehumanized as sexual objects, things, or commodities. (2) Women are presented as sexual objects who enjoy humiliation or pain; or as sexual objects experiencing sexual pleasure in rape, incest, or other sexual assault; or as sexual objects tied up, cut up, mutilated, bruised, or physically hurt. (3) Women are presented in postures or positions of sexual submission, servility, or display. (4) Women's body parts—including but not limited to vaginas, breasts, or buttocks—are exhibited such that women are reduced to those parts. (5) Women are presented being penetrated by objects or animals. (6) Women are presented in scenarios of degradation, humiliation, injury, or torture, shown as filthy or inferior, bleeding, bruised, or hurt in a context that makes these conditions sexual. The use of men, children, or transsexuals in the place of women is also pornography for purposes of this law. (as in Gillespie et al., 1994, p. 44)

A 1994 issue of *Ms.* magazine contained a discussion of pornography by several prominent feminist researchers, authors, and activists, led by editor

Marcia Ann Gillespie. The purpose was to air diverse views on the issue or as Gillespie stated, "to get feminists talking *to* instead of *at* each other—and listening; to get us thinking and sharing our thoughts and feelings and fears, our questions and concerns" (p. 33). In that discussion, Norma Ramos, attorney and antipornography activist, stated that pornography is "evidence of women's second-class status. It is a central feature of patriarchal society, an essential tool in terms of how men keep power over women" (as in Gillespie et al., 1994, p. 34).

Representing another viewpoint is Nadine Strossen, author of the book *Defending Pornography* (1995), and one of the most outspoken critics of antipornography efforts. In Strossen's view, "Pornography is a vague term. In short, it is sexual expression that is meant to, or does, provoke sexual arousal or desire" (p. 18). She goes on to critique others' definitions: "In recent times, the word 'pornography' has assumed such negative connotations that it tends to be used as an epithet to describe—and condemn—whatever sexually oriented expression the person using it dislikes. As one wit put it, 'What turns *me* on is erotica, but what turns *you* on is pornography!'" (p. 18). In her book, Strossen differentiates between pornography that is destructive and degrading and that which is merely sexually arousing. She still considers the latter pornography, but acceptable pornography.

Types of Readily Accessible Pornography

One other distinction in terminology is important before going further. *Hard-core pornography* depicts or describes intercourse and/or other sexual practices (e.g., oral sex, anal sex). In *soft-core pornography,* such acts are implied but not fully or explicitly acted out on a screen or displayed on a page. According to Malamuth and Billings (1984), "both soft- and hard-core pornography present women as animalistic and in need of control. Women also are portrayed as easily accessible objects intended for possession. This allows men to commoditize women and appropriate what women produce, undercompensating them or not compensating them at all" (pp. 122–123).

In the next few paragraphs, we present divergent viewpoints on pornography. But before doing so, we have some questions for you to consider: Before you dismiss or downplay this discussion because you don't believe yourself to be a consumer of pornography, think again. If you adopt a broad definition of pornography as material that provokes sexual desire, then what can be considered pornographic takes on a much wider frame, doesn't it? For example, do you consider television's *Baywatch* pornography? How about *Playboy* and *Penthouse* magazines? Are they somehow in a different, more acceptable category than *Hustler* magazine? If the depictions in *Playboy* are sexually arousing, then do they qualify as pornographic? How about the swimsuit issue of *Sports Illustrated*? (Uh-oh, we've just tread on some *really* sacred ground.) Believe it or not, there is considerable opinion that the swimsuit issue actually is soft-core porn, just packaged in a sports magazine to make it appear more socially acceptable (Davis, 1997). What about the stripping and dancing in so-called gentleman's clubs? Is this erotic, but not pornographic, even though it may be sexually arousing to the viewers? Do you see a difference between what is erotic versus what is pornographic?

We continue to go through this exact process as we struggle in our own minds as to what should and should not be considered pornographic. Here are more questions for you: Just because something might be pornographic, is it necessarily harmful, degrading, and dangerous for society? Does pornography serve some useful purpose? We have our own personal answers to all these questions, but what's most important for our discussion here is this: Concerned adults must deal with these questions and others about pornography carefully and thoughtfully. Sexually explicit, arousing material is all around us and available for our consumption any hour of the day, especially as *cyberporn* on the Internet (Burr, 1997; Robischon, 1998). What you consume, what you believe consenting adults have the right to consume, and what adults should protect children from consuming are very important decisions each individual should make.

Multiple Camps for a Complex Issue

As we've said, there are different ways of looking at the issue of pornography. One thing to remember is that the two main camps we discuss below aren't really opposing sides of the issue. It's similar to the debate over reproductive rights: The pro-life camp isn't really the opposite of the pro-choice camp. The pro-choice stance isn't really a pro-abortion or pro-death (the opposite of pro-life) view; it's about one's right to make decisions about one's body. Just as many people hold a mixture of views termed pro-life *and* pro-choice, one can be in more than one camp regarding pornography. The two main groups—antipornography and anticensorship—both talk about the topic of pornography, but they talk about it in very different ways. The people do not consider themselves pro-censorship; the anticensorship people do not consider themselves pro-pornography. As journalist Maureen Dezell (1993) explains, "The American feminist movement's battle over censorship— those who favor legal limits on pornography versus those who oppose them—has escalated dramatically. Anti-porn feminists have won significant victories. Anti-censorship feminists—who've long maintained that it is people, not books or pictures, that harm women, and that women have historically been targets of censure when censorship is condoned—find their ideological opponents' growing influence alarming" (p. 2).

Voices from the AntiPornography Camp

Andrea Dworkin (1986), in an address before the Attorney General's Commission on Pornography, stated the following (be forewarned about the language and graphic descriptions):

> In this country where I live, every year millions and millions of pictures are being made of women with our legs spread. We are called beaver, we are called pussy, our genitals are tied up, they are pasted, makeup is put on them to make them pop out of a page at a male viewer. Millions and millions of pictures are made of us in postures of submission and sexual access so that our vaginas are exposed for penetration, our anuses are exposed for penetration,

our throats are used as if they are genitals for penetration. In this country where I live as a citizen real rapes are on film and are being sold in the marketplace. And the major motif of pornography as a form of entertainment is that women are raped and violated and humiliated until we discover that we like it and at that point we ask for more. (p. 277)

Dworkin's descriptions may sound harsh, but many of us are shielded from such degrading images of women. That doesn't mean those images don't exist; they are readily consumed by people every day. In fact, the pornography industry is a multibillion-dollar moneymaker—some estimates place it at $10 billion a year (Peach, 1998; Steinem, 1997). With the pervasiveness and easy accessibility of the Internet, coupled with the slow responses of governments to regulate what appears in cyberspace, the porno industry is experiencing record success and profits. How naive is it of all of us to think that the consumption of pornography doesn't have some measure of an effect on us—our views of the sexes, our expectations for how women and men ought to be treated and ought to behave toward one another?

But don't get the idea that Dworkin is in favor of censorship; she and MacKinnon believe that the pornography issue really has nothing to do with censorship—it has to do with respect. As Dworkin explains in the 1994 *Ms.* discussion, "The mindset has to change. It's not a question of looking at a magazine and censoring the content. It's a matter of looking at the social reality, the subordination of women necessary to create the magazine, and the way that the magazine is then used in the world against women" (as in Gillespie et al., 1994, pp. 37, 38). Law professor and author Mari Matsuda (1994) commented about the censorship issue, in relation to pornography: "We need to get away from male-centered notions of free speech. We should say that pornography, sexual harassment, racist speech, gay-bashing, anti-Semitic speech—speech that assaults and excludes—is not the same as the forms of speech deserving protection. Why is it that pornography, which undermines women's equality, is singled out for absolute protection?" (as in *Pornography*, 1994, p. 42). Gloria Steinem holds a similar view, expressed in an article responding to the 1997 film *The People vs. Larry Flynt,* in which she asked the question "Why can feminists speak against everything from wars and presidents to tobacco companies, yet if we use our free speech against pornography, we are accused, in Orwellian fashion, of being against free speech? (p. 76)

Voices from the AntiCensorship Camp

Strossen (1995) describes herself as a feminist who is "dedicated to securing equal rights for women and to combating women's continuing second-class citizenship in our society," but she "strongly opposes any effort to censor sexual expression" (p. 14). She and other activists, including Leanne Katz, Executive Director of the National Coalition Against Censorship, believe that if you suppress women's sexuality, you actually oppress them. Strossen describes the position of many members of the anticensorship camp as follows: "We are as committed as any other feminists to eradicating violence and discrimination against women. But we believe that suppressing sexual words and images will not advance these crucial causes. To the contrary, we are convinced that censoring sexual expression actually would do more harm than good to women's rights and safety" (p. 14).

Performance artist Holly Hughes revealed her views of pornography and censorship in the same issue of *Ms.*, explaining that being a consumer of pornography doesn't mean that "I'm going to go out and do everything I see. To be anticensorship doesn't mean that you are not offended. But the antidote to speech that you find disturbing is more speech" (as in *Pornography*, 1994, p. 43).

Author Sallie Tisdale (1992), in an article for *Harper's Magazine* entitled "Talk Dirty to Me: A Woman's Taste for Pornography," provides an interesting, more personal glimpse into the anticensorship view. She describes her journeys into adult video stores, the fear and discomfort she feels while selecting porn tapes, and the bashful way she later views these films at home. She believes the tapes have educational value, that she learns a great deal about her own sexuality from them, and she's certainly not in favor of any efforts to censor her viewing pleasure. But she makes a distinction between viewing consensual sex in a film versus viewing violence against women or degrading images of them. She explains: "What I like about pornography is as much a part of my sexuality as what I do, but it is more deeply psychological. What I *do* is the product of many factors, not all of them sexually motivated. But what I *imagine* doing is pure—pure in the sense that the images come wholly from within, from the soil of the subconscious. The land of fantasy is the land of the not-done and the wished-for. There are private lessons there, things for me to learn, all alone, about myself" (p. 38).

While we would not put Malamuth and Billings (1984) in the anticensorship camp, they describe others' views that coincide with Tisdale's: "Some of those who see pornography as sexual communication interpret its function in light of consumers' needs. Accordingly, pornography affects only the realm of fantasy or provides desirable information often lacking in many people's sex education" (p. 118). In the view of one researcher Malamuth and Billings cite, porn may have "important positive instructional functions" (p. 119).

Where to Put Up Your Tent

If you're having trouble deciding which camp to align yourself with, you're not alone. Elements of both positions have merit, we realize. There are well-known, outspoken feminists who adopt what could be perceived as a middle position. One such person is Marilyn French, author of eight books including *The War Against Women* (1992). In the *Ms.* magazine discussion, French admitted that she viewed the Dworkin-MacKinnon ordinance against pornography as a form of censorship. She suggested: "There may be some of us who would defend the First Amendment rather than see these [pornographic] magazines end—I'm one of them. But the problem is never, never going to be solved unless we start thinking about what this stuff means to *men*. You cannot make a movie or write a book that defends the practices of the Holocaust or that exalts black slavery. But you can make a movie, you can write a book that shows any kind of torture, enslavement, or murder of women. How come?" (as in Gillespie et al., 1994, p. 36).

The Crux of the Matter: Pornography is Personal

We have two purposes in presenting this material on pornography to you: first, to help you better understand the complexities of the issue through a discussion of diverse viewpoints; and second, to challenge you to think about the role of pornography in your own life. Now before you start to think, "Hey, don't accuse me of looking at that kind of stuff," we realize, as we've said before, that many of you reading this text think of pornography only in a hard-core sense and that you choose not to consume it. But what concerns us more, as writers and teachers of gender communication courses, is the more subtle, soft-core porn that permeates our existence because even soft-core porn includes stereotyping of women as subordinate sex objects and men's playthings (Jensen, 1991).

The barrage of sexual images we consume daily—in song lyrics and music videos (as we explore in the next and final section of this chapter), television and film images, advertisements in magazines and newspapers, images in comic books, cartoon strips, and cyberspace—simply *have* to have some effect. No one is superhuman enough to be immune to the effects of these images. We really do believe, as research shows and our students confirm for us consistently, that the amount of sexual images we consume in mediated messages shapes our views of the sexes (Jansma, Linz, Mulac, & Imrich, 1997; Senn, 1993). Mediated messages affect how we believe we are supposed to behave toward one another, what we expect from each other in relationships (both platonic and romantic), how we communicate our desires and needs (especially in sexual situations), and how much respect we develop for ourselves and others.

Here's an example to make this stance more concrete; you might think it an extreme case, but it involves a male student just like someone sitting in one of your classes. A few years back one of the TV news magazine shows did a story on a pornography-users' support group, a group of about 30 or so male students at Duke University that began as a small group of guys in a campus dorm having regular discussions about sex and the effects of pornography on their lives. The camera taped one of the weekly discussions, and the men's revelations were startlingly honest. Viewers at the time were shocked that pornography could so permeate these young men's lives, so debilitate their relationships with women and their feelings of self-esteem. One student's admission was particularly painful and memorable: He described a sexual encounter with a woman he was very interested in. They'd been out a couple of times but had not had sex. He was highly attracted to the woman and really wanted to be intimate with her, but described to the discussion group his embarassment over realizing that he was unable to become aroused and get an erection. He then explained how he enabled himself to function in the situation by imagining the woman beneath him as a pornographic image of a woman from a magazine.

When he shut his eyes, tuned out the real person he was with, and vividly imagined the graphic magazine picture, only then did he become aroused. He was not only worried that this signaled his sexual future—that he was doomed to a life of being aroused not by real people, but by mediated images—but also mortified at the impersonal, at-a-distance way he behaved with the woman. He could not continue the relationship after this experience and had had no other sexual encounters at the time the group met.

What's your reaction to this story? Do you know people who seem to be more comfortable with pornography than with real lovers or with their own sexuality? Should sexual fantasy and reality blend, rather than exist as separate entities that debilitate one's ability to function? We worry on a macro or societal level about how pornographic images—hard- and soft-core—harm women and men, how they keep women "in their place," as sexualized commodities to be purchased and used for gratification, and how they add to the pressure men feel to be sexual performers. But we worry more on a micro level; we worry about people like the former Duke students who might now be considered as sex addicts. We wonder how some men can say that they respect their wives when they regularly frequent strip clubs or adult film houses, become aroused by the dancers or images, and then come home expecting to have sex with their wives. What's the role of pornography in these men's lives? And we cannot help but believe (as the research has begun to document) that the enormous problem of violence, such as date rape and sexual assault, that occurs between persons in romantic situations is somehow connected to the all-pervasive, ready-and-waiting-for-your-consumption pornography.

WE COULD MAKE BEAUTIFUL MUSIC TOGETHER . . .

The July 21, 1997, cover of *Time* featured the popular singer Jewel, with a caption that read "Jewel and the Gang: Macho music is out. Empathy is in. And the all-female Lilith festival is taking rock's hot new sound on the road." While the music industry has traditionally been a male-dominated domain, female musicians in the 1990s and beyond are enjoying unprecedented success. Even though by most estimations men still outnumber women in the music business, the percentages continue to change (Christenson, 1993). The Lilith Fairs, which began in the summer of 1997, are highly successful all-women, multi-city tours that highlight the musical achievements of female artists and bands, including fair creator Sarah McLachlan, Luscious Jackson, Jewel, Joan Osborne, Liz Phair, Lauryn Hill, Paula Cole, the Indigo Girls, Sheryl Crow, Mary Chapin Carpenter, Erykah Badu, Lisa Loeb, Fiona Apple, Tracy Chapman, Suzanne Vega, Shawn Colvin, Missy "Misdemeanor" Elliott, Emmylou Harris, Meredith Brooks, Cassandra Wilson, Tracy Bonham, and Natalie Merchant. In the words of a *Time* magazine reporter, "Lilith Fair is a coming-out party, a chance for this generation of female singer-songwriters to meet and greet each other, jam onstage together, share audiences and, perhaps, start a folk-pop revolution" (Farley, 1997, p. 62). However, Lilith Fair is not without its critics, among them musicians Ani DiFranco, Courtney

Love, and Tori Amos, who view the tours as evidence of gender separatism (Willman, 1998).

It's obvious that music is a powerful force in our culture; its influence pervades our existence. In this final section of the chapter, we examine how song lyrics and music videos communicate images of women and men.

From Pop to Rock to Rap to Country: The Women and Men of Song Lyrics

Sometimes when you listen to a song you want to concentrate on the lyrics; you attend to the words from a more critical standpoint. But other times you simply like the rhythm, beat, and musical performance, so you tune out the lyrics. Have you ever read the lyrics to a particular song and said to yourself, "Oh, *that's* what they're saying"? That's much easier to do nowadays, with full transcripts of words often accompanying new CDs or tapes. Sometimes, however, you find yourself humming or singing along with a song on the radio or on a favorite CD when you suddenly realize what the words really are. You become acutely aware that what you're singing with or listening to isn't something you'd like to repeat in *any* company, especially mixed company.

> *I don't know if I'd call it a victory celebration. It's celebrating what we are—the fact that after centuries of women's voices and ideas being suppressed, we've finally come into a time where women can be heard and respected and loved for what they say. That's something worth celebrating.*
>
> Sarah McLachlan, singer/songwriter, about the concert tour Lilith Fair

There are just about as many ways to process music as there are people who listen to it. But consider the possibility that music, specifically song lyrics depicting the sexes, may have more impact on you than you realize.

Hearing the Beat Versus *Listening* to the Words

In research about the content and impact of song lyrics, music scholar Peter Christenson (1993) contends, "Even though the 'message' of popular music resides as much in its 'sound' as in its words, and even though lyrics are often—perhaps usually—ignored during the listening process, the words matter" (p. 2). Media scholar Roger Desmond (1987) explains how lyrics are often redundant within songs so that they form a "hook" or memorable strain that runs through the listener's mind long after the song has played. (We all know that once we get "hooked" by a certain refrain of a song, it's hard to get "unhooked.") The repetition of songs in a typical radio day and on CDs is likely to greatly reinforce lyrics in listeners' psyches. So what do these lyrics communicate about women and men?

Researchers Freudiger and Almquist (1978) conducted an important study of images and sex-role depictions of men and women in song lyrics of three genres of popular music. Although this study was done in the '70s, it is the only content analysis of song lyrics to date that takes into account both the sex of the singer and the type of music. Freudiger and Almquist examined the top 50 hits on the *Billboard* country, soul, and easy listening charts and found, first, that women were more the focus of song lyrics than men across all three musical genres. Second, women were rarely criticized and were most often positively portrayed in these lyrics, but they were described primarily in stereotypes of submissiveness, supportiveness, and dependency. In contrast, when men were mentioned in lyrics—especially songs written from a female perspective—their portrayals were more negative and critical, especially in country lyrics. Men's depictions reflected stereotypical traits of aggression, consistency, action, and confidence.

Research in the late 1980s identified stereotypical portrayals of women in American popular music, portrayals that are still prevalent today. Communication scholars Susan Butruille and Anita Taylor (1987) detected "three recurring images of women: The Ideal Woman/Madonna/Saint, the evil or fickle Witch/Sinner/Whore, and the victim (often dead)" (p. 180). Some of these images date back to early religious customs and beliefs about the sinful versus virginal nature of woman. As communication researcher Janet Wyman (1993) suggests, "The virgin/whore dichotomy is destructive to women not only because it polarizes, and thus limits their sexual identity, but because neither category is particularly flattering. The virgin/whore dichotomy stifles the social power of women since both the virgin and the whore are powerless positions" (pp. 6–7). Interestingly enough, one explanation for the popularity of the late Tejano singer Selena was her ability to combine saint and sinner, meaning that she presented a sexual, sensual image through dress and demeanor along with a "good girl" quality and a strong connection to family (Willis & Gonzalez, 1997).

With the wave of rising popularity of female singers and all-women bands, are depictions of the sexes changing in lyrics? Some scholars contend that this popular music is just as focused on romantic relationships as music has always been, but that the newer female artists' bold representations of brutality and degradation they've experienced in relationships communicate an unprecedented honesty. As one of our students recently put it, "I really like the new women musicians, but *man*, their songs are depressing." For example, Liz Phair's "Johnny Feelgood" is about a woman's obsession with an abusive man, Ani DiFranco's "Lost Woman Song" asserts a woman's right to an abortion, and Tori Amos's "Silent All These Years" and Fiona Apple's "Sullen Girl" describe recovery after rape (Browne, 1998; Farley, 1997; Papazian, 1996).

Sex and Degradation in Songs

Christenson (1993) discusses similarities and differences in the way men and women are depicted in song lyrics. He suggests that both sexes are often portrayed as emotional and dependent, stemming from "the natural tendency of popular music songs, no matter who is singing them, to take on a sad, bittersweet tone" (p. 15). But he does see persistent sex-role stereotypes and negative depictions of women in modern popular music. His insightful comparison of sexual imagery in songs by the Rolling Stones, Donna Summer, and Marvin Gaye with imagery in the songs of such 1980s and '90s groups as 2 Live Crew, Motley Crue, and Guns 'n Roses reveals a trend toward more explicit and graphic representations of sexual activity and more dramatically degrading images of and actions toward women.

> *Basically I write for the females, because we go through the most stuff. But even though I'm speaking from a woman's point of view, guys can relate, because they know the dirt that they do.*
>
> Missy "Misdemeanor" Elliot, singer/songwriter

Popular culture researchers Harding and Nett (1984) asserted that rock music provided the most derogatory, sexist images of women among all forms of popular music. However, more recent opinion suggests that rap music has overtaken rock as the most misogynistic form (hooks, 1992; Leland, 1992). Although some rap and hip-hop artists focus on racial and political issues and attempt to show positive images of relationships in their music, other artists are notorious for their depictions of women as virtual sex slaves to men. A study of listeners' reactions to music revealed that subjects believed sexually explicit rap music to be more patently offensive than sexually explicit nonrap music (Dixon & Linz, 1997). The study's authors suggest that because rap artists tend not to use "softening strategies" (such as poor pronunciation of offensive words, excessive loudness of music to muffle explicit language, and double entendres to soften offensive ideas), the rap songs used in the study may have seemed more blatant in their offensiveness when compared to nonrap songs (p. 234). Some of the lyrics depicting men as brutal terrorizers and users of women communicate skewed, nonrepresentative images that do nothing to improve relationships between the sexes.

As examples, have you ever read the words to 2 Live Crew's "S & M" (sadism and masochism) and "Dopeman" by N.W.A. (Niggaz With Attitude)? On the rock front, have you ever really listened to the words in Nine Inch Nails' "Closer," Motley Crue's "Same Ole' Situation," or "Stone Cold

Women are really empowering themselves in politics and in every facet of life now. Music tends to represent what's going on with youth, and the youth of America felt really frustrated a few years ago, and you had these angry alterna-bands. Now you have a lot of females who are stepping up to represent women in America or women in the world, becoming role models for young girls.

Sheryl Crow,
singer/songwriter

Bush" by the Red Hot Chili Peppers? These are examples of lyrics on tapes or CDs that typically receive parental advisory labels (Christenson, 1992). If you listen to any of these songs, you might be surprised, even appalled, at the language and brutal imagery the lyrics convey. Is it wise to say, "Oh the words don't really matter; it's got such a great sound, I just really like song"? If the words don't matter, if they don't communicate anything, then why aren't these songs instrumentals? Why include words at all if the words don't mean anything?

It's interesting to consider what effects song lyrics have on your perceptions or expectations of members of your same sex and the opposite sex. If you can easily remember the lyrics to a popular song (as opposed to formulas for your math exam), it's clear that they're permeating your consciousness on some level, right? So while we might not regulate our relationships according to what we hear depicted in song lyrics, those lyrics do affect all of us in some way. Do you think your own sex-role attitudes and gender communication can be shaped or affected by the messages contained in song lyrics? What about the effects of graphically violent and sexually explicit messages on noncritical consumers, meaning adolescents and children? Can children actually learn brutality through music? We can agree that music is not the sole or primary socializing agent of children, but along with violent, degrading images children view in other forms of media, it's safe to say that some popular music contributes to the problem.

Sex Kittens and He-Men in Music Videos

What happens when visual images in music videos reinforce the messages of song lyrics? As one researcher put it, "Music videos are more than a fad, more than fodder for spare hours and dollars of young consumers. They are pioneers in video expression, and the results of their reshaping of the form extend far beyond the TV set" (Aufderheide, 1986, p. 57). Since MTV went on the air in 1981 and quickly infiltrated American households, the music video industry has skyrocketed (Vivian, 1999). So have profits in the music industry—an industry that wasn't floundering, but that wasn't booming either prior to the innovation of music video. Nowadays the music video industry has sparked so much attention and has become such a vehicle for boosting recording sales that popular music artists feel compelled to create and market videos to accompany their songs.

Sexes and Races in Music Video

As media scholar Joe Gow (1996) explains, although music video has been praised for its innovativeness, it has also been criticized for its stereotypical depictions of relationships between women and men and between people of different racial groups. In fact, not too long after music video was introduced into this country (having first emerged in Europe in the 1970s), researchers began to investigate the extent of sex-role stereotyping in music videos (Peterson, 1987; Seidman, 1992; Sherman & Dominick, 1986).

Music video researcher Richard Vincent (1989) found that music videos predominantly depicted women as decorations and sex objects and that female artists most often portrayed themselves and other women in their videos in seductive clothing, with Tina Turner and Madonna heading up this list. Media specialists Brown and Campbell (1986) assessed race and sex differences in music videos airing on MTV and *Video Soul*, a music video program broadcast by the Black Entertainment Television cable channel. Results revealed "indications of persistent stereotypes of women as less active, less goal-directed, and less worthy of attention" (p. 101). Women of both races were significantly less often portrayed in professional settings in comparison to men of both races, a finding corroborated by subsequent research (Seidman, 1992). Brown and Campbell concluded, "White men, primarily by virtue of their greater numbers, are the center of attention and power and are more often aggressive and hostile than helpful and cooperative. Women and blacks are rarely important enough to be a part of the foreground" (p. 104). Media researchers Sherman and Dominick (1986) found similar results; they concluded, "Music television is a predominantly white and male world. Men outnumber women by two to one" (p. 84).

Research in the 1990s found little evidence of increased sex equity in music video. Scholars Rita Sommers-Flanagan, John Sommers-Flanagan, and

Britta Davis (1993) analyzed 40 music videos broadcast on MTV and found the following:

1. Men appeared in videos twice as often as women.
2. Men were significantly more aggressive and dominant in their behavior than women.
3. Women were significantly more sexual as well as subservient in their behavior.
4. Women were often targets of explicit and aggressive sexual advances.

> *I don't think having a naked woman strapped to a rack is sexist at all. And I don't think the fact that we pretend to slit her throat is violent. It's all show biz; it's entertainment. Can't everyone understand that?*
>
> Blackie Lawless,
> member of rock band
> W.A.S.P.

The researchers concluded "we are still a very male-dominated culture" (pp. 751–752).

Joe Gow's (1996) study of the 100 most popular MTV videos of the early '90s produced more bad news for women. In the videos he analyzed, five times as many men as women held lead roles. Women most often appeared performing their music for the camera (termed "posers" by Gow) or dancing while lip-synching the song, suggesting that "for women to star in music videos they had to affect an attitude or demonstrate physical talents, rather than exhibit the musical skills typically displayed by the men who appeared in lead roles" (p. 159). Thus, women's roles in these videos indicated "a much greater emphasis upon personal appearance" (p. 159). Men were most often shown performing in earnest in recording studios or on sound stages, but they also held several other lead roles in comparison to the narrow range of roles for women.

Music Video: Sex, Sex, and More Sex

Research on the sexualization of music video has focused on sexual content that degrades or demeans women, in particular. Perhaps you have seen the documentary film *Dreamworlds: Desire/Sex/Power in Rock Video*, by Sut Jhally (1990), which explores music video's hypersexualized images of women. In many videos, especially rock videos, women appear as mere sex objects designed to please men—as "legs in high heels" according to Jhally.

The fact that so much sexual imagery and activity appears belies industry executives' attempts to "clean up" music video. In 1990, when MTV executives screened Madonna's "Justify My Love" video, they found images more common to triple-X-rated movies than to music videos, so they refused to air the video (Rich, 1998). This was a huge decision because Madonna was considered the "queen," a pioneer in the music video industry, a performer who helped make MTV as much as it helped make her. For the major television outlet for music video to censor her artistic expression was an enormous development (one that, needless to say, did not go over well with Madonna). However, slowly but surely, standards have evolved and videos continue to explore more sexual territory. As Gow (1996) contends, "It appears that the changes implemented by MTV executives in the late 1980s had little impact upon portrayals of women in the videos shown on the popular network . . ." (p. 160).

One team of media researchers compared rock, country, and Christian music videos for religious imagery and sexual imagery, which the study described as provocative clothing, physical contact, sexually suggestive dance movements, depictions of heterosexual and homosexual dating, using a musical instrument in a sexual way, and depictions of sadomasochism (McKee & Pardun, 1996). They found that sexual imagery was very prevalent; however, sexual and religious imagery in combination frequently occurred as well. Of the three types of music videos, country music videos contained the most amount of sexual imagery compared to rock or contemporary Christian videos. This finding contrasts with those of other studies, which have found that country music videos tend to contain more images of romantic love, including relationship endings, than sexual images (Porter, 1993; Wilson, 1996).

Is Seeing Believing Or Is Hearing Believing?

Do music videos have an impact beyond that of song lyrics? As Desmond (1987) points out, "Music videos, with their capacity for both verbal and visual coding, and their tendency to dramatize the themes of lyrics, do add a potential for learning and arousal beyond the realm of music lyrics" (p. 282). While disagreement exists as to the exact added effects of visual images produced by music videos, there is considerable agreement that the combined visual and auditory channels have profound effects on memory and recall. And for some, this is a real concern when the lyrics and accompanying video images are sexist, racist, violent, and degrading. Calling it "concern" is an understatement for many feminists who believe that music videos and degrading song lyrics the music industry regularly distributes and profits from are among the most serious contributors to women's lowered status and violence against women in our culture.

Media scholar Susan Douglas (1995b), whose work we discussed in the section on prime-time television, describes her concerns about music video and its effects on future generations:

> What will be dramatically different for my little girl is that she will be less sheltered from images of violence against women than I was. Now the actual or threatened violation of women permeates the airwaves and is especially rampant on a channel like MTV. The MTV that initially brought us Culture Club, "Beat It," and Cyndi Lauper switched, under the influence of market research, to one of the most relentless showcases of misogyny in America. If MTV is still around in ten

years, and if its images don't change much, my daughter will see woman after woman tied up, strapped down, or on her knees in front of some strutting male hominid, begging to service him forever. These women are either garter-belt-clad nymphomaniacs or whip-wielding, castrating bitches: they all have long, red fingernails, huge breasts, buns of steel, and no brains; they adore sunken-chested, sickly looking boys with very big guitars. Worse, they either want to be or deserve to be violated. Anyone who doesn't think such representations matter hasn't read any headlines recently recounting the hostility with which all too many adolescent boys treat girls, or their eagerness to act on such hostilities, especially when they're in groups with names like Spur Posse. (pp. 302–303)

Music video is a pervasive form of media, particularly in the lives of middle- and high-school and traditionally-aged college students. However, it is not as pervasive or intrusive into your day as music that you hear on the radio as you're driving to class or to work, or that you turn on instantly when you walk in the door of your dorm room or home. Turning on the television and tuning in to music videos implies more conscious choice and more action than merely listening to background music. But think for a moment about the whole effect—the very powerful effect of combining visual images with musical sound, a beat, and lyrics. Whether or not you actually watch every second of the average three-minute music video or really attend to the lyrics in a song, you still receive the message. Somewhere your brain is processing the information, sometimes on a conscious level, but most times on a subconscious level.

Do you think that taking in so many stereotypical, sexist messages has some effect on you? We encourage you to think about how the music you listen to and videos you watch (if you watch them) affect your view of self, your attitudes about sex roles in society, the expectations you form (especially of members of the opposite sex), and your gender communication within relationships.

CONCLUSION

You may not feel you have reached media expert status, but we suspect that you know more about the forms of media that surround you every day than you did before you read this chapter. When you think about the many media outlets and methods that have the potential to influence you, it's almost overwhelming. But rather than feeling overwhelmed by media influence, your knowledge can empower you to better understand the effects of media messages about the sexes. We hope that you not only have an increased knowledge about mass communication, but that you are able to more critically assess the role media play in your life. That critical assessment enables you to make thoughtful choices about just how much you will allow the media to affect you.

Think about whether you have some standards for romantic relationships between women and men, for example, and where those standards came from. Do your expectations reflect romance as portrayed in movies or between characters on television? When you think about communication between marital partners, do you think about your parents, your married friends, or married characters on soap operas or prime-time television shows? If you were to describe someone's relationship or use it as an example, would you mention a couple from real life or would you call it a "Mulder-Scully" or "Dharma and Greg" kind of pairing?

When you're feeling down, are there certain songs and musical artists that either help you feel your pain more fully or that help raise your spirits? Have you ever watched TV characters go through some trauma, such as the death of a loved one, an angry exchange between friends, or the breakup of an important relationship, and then later used how the characters talked about the experience in your own life events? We encourage you to take more opportunities to consciously decipher media influence, particularly in reference to gender communication. The more you understand what's influencing you, the more ready you'll be to dive into new relationships or to strengthen your existing ones.

Key Terms

hypodermic needle theory
direct effects theory
uses and gratifications
   theory
agenda-setting theory
cultivation theory
stereotyping
female gender-role
   stereotypes
mixed signal advertising
male gender-role
   stereotypes

power babe commercials
Rambo and Himbo
   depictions
voice-overs
feminized or
   reconstructed male
feminization of prime-
   time television
mock-macho sitcom
playful patriarch
social issues
   programming

news magazine shows
gender-bending
pornography
obscenity
erotica
hard-core pornography
soft-core pornography
cyberporn

Discussion Starters

1. On a piece of paper, list the different forms of media we mentioned in the opening case study of this chapter. Then rank order these media, with a 1 ranking indicating the form of media you use the most, 2 indicating the second most used form of media, and so on. After you've ranked the items on the list, review your ranks. You should have a fairly accurate profile of yourself as a media consumer. Do any of the ranks surprise you? Is there a form of media that you believe you consume too much at present? Which one(s) and why?

2. When your favorite magazine arrives at your door or when you decide to buy the newest edition of it at the store, don't plunge into it right away. Try this exercise first. Thumb through the magazine, paying special attention to the advertisements. How many ads depict members of your same sex? How many depict members of the opposite sex? Analyze an ad the way we did for the woman on the beer bottle billboard. Do you see the ad in a different light after having analyzed it in this manner? What does the ad communicate about the sexes?

3. What's your favorite prime-time television show? Think of several reasons why this show is your favorite. Do your reasons have more to do with the characters, the setting or scenery, the plot lines, or something else? Now think about a prime-time television show that you watched and just hated. What was so irritating about that show? Are there any gender issues affecting your decision about most and least favorite TV shows?

4. After having read the section in this chapter about talk shows, try to watch one or record one on videotape. If you don't have the necessary equipment, ask a friend to record a talk show for you. What issue is being discussed on the talk show? Is the host of the talk show a man or a woman? Do you think the sex of the host makes a difference? Would an opposite-sex host have put a different spin on the topic of the particular show you watched? If so, why? Can you see the agenda-setting function of media at work in this talk show?

5. This is an old exercise, but it's always revealing and interesting. At a gathering of some friends or when on break with a few co-workers, ask everyone to come up with their top 5 or top 10 favorite movies of all time. The fun part comes when you find out why each person chose the movies on his or her list. You find out if people are drawn to a certain film genre, such as action or romance, or if it's the actors that make the difference. You can search for trends based on the sex of persons sharing their lists. It's also interesting to see which films are common across different people's lists.

6. Have your views on pornography changed at all as a result of the information in this chapter? Think about the different definitions of pornography and decide which one you are the most comfortable with. Then think about media you consume—from magazine ads to television shows to films to music videos. How much of this media you consume could be classified as pornographic? What role, if any, has pornography played in your developing understanding of the sexes?

7. Assess your music collection. Who do you listen to—predominantly artists of the same sex as you or of the opposite sex? If there's a pattern, why do you think the pattern exists? Then pick one album, CD, or cassette tape and play the cut on it that you are the least familiar with. Listen carefully and try to take in every word of the song lyric. Did you hear anything for the first time? Did you realize that this song was actually on this tape?

8. Think about the most sexist music video you've ever seen. What makes this video memorable? Was it sexist toward men, toward women, or both? How was the sexism conveyed in the video? Who was the artist in the video? What do you think the connection is between the artist and the sexism inherent in that artist's video?

References

ALLAN, K., & COLTRANE, S. (1996). Gender displaying television commercials: A comparative study of television commercials in the 1950s and the 1980s. *Sex Roles, 35,* 185–196.

ATKIN, D. (1991). Sex in prime-time television: 1979 versus 1989. *Journal of Broadcasting and Electronic Media, 35,* 517–523.

AUFDERHEIDE, P. (1986). Music videos: The look of sound. *Journal of Communication, 36,* 57–77.

AXELROD, J. (1993). Sexual harassment in the movies and its effect on the audience. In G. L. Kreps (Ed.), *Sexual harassment: Communication implications* (pp. 107–117). Cresskill, NJ: Hampton.

BAKER WOODS, G. (1995). *Advertising and marketing to the new majority.* Belmont, CA: Wadsworth.

BITTNER, J. R. (1989). *Mass communication: An introduction* (5th ed.). Englewood Cliffs, NJ: Prentice Hall.

BOWERS, M. (1997, May 23). *Thelma & Louise* debuts. *Entertainment Weekly,* 74.

BROWN, J. D., & CAMPBELL, K. (1986). Race and gender in music videos: The same beat but a different drummer. *Journal of Communication, 36,* 94–106.

BROWNE, D. (1998, August 14). Modern maturity. *Entertainment Weekly,* 78–79.

BURR, T. (1997, July 18). Down and dirty. *Entertainment Weekly,* 92.

BUTLER, R. W. (1997, August 24). Films hold misogyny to light. *Corpus Christi Caller Times,* p. F5.

BUTRUILLE, S. G., & TAYLOR, A. (1987). Women in American popular song. In L. P. Stewart & S. Ting-Toomey (Eds.), *Communication, gender, and sex roles in diverse interaction contexts* (pp. 179–188). Norwood, NJ: Ablex.

CAGLE, J. (1998, May 8). As gay as it gets? *Entertainment Weekly,* 26–32.

CHRISTENSON, P. G. (1992). The effects of parental advisory labels on adolescent music preferences. *Journal of Communication, 42,* 106–113.

CHRISTENSON, P. G. (1993, February). *The content of popular music.* Paper presented at the meeting of the Western States Communication Association, Albuquerque, NM.

CHRISTENSON, P. G. (1994). Childhood patterns of music uses and preferences. *Communication Reports, 7,* 136–144.

CLARK, K. R. (1993, January 6). Role models. *Dallas Morning News,* pp. 5C, 14C.

COMSTOCK, G. (1983). Television and American social institutions. In J. C. Wright & A. C. Huston (Eds.), *Children and television* (3rd ed.). Lexington, MA: Ginn.

COMSTOCK, J., & STRZYZEWSKI, K. (1990). Interpersonal interaction on television: Family conflict and jealousy on prime-time. *Journal of Broadcasting and Electronic Media, 34,* 263–282.

COURTNEY, A. E., & WHIPPLE, T. W. (1974). Women in TV commercials. *Journal of Communication, 24,* 110–118.

COURTNEY, A. E., & WHIPPLE, T. W. (1983). *Sex stereotyping in advertising.* Lexington, MA: Lexington Press.

CRAIG, R. S. (1992, October). *Selling masculinities, selling femininities: Multiple genders and the economics of television.* Paper presented at the meeting of the Speech Communication Association, Chicago, IL.

CULLEY, J. O., & BENNETT, R. (1976). Selling women, selling blacks. *Journal of Communication, 26,* 160–174.

DAMBROT, F. H., REEP, D. C., & BELL, D. (1988). Television sex roles in the 1980s: Do viewers' sex and sex role orientation change the picture? *Sex Roles, 19,* 387–401.

DAVIS, L. R. (1997). *The swimsuit issue and sport: Hegemonic masculinity in Sports Illustrated.* Albany: State University of New York Press.

DEGRAZIA, E. (1992). *Girls lean back everywhere: The law of obscenity and the assault on genius.* New York: Random House.

DESMOND, R. J. (1987). Adolescents and music lyrics: Implications of a cognitive perspective. *Communication Quarterly, 35,* 276–284.

DEZELL, M. (1993, July). Porn wars. *Boston Phoenix,* 2–8.

DIXON, T. L., & LINZ, D. G. (1997). Obscenity law and sexually explicit rap music: Understanding the effects of sex, attitudes, and beliefs. *Journal of Applied Communication Research, 25,* 217–241.

DOBOSZ, A. M. (1997, November-December). Thicker thighs by Thanksgiving. *Ms.*, 89–91.

DOHERTY, T. (1988). *Teenagers and teenpics: The juvenilization of American movies in the 50s*. Boston: Unwin Hyman.

DOMINICK, J. R. (1998). *The dynamics of mass communication* (6th ed). New York: McGraw-Hill.

DORR, A., & KUNKEL, D. (1990). Children and the media environment: Change and constancy amid change. *Communication Research, 17*, 5–25.

DOUGLAS, S. J. (1995a). Sitcom women: We've come a long way. Maybe. *Ms.*, 76–80.

DOUGLAS, S. J. (1995b). *Where the girls are: Growing up female with the mass media*. New York: Random House.

DOW, B. J. (1996). *Prime-time feminism: Television, media culture, and the Women's Movement since 1970*. Philadelphia: University of Pennsylvania Press.

DREWNIANY, B. (1996). Super Bowl commercials: The best a man can get (or is it?) In P. Lester (Ed.), *Images that injure* (pp. 87–92). Westport, CT: Praeger.

DWORKIN, A. (1986). Pornography is a civil rights issue. In A. Dworkin (Ed., 1993) *Letters from a war zone*. Brooklyn, NY: Lawrence Hill.

FALUDI, S. (1991). *Backlash: The undeclared war against American women*. New York: Crown.

FARLEY, C. J. (1997, July 21). Galapalooza! Lilith Fair—a traveling festival featuring female folk-pop stars—is rocking the music world. *Time*, 60–64.

FAWCETT, A. W. (1993, October 4). Narrowcast in past, women earn revised role in advertising. *Advertising Age*, pp. S1, S10.

FINE, M. G. (1981). Soap opera conversations: The talk that binds. *Journal of Communication, 31*, 97–107.

FISKE, J. (1987). *Television culture*. New York: Methuen.

FRENCH, M. (1992). *The war against women*. New York: Summit.

FREUD LOEWENSTEIN, A. (1993, November-December). Sister from another planet probes the soaps. *Ms.*, 76–79.

FREUDIGER, P., & ALMQUIST, E. M. (1978). Male and female roles in the lyrics of three genres of contemporary music. *Sex Roles, 4*, 51–65.

GAGNARD, A. (1986). From feast to famine: Depiction of ideal body type in magazine advertising: 1950–1984. In E. F. Larkin (Ed.), *Proceedings of the Nineteen Eighty-Six Conference of the American Academy of Advertising* (pp. R46–R50). Charleston, SC: American Academy of Advertising.

GARST, J., & BODENHAUSEN, G. (1997). Advertising's effects on men's gender role attitudes. *Sex Roles, 36*, 551–572.

GERBNER, G., GROSS, L., ELEEY, M. F., JACKSON-BEECK, M., JEFFRIES-FOX, S., & SIGNORIELLI, N. (1977). TV violence profile no. 8: The highlights. *Journal of Communication, 27*, 171–180.

GERBNER, G., GROSS, L., MORGAN, M., & SIGNORIELLI, N. (1980). The "mainstreaming" of America: Violence profile no. 11. *Journal of Communication, 30*, 10–29.

GILLESPIE, M. A., DWORKIN, A., SHANGE, N., RAMOS, N., & FRENCH, M. (1994, January-February). Where do we stand on pornography? *Ms.*, 33–41.

GLENN, R. J. III. (1992, November). *Echoes of feminism on the big screen: A fantasy theme analysis of "Thelma and Louise."* Paper presented at the meeting of the Speech Communication Association, Chicago, IL.

GOLDBERG, R. (1998, November). If not now, when? *Premiere*, 86–88.

GOLDMAN, R., HEATH, D., & SMITH, S. L. (1991). Commodity feminism. *Critical Studies in Mass Communication, 8*, 333–351.

GOW, J. (1996). Reconsidering gender roles on MTV: Depictions in the most popular music videos of the early 1990s. *Communication Reports, 9*, 151–161.

HALL, C. C. I., & CRUM, M. J. (1994). Women and "body-isms" in television beer commercials. *Sex Roles, 31*, 329–337.

HANKE, R. (1998). The "mock-macho" situation comedy: Hegemonic masculinity and its reiteration. *Western Journal of Communication, 62*, 74–93.

HARDING, D., & NETT, E. (1984). Women and rock music. *Atlantis, 10*, 60–77.

HEATON, J. A., & WILSON, N. L. (1995, September/October). Tuning in to trouble. *Ms.*, 44–51.

HOERRNER, K. L. (1996). Gender roles in Disney films: Analysing behaviors from Snow White to Simba. *Women's Studies in Communication, 19*, 213–228.

HOFFMAN, A. (1997, October). *Thelma & Louise:* What do you do when the American dream fails you? *Premiere*, 69.

HOOKS, B. (1992). *Black looks: Race and representation.* Boston: Sound End Press.

HUANG, T. (1998, March 9). "Ally" oops: Sitcom's fans are happy to see somebody else jumping through hoops. *Dallas Morning News*, pp. 1C, 2C.

IRWIN, B. J., & CASSATA, M. (1993, November). *Cultural indicators: Families on daytime television.* Paper presented at the meeting of the Speech Communication Association, Miami, FL.

JACKSON, K. (1991, September 14). Have you come a long way, baby? *Dallas Morning News*, pp. 1C, 3C.

JACOBS, A. J. (1998, October 23). When gay men happen to straight women. *Entertainment Weekly*, 20–27.

JANSMA, L. L., LINZ, D. G., MULAC, A., & IMRICH, D. J. (1997). Men's interactions with women after viewing sexually explicit films: Does degradation make a difference? *Communication Monographs, 64*, 1–24.

JAPP, P. M. (1991). Gender and work in the 1980s: Television's working women as displaced persons. *Women's Studies in Communication, 14*, 49–74.

JENSEN, K. B. (1987). Qualitative audience research: Toward an integrative approach to reception. *Critical Studies in Mass Communication, 4*, 21–36.

JENSEN, S. (1991, January-February). Pornography does make women sex objects. *Utne Reader*, 13.

JHALLY, S. (1990). *Dreamworlds: Desire/sex/power in rock video.* [Videotape] Amherst: University of Massachusetts Communication Service Trust Fund.

KALISH, D. (1988, March). Which sex speaks louder? *Marketing & Media*, 30–31.

KANG, M. (1996). The portrayal of women's images in magazine advertisements: Goffman's gender analysis revisited. *Sex Roles, 35*, 979–996.

KANNER, B. (1990, May 21). Big boys don't cry. *New York*, 20–21.

KILBOURNE, J. (1998). Beauty and the beast of advertising. In L. J. Peach (Ed.), *Women in culture: A women's studies anthology* (pp. 127–131). Malden, MA: Blackwell.

KIM, A. (1995, January 20). Star trip: A new "Trek," a new network, a new captain—and (red alert!) she's a woman. *Entertainment Weekly*, 14–20.

KLAWANS, S. (1991, June 24). Films: *Thelma & Louise. The Nation*, 862–863.

KOLBE, R. H. (1991). Gender roles in children's television advertising: A longitudinal content analysis. *Current Issues in Advertising Research*, 196–205.

KRENDL, K., CLARK, G., DAWSON, R., & TROIANO, C. (1993). Preschoolers and VCRs in the home: A multiple methods approach. *Journal of Broadcasting & Electronic Media, 38*, 293–310.

KROLL, J. (1991, June 24). Back on the road again. *Newsweek*, 67.

LANIS, K., & COVELL, K. (1995). Images of women in advertisements: Effects on attitudes related to sexual aggression. *Sex Roles, 32*, 639–649.

LARSON, M. (1989). Interaction between siblings in primetime television. *Journal of Broadcasting and Electronic Media, 33*, 305–315.

LAZIER, L., & GAGNARD KENDRICK, A. (1993). Women in advertisements: Sizing up the images, roles, and functions. In P. Creedon (Ed.), *Women in mass communication* (2nd ed.) (pp. 199–219). Newbury Park, CA: Sage.

LEE, M. (1995, November). No more waifs. *The Progressive*, 13.

LELAND, J. (1992, June 29). Rap and race. *Newsweek*, 47–52.

LEMISH, D. (1985). Soap opera viewing in college: A naturalistic inquiry. *Journal of Broadcasting & Electronic Media, 29*, 275–293.

LEO, J. (1991, June 10). Toxic feminism on the big screen. *U.S. News and World Report*, 20.

LIN, C. A. (1997). Beefcake versus cheesecake in the 1990s: Sexist portrayals of both genders in television commercials. *Howard Journal of Communications, 8*, 237–249.

LINDLOF, T. R. (1987). *Natural audiences: Qualitative research of media uses and effects.* Norwood, NJ: Ablex.

LINDLOF, T. R. (1991). Qualitative study of media audiences. *Journal of Broadcasting and Electronic Media, 35*, 23–42.

LIU, W. Y., INOUE, Y., BRESNAHAN, M. J., & NISHIDA, T. (1998, November). *Eat, drink, man, woman: Sex and occupational role stereotypes in prime time commercials in Japan and Taiwan.* Paper presented at the meeting of the National Communication Association, New York, NY.

LIVINGSTONE, S., & LIEBES, T. (1995). Where have all the mothers gone? Soap opera's replaying of the Oedipal story. *Critical Studies in Mass Communication, 12,* 155–175.

LOOHAUIS, J. (1994, March 16). Now, here's a pause that really refreshes. *Dallas Morning News,* pp. 5C, 13C.

LUONG, M. A. (1992, October). *Star Trek: The Next Generation: Boldly forging empowered female characters.* Paper presented at the meeting of the Speech Communication Association, Chicago, IL.

LYSONSKI, S., & POLLAY, R. W. (1990). Advertising sexism is forgiven but not forgotten: Historical, cross-cultural and individual differences in criticism and purchase boycott intentions. *International Journal of Advertising, 9,* 317–329.

MACKAY, N. J., & COVELL, K. (1997). The impact of women in advertisements on attitudes toward women. *Sex Roles, 36,* 573–583.

MACKINNON, C. A. (1993). *Only words.* Cambridge, MA: Harvard University Press.

MACKLIN, M. C., & KOLBE, R. H. (1984). Sex role stereotyping in children's advertising: Current and past trends. *Journal of Advertising, 13,* 34–42.

MALAMUTH, N. M., & BILLINGS, V. (1984). Why pornography? Models of functions and effects. *Journal of Communication, 34,* 117–129.

MANDZIUK, R. (1991, February). *Cementing her sphere: Daytime talk and the television world of women.* Paper presented at the meeting of the Western States Communication Association, Phoenix, AZ.

MARACEK, J., PILIAVIN, J. A., FITZSIMMONS, E., KROGH, E. C., LEADER, E., & TRUDELL, B. (1978). Women as TV experts: The voice of authority? *Journal of Communication, 28,* 159–168.

MASLIN, J. (1994, January 20). Women getting scary in pop culture. *New York Times.*

McKEE, K. B., & PARDUN, C. J. (1996). Mixed messages: The relationship between sexual and religious imagery in rock, country, and Christian videos. *Communication Reports, 9,* 163–171.

MILNER, L. M. (1994). Multinational gender positioning: A call for research. In E. G. Basil (Ed.), *Global and multinational advertising* (pp. 83–102). Hillsdale, NJ: Laurence Erlbaum.

MINOW, N. N. (1991). Television: How far has it come in 30 years? *Vital Speeches, 57,* 121–125.

MOORE, M. L. (1992). The family as portrayed on prime-time television, 1947–1990: Structure and characteristics. *Sex Roles, 26,* 41–61.

MUMFORD, L. S. (1995). *Love and ideology in the afternoon: Soap opera, women, and television genre.* Bloomington: University of Indiana Press.

MYERS, P. N., JR., & BIOCCA, R. A. (1992). The elastic body image: The effect of television advertising and programming on body image distortions in young women. *Journal of Communication, 42,* 108–133.

NICHOLSON, J. (1992, Summer/Fall). The advertiser's man. *Adbusters,* 21–26.

O'DONNELL, W. J., & O'DONNELL, K. J. (1978). Update: Sex-role messages in TV commercials. *Journal of Communication, 28,* 156–158.

OLSON, B., & DOUGLAS, W. (1997). The family on television: An evaluation of gender roles in situation comedy. *Sex Roles, 36,* 409–427.

PALMGREEN, P., & RAYBURN, J. D. II. (1985). A comparison of gratification models of media satisfaction. *Communication Monographs, 52,* 334–346.

PAPAZIAN, E. (Ed.) (1990). *TV dimensions '90.* New York: Media Dynamics.

PAPAZIAN, E. (1996, November-December). Woman on the verge. *Ms.,* 38–45.

PARISH PERKINS, K. (1994, January 13). Is television's "gender gap" also a gap in quality? *Dallas Morning News,* p. 7E.

PATTERSON, P. (1996). Rambos and Himbos: Stereotypical images of men in advertising. In P. Lester (Ed.), *Images that injure* (pp. 93–96). Westport, CT: Praeger.

PEACH, L. J. (1998). Women and popular culture I: Advertising, print media, and pornography. In L. J. Peach (Ed.), *Women in culture: A women's studies anthology* (pp. 119–127). Malden, MA: Blackwell.

PETERSON, E. E. (1987). Media consumption and girls who want to have fun. *Critical Studies in Mass Communication, 4*, 37–50.

Pornography: Does women's equality depend on what we do about it? (1994, January-February). *Ms.*, 42–45.

PORTER, S. B. (1993, February). *"If it weren't for country music I'd go crazy": An analysis of subject matter content and production styles of country music videos*. Paper presented at the meeting of the Western States Communication Association, Albuquerque, NM.

PRATKANIS, A., & ARONSON, E. (1992). *Age of propaganda: The everyday use and abuse of persuasion*. New York: W. H. Freeman.

PRESS, A. L. (1991a). *Women watching television: Gender, class, and generation in the American television experience*. Philadelphia: University of Pennsylvania Press.

PRESS, A. L. (1991b). Working-class women in a middle-class world: The impact of television on modes of reasoning about abortion. *Critical Studies in Mass Communication, 8*, 421–441.

RAEBACK-WAGENER, J., EICKENHOFF-SCHEMECK, J., & KELLY-VANCE, L. (1998). The effect of media analysis on attitudes and behaviors regarding body image among college students. *Journal of American College Health, 47*, 29–40.

RAKOW, L. F. (1992). "Don't hate me because I'm beautiful": Feminist resistance to advertising's irresistible meanings. *Southern States Communication Journal, 57*, 132–142.

RAYBURN, J. D., PALMGREEN, P., & ACKER, T. (1984). Media gratifications and choosing a morning news program. *Journalism Quarterly, 61*, 149–156.

RICH, J. (1998, November 20). Madonna banned. *Entertainment Weekly*, 152.

RICHMOND-ABBOTT, M. (1992). *Masculine and feminine: Gender roles over the life cycle* (2nd ed.). New York: McGraw-Hill.

ROBISCHON, N. (1998, January 9). Porn to lose—maybe. *Entertainment Weekly*, 81.

ROWE, K. (1990). Roseanne: Unruly woman as domestic goddess. *Screen, 31*, 408–419.

RUBIN, A. M. (1985). Uses of daytime television soap operas by college students. *Journal of Broadcasting and Electronic Media, 29*, 241–258.

RUBIN, A. M. (1986). Uses and gratifications. In J. Bryant & D. Zillmann (Eds)., *Perspectives on media effects*. Hillsdale, NJ: Lawrence Erlbaum.

SAPOLSKY, B. S., & TABARLET, J. O. (1991). Sex in primetime television: 1979 versus 1989. *Journal of Broadcasting and Electronic Media, 35*, 505–516.

SCHICKEL, R. (1991, June 24). Gender bender. *Time*, 52–56.

SCHRAG, R. L. (1990). *Taming the wild tube: A family's guide to television and video*. Chapel Hill: The University of North Carolina Press.

SCODARI, C. (1998). "No politics here": Age and gender in soap opera "cyberfandom." *Women's Studies in Communication, 21*, 168–187.

SEIDMAN, S. A. (1992). An investigation of sex-role stereotyping in music videos. *Journal of Broadcasting and Electronic Media, 36*, 209–216.

SENN, C. Y. (1993). Women's multiple perspectives and experiences with pornography. *Psychology of Women Quarterly, 17*, 318–341.

SHAPIRO, L. (1991, June 17). Women who kill too much. *Newsweek*, 52–56.

SHERMAN, B. L., & DOMINICK, J. R. (1986). Violence and sex in music videos: TV and rock and roll. *Journal of Communication, 36*, 79–93.

SILVERSTEIN, B., PERDUE, L., PETERSON, B., & KELLY, E. (1986). The role of mass media in promoting a thin standard of bodily attractiveness for women. *Sex Roles, 14*, 519–532.

SOMMERS-FLANAGAN, R., SOMMERS-FLANAGAN, J., & DAVIS, B. (1993). What's happening on music television? A gender role content analysis. *Sex Roles, 28*, 745–753.

STEINEM, G. (1983). Erotica vs. pornography. In G. Steinem (Ed.), *Outrageous acts and everyday rebellions* (pp. 219–230). New York: Holt, Rinehart and Winston.

STEINEM, G. (1997, March-April). What's wrong with this picture? *Ms.*, 76.

STROSSEN, N. (1995). *Defending pornography: Free speech, sex, and the fight for women's rights*. New York: Scribner.

SULLIVAN, G. L., & O'CONNOR, P. J. (1988). Women's role portrayals in magazine advertising: 1958–1983. *Sex Roles, 18*, 181–189.

SVETKEY, B. (1992, March 6). "Star" struck. *Entertainment Weekly*, 20.

TEDFORD, T. L. (1993). *Freedom of speech in the United States* (2nd ed.). New York: McGraw-Hill.

TISDALE, S. (1992, February). Talk dirty to me: A woman's taste for pornography. *Harper's*, 37–46.

TRAUBE, E. (1992). *Dreaming identities: Class, gender, and generation in 1980s Hollywood movies*. Boulder, CO: Westview.

TUCHMAN, G. (1979). Women's depiction by the mass media. *Signs, 4*, 528–542.

UNGER, R., & CRAWFORD, M. (1996). *Women and gender: A feminist psychology* (2nd ed.). New York: McGraw-Hill.

VANDE BERG, L. R. (1993, November). *Not quite boldly going where no one has gone before: Star Trek and the next generation*. Paper presented at the meeting of the Speech Communication Association, Miami, FL.

VANDE BERG, L. R., & STRECKFUSS, D. (1992). Prime-time television's portrayal of women and the world of work: A demographic profile. *Journal of Broadcasting and Electronic Media, 36*, 195–208.

VAN EVRA, J. (1990). *Television and child development*. Hillsdale, NJ: Lawrence Erlbaum.

VINCENT, R. C. (1989). Clio's consciousness raised? Portrayal of women in rock videos, re-examined. *Journalism Quarterly, 66*, 155–160.

VIVIAN, J. (1999). *The media of mass communication* (5th ed.). Boston: Allyn & Bacon.

WELLS, W., BURNETT, J., & MORIARTY, S. (1998). *Advertising principals and practice*. Upper Saddle River, NJ: Prentice Hall.

WHIPPLE, T. W., & COURTNEY, A. E. (1980). How to portray women in TV commercials. *Journal of Advertising Research, 20*, 53–59.

WHIPPLE, T. W., & COURTNEY, A. E. (1985). Female role portrayals in advertising and communication effectiveness: A review. *Journal of Advertising, 14*, 4–8.

WHITE, S. E. (1995). A content analytic technique for measuring the sexiness of women's business attire in media presentations. *Communication Research Reports, 122*, 178–185.

WHITMIRE, T. (1996, September 8). Soap opera study finds plenty of sex, not much talk of birth control. *Corpus Christi Caller Times*, p. A7.

WILLIS, J., & GONZALEZ, A. (1997). Reconceptualizing gender through intercultural dialogue: The case of the Tex-Mex Madonna. *Women & Language, 20*, 9–12.

WILLMAN, C. (1998, June 19). A fair to remember. *Entertainment Weekly*, 28–37.

WILSON, B. J., LINZ, D., DONNERSTEIN, E., & STIPP, H. (1992). The impact of social issue television programming on attitudes toward rape. *Human Communication Research, 19*, 179–208.

WILSON, J. L. (1996, October). *Country music videos: Women gaining ground?* Paper presented at the meeting of the Organization for the Study of Communication, Language, and Gender, Monterey, CA.

WYMAN, L. M. (1993, November). *The virgin/whore dichotomy of sexual powerlessness: Vampire bitches, brides, and victims in Bram Stoker's Dracula*. Paper presented at the meeting of the Speech Communication Association, Miami, FL.

ZINN, L. (1991, November 4). This Bud's for you. No, not you—her. *Business Week*, 86–87.

PART THREE

LET'S TALK: INITIATING AND DEVELOPING RELATIONSHIPS

ALL FILMS
STARS
TO THE
STAIRWAY
GIRLS NUDE GIRLS
PEEP MOVIES
GIRLS NUDE GIRLS
VIDEO MOVIES
GIRLS NUDE GIRLS
LIVE THEATRE
GIRLS NUDE GIRLS
TO THE
STARS
STAIRWAY
WELCOME
SEX ACTS
VIDEO PEEPS
UPPER LEVEL

CHOOSING AND USING GENDERED LANGUAGE

CASE STUDY: WATCH YOUR LANGUAGE

For most of 1998, American airwaves and newspapers were riveted to one particular story—the sex scandal surrounding President Bill Clinton and a former White House intern, Monica Lewinsky. Month after month, despite other national and international events of importance to the general health and security of the country, allegations of an extramarital affair and the ensuing cover-up dominated the headlines. One of the more interesting aspects of following developments in the ongoing investigation was television news personalities' attempts at "watching their language." The sexual innuendoes were extremely tempting and many times unintentional, as, for example, one news talk show guest who described the scandal as "a seminal moment in the Clinton presidency." One comment that emerged during the scandal coverage had particular resonance for the topic of this chapter. A political pundit on a cable newscast was discussing possible ramifications of forcing Secret Service agents and government attorneys to testify to the grand jury about what they may have witnessed between the president and the intern (MSNBC, August 4, 1998). His comment was as follows: "With all the rulings in this investigation, future presidents will have no one to talk to in confidence but their personal attorneys and their wife." Anything objectionable in the language of that statement?

Besides the awkwardness of the phrase "their wife," meaning the use of a plural pronoun with a singular noun, the political pundit obviously had men—and only men—in mind when thinking of future presidents. He had only married men in mind, too, because he was describing what he saw as diminishing legal privilege in the country, privilege extended only to spouses and personal attorneys. Was the language acceptable because perhaps the pundit was merely reflecting the situation at the time, which involved a married male president? Or was his language reflective of limited thinking, revealing a sexist attitude or preference for male presidents? Most of our traditionally-aged students believe that a woman will be elected president of the United States within their lifetimes. How might the pundit's statement be rephrased to have included the potential for future presidents who could be female or single?

This chapter is not about politics or sex scandals. Instead it is an in-depth examination of language because *the language we choose to use reveals to others who we are.* As linguist Jennifer Coates (1998) explains: "It has been understood for a long time that language and identity are crucially intertwined, . . . but it is only recently that researchers in language and gender have begun to explore the way that language practices accomplish gender" (p. 79).

Hot Topics

- The power of *choosing* and *using language*
- The definition of *sexist language*
- The *interrelationship* between *language* and *thought*
- Reasons for using *nonsexist language* in your gender communication
- Sexism in *generic pronouns, antimale language, man-linked terms, sex marking,* and *feminine suffixes*
- Demeaning *animal, food,* and *plant* terms for women and men
- Male-dominated imagery within *religious language*
- *Sexual language* and what it communicates about men and women
- How choices for *married names, euphemisms, metaphors,* and *insults* can reflect sexism
- New thinking about *parallelism, order,* and *references to relationships*
- Outdated *titles* and *salutations*
- The *Relational* and *Content Axiom* of communication
- Current research into the sexes' views about the *functions* of conversation
- *Vocal properties* and *linguistic constructions* that communicate *tentativeness*
- Ways women and men *manage conversation*
- *Profanity* and *color* terms used differently by men and women

CHOOSING YOUR LANGUAGE

The *choosing* and *using* aspects in the chapter title refer to our view of using language by choice. Many people use language by default—they talk the way they've always talked, simply because they've always talked that way. These people never think about the influence of language on their view of self, their relationships, and their communication. After reading this chapter, maybe you won't be one of these people. This chapter puts language under the microscope to examine its powerful influences on communication. We explore language in a way that parallels the definition of gender communication: communication *about* and *between* women and men. We first focus on language that is used to communicate *about* the sexes—language others use to communicate about you, as well as language you might use to communicate about others. The latter part of the chapter explores language from the *between* standpoint, in terms of how sex and gender affect your choice of language as you communicate with others. The goal here is to focus on language and its important role in gender communication, to expand your options in terms of language choice, and to challenge you to choose and use language in a more inclusive way to enhance your personal effectiveness in gender communication and your relationships.

Students sometimes suggest that, rather than wasting time talking about language, people should concentrate on issues that have more serious consequences on people's lives—such as equal pay for equal work and reproductive and family rights. We agree that equal opportunity, wage gaps, and other political and economic issues affecting the sexes are extremely important. But politics and economics aren't the focus of this text; gender communication *is.* Think about it this way: If language is at the very base of our culture, and if that language is flawed or biased, then that flawed, biased language is what we use to communicate about so-called bigger issues. Why not address problems in the very language of the issues?

Another response we hear occasionally when we have classroom discussions or make professional speeches about language and gender is that a given element of sexist language, such as using *he* as a pronoun to stand for all people, is just such a picky, minor thing to spend one's energy on. What's the big deal? You may share or understand that view, but the multiple examples of outdated, sexist, exclusive language we expose in this chapter should show you the magnitude of the problem. Keep in mind that while each form of sexist language is important, the cumulative effect of this language on our culture is enormous.

LANGUAGE: A POWERFUL HUMAN TOOL

What Is Language? What Is Sexist Language?

A *language* is a system of symbols (words or vocabulary) governed by rules (grammar) and patterns (syntax) common to a community of people. Authors Graddol and Swann (1989) suggest that language is both personal and social, that it is a "vehicle of our internal thoughts" as well as a "public resource" (pp. 4–5). Our thoughts take form when they are translated into language, but sometimes language is inadequate to truly express our thoughts or, particularly, our emotions. Have you ever seen or felt something that you just could not put into words? When you want to extend yourself to someone else, to communicate who you are and what you think and feel, language becomes incredibly important.

Noted Australian gender scholar Dale Spender (1985) describes language as "our means of ordering, classifying and manipulating the world. It is through language that we become members of a human community, that the world becomes comprehensible and meaningful, that we bring into existence the world in which we live" (p. 3). Language has power because it allows us to make sense out of reality, but that power can also be constraining. If you don't have a word for something, can you think about it? Have you ever considered that maybe your thinking might be limited by your language? There might be a whole host of "realities" that you have never thought of because there are no words within your language to describe them.

Two researchers who investigated this notion were Edward Sapir and his student Benjamin Lee Whorf. They developed what has come to be called the *Sapir-Whorf Hypothesis,* which suggests an interrelationship between language and thought. Whorf (1956) hypothesized that "the forms of a person's thoughts are controlled by inexorable laws of pattern of which he [she] is unconscious" (p. 252). In this view, human thought is so rooted in language that language may actually control what you can think about. Language and gender scholar Julia Penelope (1990) put it this way: "What we say *is* who we are" (p. 202). Gloria Steinem (1995) believes that "Clearly, the choice of what words we may use determines what dreams we are able to express" (p. 95).

Thus, language is a powerful tool in two ways: it affects how you think, shaping your reality; and it allows you to verbally communicate what you think and feel, to convey who you are to others. Recalling the terminology discussion in Chapter 1, we defined *sexism* as attitudes, behavior, or both that denigrate one sex to the exaltation of the other. It follows, then, that *sexist language* is verbal communication that conveys those differential attitudes or behaviors. As Bobbye Sorrels (1983) puts it in *The Nonsexist Communicator,* "A basic sense of fairness requires the equal treatment of men and women in the communication symbols that so define the lives of the people who use them. Sexist communication limits and devalues all humans . . ." (pp. 2–3).

Much of what research has exposed as sexist language reflects women's traditional lower status or the patriarchal nature of our society. Our intent in this chapter is to explore the English language, wonderful and flawed as it is— not to blame anyone, to suggest that men use language purposefully to oppress women and maintain their status, or to make readers feel defensive about how they use language. We all inherited a male-dominated language, but it is not some mystical entity that cannot be studied or changed. In fact, English has changed a great deal, according to three of the most influential language scholars in the country. Casey Miller, Kate Swift, and Rosalie Maggio (1997) discuss many advances within recent American culture, citing such sources as the 1996 *American Heritage Book of English Usage* and the third edition of the *American Heritage Dictionary,* which document successful efforts at ridding sexism from the language.

Language may control some people, but it need not control you. Think of language as something that has tremendous influence on us, but remember that we can *choose* how to use it and how to influence *it.* In this chapter, we examine various aspects of language that research has deemed sexist, as well as efforts individuals have made to reform the sexism. Some of these reforms you've already learned, so you may think there was never another way of expressing the ideas in question. After reading this chapter, you may decide that other aspects of your language usage are a bit outdated. Or you may realize that some ways you've used language in the past could be taken as sexist, but you simply didn't realize it until now. That happens to the best of us.

WHY USE NONSEXIST LANGUAGE?

Reason 1: Nonsexist Language Reflects Nonsexist Attitudes

Even though we aren't sure about the exact relationship between language and thought, it's clear that a relationship exists. So if you communicate in a sexist manner—whether or not you are aware that a particular usage is sexist and regardless of your intentions—it is possible that you hold some form of sexist attitudes. That conclusion may seem pretty strong, but if thoughts are indeed influenced by language and if language affects the quality of thought, then sexist language may be linked to sexist thoughts. Sorrels (1983) explains: "With an English language that portrays males as the norm and females as abnormal or subnormal, those who analyze and practice the language must believe that females have less value than males" (p. 2). Stop and think for a moment: Can you safely say that your communication—both oral and written—is free from sexist language? The tougher question is: If your communication contains some sexist usages, could someone claim that you hold sexist attitudes?

Reason 2: Nonsexist Language Is Basic to the Receiver Orientation to Communication

Hardly any other topic we discuss in this text pertains more to the principles of receiver orientation to communication (explained in Chapter 1) than the topic of sexist language. Simply put, if a listener perceives your language to be sexist, then, from a receiver orientation to communication, your language in that situation *is* sexist. For example, if you say, "If a person needs help, he should feel that he can call on me to be his friend," a listener may interpret your use of male pronouns in reference to "a person" as sexist because it might insinuate (1) that only men are persons, and (2) that only male friends can call on you for help. You may not mean anything sexist or demeaning in your message, but if your message is interpreted by a listener as sexist, you can't erase it, can you? The communication is *out there,* and undoing it or convincing a listener that you meant otherwise takes 10 times as long as if you'd applied a little forethought before speaking.

Reason 3: Nonsexist Language Is Contemporary

One set of goals within higher education is that upon graduation, students will be able to think, write, and converse in a manner befitting a highly educated person. Using outdated, sexist language undermines that goal. The reality we all share is that the roles women and men can fulfill have changed a great deal. Since these changes have occurred and are likely to keep occurring, language should evolve to reflect current society. In addition, since the 1970s, research and publication standards have been explicit about nonsexist language usage. For example, in 1977 the American Psychological Association included *Guidelines for Nonsexist Language in APA Journals* in its style manual and has continued to reprint this material in each subsequent edition. This means that something rarely gets into print if it violates current standards regarding nonsexist language. Probably some of your college professors— maybe even your high school teachers—instructed you in nonsexist language practices for your writing. Maybe they talked to you about ridding your speaking of sexism as well. We encourage you to inventory your spoken and written language in efforts to exorcise the sexism, if you haven't done so already, so that you will be viewed as educated and contemporary.

Reason 4: Nonsexist Language Is Unambiguous

Identify the sex of the person being referred to in the following statement: "If a person wants to be treated as an adult, he must earn the respect worthy of such treatment." Is the "person" a man (only), a woman (only), or a human being of either sex? Or does the pronoun mean all human beings? Compare this first statement with the following one: "If a person wants to be treated as an adult, she must earn the respect worthy of such treatment." Has the meaning of the statement changed? Are we talking about one person—a woman— or all persons? Some might say that the second statement leaves men out completely. These statements illustrate the kind of confusion sexist language causes. How can the term *man* mean one male person and at the same time all persons? Avoiding such terms reduces ambiguity and confusion in spoken and written communication.

Reason 5: Nonsexist Language Strengthens Expression

Another benefit of nonsexist language usage is an enhanced writing style. Linguist Rosalie Maggio (1988; 1992), author of two books containing alternatives for biased English words and phrases, suggests: "One of the most rewarding— and, for many people, the most unexpected—side effects of breaking away from traditional, sexist patterns of language is a dramatic improvement in writing style" (1988, p. 164). Some students balk at our suggestion that they rid their talk of even the most subtle forms of sexism. They hold the belief that nonsexist language is cumbersome, that it "junks up" one's speaking and writing with a "bunch of extra words," just to "include everybody." However, once they begin to practice simple methods of avoiding sexist, exclusive means of expression, they readily admit that it does make their communication more clear and dynamic.

Reason 6: Nonsexist Language Demonstrates Sensitivity

Sensitivity seems like an obvious reason for using nonsexist language, but it may be more obvious in spirit than in practice. While you may hold a basic philosophy that variations among people are worthy of respect, you may communicate in a manner that contradicts your philosophy—either out of ignorance (because you just didn't know any better) or nonchalance (thinking that sexist communication is just "no big deal"). Maybe you simply feel that subtle forms of sexist language that have developed into habits will take too much time and effort to change and that people will realize you didn't intend to be insensitive. Maybe you believe that if people get the wrong impression of you from your language, they'll either take the time to learn differently or if not, they aren't worth your energy in the first place. But remember that spoken and written communication are ways of extending oneself into the world, of getting to know others and being known by them. If you desire to present yourself as a caring, sensitive individual who believes in a basic system of fairness for all persons, then doesn't it seem logical that your language reflect that desire?

SEXIST LANGUAGE: FORMS, PRACTICES, AND ALTERNATIVES

There are more ways to communicate a sexist attitude than you probably imagined, ranging from very overt to very subtle. This section is divided into two main areas: *forms* of sexist language and sexist *practices* that involve language. The first designation refers to language that is sexist in and of itself. In the second aspect, it's not the words themselves that are sexist, but the traditions inherent in how we *use* language. When we explain each sexist form or practice, we also offer a nonsexist alternative. As you work through this information, take inventory of your own communication habits by asking, "Does my communication contain any of these sexist language forms or practices?" If you find that it does, you will want to note the nonsexist alternatives.

Forms of Sexist Language

The Perpetual Pronoun Problem

Think about what you were taught regarding pronouns. If you were taught that the masculine pronoun *he* (and its derivatives *his, him,* and *himself*) was perfectly acceptable as a generic term for all persons, both female and male, then you got an outdated lesson. Research since the 1970s provides convincing evidence that the generic *he* just isn't generic at all; it's masculine and conjures up masculine images (Gastil, 1990; Hamilton, 1988; Moulton, Robinson, & Elias, 1978; Ng, 1990).

One of the most illuminating early studies on this topic was conducted by gender psychologist Wendy Martyna (1978) who investigated college students' use of pronouns by asking them to complete sentence fragments, both orally and in writing. The students were required to provide pronouns to refer to sex-indefinite nouns, as in the statement, "Before a judge can give a final ruling, _____." Fragments depicting typically male occupations or roles included such terms as *doctor, lawyer, engineer,* and *judge;* feminine referents included *nurses, librarians, teachers,* and *babysitters;* neutral fragments used such nouns as *persons, individuals,* and *students.* The participants also were asked to reveal what particular image or idea came to mind as they chose a certain pronoun to complete a sentence.

In a nutshell, college students in Martyna's research continually read sex into the subjects of sentence fragments and responded with sex-specific pronouns. The nurses, librarians, teachers, and babysitters were predominantly *she*s, while the doctors, lawyers, engineers, and judges were *he*s. The neutral subjects most often received the pronoun *they.* If the pronoun *he* had truly been a term indicating all persons, then *he* would have been the pronoun of choice no matter what role the sentence depicted. When Martyna questioned her students about the images that came to mind when reading the fragments, their answers supported their pronoun choices.

Martyna's results underscore the fact that people (at least in American culture) can hardly function without knowing the sex of a person. If they aren't told the sex, they generally assign one based on stereotypes and, granted, on the numbers of persons in our society who hold the majority of certain positions and roles. So, if you argue that when you say *he* you are including everyone and that neither sex is insinuated, listeners may tell you that you are referring to men only and excluding women completely. Further, your language implies that male is the standard; if this were not the case, then why didn't you use *she*? From a receiver orientation to communication, your listeners have a point.

If you think that Martyna's study is so dated that the results couldn't apply to today's college students, think again. At an east coast and a west coast university, we repeated and extended Martyna's study, hoping to find that college students in the 1990s were attuned to the problem of sexist pronouns (Ivy, Bullis-Moore, Norvell, Backlund, & Javidi, 1995). On the contrary, the results were virtually the same as Martyna's. For terms such as *lawyer, judge,* and *engineer,* students responded predominantly with masculine pronouns. Most of the students' imagery was sex-typed, too, meaning that many of them reported thinking of women when they saw or heard the term *librarian* and men when they saw the term *lawyer.* The only change in our results was that students did not connect the stereotypical female roles with feminine pronouns as often as they connected stereotypical masculine roles with male pronouns.

In the second part of our study, we examined psychological attitudes toward appropriate sex roles and asked subjects about their exposure to nonsexist language instruction in both high school and college. Neither attitudes nor education had any bearing on students' use of language. We did discover, however, that students received mixed messages regarding pronoun usage in both their high school and college educations. For every lesson that taught them to use inclusive, nonsexist pronouns, students recalled a counterlesson telling them that the pronoun *he* was an acceptable substitute for all persons. One thing our study taught us was this: People aren't getting a clear message about nonsexist language. If you are among the few who have been taught something about this topic, what you have been taught is probably contradictory and confusing. That contradiction may lead people to rely on stereotypes in their language, especially when selecting a term to stand for everyone.

Besides the fact that generic masculine pronouns aren't really generic, other negative consequences of using this form of exclusive language have emerged from research. Studies show that exclusive pronoun usage does the following:

1. It maintains sex-biased perceptions.
2. It shapes people's attitudes about careers that are appropriate for one sex but not the other.
3. It causes some women to believe that certain jobs and roles aren't attainable.
4. It contributes to the belief that men deserve more status in society than women do (Briere & Lanktree, 1983; Brooks, 1983; Ivy, 1986; Stericker, 1981).

The Pronoun Solution

Is there a pronoun that can stand for everyone? Some scholars have attempted to introduce new words or *neologisms* into the language primarily for the purpose of inclusivity. Such neologisms as *gen, tey, co, herm,* and *heris* are interesting, but they haven't had much success in being adopted into common usage. If you want to refer to one person—*any* person of either sex—the most clear, grammatical, nonsexist way to do that is to use either *she or he, he/she,* or *s/he* (Kennedy, 1992). Other ways to avoid excluding any portion of the population in your communication are to omit a pronoun altogether, either rewording a message or substituting an article (*a, an,* or *the*) for the pronoun; use *you* or variations of the indefinite pronoun *one;* or (c) use the plural pronoun *they* (Maggio, 1988; Miller, Swift, & Maggio, 1997). But be careful with that last suggestion. While it is quite common in conversation to hear singular nouns with plural pronouns (e.g., "If a student wants good grades, they have to work hard"), some instructors and writers view this as nongrammatical.

Antimale Bias in Language

English scholar Eugene August (1992) describes three forms of antimale language in English: gender-exclusive language, gender-restrictive language, and language that evokes negative stereotypes of males. First, August explores the equating of *mother* and *parent,* suggesting that the terms are often used interchangeably, whereas the term *noncustodial parent* is almost always synonymous with *father.* He suggests that males are also excluded from victim language, such as in the expressions *wife abuse* and *innocent women and children.* This language insinuates that males cannot be victims of violence, rape, and abuse. The second category, gender-restrictive language, refers to language that limits men to a social role. August's examples include language that strongly suggests to boys the role they are to play and chastises them if they stray from that role or do not perform as expected (e.g., *sissy, mama's boy, take it like a man,* and *impotent*). In the final category, August claims that "negative stereotyping is embedded in the language, sometimes it resides in people's assumptions about males . . ." (p. 137). As evidence of this tendency, August cites terms linked to crime and evil, such as *murderer, mugger, suspect,* and *rapist*—terms he contends evoke male stereotypes that are "insulting, dehumanizing, and potentially danger-ous" (p. 132). In reference to the term *rape,* August discusses the fact that the majority of rapes are committed by males upon female victims; however, the bias comes in with the assumption of a female victim, ignoring the many rapes of male victims in our culture (especially among prison populations).

Manmade Everything

Man-linked terminology, that is, words or phrases that include *man* in them as though these terms should operate as generics, is a form of sexist language that appears to be diminishing along with generic pronouns (Miller, Swift, & Maggio, 1997; Steinem, 1995). The term *man* or its derivative *mankind* in reference to all persons is similar to the problematic usage of *he.* (Even more confusing is the term *he-man*!) Ambiguity and confusion arise when one doesn't know whether the term refers to a set of male persons or to all persons in general (Graddol & Swann, 1989). This confusion led the National Council of Teachers of English sev-eral years ago to conclude, "Although 'man' in its original sense carried the dual meaning of adult human and adult male, its meaning has come to be so closely identified with adult male that the generic use of 'man' and other words with masculine markers should be avoided whenever possible" (NCTE, 1975, p. 2).

Originally, *man* was derived from a truly generic form, similar to the term *human.* The terms for female-men (*wifmann*) and male-men (*wermann*) devel-oped when the culture decided that it needed differentiating terms for the sexes (McConnell-Ginet, 1980). Maggio's (1988) dictionary of gender-free ter-minology provides Greek, Latin, and Old English terms for human, woman, and man. In Greek, the terms are *anthropos, gyne,* and *aner;* in Latin, *homo, fem-ina,* and *vir;* and in Old English, *man, female,* and *wer* (pp. 176–177). The prob-lem is that *man* has developed into a designation for *male* persons, not *all* per-sons. As with pronouns, research shows that masculine mental images arise when the term *man* is used. Again, not only does this term exclude women and make them invisible, but it reinforces the male-as-standard problem.

Even though the word *human* contains *man,* it is derived from the Latin *homo,* meaning all persons. The term *human* does not connote masculine-only imagery like the term *man* does (Graddol & Swann, 1989; Maggio, 1988). Man-linked terms include expressions such as *man the phones* or *manned space flight* as well as numerous words that have *man* attached to or embedded within them (e.g., *re-pairman*), which convert the term into a role, position, or action that an individual can assume or make. Unfortunately, people see the masculine part of the term and instantaneously form perceptions that the word describes something mascu-line only. If you are thinking, "People make too big a deal of this 'mailman, fire-man, policeman' thing," then check out Figure 5–1 just to see how many com-monly used man-linked terms there are. Maggio (1988) cautions, however, that not all words containing *-man* or *-men* are sexist. Some examples she provides are *amen, emancipate, manager, maneuver, manipulate, ottoman,* and *menstruation.*

Alternatives to *man* (e.g., *people, persons, individuals*), the simplest being *hu-mans* (and its derivatives *human beings, humanity,* and *humankind*), are becoming

FIGURE 5-1. Man-Linked Terminology and Alternatives

Term	Alternatives
adman	advertising executive; ad executive
airman	aviator; pilot
anchorman	anchor; newscaster
bail/bondsman	bail or bond agent
bogeyman	bogey; bogey monster
base man	base player
bellman/bellboy	attendant; luggage handler; bellperson
businessman	businessperson; business executive or leader
cameraman	camera operator
cattleman	rancher; cattle owner
caveman	prehistoric person; neanderthal
chairman	chair; chairperson
churchman	churchgoer
committeeman	committee member
congressman	senator; representative; legislator; congressperson
con man	con artist
councilman	council member
doorman	doorkeeper; porter
draftsman	drafter
everyman	common person; typical or ordinary person
fisherman	fisher
foreman	supervisor; foreperson
frenchman (other nations)	french native (native of other nations)
freshman	first-year student
frontiersman	pioneer; settler
garbageman/trashman	garbage or trash collector; sanitation worker
G-man	government or federal agent
groomsman	wedding or groom's attendant
gunman	killer; assassin; shooter
handyman	odd jobber; repairer
hit man	hired killer; hired gun
layman	layperson; laity; lay worker
mailman/postman	mail carrier; postal worker
man	human; humans; person; persons; people
man about town	worldly person; socialite; jet-setter
man a post	fill a post; staff a post
man-eating	flesh eating; carnivore
man for all seasons	all-around expert; Renaissance person
manhandle	mistreat; rough up
manhole	sewer; utility hole
manhood	pride; strength
man-hours	staff hours
manhunt	chase; fugitive search
man in the moon	face in the moon
mankind	humankind; humanity
manmade	artificial; handmade; synthetic
manned space flight	space flight
man of few words	silent type
man of the house	homeowner
man of the world	sophisticate
man-of-war	warship
man on the street	average person; common person
man overboard	overboard; person overboard
manpower	staff power; work force
manservant	servant; butler; valet; maid
man the phones	answer the phones
man-to-man	one-to-one; person-to-person
man your battle stations/positions	assume your battle stations; go to your positions
marksman/rifleman	sharpshooter
may the best man win	may the best person win
men working	people working; workers
modern man	modern people; modern civilization
no-man's land	limbo; dead zone; void
one-upmanship	going one better; one-up tendency; dominance
patrolman	patroller; patrol officer; trooper
penmanship	handwriting
policeman	police officer; cop
Renaissance man	Renaissance person; all-around expert
repairman	repairer; servicer; technician
salesman	salesclerk; clerk; salesperson
self-made man	independent person; self-made person; entrepreneur
serviceman (military)	soldier; member of the armed forces
snowman	snow figure or person
spaceman	astronaut; space explorer
spokesman	spokesperson; speaker
sportsman	sports enthusiast; athlete; good sport
statesman	politician; citizen; patriot
stunt man	stunt person; stunt performer; daredevil
under/upperclassman	undergraduate; first-year student; sophomore, etc.
unman	unnerve; frighten; disarm
unmanned	unstaffed; uninhabited
unsportsmanlike	unsporting; unfair
watchman	guard; security guard; sentry
workman's compensation	worker's compensation
workmanship	work; handiwork; artisanry

J'm just a person trapped inside a woman's body.

Elaine Boosler, comedian

more commonplace in everyday language usage (Miller, Swift, & Maggio, 1997). Figure 5-1 shows some of these alternatives. Note that only a few call for the addition of *person* to the term; some feel this change has come to stand for a feminine form of a word rather than a generic term (Aldrich, 1985). They think a term such as *chairperson*, for example, automatically signifies a woman. Some of the alternatives to masculine terms may seem awkward or even ridiculous, but over time you will probably come to wonder how anyone could argue with such simple changes.

The Lady Doctor and the Male Nurse

A subtle form of sexist language termed *marking* involves placing a sex-identifying adjective in front of a noun to designate the reference as somehow different or deviant from the norm (LaRocque, 1997; West, 1992). Examples of this practice include *woman doctor, male secretary, female boss, male nurse*, and *lady lawyer*. Such sex marking is limiting and discriminatory, and needless to say, extraneous. Why does one need to point out the sex of a doctor, lawyer, or boss? The implication is that one incarnation of a role or position is the norm, whereas the opposite sex in that role or position is an aberration or "not normal." Such language can have an isolating, chilling effect on the person who is "not the norm." The use of marking terms appears to be changing as more people enter professions previously dominated by one sex or the other and as people take on roles that go against the status quo. For example, along with the dramatic increase in the numbers of men who become nurses has come a decrease in language such as *male nurse*.

References to sports teams commonly reflect this sexist practice. Male teams or groups use the generic or mascot name (e.g., Professional Golf Association; Longhorns) and female teams or groups are marked by sex (e.g., Ladies' Professional Golf Association; Lady Longhorns) (Miller, Swift, & Maggio, 1997). If there were no sexism in language, these associations would either not be identified by sex at all or would have parallel names, such as the Men's National Basketball Association (MNBA) and the Women's National Basketball Association (WNBA). (Would that lead to the formation of the "Gentlemen's Professional Golf Association"?!) Some argue that this practice merely reflects the fact that male teams existed long before female teams and thus were assigned the generic or mascot name. But is it more important to hold on to tradition (especially if that tradition may be exclusive and sexist) or to use language that reflects equality and the contemporary state of things? Some university athletic programs have resisted change, but others have worked to counter the sexism, insisting that references to teams be parallel and include no sex-based markers. This is more easily accomplished in some sports where there is more of a tradition of equity, such as in women's and men's tennis, than others.

How's Trix?

Adding a suffix such as *-ette, -ess, -enne,* or *-trix* to form a feminine version of a supposed male term is another subtle form of sexist language that appears to be making its rightful exit from common usage (Miller, Swift, & Maggio, 1997). Like other forms, the suffix "perpetuates the notion that the male is the norm and the female is a subset, a deviation, a secondary classification. In other words, men are 'the real thing' and women are sort of like them" (Maggio, 1988, p. 178). Does it really matter if the person waiting on a table at a restaurant is female or male? Does someone who is admired need to be called a *hero* or a *heroine*? Such terminology makes a person's sex too important, revealing a need to know the sex to determine how to behave or what to expect. That kind of thinking perpetuates sexual stereotypes and heightens misunderstanding between men and women; thus, such usage is diminishing in contemporary communication.

How can sexist suffixes be avoided? Figure 5–2 provides a list of appropriate alternatives to words with feminine endings. One can simply use the original term and omit the suffix. If there is a legitimate reason for specifying sex, a pronoun can be used, as in "The actor was performing her monologue beautifully, when someone's watch alarm went off in the theater."

FIGURE 5-2. Feminine Suffixes and Alternatives

actress	actor
adulteress	adulterer
ambassadress	ambassador
anchoress	anchor
authoress	author
aviatrix or aviatress	aviator
bachelorette	bachelor or single person
comedienne	comedian
equestrienne	equestrian
governess	governor
heiress	heir
heroine	hero
hostess	host
justess	justice
laundress	laundry worker
majorette	major
murderess	murderer
poetess	poet
sculptress	sculptor
songstress	singer
starlet	star
stewardess	flight attendant
suffragette	suffragist
usherette	usher
waitress	waiter, waitron, waitstaff, or server

Chicks, Cupcakes, and Clinging Vines

There are many derogatory terms for human beings, unfortunately. But did you know that using animal, food, and plant terms as labels for men and women can be interpreted as demeaning and sexist? Figure 5–3 lists some of these terms. Note that the lists of terms for women are longer than men's, because these kinds of references are used more often to demean and make objects out of women (Lakoff & Johnson, 1981). Keep in mind one important point: This is one of those categories of language usage that is especially

FIGURE 5-3. Animal, Food, and Plant Terms for Persons

Animal Terms		*Food Terms*		*Plant Terms*	
WOMEN	MEN	WOMEN	MEN	WOMEN	MEN
fox, vixen	fox, wolf	honey	honey	rose, rosebud	pansy
pig, hog, sow	pig	sugar	sugar	clinging vine	
lamb	lamb	cookie	cookie	buttercup	
dog	dog	pumpkin	pumpkin	sweet pea	
bitch	stag (party)	honey buns	honey buns	petunia	
tiger	tiger	cupcake	cupcake	daisy	
pussy	pussy	baby cakes	beefcake	honeysuckle	
cat (cat fight)	cat, tomcat	cheesecake	big cheese	violet	
sex kitten	ass, jackass	candy	candy ass		
kitty	gorilla, big ape	cutie pie	cutie pie		
dumb ox	big ox	muffin	(stud) muffin		
chicken	chicken	jelly roll	meathead		
chick	cock	tomato	hot dog		
chickadee	turkey	sugar lips	top banana		
bird	old goat	peach	cream puff		
silly goose	snake	cherry	wiener,		
bunny	worm	lamb chop	weenie		
mouse	rat	pudding			
beaver	weasel	dish			
filly	stud	brown sugar			
old mare	buck	marshmallow			
black widow	bear or	tart			
cow	teddy bear				
heifer	bull				
broad (pregnant	squirrel				
cow)					
hen ("he's					
henpecked")					
shrew (a mouse-					
like mammal)					
claws ("her					
claws are out")					

connected to the context of the communication, as well as to the relationship between the person doing the naming and the person being named. To clarify what we mean, here's an example that occurred at a university where one of your textbook authors used to teach.

On a day when a couple of groups were to give their final presentations for a class, students were nervously congregating in the hallway outside the classroom. They were nicely dressed (wanting to create that ever-important favorable impression on the teacher) and were going over their notes together one last time before the presentation. When a male classmate came down the hall, he saw one of the female presenters and said, "Wow, you look like a delicious piece of cheesecake today." The woman did not feel complimented; the comment made her flustered, embarrassed, even more nervous before her presentation, and, later, quite angry. When she confronted the male student, he explained that he had no intention of offending her. Just the opposite, he meant to compliment her and had no idea that his words would make her feel bad. How does this example register with you? Was the guy a victim of circumstance, a complete jerk, or just an ignoramus? Was he at fault with his timing, but not his words, because he meant to be nice? Maybe she was just nervous and didn't take him the "right" way?

From a receiver orientation to communication, her interpretation carried more weight than his intentions. The male student was at fault not because he was complimenting a woman, but because his language objectified her and communicated inappropriate sexual overtones—comparing a woman to something soft, sweet, and edible. His "cheesecake" comparison reduced a person who was intelligent, competent, worthy of respect, and concerned about her class assignment to something trivial. Not only did these two people not have a sexual or romantic relationship, the educational context and the woman's already nervous state made the comment extremely insensitive and inappropriate. If you deem this example exaggerated, look again at Figure 5–3 and imagine these terms being directed at someone you love, either a

> *There's something you get from a chick you can't have with any other being on the planet, and that is something super special. I mean, if there were nothing but old whores and nasty, old, hard women, I'd be out looking for some young, sweet, little fifteen-year-old boy.*
>
> *Don Johnson, actor*

woman or a man. Is it easier now to envision how these terms could be demeaning?

Maggio (1988) points out, "Using animal names to refer to people is neither sensitive nor very socially attractive. Names of foods are also used for people, and while many of them purport to be positive, ultimately they are belittling, trivializing, and make objects of people" (pp. 182–183). Feminist scholars Thorne, Kramarae, and Henley (1983) state their opposition more strongly: "Men's extensive labeling of women as parts of body, fruit, or animals and as mindless, or like children—labels with no real parallel for men—reflects men's derision of women and helps maintain gender hierarchy and control" (p. 9). Only in certain contexts and within certain relationships—those in which two people's feelings and regard for each other are mutually understood—should animal, food, and plant terms for persons be construed as endearments.

Speaking of a Higher Power . . .

Saying that the topic of sexism in religious language is "sticky" is the understatement of the year. It is not our intent here to uproot your religious beliefs (or even to assume you have religious beliefs that need uprooting), but merely to engender awareness of the perpetuation of patriarchy through religious language.

In their book about language and women, Miller and Swift (1976) explain in a chapter on the language of religion that "Since the major Western religions all originated in patriarchal societies and continue to defend a patriarchal world view, the metaphors used to express their insights are by tradition and habit overwhelmingly male-oriented" (p. 64). These authors explain that within the Judaeo-Christian tradition, religious scholars for centuries have insisted that the translation of such an abstract concept as a deity into language need not involve a designation of sex. According to Miller and Swift, "the symbolization of a male God must not be taken to mean that God really is 'male.' In fact, it must be understood that God has no sex at all" (p. 64). To one dean of the Harvard Divinity School, masculine language about God is "a cultural and linguistic accident" (Stendahl, as quoted in Miller & Swift, 1976, p. 67). As one rabbi put it, "I think of God as an undefinable being; to talk about God in gender terms, we're talking in terms we can understand and not in terms of what God is really like" (Ezring, as in Leardi, 1997, p. H1).

The problem, at least for religions relying on Biblical teachings, is that translations of scriptures from the ancient Hebrew language into Old English rendered masculine images of deity, reflecting the culture of male superiority at the time (Kramarae, 1981; Schmitt, 1992). Thus, the literature is dominated by the pronoun *he* and by such terms as *father, son,* and *kingdom.* Linguistic scholars contend that much of the original female imagery was lost in modern translation or was omitted from consideration by the canonizers of the Bible (Miller & Swift, 1976; Spender, 1985). Language scholar Julia Penelope (1990) reviews Old Testament lists of sons who were begat by their fathers and suggests "The women and daughters who must have participated remain nameless and invisible" (p. 191). The Old Testament says that humans were created in God's image—both male and female. It is interesting, then, that we have come to connect masculinity with most religious images and terms. Also interesting, as August (1992) contends, is the "masculinization of evil," the fact that male pronouns and images are most often associated with Satan, such as a reference to the *Father of Lies*. August says "Few theologians talk about Satan and her legions" (p. 139).

Are you uncomfortable enough at this point in your reading to say to yourself, "Come on now; you're messing with religion. Enough is enough"? That's understandable, because religion is a deeply personal thing. It's something that a lot of us grew up with; thus, its images and teachings are so ingrained that we don't often question them or stop to consider where some of the traditions originated. However, questioning the language of religion doesn't mean that one is questioning his or her faith. In fact, a few Christian sects have begun to lessen male dominance in their communication. The masculinity *and* femininity of God are beginning to receive equal emphasis, as in one version of the Apostles' Creed which begins with "I believe in God the Father and Mother almighty, maker of heaven and earth." These kinds of attempts are interesting and increasing in number, but they are unnerving to many people (Leardi, 1997). The root of the problem that once again surfaces is that many people need to dichotomize, to designate everything—even God—as masculine or feminine. Even if you envision some form of deity as a spiritual entity without femininity or masculinity, it is likely very difficult to talk about that spiritual entity in ways that break out of sex-typed language.

Reduced to a Body Part

Sexual language profoundly affects how women and men perceive the sexes, as well as how they communicate with one another. Most of us know that reducing a human being to his or her sexuality is a loathsome, degrading practice that can be personally devastating to the recipient or target of such language. While most of us refrain from this practice, think about how many times a group of people will see someone walk by and make comments that turn the person into an object by reducing her or him to mere sexuality. One attempt to justify this behavior is the claim, "We were just admiring the person." Most of us would rather be deprived of this kind of admiration.

We defer a good deal here to the important work of linguist Robert Baker in the 1980s who was interested in "how women are conceived of in our culture" (1981, p. 166). Although men also are described in sexualized terms, there are significantly fewer sexual terms that identify men than women. For example, one study uncovered 220 terms for sexually promiscuous women and only 22 terms for sexually promiscuous men (Stanley, 1977). Baker contends that the following categories of terms are recognized as "more or less interchangeable with 'woman'" (p. 167):

1. Neutral terms, such as *lady, gal,* and *girl*
2. Animal terms
3. Words that describe playthings or toys, such as *babe, baby, doll,* and *cuddly*
4. Clothing terms, such as *skirt* or *hem*
5. A whole range of sexual terms

In my young days, I used to pick up sluts, and I don't mean that nastily. It's more a term of endearment, really, for girls who know how to speak their minds.

Kevin Costner,
actor & director

In reference to Baker's category 5, think of how many terms exist in our language that are based on anatomy, but that may be used to describe the whole person. Some of the less graphic terms that describe women's anatomy or sexual behavior and that are interchangeable with the word *woman* include snatch, twat, pussy, beaver, cherry, a piece, box, easy, some (as in "getting some"), slut, whore, and a screw or lay. Here's some male sexual lingo: prick, cock, male member, dick, tool, and a screw or lay. Obviously, there are more terms than these, but we leave those to your imagination rather than putting them in print.

Baker contends that only men use the terms falling into his categories 2 through 5. He believes that men think about women as "certain types of animals, toys, and playthings; . . . they [men] conceive of women in terms of those parts of their anatomy associated with sexual intercourse . . ." (1981, p. 168). Anthropologist Michael Moffat (1989) studied university dormitory residents' use of language and found that one-third of young men in the study, in conversations with other men, consistently referred to women as "chicks, broads, and sluts," reflecting what Moffat termed a "locker-room style" of communication about women (p. 183). We don't believe that only men use sexually demeaning terminology in reference to women. We've heard women call or refer to other women by a few of the terms listed above, but typically just the ones that imply sexual promiscuity (e.g., slut, easy, etc.). Do you agree that conceiving of a person in sexual terms is demeaning? And, since evidence and experience indicate that women more often than men are thought of, talked about, and communicated to in sexual terms, do you see how this form of language is sexist?

Another form of sexual language describes sexual activity. The main emphasis in this category is on verbs and their effect on the roles women and men assume during sexual activity. Here are some of Baker's synonyms for sexual intercourse, as generated by his students in the early 1980s: screwed, laid, had, did it, banged, slept with, humped, and made love to. Feminist theorist Deborah Cameron's (1985) discussion of sexual language adds the verb poked to the list. Our students have generously offered such contemporary references as "hooked up with," "got some from," "made [someone]," "took," and even "mated."

The sexism in these descriptions comes from the placement of subjects that precede some of the verbs and the objects that follow them. According to

> ## *RECAP*
> ---
> language, Sapir-Whorf Hypothesis, sexist language, receiver orientation, generic pronouns, neologisms, antimale bias, man-linked terms, marking, feminine suffixes, animal, food, and plant language, religious language, sexual language

Baker, sentences like "Dick screwed Jane" and "Dick banged Jane" describe men as the doers of sexual activity, while women are almost always the recipients. When a female subject of a sentence appears, the verb form changes into a passive rather than an active construction, as in "Jane was screwed by Dick" and "Jane was banged by Dick"—the woman is still the recipient (pp. 175–176). Baker labels "inadequate" the argument that the male-active, female-passive linguistic trend is a reflection of the outward nature of men's genitalia and the inward nature of women's (p. 177). If active sexual roles in women were the norm or more accepted, then Baker contends that the verb "to engulf" would be in common usage. Cameron (1985) proposes that the term *penetration* as a synonym for the sexual act suggests male origins; if a woman had set the term, it might have been *enclosure.*

Our students heading into the 21st century believe that the dichotomy of male-active, female-passive sexuality is rapidly changing, as is the corresponding language. They offer a few active constructions for women's sexual behavior (largely related to women being on top in heterosexual intercourse, such as in the language *to ride*). However, they admit that, even in our postmodern times, more negative judgments are communicated about women who behave actively or dominantly in intercourse than about men who behave submissively. Changes are taking place in the sexual arena, but the language hasn't kept pace. If the very language that describes sexual intercourse still predominantly portrays men in dominant, active roles and women in submissive, passive roles, then that parallels the current sexism in society.

Sexist Linguistic Practices

The Name Game

Many women and men alike believe that parts of their identities are connected to the names they've had all their lives. So why should a woman be expected to give up her last name, part of her identity, to adopt her husband's? The practice of wives taking husbands' names isn't necessarily sexist; what is sexist is the expectation that a woman is *supposed to* or *has to* take a man's last name. To some people, assuming the husband's last name identifies a woman as property, which is the historic intent behind the practice. But have you ever realized that *all* last names are male since a woman's birth name is, almost without exception, the last name of her father? If a baby isn't given the father's last name,

I bet that women who keep their own names are less apt to keep their husbands.

Andy Rooney, commentator on CBS's 60 Minutes

it is given the last name of the mother, which is the last name of the mother's father, and so on. Some have altered this process to give themselves an autonomous identity. For example, feminist author Julia Penelope used to be Julia Stanley, but she dropped her father's last name "Stanley" and began using her middle name "Penelope" as a last name (Spender, 1985).

Only recently in this country have women readily chosen to retain their maiden names when marrying rather than adopting their husbands' last names—a choice that has caused many a prenuptial argument. A recent study shows that many Americans hold mixed perceptions of married women who use their maiden names. A language professor surveyed over 10,000 people in 12 states and discovered that married women who kept their maiden names were perceived as "more likely to be independent, less attractive, less likely to make a good wife or mother, more feminist, younger, better educated, more likely to work outside the home, more outspoken, more self-confident, less likely to enjoy cooking, and less likely to go to church" (Murray, as in "'Feminist' stereotype persists," 1998, p. H1).

If you're a female reader expecting to marry some day, what do you think would happen if you asked your future husband to take *your* last name? If you're a male reader, what would happen if you future wife asked you to take *her* last name rather than taking yours? Do you know of men who have taken their wives' last names? We can't think of any married couples who go by only the wife's last name, such as Jane Smith and Joe Jones becoming Jane and Joe Smith. We do know many couples who use both last names or have combined them into a new family name, because the naming game can get really tense when children come along. But we have found that, in most cases, the wife uses the combined last name while the husband uses only his last name, such as in Jane Smith Jones and Joe Jones.

Euphemisms and Metaphors

The English language contains a great many expressions about the sexes that go seemingly unnoticed, but that form subtly sexist patterns. These expressions are usually in the form of metaphors or euphemisms—more comfortable substitutes for other terms. We find traditionally-aged college students hesitant to refer to themselves as *men* and *women,* as though there were some future, magical age when those terms fit. The term *man* is used inconsistently—males hear "Take it like a man" and "He's a real man's man," but they're *boys,* then *guys* until they're old (whatever *old* means), and then they become *men.*

One of the most influential authors on the topic of euphemistic language is Robin Lakoff, whose research in the 1970s continues to have impact today. Lakoff (1975) explored euphemisms for the word *woman,* such as *lady* and *girl,* and their

connotations. Depending on the context, these three terms can either be synonyms or opposites (Kruh, 1992). While many people think of *lady* as a term of respect that puts a woman on a pedestal, to some it suggests negative qualities, such as being frail, scatterbrained, sugary sweet, demure, flatterable, and sexually frigid or repressed. If you're a female reader, maybe you can recall instances in which your mother, father, or other authority figure warned you to "Act like a lady!" Did you know what that meant, and did you then know how to act?

Connotations of the word *girl* have changed a great deal in recent years. Many adult women in the '70s and '80s reported feeling patronized and disrespected when referred to as *girls*. The term connoted childishness, innocence, and immaturity—and most women don't want to be thought of in those terms. However, in the 1990s more positive meanings for *girl* have emerged (especially for women in their teens and 20s). Some of this trend is related to what *Time* magazine refers to as "alternative culture's Riot Grrrl movement, an effort by new female bands in the early '90s to reclaim the brash, bratty sense of self-control that psychologists claim girls lose just before puberty" (Bellafante, 1998, p. 60). England's Spice Girls and the slogan "girl power" are among the contributors to this shift in language. However, a positive view of *girl* isn't held only by young women. A colleague who recently became a good friend of one of your text's authors made her feel accepted in a circle of older friends by calling her a long-standing insider name, "pig"—which stands for "pretty interesting girl."

Part of the euphemistic confusion is that there's no acceptable female equivalent term for *guy*. When males are called *guys*, females are called *girls*, rather than *gals* or *women* (or *dolls*, as in the musical "Guys and Dolls"). As

It's okay to say "girls." Women want to be called girls. You can't say, "To all the old ladies I've loved before."

Enrique Iglesia, son of
Julio Iglesia, singer

Miller and Swift (1988) suggest, the female terms have "psychic overtones; of immaturity and dependence in the case of 'girl;' of conformity and decorum in the case of 'lady;' of sexuality and reproduction in the case of both 'female' and 'woman'" (p. 67).

Think about what would happen if you were to say to a group of men, "Good morning, boys!" It could be seen as a friendly greeting in reference to male camaraderie or a derogatory, condescending euphemism for men. So which terms are most appropriate really depends on the context in which you find yourself.

Fightin' Words

Whether or not you personally have ever resorted to insults or name-calling, it's hard to disagree with the fact that there are plenty of these terms in our language to go around. In Chapter 2 we said that one of the worst insults that can be directed at a man in our culture is to call him by a feminine term. Let's examine some of the main derogatory terms used for men: *bastard, son of a bitch, motherfucker, queer, faggot* or *fag, fairy,* and *queen.* Why are these seen as male terms when most of them have to do with women?

A *bastard* is a term that, by definition, describes a child who doesn't know who his or her father is. The term implies that the mother was unmarried and perhaps someone who "slept around." Granted, this term doesn't put fatherhood in the best light either, but the clinical interpretation of the term implies that the mother figure is really the person at fault. If a man is called a *son of a bitch,* it indicts both the mother and the son, because the term *bitch* is used more often to demean a woman than to describe a female dog. Most people agree that the worst term in this category is *motherfucker.* There could hardly be a more disgusting term with more taboo imagery than one that accuses someone of having had intercourse with his or her mother. However, we should add that, particularly among African-Americans, this term (with the pronunciation *muthafuka*) has a quite different, and many times positive, meaning (Kochman, 1981).

The last four terms in the above list are derogatory, first, because they are negative terms for homosexuals, primarily homosexual men. Second, all but one are terms for women that become derogatory when applied to men. The exception is the term *faggot,* defined in the dictionary as a bundle of sticks, and its shortened version *fag,* which actually means to become tired. Occasionally, terms that imply masculinity are derogatory when leveled at women, such as in *bull dyke* or *butch.* But most of the name-calling directed at women is done via terms that demean their anatomy or exaggerate their sexuality.

A Parallel Universe

Symmetry in language refers to the use of gender-fair, *parallel* terms when referring to the sexes. Maggio (1988) cites three ways in which terms are asymmetrical and sexist. The first involves words that may appear parallel, but in actuality are not parallel (or equal). An example that seems to be on its rightful way out is the dreaded statement "I now pronounce you man and wife" (LaRocque, 1997; Miller, Swift, & Maggio, 1997). If you don't see anything wrong with this last statement, look closer. The man is still a man, but the woman is now a wife, with the connotation that she is relegated to that one role while he maintains a complete identity. What if the traditional statement was, "I now pronounce you woman and husband?"

A second violation relates to terms originally constructed as parallel whose meanings have changed with common usage and time so that the feminine form has a negative connotation. Examples include *governor/governess*, *master/mistress, sir/madam,* and *bachelor/spinster* or *old maid.* A man who governs is a *governor,* but a *governess* has come to mean a woman who takes care of someone else's children. You can certainly see the gap between meanings in the second and third examples—*mistress* and *madam* have taken on negative connotations while the masculine forms still imply power and authority. The last example is dramatic—as men grow older and stay single, they remain *bachelors* while women degenerate into *spinsters* and *old maids.* While this is changing, the tendency in our culture to compliment a man for his ability to stay single while ridiculing a woman for being unmarried is still quite real (Connelly, 1998).

A final category of parallel construction involves acceptable words with usages that are unacceptable because they alter the equality (Lakoff, 1975; Maggio, 1988). A prime example is the way journalists referred to American soldiers taken hostage in the Persian Gulf War, such as in the following news report: "A small number of American soldiers were taken captive by the Iraqi soldiers; one of the prisoners is believed to be a woman." Granted, this may have been the first time in America's military history that a female soldier was a POW—the first time on record, anyway. But do you see how that news report depicted the female prisoner as though men were the norm and she was the aberration? Maggio (1988) offers a similar example in the statement, "Seventy people were killed in the derailment yesterday including fourteen women" (p. 169). Adhering to parallelism principles would result in the statement "Seventy people were killed in the derailment yesterday—fourteen women and fifty-six men."

Out of Order

Have you heard the traditional saying "ladies first"? While many people still operate by this standard in things like opening doors, the "ladies first" pattern isn't predominant in the language, nor should it be. If you believe in equality for the sexes, then references to the sexes should reflect that equality, right? But when you put language under the microscope, you find that male terms are almost always communicated first and female terms second, as in the following: his and hers; boys and girls; men and women; men, women, and children; male and female; husband and wife; Mr. and Mrs. Smith; the Duke and Duchess of Windsor; king and queen; the President and First Lady; brothers and sisters. Three exceptions include the traditional greeting, "ladies and gentlemen," references to the "bride and groom," and a mention of someone's parents, as in "How are your mom and dad doing?" Always putting the masculine term first is a subtle indication of giving precedence to men (Frank & Treichler, 1989; Miller & Swift, 1988). So try to alternate which term you say or write first when you use these constructions in communication. If you're sharp you've noticed that, in this text, for every "women and men" and "she or he," a "men and women" and "he or she" appears. It's a small thing to correct in one's language and few may notice, but it will make your communication more gender-sensitive.

"May I Introduce . . . ?"

A practice related to the marital naming problem is one of referring to a person according to his or her relationship to someone else. Research shows that women are often identified, introduced, and engaged in conversation based on their connections to men (Lakoff, 1975; LaRocque, 1997; Maggio, 1988; Thorne, Kramarae, & Henley, 1983). Maggio (1988) believes that "one of the most sexist maneuvers in the language is the way we oblige women to label themselves in relationship to a man" (p. 171). For example, it is common to hear a reference made to "Mary, John's wife," or a woman is likely to be introduced as "This is Mary, John's wife." Less often do you hear a man introduced as "This is John, Mary's husband." We realize that in these situations, a choice of language may be reliant on whose company or circle of friends the couple is in. But if you want to avoid statements like "This is Sandy, Wayne's girlfriend of two years," try the nonsexist phrasing, "This is Sandy; she and Wayne have been together for two years." Another way (the best way) to avoid this problem is to simply introduce Sandy as herself, without any reference to Wayne at all.

Yet another related practice is most obvious in newspaper wedding announcements. Quite often the bride is identified as the "daughter of Mr. and Mrs. So-and-So," while the groom is identified by where he went to school and his profession. There are some indications that this practice is changing, though. A quick glance at wedding pages of newspapers shows a greater frequency of both grooms' and brides' occupations being mentioned, but the identification of a bride via her parents (father first) doesn't seem to be changing much, even with the high incidence of divorce and later-in-life marriages.

Titles and Salutations

The accepted male title is *Mr.*, which doesn't reflect a man's marital status. Mr. Joe Schmoe can be single, married, divorced, or widowed. Among the titles for women, *Miss, Mrs.*, and *Ms.*, what differentiates the first two is marital status, but that's only a fairly recent usage. Until the 19th century, the two terms merely distinguished female children and young women from older, more mature women (Spender, 1985). History isn't clear about why the function of the titles changed, but some scholars link it to the beginning of the industrial revolution when women began working outside the home. Supposedly, that working status obscured a woman's tie to the home, so the titles provided clarity (Miller & Swift, 1976). The patriarchal nature of language deemed it necessary for people to be able to identify whether or not a woman was married, but it was not necessary to know a man's relationship to a woman. As Spender describes it, "The practice of labeling women as married or single also serves supremely sexist ends. It conveniently signals who is 'fair game' from the male point of view" (p. 27).

To counter this practice, women began to use the neologism *Ms.* a few decades ago, although the term has existed as a title of courtesy since the 1940s (Miller & Swift, 1976). People of both sexes resisted the use of *Ms.* when it first came on the scene, claiming that it was hard to pronounce. But is it any harder to pronounce than *Mrs.* or *Mr.?* Some women today choose not to use the title because they believe it links them with feminists, a connection they consider undesirable. Others use *Ms.* just exactly for that reason—its link with feminism—and to establish their identities apart from men. Our male and female students alike report that *Ms.* is well accepted and commonly used, although some mistakenly believe that *Ms.* is a title referring exclusively to divorced women.

Regarding written salutations and greetings, for many years the standard salutation in a letter to someone you did not know (and did not know the sex of) was "Dear Sir" or "Gentlemen." If you only knew the last name of a person in an address or if the first name did not reveal the sex of the person, the default salutation was "Dear Mr. So-and-So." But that sexist practice has changed because of questions about why the masculine form should stand for all people. The terms *Sirs* and *Gentlemen* no more include women than the pronoun *he* or the term *mankind.*

What are your nonsexist options for salutations? Sometimes a simple phone call or e-mail to the organization you are contacting will enable you to specify a greeting. An easier way to fix this problem is to use terms that don't imply sex, such as: (Dear) Officers, Staff Member, Personnel, Members of the Department, Managers, Resident, Subscriber, Directors, Executives, Professional Persons, and the like. It may seem awkward the first time you use terminology like this. If it is more comfortable for you to use a sex-identified reference, then use inclusive terms such as *Ms./Mr., Sir or Madam,* and *Madams and Sirs.* We suspect that a man's reaction to *Dear Madam or Sir* won't be as negative as that of a woman who sees *Dear Sir* in her letter. Other alternatives include omitting a salutation altogether, opting for an opening line that says "Greetings!" or "Hello!" or structuring a letter more like a memo, beginning with "To the Director," "Regarding your Memo of 9/7," or "TO: Friends of the Library" (Maggio, 1988, p. 184). We caution against using the trite, overused "To Whom It May Concern"; your letter may end up in the trash simply because "no one was concerned."

RECAP

married names, euphemisms, metaphors, insults, symmetrical or parallel language, order of terms, references to relationships, titles, salutations

USING LANGUAGE: ONCE YOU CHOOSE IT, HOW DO YOU USE IT?

Now that you understand what we mean by choice in language, now comes the real challenge: the actual usage of language in everyday interactions with others. We now move on to the *between* aspect of language—communication *between* the sexes, not *about* them. Experience and research tell us that men and women often have difficulty communicating with each other. Before we explore *how* women and men communicate, let's get an understanding of *why* they communicate. Our own research and that of others led to the development of a supposition to help explain why gender communication is so complex. First, we backtrack briefly to review the research of some communication theorists whose work forms the basis for our supposition.

An Axiom of Communication

Three communication scholars in the 1960s developed a set of *axioms* or basic rules about how human communication operates. One of Paul Watzlawick, Janet Helmick Beavin, and Don Jackson's (1967) axioms proposed that "Every communication has a content and a relationship aspect such that the latter classifies the former and is therefore a metacommunication" (p. 54). The *content* aspect of communication is what is actually said or the information imparted from one communicator to another. The *relational* aspect of the message is termed *metacommunication* (communication about communication) because it tells the receiver how the message should be interpreted and communicates something about the nature of the relationship between the interactants. For example, a simple "hello" to someone in a warm tone of voice conveys a sense of friendship and familiarity, whereas a hollow, perfunctory tone may indicate a more formal and impersonal relationship. Tone of voice, in this case, serves as metacommunication, that is, it indicates how the message should be interpreted and gives clues about the relationship. The content element is generally conveyed via verbal communication, while the relational element primarily takes the form of nonverbal communication. Watzlawick, Beavin, and Jackson suggested that rarely do interactants deliberately define the nature and state of their relationship; thus, the relational elements of messages are usually conveyed in subtle, unspoken, and unconscious ways.

Even the simplest of exchanges has a relational and a content dimension. If a complete stranger walked toward you on the sidewalk, made eye contact, and said "Hi; how's it going?," you might reply with some minimal greeting like "Okay, thanks." But if someone you knew were walking down the hallway at school and extended the same greeting, although you might answer the same way, your response would probably sound and look different from the exchange with the stranger. In both interactions, the content of the message is a basic greeting, but the relational aspects signal a difference in the relationship between you and the stranger versus you and the school acquaintance.

Women, Men, and the Relational Versus Content Approach to Communication

Stemming from Watzlawick, Beavin, and Jackson's axiom, we suggest that a fundamental difference exists in what women and men believe to be the function or purpose of communication. (Granted, this is a generalization and there are exceptions.) Specifically, men approach conversation more with the intent of imparting information (content aspect) than to convey cues about the relationship (relational aspect). In contrast, women view conversation as functioning more as an indication of relationship than as a mechanism for imparting information. This does not mean that every time a man speaks, he is conveying information only; on the contrary, *every* message carries content and relational meanings. This also does not mean that women only communicate relationally, without ever exchanging any real information. What it does mean is that men may use communication primarily for information exchange rather than for relationship development. Think about it: The development of male friendships comes more often in the form of *doing*, rather than *talking*. Women like to *do* as well as *talk*, but their relationships with other women are more often maintained via conversation than by doing things together. This represents a fundamental sex difference before women and men even meet, and it may set us up for conflict when we communicate.

Here are some examples (drawn from actual accounts of students and friends) to illustrate this supposition—what we term the *relational versus content approach to communication*. Upon hearing an explanation of the relational versus content approach, a colleague said "Is this like the other morning when my wife and I woke up before we had to actually get up, and she said, 'Let's just lie here and talk,' and I didn't have anything to talk *about*?" In a similar account, a friend explained that a man she'd been seeing gave her the "silent treatment" one evening when they decided to spend some time at her house rather than going out. She asked him a couple of times if anything was wrong and he politely replied "No," but he continued to be quiet. In frustration, she finally accused him of holding something back; she assumed he didn't care about her or they would be talking. His response was that he just didn't have anything to say, but that obviously he must care about her because "After all, I'm *here* aren't I?" A student recalled a recent argument he'd had with his partner: "We'd been talking about something that happened a few nights before and it led to an argument. When I felt that I'd explained my side of the story sufficiently and that we'd argued enough, I simply said 'There's nothing more to say. End of discussion.' This made her furious and I couldn't figure out why. She wanted to continue talking about the incident, my side of it, her side of it, what the argument meant about our relationship, and I just wanted the conversation *over*."

Another example from some married friends depicts an exchange between spouses. See if you can spot relational and content approaches operating here. Both spouses work full-time jobs; on this particular day, the wife had arrived home just before the husband did and the conversation went as follows:

WIFE: Hi honey; how was your day?
HUSBAND: Fine.
(Long Pause.)
W: Well, did anything interesting happen at work today?
H: Nope; just the same old, same old.
(Long Pause.)
W: Well, what about that deal you were going to talk to Bob about? Did you guys talk?
H: Yeah, we talked, but nothing much came out of it.
(Silence.)

Let's analyze this brief, fairly ordinary conversation. The wife's three verbalizations were in the form of questions designed to draw the husband into a conversation; the husband's verbalizations were brief responses to his wife's queries. Research indicates that it is typically the woman in a male-female pair who initiates conversation and offers verbalizations and nonverbal cues in attempts to keep conversation going (Carli, 1990; Fishman, 1983). The husband didn't make any overt attempt to extend the conversation. If the wife hadn't continued to ask questions, it's likely that the conversation would have ended after the first question-and-answer sequence. The information imparted (content element) was logical; the questions received appropriate answers. However, the relational elements may speak volumes.

Depending on the relational history of this couple, along with how the words were said and other nonverbal cues such as facial expressions and eye contact (or the lack of it), a couple of interpretations are plausible. One is that this is just a typical, ritualistic conversation between couples at the end of a long, tiring workday. Basic information is exchanged and there is no real need for relationship maintenance via this particular conversation. Another interpretation is that the husband wants to maintain and strengthen his relationship with his wife, but he simply doesn't want to do this kind of maintenance during the first 10 minutes at home after a tiring day at work. Yet another interpretation might be that there is a real communication problem in this relationship. The wife's attempts at conversation might signal her need for relationship involvement; the husband's thwarting of her efforts might signal a lack of relationship engagement on his part. Both approaches could signal bigger problems ahead.

This example illustrates men's and women's different views as to the uses or functions of conversation. Many times women want to talk just to reinforce the fact that a relationship exists and that the relationship is important. What is actually being said is usually less important than the fact that a conversation is taking place. Conversely, men generally approach conversation from a functional standpoint. A conversation functions as a means of exchanging information or content, not as some reinforcement of the relationship.

No wonder men often think that women talk on and on about nothing. No wonder women often think that men's relationships (and sometimes, men themselves) are superficial. What's going on here? It's not that women are insecure chatterboxes who have nothing better to do than carry on long, pointless conversations because they need relational reinforcement. And it's not that men are relationally aloof clods who don't need relationship reinforcement or can't manage even a simple conversation to save their souls. What's going here is that, in general, women and men use communication for different purposes and get their "relational goodies" in dramatically different ways.

What Does the Research Say?

Research and theory support the supposition that men and women approach conversation from different functional perspectives. However, some of the terminology and research approaches vary across disciplines.

Videotaped Conversation Research

To test the relational versus content supposition, we conducted two experiments to see if observers would assign different purposes or reasons for why people were engaged in conversation. Both involved scripted, videotaped conversations (authored and enacted by undergraduate students enrolled in a gender communication class) between two opposite-sex classmates. In the first study, the video depicted acquaintances chatting before class started, with the male student recognizing the female classmate as someone from a previous class. They slowly remembered each other and the past class, discussed problems with the current class, and ended the conversation with the female student agreeing to loan her class notes to the male student. At various points, a facilitator stopped the tape during breaks in the conversation and asked subjects to complete items on a questionnaire. When asked "What do you think the purpose of this conversation is?" most of the female respondents indicated relational purposes, while male respondents attributed content purposes. Female subjects reported that the purpose was "to become friends rather than just acquaintances," "he was really trying to get to know her better," and "to introduce something larger, perhaps a date or to study together for a test." The few male subjects who perceived relational elements in the conversation offered comments like "to get to know each other better" and "acknowledging that she is alive and feeling her vibes, to see if he's got a shot."

A different group of students responded to a second video in which the same before-class setting was used, but the topic of conversation and the relationship of the interactants was altered. The script involved a female student telling a male friend about a club she'd been to and about a party she was going to with some friends. The conversation ended just before class started, with the guy deciding to go to the party with the female student and her friends. As in the first study, female subjects saw primarily relational purposes in the conversation, offering such comments as "They're establishing 'extra interest' at this point" and "It seems like they're trying to get to see each other outside of class, as maybe more than just friends." Male subjects attributed content purposes more than relational ones, revealed by comments like "She's telling him about a party," and "They're catching up on what they've been doing." While these studies are from the perspective of an observer or eavesdropper rather than someone involved in the conversation, the findings do lend preliminary support for the relational versus content approach to communication.

Research into Interpersonal Communication Motives

Interpersonal communication researchers have explored the purposes of talk, specifically persons' motives for engaging in conversation. Rubin, Perse, and Barbato (1988) propose that while interpersonal communication research is thorough in its examination of *how* interaction occurs, it is less thorough in attempting to understand *why* people choose to interact, that is, their interpersonal motives. Thus, Rubin and colleagues studied over 500 subjects ranging in age from 12 to 91, attempting to discover whether people communicated for such purposes as wanting to be included by others, extending and receiving affection, simple relaxation, a need for companionship, or to control situations and people. They detected a significant sex difference: Female subjects reported being "more likely to talk to others for pleasure, to express affection, to seek inclusion, and to relax" (p. 621). Men reported communicating more to exert control over a situation rather than to express affection or seek inclusion. Results from this study support the contention that, in many cases, men's and women's motives or purposes for engaging in conversation differ.

Human Development Theory

Going back to Chapter 2's discussion of human development, recall that Carol Gilligan (1982) views female development almost entirely within the context of relationships. Gender-role identity development includes the ability or inability to identify with the primary caregiver—usually the mother. As a female child develops she identifies with the mother figure; her identity is steeped in her relationship with the mother from the start. A male child, on the other hand, must develop his identity separately from an identification with his mother. Thus, according to this theory, the sense of development via relationships is not as innately ingrained for male children as it is for female children. Communication researchers Wood and Lenze (1991) suggest that "distance or separation from others tends to be threatening to female identity in the same way that close connections to others jeopardize male identity" (p. 5). Gilligan's theory supports the relational versus content approach to communication in that the very way men and women develop from infancy might set up an eventual communication difference between the sexes. Women's identity develops out of connectedness and affiliation, whereas men's identity develops from a sense of independence and separation. It follows, then, that women would use conversation as a vehicle of relationship development in a way that is neither preferable nor natural for men.

Tannen's Contributions

In her first book, *That's Not What I Meant!*, sociolinguist Deborah Tannen (1986) describes communicative sex differences in terms of messages (the actual content) versus metamessages (cues about how to interpret messages and about the relationship), using similar language to Watzlawick et al.'s (1967) axiom. She posits that "women are often more attuned than men to the metamessages of talk. When women surmise meaning in this way, it seems mysterious to men, who call it 'women's intuition' (if they think it's right) or 'reading things in' (if they think it's wrong). The difference in focus on messages and metamessages can give men and women different points of view on almost any comment" (Tannen, 1986, as in Coates, 1998, pp. 435–436; 437). In her second book *You Just Don't Understand*, Tannen (1990) describes male and female talk in ways that parallel the relational versus content supposition. The female style, termed *rapport-talk* is women's "way of establishing connections and negotiating relationships" (p. 77). Male style or *report-talk* "is primarily a means to preserve independence and negotiate and maintain status. This is done by exhibiting knowledge and skill, and by holding center stage through verbal performance such as story-telling, joking, or imparting information" (p. 77).

What's Preferable—Relational or Content Communication?

Neither the relational nor the content approach is necessarily preferable. Remember that in every message—no matter how brief or trivial—both content and relational elements exist. The difference seems to lie in a person's view of the function or purpose of a given message. Watzlawick, Beavin, and Jackson believed that healthy relationships evidenced a balance of content and relational aspects. To them, a "sick" relationship could be characterized by communication that focuses too heavily on the relational dimension, such that even the simplest messages become interpreted as "statements" about the relationship. Likewise, relationships in which communication has degenerated into a mere information exchange rather than clueing one another in to the state of the relationship could also be termed "sick" (p. 53).

In Chapter 2 we discussed gender transcendence; throughout this textbook we encourage you to expand your choices of behavior into a more fully developed repertoire of communicative options. Thus, it follows that, while an understanding of male and female approaches to talk is illuminating, an

---

RECAP

axiom of communication, relational approach, content approach, interpersonal communication motives, human development theory, gender-role identity, metamessages, rapport talk, report talk

---

important goal is to develop an integrated or balanced approach derived from the best attributes of both. Such an approach recognizes that certain times, situations, and people require different kinds of communication. The skill comes in learning which communicative approach—relational or content—is best, given the dictates of the situation. In this manner, men could strengthen their male friendships through conversation rather than relying primarily on action or shared activities. Such conversation would provide good experience that could carry over into their relationships with women. Likewise, more women could realize that, in many of their relationships with men—relationships of all types and levels of intimacy—talk may not be the primary way to develop the relationship. Women might become more comfortable in approaching conversation with men on more of a content-exchange basis, rather than expecting the conversation to reveal how men feel about them or how men view the relationship. The ideal would be to respond to each other in the most effective manner possible, unencumbered by what is expected or stereotypical for persons of our sex.

LANGUAGE USAGE BETWEEN WOMEN AND MEN

This final section of the chapter examines ways in which language is used in communication *between* women and men—the *how* we communicate. Studies have produced contradictory results regarding some linguistic patterns of the sexes, but a general, unsettling research trend labels feminine patterns as weaker, more passive, and less commanding of respect in comparison to masculine styles. Some view linguistic sex differences as profound enough to form *genderlects,* defined as "speech that contains features that mark it as stereotypically masculine or feminine" (Hoar, 1992, p. 127).

Vocal Properties and Linguistic Constructions

Vocal properties are aspects of the production of sound related to the physiological voice-producing mechanism in humans. *Linguistic constructions* reflect speech patterns or habits; they are communicative choices people make.

How Low Can You Go?

The *pitch* of a human voice can be defined as the highness or lowness of a particular sound due to air causing the vocal chords to vibrate. Physiological structures related to voice production are configured so women tend to produce higher-pitched sounds, while men tend to produce lower-pitched sounds. Thus, most women's speaking voices are higher in pitch than most men's. But scholarly evidence, especially in the area of singing voices, has uprooted some notions about physiological sex differences and voice production, suggesting that vocal sex differences may have more to do with social interpretations than with physiology alone (Brownmiller, 1984; Graddol & Swann, 1989). Research indicates that women and men have equal abilities to produce high pitches, but that men have been socialized not to use the higher pitches for fear of sounding feminine (Henley, 1977; Kramer, 1977; Pfeiffer, 1985).

In comparison to the low melodic tones that most men are able to produce, the so-called high-pitched female whine has drawn long-standing societal criticism (McConnell-Ginet, 1983) which has led to, as Cameron (1985) puts it, "a widespread prejudice against women's voices" (p. 54). In a patriarchal society such as ours, men's lower-pitched voices are deemed more credible and persuasive than women's. Gender scholar Nancy Hoar (1992) suggests, "Women who aspire to influential positions are often advised to cultivate lower-pitched voices, voices that communicate authority" (p. 130). Men who possess higher-pitched voices are often ridiculed for being effeminate. Their "feminine" voices detract from their credibility and dynamism, unless another physical or personality attribute somehow overpowers or contradicts that judgment. (Mike Tyson, former heavyweight boxing champion, is one example of this.)

Indications of Tentativeness

Several vocal properties and linguistic constructions have been linked to *tentativeness* in human communication. A great deal of research shows that women use far more tentativeness in their communication than men, and this tentativeness can undermine women's messages, making them appear uncertain, insecure, incompetent, powerless, and less likely to be taken seriously (Carli, 1990; Graddol & Swann, 1989; Lakoff, 1975; McConnell-Ginet, 1983). However, other more recent studies suggest that factors such as culture, status and position in society, the goal or intent of the communicator (e.g., to create rapport between interactants, to facilitate conflict), and the nature of the group in which communication occurs (same-sex or mixed-sex) have much more impact than sex on stylistic variations (Johnson & Aries, 1992; Maltz & Borker, 1992; Nichols, 1992; Swann, 1992; Weatherall, 1998; Yaeger-Dror, 1998).

One vocal property that indicates tentativeness is *intonation,* described by sociolinguist Sally McConnell-Ginet (1983) as "the tune to which we set the text of our talk" (p. 70). Research is contradictory as to whether rising intonation (typically associated with asking questions) is more indicative of a female style than a male style. Back in the '70s, Robin Lakoff contended that the rising intonation pattern was unique to English-speaking women whose intent was to receive confirmation from others. An example can be found in the simple exchange, "What's for dinner tonight?" followed by the answer, "Spaghetti?" The intonation turns the statement or answer into a question, as if to say, "Is that okay with you?" However, research conducted by language and education expert Carole Edelsky (1979) indicated that the interpretation of a rising intonation depended upon the context in which it was used. In certain contexts in her research, female subjects used the rising intonation pattern more than men; in other contexts, no patterns of sex differences emerged. Contradictory research findings led feminist scholar Julia Penelope (1990) to conclude the following: "Women are said to use . . . structures that are servile and submissive ('polite'), tentative, uncertain, emotionally exaggerated, and self-demeaning. These alleged traits represent a stereotype of how women talk, *not* the way we do talk" (pp. xxii–xxiii).

A linguistic construction related to tentativeness is the *tag question,* as in the example "This is a really beautiful day, don't you think?" The primary function of the tag question is to seek agreement or a response from a listener (Fishman, 1980; Zimmerman & West, 1975). Lakoff (1975) believed that tag questions served as an "apology for making an assertion at all" (p. 54). She attributed the use of tag questions to a general lack of assertiveness or confidence about what one is saying, a usage her research showed was more related to a female style than a male style. Some research supports a connection between women's style and the use of tag questions (Carli, 1990; Zimmerman & West, 1975), but other research finds no evidence that tag questions occur more in female speech than in male speech, nor that tag questions necessarily function to indicate uncertainty or tentativeness (Holmes, 1990; Roger & Nesshoever, 1987). Tag questions may operate as genuine requests or to "forestall opposition" (Dubois & Crouch, 1975, p. 292). As Spender (1985) points out, it is inappropriate to view tag questions as always indicating hesitancy, as evidenced by her example, "'You won't do that again, *will you?*'" (p. 9).

Qualifiers, hedges, disclaimers, compound requests, and *intensifiers* are other linguistic constructions generally interpreted as indicating tentativeness and stereotypically associated with women's speech. Lakoff (1975) claimed that these constructions indicated women's general uncertainty and inability to "vouch for the accuracy of the statement" (p. 53). *Qualifiers* include "well," "you know," "kind of," "sort of," "really," "perhaps," "possibly," "maybe," and "of course." *Hedging* devices include such terms as "I think/believe/feel," "I guess," "I mean," and "I wonder" (Carli, 1990; Holmes, 1990; Spender, 1985). *Disclaimers* are typically longer forms of hedges that act as prefaces or defense mechanisms when one is unsure or doubtful of what one is about to say (Beach & Dunning, 1982; Hewitt & Stokes, 1975). Disclaimers generally weaken or soften the effect of a message. Examples of disclaimers include such statements as "I know this is a dumb question, but . . . ." and "I may be wrong here, but I think that . . . ." *Compound requests* typically involve negative constructions and are longer, more complex requests for action or assistance. Again, according to Lakoff (1975), they signal tentativeness and are more characteristic of women's speech than men's. The question, "Won't you please come with me tonight?" is a compound request compared with the simple or direct construction "Come with me tonight."

Documentation of *intensifiers* by language scholars dates back as far as 1922 when linguist Otto Jespersen studied women's use of exaggeration, specifically in the form of the term *vastly*. He concluded that women's communication was much more prone to hyperbole than men's. Lakoff (1975) focused on the word *so*, claiming that more women than men use such constructions as "I like him *so* much" (p. 55). Penelope (1990) adds *so much, such,* and *quite* as ways of signaling a feeling level or intensifying what one is saying (p. xxii). In Carli's (1990) study, women exhibited more tentativeness than men in the form of disclaimers, hedges, and tag questions but only in mixed-sex conversations, not in same-sex conversations. However, women used more intensifiers in same-sex than mixed-sex conversations.

Two linguists, Janet Holmes (1990), who studied speech patterns in New Zealand, and Deborah Cameron (1985), who studied tentativeness in Londoners' speech patterns, conclude that sex-typed interpretations of tentativeness must be made within the given context in which the communication occurs, as do researchers in the United States (Mulac & Lundell, 1986; Ragan, 1989; Sayers & Sherblom, 1987). Holmes (1990) discovered, for example, that men and women were equally as likely to use tentative linguistic devices, depending upon the needs or mandates of the particular situation. Cameron (1985) found that male subjects exhibited tentative communication when placed in certain roles, such as facilitators of group interaction. Male and female subjects in O'Barr and Atkins's (1980) study of courtroom communication used the entire range of tentativeness indicators with equal frequency, with the exception of tag questions.

An overabundance of tentative forms of expression in one's communication can be interpreted as a sign of uncertainty and insecurity. But tentative language may also have positive, facilitative uses; these kinds of expressions need not be identified with one sex or the other. As Deakins (1992) suggests, "women's style" or "powerless style" may be "interpreted as cooperative, consensual, and leaderless" (p. 155). For example, a manager holding a high status position within an organization might use disclaimers or hedges in attempts to even out a status differential, foster a

RECAP

genderlects, vocal properties, linguistic constructions, pitch, tentativeness, intonation, tag questions, qualifiers, hedges, disclaimers, compound requests, intensifiers sense of camaraderie among staff members, and show herself or himself as open to employees' suggestions and ideas.

Managing to Converse

Have you ever considered how conversation is organized or "managed"? *Conversation management* involves several variables, but one interesting vein of research surrounds indicators of conversational dominance.

Conversation typically occurs in *turns*, meaning that one speaker takes a turn, then another, and so on, such that interaction is socially organized (Sacks, Schegloff, & Jefferson, 1978). Noted sociologists Candace West and Don Zimmerman have conducted significant research into how turn-taking is accomplished. A speaker's interjection into a conversation is her or his *turn at talk*, which involves not only duration but "the right and obligation to speak allocated to a particular speaker" (West & Zimmerman, 1975, as in Coates, 1998, p. 166). *Topic control* is fairly self-explanatory; a speaker initiates a topic and works to see that that topic continues to be the focal point of discussion. *Talk time*, sometimes referred to as *air time* or *verbosity*, refers to how long a speaker takes to accomplish one turn at talk.

When people take turns at talk, they may experience *overlaps* defined as "simultaneous speech initiated by a next speaker just as a current speaker arrives at a possible turn-transition place" and *interruptions*, which are "deeper intrusions into the internal structure of the speaker's utterance" (West & Zimmerman, 1983, pp. 103–104). A range of interpretations has been made of interruptions and overlaps, including that they indicate disrespect, restrict a speaker's rights, serve as devices to control a topic, and indicate an attitude of dominance and authority (Marche & Peterson, 1993). Overlaps are considered less egregious than interruptions because overlapping someone's speech may be seen as supportive, as in trying to reinforce or dovetail off of someone's idea. Interruptions more often indicate dominance and power play because they cut off the speaker in midstream and suggest that the interrupter's comment is somehow more important or insightful.

In the most widely cited study of adult conversations, Zimmerman and West (1975) found few overlaps and interruptions within same-sex interactions. However, in cross-sex conversations, more interruptions occurred than overlaps, and 96 percent of the interruptions were made by males. West and Zimmerman (1975) compared their findings for male and female interruptive behavior to that seen in parent-child interaction; they suggest that "the use of interruptions by males is a *display* of dominance or control to the female (and to any witnesses), just as the parent's interruption communicates an aspect of parental control to the child and to others present" (as in Coates, 1998, p. 172).

Other early research revealed definite evidence of male conversational dominance in terms of initiating topics, working to maintain conversation around those topics, talking more often and for longer durations, offering minimal responses to women's comments, and using more declaratives than questions (Edelsky, 1981; Fishman, 1983). However, later studies have explored beyond sex effects to examine the complexity of dominance in such contexts as face-to-face interaction, same-sex and mixed-sex dyads and groups, and electronic conversations. Researchers now suggest that many nonverbal, contextual, and cultural factors, such as perceptions of power and status, seating arrangements, and sex-typed topics, affect judgments of dominant or powerless styles (Deakins, 1992; Herring, Johnson, & DiBenedetto, 1998; Hoar, 1992; Maltz & Borker, 1998; Smythe & Huddleston, 1992; Swann, 1998; Tannen, 1994).

As an example of a cultural effect on conversation management, Thomas Kochman, in his insightful and oft-cited book *Black and White Styles in Conflict* (1981) discusses the expressiveness and responsiveness indicative of what he describes as a black style of communication. Kochman explains, "Black presentations are emotionally intense, dynamic, and demonstrative; white presentations are more modest and emotionally restrained" (p. 106). The cultural dimensions of a given exchange affect one's views of what constitutes an interruption, for example (Tannen, 1994). In Kochman's view, "Black speakers tend to infer from the absence of a response that the whites to whom they are speaking are not listening. White speakers tend to infer from various responses which blacks consider necessary and appropriate interpolations to an ongoing performance . . . that blacks are constantly interrupting them" (p. 112). One person's expressiveness or responsiveness might be another's rudeness or power play.

Television news talk shows such as CNN's *Larry King Live,* MSNBC's *The Big Show,* and Fox News' *The Crier Report* are prime opportunities to observe conversation management (or, many times, mismanagement). The displays of vocal dominance and competitiveness among male and female guests is fascinating in these forums. Many times, male speakers dominate female speakers. However, the more seasoned female guests have learned techniques to control the topics they respond to and raise with hosts, hold their turns at talk longer, and minimize interruptions from other guests, the host, or both. Some speakers have so cleverly mastered the art of breathing that they never seem to breathe at normally expected places (perhaps never breathing at all!), never seem to need pauses to collect their thoughts, and are quite successful at fending off would-be interrupters. Perhaps we as authors know too well what to look for, but the women on these shows who fare the best (meaning that they are equal participants with their male counterparts) tend to have lower-pitched voices and greater potential for volume, volume that they can increase as someone attempts to interrupt or overlap their comments. They tend to vary their rate of speech and pace their breathing in ways that discourage interruption.

Take a break some time from all that studying you do every night and tune in to one of these programs. See if you detect the elements we describe, as well as other linguistic and vocal devices that manage conversation. What makes some people effective at interrupting others? Why are some successful at warding off interruptions? Do you believe that interruptions are power plays or simply expected elements of everyday conversation? Do you think that dominance behaviors such as those we've described here are necessarily male or masculine conversational devices? Is it "just like a woman" to wait for her turn at talk, rather than to speak up and offer her input? Are the sexes limited or stereotyped by such designations of "appropriate" behavior? Do you think your own patterns of conversation management are connected to your sex, or are other factors at work? Do you think you can use different patterns of conversational management to enhance your communication with others?

Choosing Those All-Important Words

Profane—Not Profound

Here's a question for you: In the 21st century, will it still be more acceptable for men than women to say "shit," "damn," "hell," and other colorful metaphors and curse words? Profanity has long been considered a man's behavior (if it's considered *anyone's* behavior). Lakoff (1975) suggested that if profanity makes one's opinions more forceful and believable, but such usages are unacceptable for women, then the ability to use profanity only enhances men's position of strength. She wrote that women's language encourages them to remain "little ladies" and that a woman violates this "ladylike" demeanor if she uses profanity or an overabundance of slang. In testing this argument, Lakoff offered two versions of the same statement, asking readers to label them as being spoken by a man or a woman. The statements were: "Oh dear, you've put the peanut butter in the refrigerator again," and "Shit, you've put the peanut butter in the refrigerator again" (p. 10). The results supported her position.

Gender linguist Constance Staley conducted a fascinating study of male and female college students' uses of profane and hostile language in 1978. Her research found that female subjects held the perception that men used profanity and hostile language to a much *greater* degree than male subjects indicated they actually used. In contrast, male subjects thought that women used *far less* profanity than female subjects reported actually using. Gender and language expert Julia Penelope (1990) specifically addressed forms of language she termed "the slang of sexual slurs" and concluded that it appears to be unacceptable even in modern society for women to use sexual slang or to hear it used. Men are permitted to use such language, but with one restraint: "they rarely exhibit the full range of it in the company of women" (p. 46).

One of the problems people face when they have discussions about sex—with a dating or marital partner, with their children, with *anyone*—is that the language describing body parts and sexual activity is either completely clinical or "gutter" (Potorti, 1992). In other words, it's sometimes hard to talk frankly about sex-related topics, even though those kinds of discussions are important, because the embarrassing choices are to use awkward medical-book terminology that may not be understandable to both speaker and listener, to use "gutter terms" or graphic slang that may be offensive and is likely to demean the very topic you are discussing, or to keep the discussion vague by using inferences rather than specific language, again risking misunderstanding. If people have difficulty expressing themselves on sexual topics, it's understandable when you consider the language that currently exists for our use.

Is It Mauve, Puce, or Aubergine? (or Just Purple?)

We recall a funny conversation in which two men were talking about the colors of NFL teams' uniforms. "Nothing could be uglier than that sick orange and brown the Tampa Bay Buccaneers wear." "Yeah, but how about that weird blue on the Miami Dolphins' uniforms?" We're glad to say that the Buccaneers have since changed their uniforms (not much of an improvement, many argue) and that the spouse of one of the men in the conversation chimed in with, "That weird blue is called 'teal,' and it's an appropriate color for a team based at the ocean."

Very little is written about this topic, but most often color language is relegated to the women's realm (Berlin & Kay, 1969). Lakoff (1975) contended that "Women make far more precise discriminations in naming colors than do men; words like beige, ecru, aquamarine, lavender, and so on are unremarkable in a woman's active vocabulary, but absent from that of most men" (pp. 8–9). Research offers few explanations for why women tend to provide more categories for colors than men. One explanation relates to the tendency for more men than women to be color blind. But this doesn't explain why men who aren't color blind don't tend to use many variations of color terms. Another explanation is simply that the whole topic of color may be more important to women than to men because women have traditionally been more closely linked with home decoration and fashion. Some of our younger students, though, believe that the trend for women to use more color terms than men is changing among persons of their generation.

CONCLUSION

In this chapter on language, we've explored some influences existing in your world that profoundly affect your gender communication. You first have to understand how you are influenced before you can choose to lessen or negate the influence. This chapter has given you more than a few things to think about, because when you put something under a microscope, you see it in a whole new way. We tossed a lot at you for one main reason: so that you won't use language by default or habit but instead *choose* to use language that accurately reflects who you are and how you think. Now that you've read this material, do you understand what we meant by the *cumulative effect* we alluded to in the introductory paragraphs of this chapter?

This chapter challenged you to more fully consider how communication is used to talk *about* the sexes, as well as why and how communication occurs *between* them. We first explored the nature of language and some reasons for using nonsexist language; then we reviewed several forms and practices related to sexist language usage, as well as nonsexist alternatives. In shifting to the *between* dimension, we examined relational and content approaches to communication to determine whether the sexes view communication as serving different functions or purposes. We shifted focus to vocal properties, linguistic constructions, and word selections that continue to be studied for what they might reveal about the sexes and how we communicate. The sections on sexual language and profanity no doubt included more vivid terms than you're used to seeing in college textbooks. As we said in the introduction to this chapter, the goal was to focus on language and its important role in gender communication, to offer ways that you can expand your linguistic options, and to challenge you to *choose* and *use* language in a more inclusive and unbiased way in order to enhance your personal effectiveness in gender communication and your relationships.

Key Terms

language	order of terms	pitch
Sapir-Whorf Hypothesis	references to	tentativeness
sexist language	relationships	intonation
receiver orientation	titles	tag questions
generic pronouns	salutations	qualifiers
neologisms	axiom of communication	hedges
antimale bias	relational approach	disclaimers
man-linked terminology	content approach	compound requests
marking	interpersonal	intensifiers
feminine suffixes	communication	conversation management
animal, plant, and food	motives	turn-taking
terms	human development	topic control
religious language	theory	talk time
sexual language	gender-role identity	overlaps
married names	metamessages	interruptions
euphemisms	rapport talk	profanity
metaphors	report talk	color language
insults	genderlects	
symmetrical or parallel	vocal properties	
construction	linguistic constructions	

Discussion Starters

1. What were you taught in junior high or high school about *sexist language*? Do you remember any reactions you had at the time to what was taught? If you received no instruction on nonsexist language usage, why do you think this information wasn't included in your education? Have you been taught something similar or contradictory in college about sexist language? (Or maybe nothing at all?) How do previous teachings on this topic coexist with the information in this chapter?

2. Think again about the *receiver orientation to communication*. Do you believe that adopting a receiver orientation to communication puts more pressure on people to be nonsexist? If so, do you believe that this pressure is a good thing or that it may have a negative effect on communication?

3. Why do you think a *neologism* like *Ms.* made its way into the language, but nonsexist pronouns like *tey, gen,* and *herm* have not? What does it take, in your opinion, for a new term to be accepted in society? If you wanted to introduce new words into the language, what would they be and how would you go about it?

4. Sexism in *religious language* is one of the more difficult topics to explore and discuss. For some people, it is an affront to put the language used to convey their deeply personal religious beliefs under the microscope. What are your views on this subject? Do you think that male-dominated religious language should be examined? Or do you think religious language should be an exception within the larger topic of sexist language?

5. Names are important parts of our self-identities. If you are single now but get married in the future, how will you handle the name-taking problem? If you are a heterosexual male, have you always wanted your future wife to take your last name? Have you always assumed that a woman you would marry would want to take your last name? What if she insists on keeping her last name? How will you react? If you are a heterosexual female, what do you think about women keeping their last names upon marriage? If you become engaged, what will you say to your future husband about taking his last name? Does it seem too radical to suggest that you hyphenate your two last names? What about the suggestion that he take *your* last name?

6. Think of two people—a woman and a man—whose communication styles most closely (or stereotypically) correspond to the *relational and content approaches* presented in this chapter. What are the most marked aspects of each person's communication that make them stand out in your mind as examples?

7. Research in the '70s and '80s concluded that many stylistic properties of women's speech caused them to communicate *tentativeness* and *powerlessness.* Do you agree with the research on this topic? Do you see evidence of powerlessness in the communication of women (and men) with whom you come into contact? What kind of values underlie labeling one style "dominant" and another style "powerless"? What do you think of the more current research that suggests that what has been termed "powerless" might actually be affiliative, supportive, other-oriented, and facilitative?

8. In light of the information on *conversation management,* assess your own style of communication. How often do you communicate in questions versus statements? Do you use questions because you earnestly want the answers or to ensure you'll get a response and the conversation will continue? Do you use statements to control conversation and establish your sense of importance in the world? Are you more likely to be interrupted or to interrupt someone else? Do you have a lot of *tag questions, hedges,* and *disclaimers* in your communication? Think about classroom communication: Do you find yourself saying things like, "This might be a dumb question, but . . ." or "I could be wrong, but . . ."? If so, do you believe that these elements weaken your effect or make you appear tentative or powerless? Why or why not?

References

ALDRICH, P. G. (1985, December). Skirting sexism. *Nation's Business,* 34–35.

AMERICAN PSYCHOLOGICAL ASSOCIATION. (1994). Guidelines to reduce bias in language. In *Publication manual of the American Psychological Association* (4th ed.). Washington, D.C.: Author.

AUGUST, E. R. (1992). Real men don't: Anti-male bias in English. In M. Schaum & C. Flanagan (Eds.), *Gender images: Readings for composition* (pp. 131–141). Boston: Houghton Mifflin.

BAKER, R. (1981). "Pricks" and "chicks": A plea for "persons." In M. Vetterling-Braggin (Ed.), *Sexist language: A modern philosophical analysis* (pp. 161–182). New York: Rowman & Littlefield.

BEACH, W. A., & DUNNING, D. G. (1982). Pre-indexing and conversational organization. *Quarterly Journal of Speech, 67,* 170–185.

BELLAFANTE, G. (1998, June 29). Feminism: It's all about me! *Time,* 54–62.

BERLIN, B., & KAY, P. (1969). *Basic color terms: Their universality and evolution.* Berkeley: University of California Press.

BRIERE, J., & LANKTREE, C. (1983). Sex-role related effects of sex bias in language. *Sex Roles, 9,* 625–632.

BROOKS, L. (1983). Sexist language in occupational information: Does it make a difference? *Journal of Vocational Behavior, 23,* 227–232.

BROWNMILLER, S. (1984). *Femininity.* New York: Simon & Schuster.

CAMERON, D. (1985). *Feminism and linguistic theory.* New York: St. Martin's.

CARLI, L. L. (1990). Gender, language, and influence. *Journal of Personality and Social Psychology, 59,* 941–951.

COATES, J. (Ed.) (1998). *Language and gender: A reader.* Malden, MA: Blackwell.

CONNELLY, S. (1998, August 2). Single women still viewed as incomplete. *Corpus Christi Caller Times,* p. H1.

DEAKINS, A. H. (1992). The *tu/vous* dilemma: Gender, power, and solidarity. In L. A. M. Perry, L. H. Turner, & H. M. Sterk (Eds.), *Constructing and reconstructing gender: The links among communication, language, and gender* (pp. 151–161). Albany: State University of New York Press.

DUBOIS, B. L., & CROUCH, I. (1975). The question of tag questions in women's speech: They don't really use more of them, do they? *Language in Society, 4,* 289–294.

EDELSKY, C. (1979). Question intonation and sex roles. *Language in Society, 8,* 15–32.

EDELSKY, C. (1981). Who's got the floor? *Language in Society, 10,* 383–421.

'Feminist' stereotype persists about wives who choose to keep maiden name. (1998, July 12). *Corpus Christi Caller Times,* pp. H1, H3.

FISHMAN, P. M. (1980). Conversational insecurity. In H. Giles, W. P. Robinson, & P. M. Smith (Eds.), *Language: Social psychological perspectives* (pp. 127–132). New York: Pergamon.

FISHMAN, P. M. (1983). Interaction: The work women do. In B. Thorne, C. Kramarae, & N. Henley (Eds.), *Language, gender, and society* (pp. 89–101). Rowley, MA: Newbury.

FRANK, F. W., & TREICHLER, P. A. (1989). *Language, gender, and professional writing: Theoretical approaches and guidelines for non-sexist usage.* New York: Modern Language Association.

GASTIL, J. (1990). Generic pronouns and sexist language: The oxymoronic character of masculine generics. *Sex Roles, 23,* 629–641.

GILLIGAN, C. (1982). *In a different voice.* Cambridge, MA: Harvard University Press.

GRADDOL, D., & SWANN, J. (1989). *Gender voices.* Cambridge, MA: Basil Blackwell.

HAMILTON, L. C. (1988). Using masculine generics: Does generic "he" increase male bias in the user's imagery? *Sex Roles, 19,* 785–799.

HENLEY, N. M. (1977). *Body politics: Power, sex, and nonverbal communication.* Englewood Cliffs, NJ: Prentice-Hall.

HERRING, S. C., JOHNSON, D. A., & DIBENEDETTO, T. (1998). Participation in electronic discourse in a "feminist" field. In J. Coates (Ed.), *Language and gender: A reader* (pp. 197–210). Malden, MA: Blackwell.

HEWITT, J. P., & STOKES, R. (1975). Disclaimers. *American Sociological Review, 40,* 1–11.

HOAR, N. (1992). Genderlect, powerlect, and politeness. In L. A. M. Perry, L. H. Turner, & H. M. Sterk (Eds.), *Constructing and reconstructing gender: The links among communication, language, and gender* (pp. 127–136). Albany: State University of New York Press.

HOLMES, J. (1990). Hedges and boosters in women's and men's speech. *Language and Communication, 10,* 185–205.

IVY, D. K. (1986, February). *Who's the boss?: He, he/she, or they?* Paper presented at the meeting of the Western Speech Communication Association, Tucson, AZ.

IVY, D. K., BULLIS-MOORE, L., NORVELL, K., BACKLUND, P., & JAVIDI, M. (1995). The lawyer, the babysitter, and the student: Inclusive language usage and instruction. *Women & Language, 18,* 13–21.

JESPERSEN, O. (1922). *Language: Its nature, development, and origin.* New York: Holt.

JOHNSON, F. L., & ARIES, E. J. (1992). The talk of women friends. In J. Coates (Ed.), *Language and gender: A reader* (pp. 215–225). Malden, MA: Blackwell.

KENNEDY, D. (1992). Review essay: She or he in textbooks. *Women & Language, 15,* 46–49.

KOCHMAN, T. (1981). *Black and white styles in conflict.* Chicago: University of Chicago Press.

KRAMARAE, C. (1981). *Women and men speaking.* Rowley, MA: Newbury.

KRAMER, C. (1977). Perceptions of female and male speech. *Language and Speech, 20,* 151–161.

KRUH, N. (1992, April 29). What name should you wear? Girl, lady or woman—the terms mean more than you think. *Dallas Morning News,* pp. 1C, 2C, 3C.

LAKOFF, G., & JOHNSON, M. (1981). *Metaphors we live by.* Chicago: University of Chicago Press.

LAKOFF, R. (1975). *Language and woman's place.* New York: Harper & Row.

LAROCQUE, P. (1997, April 7). Sexism slips into language. *Dallas Morning News,* p. 13A.

LEARDI, J. (1997, September 28). Is God male or female? For some, issue of God and gender is subject to debate. *Corpus Christi Caller Times,* pp. H1, H3.

MAGGIO, R. (1988). *The nonsexist word finder: A dictionary of gender-free usage.* Boston: Beacon.

MAGGIO, R. (1992). *The bias-free word finder.* Boston: Beacon.

MALTZ, D. N., & BORKER, R. A. (1998). A cultural approach to male-female miscommunication. In J. Coates (Ed.), *Language and gender: A reader* (pp. 417–434). Malden, MA: Blackwell.

MARCHE, T. A., & PETERSON, C. (1993). The development and sex-related use of interruption behavior. *Human Communication Research, 19,* 388–408.

MARTYNA, W. (1978). What does "he" mean? Use of the generic masculine. *Journal of Communication, 28,* 131–138.

McCONNELL-GINET, S. (1980). Linguistics and the feminist challenge. In S. McConnell-Ginet, R. Borker, & N. Furman (Eds.), *Women and language in literature and society* (pp. 3–25). New York: Praeger.

McCONNELL-GINET, S. (1983). Intonation in a man's world. In B. Thorne, C. Kramarae, & N. Henley (Eds.), *Language, gender, and society* (pp. 69–88). Rowley, MA: Newbury.

MILLER, C., & SWIFT, K. (1976). *Words and women: New language in new times.* Garden City, NY: Doubleday.

MILLER, C., & SWIFT, K. (1988). *The handbook of nonsexist writing* (2nd ed.). New York: Harper & Row.

MILLER, C., SWIFT, K., & MAGGIO, R. (1997, September-October). Liberating language. *Ms.,* 50–54.

MOFFAT, M. (1989). *Coming of age in New Jersey.* New Brunswick, NJ: Rutgers University Press.

MOULTON, J., ROBINSON, G. M., & ELIAS, C. (1978). Sex bias in language use: "Neutral" pronouns that aren't. *American Psychologist, 33,* 1032–1036.

MULAC, A., & LUNDELL, T. L. (1986). Linguistic contributors to the gender-linked language effect. *Journal of Language and Social Psychology, 5,* 81–101.

NATIONAL COUNCIL OF TEACHERS OF ENGLISH. (1975). *Guidelines for nonsexist use of language in NCTE publications.* Urbana, IL: Author.

NG, S. H. (1990). Androcentric coding of *man* and *his* in memory by language users. *Journal of Experimental Social Psychology, 26,* 455–464.

NICHOLS, P. C. (1992). Black women in the rural south: Conservative and innovative. In J. Coates (Ed.), *Language and gender: A reader* (pp. 55–63). Malden, MA: Blackwell.

O'BARR, W. M., & ATKINS, B. K. (1980). "Women's language" or "powerless language?" In S. McConnell-Ginet, R. Borker, & N. Furman (Eds.), *Women and language in literature and society* (pp. 93–110). New York: Praeger.

PENELOPE, J. (1990). *Speaking freely: Unlearning the lies of the fathers' tongues.* New York: Pergamon.

PFEIFFER, J. (1985). Girl talk, boy talk. *Science, 85,* 58–63.

POTORTI, P. (1992). Personal communication, October.

RAGAN, S. L. (1989). Communication between the sexes: A consideration of sex differences in adult communication. In J. F. Nussbaum (Ed.), *Life-span communication: Normative processes* (pp. 179–193). Hillsdale, NJ: Lawrence Erlbaum.

ROGER, D., & NESSHOEVER, W. (1987). Individual differences in dyadic conversational strategies: A further study. *British Journal of Social Psychology, 26,* 247–255.

RUBIN, R. B., PERSE, E. M., & BARBATO, C. A. (1988). Conceptualization and measurement of interpersonal communication motives. *Human Communication Research, 14,* 602–628.

SACKS, H., SCHEGLOFF, E. A., & JEFFERSON, G. (1978). A simple systematic for the organization of turn taking for conversation. In J. Schenkein (Ed.), *Studies in the organization of conversational interaction* (pp. 7–55). New York: Academic Press.

SAYERS, F., & SHERBLOM, J. (1987). Qualification in male language as influenced by age and gender of conversational partner. *Communication Research Reports, 4,* 88–92.

SCHMITT, J. J. (1992). God's wife: Some gender reflections on the Bible and biblical interpretation. In L. A. M. Perry, L. H. Turner, & H. M. Sterk (Eds.), *Constructing and reconstructing gender: The links among communication, language, and gender* (pp. 269–281). Albany: State University of New York Press.

SMYTHE, M. J., & HUDDLESTON, B. (1992). Competition and collaboration: male and female communication patterns during dyadic interactions. In L. A. M. Perry, L. H. Turner, & H. M. Sterk (Eds.), *Constructing and reconstructing gender: The links among communication, language, and gender* (pp. 251–260). Albany: State University of New York Press.

SORRELS, B. D. (1983). *The nonsexist communicator.* Englewood Cliffs, NJ: Prentice-Hall.

SPENDER, D. (1985). *Man made language* (2nd ed.). London: Routledge & Kegan Paul.

STALEY, C. (1982). Sex related differences in the style of children's language. *Journal of Psycholinguistic Research, 11,* 141–152.

STANLEY, J. P. (1977). Paradigmatic woman: The prostitute. In D. L. Shores (Ed.), *Papers in language variation.* Birmingham: University of Alabama Press.

STEINEM, G. (1986). *Outrageous acts and everyday rebellions.* New York: Signet.

STEINEM, G. (1995, September-October). Words and change. *Ms.,* 93–96.

STERICKER, A. (1981). Does this "he or she" business really make a difference? The effect of masculine pronouns as generics on job attitudes. *Sex Roles, 7,* 637–641.

SWANN, J. (1998). Talk control: An illustration from the classroom of problems in analysing male dominance of conversation. In J. Coates (Ed.), *Language and gender: A reader* (pp. 184–196). Malden, MA: Blackwell.

TANNEN, D. (1986). *That's not what I meant!* London: Dent.

TANNEN, D. (1990). *You just don't understand.* New York: William Morrow.

TANNEN, D. (1994). *Gender and discourse.* New York: Oxford University Press.

THORNE, B., KRAMARAE, C., & HENLEY, N. (Eds.). (1983). *Language, gender and society.* Rowley, MA: Newbury.

WATZLAWICK, P., BEAVIN, J. H., & JACKSON, D. D. (1967). *Pragmatics of human communication.* New York: W. W. Norton.

WEATHERALL, A. (1998). Re-visioning gender and language research. *Women & Language, 21,* 1–9.

WEST, C. (1992). When the doctor is a "lady": Power, status and gender in physician-patient encounters. In J. Coates (Ed.), *Language and gender: A reader* (pp. 396–412). Malden, MA: Blackwell.

WEST, C., & ZIMMERMAN, D. H. (1975). Women's place in everyday talk: Reflections on parent-child interaction. In J. Coates (1998) (Ed.), *Language and gender: A reader* (pp. 165–175). Malden, MA: Blackwell.

WEST, C., & ZIMMERMAN, D. H. (1983). Small insults: A study of interruptions in cross-sex conversations between unacquainted persons. In B. Thorne, C. Kramarae, & N. Henley (Eds.), *Language, gender, and society* (pp. 102–117). Rowley, MA: Newbury.

WHORF, B. L. (1956). Science and linguistics. In J. B. Carroll (Ed.), *Language, thought, and reality.* Cambridge, MA: Massachusetts Institute of Technology Press.

WOOD, J. T., & LENZE, L. F. (1991). Gender and the development of self: Inclusive pedagogy in interpersonal communication. *Women's Studies in Communication, 14,* 1–23.

YAEGER-DROR, M. (1998). Factors influencing the contrast between men's and women's speech. *Women & Language, 21,* 40–46.

ZIMMERMAN, D. H., & WEST, C. (1975). Sex roles, interruptions and silences in conversation. In B. Thorne & N. Henley (Eds.), *Language and sex: Difference and dominance* (pp. 105–129). Rowley, MA: Newbury.

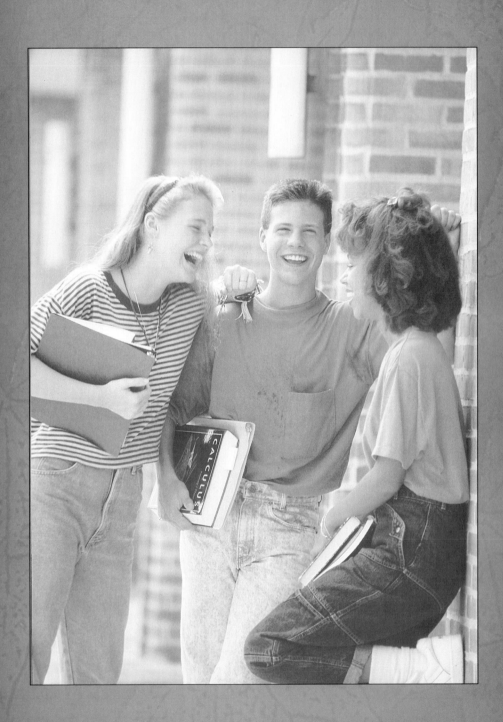

CHAPTER SIX

GENDER AND RELATIONSHIPS

Developing Potential into Reality

CASE STUDY: CHOOSING AND BEING CHOSEN

One of the toughest and most self-esteem–threatening rituals boys and girls face growing up is the choosing game. "Will they choose me for the team?" "Why am I always the last chosen?" "Will I be asked to the prom?" "Will they vote for me?" "How can I get a date?" This game doesn't slow down in college. "I don't want to be in *his* group!" "Will I like my roommate?" "Will the professor call on me in class?" "No one ever asks me!" "Who wants me for their friend?" "Will I get the job?" Students face a multitude of situations where choosing and being chosen is a fact of life. For some other students, the problem is having too many choices, being chosen too many times. For others, the opposite is true. This choosing game is a very energy-consuming activity. The choices you make and the choices others make about you impact how you feel about yourself and your relationships. Given that fact, the questions become: How can I make good choices? How can I help other people to make effective choices about me?

This chapter examines the bases of choices. When we talk with students about the relationship choice process or who chooses whom and why, it seems to come down to one thing: not physical appearance, not opposites attract, but *information*. Students choose students they *know the most about*. And what is the source of this information? *Communication*. The initiation of relationships depends more on information gathered through the communication process than on any other factor, even physical appearance (no matter what the media and the fashion industry would have you believe).

The basic process works like this. You observe, you communicate, you evaluate, you make choices, you act. How relationships develop and change and who takes responsibility for these tasks are questions many of our students have pondered, yet most are not fully aware of the information they use to make their choices. Understanding how the process works and, more importantly, understanding the differences in how women and men deal with these relational issues are critical to long-term personal effectiveness in gender communication. Rather than hoping or believing that if you wait long enough or experiment enough, the perfect friend, dating partner, or mate will find his or her way to you, this chapter suggests a more proactive (rather than reactive) strategy. Relationship initiation and development are based on *choice—choosing* and *being chosen.* You clearly can't have close, personal relationships with everyone, so you must choose. On the flip side, it is very flattering to be chosen and can be very painful not to be.

Hot Topics

- *Barriers* or *roadblocks* to relationship initiation
- How relationships get started in *cyberspace.*
- *Choosing* and being *chosen* in relationships
- The role of *attraction* and *information* in *initiating* relationships
- *Stages* of relationship development
- *Strategies* for relationship initiation
- How sex differences in personal communication skills such as *self-disclosure, empathy, listening,* and *nonverbal expressiveness* and *sensitivity* influence relationship development
- *Movement* and *change* in the stages of relationship development and deterioration
- *Dysfunctional beliefs* about relationship development
- *Stabilizing* a relationship at the appropriate level

BETTER INFORMATION = BETTER CHOICES

Information and *choice.* These two words form the linchpins of this chapter. The information you gather may be based in verbal or nonverbal, conscious or unconscious, or intentional or unintentional communication. What you know informs your communication behavior and forms what you choose. At various points in a developing relationship, you will make decisions about the future of the relationship (we refer to these instances as "choice points"). To illustrate, imagine that you have a superficial friendship with someone at work. However, you decide a more personal friendship with this person is possible. By making that decision, you have exercised some control over the direction of the relationship. You've decided to accelerate the rate of change and move the relationship from one level to another. Each of us has faced decisions such as whether to turn an acquaintance into a friend, a friendship into something deeper, or a romantic relationship *back* to a friendship. Choice points such as these occur frequently and the decisions that arise from them have an obvious impact on the quality of the relationship. Given the importance of information in making these choices, the more you know about making effective choices, the more effective communication can be.

These choice points occur over the life of the relationship. Initiating a relationship, making a new friend, falling in love, and other relationship beginnings are great experiences. When a relationship works, it is an exhilarating feeling. When it doesn't, or when things change for the worse, the feelings can be quite painful. This evolution of feelings is a natural part of relationship change and development, and evolution provides the relational partners with a number of choice points as the relationship develops. Most researchers agree that relationships go through relatively identifiable stages, and it is intriguing to analyze the apparently different roles played by men and women in the movement between stages.

People react differently to various choice points in relationship development. Some may miss the excitement of a brand new relationship, think the relationship is over, and choose to start looking for someone new. Others hang in there, knowing the relationship will continue to develop. Why do some people choose to stay and others leave? Do you think men are more likely to leave, while women are more likely to stay? Who is more likely to talk with their friends about relationship changes? For our male readers, how many times have you gone to your male friends to talk about relationship problems and choices? If you are a woman, how many conversations like this have you had with female friends? Do you think women have more conversations like this than men? Who makes better choices at the various stages of relationship development?

Mark Knapp (1978) was among the first interpersonal communication researchers to write extensively about the relationship development process. He asked some interesting questions about these stages:

1. Are there regular and systematic patterns of communication in each stage on the road to a relationship or its deterioration?
2. How do people talk to each other when they are building, maintaining, or tearing down a relationship?
3. What determines how fast or slow a relationship progresses or dissolves?

These questions are useful guides as you attempt to make sense of the relationship change process. Knowledge of the relationship change process is an example of "forewarned is forearmed." If you know what to expect, if you know what sex differences exist, and if you have the knowledge and skill to help move a relationship from stage to stage, you will have achieved real progress on the road to increased personal effectiveness in gender communication. We describe three stages in this chapter and have given each stage a label. As we explore each stage, compare your own relational history with the information for added insight.

Before getting into the specifics of this chapter, let's clarify our use of the terms *relationship* and *relational partner*. There are all kinds of relationships and the word *relationship* is widely used. When we use the word *relationship* in our gender communication classes, students typically think of dating or romantic relationships rather than other kinds. We will discuss some elements that pertain to relationships in general—all kinds of relationships. Other elements are more relevant to dating or romantic relationships than to other types, and we specifically identify those instances. When we use the term *relational partner* in those specific references to dating relationships, it does not imply the same permanence implied by the term *marital partner*. It is simply a means of identifying the two people in a relationship.

This chapter considers relationships, relational partners, and relationship development from the point of view of choice and information. Have you ever considered relationship initiation from the standpoint of choosing and being chosen? Probably not, because it's a different approach. As you read this chapter, think about strategies you currently use to begin and develop relationships, strategies you have seen others use, and what factors seem to contribute to success. It is possible to become more successful despite abundant evidence of relationship failure. Some relationships are going to fail and, although the experience can be painful, it is to be expected.

RELATIONSHIP ROADBLOCKS

Sometimes relationships just don't go well. At times, barriers arise that get in the way of a successful beginning to a relationship. What *does* get in the way of a good relationship, and what can you do about it?

Roadblock 1: High Expectations

Chapter 4 discussed the impact of the media on our behavior. MTV, movies, and television shows set us up for unrealistic expectations. The media frequently depict attractive, beautiful people engaged in fun, seemingly carefree, highly physical romantic relationships. The media rarely show these relationships six months later, as they have developed over time, nor do they typically depict the work necessary to make relationships successful. Women may fantasize about the perfect man and men may fantasize about the perfect woman, but we know that nobody's perfect, so sometimes when we set high expectations for others and our relationships, we are really setting ourselves up for a fall.

Roadblock 2: This Should Be Easy

You know now that communication isn't a natural thing that you can do successfully just because you've been communicating all your life. So, why do we sometimes think it ought to be easy to just relax and talk to someone? Why, in reality, is communication so difficult in relationships—especially in really important relationships? Effective communication isn't easy and the more you have riding on the success of your relationship, the more difficult communication seems to be (Grove, 1991).

Roadblock 3: Fear of Failure

This is the reverse of Roadblock 2. Chapter 1 described your relational "batting average" and the fact that no one can be successful all of the time. But how many people do you know who are so afraid of failure—failure to initiate and keep a relationship going—that they don't even try to make friends? Failure is part of the relational process, however painful it might be. And, even though it is a cliché, we do learn from failure.

Roadblock 4: If I Just Relax, a Good Relationship Will Find Me

It does seem that the more we want something, the harder it is to get. The more we try to make friends, the less friendly people seem to become. And there are those times when you aren't thinking about dating anyone, when you least expect to meet someone wonderful, and—bingo—Ms. or Mr. Right (or Right Now) comes into the picture. There's no outguessing this process, but you may be setting yourself up for some lonely times if you merely wait and expect friendship or romance to find you. A proactive, balanced approach of introspection, planning, patience, communication skill development, and maybe a bit of faith is likely to generate better results than just waiting for something to happen.

Roadblock 5: The "Bozo Pill"

Some people get really tongue-tied when they talk to someone they are attracted to and interested in. Nothing seems to work, weird sentences come out of their mouths, they break into a sweat, and things generally go from bad to worse. Men and women alike, who are articulate in every other situation, suddenly get an attack of the "Bozos" when they face an attractive person. Sometimes they can't even remember their own names to introduce themselves. Has this ever happened to you? What did you do about it at the time? What *should* you have done? The "Bozos" probably happen to all of us at one time or another.

Roadblock 6: It's Got to Happen Now!

As Carrie Fisher wrote in *Postcards from the Edge*, "Instant gratification takes too long." Some people express a desire to have a remote control for relationships, so they can zip and zap, getting what they want when they want it. Probably all of us could use a bigger dose of patience in our relationships. Solid, successful relationships of all kinds take time to nurture and develop. Wanting too much too soon (and sometimes getting it) can be a big problem. Not taking adequate time to nurture a relationship can sabotage a potentially wonderful relationship before it has had its chance.

Roadblock 7: Giving Up Too Much Just to Have a Dating Relationship

University residence hall advisors describe a problem that they see regularly, the fact that some students (more often female than male) are too willing to compromise themselves sexually or in other ways in order to get a dating relationship started. Are women more prone than men to want dating or romantic relationships, or is this just a stereotype? Women often feel a tension between the traditional message that they should have a man in their lives and the modern messages of careerism and autonomy. Sometimes this desire for acceptance causes people to do things they really don't want to do. No one should have to bend to pressure or be motivated by the desire to impress another person or to achieve some form of social status.

Do any of these roadblocks to beginning relationships sound familiar to you? Do they sometimes keep you from making effective relational choices? Might they keep you from being chosen for relationships as often as you would like? Think about how you would answer these questions as you continue to read about gender communication in relationship initiation.

STAGE 1: IS THERE A RELATIONSHIP GOLD MINE OUT THERE? PROSPECTING AND BEING A PROSPECT

Finding and initiating relationships is a process similar to prospecting. Like a prospector, you are looking for something that will add value to your life (if not actually make you rich!). Like a prospector, you go out into the "field" and examine "samples" for possible value to you. If a sample (person) looks interesting, you can examine him or her more closely. There is (at least) one big difference—while you are examining prospects, they could be examining you. You are a prospect as well as a prospector.

Prospecting—whether for gold or for a relationship—is an active process. This is very different than the wait-for-something-to-happen belief epitomized by the expression, "If it's meant to be, it will be." The proactive approach presented here puts you in charge of your relational life; you neither wait for something to happen nor blame something or someone if it doesn't happen. A proactive approach may increase your opportunity to turn relational potential into reality. Did you ever see the bumper sticker, "So many men, so little time?" In your lifetime, you have the potential to initiate and develop hundreds of relationships. Whether you entered college right out of high school or started your college career later in life, college is a prime time for experiencing various kinds of relationships, and it presents numerous opportunities for relationship initiation.

The first part of stage 1 in relationship development, normally, is seeing others and being seen. Information gathered through observations guides your first choices, and it is the natural place for us to begin our discussion. When men and women go prospecting, what do they look for? What features catch the eye and spark the imagination? We like to ask our male and female students, separately, what they look for in the opposite sex. The sexes' responses are amazingly similar. Both sexes seem to look for people who are physically appealing (but not so exceptionally gorgeous that they are unapproachable), who look nice (usually that means nonthreatening, well-groomed, etc.), who show an appropriate degree of self-confidence, who smile a lot and have a good sense of humor, who aren't too afraid or too macho to show interest, and who will impress their parents and friends. An *Ebony* magazine cited the following attributes as important in the attraction process: appearing approachable, increasing an intrigue factor (meaning that you project yourself as an interesting and captivating person), dressing to enhance not entice, not getting lost in the crowd, having good conversational skills, exuding confidence, combining independence with a touch of vulnerability, staying in good physical shape, having a good sense of humor, and being positive about life in general (Turner, 1990, pp. 27–28, 30). It's interesting that neither our students' list nor the *Ebony* list contains comments about being "Joe Stud" or looking like "Molly Model." The characteristics of a good prospect appear to be quite similar for both sexes.

Cyber-Territory

Obviously, seeing a person is not the only way relationships begin. The Internet has vastly increased opportunities for relationship development. Reporter Tom Maurstad (1996), writing about the relationship possibilities on the Internet, quotes psychologist Neal Goldsmith: "Whatever the special interest you want to name, there are people out there" (p. A18). Communication scholar Malcom Parks, who has researched relationship formation on the Web states: "One of the great things about the Net, for both good and bad, is that it allows you to find and communicate with people of a common interest unusually quickly and on a tremendous scale" (Maurstad, 1996, pp. A17–A18).

Interestingly, some research appears to indicate that gender differences in communication are diminished though computer-mediated communication. Educational researcher McConnell (1997) found women were at less of a disadvantage in computer-mediated communication and could be more participative and more direct than in face-to-face communication. Sociologists Cooper and Sportolari (1997) found that computer networks reduce the importance of physical traits, increase the significance of rapport and similarity, and allow more freedom from gender role constraints. However, many of the common gender stereotypes hold true on the Internet. Men still tend to be more critical and more interested in sex. Internet observer Sutton (1996) found that online communication is male dominated and male oriented. "Generally, men tend to use strong assertions, self-promotions, authoritative orientation, challenge and sarcasm, while women use apologies, questions, personal orientation, and explicit justification in their discourse" (p. 178).

In their research, Adelman and Ahuvia (1992) analyzed videotapes and print ads in addition to Internet communication in their review of mediated channels for mate seeking. They found that mediated channels not only sharply increased the opportunity for meeting eligible people, but also had an impact on how their users understood romantic relationships. Mediated channels allow for (even encourage) inappropriate or excessive self-disclosure and more explicit conversations related to social exchange. These two differences from nonmediated communication can have a potential negative effect when the two people begin to communicate in person.

One of the most interesting aspects of Internet communication is the possibility for identity alteration and gender bending. As Sutton (1996) said, "For once in your life, you can be sure that people are paying attention to what you're saying, and not the way you look or how nicely you dress" (p. 171). You are your words, however you choose to define yourself. It is possible for people to take on totally different identities, to present themselves as a member of the other sex, and to "walk on the wild side" in relative safety. The possibilities for experimentation are endless! On the other hand, you may never know exactly with whom you are communicating; the other person may be experimenting as well. People who meet on the Internet must be careful if they arrange to meet in person. More than one Internet relationship failed to survive the first face-to-face meeting. However, we have students who spend hours on the Internet, go out on computer dates, develop deep relationships, and in some cases, fall in love. Internet relationships can be as meaningful and significant as in-person relationships. While it is clear the Internet may moderate the effects of gender, gender differences in mediated communication are still present and need to be taken into account (Yates, 1997).

As a society, we are only beginning to realize the power of the Internet, but the relationship possibilities are truly mind-boggling. Future research will tell us more about its impact, but it is clear that the Internet has greatly increased the opportunity to develop relationships.

The Role of Attraction in Relationship Initiation

Just what *is* attraction? According to students, it can be "lust," "a sort of chemistry between you and another person," "wanting to have sexual intercourse with another person," "liking someone—not just physically, but for personality traits." You can see from these responses that some people use the term to apply to platonic friendships, in which one person is attracted to another on a non-physical, nonsexual basis, whereas others correlate attraction with sexual interest. For the sake of simplicity in this chapter, when we refer to *attraction*, we mean the basic interest in pursuing a relationship with another person—type unspecified.

> *I've gone for each type. . . I don't really have a type. I have to say that men in general are a good thing.*
>
> *Jennifer Aniston, actor*

The Territory Ahead

Where does attraction start? Its source can be found in a nonverbal communication concept known as *proximity*. Proximity relates to the space (territory) around you and the physical distance between you and someone else, the amount of time you spend physically near that person, how easily you can gain access to her or him, and how physical closeness affects the relationship. While it is possible to be attracted to someone you've never met and will likely never meet, realistically you are more likely to be attracted to someone if you perceive that there are opportunities to be around that person. Early research identified proximity as the most influential variable in attraction (Berscheid, 1985). More recent research and conceptualization refines the idea of physical distance (proximity) into that of *communication distance.* Communication distance is the "number of members of their communication networks an initiator and his or her potential partner would have to go through to reach each other" (Berscheid & Reis, 1998, p. 204). This concept extends proximity by taking into account social context, patterns of expectations, and electronically mediated communication. In other words, you are more likely to be attracted to people you have the *opportunity* to interact with.

Have you ever heard the old saying, "There's one right person in the world for you"? If you believe this, did you ever wonder why that right person probably went to the same school as you, knew the same people you knew, or had the same interests? Why wasn't she or he born in Calcutta? For another example, have you ever been involved in a long-distance romantic relationship? If you have, then you know firsthand the effects of proximity and the importance of being able to gain access (even computer-assisted access) to your relational partner. Simply put, it's hard (and fairly self-defeating) to maintain your attraction for a person if you have no opportunity to interact with that person.

Consequently, proximity can increase or decrease your opportunity for attraction—that's simple enough. Now it's a matter of turning proximity to your advantage. Have you ever stationed yourself in the hallway to get a chance to talk with a certain special person? Or have you ever taken up a dangerous sport or a crazy hobby, just because a certain person participates in that activity? This is the "just-happened-to-run-into-you-at-the-gym" approach. If you have done any of these things, then you've been putting proximity to work for you.

Besides proximity, many other nonverbal communication cues are present in the initial phase of any attraction. Simply defined, *nonverbal communication cues* are those aspects of communication (vocal tone, gestures, eye contact, etc.) that function without words or to help us understand the spoken word. Some of these cues may function at a primal level. For example, magazine columnist Sherry Cohen (1995), suggests that chemistry may be at the heart of attraction. She describes "pheromones," chemicals that appear to be nature's perfume. Perhaps you have found yourself strangely attracted to someone who ordinarily would not interest you or who may even be wrong for you, and you can't quite understand why. It may be the pheromones Cohen describes. Of course, pheromones can work in your favor as well. However, since they are not based in communication, this topic will be left to the chemistry writers. In this chapter, we will be referring to other nonverbal cues that apply to attraction.

Scanning the Prospects

Earlier we mentioned that one prospecting strategy for gathering information and reducing uncertainty about other people is to go out and observe them. You look at others; they look at you. In a large number of social situations the opening gambit in attraction is "the look." Here's a stereotypical set-up: A man looks at a target woman who notices his glance. If she wants to encourage him, she will glance back, then look down. A few seconds later, she'll look again to see if he is still looking. Usually it is the man who maintains the greater degree of eye contact, with the woman looking just often enough to indicate an interest. As the opportunity presents itself, the man will do a quick body scan. This scene is stereotypical; it is not the way it *has* to be.

A few years ago, Nancy (a friend of one of your textbook authors) liked to have some fun with the eye contact game at clubs with friends. If she happened to approach and pass a guy in a club, she would turn to glance back at him just about the same time he was turning around to check out the rear view. She would meet his eyes, then drop her gaze to a few inches below his belt buckle, then look back at his eyes. Most guys were very confused by this approach, but it was truly fascinating to watch the reactions!

Recent research reported by Debi Howell (1996) suggests that women may play the dominant role in scanning prospects. While men do most of the physical approaching in initiating a relationship, (for example, walking over to a woman to start a conversation) men usually only approach after the woman has indicated, nonverbally, that the approach would be welcome. Howell suggests women initiate the contact over two-thirds of the time by making eye contact with a man in whom they are interested and either smiling or prolonging the eye contact to indicate approachability. Men usually will not approach a woman who has not given them a nonverbal expression of interest. How does this idea match with your experience?

Are the sexes different, in terms of how much importance they place on physical appearance? Social psychologist Alan Feingold (1990) found approximately 50 studies supporting the notion that men value physical attractiveness more than women when deciding to initiate and develop heterosexual romantic relationships. What can you make of this sex difference? How does it affect you when it comes to initiating relationships or in relationships initiated with you? Just the knowledge that women and men tend to look for and be attracted to different things is empowering. A woman may find a man's emphasis on looks frustrating, so what are her options? She can set her frustrations aside and use the realization to her advantage by concentrating on her looks when trying to attract a man. Or she can find a male relational partner whose emphasis on and standards for physical attractiveness match her own.

How is this information empowering to men? It may be obvious that a male who knows that women generally place less emphasis on physical characteristics than other qualities (personality, intelligence, kindness and sensitivity, sense of humor, etc.) would find it to his advantage to work on developing these qualities rather than concentrating energy on how he looks. Women are often baffled by men's competitiveness and vanity about looks, being fit, physical signs of aging, and the like. Most women believe that women put far less pressure on men to look good than men put on women. Many women conclude that men are concerned about appearance more out of a need to impress other *men* than a need to impress women. Do you agree?

The Self as Prospect

You are prospecting, but so are other people. Do you consciously try to present a certain image to others so as to be seen as a better "sample"? How do you see yourself? How do you communicate your self-image and value to others, particularly those persons with whom you'd like to have a relationship? Do you project an androgynous, masculine, or feminine image?

Researchers have studied the process of presenting oneself to the public. Noted scholar and social critic Erving Goffman (1959) viewed people as constantly staging dramas that let them display their self-images and project their definitions of situations. The 1998 movie, *How Stella Got Her Groove Back*, depicted people working to project very attractive images. Everyone projects some type of image, and your awareness of the number of times you project your image to someone else may be increasing. You project a self-image regularly, but the question is the degree to which you are consciously aware of what you are projecting.

Understanding your self-image and consistently projecting that image to people will help to reduce uncertainty, both for yourself and others. We don't mean you should find an image and stick with it until you die. In fact, there will be times when you may experiment because you don't know exactly what you want your image to be. For example, a man might test out being the "sensitive listener" rather than attempting to lead all the time. If he decides that this isn't the real him, he might go a different route with the image he wants to project. However, most people do not value a high level of inconsistency.

Placing self-image in the context of gender communication, think about times when you've felt burned by someone who projected a totally different image of himself or herself than was really true. Maybe this person portrayed his or her notion of the ideal masculine man or feminine woman in the hopes of attracting you. When you discover this inconsistency, it's not only confusing, it can be maddening and abusive. Have you ever fallen into the trap of pretending to be some image of an ideal, or who you *thought* you were supposed to be as a woman or a man, instead of the person you really *are*? Projecting false images is hard work and ultimately unsatisfying. What do you do if someone falls in love with your false image?

Another interesting point regarding image and physical attractiveness is that you may see someone you deem attractive but remain unattracted to that person. The research of social psychologists Bar-Tal and Saxe (1976) produced a fascinating observation of human behavior that has come to be known as the matching hypothesis. Their research indicates that while you may appreciate the appearance of someone who is stunningly good looking, you usually have relationships with (and even partner with) people you feel are similar in image and attractiveness to you. An average looking man may appreciate the physical appearance of a very good looking woman, but he is more likely to be attracted to a woman he believes is at a level of attractiveness similar to his own. Thus, it may be that we need to present a physical image in line with how we see ourselves and in line with the kind of people we want to attract.

While initial attraction to a dating partner or potential spouse is usually based on a response to someone's physical appearance, decisions about whether the attraction continues are based on further information. For example, a woman may be attracted to a man's looks initially, but, given more information, she may find herself saying, "What did I ever find attractive in him?" A man may not be physically attracted to a woman at first, but over time and given more information, her looks become incredibly attractive. Then he may find himself wondering, "Did her looks change somehow, or is it just how I *see* her now?" The nonverbal aspects of attraction remain a fascinating subject, but they are only the beginning. Words are next.

Learning about the Prospect

What do people look for? A recent poll in *Parents* magazine found that 78 percent of its respondents said a person should be caring and considerate, 68 percent cited a good sense of humor, 58 percent looked for compatible interests, 57 percent wanted a good conversationalist, 55 percent cited intelligence, 50 percent wanted a good sexual partner, and 49 percent cared about romance. Only 15 percent said the person must have a good figure or a good physique, and only 11 percent said the person should have an attractive face. The list clearly does not focus on appearance, but on information related to aspects other than physical characteristics. How do you get this information?

As you perceive other people and begin to learn about them, understanding the role of information in this process may be helpful. Recall our previous discussions in this text about uncertainty. To briefly review, communication researchers have detected that one of the primary things people do upon meeting someone new who interests them is to reduce uncertainty (Berger & Calabrese, 1975; Berger & Douglas, 1981; Douglas, 1990). We want to know what this person might be like in a friendship or romantic relationship. With some new people, you may make a decision in only a few seconds that the potential for a relationship just isn't there. With others, you decide just as quickly that further interaction is desirable. And while you're making those decisions, the other person is likely doing the same about you. Reducing uncertainty by gaining information enables *choice*—the choice you will make about whether or not to initiate a relationship with someone, as well as the choice someone else will make about you.

Strategies to Learn More

How exactly do people gather information and reduce their uncertainty? Communication scholars Berger and Calabrese (1975) describe three general strategies for reducing uncertainty, all of which are based on information. The strategies are progressive, meaning that people usually start with the first and progress through the other two. Anywhere along the line, however, you can choose to break off the search for information if you deem it too risky or if you discover something that leads you to think the relationship will not be rewarding.

First, people engage in *passive strategies.* You do this when you just watch people without them knowing it. If you are thinking about making friends with someone, you may watch to see who that person hangs out with and what they do. The more observations you make, the more information you gain and the more you know.

The second category of strategies is *active strategies.* An active strategy requires more action than observation and typically involves a third party or another indirect means of gaining information. The most obvious tactic is to ask other people about someone—what the person is like, what he or she does, if the person is involved with someone at the time, and so on. In a study of the dating behaviors of college students by sociologists Knox and Wilson (1981), female and male subjects alike reported that they learned about their current dating partner through a third party. As another active strategy, you can also stage situations to gain information about how another person responds. Haven't you seen (or arranged) situations where one friend sets up another friend who's interested in someone?

The most direct method is referred to as an *interactive strategy,* one that involves asking the interesting party direct questions or engaging her or him in conversation, either one-on-one or in a group. This strategy is considered the most risky, and it takes self-confidence and nerve for most of us, but it seems to be the most reliable, straightforward, and time-efficient method of getting information. It's unwise to assume interactive strategies are for men's use only; women as well as men can actively seek to get to know someone and can make the first move toward getting a relationship started.

The two factors in our discussion of the Prospecting Stage—attraction and information—are factors over which you have some control. Granted, some aspects of physical appearance aren't alterable, even given the advances of modern medicine. Some of us will always be vertically challenged. But a great deal about your appearance, as well as how you communicate information and attraction, can become empowering strategies that will turn your relationship potential into reality.

RECAP

---

choosing, information, choice points, relational partner, prospecting, attraction, proximity, uncertainty, being chosen, reduction, interest, eye contact, image, information gathering strategies, passive, active, interactive strategies

STAGE 2: TESTING THE PROSPECT—CONVERSATIONS

There is no clear-cut line between the first and second stages; each merely has some identifying characteristics. Stage 2 consists of the opening interactions of a relationship. Each person has made the initial choice in favor of the other person and each has indicated a willingness to begin to interact and learn about each other. In this stage, people expend a good deal of energy trying to get the other person to think well of them. Here are a few strategies that help accomplish that goal.

Digging In and Discovering More

As you develop an interest in a person and want to begin a conversation, what do you do? What are the best ways to develop an effective conversation? Your interest, and we use the word *interest* as an extension of attraction, leads to further developments in the communication process. You may be interested in certain qualities of the person, and finding out about these qualities usually takes more active conversational strategies than the elements of attraction, such as proximity and physical appearance, required. This step requires more information—information that can really only be learned through conversation.

Conversation Starters

Conversations have to start somewhere and there has to be an opening line. Everyone laughs at the old pick-up lines of the 1960s and 1970s, lines like "What's your sign?," "Haven't I seen you somewhere before?," and "What's a nice girl like you doing in a place like this?" In fact, a book from 1970 entitled *How To Pick Up Girls!* offered a list of opening lines that guaranteed men success with women. Here are a few of the more laughable ones: "You're Miss Ohio aren't you? I saw your picture in the paper yesterday." "Do you have change for a 10?" "What kind of dog is that? He's great looking." "Here, let me carry that for you. I wouldn't want you to strain that lovely body of yours." "Please pass the ketchup." "Didn't I meet you in Istanbul?" (Weber, 1970, pp. 72–78).

Opening lines can be funny to think and talk about, but they can reduce effective communication down to a gimmick. Packaged opening lines are inconsistent with the principles underlying the receiver orientation to communication because they generally ignore the process of adapting one's communication to the situation and the receiver of the message. So why would someone use a line on someone else? Sometimes it is simply easier—people who might be nervous sometimes resort to trite beginnings just to get the ball rolling. Because of these reasons, we also grant that lines or conversational openers may be useful at times. In addition, opening lines could simply be intended as conversation starters, not necessarily as efforts to pick up or hit on someone. Conversational beginnings that reflect a thoughtful, sincere attempt at interaction can serve as icebreakers between you and someone you are interested in. Maybe you know some things to say that have received relatively positive responses in past conversations. If you define lines in this way, then they can become part of an effective communication repertoire. But are conversation starters more associated with male behavior than female?

Gender psychologists Kleinke, Meeker, and Staneski (1986) found that over 90 percent of their subjects believed it was just as appropriate for a woman to open a conversation with a man as the reverse. In this study, college students generated examples of conversation starters that they had heard or used, including things men might say to women and vice versa. Then the researchers surveyed over 250 college students' preferences for these openers, divided into general

> *Germ phobia is a problem. You have to be selective. It's pretty darn dangerous out there. It's like Vietnam! Dating is my personal Vietnam!*
>
> *Donald Trump,*
> *businessperson*

and situation-specific categories. Here are the five most preferred general openers (in descending order) for women who initiate conversation:

1. "Since we're both sitting alone, would you care to join me?
2. "Hi."
3. "I'm having trouble getting my car started. Will you give me a hand?"
4. "I don't have anybody to introduce me, but I'd really like to get to know you."
5. "Can you give me directions to (anywhere)?"

The top five least preferred openers were these:

1. "Didn't we meet in a previous life?"
2. "It's been a long time since I had a boyfriend."
3. "Hey baby, you've got a gorgeous chassis. Mind if I look under the hood?" (We're *not* kidding.)
4. "I'm easy. Are you?"
5. "What's your sign?"

Do you notice how the first five are really just common ways to get someone talking, rather than suggestive, manipulative lines that make the other person feel uncomfortable or set up? The five preferred openers that men might use on women are as follows:

1. "Hi."
2. "Hi. My name is ___."
3. "I feel a little embarrassed about this, but I'd like to meet you."
4. "That's a very pretty (sweater, dress, etc.) you have on."
5. "You have really nice (hair, eyes, etc.)."

The five least preferred general openers (with the very least preferred listed first) from this study were these:

1. "Is that really your hair?"
2. "You remind me of a woman I used to date."
3. "Your place or mine?" (Some things *never* change.)
4. "I'm easy. Are you?"
5. "Isn't it cold? Let's make some body heat."

Kleinke, Meeker, and Staneski's studies revealed that both women and men tended to agree that cute, flippant conversational openings were less effective than direct or nonthreatening and innocuous ones. We leave it up to your discretion how to use this information, like other topics covered in this chapter. If some of the conversation openers cited here from the research didn't strike you as lines at all, then perhaps you can put them to use.

You Tend to Like People Who Are Like You

Perhaps you have heard the cliché, "opposites attract." Probably more accurate is the notion that opposites attract, but the attraction typically doesn't last. Some people may be interested in others who are radically different from them—mainly because the differences are intriguing. But often these relationships don't last because as the initial intrigue fades, the differences become obstacles, sometimes insurmountable. Research indicates that under most circumstances, you will generally be more interested in someone who holds attitudes, beliefs, and values similar to yours than someone whose attitudes (and especially values) are quite different (Lydon, Jamieson, & Zanna, 1988; Shaikh & Kanakar, 1994; Sharma & Kaur, 1995). Social psychologists Berscheid and Reis (1998) put it bluntly: "The most basic principle of attraction is familiarity. As opposed to the unfamiliar, familiar people usually are judged to be safe and unlikely to cause harm" (p. 205). This familiarity tends to breed comfort in initial relationships. Research on dating partners and with college roommates found that for both the partners and the roommates similarity in the emotional dimensions of the relationship (comfort, ego support, conflict management, sincerity, and warmth) were more important than other dimensions of attraction and contributed to greater relationship satisfaction (Burleson, Kunkel, & Birch, 1994; Varnadore, Howe, & Brownlow, 1994).

Generally, when you look around a room, you gravitate toward people you think are like you and who appear nonthreatening. For example, some years ago, one of your text's authors accepted a position at a new university. Early in his first semester, the college held a reception for new faculty. Upon arriving at the reception, he and his wife saw another couple that appeared to be of the same age who were dressed similarly, and made a beeline toward them. The other couple had exactly the same thought and it turned out that the four became very good friends. This type of example has basis in interpersonal research. Psychologists Aboud and Mendelson (1998) found that among teens, similarities in appearance, sex, age, and race highly influenced interpersonal attraction and choices for beginning conversations. Given a choice, we tend to move toward people we see as being similar to ourselves. So how do you turn this information into a strategy—both for choosing and being chosen?

Remember proximity? It's a good idea to place yourself in the company of people who are similar to you and to learn to what extent those similarities exist. For example, if you think that bar or club scenes are great opportunities for socializing with fun people, you are more likely to find someone with similar attitudes if you look for them in a bar or club than elsewhere. If your religious values are such that you believe attending church is important, then your chances of finding someone with similar values and beliefs are greater in a church setting than other places.

Information gained through these shared interests might form the basis for a decision of whether or not to initiate a relationship with a person. It may not be the case that you intend to initiate a friendship or romantic relationship upon first encountering someone. However, if you do a class project with that person, attitudes, values, and beliefs might surface from extended contact that can inform your relational decision making. When you are in the company of someone attractive who you believe is similar to you, emphasize those similarities. You should even emphasize nonverbal communication similarities. Social psychologists Depaulo and Friedman (1998) indicate that individuals who are attracted to each other demonstrate synchronicity in their nonverbal communication. They are likely to have similar types of gestures, posture, eye contact, and expressions. Generally, it will be to your benefit to let someone know that you see things (figuratively and literally) the same way she or he does.

You Tend to Like People Who Like You

Reciprocity of liking sounds like jargon, but what it basically means is that you are apt to be more interested in someone who likes you than someone who seems neutral or indifferent toward you, or who doesn't like you. Most attraction theorists view expression of liking and esteem as a valuable reward that the recipient is likely to reciprocate (Berscheid & Reis, 1998). Psychologist Kenny (1994) analyzed 10 studies related to attraction and concluded that increased liking becomes more pronounced as the relationship develops if the participants verbalize their esteem and liking.

If this sounds fairly commonsensical, think again. Sometimes you may find yourself liking someone because he or she doesn't seem to respond to your attempts at friendship or won't give you the time of day on a romantic level. This is the trap of the challenge—in most instances it is a poor use of time and energy to try to initiate a relationship with someone who just isn't interested. On occasion, you may have a positive outcome to such a challenge, but more times than not it causes the ego to deflate rather than inflate.

If you are choosing to initiate a relationship with someone, how do you convey your interest? Do you express curiosity about the other person's background or opinions? Do you compliment her or him, or show a concern for his or her well-being? For example, assume you've been introduced to someone a couple of times in social settings. With each occasion, you come to believe the person could become a good friend. How do you convey your interest? Is it common for you to ask the person about herself or himself, including questions about hometown, occupation, hobbies, and the like? Are you more likely to talk about yourself or about nonthreatening topics, such as the weather or sports, rather than to ask the other person questions? Maybe your pattern is more connected to doing mutual activities with another person until the proximity and shared activity just seem to develop into friendship.

On the "being chosen" flip side, is it typical of you to be unaware when someone really does like you? How do you detect that someone is interested, either on a friendship or romantic level? No matter the type of relationship being initiated, interest is usually conveyed via nonverbal channels. After all, few people are likely to walk up and say "Hey; I like you; let's start a relationship." If people are interested in getting to know each other better, first they will probably increase their proximity to each other, both in terms of how often they see each other and how close they get physically when interacting. Other cues of liking, or *immediacy* as nonverbal scholar Albert Mehrabian (1981) termed it, will be present as well, including increased eye contact and head nodding, more direct body position and forward body lean, more animated facial expression, increased touch, increased conversational time, and even the use of more variation in vocal expression.

Mehrabian (1981) also discovered that immediacy involves sex differences. He found that men tended to display indirect nonverbal cues (such as turned out body positions, less eye contact, etc.) even with people they really like. Women display some indirect cues when interacting with less-liked individuals, but they use far more nonverbal immediacy indicators with people they like than men use. More recent research by Sanders, Wiseman, and Matz (1990) found women exhibit more immediate nonverbal behaviors (smiling, eye contact, and proximity) than men. In relationship initiation contexts, this finding has led some people to claim that women are transparent, especially heterosexual women when they are romantically attracted to men. In many instances, this is frustrating for women who cannot detect their effect on men due to the lack of men's nonverbal immediacy cues.

When the cues are detected, men and women tend to interpret the same cues in different ways. Research reported by communication scholar Mongeau (1992) found that men perceive a women's behavior as reflecting greater sexual interest and relational intimacy than women perceive in men's behavior. Men and women rating the same behavior had significant differences—the female saw friendliness and interest, while the men saw more sexual connotations. Abbey (1991) analyzed six studies on the same phenomenon and concluded that "regardless of the situation, men attribute more sexuality to other men and women than do females" (p. 99). This tendency, oddly enough, has implications for occupations such as grocery store clerks. Newspaper reporter Kim Curtis (1998) filed a story about clerks in a major food chain who objected to the store's rule of smiling at and making eye contact with customers. Too many male customers mistook friendliness for flirtation and not only propositioned the clerks, but also, in some cases, followed them around the store.

Flirting behavior research has analyzed this gender difference in perception. Communication researchers Egland, Spitzberg, and Zormeier (1996) report on flirting between cross-sex friends and found that for many people, flirting is an enjoyable and ego-enhancing activity, though care needs to be taken with its implication for the relationship. Women and men appear to interpret flirting behavior differently as well. Sociologist Montgomery (1990) reported that the way you interpret flirting by a member of the opposite sex is usually consistent with the way you perceive your own motive for flirting, and this is consistent with the tendencies noted above. Men interpret women's flirting as communicating sexual interest, whereas women interpret men's flirting as communicating friendship and liking. In any given situation, both interpretations may be wrong. An awareness of these tendencies can keep both men and women from reaching the wrong conclusions about nonverbal cues.

Communication Competence

As conversations develop, a judgment of *communicative competence* appears to outweigh other factors (such as appearance, similarity, etc.) in determinations of how satisfying a relationship will be. Communication researchers Zakahi and Duran (1984) investigated the effects of perceptions of communication competence and physical attractiveness on judgments of communication satisfaction within a relationship. They found only 5 percent of subjects' judgments of relational satisfaction were related to physical appearance, whereas 32 percent were related to communicative competence. From these findings, they conclude, "Although physical attractiveness may be the primary predictor of initial interaction, it does not appear to be as important as communication skills once the relationship is underway" (p. 56). Researchers Bell and Roloff (1991), who studied the communication competence of individuals marketing themselves as potential romantic partners, found similar results. Subjects who were high in competence reported less loneliness, had greater relationship options, and reported greater levels of relationship development. Communication researchers Logo and Ashmore (1992) commented on the role of social communication skills as moderating the impact of physical attractiveness. So it is more important to work on your competence (or personal effectiveness) in gender communication than your physical appearance.

How do you do that? What do you work on? Although many factors come into play, one seems to make the most difference in the developing relationship: listening. Since we are major proponents of the receiver orientation to communication, it's no surprise that we believe listening ability more significantly controls the direction of a relationship than speaking ability. But here we refer to a special kind of listening— the skill of listening to confirm someone else's self-concept (Cissna & Keating, 1979; Leaper, Carson, Baker, & Holliday, 1996; Lifshitz & Shulman, 1983).

Have you ever said something to someone whose lack of response made you feel like you were completely invisible? Or maybe the person responded with her or his own ideas, never acknowledging yours (zero empathy). On a more positive note, have you ever found yourself talking more and about more personal things to someone, only to stop and wonder how you got to that depth in the conversation? In both positive and negative circumstances, the quality of the listening most likely brought about the result.

Communication scholar Evelyn Sieburg (1969) described some basic aspects of *listening to confirm:*

1. Directly acknowledging another person's communication and responding to it verbally and nonverbally.
2. Giving a supportive response by expressing understanding and reassurance.
3. Clarifying the content, feelings, or both expressed in the other's message by asking questions, paraphrasing what the other person said, or encouraging more communication.
4. Expressing positive feelings that communicate support and confirmation of the other person.

Listening to confirm is not a common event. All too often one person (frequently male) monopolizes the conversation while the other person, frequently female, just listens (or pretends to). This is not the definition of a good conversation. Impressing the other person with your verbal ability usually will not result in a judgment of communication competence leading to a developing relationship. Confirming listening, on the other hand, is a powerful motivator in the decision to continue a relationship and build positive relationships (Rosenfeld & Richman, 1997). If the other person can listen to you in a confirming, supportive manner, then you will be more likely to want that relationship to continue.

Does one sex appear to value this style of listening more than the other? Communication researchers Richmond, Gorham, and Furio (1987) asked male and female college students to indicate how likely they would be to use a variety of communication strategies to get to know someone better—someone they might want to date. Female subjects in the study preferred such conversational strategies as asking questions in order to elicit disclosure from the other person, listening intently and paying close attention to the other person's responses, allowing the other person to control the conversation and future activities, and generally showing empathy and sensitivity to someone's concerns. Male subjects preferred such strategies as actively communicating to make the other person feel important and to validate the other's self-concept, putting themselves in positions to be included in future events, presenting a positive, interesting image of themselves to the other person, and taking charge of conversations and planning future activities. On all but three possible strategies, female and male subjects responded significantly differently in terms of how likely they were to employ various strategies. Where does listening appear?

This research is useful if you are interested in getting a relationship off the ground. Understanding what men and women might do to be liked is empowering information. Sometimes a woman might interpret a man's proactive communication as a signal of self-absorption. That might be a correct interpretation in a given situation, but his style or strategy might really indicate a desire to be liked rather than to be the focus of attention. A man might interpret a woman's reactive, responsive style as timidity or as a lack of confidence, when, in reality, the woman is employing a commonly used strategy. Her style may have nothing to do with her level of confidence.

Developing a full range of communication strategies can make a person a more personally effective communicator, friend, and relational partner. Well-rounded, flexible individuals develop the ability to respond with the best strategy for the situation, independent of one's sex.

Deciding to Continue

By now in the development of a relationship, first conversations have been successful enough to make you feel there is real potential with someone. Communication researchers Redmond and Vrchota (1997), in analyzing the effect of initial interactions on attraction, found that most decisions about attraction were made in the first few minutes of a conversation between two people. Enhancing the positive qualities of these initial interactions will increase the possibility that both individuals will make a positive choice.

Once you have made the decision to continue, you look for information and communication behavior that will suggest to you that the relationship has longer-term potential. By *longer-term potential,* we mean you will come to the point at which you decide whether or not to move any relationship—platonic, romantic, and so on—into a deeper phase with more long-lasting effects. On what do you base this decision?

At this point, the question, "Am I getting what I want out of this relationship?" becomes a major factor. It's highly likely you and the other person in your relationship are both asking this question. Not only that, you're both comparing what you're getting out of the relationship with what you think the other person is getting out of it.

In 1959, a social science researcher, George Homans (1959), proposed an interpersonal theory known as *social exchange.* Homans viewed interpersonal interaction from an economic perspective, proposing that one

> *If you never want to see a man again, say, "I love you. I want to marry you. I want to have children"--they leave skid marks.*
>
> *Rita Rudner, comedian*

could view relationships as deals or bargains in which parties compared the costs likely to be incurred (e.g., time, money, effort) with the rewards likely to be received (companionship, heightened self-esteem, acceptance). According to this theory, one is more likely to stay in relationships that minimize costs and maximize rewards.

Feminist scholars have been critical of social exchange theory as a cogent explanation of why relationships continue. One basis for this criticism stems from the view that different standards apply to men and women regarding what counts as costs and rewards. In our society, women often feel significant pressure to be in a dating or romantic relationship or a marriage because for centuries women's relationships with men have legitimized their existence. Even though these notions are changing, some women still believe that any relationship—no matter how destructive or costly—is better than no relationship at all. For women in costly relationships, the reward of just having a man in one's life outweighs the costs or toll the relationship may take.

Another criticism maintains that social exchange theory actually fosters greater male power in relationships. As feminist psychologists Unger and Crawford (1996) explain, men more often than women bring resources such as money, education, and prestige to relationships—resources that are more highly valued in our society than emotional nurturance, for example. This places the man in the power position, which implies that he holds rights to financial decision making. A problem occurs, according to Unger and Crawford, when that decision-making right about money is extended to decision making about other things. Another problem occurs when a woman brings more earning power to a relationship. Because of remnant societal attitudes about sex roles, the woman's resource contribution may not necessarily identify her as the powerholder and decision maker.

There is merit in the criticism of social exchange theory, but the criticisms may have actually increased the practical value of the theory when it comes to making a decision to continue a relationship. The criticisms can cause people to take a longer look at what they deem to be the rewards and costs of any romantic relationship or friendship. Then they can compare their own cost-reward criteria to another person's and to that of society in general. Setting your own terms for costs and rewards will help you determine what exchange must be present for you to continue in relationships.

Sometimes the best way to discover cost-reward information about one another is to simply talk about it, to ask one another, "What's important to you in this relationship?" Having a discussion like this just may not seem normal or comfortable for you in the beginning stages of relationships. But, at some time and in some way, you will want to ask some important questions. How will you negotiate the difference? More generally, how will each of you react if relational rewards aren't being realized or the costs are running too high? It's wise to discover how people view these kinds of issues so you can negotiate ways to bring the costs and rewards into balance.

RECAP

affinity seeking, opening lines, reciprocity of liking, communication competence, listening to confirm, social exchange theory, decision-making, attitude and value similarity, confirmation

---

STAGE 3: DEVELOPING THE CLAIM AND ESTABLISHING THE RELATIONSHIP

After relationships are established, they may stabilize at a particular level. Sometimes this may work; sometimes not. This natural tendency for relationships to reach a level and stay there generates two questions: How do you effectively stabilize a relationship at the level you want? How do you change the level when change is what you want? Many of the communication behaviors and strategies that assisted you in getting to stage 3 will also be valuable as the relationship continues to develop (Dindia, 1992). Most communication skills discussed in this section will apply at each stage of the relationship.

As we begin to answer these questions, an examination of a relationship that has ended can provide some insight. Maybe one of your relationships ended because one or both of you wanted to change the level, but you couldn't agree on a new level. Did it end because one person saw no possibility for change and the relationship just no longer met her or his needs, or did it end just out of neglect? Look at these questions again in light of gender communication. Which relationships tend to be the ones you would like to change, same-sex or other-sex? Who seems to take responsibility for relationship change—women or men?

Personal Communication Skills

This section focuses on personal communication skills that can help stabilize a relationship or move it to a different level. While literally dozens of communication variables can affect the outcome of a relationship, we describe four that are most central to the relationship development process. In describing self-disclosure, empathy, listening, and nonverbal expressiveness and sensitivity, we explore some traditional sex differences and how members of each sex might expand their communication behavior repertoire to become more personally effective.

Self-Disclosure

You probably know by now that it's hard to make effective decisions or act effectively toward another person without accurate and useful information. Women and men both need information, but each sex asks for, gives, and emphasizes different kinds of information. The most common means of actively sharing information is known as *self-disclosure.*

While many definitions of self-disclosure exist, most are similar to one offered by interpersonal communication authors Judy Pearson and Brian Spitzberg (1990). They define self-disclosure as "communication in which a person voluntarily and intentionally tells another person accurate information about himself or herself that the other person is unlikely to know or find out from another source" (p. 142). This definition reinforces our earlier focus on the importance of information and uncertainty reduction in initiating a relationship.

The conventional wisdom is that women like to self-disclose more than men, especially about relationships. Women are stereotypically seen as more willing to convey information about themselves to others. Conversely, men are stereotyped as strong, silent types. Interestingly enough, these stereotypes are supported by some of the disclosure research. For example, interpersonal communication researchers Greenblatt, Hasenauer, and Friemuth (1980) reported that women disclosed more and received more disclosure than men. They also found that men disclosed more often and more openly to women than to other men. Specifically, in terms of the depth and breadth of information the participants share with one another, female-female relationships have been ranked first in several studies, followed by male-female relationships. Male-male relationships rated lowest on degree of intimacy and amount of disclosure (Derlega, Winstead, Wong, & Hunter, 1985; Henley, 1986; Ickes, 1985). Communication researchers Derlega, Metts, Petronio, and Margulis (1993) noted an interesting exception to the disclosure norm in their analysis of first dates. Given the general expectation that men take the initiative in dating and other aspects of the initiation of a relationship, men also may set the tone and level of self-disclosure during the first date. Many women wait for the man to take the lead, even in self-disclosure. Psychologists Shaffer, Pegalis, and Bazzini (1996) found that the only time highly masculine men exhibited high levels of disclosure was in first dates with women they anticipated dating again.

Winstead (1986), a gender researcher, suggests that these trends may reflect a self-fulfilling prophecy, in that some people consciously or unconsciously live up to the sexual stereotypes. However, we should note that not all research supports the stereotype. Communication researchers have found that men and women had very similar levels of disclosure on many topics such as religious views, ambitions and goals, career choice, health, and so on. However, women were much more likely to take risks in their disclosure, particularly by relating sensitive feelings and personal problems (Dindia & Allen, 1992; Sanders, Wiseman, & Matz, 1990).

Why are women considered better people to disclose to? Women are usually seen as more supportive and responsive (and as better listeners), which encourages others to open up to them. Thus, they are more likely to be the targets of others' disclosure. Interpersonal communication researchers Petronio, Martin, and Littlefield (1984) found women feel it more important than men that the receiver of disclosure "be discreet, trustworthy, sincere, liked, respected, a good listener, warm, and open" (p. 270). In addition, these researchers reported women feel more strongly than men that it is important for a discloser to feel accepted, to be willing to disclose in an honest and frank manner without being anxious, and to not be provoked into giving information. Perry, Turner, and Sterk (1992) make the point that for most women, disclosure functions as an invitation to more disclosure, while men tend (even in disclosure) to be competitive and to trade disclosures. Psychologists Stephens and Harrison (1985) identified the feminine communication style as characterized by emotional sensitivity, sympathy, and consideration. Men tend to preserve a masculine image; disclose more about their own strengths (such as professional or athletic successes); and use a dominant, assertive, and aggressive communication style. Given that, who would you rather disclose to? Men who adhere to a strong, masculine gender role not only disclose less than androgynous men and women, but are much less likely to be targets of others' disclosure (Greenblatt, Hasenauer, & Friemuth, 1980). If a man is interested in information to use in developing effective relationships, then the masculine gender role may inhibit that goal.

When you think about yourself as a target of disclosure, it may be helpful to consider how you respond to someone's disclosure. For example, if you are listening to a strong, silent–type man's disclosure, what type of response style might match his particular needs? Both sexes may need to adjust their response style to more fully match the needs of the sender, since this is an integral part of the receiver orientation to communication.

For several reasons, men often have difficulty disclosing to other men. Psychologist Sidney Jourard (1971) described the effect of this on men's health in a book chapter entitled, "The Lethal Aspects of the Male Role." Jourard's research determined that men who have difficulty expressing their feelings also had higher levels of stress-related diseases compared to men who were able to disclose more fully. Nondisclosure not only affects relational health, but personal health as well. More recent research supports this finding, noting that male role stress has not significantly declined since Jourard's chapter was published (Copenhaver & Eisler, 1996).

One potential reason for less male disclosure was suggested by researchers Derlega and associates (1993), who found that North American white males are likely to believe that task accomplishment is a more important goal and emotional control facilitates it. Two (or more) men together are likely to work on the task while maintaining an air of composure even when things are not going well. Perhaps this is changing. Research reported by Parker and Parrott (1992) found that younger men were more likely to engage in disclosure about feelings than elderly men and more likely to engage in disclosure with friends.

Since the stereotypical masculine role implies that men don't disclose to other men, men rely more on women as outlets for disclosure. Men are generally open only with lovers and other women, according to research. As Snell, Miller, and Belk (1988) contend, "Men, it seems, are dependent upon women listeners for emotional self-expression" (p. 69). In self-disclosing conversations, men may express uncertainties, vulnerabilities, and weaknesses that they would rarely disclose to another man. As a result, many men select women as the targets of emotional disclosure because it is unlikely that they will find a male partner with whom to share these issues. If you are a female reader, would you say in your conversations with men the amount and level of disclosure is equal? If not, which way is the scale tipped? For either sex, do you find yourself falling into the stereotypical disclosure patterns?

There are reasons for the differences in men and women regarding disclosure. Social pressure on both sexes regarding the appropriateness of disclosure can be pronounced. One study found that women were judged more positively when disclosing more information because disclosure is attributed to their high degree of affiliation and supportiveness. Men were rated as *less* competent by both men and women when showing a high level of disclosure (Jones & Bruner, 1984). That's not good news. In other research, a man who hid his fears was judged more appealing to some women than a man who was more emotionally forthright (Zillman, Weaver, Mundorf, & Aust, 1986). Women are reinforced for disclosing, which generates more disclosure. The opposite seems to be the case for men; they receive more negative reinforcement, especially from peers, so they disclose less. Do women generally react supportively when a man discloses personal information, especially if it has to do with fears and uncertainties, or do they think him "less of a man" because of what he said? How do men typically react when a male friend discloses fears and uncertainties? Perhaps both men and women need to look at how supportive and responsive they are to men's disclosure since responses can either encourage or discourage the sharing of personal information.

Beyond socialization, do other reasons exist as to why men keep their thoughts to themselves? Here's one explanation: Some men are generally inexpressive as a means of maintaining power and control (referred to as the "Clint Eastwood" effect). They see giving information as giving up control. In an era where information is power, giving out too much information may give others too much power. The business world reinforces this attitude—the term *businesslike* has the connotation of being "without feelings." In relationships, however, balance of power and disclosure appear to assist in the development of satisfying friendships, romantic relationships, marriages, and working relationships with peers. But some men excuse the withholding of information by saying, "We don't tell women (or anyone) things because we don't want them to worry." Many people, especially women, see that as a fear of intimacy and as a move to increase relational distance.

The content of disclosure is also important to relational development, and there are clear differences between the sexes on what might be defined as disclosure (Derlega, Durham, Gockel, & Sholis, 1981). Some men may think they are disclosing when they talk about work. After all, for many men, that's what is most important in their lives. Women tend to talk about the self when expressing feelings about people or personal issues. Gender scholar Barbara Bate (1988) suggests that each sex gives "information that the sender considers essential to intimacy and the receiver finds pointless" (p. 186).

Following up this point on the relationship between intimacy and disclosure, magazine reporter Tavris (1992) makes the case that in present-day relationships, the feminine model has become the dominant one. She contends that women appear to

> be better than men at intimacy because intimacy is defined as what women do; talk, express feelings, disclose personal concerns. Intimacy is rarely defined as sharing activities, being helpful, doing useful work, or enjoying companionable silence. Because of this bias, men rarely get credit for the kinds of loving actions that are more typical of them. (p. 100)

Does disclosure need to be based in words? Perhaps men disclose themselves partially through what they do with their partners—some men who have difficulty disclosing with words attempt to disclose through actions. Wood and Inman (1993) make a case for considering male joint activities (basketball, watching sports together, etc.) as a path to closeness in male friendships—men seek and express intimacy in nonverbally expressive ways. While this may be an overgeneralization, if certain forms of disclosure are important to your relational partner or friend, perhaps they should be important to *you*.

A number of researchers suggest that a positive combination of femininity and masculinity contributes to a person's ability and willingness to form satisfying relationships. Studies identify androgynous people as being more flexible and adaptable, which allows for a potentially broader range of encounters, a higher level of self-disclosure, and a decreasing potential for loneliness (Wheeless & Lashbrook, 1987; Wheeless, Zakahi, & Chan, 1988). Thus, it appears that it is not just your sex, but how you play out your gender role that makes a difference.

So what does all this mean? Here's what it could mean to you:

1. There are differences in the way men and women (and feminine, androgynous, and masculine individuals) give and receive disclosure.
2. Each sex needs to understand its own general tendencies in giving and receiving disclosure, as well as the tendencies of the other sex. Knowledge of these tendencies may help you compensate for them.
3. Each sex needs to understand what constitutes disclosure for the other and to react in a manner that supports the disclosure and the discloser.
4. This understanding can help each person expand his or her disclosing repertoire.
5. Effective use of self-disclosure is central to relationship acceleration or movement from one stage to another.

Progress on these five points is important to the development and growth of any relationship. Now let's turn to more detail on how you might respond to someone's self-disclosure.

The Big "E": Empathy

Understanding and responding effectively to another person is critical to long-term relational effectiveness. You probably value people who seem to understand you and you probably want to increase contact with them. Most researchers view this type of deep understanding as *empathy*.

Empathy is a difficult concept to define; yet a basic understanding of the concept is needed to begin our discussion. Interpersonal communication researchers Stiff, Dillard, Somera, Kim, and Sleight (1988) described three relevant dimensions of empathy. These included *perspective-taking*, described as a cognitive ability to adopt the viewpoint of the other person; *emotional contagion*, described as happening when one person experiences an emotional response parallel to that of the other person; and *empathic concern*, described as a sympathetic and altruistic concern for the other person (p. 199). Empathy seems to be a concept (and skill) that expresses a full understanding of and concern for the other individual at both cognitive (content) and emotional-relational dimensions of the relationship.

> *J don't put a gender tag on empathy. J've seen films and read books by men that J would have sworn were written or filmed by women. J think there's elements of the masculine and feminine in all of us.*
>
> *Natalie Merchant,*
> *singer/songwriter*

Recent research underscores the power of empathy for enhancing the quality of close relationships. Researchers Bissonnette, Rusbult, and Kilpatrick (1997) found that the ability to correctly infer a partner's thoughts and feelings and to respond supportively provides the foundation for other relationship-enhancing behaviors, including accommodation, social support, intimacy, and effective communication. Communication researcher Mark Redmond (1985) added a critical point to this discussion. It is not enough to be empathic; the other person must perceive you as having empathy. It does you no good to have empathy if the other person never finds out you do.

How do women and men show empathy in relationships? It's unwise to assume that members of the opposite sex see the world in the same way you do. Nor can you assume that someone of the opposite sex will express empathy in the same way you do. The stereotype suggests women are more empathic than men; however, research has found mixed results regarding differences, according to both gender and sex. One study found no significant differences between the sexes related to empathetic ability (Brehm, Powell, & Coke, 1984). Other research focused on gender differences rather than sex. Psychologist Sandra Bem (1974) found that traditionally feminine participants demonstrated more apparent empathy than less traditional women because traditionally feminine women are socialized to exhibit supportive responses. Psychologists

ROSE IS ROSE reprinted by permission of United Feature Syndicate, Inc.

Fong and Borders (1985) found androgynous individuals were more empathic, regardless of sex. More recent research has suggested there are no significant differences between women and men in empathic ability (Graham & Ickes, 1997), but there seems to be differences in the extent to which men and women are willing to use their abilities in interpersonal communication—women are more willing to demonstrate empathy and do so more often (Reis, 1998). An important part of the movement toward more androgyny is the expansion of your abilities to both feel and express empathy for others.

The ability to both feel and express empathy is a fundamental skill to add to your communication repertoire as you move to more androgynous communication. The expression of empathy can do much to strengthen and deepen a relationship. Interpersonal communication researchers Pearson and Spitzberg (1990) identify communication behaviors that express empathy, including inviting additional comments from someone who is disclosing, identifying areas of agreement, providing clear verbal responses, and providing affirming feedback. As you contemplate developing a relationship, empathy will play a significant role because it helps deepen a relationship and move it from one stage to another. In general, both men and women tend to trust and disclose more to persons who can effectively demonstrate empathy.

Are You Listening?

Listening is closely related to empathy in that both enhance disclosure, increase trust, and decrease psychological distance between people. Listening and responding to disclosure are obviously important in encouraging or discouraging further disclosure. Listening and responding, however, have been identified as "what women do." Gender researchers Borisoff and Merrill (1998) describe how the phenomenon of listening is portrayed as a passive (thus female) behavior, while speaking is portrayed as active (thus male). Many men and many women behave in conversations as if this inaccurate portrayal were true: It is the man's job to talk, the woman's job to listen.

> *Listening to a woman is almost as bad as losing to one. There are only three things that women are better at than men: cleaning, cooking, and having sex.*
>
> *Charles Barkley, basketball player*

Beyond this basic difference, other differences in listening patterns exist. These differences can help or hurt relationship maintenance and development. In her book, *You Just Don't Understand*, Deborah Tannen (1990) discusses gender differences in listening. As we discussed in Chapter 5, men and women seem to have very different styles: Men focus on the content of what is said, and women on the relationship between the interactants. For example, when someone discloses a personal problem or issue, men seem to listen for solutions and to give advice to solve the problem. This may or may not be what the speaker wants. Women, on the other hand, tend to listen to reflect understanding and support for the other person. As you might guess, this behavior makes both sexes feel more understood. This basic difference also leads to a difference in the amount of effort each sex puts into listening. Men tend to tune things out that they can't solve right away or wonder why they should even listen if there isn't a problem to solve. Women tend to become more involved and connected to the speaker and see listening as something important to do for the other person. Communication researcher Melanie Booth-Butterfield (1984) concludes from her studies that women and men "learn to listen for different purposes and have different listening goals. The primary contrast appears in task versus interpersonal understanding; males tend to hear the facts while females are more aware of the mood of the communication" (p. 39).

This difference can lead to frustration between the sexes. For example, if a man uses male listening behavior with a woman and begins to offer immediate solutions to a concern she is expressing, she may feel that he is dismissing and trivializing those concerns. Men tend to listen to solve problems, not to express support. A woman may react to this rush to a solution by dismissing him as "someone who just doesn't understand." If she rejects the solutions proposed, the man may feel misunderstood. After all, he was just trying to help. Whether attention or advice, it's a good idea to find out what the other person wants in a conversation so that you can apply the appropriate listening behavior.

As we look at expanding our repertoire of communication behaviors, men may need to pay closer attention to listening and to the nonverbal cues that support listening. One suggestion is for men to make more listening noises such as "uh-huh," "yeah," and other encouragers so the other person feels listened to. These noises, called *back-channeling* by a variety of researchers (Aries, 1996), serve to draw out more information from the speaker.

Listening is also related to power (Tannen, 1990). Men tend to use talk to establish status, whereas women use listening to empower others. If men do see things as "one-up, one-down" in listening, then careful listening can be seen as a loss of power and control (e.g., "If I hop to what she says, then I'm subordinate."). This is a real issue for some men (Warshaw, 1992). However, if each sex holds the same value expressed in Chapter 1, that of equality of power, then listening can be used to support and strengthen the closeness of a relationship. It does not need to be a source of power differences.

As in disclosure, an awareness of the different styles of listening behavior can do much to increase the likelihood that you will apply the appropriate listening behavior to match your (and the other person's) intent in the situation. As each sex develops an awareness of its own tendencies and an understanding of each other's tendencies in listening, then listening can be used effectively to generate the kind of relationship both people want (Bostrom, 1997).

Nonverbal Communication Expressiveness and Sensitivity

An integral component of the receiver orientation to communication, as well as one of the most useful skills in demonstrating empathy and effective listening, is *nonverbal communication expressiveness* and *sensitivity*. Albert Mehrabian (1970) first described these skills in terms of nonverbal *immediacy,* as discussed earlier in the chapter. Generally, as one person in a relationship uses more immediate and direct nonverbal communication, the other person feels support and is more likely to value the interaction and the relationship.

Would it surprise you to learn that women tend to use more immediate nonverbal communication than men? We suspect not, since you probably know by now that women's behaviors, both verbal and nonverbal, tend to emphasize their connection to and affiliation with others. Again, it's not that women value relationships more than men, but that women more actively communicate the importance of relationships by utilizing nonverbal channels to adapt to their partner, accommodate his or her nonverbal style, and adopt greater nonverbal expressiveness (Burgoon, 1994).

This point of view is supported by social psychologists Depaulo and Friedman (1998), who, in summarizing trends in research, stated "in general, women are more open, expressive, approachable, and actively involved in social interactions than are men. Their faces are more legible than men's, and they smile and gaze at other people and approach them more closely than men" (p. 11). This appears to be true across the age span. Tannen (1994) analyzed the conversations of children and young adults of both sexes to compare nonverbal cues during conversation. At each of the four age levels studied (second-, sixth-, and tenth-grade students, and 25-year-old adults), girls and women sit closer to each other, align their bodies more directly facing each other, have greater eye contact, and touch more. At each age level, boys and men sit at angles to each other, look more at their surroundings than each other, and give the impression of restlessness and diffused attention. Boys and men appear to be less engaged. However, Tannen points out that the appearance of disengagement does not necessarily mean the conversation is disengaged. In fact, the tenth-grade boys engaged in very disclosing conversation. Tannen concludes that conversational engagement patterns are different between men and women. These differences may lead to negative evaluation misunderstood or measured by the standard of immediacy. Again, an awareness of these differences can assist both men and women in using nonverbal communication to support their goals for the conversation.

Tannen's descriptions fit with earlier research that found men tend to talk at angles to each other and don't look directly at each other, use more signals of power, and are less immediate in conversations with other men. Women, in conversations with other women and with men, are more likely to face people physically and look directly at others (Ellyson, Dovidio, & Fehr, 1981; Hall, 1984; Mulac, Studley, Wiemann, & Bradac, 1987; Tannen, 1990). Women also display more general immediacy behaviors than men, such as forward lean, direct body orientation, head nodding, smiling, and touching (Deutsch, LeBaron, & Fryer, 1987; Fugita, Harper, & Wiens, 1980; Jones, 1986). Part of the explanation for this difference in behavior relates to the basic idea that a person in a subordinate position usually makes more eye contact than a person in a dominant position (Hickson & Stacks, 1993). Beyond that explanation, women appear to be more comfortable with greater levels of eye contact than men.

An overuse of these behaviors can make the other person uncomfortable—if you concentrate too much on being responsively correct you may not be able to really listen. Communication researchers Sabatelli and Rubin (1986) define nonverbal expressiveness as "an individual's spontaneous tendency to accurately communicate his or her emotional state to others via nonverbal channels" (p. 121). Note the word *spontaneous*. Results from their study indicate that those people who display nonverbal information in an automatic and uncensored manner create more favorable impressions on others. They also found, interestingly enough, that even negative uninhibited nonverbal responses result in more attractive perceptions of a person than awkward and censored nonverbal signals.

It's hard to practice your nonverbal expressiveness so it appears natural and unrehearsed to others—that's almost a contradiction in terms. But becoming more nonverbally expressive and sensitive doesn't come naturally for many of us; we have to learn what skills work and when to use them, and then practice their use. With enough practice and positive reinforcement from others, your nonverbal sensitivity and expressiveness can become a more natural element of your communication repertoire.

Spending some time watching other people and comparing their use of immediate nonverbal cues to your own might cause you to become more self-aware. Do you think it would improve your relationships if you were more nonverbally expressive and sensitive? For female readers, it also might be a good idea to think about how you would react to a man who uses a higher degree of immediacy cues than the average. At what point might the use of these cues make you uncomfortable? If both members of any kind of relationship are interested in developing an effective relationship, then attention to nonverbal cues and their use will play a significant role.

Effective use of the four skills just discussed—self-disclosure, empathy, listening, and nonverbal expressiveness and sensitivity—will likely lead to greater feelings of closeness and less psychological distance between persons in a relationship. When issues arise that cause you to make decisions about a relationship (sometimes referred to as "decision points"), these basic communication skills can do much to help you implement effective choices. These four skills can also serve as relationship accelerators, meaning that when they are used well, they can accelerate the movement between stages in a relationship.

Opening a New Vein

It seems that everyone wants relationship satisfaction and will work to achieve it. Each of us has a strong motivation for the perfect relationship, but we may not have the knowledge and skill to effectively advance in that direction.

When Things Change

Everyone faces countless decisions in relationships from the abstract (e.g., Where is this relationship going? Where do I want it to go?) to those made on the spur of the moment (e.g., You have an opportunity to ask a co-worker to have a cup of coffee with you, opening up the possibility of a friendship rather than just a professional relationship). These decisions offer many possibilities for growth, development, and change. But some people fear change because they believe it signals the beginning of the end for the relationship. For example, a woman and a man may have a new, intense relationship. If the intensity changes, one or both may view it with alarm and believe "something must be wrong." It doesn't have to be. Change and evolution in relationships are natural and expected, and probably should be viewed as a sign of potential growth rather than decline.

In addition to being expected, change sometimes can be desired. It is possible to communicate so that you influence the amount and rate of change. For example, have you ever felt dissatisfied with a relationship and wanted to move it to a deeper level? Are there strategies you could follow to accelerate the rate of change in a relationship? Are there male-female differences regarding movement in relationships? These are provocative questions.

In her book, *The Ship That Sailed Into the Living Room,* Sonja Johnson (1991) presents an insightful view that casts the relationship itself as a third entity, separate from the two people involved. Johnson describes the "relation Ship" as a large object between the two people that comes with its own expectations and rules. For example, people in relationships are supposed to do things like "work on the relationship." Johnson says the Ship virtually "shouts" orders at the two people in it. Johnson's perspective—that it is the relationship that deserves to be examined and possibly changed, not either of the people involved—sheds light on two important and helpful factors: (1) each relationship comes with its own built-in patterns of expectations; and (2) change and movement need to focus on the patterns in the *relationship*, not the *individuals*.

This is a useful perspective. When you say to someone, "We have a relationship," do patterns of expectations arise almost automatically? Are the expectations the same for men as for women? Can the female member of the relationship say as easily as the male "I'm going out to get a beer; see you later." While this is a superficial example, perhaps many relation Ships come with different expectations for men and for women, different expectations regarding control, emotions, amount of time spent together, quality of communication, basic treatment of each other, and so forth.

Helping Change Happen

What can be done to propel a relationship from one level to another? Are women and men likely to use similar strategies or different ones? As you read this material, consider your own relationships and *think* about whether change or movement is on the horizon in them.

A study by interpersonal communication researcher James Tolhuizen (1988) investigated communication strategies used to change casual dating relationships into serious dating relationships. While his research focused on dating relationships, the strategies he identified are applicable to most other contexts. These strategies include the following (listed in descending order of use):

1. Increased amount of contact.
2. Relationship negotiation (i.e., direct discussion about the relationship, feelings in the relationship, and the future).
3. Social support and assistance (e.g., asking for advice, information, and support from others in attempts to intensify a relationship).
4. Increased rewards.
5. Direct definitional bid (e.g., "Here's what I think we should do with this relationship.").
6. Accepting a direct definitional bid.
7. Tokens of affection.
8. Personalized communication through verbal expressions of affection.
9. Suggestive actions (i.e., flirting).
10. Nonverbal expressions of affection.
11. Social enmeshment (e.g., "I want you to meet my family.").
12. Changing/improving one's personal appearance.
13. Increased sexual intimacy.
14. Adapting self-presentation (i.e., altering how you communicate yourself to others).

While this a rather lengthy list, we have included it because you probably will recognize at least some of the strategies as familiar.

In studying men's and women's use of these strategies, Tolhuizen found that men reported using direct definitional bids (e.g., "Let's have this kind of relationship") and verbal expressions of affection more than women. Women reported using the strategies of relationship negotiation and accepting a definitional bid. Tolhuizen contends that "these results depict males as being more direct and more willing to explicitly express feelings of affection, and females as being less direct, more responsive, and more concerned with the relationship" (p. 5). Perhaps this information on the strategies Tolhuizen described will begin to answer questions you might have about relational change. Try to monitor your own behavior and look for these strategies in your friendships with women and men. See if you employ any of these strategies in attempts to move relationships from one level to another.

When Change is NOT the Goal

Relationships don't always have to change. In fact, in many instances, relationships stabilize at one level or another (Shea & Pearson, 1986). People seek comfort in the familiar and in relationships from which consistent benefits can be drawn. Change usually comes about when one person or the other feels that the relationship no longer meets their needs and that some change may be necessary. If the relationship has a long history, it will be more difficult to change. For example, if you have recently moved away from home to go to college, what has been your experience when you return and talk to old friends? Did they treat you as they used to treat you, in spite of the fact you have probably changed since you left? Relationships, once they get a momentum going, can be difficult to change. That's why we suggest each person be aware of how the relationship begins—the patterns developed in the beginning are the ones that are likely to continue. The longer the patterns have been in place, the more difficult they will be to change.

> *I've always been the one to push and shove and say, "Sorry, that's it darlin', it's all over, goodbye. Take twenty Valiums and have a stomach pump and that's the end of it."*
>
> *Rod Stewart, singer*

Do men and women approach strategies for relational stability similarly? Interpersonal communication researchers Baxter and Wilmot (1983) explored this question and found that women tend to be more relationally oriented and thus more likely to discuss their relationships. Remember the value "Talking about it makes it better"? Baxter and Wilmot's research suggests that direct conversations about the desired level of the relationship is important to the relationship's stability, but women may be more inclined than men to make these conversations happen. It may be awkward to sit down with a friend and say "Let's talk over our relationship and where we want it to go." Despite the awkwardness, that approach may be valuable in developing the potential that exists in the relationship. Deciding to have the conversation is a good choice to make.

CONCLUSION

The topics explored in this chapter represent a significant challenge for most of us—the challenge of turning relationship potential into reality. To borrow Sonja Johnson's term, the "relation Ships" that sail into your life can change you in powerful and significant ways. Friendships, work relationships, romantic relationships, and marriages can all have a significant impact on you. This chapter has explored the other side of that process: your influence on relationships and choices related to their initiation and development. A consistent theme in this text has been the acquisition of awareness—awareness of how various factors (e.g., biology, sociology, language, and media) influence you and influence your choices, awareness of how you can gain control over or manage those influences and, in this chapter, awareness of how choices may influence the development of relationships.

Becoming more personally effective in initiating and creating the type of relationships you desire is a worthwhile, important goal. In this chapter, we began with a view of relationship development as "prospecting" and followed through with thoughts on finding prospects, testing the prospect, and developing the "claim." Understanding the skills associated with moving a relationship from one level to another and understanding women's and men's tendencies in relational change can give you greater insight into how positive change might be brought about. And it can keep you from getting the relationship "shaft."

The final section of this text connects these concepts to some specific contexts in your life—friendships, romance, family life, work, and education. Effective gender communication in these contexts involves applying the concepts described in the chapters you have just read. The more you understand about relationships, the more you can take charge of your relational future and optimize your chances for successful, satisfying relationships.

Key Terms

choosing
being chosen
choice points
information
proximity
attractor
interest
prospecting
eye contact
uncertainty reduction
image
information gathering
    strategies
relational partner

opening lines
affinity seeking
decision-making
attitude and value
    similarity
reciprocity of liking
communication
    competence
social exchange theory
self-disclosure
intimacy
empathy
perspective-taking
emotional contagion

empathic concern
listening
nonverbal expressiveness
nonverbal sensitivity
immediacy
relational movement and
    change
accelerators and
    decelerators
stages of relationships
relationships
relational stability
movement strategies

Discussion Starters

1. Some people believe the initiation of a dating or romantic relationship should be men's work. Do you think women should be able to initiate dating relationships in the same ways men can? If you believe they can, and you are a woman, have you ever initiated a relationship with a man? If you are a man who has been "chosen" by a woman, how did you feel when she initiated a relationship with you?

2. Think about the role of information in the initiation of relationships. What information do you use to make decisions about people when initiating a friendship? Do you need different kinds of information when initiating a dating relationship than a friendship with someone? What information about yourself as a potential relational partner do you think is most important? What's the most important information to learn about someone else as a potential relational partner?

3. What are some of the most unusual or funny examples you have seen of men trying to be attractive by appearing "too" masculine? Of women trying to appear "too" feminine? Do think there is such a thing as "too" masculine or feminine?

4. We've noticed that some students present a particular *image* of themselves in classes, but we imagine that they are really different than that image when they are with their friends. Do you personally choose an image you want to project in class and then actually project it? Have you ever tried to purposefully alter the image you convey? Do you project one image to the same sex and another to the opposite sex?

5. Recall a time when you or a close friend were at the point of deciding whether to continue or put a halt to a relationship that was trying to get off the ground—the third stage of relationship initiation discussed in this chapter. Do you recall what factors made the difference or helped you make your decision? Did you (or your friend) make a wise decision at the time? If not, what do you wish had been done differently?

6. How do people signal you that they want to *change the level* of the relationship? Do men use different signals than women? Are the signals usually nonverbal in nature? Do people ever say to you—"I'd like to change our relationship?" Have you ever said that?

7. What strategies have you used to change the level of a relationship? How do your strategies compare with what we have described in this chapter?

8. Do you know men who disclose more than the average amount of personal information? What are some reactions to these men? Is it the same or different than the reaction a woman gets when she discloses more that average?

9. Think about whether or not you believe that there is such a thing as women's intuition. If you believe it exists, how might you account for this phenomenon? Is there a men's intuition? What is the relationship of intuition to communication, both verbal and nonverbal?

References

ABBEY, A. (1991). Misperception as an antecedent of acquaintance rape: A consequence of ambiguity in communication between men and women. In A. Parrot & L. Bechhofer (Eds.), *Acquaintance rape: The hidden crime* (pp. 96–111). New York: Wiley.

ABOUD, F. E., & MENDELSON, M. J. (1998). Determinants of friendship selection and quality: Developmental perspectives. In N. Burkowski (Ed.), *The company they keep: Friendship in childhood and adolescence.* New York: Cambridge University Press.

ADELMAN, M. B., & AHUVIA, A. C. (1992). Mediated channels for mate seeking: A solution to involuntary singlehood? *Critical Studies in Mass Communication, 8,* 273–289.

ARIES, E. (1996). *Men and women in interaction: Reconsidering the differences.* New York: Oxford University Press.

BAR-TAL, D., & SAXE, L. (1976). Perceptions of similarity and dissimilarity of attractive couples and individuals. *Journal of Personality and Social Psychology, 33,* 772–781.

BATE, B. (1988). *Communication and the sexes.* Prospect Heights, IL: Waveland.

BAXTER, L. A., & WILMOT, W. W. (1983). Communication characteristics of relationships with differential growth rates. *Communication Monographs, 50,* 264–272.

BELL, ROBERT A., & ROLOFF, M. E. (1991). Making a love connection: Loneliness and communication competence in the dating marketplace. *Communication Quarterly, 39,* 58–74.

BEM, S. (1974). The measurement of psychological androgyny. *Journal of Consulting and Clinical Psychology, 42,* 155–162.

BERGER, C. R., & CALABRESE, R. J. (1975). Some explorations in initial interaction and beyond. Toward a developmental theory of interpersonal communication. *Human Communication Research, 1,* 99–112.

BERGER, C. R., & DOUGLAS, W. (1981). Studies in interpersonal epistemology III. Anticipated interaction, self-monitoring, and observational context selection. *Communication Monographs, 48,* 183–196.

BERSCHEID, E. (1985). Interpersonal attraction. In G. Lindzey & E. Aronson (Eds.), *Handbook of social psychology* (3rd ed.). New York: Random House.

BERSCHEID, E., & REIS, H. T. (1998). Attraction and close relationships. In D. T. Gilbert, S. T. Fiske, & G. Lindzey (Eds.), *The handbook of social psychology* (4th ed., vol. 2, pp. 193–281). New York: McGraw-Hill.

BISSONNETTE, V. L., RUSBULT, C. E., & KILPATRICK, S. D. (1997). Empathic accuracy and marital conflict resolution. In W. Ickes (Ed.), *Empathic accuracy* (pp. 251–281). New York: Guilford.

BOOTH-BUTTERFIELD, M. (1984). She hears . . . he hears: What they hear and why. *Personnel Journal, 44,* 36–42.

BORISOFF, D. E., & MERRILL, L. (1998). *The power to communicate: Gender differences as barriers* (3rd ed.). Prospect Heights, IL: Waveland.

BOSTROM, R. N. (1997). The process of listening. In O. D. W. Hargie (Ed.), *The handbook of communication skills* (2nd ed., pp. 236–258). London: Routledge.

BREHM, S. S., POWELL, L., & COKE, J. S. (1984). The effects of empathic instructions upon donating behavior: Sex differences in young children. *Sex Roles, 10,* 415–416.

BURGOON, J. (1994). Nonverbal signals. In M. L. Knapp & G. R. Miller (Eds.), *Handbook of interpersonal communication* (2nd ed., pp. 229–285). Thousand Oaks, CA: Sage.

BURLESON, B. R., KUNKEL, A. W., & BIRCH, J. D. (1994). Thoughts about talk in romantic relationships: Similarity makes for attraction (and happiness, too). *Communication Quarterly, 42,* 259–273.

CISSNA, K. N. L., & KEATING, S. (1979). Speech communication antecedents of perceived confirmation. *Western Journal of Speech Communication, 43,* 48–60.

COHEN, S. S. (1995, October). The mystery of attraction. *Corpus Christi Caller Times.* pp. G1, G3.

COOPER, A., & SPORTOLARI, L. (1997). Romance in cyberspace: Understanding online attraction. *Journal of Sex Education & Therapy, 22,* 7–14.

COPENHAVER, M. N., & EISLER, R. M. (1996). Masculine gender role stress: A perspective on men's health. In P. M. Kato & T. Mann (Eds.), *Handbook of diversity issues in health psychology* (pp. 219–235). New York: Plenum.

CURTIS, K. (1998, September 3). Safeway clerks object to service with a smile. *Yakima Herald-Republic.* p. 7A.

DEPAULO, B. M., & FRIEDMAN, H. S. (1998). Nonverbal communication. In D. T. Gilbert, S. T. Fiske, & G. Lindzey (Eds.), *The handbook of social psychology* (4th ed., vol. 2, pp. 3–40). New York: McGraw-Hill.

DERLEGA, V. J., DURHAM, B., GOCKEL, B., & SHOLIS, D. (1981). Sex differences in self-disclosure: Effects of topic content, friendship, and partner's sex. *Sex Roles, 7,* 433–447.

DERLEGA, V. J., METTS, S., PETRONIO, S., & MARGULIS, S. T. (1993). *Self-disclosure.* Newbury Park, CA: Sage.

DERLEGA, V. J., WINSTEAD, B. A., WONG, P., & HUNTER, S. (1985). Gender effects in initial encounters: A case where men exceed women in disclosure. *Journal of Social and Personal Relationships, 2,* 25–44.

DEUTSCH, F. M., LeBARON, D., & FRYER, M. M. (1987). What is in a smile? *Psychology of Women Quarterly, 11,* 341–352.

DINDIA, K. (1992, November). *A typology of relational maintenance and change strategies.* Paper presented at the meeting of the Speech Communication Association, Chicago, IL.

DINDIA, K., & ALLEN, M. (1992). Sex differences in self-disclosure: A meta-analysis. *Psychological Bulletin, 112* (1), 106–124.

DOUGLAS, W. (1990). Uncertainty, information-seeking, and liking during initial interaction. *Western Journal of Speech Communication, 54,* 66–81.

EGLAND, K. I., SPITZBERG, B. H., & ZORMEIER, M. M. (1996). Flirtation and conversational competence in cross-sex platonic and romantic relationships. *Communication Reports, 9,* 105–118.

ELLYSON, S. L., DOVIDIO, J. F., & FEHR, B. J. (1981). Visual behavior and dominance in women and men. In C. Mayo & N. M. Henley (Eds.), *Gender and nonverbal behavior* (pp. 63–94). New York: Springer-Verlag.

FEINGOLD, A. (1990). Gender differences in effects of physical attractiveness on romantic attraction: A comparison across five research paradigms. *Journal of Personality and Social Psychology, 59,* 981–993.

FONG, M. L., & BORDERS, L. D. (1985). Effects of sex role orientation and gender on counseling skills training. *Journal of Counseling Psychology, 32,* 104–110.

FUGITA, B. N., HARPER, R. G., & WIENS, A. N. (1980). Encoding and decoding of nonverbal emotional messages: Sex differences in spontaneous and enacted expressions. *Journal of Nonverbal Behavior, 4,* 131–145.

GOFFMAN, E. (1959). *The presentation of self in everyday life.* Garden City, NJ: Doubleday.

GRAHAM, T., & ICKES, W. (1997). When women's intuition isn't greater than men's. In W. Ickes (Ed.), *Empathic accuracy* (pp. 117–143). New York: Guilford.

GREENBLATT, L., HASENAUER, J. E., & FRIEMUTH, V. (1980). Psychological sex type and androgyny in the study of communication variables. *Human Communication Research, 6,* 117–129.

GROLLER, L. (1990, February). What's the attraction? Americans reveal what they look for when sizing up the opposite sex. *Parents, 36.*

GROVE, T. G. (1991). *Dyadic interaction: Choice and change in conversations and relationships.* Dubuque, IA: Wm. C. Brown.

HALL, J. A. (1984). *Nonverbal sex differences: Communication accuracy and expressive style.* Baltimore: Johns Hopkins University Press.

HENLEY, N. (1986). *Body politics: Power, sex, and nonverbal communication.* New York: Touchstone.

HICKSON, M. I., & STACKS, D. W. (1998). *Nonverbal communication: Studies and applications* (4th ed.). Los Angeles, CA: Roxbury.

HOMANS, G. C. (1959). *Social behavior: Its elementary forms.* New York: Harcourt, Brace & World.

HOWELL, D. (1996, March 24). Women play the dominant role in courtship today: Researcher finds 52 ways males, females flirt to attract attention of potential mate. *Corpus Christi Caller Times,* pp. G1, G3.

ICKES, W. (1985). *Compatible and incompatible relationships.* New York: Springer-Verlag.

JOHNSON, S. (1991). *The ship that sailed into the living room: Sex and intimacy reconsidered.* Estancia, NM: Wildfire Books.

JONES, S. E. (1986). Sex differences in touch communication. *Western Journal of Speech Communication, 50,* 227–241.

JONES, T. S., & BRUNNER, C. C. (1984). The effect of self-disclosure and sex on perceptions of interpersonal communication competence. *Women's Studies in Communication, 7,* 23–37.

JOURARD, S. (1971). *The transparent self.* Princeton, NJ: Van Nostrand.

KENNY, D. A. (1994). Using the social relations model to understand relationships. In R. Erber & R. Gilmour (Eds.), *Theoretical frameworks for personal relationships* (pp. 111–127). Hillsdale, NJ: Erlbaum.

KLEINKE, C. L., MEEKER, F. B., & STANESKI, R. A. (1986). Preference for opening lines: Comparing ratings by men and women. *Sex Roles, 15,* 585–600.

KNAPP, M. (1978). *Social intercourse: From greeting to good-bye.* Boston: Allyn & Bacon.

KNOX, D., & WILSON, K. (1981). Dating behaviors of university students. *Family Relations, 30,* 255–258.

LEAPER, C., CARSON, M., BAKER, C., & HOLLIDAY, H. (1996). Self-disclosure and listener verbal support in same-gender and cross-gender friends' conversations. *Sex Roles, 33,* 387–404.

LIFSHITZ, P., & SHULMAN, G. M. (1983). The effect of perceived similarity/dissimilarity on confirmation/disconfirmation behaviors: Reciprocity or compensation? *Communication Quarterly, 31,* 85–94.

LOGO, L. C., & ASHMORE, R. D. (1992). *The perceived relationship between physical attractiveness and social influence effectiveness.* Paper presented at the meeting of the Speech Communication Association, Chicago, IL.

LYDON, J. E., JAMIESON, D. W., & ZANNA, M. (1988). Interpersonal similarity and the social and intellectual dimensions of first impressions. *Social Cognition, 6,* 269–286.

MAURSTAD, T. (1996, November 17). Strange desires can be fulfilled via the Internet: Cyberspace is making it easier to find people with like interests. *Corpus Christi Caller Times,* pp. A17, A18.

McCONNELL, D. (1997). Interaction patterns of mixed sex groups in educational computer conferences. *Gender and Education, 9,* 345–363.

MEHRABIAN, A. (1970). A semantic space for nonverbal behavior. *Journal of Counseling and Clinical Psychology, 35,* 248–257.

MEHRABIAN, A. (1981). *Silent messages: Implicit communication of emotions and attitudes.* Belmont, CA: Wadsworth.

MONGEAU, P. A. (1992, November). *Relational communication in male- and female-initiated first dates.* Paper presented at the meeting of the Speech Communication Association, Chicago, IL.

MONTGOMERY, B. M. (1990). *Sociable versus sexual flirting: The influence of gender.* Unpublished manuscript, University of New Hampshire.

MULAC, A., STUDLEY, L. B., WIEMANN, J. M., & BRADAC, J. J. (1987). Male/female gaze in same-sex and mixed sex dyads. *Human Communication Research, 13,* 323–343.

PARKER, R., & PARROTT, R. (1992, November). *An exploratory study of the functions of self-disclosure: The role of age, gender, and social support networks.* Paper presented at the meeting of the Speech Communication Association, Chicago, IL.

PEARSON, J. C., & SPITZBERG, B. H. (1990). *Interpersonal communication: Concepts, components, and contexts* (2nd ed.). Dubuque, IA: Wm. C. Brown.

PERRY, L. A. M., TURNER, L. H., & STERK, H. M. (Eds.) (1992). *Constructing and reconstructing gender: The links among communication, language, and gender.* Albany: State University of New York Press.

PETRONIO, S., MARTIN, J., & LITTLEFIELD, R. (1984). Prerequisite conditions for self-disclosing: A gender issue. *Communication Monographs, 51,* 268–272.

REDMOND, M. V. (1985). The relationship between perceived communication competence and perceived empathy. *Communication Monographs, 52,* 377–382.

REDMOND, M. V., & VRCHOTA, D. A. (1997). The effects of varying lengths of initial interaction on attraction. *Communication Reports, 10,* 47–53.

REIS, H. T. (1998). Gender differences in empathy and related behaviors: Context and process. In D. Canary & K. Dindia (Eds.), *Sex, gender, and communication: Similarities and differences.* Mahwah, NJ: Lawrence Erlbaum.

RICHMOND, V. P., GORHAM, J. S., & FURIO, B. J. (1987). Affinity-seeking communication in collegiate female-male relationships. *Communication Quarterly, 35,* 334–348.

ROSENFELD, L. B., & RICHMAN, J. M. (1997). Developing effective social support: Team building and the social support process. *Journal of Applied Sport Psychology, 9,* 133–153.

SABATELLI, R. M., & RUBIN, M. (1986). Nonverbal expressiveness and physical attractiveness as determiners of interpersonal perception. *Journal of Nonverbal Behavior, 10,* 120–133.

SANDERS, J. A., WISEMAN, R. L., & MATZ, S. I. (1990). The influence of gender on reported disclosure, interrogation, and nonverbal immediacy in same-sex dyads: An empirical study of uncertainty reduction. *Women's Studies in Communication, 13,* 85–108.

SHAFFER, D. R., PEGALIS, L. J., & BAZZINI, D. G. (1996). When boy meets girl (revisited): Gender, gender-role orientation, and prospect of future interaction as determinants of self-disclosure among same- and opposite-sex acquaintants. *Personality and Social Psychology Bulletin, 22,* 495–506.

SHAIKH, T., & KANAKAR, S. (1994). Attitudinal similarity and affiliation need as determinants of interpersonal attraction. *Journal of Social Psychology, 134,* 257–259.

SHARMA, V., & KAUR, T. (1995). Interpersonal attraction in relation to similarity and help. *Psychological Studies, 39 (2–3),* 84–87.

SHEA, C., & PEARSON, J. (1986). The effects of relationship type, partner intent, and gender on the selection of relationship maintenance strategies. *Communication Monographs, 53,* 352–363.

SIEBURG, E. (1969). *Dysfunctional communication and interpersonal responsiveness in small groups.* Unpublished doctoral dissertation, University of Denver, Denver, CO.

SNELL, W. E., MILLER, R. S., & BELK, S. S. (1988). Development of the emotional self-disclosure scale. *Sex Roles, 18,* 59–73.

STEPHENS, T. D., & HARRISON, T. M. (1985). Gender, sex-role identity, and communication style: A Q-sort analysis of behavioral differences. *Communication Research Reports, 2,* 53–61.

STIFF, J. B., DILLARD, J. P., SOMERA, L., KIM, H., & SLEIGHT, C. (1988). Empathy, communication, and prosocial behavior. *Communication Monographs, 55,* 198–213.

SUTTON, LA. (1996). Cocktails and thumbtacks in the old West: What would Emily Post say? In L. Cherny & E. R. Weise (Eds.), *Wired women: Gender and new realities in cyber space* (pp. 169–187). Seattle: Seal.

TANNEN, D. (1990). *You just don't understand: Women and men in conversation.* New York: William Morrow.

TANNEN, D. (1994). *Gender and discourse.* New York: Oxford University Press.

TAVRIS, C. (1992, February). The man/woman thing: Moving from anger to intimacy. *Mademoiselle,* 98–101, 135.

TOLHUIZEN, J. H. (1988, November). *Intensification strategies in dating relationships: Identification, structure and an examination of the personality correlates of strategy preferences.* Paper presented at the meeting of the Speech Communication Association, New Orleans, LA.

TOLHUIZEN, J. H. (1992, November). *The association of relational factors to intensification strategy use.* Paper presented at the meeting of the Speech Communication Association, Chicago, IL.

TURNER, R. D. (1990, October). How to attract the opposite sex. *Ebony,* 27–28, 30.

UNGER, R., & CRAWFORD, M. (1996). *Women and gender: A feminist psychology.* (2nd ed.). New York: McGraw-Hill.

VARNADORE, A. E., HOWE, S. C., & BROWNLOW, S. (1994, March). *Why do I like you? Students' understanding of the impact of the factors that contribute to liking.* Paper presented at the meeting of the Southeastern Psychological Association, New Orleans, LA.

WARSHAW, R. (1992, August). Why won't he listen?!!!! *New Woman,* 67–70.

WEBER, E. (1970). *How to pick up girls!* New York: Bantam Books.

WHEELESS, V. E., & LASHBROOK, W. B. (1987). Style. In J. C. McCroskey & J. Daly (Eds.), *Personality and interpersonal communication* (pp. 243–277). Beverly Hills, CA: Sage.

WHEELESS, V. E., ZAKAHI, W. R., & CHAN, M. B. (1988). A test of self-disclosure based on perceptions of a target's sex and gender orientation. *Communication Quarterly, 36,* 109–121.

WINSTEAD, B. A. (1986). Sex differences in same-sex friendships. In V. Derlega & B. A. Winstead (Eds.), *Friendship and social interaction.* New York: Springer-Verlag.

WOLF, N. (1991). *The beauty myth.* New York: William Morrow.

WOOD, J. T., & INMAN, C. C. (1993). In a different mode: Masculine styles of communicating closeness. *Journal of Applied Communication Research, 21,* 279–295.

YATES, S. J. (1997). Gender, identity, and computer mediated communication. *Journal of Computer Assisted Learning, 13,* 281–290.

ZAKAHI, W. R., & DURAN, R. L. (1984). Attraction, communicative competence, and communication satisfaction. *Communication Research Reports, 1,* 54–57.

ZILLMAN, D., WEAVER, J. B., MUNDORF, N., & AUST, C. F. (1986). Effects of opposite-gender companions' affect to horror on distress, delight, and attraction. *Journal of Personality and Social Psychology, 51,* 586–595.

PART FOUR

THE CONTEXTS FOR OUR RELATIONSHIPS: PERSONAL EFFECTIVENESS IN ACTION

CHAPTER SEVEN

GENDER COMMUNICATION
"Just among Friends"

CASE STUDY: ARE FRIENDSHIPS CHANGING?

Maybe things are changing. This case study describes the experience of the male author of this text. When Phil was in high school and college, the prevailing attitude among most guys was that girls (women) were basically for one thing and that wasn't friendship. Phil was in a fraternity during college, and while it was a valuable experience, his friendships with fraternity brothers didn't do much to change his general stereotype of women. Women were "things" to be pursued, and most of his conversations with buddies revolved around real, imagined, or partial conquests. Few of Phil's friends had any female friends, a situation that could be considered somewhat typical for men in the late 1960s.

Have things changed in the past three decades? Now Phil is the father of three sons, aged 19, 22, and 26. Each is unique, but they all have something in their lives that is very unlike Phil's experience at that age: female friends. It's not unusual for groups of Phil's sons and their buddies—including both female and male friends—to descend on the home front. No one in these groups is a couple; they are just friends who are out having a good time together. Phil's sons have had female friends for most if not all of their lives, developed through shared class experiences, activities, and sports. They and their male friends don't seem to attach sex object definitions to women—particularly their female friends. There appears to be a more natural, personal acceptance of individuals as individuals, regardless of sex. As a father, Phil appreciates the kinds of friendships his sons have and, frankly, wishes it had been that way when he was their age.

This example of one person's experience is not enough to draw conclusions. Have things changed regarding the possibility of rewarding friendships with members of the opposite sex? Perhaps you can do some research to see if Phil's experience matches that of other people of his age. Talk with a baby boomer and ask if he or she has observed changes in the patterns of male-female friendships. We bet you'll find the answer is "yes." Evidence from our own experience and from that of our students indicates things have definitely changed for the better.

It is the purpose of this chapter to explore the aspects of communication knowledge and skill that will lead to increased personal effectiveness in the specific contexts of same-sex and cross-sex friendship. This chapter is consistent with what we've said throughout the text—both sexes can expand their repertoire of communication behaviors to become more effective in gender communication. An increased range of behaviors, an orientation to the receiver (the friend), and increased personal effectiveness can all lead to greater satisfaction, fewer conflicts, and deeper friendships.

Hot Topics

- Changing *patterns* of friendship
- The friendship *socialization* process
- Issues and possibilities in *same-sex* friendship
- Why men form *friendships* with other men
- Research on men's *communication patterns* in friendships
- *Intimacy and disclosure* in male-male as compared to female-female friendship
- *Support, intimacy,* and *competitiveness* in female friendships
- *Increasing your ability* to develop meaningful friendships with women and men
- Issues that *enhance and detract* from satisfying cross-sex friendships
- *Developing* stronger friendships

OPENING ISSUES

Friendship Defined

How is friendship defined? Aristotle described a friend as "a single soul who resides in two bodies." More modern definitions are not so poetic. In the 1970s, social science researcher John Reisman (1979) spoke of the difficulty of defining friendship. He described a friend as "someone who likes and wishes to do well by someone else and who believes those feelings and good intentions are reciprocated" (p. 108). Although this may not sound like a very profound definition, it is representative of others we have read and seems to express the central characteristics of friendship.

Friendships are a unique class of relationships. Reisman contrasts friendships with other social relationships, such as marriages, business partnerships, family ties, and the like. Each of these relationships is embedded within social structures and is reinforced by those structures. We're not saying these relationships are easily maintained, but they do involve a social structure that is conducive for relationship maintenance. This is not the case with friendship; friends have to set up social structures, such as a weekly bowling night or study session, a pattern of telephoning, happy hours, and so on as vehicles of relationship maintenance. If someone takes friendship for granted, assuming that this form of relationship does not require as much attention and maintenance as other types, that person could find himself or herself friendless. Attending to the friendship helps make it better.

Learning to Be Friends

Sex differences in friendship development show up early in children, indicating that society extends its influence to teaching children how to be friends. Reisman (1990) found that, beginning about age seven, boys form extended friendship networks with other boys while girls cluster into exclusive same-sex friendship dyads. In those dyads, girls acquire the social skills of communicating their feelings and being nurturing. In contrast, boys learn to follow rules and to get along with groups of people. In varying degrees, this tendency remains into adulthood. Women tend to form small, intimate groups while men tend to form clubs and societies with a hierarchical structure (Diamond & Karlen, 1980).

Reisman (1990) also examined self-disclosure and the changing patterns of friendship through the formative years. He found that male adolescents reported they disclosed about the same amount of information with friends of either sex, but female adolescents reported less self-disclosure with boys than with other girls. This appears to change as persons leave their teen years. Young male adults reported higher levels of self-disclosure with members of the opposite sex than with their same sex. Females reported similar levels of disclosure with both males and females. Does this correlate with your experience? If you are a male reader, has your disclosure and friendship pattern changed since you were a teenager? Have you shifted some of your disclosure to women? If you are a female reader, have your patterns of friendships changed as you have moved into early adulthood? Since male-male friendships and female-female friendships develop differently, is one better than the other?

Male Friendships Are Best

It wasn't too many years ago that friendship was seen as an almost exclusively male prerogative. People believed that women apparently just did not have the same friendship bonding capacity that men did. From Ancient Greece and the story of Damon and Pythias, to more modern perspectives as indicated in Simone de Beauvoir's comment that "women's feelings rarely rise to genuine friendships" (Brenton, 1975, p. 142), the belief has persisted that women cannot experience the same quality of friendship as men can. Look up the word *friend* in a thesaurus or dictionary. One thesaurus lists six examples of friendships—all male (Morehead, 1985). Author Lionel Tiger (1969), in a well-known book about the male experience, maintained that men, not women, have a strong predilection to form deep, enduring same-sex bonds. Men have faced common hazards over evolutionary history; these common hazards and pressures have given men a capacity for close friendships that women cannot duplicate (Wright, 1982). Do you agree with these researchers and writers?

Female Friendships Are Best

A different perspective has developed since about 1970. The past two decades have brought about a distinct shift in thinking regarding the qualities of same-sex and cross-sex friendship. A commonly accepted belief that has emerged in the past few years is that women actually have a greater capacity for developing strong, supportive friendships than men. As we discussed in Chapter 6, women have the ability to achieve more intimacy through increased self-disclosure and through the sharing of emotions. Men are criticized for lacking the ability to disclose themselves effectively and to form truly open relationships with other men. This point of view was supported by recent research by Elkins and Peterson (1993), who found that "friendships that involved at least one woman were more satisfying than friendships that did not . . . The consistently least satisfying friendships described were between two men" (p. 506). The accepted standard for "correctness" in friendships appears to have shifted from male superiority to female superiority. This is an overgeneralization, but it seems to reflect recent perspectives and research on this topic.

Are we then insinuating that women's friendships are to be emulated, to be held up as the model for men to follow in their friendships? Not really, because we believe that the sexes can learn from each other. Women and men can develop greater appreciation for and understanding of the qualities of the friendship style of the opposite sex. This appreciation and understanding will likely lead to better friendships.

What about Male-Female Friendships?

Friends of both sexes are important to our overall satisfaction with life. Many of you may not have too much trouble with friends of your same sex, but what about cross-sex friendship? Is it possible to be friends with someone of the opposite sex? Or is female-male friendship just a prelude to something more intimate? A movie of a few years ago, *When Harry Met Sally,* asked that question. The movie's answer was, "yes and no." Harry and Sally became friends, but the friendship did lead them to become lovers. The dramatic tension of the movie was reflected in the questions, "Will they?" and "What happens after they do?" Countless television sitcoms follow this plot line as well, revealing society's general attitude toward cross-sex friendship. Is love the inevitable outcome for all male-female friendships? Of course not, though perhaps you have heard people advocate limited or no friendships with the opposite sex, just because of that possibility. Clearly, limiting one's friends to 50 percent of the population is a bad move. As much as male friends are important to a man and female friends to a woman, friendships with the opposite sex have their place and their own importance.

What about Androgyny?

Earlier in this text, we discussed the concept of androgyny and defined an androgynous person as an individual with a combination of traditional male and traditional female characteristics. We also suggested that an androgynous person may have a more complete communication repertoire to bring to a relationship. This appears to hold true for friendships as well. Research by Jones, Bloys, and Wood (1990) found that androgyny is associated with characteristics that enhance the development and maintenance of relationships. These characteristics include an orientation to communication, positive view of the friend's attributes, reliable trust, less expressed loneliness, and greater satisfaction. Individuals with undifferentiated gender roles are the most at risk because they do not recognize their friends' needs, have a diminished sense of trust, do not feel positive, and express greater loneliness. They found that androgynous men had more and better close male friends. Androgynous women had the greatest number of cross-sex friends and expressed a strong sense of trust in male friends. In similar research, Narus and Fischer (1992) found that androgyny is associated with greater sociability, ease of dyadic communication, and social competence. Thus, androgyny seems to allow for stronger and more satisfying friendships.

Are the Differences Real?

In the chapter that follows, we present a number of research studies that analyze the differences between men, women, and the qualities of their friendships. Many of these research studies point to differences that have given rise to cultural acceptance of stereotypes related to friendships. "Men do things together, women talk." "Women deal with feelings more than men." "Men don't have close friendships." In a recent review of this research, communication researcher Paul Wright (1998) maintains that similarities outweigh the differences. He asks the question, "Do we need one or two models to describe friendships?" He answers his own question by saying, "The answer is that one model will do nicely because differences in women's and men's friendships emerge in a context of more fundamental similarities" (p. 47). He allows that differences do exist, but they can be explained by structural and cultural factors, not by any real differences between men and women. His is a provocative point of view. As you read the material below, compare it with your experiences in friendships. Perhaps you have experienced the differences between men's and women's friendships; perhaps your experience is closer to the position now held by Wright that the differences are outweighed by the similarities.

We presented this consideration of changes in friendship patterns, definitions, socialization, and qualities for two reasons. First, we want you to become more aware of how your own friendship patterns have been influenced throughout your life and how they may influence you. Second, we sought to offer a brief explanation for the divergent approaches each sex brings to communication and friendships. This understanding is empowering, in that you can exert more control over an influence once you are aware of its existence.

COMMUNICATION IN SAME-SEX FRIENDSHIPS: FROM BUTCH AND SUNDANCE TO THELMA AND LOUISE

Chapter 6 pointed out that women and men approach communication differently, and these differences affect how relationships develop. The same point seems to be true regarding friendships; there are differences in all three possible combinations—male-male, female-female, and female-male. Specific differences exist in what women want and get from their female friends, compared to what men want and get from their male friends, compared to what each sex wants and gets from opposite-sex friends. In this section of the chapter, we focus on same-sex friendships, operating from an assumption that understanding gender differences can lead to improved friendships.

Many assume same-sex friendships to be easier than opposite-sex friendships. Same-sex friendships do not, for the most part, experience the same tensions as opposite-sex friendships; tensions such as issues of romance versus friendship, sexuality, jealousy, emotional intensity, and how others perceive the relationship. If these tensions appear in same-sex friendships, it is assumed they will be easier to deal with, or the relationship might be a special case (such as a homosexual same-sex friendship) (Arnold, 1995). Same-sex relationships are assumed to operate on a higher level, one that is more purely friendship.

Another assumption about same-sex friendships is that they are egalitarian. Veniegas and Peplau (1997) studied the variables of power and friendship quality in same-sex friendships. The popular assumption seems to be that same-sex friendships are invariably equal. Both women and men rated equal-power friendships as more emotionally close, satisfying, enjoyable, disclosing, and rewarding than unequal-power friendships. Thus the assumptions made about same-sex friendships appear to be different from those made about cross-sex friendships.

Male-Male Friendship: Issues and Possibilities

As we said in the introduction to this chapter, friendships between men seem to have evolved from the standard of true friendship to something that both male and female writers have begun to critique in recent decades. Part of this critique extends to mild teasing about "male bonding" activities and extends to more serious accusations of men's friendships as "impoverished" (Nardi, 1992). In this section, we review attributes of men's friendships as described by various researchers. Then we suggest some ideas for the development of deeper and more satisfying friendships between men.

> *The fastest way to a man's heart is through his chest.*
>
> *Roseanne, actor & talk show host*

"Doing" versus "Talking"

We ask our male readers, "Why do you form friendships with other men?" If you follow the typical pattern, you form them so that you have *something to do* and *someone to do it with.* Research has shown that while men and women typically have similar numbers of friends and spend similar amounts of time with friends, men's friendships with other men serve very different purposes than women's friendships with other women (Caldwell & Peplau, 1982). Men's friendships begin with, are sustained by, and sometimes dissolve over activities and doing things together (Brehm, 1985; Farr, 1988; Rawlins, 1992). In studying friendship, sociologists in the 1970s found that men value doing things together more than having someone to talk to (Crawford, 1977; Weiss & Lowenthal, 1977). Through these shared experiences and activities, men are able to develop feelings of closeness and to express their commonality with male friends. In essence, activities create a vehicle for male friendship development and maintenance. Think of the war stories or fishing tales that your father, uncle, or grandfather may tell. Men do talk and may value talk as much as women do (Duck & Wright, 1993), but the content of these stories is generally different than the kind of talk between women. While they might not readily admit it or talk about it, shared conquests (or defeats) in battle or sports are significant male bonding events for men. In his analysis of male friendships in sports, titled *Like Family,* sociologist Messner (1992) interviewed 30 professional athletes about their friendships with teammates and competitors. The interviews were filled with stories of friendships forged through fierce competition both with teammates and with the opposition. Messner found these men developed what he termed "covert intimacy," characterized by doing together and talking about what they do together, rather than by mutual talk about their lives.

Bruess and Pearson (1997) extended the analysis of "doing" versus "talking" by examining friendship rituals. Rituals are repeated events in a friendship such as "When we get together, we always . . ." Rituals in male-male friendships tended to consist of the guys' night out, which one group reported as barbecuing steaks, smoking cigars, and watching boxing on television. For men, rituals tended to be important as they allow for a familiar, structured pattern to the friendship that reduced uncertainty and in some situations, facilitated the friendship without the necessity for a great deal of conversation. As it turns out, this may not be a disadvantage. Burelson and Samter (1996) found that people were likely to choose, and be satisfied with, individuals having similar levels of social-cognitive and communication skills. Low-skill pairs were just as satisfied as high-skill pairs. The key was the matching level of communication skills. Men with lower communication skills who are more oriented to doing than talking had satisfying friendships. Amount of talk was not necessarily associated with relationship satisfaction.

As you are no doubt aware, women don't generally base their friendships around activities, but prefer conversation and an exchange of thoughts and feelings (Brehm, 1985). We talk more about female-female friendships in a subsequent section, but you should be aware of the basic contrast here. Think about your own friendships with men. (For female readers, think about friendships between men you know.) Were most of these male friendships initiated through an activity, such as a sport, drinking beer, hunting, working on cars, and the like? Is most of your time with male friends spent in these kinds of activities? Have you ever had a friendship end because you (or the other guy) lost interest in the activity that bonded you together?

Belonging to a Group

Men also form group friendships through participation on teams, member-ships in clubs and fraternities, involvement with work or study groups, and the like. Sociologists Orosan and Schelling (1992) describe men's friendships as group oriented, competitive, and fairly hierarchical. Communication schol-ars Bate and Bowker (1997) describe boys' friendships as occurring in large networks where they learn to follow rules and get along with all kinds of peo-ple, even ones they don't like. These organized friendships centered around group activities give men a sense of belonging (Strikwerda & May, 1992). Many men place great emphasis on the group and being one of the guys. For centuries, men have used group belongingness as a source of power and con-nection. Sociologist Spain (1992) states

> The religious ceremonies, initiation rites, and discussions taking place within the walls of men's huts are protected by secrecy. Controlling access to secret rituals thus becomes one way of distinguishing insiders from out-siders. Insiders—all men—have access to highly valued social resources, while outsiders—primarily women—are excluded from such access. (p. 61)

Each of us feels a need to belong, but for some, belonging has a price. This sense of belonging is so important to some men that they sometimes place being a team player above their own self-respect, to the point of humiliation. The fraternity initiation ritual that the male co-author of your text went through was difficult and sometimes humiliating, but it was required to join. The need to belong, to be accepted in a group of other men, can hold a great deal of control over a man's behavior.

Getting Ahead

Doing things together and belonging to a group are just two motivations for friendships between men. Psychologist Suzanna Rose (1985) explored what she referred to as the *homosocial norm* of seeking social enjoyment through the company of the same sex. A homosocial norm is the societal pressure that en-courages men to seek out other men for friendship. Rose suggests that since men control the power and rewards in the society, men value friendship with other men more than with women because a man can attain more social and economic rewards from other men. This isn't as manipulative as it seems at first glance. It doesn't mean that men necessarily form friendships with other men for the sole purpose of furthering their own achievement, although for some men this is the primary motivation. A more accurate explanation is that often, in forming friendships with other men, men look beyond mere commonality and the opportunity to share activities to consider other, possibly lucrative, benefits of friendship. What do you think of this contention? Do you know men who use male friendships for personal gain? Do you view this approach as a use or an abuse?

Communication researchers Hickson and Stacks (1993) report that when men meet for the first time, they are likely to disregard physical appearance and begin with a mutual attempt to determine the major interests of the other man. Hickson and Stacks also found that if a man is not interested in sports, the possibility of a relationship is lessened for many men. In the business world, if another man cannot help you get ahead, the possibility of a friendship may likewise decrease—not disappear necessarily, but decrease. Thus, these three motivations—doing things together, using friendships to get ahead, and needing to belong—go a long way in explaining friendships between men.

Closeness and Intimacy in Male-Male Friendship

Feelings of closeness are important in any friendship (Rawlins, 1992), and the expression of closeness between men has changed dramatically over the years. In his analysis of men's friendships, Peter Nardi (1992) makes the point that same-sex friendships between men were highly revered in ancient Greece and during the European Renaissance. He quotes Daniel Webster who, in 1800, called his best male friend "the partner of my joys, grieves, and affections, the only participator in my most secret thoughts." Men's friendships in the 19th century could be characterized by a high degree of romance. Nardi states: "Romantic friendships could be erotic but not sexual, since sex was linked to reproduction. Because reproduction was not possible between two men, the close relationship was not interpreted as being a sexual one" (p. 2). It wasn't until the concept of homosexuality came to have sharper definition in the late 19th century that a stigma came to be attached to same-sex romantic friendships.

It appears that the concept of closeness in men's friendships has changed a great deal. How do men become close now? If you are a man reading this, would you say that shared activities bring you close to your male friends? Most men would like to have close male friends, but the issue of closeness or intimacy is the one most commonly highlighted as a problem in male-male friendship.

Levinson (1978), a popular author on men's friendships, concluded via interviews with 40 men that "most men do not have an intimate male friend of the kind they recall fondly from boyhood or youth. Close friendship with a man or woman is rarely experienced by the American male" (p. 335). Holding a similar viewpoint, another friendship author comments, "To say that men have no intimate friends seems on the surface too harsh . . . But the data indicate that it is not far from the truth . . . Their relationships with other men are superficial, even shallow" (Pogrebin, 1987, p. 253). Feminist author Alice Walker (1989) has one of her characters (Mr. Hal) make the following remarks:

> Life is so very different when you have a good friend. I've seen people without special friends, close friends. Other men, especially. For some reason men don't often make and keep friends. This is a real tragedy, I think, because in a way, without a tight male friend, you never really are able to see yourself. That is because part of shaping ourselves is done by others; and a lot of our shaping comes from that one close friend who is something like us. (p. 114)

This is a rather sad commentary on male-male friendship. Do men cringe at the thought of intimacy with other men? It appears so, but why?

Why Not Intimacy?

Gender researchers Strikwerda and May (1992) offer this explanation: "Men in America are clearly stymied in pursuing intimacy with other males because of fears involving their sexuality, especially culturally inbred homophobia . . . The taboo against males touching, except in firm public handshake, continues these teenage prohibitions" (p. 118). Bate and Bowker (1997) state that "the pressure to avoid the stereotype of being gay or lesbian keeps many heterosexual individuals from communicating as they might with people they would enjoy having as close friends" (p. 171). Students confirm this point. Many of the men in our classes admit that they have a good deal of difficulty with intimacy, especially when it is operationalized in the form of hugging or otherwise expressing affection for a male friend. Floyd and Morman (1997), in their research regarding affection in nonromantic relationships, found that in situations where misattribution of the motives for affection is possible, such as male friendships, involved individuals are more reluctant to express affection and thereby run the risk of being seen as "odd." This is a common reaction, and an unfortunate one. Psychologist Rabinowitz (1991) provided a case study detailing the therapeutic benefits and psychological risks associated with hugging in men's therapy groups. Under the right conditions, he reported that embracing can aid therapeutic efforts by creating a sense of trust, inclusion, and acceptance.

The group nature of many male friendships also works against intimacy and closeness and can actually be a way of avoiding intimacy for some men. Strikwerda and May (1992) explored the role of the group, describing male friendship as comradeship. Comrades tend not to reflect on their relationship; they are more bound to each other because of groupness than out of individual concern. Strikwerda and May suggest that "What passes for intimate male bonding is really the deep loyalty of comradeship, which is based on so little information about the person to whom one is loyal that it is quite fragile and likely to change . . ." (p. 114). Feminist scholar Mary Daly (1978) contrasts comradeship and male friendship with sisterhood and female friendship. Comradeship, because of its lack of reflection, can have destructive consequences. She gives examples of mob behavior in males and the involvement of fraternities in college rapes. Daly contends that "male bonding/comradeship requires the stunting of individuality" (p. 379). Because of the fragile nature of comrade relationships, a writer for *Esquire* magazine termed male-male friendships "serial friendships" (Bing, 1989, p. 51).

Male friendships may in some instances be based on the apparent opposite of intimacy—fighting. Linguist Deborah Tannen (1994) describes a number of historical and modern male bonding patterns that are either based in physical combat against each other or in strong, verbal arguing. She reports that some men appear to develop powerful friendships with other men with whom they have fought.

For many men, male friends are important but replaceable, and they have more numerous but less intimate same-sex friendships than women (Basow, 1992). Communication scholars Davidson and Duberman (1982) suggest that, even if some level of intimacy is achieved, society doesn't accept it very well. If a man manages to have a true emotional attachment to another man, a lot of subtle pressures are placed on him to eliminate it. These researchers contend that "For many men, maintaining one's lawn is more important than maintaining one's friendships" (p. 811).

Regarding male intimacy (or the lack thereof), you might be thinking, "But what about the experience of just sitting at a bar, drinking a beer, and just 'BS-ing?' At the end of the evening, you shake hands and head out. Isn't that closeness? I really enjoy those times." Granted, those can be close, good times, but do they actually create intimacy? Wright (1982) suggests that many people think so. In describing male-male friendships, he finds "for the most part the characteristics of loyalty, fellow feeling, and concern for the other's interests have been stressed much more heavily than intimacy in male friendships. Moreover, the presence of these characteristics has been thought to make male friendship superior to female friendship" (p. 110). Similar results were found by communication researchers Wood and Inman (1993), whose evidence showed that men regard practical help, mutual assistance, and companionship as marks of caring. Reisman (1990) concedes that women develop a feeling of closeness to one another by talking, but contends that men gain an equally intimate feeling by sharing activities. Communication researchers Floyd and Parks (1995), in their analysis of same-sex friendships, found that shared activities were no more important to men than to women. But shared activities may lead to shared perceptions of intimacy. Results of a study conducted by communication researchers Caldwell and Peplau (1982), and corroborated by more recent research by Botschner (1996) indicated that many men thought their friendships with other men were intimate; these men felt just as close, as supported, and as satisfied in their male friendships as women did with their female friends.

Disclosure in Men's Friendships

In addition to differences in the way same-sex friends accomplish intimacy, differences also exist in both the amount and type of disclosure exchanged between same-sex friends. Research generally concludes that men practice less self-disclosure in their same-sex friendships than women (Clark & Reis, 1988; Fox, Gibbs, & Auerbach, 1985; Hacker, 1981; Reis, 1984). As we described in Chapter 7, disclosure is a building block of intimacy.

Wright (1982) explored the relationship between disclosure and the development of friendship. He found that pairs of minimally acquainted same-sex subjects made a better start toward becoming friends if one of them revealed highly intimate things about himself or herself than if he or she revealed only nonintimate things. This was true for both men and women. However, here's a revealing point from the study: It was necessary to solicit *half again* as many male subjects to obtain the number necessary to complete the experiment because so many men refused to follow instructions that led them into intimate self-disclosure. In Wright's words, "men who disclosed intimate things about themselves became better friends if they ever overcame their reluctance to engage in intimate self-disclosures. None of the women in the experiment showed a similar reluctance to disclose intimate items of information" (p. 8). Perhaps the message to men about disclosure is, "Try it, you'll like it."

Some authorities go so far as to say that men avoid disclosure in their friendships because some topics are too feminine for male conversation. Herb Goldberg, the author of *The New Male* (1979) contends that many men view the following topics as too feminine and, thus, to be avoided in men's conversations: emotional expression, giving in to pain, asking for help, paying too much attention to diet, self-care, dependency, touching, and alcohol abstinence. Not all men avoid these topics. Psychologists Schiedel and Marcia (1985) found men with a higher level of femininity expressed higher levels of intimacy with more comfort than men low in femininity. Men who fear anything feminine in themselves avoid expressiveness about feminine topics and intimacy. Goldberg believes the avoidance of this type of personal topic is destructive to men.

Perhaps men don't disclose as much as women because men's style of conversation does not suggest disclosure. In an examination of this notion, Haas and Sherman (1982) concluded that talking about sports may be more appropriate for an excited pattern of conversation—one containing stylistic devices more commonly associated with men's communication, such as topic dominance and the use of interruptions. In contrast, discussions in female same-sex friendships of topics such as family, other relationships, and the like may typically occur in a more reflective, supportive mode that has been identified with women's style (Thorne & Henley, 1975; Parker & de Vries, 1993). Communication researcher Martin (1997) analyzed transcripts of friendship conversations between couples with all obvious gender identifiers removed. She found that respondents were able to accurately judge the sex of the conversants from the topic discussed, occurrence of dysfluencies, presence of gossip, and the openness of the discussion. Sex-related differences in patterns of conversation appear to exist.

Parker and de Vries (1993) also found that men's same-sex friendships were characterized by less giving and receiving of affective communication such as support, empathic understanding, deepening other's self-awareness, and authenticity. The male friendship style tends not to include conversation around supportive or emotional topics. A more recent study by Beeler (1995), analyzing the friendships of 50 pairs of male friends, found a higher level of disclosure than expected. She concluded that, at least for the men in her study, "friendship closeness is a combination of the fundamental female intimacy requirements and the male's notion of activities engaged in" (p. 17). This conclusion directly relates to the relational versus content approaches to talk, a topic we explored in Chapter 5. Since evidence is beginning to indicate that men tend to approach conversation more from a content function and less from a relational function, the lack of disclosure in order to increase closeness in a friendship may be related to a perception of what purpose talk serves. Next time you watch television, compare characters' conversations in such shows as *King of the Hill* and *Ally McBeal*. Do the amounts, topics, and styles of self-disclosure among male characters differ from that of female characters?

Thus far, it appears men may not be as capable as women when it comes to disclosure in a same-sex friendship; most folk wisdom would agree. However, some research suggests preference, not capability, is responsible for the difference. Reisman's (1990) male subjects described their same-sex friendships as being as high in disclosure as female subjects described theirs. In addition, he found male college students believe they have the capability of disclosing at the same high level as women. Perhaps males may *prefer* not to be as disclosing with their male friends as they are with their female friends, dating partners, or spouses. The purposes of friendship for men and the social pressures men face explain at least part of it.

Men's studies researcher James Doyle (1989) speaks to this issue:

> Why should men—granted, some men more than others—hold back their feelings, create false appearances about how they feel, or withhold their real emotions from the very individuals who they openly call their best male friends, their buddies? One possible answer lies in the proscriptive norm that most males in our society subscribe to—under no circumstances let down your emotional guard in the company of other men. To do so would more than likely get one branded as an emotional weakling, a sissy, or the latest in unkind cuts delivered to a man these days, a wimp. (p. 252)

Some men equate disclosure with vulnerability—the belief that if a man discloses his thoughts and feelings, to women or to other men, he has put himself in a one-down, powerless position. Since powerlessness is undesirable, actions linked to powerlessness are to be avoided, even at the cost of closeness in friendship (Lombardo & Lavine, 1981).

So, we are left with two conflicting lines of thought regarding intimacy and disclosure. On the one hand, sources claim that male-male friendships are deficient due to a lack of intimacy derived through personal disclosure. On the other hand, some argue that the type of closeness men achieve through activities is just as legitimate and beneficial as any other type of closeness. Perhaps we could suggest a combination of perspectives. Intimacy in male-male

---

RECAP

friendship, androgyny, closeness, homophobia, intimacy, doing versus talking, contexts, same-sex friendships, cross-sex friendships, friendship socialization, male bonding, homosocial norms, comradeship, disclosure

---

friendships requires the sharing of activities and experiences, but may likely be enhanced by disclosure of personal information and treatment of the other person as a unique, irreplaceable individual.

How do you react to these lines of thought? (If you are a woman reading this, think of a male friend of yours as we asked you to do earlier; then attempt to answer these questions according to his experiences.) For the men, do you have male friendships that are characterized by the three things we just mentioned? Would you use the word *intimate* to describe a close friendship with another man, or does that word conjure up a meaning too close to sexual intimacy, striking a possible homophobic reaction in you? Concerning disclosure, what topics do you avoid in your friendships with other men? What would happen if you tried to talk over some of these topics with close male friends? Could there be a consequence to the friendship if you don't bring them up? Are your male friends unique or are they replaceable? Giving thought to the questions of intimacy and disclosure in male friendships may lead to some changes in the way these friendships develop. It may also cause men to think about the quality of their friendships with other men.

Female-Female Friendship: Issues and Possibilities

Many women can attest to the fact that since the earliest days they can remember as girls, same-sex friendships have been sustaining, highly significant forces in their lives. However, until only recently, little research specific to female friendship was available. In fact, sociologist Lionel Tiger (1969) argued that women were not genetically programmed to bond with one another! Psychologists Block and Greenberg (1985) noted the absence of research a few years ago: "It is rare to read of the electricity that suffuses female friendship, of the feelings women develop for one another that intensify their existence. Friendship remains a vast, fertile area of women's lives that is unexplored" (p. 1). In her review of friendships between women, O'Connor (1992) titles the first chapter in her book, *Friendships between Women*, "Women's friendships: The underexplored topic?" More academic and popular attention has been paid to female friendships in recent years; feminist scholars and researchers have described friendships between women with far more detail and insight than we can recount here (Arliss & Borisoff, 1993; Block & Greenberg, 1985; Briles, 1987; Eichenbaum & Orbach, 1988; Gibbs-Candy, Troll, & Levy, 1981; Johnson, 1991; O'Connor, 1992).

The women's movement has given more status to friendships between women and has emphasized their value. Psychologists Eichenbaum and Orbach (1988) state that it wasn't until the 1970s that general society recognized the significance of women's friendship. To overgeneralize somewhat, it seemed that until that point, friendships between women had to be interspersed between relationships with men and family commitments. The increased attention to women's friendships not only coincides with changing perceptions of their importance, it also coincides with the changing roles of women in general society. Friendships between women, once viewed as well down on the priority list for most women, has moved up. Let's explore some of the more prominent features, both positive and negative, that characterize female-female friendship.

The Value of Women's Friendships

Earlier, we mentioned historical changes in men's friendships and commented on the intensity of these friendships in the 19th century. Women's friendships showed parallel or even greater intensity. O'Connor (1992), in summarizing Smith-Rosenberg's (1975) work, states:

> women shared joys , sorrows and tasks; they encouraged each other; enjoyed each other's company; valued each other; regularly slept together and showed what to us appears to be an almost shocking level of physical demonstrativeness and florid verbal expressiveness. (p. 13)

The power of these relationships was a very real aspect of women's lives. Given the social restrictions on male-female interactions at the time, and given that fact the women inhabited a world primarily made up of other women and children, close friendships between women became an accepted form of social interaction, albeit one generally discounted by men (O'Connor, 1992).

Well-known author and gender researcher Shere Hite (1989) conducted an intense study of women and their relationships. She reports that approximately 95 percent of single women and 87 percent of married women in her study described their same-sex friendships as "some of the happiest, most fulfilling parts of their lives" (p. 457). Many women feel that their friendships with other women are more intimate, rewarding, and accepting than their relationships with men (Basow, 1986; Fitzpatrick & Bochner, 1981). Eichenbaum and Orbach (1988) state that "connectedness, attachment, affiliation, and selflessness have been and still are largely the foundations of women's experience" (p. 11). They also suggest that an individual woman "creates and maintains a sense of self through her connections with others. Women live in a network of relationships and know themselves through these relationships" (p. 179). Block and Greenberg (1985) describe women's friendships as having an atmosphere of discovery and delight. Some women would like to have this type of relationship with men, but the response of men inhibits this. O'Connor (1992) found that most of the married women in the studies she analyzed would have preferred to have shared their victories and defeats and routine activities with their husbands rather than their friends. But the husbands simply were not interested, thus increasing the potential importance of female friendships.

Women also appear to develop friendships that function on multiple levels, as opposed to many male friendships that operate around one activity or issue. Carol Gilligan (1982), in her discussion of friendships, characterizes female friendships as developing an intertwined series of obligations and responsibilities, which draws the participants into a friendship that bonds at multiple levels. Women focus on the individuals involved in the friendship and the pattern of interconnectedness between them. This pattern encourages mutual support, emotional sharing, and increased acceptance (Rawlins, 1992). Earlier, we briefly discussed rituals in friendships between men. Bruess and Pearson (1997) found that women had far more rituals such as conversation, emotional expression, and shared support in their friendships than did men in every category examined except shared activities. The rituals and patterns women develop in their friendships show a marked difference from the patterns men develop in their friendships.

Closeness and Intimacy in Women's Friendships

Author Pamela Sattran (1989) believes "today's friendships between women are no longer stand-ins for family, but may be the most intimate, profound, and most durable relationships in our lives" (p. 159). Other friendship research indicates that women value and desire relationships that emphasize intimacy, emotional sharing, and the discussion of personal problems (Brehm, 1985; Caldwell & Peplau, 1982; Lyness, 1978). Weiss and Lowenthal (1977) found that female friends tend to emphasize reciprocity, as exemplified by helping behaviors, emotional support, and confiding in one another. Sprecher and Sedikides (1993) found that women communicated more total emotion than did men, and specifically expressed greater levels of positive emotions related to affection, including love, liking, joy, and contentment. Friendship researcher William Rawlins (1993) suggests that women have a greater intimacy competence. This stems from the tendency for women to embrace the intimacy challenge and to learn how to communicate closeness with female friends quickly. Communication researcher Paul Wright (1982), in a widely quoted comment, stated, "The intimacy characteristic of female friendship is typified by the tendency for female friends to interact in a face-to-face configuration, whereas male friends tend to position themselves side-by-side" (p. 16)). However, Wright himself (1998) now believes that overstates the differences. Sherrod (1989), in his summary of intimacy research put it this way:

> Thus, while women and men seek the same abstract qualities in a best friend—intimacy, acceptance, trust, and help—the specific expectations of best friendship differ consistently in each sex. The typical woman tends to look for an intimate confidante, someone who shares the same feelings, while the typical man tends to seek a partner for activities, someone who shares his interests. (p. 167)

While verbal communication is most often linked in research to the creation of intimacy in female friendship, nonverbal communication may actually be more relevant. Since research documents women's greater nonverbal sensitivity, it follows that female friends rely heavily on nonverbal cues to respond to people, events, or other stimuli and to communicate attitudes, feelings, and emotions. Female subjects in Davidson and Duberman's (1982) study relied heavily on nonverbal communication, including touching, eye contact, smiling, and posturing, for both the sending of information and the interpretation of a female friend's communication. One of their subjects revealed, "My friend has certain gestures, like grimacing, raising her eyebrows, or touching me lightly, to communicate with me on a nonverbal level. We often read each other's minds. Sometimes we just look at each other and start laughing and know why" (p. 818).

As a similar example, the female co-author of your textbook and her best friend, Claire, developed a special nonverbal signal while in graduate school together. When one wanted to "clue" the other about something interesting going on or about someone who deserved notice, they would do so nonverbally to be more subtle than pointing something out aloud. One friend would make direct eye contact with the other, then dart the eyes back and forth from the friend to the stimulus. The eye behavior indicated the direction and location of what the other was supposed to notice. We don't mean to insinuate by these examples that men don't develop nonverbal signals with their buddies, but it does seem that women are notorious for developing complete and very private signal systems with their close friends. Tapping the signal system heightens the intimacy of the friendship.

Disclosure in Women's Friendships

How important is disclosure to same-sex friendships? Reisman (1990) points out that individuals of both sexes who rate their friendships low in disclosure also tend to rate them low in closeness and satisfaction. Since friendships between women are usually characterized by greater intimacy, this implies a greater amount of disclosure in these relationships than in male-male friendships. Research bears this out by concluding, in general, that women are more intimate or self-disclosing in their same-sex friendships than men (Clark & Reis, 1988; Fox, Gibbs, & Auerbach, 1985; Hacker, 1981; Reis, 1984).

Davidson and Duberman investigated three content levels of communication: (1) a *topical* level in which discussion focuses on topics "external to the individuals and the dyadic relationship"; (2) a *relational* level in which discussion focuses on the relationship between the two interactants; and (3) a *personal* level involving discussion about one's feelings, thoughts, and private life. The results of the study indicated that female subjects discussed twice as many personal topics and three times the relational topics when compared to male subjects. Male subjects believed the topical level to be most important in their communication.

In an older but related study, Crawford (1977) reported women were more than twice as likely as men to be able to name a close friend with whom they could disclose, other than their spouse. The women in Crawford's sample stressed that trust and having someone to talk with were most important in their friendships, while men spoke of having someone to do something with.

Beyond the amount of disclosure, greater intimacy also implies possible differences in what friends talk about and how. Social scientists Aries and Johnson (1983) found what you might expect concerning women's disclosure: Female subjects talked primarily about personal and family matters, in greater depth and with more detail than male subjects. This gender difference appeared to remain constant throughout most subjects' lives. In an analysis of conversational topic differences between same-sex friendships, communication researchers Haas and Sherman (1982) found the following:

> Women's talk tended to focus on family, relationship problems, men, health, pregnancy and menstruation, food, things they've read, movies, television, clothing . . . Men talked more about women, sex, money, news, sports, hunting, and fishing. The most frequently talked about topic for either sex was the other sex. Men also were less likely to report that they spoke "frequently" about topics than women. (p. 341)

O'Connor (1992) cautions against using intimacy and disclosure as the defining characteristics of female friendships. The danger, as she describes it, is that if we define women's friendships as operating primarily at a feeling level and "exclude any discussion of ideas or involvement with the world, they abdicate any attempt in changing that world" (p. 31). A definition of friendship in terms of confiding does nothing to challenge power relationships between women and men.

For our readers who are women, do these research findings reflect your experience with female friendship? Do you choose female friends because of the potential for being able to share feelings? Do you think your communication patterns with female friends has changed over time? As we have said at a number of places within this text, information is the key to understanding the other person. Disclosure is the primary vehicle through which information is shared, and the use of disclosure has a clear impact on same-sex friendships. We ask you to examine the degree of disclosure you allow or seek in your same-sex friendships.

Competitiveness in Women's Friendships

When you think about competitiveness, you might first think of it as a prime descriptor of how men approach the world, including their relationships with women and other men, their jobs, involvement in sports, and so on. Competitiveness still drives many men's communication and behavior, but it has become a recent descriptor of women's behavior. In their book, *Between Women: Love, Envy, and Competition in Women's Friendships*, Eichenbaum and Orbach (1988) report that "According to popular culture, women don't trust each other, women don't work well for other women, and women are inherently in competition for the available men" (p. 2). They describe the destructive envy and competition between women as follows:

> (Women) find themselves acutely aware of the successes and achievements of other women. Women gauge and measure themselves in relation to friends, coworkers, neighbors. How does she manage a job, a relationship, and children? How does she manage to keep herself looking so well and fit when I feel exhausted? (p. 11)

Judith Briles (1987), in her book *Women to Women: From Sabotage to Support,* spoke even more emphatically about this issue. She believes that women's competitive sabotage of each other is the single most significant problem in female friendship.

Block and Greenberg (1985) point to the nature of intimacy—one of the most positive values of women's friendships—as a contributing factor in the problems women face in friendships. Here's their description of the downside of intimacy:

> Because women are so often uninhibited about sharing their genuine feelings and concerns with each other, they are often able to move beyond competitive barriers. Women offer support for each other during their worst times as well as their best; they will admit weaknesses and faults to each other and will share defeats as well as victories. In short, women dare to be vulnerable with each other. And this vulnerability brings with it the joy and pain of intimacy. Like mother-daughter relationships, female friendships are seldom bland. They are intensely loving, sustaining, and supportive; when they have gone amiss, they are envious, deceitful, and treacherous. Intimacy, it appears, breeds intensity of feelings. (p. 3)

Women's relationships with men can create or heighten competitiveness between women and can interfere with female friendship. Wright (1982) suggests, "If two women have made arrangements to get together and one of them subsequently has an opportunity to get together with a man, the women's date is automatically canceled" (p. 3). Some women do operate on the premise that a friendship with another woman generally takes second place to any relationship with a man, particularly a romantic relationship.

Besides the opposite sex, many other outside factors impact women's friendships in ways different than men's. Feminist researcher Blieszner (1994) discusses oft-neglected but important structural factors such as power, networks, social opportunity, and the like that can be disadvantageous to many women's friendships. Lack of access to communication networks or inequities of power can do much to increase competitiveness between women. Have you ever seen this happen? We believe structural issues and other dynamics within female friendship are changing. But maybe we're just being optimistic. It seems, however, as more women enter the workforce, achieve more, and gain greater recognition, they focus more attention on their jobs and place more value on co-worker relationships, especially those with female co-workers. This

---

RECAP

friendship value, closeness, trust, sharing feelings, intimacy, affection, competitiveness, structural factors, relationship upheaval

---

change affects their tendencies to talk only about men, families, and relationship issues; many professional women discuss their jobs and careers at length. Likewise, this change in women's talk is reflected in their valuing one another. Our experience, informed by the comments of our students, leads us to believe women are much less likely today to drop a commitment with a female friend for the opportunity to be with a man. What does your experience tell you about this issue? Do you see more women today, maybe compared to when you were in high school, acknowledging the importance of female friendships and honoring their commitments to those relationships? Or does the "cancel the female plans at the drop of a male hat" type of friendship still predominate?

You might be wondering what factors contribute to the problem of women's competitiveness. Eichenbaum and Orbach (1988) point to a social climate of changing women's roles for one explanation. They claim that today, because of uncertainties that liberations have brought about, enormous misunderstandings can exist between women, described as "messy uncomfortable bits one wishes would just disappear, the hurt, the envy, the competition, the unexpressed anger, the feelings of betrayal, and the experience of abandonment" (p.11). This explanation seems logical in that as society shifts its notions of what are expected and acceptable roles for women and men, relationships within and between the sexes will undergo upheaval as well.

Same-sex friendships for both men and women offer unique problems and potentials. Our goal in this section has been to introduce you to the major issues in each type of same-sex friendship and to suggest ways to increase your friendship satisfaction potential. Same-sex friendships are important to each of us, but so are cross-sex friendships. Let's turn our attention to the issues surrounding these sometimes troubling, but often fulfilling friendships.

CROSS-SEX FRIENDSHIP: IS IT POSSIBLE TO BE "JUST FRIENDS"?

For some people, "friends of the opposite sex" is an oxymoron (like "death benefits"). As we mentioned in the opening case study for this chapter, the tendency for contemporary young people to travel in herds, that is, to socialize in groups of both same- and opposite-sex friends, just doesn't match the experience of persons in earlier generations. Just a few decades ago, young men and women only socialized together as dates; rarely if ever as friends. Perhaps young men and women are leading a social change related to cross-sex friendships. Research from both the 1970s and the 1990s indicates that number of cross-sex friendships reported is highest during high school and college years; the number decreases after early adulthood (Kon & Losenkov, 1978: Werking, 1994). Will the number of cross-sex friendships you experience in college remain the same across your life?

You've probably heard that Michael Bolton tune with the repeating chorus of, "How can we be lovers if we can't be friends?" This lyric suggests that a successful love affair, dating relationship, or marriage must be based on friendship. We've all heard folk wisdom (often in the form of advice that wasn't asked for) that cautions us to like each other on a friendship level before loving each other on some other level. Granted, there's merit in such advice, but there's also merit in keeping a male-female relationship at the friendship level. In cross-sex heterosexual friendships, the constant pressure or expectation is to move the relationship beyond friendship into romance. Why can't people let cross-sex friendships alone? Why do people wonder about female-male friendship as though it weren't valid or normal, or as though it were a mere pretense for an underlying romantic or sexual motivation?

> *Women are great. When they dig you, there's nothing they won't do. That kind of loyalty is hard to find--unless you've got a good dog.*
>
> *David Lee Roth, singer*

Rawlins (1993) suggests that society actively works to create static for cross-sex friendships. You've probably heard someone say about a cross-sex friendship, "Oh yeah, their relationship is completely platonic" (wink, wink, nudge, nudge). People frequently use the word *platonic* to describe a friendship they suspect is something else altogether. Werking (1997) theorizes that since heterosexism is an organizing principle in American society, "romantic relationships between women and men appear to be the 'natural' form of male-female bond" (p. 398). The preoccupation with romantic relationships diverts both cultural conversations and research away from cross-sex friendships. Another problem is that we have few ready role models or prototypes of cross-sex friendships; each couple seems to makes up their own rules as they go. So if you've had some problems in this context, you aren't alone.

As with other aspects of friendship we've discussed, society is slowly changing its expectations and notions about the appropriateness of cross-sex friendship. While research from the 1970s suggested that both women and men preferred and actually had more same-sex friendships than cross-sex friendships, the experiences of modern students challenge those findings (Booth & Hess, 1974; Larwood & Wood, 1977). Anecdotal evidence from our students and our own friends suggests both sexes are seeking better friendships with the opposite sex. As more and more women enter various walks of life (e.g., business, politics, education), effective friendships are increasingly necessary and probable. For example, sociologist Sapadin (1988) found that 89 percent of professional men and women reported engaging in cross-sex friendships.

What Gets in the Way of Cross-Sex Friendships?

Many of us have experienced the joys that cross-sex friendships can provide, but we also know that these kinds of friendships come with their own unique complexity. Let's examine three issues that are likely to pose problems in cross-sex friendships. We are back to our "forewarned is forearmed" perspective here, meaning that a knowledge of potential problems may help you avoid them.

Perceptual Issues

Research indicates men perceive a distinct difference between same-sex and cross-sex friendships, generally related to the purposes such relationships serve (Phillips & Metzger, 1976; Wright, 1982; Wright, 1998). Men tend to view different types of friendships as serving particular needs. Women, on the other hand, tend to evaluate each of their relationships independently, without any sweeping generalizations related to sex or gender. They view relationships more holistically, meaning that one individual may fulfill friendship needs on many levels. One interesting research study analyzed the perception of existence of friendships. Rubin (1985) reported that approximately two-thirds of the women a man named as a close friend did not agree that they even had a friendship!

A related issue is the attitude women and men bring to cross-sex friendship. Wright (1982) describes folk wisdom that suggests friendships between and with women are not only different from, but inferior to, those between men. We've alluded to this folklore earlier in this chapter, but at the base of it is the suggestion that men form stronger friendships through sports, the rigors of war, the stress of work, and the like—opportunities women just don't have. An overwhelming majority of Wright's male subjects, when asked about the comparative quality of men's and women's friendships, initially responded that they had not given the matter any thought. So, perhaps one of the first things each sex may need to bring to the friendship is a realization that they may be approaching it with different attitudes.

Perceptual differences also extend to views of intimacy and the difficulty in establishing boundaries of emotional closeness and dependence (Arnold, 1995). According to research, men appear to have at least two different conceptualizations of intimacy in cross-sex friendships (Komarovsky, 1976; Rands & Levinger, 1979). First, men have greater emotional dependence than women on cross-sex friendships. As we reported in an earlier section of this chapter, men typically avoid emotional intimacy with other men; thus, they often seek it with women (Aleman, Miller, & Vangelisti, 1993). In contrast, women believe that men are insufficient to meet their emotional needs and, as a result, they create strong bonds with other women (Chodorow, 1976; Gilligan, 1982). This can lead to problems of balance in cross-sex friendships. If a man views the relationship as an outlet for meeting his emotional needs, but the woman sees it as unable to do so for her, the relationship might be headed for problems. The boundaries and parameters of the relationship may need to be discussed directly.

The second perceptual difference of intimacy relates to sexuality. Egland, Spitzberg, and Zormeier (1996) go so far as to say that sexuality is a backdrop that frames virtually all cross-sex friendships. Men apparently find it more difficult than women to develop cross-sex friendships free of romantic involvement and sexual activity (Rawlins, 1993). They also tend to form cross-sex friendships more out of sexual motivation, whereas women's motives are more often platonic (Lipman-Blumen, 1976; Rose, 1985). In some ways, this reflects a remnant attitude of past generations: that relationships with women are for one thing, and that one thing is not friendship. Gender scholars Rubin, Peplau, and Hill (1980) found men were more likely to believe in the romantic ideology of relationships and more likely to perceive a potential for romance than women. Perhaps because of this, men are more likely to view both men's and women's behaviors in a sexualized manner. In other words, men sometimes see sexual overtones when they are not present and spend more time wondering where the relationship will go than women (Abbey, 1982). In Rose's (1985) study, female subjects frequently reported that their belief that men's motives were sexual made them mistrustful of male friendship overtures and unwilling to establish friendships with men. The perceived sexual motivation led to suspicion and hesitancy.

While other perceptual differences exist, these two—perceptions of the satisfaction of emotional needs and of the possibility of romance and sexual activity—probably create the greatest potential for difficulty in cross-sex friendships. However, perceptual differences aren't the only source of problems.

Social Issues

Cross-sex friendships face a unique set of social pressures and judgments. Social perceptions range from, "It shouldn't happen at all," to "You must be fooling around," to "Sure, we can be friends." However, it is clear that cross-sex friendships do not have a strong base of social support and approval. Werking (1997) maintains that a tension exists between the cultural model of romantic male-female relationships and the everyday practice of friendship. It is difficult to be friends when the culture does not expect it. Communication researchers Bell and Healey (1992) report that it has long been acknowledged that friends look to the images, norms, and rules of society as they attempt to make sense of their connection and understand their rights, privileges, and obligations. But what images of effective cross-sex friendship exist in this society—Harry and Sally?

Bell and Healey describe how difficult it is for two individuals to initiate a relationship in the absence of an effective model, while at the same time adapting the social stereotype to their own use. Do you know of any prototypes of successful cross-sex friendships? If you do, what would you say makes these friendships successful? We suspect that no clear prototype exists in this culture for successful cross-sex friendships; the successful ones become so because the individuals involved have worked to create their own definition of success.

Few role models exist because society places clear limits on what it approves in cross-sex friendships. Rawlins (1993) discusses the perception that cross-sex friendships are socially "deviant." He describes three somewhat socially approved contexts for cross-sex friendships: "(1) between males and females who work together; (2) between non-married men and women, since 'friendship' can be viewed as a euphemism for dating and hence, a stage in the 'natural' progression to publicly acknowledge romance and possibly marriage; and (3) if sanctioned by one or both friends' spouse(s) or romantic partner(s)" (p. 61). Concerning this deviance theme, author of *Friends and Lovers* Robert Brain (1976) believes this:

> We have been brought up as "dirty old men," assuming the worst when two men are constantly and devotedly together or when a boy and girl travel together as friends—if they share the same bedroom or tent, they must be lovers. We have imbued friendly relations with a smear of sexuality, so that frank enjoyment of a friend for his or her sake is becoming well-nigh impossible. (p. 26)

Rawlins (1993) contends, "In a frustrating cultural setting, cross-sex friends must orchestrate social perceptions of their relationship as well as develop a shared private definition" (p. 61). Aleman, Miller, and Vangelisti (1993) discuss the fact that many cross-sex friendships have to be more cautious and make more conscious choices about messages because misperceptions by others may have a detrimental effect on the relationship—a clear description of the unique problems faced by cross-sex friends. Bruess and Pearson (1997), in their study of friendship rituals, found that cross-sex friendships reported fewer rituals, indicating that cross-sex friends may have more difficulty establishing acceptable public and private patterns of behavior. Together with the lack of a prototype, the issues of public and private definitions contribute to a less-than-solid base for the development of the relationship. These problems extend to virtually every friendship context. For example, O'Meara (1989) indicates that the workplace constrains cross-sex friendships. The structure of the workplace and beliefs about the nature of cross-sex relationships make it harder to develop such friendships. On the contrary, same-sex friendships appear to flourish in this context (Arnold, 1995). These issues lead Rawlins (1993) to say that managing a cross-sex friendship requires "conscious supervision" (p. 62). He advocates that cross-sex friends should openly and continually discuss relational definitions.

Interpersonal Issues

A third source of difficulties in cross-sex friendships arises from interpersonal issues between the sexes, beginning with the presence of tension in a friendship. Any interpersonal relationship will experience strain to some degree or another. O'Meara (1989) describes four challenges faced by cross-sex friendships:

1. The emotional bond challenge—the need to develop a clear definition of the emotional bond.
2. The sexual challenge—enjoyed or avoided, it needs to be dealt with.
3. The equality challenge—the need to develop a communally based relationship rather than an exchange-based relationship.
4. The audience challenge—the need to present the correct relationship picture to relevant audiences.

Research by Monsour, Harris, Kurzeil, and Beard (1994) found these challenges, present in many cross-sex friendships, presented varying degrees of difficulty for the friendship. Some couples handled them more easily than others.

Other tensions exist, and gender differences appear to be present in how they are dealt with. Wright (1982) researched strain within cross-sex friendships and found that women were less inclined to develop strong friendships with people with whom they have difficulty getting along. Men, in contrast, were more likely to form friendships (particularly with other men) under circumstances of potential conflict. In addition, when meaningful cross-sex friendships became strained or tense, women were more likely than men to either terminate the relationship or become less good friends. Men indicated that they usually ignored and worked around sources of strain while pursuing unstrained aspects of the friendships. Understandably, working around relational tension or strain is easier to do if doing things together is more the focus of your relationship than talking.

In related research, gender scholars Martin and Nivens (1987) found women in cross-sex friendships tended to internalize and blame themselves for relational failures, while externalizing or crediting others for relational success. Men tended to do the reverse. This is a significant difference, one that relates to how women and men are socialized with regard to relationships. Whether the relationship is friendly, romantic, or professional, women are often socialized to place relationships (especially with men) at the center of their lives and to assume relational problems are their fault. The female co-author of this text clearly remembers her grandmother instructing her to "not let the sun go down on your anger." "Apologize and make the relationship right again, even if it's not your fault" she used to say. (Maturity and education can undo early learning, if you put your mind to it.) Many men are not socialized to place as much importance on their relationships with women; thus, they do not typically look inward for the source of a problem. This difference in approach to strain and tension in cross-sex friendships can at the minimum cause misunderstanding; it can also lead to greater difficulties within the friendship, even to possible termination. Think about how you view strain or tension within your cross-sex friendships. Do you typically assume the blame when something goes wrong in the relationship, or do you externalize the blame? How do you cope with stress or conflict that arises in cross-sex friendships?

Interpersonal Feelings

A second potential area of interpersonal problems relates to the expression of feelings. We've mentioned this topic before, but there's another twist you should be aware of. One issue in cross-sex friendships is the *recognition* of feelings. Research indicates men seem to have a harder time recognizing the feelings of another person, particularly if the other person is female (Rubin, 1983). Men tend to have less capacity for the reciprocity of feelings, that is, the ability to assume another person's feelings (this is known as role taking). This can become a real problem for male-female friendships, one that is compounded when men don't realize they have trouble recognizing the feelings of women. In trends emerging from related research, men and women reported similar levels of intimacy and emotional recognition with their friends. But in role-play situations, women were judged to display higher levels of emotional recognition, evidenced by such behaviors as more affectionate touch, expressions of empathy, and feedback after disclosure (Buhrke & Fuqua, 1987; Caldwell & Peplau, 1982; Davidson & Duberman, 1982). Differences in the recognition of feelings can create problems for cross-sex friends if an imbalance is perceived in the amount of emotional support one derives from the relationship.

A final interpersonal issue is not research based, but stems from our own experience, corroborated by numerous experiences our students describe. A unique form of communication emerges primarily between men, a form that tends to backfire when men use it with women. In a gender communication class a few semesters back, this phenomenon received the label "jocular sparring." Here's how it typically works: A guy will see one of his buddies and greet him by saying, "Man, you look *terrible* today; where'd you get that shirt, off somebody who died?! And your hair, geez—put a hat on that shit." This harmless teasing between male friends can be directly translated into "I like you; you're my buddy." It's a less threatening way for men to communicate liking and affection for one another. Now we realize this is generalizing a bit, but women don't typically talk this way with their female friends. If a woman greeted a female friend by saying, "Hey, you look like death warmed over today—what happened?! That outfit looks like it's been through the wringer and your hair looks like the cat's been chewing on it," the female friend would likely have hurt feelings, get mad, or wonder what in the world got into her friend.

Intrafriendship teasing or jocular sparring just doesn't seem to work the same way with women as it does with men. What happens when a guy teases a female friend, assuming that she'll react the way his male friends do? For example, consider what's likely to happen if a guy greets a female friend by saying, "Not getting enough sleep lately? Your eyes look like you've been on a four-day drunk. And that outfit—did you get dressed in the dark?!" More often than not, the woman will not take the teasing lightly. She might act as though she is tossing off the comments, when in fact the teasing is probably causing her discomfort because it introduces an element of uncertainty into the relationship. (We hope you're nodding your head while you're reading this—most people find a high level of correspondence between this information and their own experiences.)

Now, this doesn't mean that women don't have a sense of humor or that they're fragile creatures who can't take teasing among friends. In fact, after a friendship foundation has been established and with greater understanding of one another's communication styles, women can often take jocular sparring (and dish it right back) in the friendly spirit intended. It's not that women can't or don't engage in teasing with both their male and female friends, but they tend not to prefer it as a form of indicating closeness or affection. When women do engage in teasing, they communicate it differently and with a different effect than when men do jocular sparring. If this sounds all too familiar and descriptive of your own experience with friends, then perhaps you will want to reassess this form of communication. Jocular sparring has the potential either to hurt or to engender a sense of playfulness and closeness in a relationship; if you desire the positive outcome, it's wise for friends to negotiate the use of this kind of communication.

These three areas—perceptual, social, and interpersonal issues—are not the only potential problems facing a cross-sex friendship, but they seem to be the most common. If you become aware of these potential problems, you might be able to understand why the other person is responding in a particular way and what you might do to keep these issues from having too negative an impact on the friendship. Now that we've explored some of the more difficult aspects of cross-sex friendship, we can turn our attention to topics that enhance effectiveness.

What Enhances Cross-Sex Friendships?

We agree with a reporter for the *New York Times* who suggested that people who have friends they can turn to in troubled times are more likely to lead healthier lives (Brody, 1992). Each of us needs friends, and one of the benefits of the changes over past decades is the increased potential for satisfying friendships between men and women. Author Pamela Sattran (1989) believes men and women are much more likely now to establish solid, long-lasting, platonic friendships than they were in the past. Research published in the mid-1980s indicated that approximately 18 percent of the American population reported having close friends of the opposite sex (Davis, 1985). We project that this figure is low compared to the experiences of people in the 1990s. While many students, both male and female, are aware of some of the problems we just discussed, they also report a desire for more and better friendships with the opposite sex. In this final section of the chapter, let's explore some strategies one might follow to increase the chance that a cross-sex friendship will develop successfully.

Defining the Relationship

One of the values we described in Chapter 1, "Talking about it makes it better," is one that we keep coming back to. Within the context of cross-sex, heterosexual friendship, it's particularly pertinent that friends define their relationship

cathy® by Cathy Guisewite

by addressing the question, "Are we just friends or is this leading to something else?" While we hope that cross-sex friendship will become so commonplace that people won't suspect the relationship of being something else, we grant that society hasn't evolved to a position of complete tolerance on this issue. The sexual dynamic between women and men is still an undercurrent, so getting past that issue or negotiating the nature of the relationship is necessary for the friendship to grow.

Rawlins (1993) insightfully describes how the friends-versus-lovers decision generates three combinations of trajectories in cross-sex friendships:

1. A person interested in "friendship as not romance" meets another person interested in "friendship as not romance."
2. Friendship as not friendship (that is, looking for romance)" meets another "friendship as not friendship."
3. Friendship as not romance" meets "friendship as not friendship" (pp. 59–60).

In these possible combinations, two people described by either (1) or (2) are unlikely to run into too many problems. Two people in situation (1) will usually follow the normal pattern of a cross-sex friendship with its attendant gender issues. Two people in situation (2) will follow the pattern of using friendship as a prelude to a romantic relationship. However, the people involved in situation (3) will need to confront the differing expectations each has for the relationship.

No matter which of the three combinations apply in a given cross-sex friendship, a mutually shared definition of the friendship is critical to long-term success. Sometimes this is relatively easy to accomplish, because circumstances (e.g., professional ethics, marital status, value discrepancies, age differences) lead to a conscious decision to be friends. In other instances, such as in situation (3) where the goals for the relationship differ for the two individuals, the decision will not be made so easily. These situations in particular will benefit from a discussion devoted to "Where is this relationship headed?" State-of-the-relationship conversations may need to take place more than once if one or both persons change their minds about intentions. Keeping each other informed about relational intentions is critical to the success of cross-sex friendships.

The question of "Where is this relationship headed?" applies to same-sex friends as well, given that it can and does occur that one person in a same-sex friendship may want to move the relationship to sexual intimacy. The same suggestions apply here as well: Clarity of intentions, open communication, and a willingness to reach a mutually agreed-upon friendship definition are important to long-term relationship success.

Cross-Sex Friends as Romance Advisors

One benefit of cross-sex friendship relates to getting first-hand information about the opposite sex. We've spoken about the curiosity women and men have about each other. That curiosity is a natural and fun part of life, but when it turns into perplexity because one relational partner cannot understand the other, then we feel like we need help. Who better to turn to than an opposite-sex friend?

It's common for men to ask their female friends to help them understand women or just to seek support, empathy, or maybe even sympathy. This applies to the guy who is frustrated over his lack of success in the dating market, to the man who wants female insight into his dating relationships, or to the married man who seeks advice about his relationship with his wife, possibly from one of her friends. At times, women remain a mystery to men, so they often feel that a female friend can help them understand women more so than a male friend. As some research we reviewed in the male-male friendship section indicates, men may not want to disclose their problems, insecurities, or concerns to other men for fear of appearing weak or vulnerable. Thus, men often find female friends to be valuable confidantes (Buhrke & Fuqua, 1987; Doyle, 1989) Likewise, women who are puzzled or troubled by some situation involving romantic entanglements with men (or the lack thereof) can find their male friends a source of support, strength, and insight.

Of course, like anything else, this advice-giving, lend-an-ear function of cross-sex friendships has its abuses as well as its benefits. For example, if your sole purpose for having an opposite-sex friend is to seek counsel on your romantic relationships, your friend may see that as unfair treatment. As we said earlier, friendships need special kinds of maintenance. Using someone merely as a source of support, a guidance counselor, a spokesperson for all men or all women, or a captive audience for your relational problems could be considered a selfish, abusive way to conduct a friendship. What if your friend needs your ear sometime? What if your friend becomes unwilling to be there for you, simply because the friendship ended up being too one-sided? These important issues warrant sensitive discussion and negotiation between cross-sex friends. If you don't talk about possible abuses of the friendship, or of any relationship for that matter, you might wind up with one less friend.

Sexual Activity between "Just Friends"

Thus far in this chapter, we have been operating under the implicit assumption that cross-sex friendships are platonic, that is, they do not include sexual activity. Cross-sex friendships sometimes do have a sexual tension. This tension may be positive or negative, depending on the perception of the individuals involved. Our culture's unspoken dividing line appears to be that as soon as two friends begin to have sexual relations, the relationship moves from friendship to some other level. Whatever level that might be, it is not just a friendship any longer, and it won't be discussed in this chapter. Perhaps it is time to question that assumption.

Is a physical relationship a logical extension of the intimacy that two people can develop? If a strong friendship includes deep sharing at the psychological level, what about the physical level? If that happens, is the relationship no longer a friendship? Definitive answers may not exist for these questions. We raise the point to start you thinking about the qualities of a cross-sex friendship and what it should or shouldn't include. Here's a related question our students ask with regularity: Is it possible to go back to being just friends after being lovers? Of course the possibility exists, but it may take some careful conversations about intentions and needs before it becomes a reality. Early on in this chapter, we referred to Reisman's (1979) claim that friendship is an ill-defined concept in this society. The question of sexual relations in a friendship further complicates the concept. Since this is one of those areas where no clear guidelines exist, we can only suggest to you our earlier advice: Talk it over.

The Future for Cross-Sex Friendship

Friendship between men and women has changed. We wonder where these changes will lead, and so we close this chapter with one thought on the direction and future of friendship between the sexes. Buhrke and Fuqua (1987) concluded the following from their research:

> Given that [our research found] women wanted more contact with men, wanted to be closer to men, and wanted more balance in their relationships with men than they did with women, one could conclude that women more highly value their relationships with men and wish to better those relationships. However, women were already more satisfied with the frequency of contact, closeness, and balance in their relationships with women. Thus it seems women want more from their relationships with men and make efforts to improve the quality of those relationships so that they are more similar to their relationships with women. (p. 349)

This is an interesting thought—that women want better relationships with men, but want them to become more like their friendships with other women. Perhaps men would like their cross-sex friendships to become more like their same-sex friendships. We suggest that neither goal is complete. It may not be a good idea to force cross-sex friendships into the mold of the familiar same-sex friendship. Indeed, the terms *cross-sex* and *same-sex* friendships tend to dichotomize the two types and exaggerate their differences while minimizing their similarities (Werking, 1994). Arnold (1994) agrees, and states, "Thus, the assumption that cross-sex friendships and same-sex friendships are two distinct types of relationships is unwarranted" (p. 242). If we classify relationships into same-sex and cross-sex, she claims we restrict our understanding of communicative practices and experience and that the presence of the categories tends to emphasize differences and ignore similarities. Perhaps she has a point, and an assumption that an opposite-sex friendship is automatically going to have more problems, or unique problems, may not be accurate. Men and women can develop more effective cross-sex friendships by learning to incorporate the patterns of the opposite sex into their communication repertoire and by treating each friendship as a unique entity, not as having come from another planet. The process takes thought, sensitivity, and a willingness to learn and change.

CONCLUSION

This chapter began with the suggestion that the type and quality of same-sex and cross-sex friendships may be changing. Optimistically, we believe this to be true. Men are seeking closer ties and greater depth to their friendships with other men. Women are seeking even closer ties with other women by confronting some of the issues that may separate them. Both sexes are learning to relate more effectively to each other. We encourage and applaud these efforts.

Each type of friendship has unique communication issues and potentials. In this chapter, we have examined some of the more critical issues that enhance friendship, as well as some that detract from it. We believe that through an analysis of the issues, an exploration of the options, and the important ability to talk with a friend about the friendship, each of you can increase your personal effectiveness in this important communication context.

Key Terms

contexts	disclosure	perceptual issues
same-sex friendship	friendship value	sexuality
cross-sex friendship	closeness	social issues
friendship socialization	trust	prototypes
male bonding	sharing feelings	interpersonal issues
homosocial norms	affection	interpersonal strain
closeness	competitiveness	reciprocity of feelings
intimacy	structural factors	role taking
homophobia	relationship upheaval	jocular sparring
comradeship	platonic relationship	relational definitions

Discussion Starters

1. In your experience, how do most male friendships seem to form? What brings the friends together? Is this different than the circumstances that bring female friends together?
2. Some researchers propose that the intimacy men achieve through doing things together is of the same quality as the intimacy achieved by women through conversation. Do you believe men and women are equally capable of forming intimate relationships? Intimate same-sex friendships? Intimate cross-sex friendships? How are women and men different in terms of accomplishing intimacy in their relationships? How are they similar?
3. Earlier in the chapter we referred to competitiveness between women. Have you seen this happening in women's friendships? Are you competitive for grades in your college classes? Are you more competitive with female classmates or male classmates? What are the benefits and the hazards of being competitive?
4. Is it possible to achieve power equity in cross-sex friendships? Does one person or the other need to take the lead? How can power and leadership be discussed within the relationship? What happens if both friends are leaders?
5. Think about the issue of sexual activity in cross-sex friendships. How is the issue dealt with in most of the cross-sex friendships you know? In your own cross-sex friendships? Is the issue discussed openly, hinted at, or avoided?
6. If you had to write down on a piece of paper the name of the opposite-sex person with whom you've had the best platonic or friendship-type relationship, whose name would come to mind first? What factors about the friendship or the person caused you to think of him or her?
7. What do you think are the biggest obstacles to effective cross-sex friendships? What do you think it will take to improve friendships between women and men? Which sex would have to change the most and why? What would the ideal cross-sex friendship look like?

References

ABBEY, A. (1982). Sex differences in attributions for friendly behavior: Do males misperceive females' friendliness? *Journal of Personality and Social Psychology, 42,* 830–838.

ALEMAN, C. G., MILLER, L. L., & VANGELISTI, A. L. (1993, February). *Focus of attention as a means of assessing power in relationships: An analysis of cross-sex romantic and friendship conversations.* Paper presented at the meeting of the Western States Communication Association, Albuquerque, NM.

ARIES, E. J., & JOHNSON, F. L. (1983). Close friendship in adulthood: Conversational content between same-sex friends. *Sex Roles, 9,* 1183–1196.

ARLISS, L. P., & BORISOFF, D. J. (1993). *Women and men communicating: Challenges and changes.* Fort Worth, TX: Harcourt, Brace, & Jovanovich.

BASDEN ARNOLD, L. (1995). Through the narrow pass: Experiencing same-sex friendship in heterosexual(ist) settings. *Communication Studies, 46,* 234–244.

BASOW, S. A. (1986). *Sex role stereotypes: Traditions and alternatives.* Monterey, CA: Brooks/Cole.

BASOW, S. A. (1992). *Gender: Stereotypes and roles.* (3rd ed.). Pacific Grove, CA: Wadsworth.

BATE, B, & BOWKER, J. (1997). *Communication and the sexes* (2nd ed.). Prospect Heights, IL: Waveland.

BEELER, B. (1995, March). *Exploring male friendships: A new definition of intimacy.* Paper presented at the meeting of the Northwest Communication Association, Coeur d'Alene, ID.

BELL, R. A., & HEALEY, J. G. (1992). Idiomatic communication and interpersonal solidarity in friends' relational cultures. *Human Communication Research, 18,* 307–335.

BING, S. (1989, August). No man is an isthmus. *Esquire,* 51–53.

BLIESZNER, R. (1994). Feminist perspectives on friendships: Intricate tapestries. In D. L. Sollie & L. A. Leslie (Eds.), *Gender, families, and close relationships: Feminist research journeys* (pp. 120–141). Thousand Oaks, CA: Sage.

BLOCK, J. D., & GREENBERG, D. (1985). *Women and friendship.* New York: Franklin Watts.

BOOTH, A., & HESS, E. (1974, February). Cross-sex friendship. *Journal of Marriage and the Family,* 38–47.

BOTSCHNER, J. V. (1996). Reconsidering male friendships: A social-developmental perspective. In C. W. Tolman & F. Cherry (Eds.), *Problems in theoretical psychology.* North York, Ontario: Captus.

BRAIN, R. (1976). *Friends and lovers.* New York: Basic.

BREHM, S. (1985). *Intimate relationships.* New York: Random House.

BRENTON, M. (1975). *Friendship.* Briarcliff Manor, NY: Stein & Day.

BRILES, J. (1987). *Woman to woman: From sabotage to support.* Far Hills, NJ: New Horizon.

BRODY, J. E. (1992). Maintaining friendships for the sake of good health. *New York Times, 141,* p. C12.

BRUESS, C. J. S., & PEARSON, J. C. (1997). Interpersonal rituals in marriage and adult friendship. *Communication Monographs, 64,*

BUHRKE, R. A., & FUQUA, D. R. (1987). Sex differences in same- and cross-sex supportive relationships. *Sex Roles, 17,* 339–351.

BUKOWSKI, W. M., GAUZE, C., HOZA, B., & NEWCOMB, A. (1993). Consistency between same sex and other sex relationships during early adolescence. *Sex Roles, 29,* 225–263.

BURELSON, B. R., & SAMTER, W. (1996). Similarity in communication skills of young adults: Foundations of attraction, friendship, and relationship satisfaction. *Communication Reports, 9,* 127–139.

CALDWELL, M. A., & PEPLAU, L. A. (1982). Sex differences in same-sex friendships. *Sex Roles, 8,* 721–732.

CHODOROW, H. (1976). Oedipal asymmetries and heterosexual knots. *Social Problems, 23,* 454–468.

CLARK, M., & REIS, H. T. (1988). Interpersonal processes in close relationships. *Annual Review of Psychology, 39,* 609–672.

CRAWFORD, M. (1977). What is a friend? *New Society, 42,* 116–117.

DALY, M. (1978). *Gyn/ecology.* Boston: Beacon.

DAVIDSON, L. R., & DUBERMAN, L. (1982). Friendship: Communication and interactional patterns in same-sex dyads. *Sex Roles, 8,* 809–822.

DAVIS, K. E. (1985, February). Near and dear: Friendship and love compared. *Psychology Today,* 24–28, 30.

DIAMOND, M., & KARLEN, A. (1980). *Sexual decisions.* Boston: Little Brown.

DOYLE, J. A. (1995). *The male experience* (3rd ed.). New York: McGraw-Hill.

DUCK, S., & WRIGHT, P. (1993). Reexamining gender differences in friendships: A close look at two kinds of data. *Sex Roles, 28,* 709–727.

EICHENBAUM, L., & ORBACH, S. (1988). *Between women: Love, envy, and competition in women's friendships.* New York: Viking.

EGLAND, K. L., SPITZBERG, B., & ZORMEIER, M. (1996). Flirtation and conversational competence in cross-sex platonic and romantic relationships. *Communication Reports, 9,* 106–117.

ELKINS, L. E., & PETERSON, C. (1993). Gender differences in best friendships. *Sex Roles, 29,* 497–508.

FARR, K. (1988). Dominance bonding through the good old boys sociability group. *Sex Roles, 18,* 259–277.

FITZPATRICK, M. A., & BOCHNER, A. (1981). Perspectives on self and other: Male-female differences in perceptions of communication behavior. *Sex Roles, 7,* 523–535.

FLOYD, K., & MORMAN, M. T. (1997). Affectionate communication in nonromantic relationships: Influences of communicator, relational, and contextual factors. *Western Journal of Communication, 61,* 279–298.

FLOYD, K., & PARKS, M. (1995). Manifesting closeness in the interactions of peers: A look at siblings and friends. *Communication Reports, 8,* 69–76.

Fox, M., Gibbs, M., & Auerbach, D. (1985). Age and gender dimensions of friendship. *Psychology of Women Quarterly, 9,* 489–501.

Gibbs-Candy, S., Troll, L. E., & Levy, S. G. (1981). A developmental exploration of friendship functions in women. *Psychology of Women Quarterly, 5,* 456–472.

Gilligan, C. (1982). *In a different voice.* Cambridge, MA: Harvard University Press.

Goldberg, H. (1979). *The new male: From self-destruction to self-care.* New York: Signet.

Haas, A., & Sherman, M. (1982). Reported topics of conversation among same-sex adults. *Communication Quarterly, 30,* 332–342.

Hacker, H. (1981). Blabbermouths and clams: Sex differences in self-disclosure in same-sex and cross-sex friendship dyads. *Psychology of Women Quarterly, 5,* 385–401.

Hickson, M. I., & Stacks, D. W. (1993). *Nonverbal communication: Studies and applications* (3rd ed.). Dubuque, IA: Wm. C. Brown.

Hite, S. (1989). *Women and love.* New York: St. Martin's.

Johnson, S. (1991). *The ship that sailed into the living room: Sex and intimacy reconsidered.* Estancia, NM: Wildfire.

Jones, D. C., Bloys, N., & Wood, M. (1990). Sex roles and friendship patterns. *Sex Roles, 23,* 133–145.

Komarovsky, M. (1976). *Dilemmas of masculinity: A study of college youth.* New York: Norton.

Kon, L., & Losenkov, V. A. (1978). Friendship in adolescence: Values and behavior. *Journal of Marriage and the Family, 40,* 143–55.

Larwood, L., & Wood, M. M. (1977). *Women in management.* Lexington, KY: Lexington Books.

Levinson, D. J. (1978). *The seasons of a man's life.* New York: Alfred A. Knopf.

Lipman-Blumen, J. (1976). Toward a homosocial theory of sex roles: An explanation of the sex segregation of social institutions. In M. M. Blaxall & B. Reagan (Eds.), *Women and the workplace* (pp. 15–22). Chicago: University of Chicago Press.

Lombardo, J., & Lavine, L. (1981). Sex-role stereotyping and patterns of self-disclosure. *Sex Roles, 7,* 403–411.

Lyness, J. F. (1978). Styles of relationships among unmarried men and women. *Sociological Abstracts, 26,* 1249.

Martin, R. (1997). "Girls don't talk about garages!" Perceptions of conversations in same- and cross-sex friendships. *Personal Relationships, 4,* 115–130.

Martin, V., & Nivens, M. K. (1987). The attributional response of males and females to noncontingent feedback. *Sex Roles, 16,* 453–462.

Messner, M. A. (1992). Like family: Power, intimacy, and sexuality in male athletes' friendships. In P. M. Nardi (Ed.), *Men's friendships* (pp. 215–238). Newbury Park, CA: Sage.

Monsour, M., Harris, B., Kurzeil, N., & Beard, C. (1994). Challenges confronting cross sex friendships: Much ado about nothing? *Sex Roles, 31,* 55–77.

Morehead, P. D. (1985). *Roget's college thesaurus in dictionary form.* New York: Signet.

Nardi, P. M. (1992). *Men's friendships.* Newbury Park, CA: Sage.

Narus, I. P., & Fischer, J. L. (1992). Strong but not silent: A re-examination of expressiveness in the relationships of men. *Sex Roles, 8,* 159–168.

O'Connor, P. (1992). *Friendships between women: A critical review.* New York: Guilford.

O'Meara, J. D. (1989). Cross sex friendship: Four basic challenges of an ignored relationship. *Sex Roles, 21,* 525–541.

Orosan, P. G., & Schelling, K. M. (1992). Gender differences in college students' definition and perceptions of intimacy. *Women & Therapy, 12,* 201–212.

Park, K. A., & Waters, E. (1989). Security of attachment and preschool friendships. *Child Development, 60,* 1076–1080.

Parker, S., & de Vries, B. (1993). Patterns of friendships for women and men in same and cross-sex relationships. *Journal of Social & Personal Relationships, 10,* 617–626.

Phillips, G. M., & Metzger, N. J. (1976). *Intimate communication.* Boston: Allyn & Bacon.

Pogrebin, L. G. (1987). *Among friends.* New York: McGraw-Hill.

Rabinowitz, F. E. (1991). The male-to-male embrace: Breaking the touch taboo in a men's therapy group. *Journal of Counseling & Development, 69,* 574–576.

RANDS, M., & LEVINGER, G. (1979). Implicit theories of relationship: An intergenerational student. *Journal of Personality and Social Psychology, 37,* 645–661.

RAWLINS, W. K. (1992). *Friendship matters: Communication, dialectics, and the life course.* Hawthorne, NY: Aldine de Gruyter.

RAWLINS, W. K. (1993). Communication in cross-sex friendships. In L. P. Arliss & D. J. Borisoff (Eds.), *Women and men communicating: Challenges and changes* (pp. 51–70). Fort Worth, TX: Harcourt, Brace, & Jovanovich.

REIS, H. T. (1984). Social interaction and well-being. In S. Duck (Ed.), *Repairing personal relationships.* London: Academic.

REISMAN, J. J. (1979). *Anatomy of friendships.* New York: Irvington.

REISMAN, J. J. (1990). Intimacy in same-sex friendships. *Sex Roles, 23,* 65–82.

ROSE, S. M. (1985). Same- and cross-sex friendships and the psychology of homosociality. *Sex Roles, 12,* 63–74.

RUBIN, L. B. (1983). *Intimate strangers: Men and women together.* New York: Harper & Row.

RUBIN, L. B. (1985). *Just friends: The role of friendship in our everyday lives.* New York: Harper & Row.

RUBIN, Z., PEPLAU, L. A., & HILL, C. T. (1980). Loving and leaving: Sex differences in romantic attachments. *Sex Roles, 6,* 821–835.

SAPADIN, L. A. (1988). Friendship and gender: Perspectives of professional men and women, *Journal of Social and Personal Relationships, 5,* 387–403.

SATTRAN, P. R. (1989, November). The evolution of women's friendships. *Working Woman,* 158–160, 190.

SCHIEDEL, D. G., & MARCIA, J. E. (1985). Ego identity, intimacy, sex role orientation, and gender. *Developmental Psychology, 21,* 149–160.

SHERROD, D. (1989). The influences of gender on same-sex friendships. In C. Hendrick (Ed.), *Close relationships* (pp. 164–186). Newbury Park, CA: Sage.

SMITH-ROSENBERG, C. (1975). The female world of love and ritual: Relationships between women in nineteenth-century America. *Signs: Journal of Women in Culture and Society, 1,* 1–29.

SPAIN, D. (1992). The spatial foundations of men's friendships and men's power. In P. M. Nardi (Ed.), *Men's friendships* (pp. 59–73). Newbury Park, CA: Sage.

SPRECHER, S. & SEDIKIDES, C. (1993). Gender differences in perceptions of emotionality: The case of close heterosexual relationships. *Sex Roles, 28,* 511–530.

STRIKWERDA, R. A., & MAY, L. (1992). Male friendship and intimacy. *Hypatia, 7,* 110–125.

TANNEN, D. (1994). *Gender and discourse.* New York: Oxford University Press.

THORNE, B. & HENLEY, N. (Eds.) (1975). *Language and sex: Difference and dominance.* Rowley, MA: Newbury House.

TIGER, L. (1969). *Men in groups.* New York: Random House.

VENIEGAS, R. C., & PEPLAU, L. A. (1997). Power and the quality of same-sex friendships. *Psychology of Women Quarterly, 21,* 279–297.

WALKER, A. (1989). *The temple of my familiar.* San Diego: Harcourt, Brace, & Jovanovich.

WEISS, L., & LOWENTHAL, M. (1977). Life course perspectives on friendship. In M. Lowenthal, M. Thurnher, & D. Chiriboga (Eds.), *Four stages of life.* San Francisco: Jossey-Bass.

WERKING, K. J. (1994, May). *Barriers to the formation of cross-sex friendship.* Paper presented at the meeting of International Network for Personal Relationships, Iowa City, IA.

WERKING, K. J. (1997). Cross-sex friendship research as ideological practice. In S. Duck (Ed.), *Handbook of personal relationships: Theory, research, and interventions* (2nd ed., pp. 391–410). Chichester: John Wiley & Sons.

WOOD, J. T., & INMAN, C. C. (1993). In a different mode: Masculine styles of communicating closeness. *Journal of Applied Communication Research, 21,* 279–295.

WRIGHT, P. (1982). Men's friendships, women's friendships, and the alleged inferiority of the latter. *Sex Roles, 8,* 1–19.

WRIGHT, P. (1998). Toward an expanded orientation to the study of sex differences in friendships. In D. J. Canary & K. Dindia (Eds.), *Sex differences and similarities in communication* (pp. 41–63). Mahwah, NJ: Lawrence Erlbaum.

CHAPTER EIGHT

BEYOND FRIENDSHIP

Gender Communication in Love, Sex, and Marriage

CASE STUDY

"You know one thing that still really bothers me? Men still have to pick up the phone to make the call." Cliff complained in class one day about something he doesn't see changing, that it is *still* the man's responsibility to pick up the phone, to put his ego on the line, and call for a date. Bonnie countered with "Wait a second, you don't know what it's like to wait by the phone, hoping for a call. That's really hard, too." This led Nicole to chime in, "Hey, if you don't like waiting for a guy to call you, call him. I know lots of women who call men for dates. I've called a few myself." At this point, an informal class poll showed that the traditional model, in spite of changing times, was still very much in evidence. Few men receive calls for dates from women (even though they'd *like* to); few women actually call men for dates (even though they know they *can*). Men feel the responsibility to do the calling, and while some women do take the initiative, most are uncomfortable with it.

As the class discussion continued, Bonnie asked, "Are things really changing? The ways things used to be still seems to be the way things are." Jawarren responded, "I think you are right. A couple of friends of mine got married this summer, and even though they had a pretty balanced relationship in college, when they graduated, got married, and he got a job, all of a sudden he's the breadwinner and she's taking care of the house! They are behaving just like their parents!" Bonnie answered, "Yeah, I know what you mean. It seems like there are lots of opportunities to change, but when it comes right down to it, there is a lot of pressure to keep things they way they've been."

Research we review in this chapter supports the idea that things haven't changed much in the area of romantic relationships. While women report feeling free to assume more active, initiating roles in platonic friendships, it is still a predominant belief that taking initiative in dating relationships is a male activity (Buhrke & Fuqua, 1987; Green & Sandos, 1983; McKinney, 1987). Despite changes to role expectations in marriage, the old model of the man holding the balance of power in the marriage and taking the lead in most decision making is still widely followed (Sollie & Leslie, 1994). It seems that despite changes in many areas of male-female relationships, romantic relationships cling to some old patterns. Do you think things have changed, in terms of female and male roles in dating and romantic relationships? Does the traditional model still make its presence felt? If so, then should it? If you think things should change, what might you do to help bring about the change? For many individuals, the traditional model in dating, romance, sex, and marriage is still powerful. As you might guess, the old model does not have to continue unchanged. But changing it, either as a society or as an individual, takes conscious effort and an awareness of options.

We could discuss a whole host of issues regarding this topic. We've selected what we consider to be the most pertinent gender-related ones to present to you. Admittedly, we tend to explore the issues related to romance more from a heterosexual than a homosexual or bisexual relationship context. This decision is based primarily on the realization that more of our students (and our readers) are likely to be heterosexual than homosexual or bisexual. The decision does not stem from a prejudicial stance since, as you've probably detected in reading this text, we consider homosexuality, bisexuality, and heterosexuality to be equally viable personal orientations. As you're reading, do what we've asked you to do before—put yourself and your experiences into your reading. Compare the research and ideas to your own views about romantic relationships and your own experiences. Maybe you'll find that your approach is on the money. Or maybe you'll find some things you want to do differently.

Hot Topics

- The difficulty in language used to describe a *romantic relationship*
- Cultural views and definitions of love
- Achieving a balance between *autonomy* and *connection*
- How relational partners cope with attempts to change one another, or the relationship
- Women's and men's fears of *commitment*
- Ways men and women *test* each other and the romantic relationship
- The sexes and *relationship termination*
- Attitudes and communication about *sexual activity* in a romantic relationship
- Describing the changing face of marriage
- Developing effective communication patterns
- Understanding the role of *power* and *empowerment* in marriage
- Moving toward *intimacy* and *satisfaction* through communication

CULTURE, GENDER, AND LOVE

Hollywood movies would have us believe romantic relationships happen almost by magic, as though we all know what it takes to make them happen and how to keep them going. Movies throughout the years have also shown us various faces of pain when romantic relationships have gone awry. Given the idealized, overdrawn images in our heads, it may sometimes come as a shock, or at least a rude awakening, to find a different reality when we embark on romantic relationships of our own. Romance and marriage bring their own unique communication and challenges to men and women who venture into them. But even when we are in the midst of a break-up, when the relationship seems doomed and we wonder why we ever wandered into such uncharted territory, we'd probably say we'd do it all over again if given the chance. Humans are innately romantic creatures, and for many of us, the opportunity for romance and love is one of life's greatest experiences.

What kinds of gender issues and communication make this relational context so special and unique? That's exactly the focus of this chapter. Few things motivate individuals more strongly than the emotions that sur-

> *A guy knows he's in love when he wants to grow old with a woman. When he wants to stay with her in the morning. When he starts calling sex "making love" and afterward wants a great big hug. When he loses interest in the car for a couple of days. It's that simple, I swear.*
>
> *Tim Allen, actor*

round romance, love, sex, and marriage, and few topics are so strongly evidenced in our cultural artifacts such as movies, television, art, books, and other media. Because romantic relationships tap such strong emotions and because our culture has such a strong interest in them, communication within them is critical and complex.

As with most other aspects of gender communication, women and men approach romance from different points of view. For women, the romance novel contains the stereotypic cultural script. These novels follow a predictable formula of "woman meets a (perfect) stranger, thinks he's a rogue but wants him anyway, runs into conflicts that keep them apart, and ends up happily in his arms forever" (Brown, 1989, p. 13, as quoted in Unger & Crawford, 1996). The man is usually cold, rejecting, even brutal at the beginning, but through the woman's love, we learn that his coldness covers his emotions. In addition to romance novels, most women learned about romance from such stories as *Cinderella* and *Snow White*. Most romantic literature and movies are aimed at women—young and old. Males do not have the same experience; instead they learn about romance (as such) from nonromantic sources such as *Playboy,* locker room talk, and action or adventure stories in which the "girl" is the reward at the end. While the culture is changing slowly, these images still predominate. They tend to lead men to focus on sex and women to focus on being swept away in a romantic rush. Clearly, neither focus is very accurate.

These romantic images remain a powerful force. Social psychologist Caryl Avery (1989) states that "Given one wish in life, most people would wish to be loved—to be able to reveal themselves entirely to another human being and be embraced, caressed, by that acceptance" (p. 27). The strength, depth, and pervasiveness of this wish does cause our culture to be highly romantic (Arliss, 1993). In Chapter 4, we described some of the media images of romance and relationships. Individuals learn about romance very early. Children learn through such stories and movies as *Beauty and the Beast, Aladdin,* and other legends of princes and princesses. By this point in your life, you've seen and read countless stories of passionate, engulfing, magical love between, typically, very attractive people. These images and legends that you grew up with may have formed powerful, albeit unrealistic models for romantic relationships. Such images lead our culture to assert pressure on finding, winning, and keeping a desirable partner. Communication researchers Hendrick and Hendrick (1992), in their extensive review of romantic love, make the point that romantic love in our culture has become the overwhelming reason for people entering into the long-term relationship of marriage. Love as a reason for marriage is a relatively recent occurrence in our culture. As recently as the early part of this century, economic and social reasons were more important than love in choosing a mate. In many parts of the world, love and romance are not significant parts of marriage. In some senses, our culture is unique.

This emphasis on romance is highly emotional, and it is clear from research that the emotions we bring to our relationships affect our behavior within the relationship (Mehta & Clark, 1994). When we are in a good mood, we tend to like people more. When we are not, we are likely to have more relationship problems. While this may seem like a commonsense notion, it has powerful implications for romantic relationships. Culture shapes our beliefs about romance in powerfully emotional ways that almost govern our perception of reality, and these beliefs may set us up for disappointment. Arliss (1993) contends that realizing the great contrast between the myth and the reality of romantic relationships may lead to a high degree of frustration, disillusionment, and even violence. It also greatly contributes to the divorce rate.

The pressure to find a relational partner also results in misperceptions and outright silly ideas, one of the most prevalent being the desire to be "drunk with love." That wonderful, dizzying feeling of falling in love is like no other. But many people almost become addicted to this feeling and want it to continue indefinitely. If the feeling fades or changes into something else (as it often does), they drop the relationship and seek the same feeling from someone else. This addiction, like any other, is unhealthy. Author Lesley Dormen (1990) examined this issue from the point of view of health—both emotional and physical. She suggests "healthy lovers know that there's a world of difference between falling in love and being in love. They don't mistake dizziness for love's beginning any more than they assume calm is love's end" and they don't have a "dreary and predictable two-part tale—exciting romance followed by the bland 'working out' required by a relationship" (p. 310).

Working out the relationship is complex. To begin with, consider the terms used to describe the nature of a romantic relationship and the two people in it. For heterosexual couples, the term *girlfriend* is still the most common usage of traditionally-aged male students, but use of *boyfriend* seems to be on the decline among their female counterparts. Instead, these women often say "the guy I'm dating" or, less often, "a man I'm seeing." Homosexual couples face the naming problem as well, if not to a more difficult degree. Most often they refer to one another as *partners*, a term that heterosexual couples have begun to co-opt, because it communicates the sense of equality and cooperativeness inherent in a partnership. Older adults especially cringe when they refer to a romantic involvement given the choices of descriptors available to them: juvenile terms (as in *boyfriend* and *girlfriend*), ambiguous and nondescript terms (e.g., *my friend*), too personal terms (*lovers*), or clinical terms (as in *significant other*, a term widely used in the 1970s).

Gender researcher Laurie Arliss (1993) believes there is a gap in our language when it comes to terms for relationships that are more than "just friends," but that are not marital (and perhaps not likely to be). We've seen a number of people stumble in introductions. A newspaper editorial once gave this example: "I'd like you to meet my . . . uh . . . " Sadly enough, the English language hasn't progressed much past calling these relationships "uh," so for the purposes of this chapter, we use the term *relational partner* to refer to members of romantic relationships. We believe this term is the best option around. It sounds a bit clinical, but to a lesser degree than *significant other*. The more this term works its way into common usage, the more people will be able to connect it with the kind of relationship it describes. We use the term *romantic relationship* to include the range of relationships between dating relationships to more long-term, committed relationships (where the term *dating* doesn't seem to fit), and nonmarital relationships that include sexual activity. One quick note: We don't mean to insinuate that marital relationships are somehow not romantic because we don't discuss this form of relationship until Chapter 10. The *romantic relationship* designation here is just to keep things simple and clear.

ISSUES AFFECTING ROMANTIC RELATIONSHIPS

In comparison to friendships, romantic relationships engender a different set of issues, perhaps more aptly described as tensions within a relationship. By *tensions*, we don't mean to imply the negative connotation you might normally associate with the word. Recall from Chapter 6 Sonja Johnson's concept of the relationShip. Romantic relationship tensions arise from the decision making a couple faces in developing and defining their relationship, not necessarily because of the individuals in the relationship. The tensions are usually framed in questions related to "Should I (we) do this or should we do that?" and "Should our relationship be this or that?" These tensions are not unique to romantic relationships, but they seem to intensify in that context.

Communication researcher Daena Goldsmith (1990) describes five types of tensions that come into play as a relationship moves into the romantic stage:

1. Whether to get involved and get to know the other person on this level.
2. Whether or not to date others, especially if the relationship is a long-distance one.
3. Trade-offs with other priorities, such as spending time with one's friends.
4. Whether or not one person's will should be imposed on the other (such as "I wish you wouldn't drink").
5. The degree of commitment.

Respondents in Goldsmith's study found these tensions to be unpleasant experiences. Some dealt with the tension by going totally one way (complete submersion into the relationship) or the other (breaking the relationship off altogether). Most people tried to find a middle ground, although it can be difficult for two people to find the same middle ground. Sometimes women tend to take one side or end of an issue, while men take the other. Identifying these issues or tensions in your own relationships may give you the opportunity to talk about them with your partner.

Communication researchers Bell and Buerkel-Rothfuss (1990) also describe a number of relational issues or tensions. They cast their list in the form of alternatives:

1. Honesty versus the protection of feelings. (Should I tell you everything I think and feel about you?)
2. Self-disclosure versus privacy. (Should I tell you my secrets?)
3. Personal autonomy versus interdependence. (How often can I pursue my own interests?)
4. Integration versus differentiation. (How alike do we need to become in our attitudes, values, and beliefs?)
5. Reciprocity versus generosity. (Do I do things for you because I care about you or do I expect something in return?)
6. Commitment versus voluntarism. (Do I do things with you because I have to or because I want to?)
7. Novelty versus predictability. (How unpredictable should I be to keep the interest going?)

These are issues that couples will likely face. Talking about them may make resolving them easier, or it may lead two people to decide that they just aren't suited for each other. The earlier the couple talks about these issues, the sooner they can make a wise decision. From these two long lists, as well as our own thoughts, we have identified a few issues or tensions to describe in more detail, including autonomy, acceptance, expressions of love, levels of commitment, testing a relationship, and ending a relationship.

Autonomy versus Connection

Philosopher Robert Nozick (1993) believes a defining characteristic of love is the declaration of *we*, and states that the primary feature of *we* is the close connection of one person's well-being with that of another person. The *connection* has its trade-off; it comes with limitations on *autonomy*. Some decisions can no longer be made alone. Noted gender researcher Letitia Peplau (1994) describes autonomy as the extent to which a person values individual pursuits apart from an intimate relationship. Desired autonomy varies widely from individual to individual, thus making autonomy one of the most difficult issues to confront within a relationship (Duck, 1988). In the early stages of romance, the tendency is to spend as much time together as possible. This creates a sense that your life together almost operates in a vacuum, sheltered from the outside world. Have you ever experienced this kind of immersion in a relationship, to the point that you may realize you haven't seen a newspaper or heard a news broadcast for days? The country could be at war and you wouldn't know it, nor would you particularly care. After a period like this, the rest of life usually intrudes and begins to whittle time away from the people in the relationship. It is at this point that a couple may experience the tension created by issues of separation and independence.

Goldsmith (1990) suggests, "Each of us wants the support and companionship that come from connection with others, yet we simultaneously want independence, privacy, an individual identity" (p. 538). Interpersonal communication researcher William Rawlins (1982) makes this issue even more complicated when he describes the freedom to be independent and the freedom to be dependent as different levels within the relationship at different points in time. At one point, the issue for a couple might be time spent in independent activities versus time spent together. At another point in the relationship, the couple might deal with autonomy and connection more abstractly in terms of identity and commitment (e.g., "Who am I? What am I doing here?"). As an issue rises and falls, an individual will feel needs in both directions at different points in time.

The Relationship Tensions

Relationship researcher Leslie Baxter (1988) contends that individuals in romantic relationships face working out the details of autonomy and connection, including negotiating the freedoms outside the relationship and the rights and responsibilities within it. This working out could be an integral part of love; as Dormen (1990) suggests, "the constant tension between individuality and fusion is love" (p. 271). How do couples manage the transition from constant togetherness that often typifies the beginning stages of romantic relationships to a more balanced blend of togetherness and separateness? How can relational partners enjoy a necessary autonomy while avoiding the possible hurt or rejection the other person might feel when the first "clues of separateness" arise? How do you avoid the possibility that issues surrounding independence won't degenerate into power struggles? Conventional wisdom in romantic relationships says self-interest should become secondary to other-interest, that roman-

It's really hard to maintain a one-on-one relationship if the other person is not going to allow me to be with other people.

Axl Rose, member of the rock band Guns 'n' Roses

tic relationships are supposed to be demonstrations of unconditional love. But you know as well as we do that conventional wisdom doesn't always match reality.

Let's work through a real-life example to better understand this first issue or tension in romantic relationships. Mary and Don met, fell in love, and spent a significant amount of time together (an understatement). Then they had the first major crisis in their relationship. Mary had a long interest in the theatre, so she auditioned for a play and was awarded a part. Rehearsals were scheduled for six nights a week for five weeks. When Don learned of this, he hit the roof. "That's too much time! You're putting a *play* ahead of me? You're putting your interests ahead of our relationship?" Don wanted Mary to quit the play. Mary felt that she would be giving up one of her real interests for the sake of the relationship, which led to some serious concerns. Would Don try to control all her activities? Would he always insist that she put the relationship above everything else, requiring her to check things with him before making decisions? On the other hand, Don felt that he needed reassurance from Mary that she was committed to the relationship. Don reacted strongly to Mary taking a part in the play because he thought it meant she didn't really care about him. Don had been dumped before; he was truly afraid for the relationship and didn't want to lose Mary or the closeness they had enjoyed. The ending to this story is that the couple was able to work through this tension via a heart-to-heart conversation (and Mary stayed in the play). One relational partner offered reassurance that the relationship was important, and the other agreed to ask questions and talk a situation out next time before jumping to angry conclusions. They both realized that negotiating time spent apart versus time spent together requires honest, loving communication so the insecurities or actions of the other person wouldn't be a dividing point.

Experiences in Relationships

Have you experienced a situation like Don and Mary's? Have you seen your friends go through it? What did you or they do to work it out? Since this balance between personal freedom and shared activities is one of the single toughest issues in a relationship, talking it out isn't easy. It's particularly problematic in the initial stages of romantic relationships, when both people want to spend all their time together and conflict is the last thing either wants. When a time-consuming activity such as a play occurs, or even when the "first night out without you" arises, a relational partner is likely to feel a degree of betrayal or have problems dealing with the contrast from doing everything together. To keep the relationship alive, relational partners might benefit from an honest, open, nondefensive conversation about the amount of time they expect to spend together versus time spent apart. Talking about this issue or tension won't necessarily ensure a perfect balance or protect the relationship from having this problem again, but it will allow partners to know each other better and it will open the door for discussions if the problem repeats itself.

The concept of power complicates the issue of autonomy. In most instances, the person with the most relational power is also the person with the most individual autonomy. Given the traditional stereotype that the man holds more power, it follows that in many relationships the man has more autonomy. Peplau (1994), in a comparison of heterosexual relationships to lesbian relationships, reviewed research that suggested lesbians, unlike heterosexual women, are not afraid to develop qualities of independence, self-actualization, and strength. The emphasis on autonomy in lesbian relationships might lead women to emphasize equality as a means of preserving independence. At least some women believe it is easier to balance equality and autonomy in a same-sex relationship than in an opposite-sex romantic relationship.

The notion that women are more likely to have problems with men's assertion of independence in romantic relationships than the reverse may be more a myth than a reality. As more women pursue career goals, as they continue to explore the range of options open to them, and as they enjoy the fulfilling companionship of friendships with other women, it is likely female dependence on men has decreased. This doesn't mean romantic relationships aren't as important to women as they once were; it simply means there is more competition for women's attention than in the past. If a heterosexual romantic relationship was based on the old model with more autonomy for the man, a change in the woman's sense of autonomy and outside options can cause a severe strain on the relationship. The change in a romantic relationship from doing everything together to doing some things with other people or alone and the discomfort that goes along with the change don't appear to be sex-typed issues.

Acceptance versus Change

A stereotypical belief in romantic relationships is, "I can change this person. I know she or he has faults, but I can fix those faults." This is such a part of relational folklore that, even though your friends will warn you that you can't change a person, deep down inside you might be saying, "I'll be the exception; I'll be the one to do it." Family communication expert Kathleen Galvin (1993) describes this phenomenon in relation to the early stages of marriage: "In the beginning, couples frequently make allowances for behavior that isn't quite acceptable because new spouses focus on what they are getting, and differences seem enhancing. Later, differences become annoying and call out for resolution" (p. 95).

How do you feel when you know another person wants to change you or change the relationship? The tendency is to resist the person's attempt or to view it as a power play designed to exert control over you. Consider an example: Anthony and Amy were in the middle of the powerful, exhilarating emotions that exist in a romantic relationship. But the intense romantic feelings subsided a bit for Amy before they did for Anthony. She didn't care for Anthony any less, but she just wasn't so caught up in the "emotional rush." Anthony was really bothered by this change in Amy; he tried several ways to recreate the initial level of feeling. Amy neither wanted nor was able to change her feelings. The more Anthony pushed to get things back to the way they were, the more Amy resisted and began to resent Anthony's pressure. It wasn't until Anthony stopped putting on the pressure and relaxed enough to accept the change in Amy that Amy regained some of her positive feelings about the relationship. They didn't return to the early phase, but the relationship attained a new level of closeness.

The importance of acceptance in this type of relationship can hardly be overemphasized. It's a great feeling to have complete confidence in another person, and it's quite disconcerting when your confidence in the other person is lacking. Humanistic psychologist Carl Rogers (1970) based much of his highly successful client-centered counseling strategies on what he called "unconditional positive regard." In describing how human beings change, Rogers pointed out the paradox that real change in people seems to be possible only when a person feels completely secure and accepted in a relationship. Nozick (1993) maintains that a fundamental source of happiness in love is to be loved for *ourselves*. It seems each of us wants to be accepted and loved for who we are—not for our money, appearance, or social position. It is within that acceptance that we can change to please ourselves and to improve the relationship.

Expressions of Love

One of the clearest expressions of a desire to move a relationship to a more intimate level is saying the words, "I love you." These words can bring a reaction of intense pleasure or of nervous questioning like, "What do you mean by that?" A consistent theme throughout this text is the need to verbalize intentions, desires, and goals with your relational partner, including the expression of love.

The statement, "I love you" itself has many different meanings. Back in the 1950s, a communication researcher named Meerloo (1952) penned this truly memorable description of the range of meanings for the phrase:

> Sometimes it means: I desire you or I want you sexually. It may mean: I hope you love me or I hope that I will be able to love you. Often it means: It may be that a love relationship can develop between us or even I hate you. Often it is a wish for emotional exchange: I want your admiration in exchange for mine or I give my love in exchange for some passion or I want to feel cozy and at home with you or I admire some of your qualities. A declaration of love is mostly a request: I desire you or I want you to gratify me, or I want your protection or I want to be intimate with you or I want to exploit your loveliness . . . "I love you,"—wish, desire, submission, conquest; it is never the word itself that tells the real meaning here. (pp. 83–84)

Who is likely to express love and under what circumstances? Contrary to romance novels, movies, and stereotypes, which tend to cast women as the first to say "I love you," research has shown otherwise. Communication researcher William Owen (1987) found that men more often initiated a declaration of love, a critical communication event in a romantic relationship. Owen offered the following reasons for this tendency:

1. It is a way to coerce commitment from women.
2. Men are less able than women to withhold their expressions of love when they feel love.
3. Women are more capable of discriminating between love and related emotions.
4. Women wait until they hear the phrase from men because they often play a reactive rather than active (or proactive) role in a romantic relationship.

The old stereotype that men in a romantic relationship don't say, "I love you" is still evident. Some men believe that actions speak louder than words ("I'm here, aren't I? I don't need to tell you that I love you."). Research, however, indicates that actually saying the words is a predictor of a positive future for love in a relationship (Dainton, Stafford, & Canary, 1994). These communication researchers found that saying "I love you," was among a group of activities positively associated with predicting long-term love, including assuring the other person of feelings, keeping a positive outlook, and practicing maintenance strategies such as being patient and forgiving, being cooperative during disagreements, and avoiding criticism. Saying it does make a difference.

Does your experience or that of your friends match this research finding? If you've ever been (or are currently) in a romantic relationship that involves love, who said the dreaded three words first—the woman or the man? Another difficult issue concerns whether or not you'll hear the statement, "I love you, too" in response to a declaration of love. Not having the sentiment reciprocated may signal an imbalance of emotion or level of commitment in a relationship, which may in turn signal relational troubled waters. Once someone has expressed love, who do you think is more likely to repeat the expression, men or women? Is it the place of one party or another to offer reassurances of love in a relationship?

Levels of Commitment

Commitment involves the decision to stay in a relationship, but it also implies a coordinated view of the future of the relationship. In many ways, being in a relationship is largely a coordination problem—a meshing of the language, gestures, and habits of daily life, primarily through attentiveness, courtesy, and a mutual desire to make the relationship work. Research findings suggest that such variables as anticipated duration of the relationship (short term versus long term), sex roles enacted by the partners, and the level and quality of disclosure within the relationship interact to influence the outcome of a relationship (Cline & Musolf, 1985; Kenrick, Sadalla, Groth, & Trost, 1990). If participants

The trouble with some women is that they get all excited about nothing--and then marry him.

Cher, actor & singer

have different views of one variable or another (e.g., the woman sees the relationship as short term while the man sees it as long term or vice versa), this difference may affect other variables and work against relational success.

In Chapter 6, we discussed stages in the development of relationships, and continued development takes continued commitment. Levels of commitment appear to be related to how well couples handle turning points in relationships. Bullis, Clark, and Slive (1993) analyzed 17 different turning points in relationship development including get-to-know time, quality time, physical separation, external competition, reunions, passion, disengagement, positive psychic change, negative psychic change, exclusivity, making up, serious commitment, sacrifice, commitment tension, relational talk, and negative and positive evaluation. They found more mature relationships with greater levels of commitment used a higher amount of relational talk as a means to handle the turning points. Relational talk and commitment seemed to feed off each other—positive relational talk increased commitment, which increased positive relational talk, and so on. While it will not work all the time, the research suggests a concept we support—talking about the relationship can have many positive effects, including increased commitment.

Crisis and Commitment

Commitment also represents a level of seriousness about one's relational partner. It indicates a deeper level of regard, possibly even intimacy, in the relationship. What are some factors related to the decision to commit? Sometimes a trial or crisis causes people to make the decision to commit to each other. Here's a real-life example (with altered names) taken from some friends' experience. Frederick and Jacquie had been going together for about three years and were considering marriage when Frederick met another woman and had a brief affair with her. This affair, however, was not just about sex, but involved some strong emotions. Because of Fred's feelings for Jacquie, he told her about his affair. As you might well imagine, this event precipitated a crisis in Jacquie and Fred's relationship. After hours of very emotional discussion, Fred and Jacquie decided they wanted to stay together. For Fred, if he wasn't going to leave Jacquie for this other women, he wasn't going to leave her for anyone. Jacquie couldn't imagine a more stressful crisis and decided that if they could get through this one, they could get through anything. The crisis resulted in a strong commitment to each other and an ongoing, successful relationship.

The stereotype about commitment suggests that women are more willing to commit to a relationship than men. Jacquie and Fred's situation fit the stereotype; however, research indicates that women and men today are having equal trouble with the commitment issue. Social psychologist Maxine Schnall (1981) calls this condition "commitmentphobia," defined as "a social disease characterized by fear of the opposite sex, inability to establish a long-term intimate relationship, unsatisfying sexual encounters and loneliness" (p. 37). She contends that commitmentphobia was "first noticed among men in the 1970s," but has "spread to the female population" (p. 37).

One reason for this trend is similar to one we described in discussing autonomy versus connection. More options mean greater flexibility and more complex decision making (Baber & Monaghan, 1988; Duck, 1988; Galvin, 1993). Some of you reading this text for a gender class may be nontraditional students who married at a young age and are now returning to college to start or complete a degree at a later point in life. It used to be more common to marry early—college-educated men and women frequently married in the last year of college or upon graduation. Indeed, only a few decades ago, it was quite common for couples to marry upon graduation from high school. For many people, getting married at age 17 or 18 is unthinkable today. Granted, teenage marriage still happens, but with nowhere near the frequency of past generations. According to Galvin (1993), "A sharp increase in age at first marriage has occurred over the last three decades—from 20 for women and 23 for men in 1955 to 24 for women and 26 for men in 1988" (p. 87).

When to Commit?

Nowadays, increasing numbers of women and men alike seem to be postponing commitment and marriage or opting not to marry at all, either for career reasons or merely for reasons of personal growth. Some people simply feel they aren't personally stable enough or just aren't ready for a serious involvement with another person. Others don't really believe in marriage, and the fidelity and commitment that comes with it. Schnall (1981) connects this trend among the generation under age 35 to a variety of societal shifts including the carryover into personal relationships of competitive, self-interested values typically associated with the marketplace; the disillusionment brought on by rising divorce rates in recent decades; and economic pressures that cause people to emphasize their jobs over one another. Another explanation involves health and sexuality—an enhanced knowledge of health risks related to sexual activity may be heightening the isolation. While you might think the fear of health risks associated with sexual promiscuity would lead to a greater incidence of committed, monogamous relationships, it also has a converse effect—that of causing people to choose abstinence or celibacy, to more deeply immerse themselves in their jobs, and to become even more fearful of connecting with another person.

We certainly aren't suggesting you have an affair or fabricate some means of testing the level of commitment in your relationship. With enough trust in one another, maybe a relationship won't have to be tested. But trusting your relational partner involves some risk—risk that the person may violate your trust and your commitment. Partners have to communicate to decide if the trust and the risk are worth it. Commitment is complicated and, like many other things we've discussed in this text, there are no quick fixes or magic formulas for success.

Secret Tests of a Relationship

We have discussed the notion of a test or crisis that may arise to challenge the level of commitment in a romantic relationship. Not all relationships involve testing, and, as you might guess, most people do not sit down with their partners and say, "Okay, it's time to test the relationship." Instead, people may generally give their partners covert tests of commitment and trust, termed "secret tests" by communication researchers Leslie Baxter and William Wilmot (1984). They provide the following six categories of tests individuals use to determine the feelings of the other person:

1. Endurance: If a partner puts up with "costly" behavior such as being criticized, receiving inconvenient requests, and the like, then one can assume a commitment to the relationship.
2. Indirect suggestion: This includes hints of increased intimacy, such as flirting, to see if the partner responds in kind.
3. Public presentation: One partner introduces the other as "my girlfriend/boyfriend" (in Baxter and Wilmot's terms) to see how she or he reacts to that label.
4. Separation: Two people separate for a while to see if the relationship can take it, although it is not clear which cliché holds most often—"absence makes the heart grow fonder" or "absence makes the heart go wander."
5. Third-party questioning: One partner asks his or her friends to find out the other person's feelings.
6. Triangle tests: This involves using someone else to make the partner jealous or setting up a situation to see if a partner would give in to temptation.

Baxter and Wilmot (1984) found women were more likely to use secret tests than men. This finding was most pronounced for separation and triangle tests, leading the researchers to suggest that "The use of tests by females more than by males may reflect their greater relationship monitoring . . . It is through secret tests that females monitor a relationship's pulse" (p. 197). Peplau (1983) reached similar conclusions about women's behavior in romantic relationships, finding that women were more pragmatic in their approaches to courtship and were more likely to analyze or monitor the development of their relationships. A study conducted by communication scholars Honeycutt, Cantrill, and Greene (1989) found that women were deemed more attentive to the relational process than men and employed a wider range of actions than men to engage in, test, escalate, and de-escalate a romantic relationship.

Bell and Buerkel-Rothfuss (1990) further investigated secret tests; however, they found little support for the argument that women are more active monitors during courtship than men. In fact, they found "males were more likely to describe their tests as deliberate ones than were females and were more likely to believe that they had acquired a better understanding of their relationships" (p. 79). Bell and Buerkel-Rothfuss also indicated that some people set up tests their partners cannot fail, particularly in relationships with romantic potential. Thus, the research evidence is contradictory about the sexes' use of secret tests in romantic relationships. Perhaps testing a relationship has more to do with personality and possibly relational history (a person's relational "track record") than with sex or gender. What's your experience with tests in a relationship? Can you recall a time when a relational partner tested your level of involvement? Have you tested someone's commitment or interest level in you? If so, what was the outcome?

Ending a Relationship

As a culture, are we getting better at resolving problems in a relationship? Listen to the responses of high school students who were asked in a recent article in *Parade* magazine (Minton, 1997) "How did you solve a problem with the opposite sex?" One 16-year-old girl said, "How I deal with a problem with the opposite sex is that I really don't. I'll most likely just call the whole thing off." A 16-year-old boy said, "One way to deal with your problems is to get a car. I promise you that the minute you're behind the wheel, a hot chick will be next to you." A 15-year-old girl stated, "I work out problems with the opposite sex by yelling, because males don't know how to listen." A 14-year-old boy said, "I have worked out my problems by sucking up. They (girls) get mad over anything, but all you have to do is give them a sad face, say you're sorry, and they will forgive you in a heartbeat." If the teens interviewed for this article are any indication, our culture is still not very good at resolving problems in relationships.

But we do know that not all relationships can be salvaged. We realize a discussion of ending relationships can be depressing, but you're probably realistic and experienced enough to know that not all relationships make it. Although we may enter a romantic relationship with a vision of forever and ever in mind, relationships often don't work out as we first imagine. Thus, it's wise to consider some effective communication strategies for ending romantic relationships.

Break-ups can cause stress and anguish for both persons involved—and that may be the understatement of the year! Social exchange theory can help us understand relational break-ups (Banks, Altendorf, Greene, & Cody, 1987; Roloff, 1981). If partners see the costs of the relationship as beginning to outweigh its rewards, then the problem may be discussed or the relationship may be terminated, or both. Communication researcher Michael Roloff (1981) contends, "If relationship problems cannot be negotiated over time, a person is likely to dissolve the relationship and eventually enter into another, more rewarding one" (p. 20).

Michael Cody (1982), an interpersonal communication scholar interested in relationship disengagement, identified the following general categories of strategies:

1. *Behavioral De-escalation*—avoiding a relational partner without offering a justification for the behavior.
2. *Negative Identity Management*—typically, a "rude" explanation of the desire to end the relationship, one that blames the partner and ignores her or his feelings.
3. *Justification*—an in-depth explanation of a partner's reasons for ending the relationship.
4. *De-escalation*—an explanation of what will possibly be gained by changing the relationship, one that implies a future relationship of some sort.
5. *Positive Tone*—showing concern for the feelings of the partner (the "dumpee"), so as to end the relationship on a somewhat positive note.

Leslie Baxter (1982), a prolific researcher in the area of relationship initiation and termination, offers some insight into how a relational partner chooses to disengage. She contends, "Both relationship closeness and perceived cause of the relationship demise affect the disengager's use of termination strategies" (p. 241). Such issues as what prompted the break-up, the duration of the relationship, how intense the relationship had become, and especially the partners' expectations for future contact affect how one approaches terminating a romantic relationship.

Who Is More Likely to End a Relationship?

Communication researchers Rubin, Peplau, and Hill (1981) report that men more often initiate relationships while women more often terminate them. (Maybe this is why so many country and western tunes depict a male jilted lover.) Findings also indicate that women tend to foresee a break-up sooner than men, but men tend to be more deeply affected by the break-up. This last result is particularly interesting, given the stereotype that suggests women are more interested in relationships, their self-esteem has a more direct connection to the success of their relationships than men's self-esteem, and they suffer more than men when a relationship ends. However, the stereotype is not supported by research. Peplau (1994) suggests that men are usually more depressed and distressed after a relationship ends. She suggests "women might be more skilled than men in managing their emotions—in this case, their feelings of romantic attraction and of hurt at the ending of a relationship" (p. 25). Unger and Crawford (1996) suggest that men fall in love more readily than women; feel more depressed, lonely, and unhappy after a breakup; and are less likely to initiate a breakup than their female partners.

Perhaps the stereotype relates more to the difference in the ways men and women express themselves regarding relationships than to an actual value placed on relationships in general. As we discussed in the chapter on friendship, women usually deal with things and make sense of their world via talk. Conversely, men typically deal with things by distracting themselves with activities or by withdrawing and isolating themselves until the situation is resolved. When men do choose to talk out a relational issue such as a break-up, the conversation is typically not as long, in-depth, detailed, and emotionally displayed as a woman's conversation on the subject. Think about how female friends talk to each other for hours, either in person or over the phone, about a relationship. They'll explore what happened, what was said, how it was said, how it made the woman feel, what she thinks she'll do next, and so on. The male equivalent of the break-up aftermath might look like this: A guy learns about his buddy's break-up. He consoles his friend by saying, "Hey, forget about her, man. She's not worth it. Let's go shoot some hoops and have a few beers. I guarantee you'll feel better." This is an overgeneralized example to expose the contrast, but does it sound familiar?

Skills in Ending a Relationship

You may be wondering whether there is a personally effective way to end a romantic relationship. Romantic relationships are so situation- and person-specific that advising an optimum termination strategy would be unwise. However, like we've said time and again, to communicate is better than not to communicate ("talking about it makes it better"). From our own experiences and those shared by our students, the worst relationship ending is the "Dear John letter" or its equivalent, the silent treatment. Even a screaming match, while traumatic, doesn't seem to carry the same sting as noncommunication or one-sided communication. It's quite painful to be told it's over without any explanation, without any chance for negotiation, and without the opportunity for the one who gets "terminated" to express her or his feelings. Many people would rather talk it out—even argue it out—than be shut out and left to wonder what went wrong, which is likely to plunge a person's self-esteem to a new low. So, the receiver orientation to communication implies that women and men would do well to think through their break-ups, to consider what strategy is best to use—given the person who will be on the receiving end of the upsetting information—and to communicate as sensitively and clearly as possible. Not only is it probable that kind of communication will lessen the blow to the other person, but it will also keep the terminator from feeling like a louse, a schmuck, or a downright terrible person for hurting someone and communicating poorly.

> *In biblical times, a man could have as many wives as he could afford. Just like today.*
>
> Abigail Van Buren,
> aka "Dear Abby,"
> advice columnist

RECAP

romantic relationship, relational partner, significant other, tensions, autonomy, connection, acceptance, change, commitment, commitmentphobia

---

The tensions in romantic relationships are by no means *all* of the issues relational partners may have to face, but they represent some of the more prominent, common, and troublesome ones examined by research. One remaining issue connected to women and men involved in romantic relationships surrounds the presence of sexual activity—more specifically, how gender communication plays a significant role in a relationship that becomes a sexual one.

GENDER ISSUES SURROUNDING SEXUAL ACTIVITY

Passionate love is one of the most intense feelings a person can experience. Anthropologists Hatfield and Rapson (1996) describe it this way: "Passionate love is a 'hot,' intense emotion, sometimes called a crush, obsessive love, lovesickness, head-over-heels in love, infatuation, or being in love" (p. 3). They go on to describe passionate love as associated with fulfillment and ecstasy generally expressed through sexual union. It is difficult to separate considerations of passionate love from considerations of sex. Freud, in fact, believed they were one and the same (as cited in Hendrick & Hendrick, 1992), and at the very least, the two are deeply intertwined. At some point in a romantic relationship, the issue of sexual activity will probably develop. Then the questions become, "What does sex mean to us?" and "What do we do about it?" Hendrick and Hendrick (1992) point out that for some individuals, sex without love is unthinkable while for others, sex is intrinsically good and should be an end in itself. Any given couple is likely to have different meanings for sex within the relationship. Regarding the second question, a number of answers are possible, ranging from "absolutely nothing" to "absolute passion." We're not making any assumptions about how the questions should be answered for obvious reasons. What's more important to us is the communication of a clear and mutually agreed-upon decision about what course to take. Sexual activity is

> *Women complain about sex more often than men. Their gripes fall into two major categories: (1) Not enough. (2) Too much.*
>
> *Ann Landers,*
> *advice columnist*

Reprinted with special permission of King Features Syndicate

an awkward topic to talk about with another person; it may be an especially uncomfortable topic to discuss with your relational partner. It's difficult, in what might be the heat of building passion, to stop and talk about the advisability of advanced sexual activity. Yet there are many reasons for doing so, not the least of which is the threat of AIDS and other sexually transmitted diseases (STDs). This section of the chapter focuses on understanding variant attitudes about sexual activity, talking about sex with a relational partner, and developing a broader repertoire of communication behavior in dealing with sexually problematic situations.

Attitudes toward Sexual Activity

In the 1970s, after the free love emphasis of the 1960s, sexual decision making was a prominent issue. It still is, though perhaps not for the same reasons. Newspaper columnist Ellen Goodman (1979) expressed a particularly thoughtful point of view about sexual decision making at the time, that retains its wisdom for current generations:

> There is often a sexual aura between people who genuinely like each other. But there may be a thousand reasons not to turn it into a romance. And reasons make the difference between the urge and the act. I find it sometimes amusing and sometimes sad that we attribute so much more power to the sexual urge than to our own restraint, or to our wider choices. If caution is just as predictable as attraction, friendship may be as valuable an alternative as love. We surely have wider options than segregation or sex. (p. 10A)

In considering your options, it may be helpful to know what some research says about the sexes' attitudes toward sexual activity. Sex-role researcher Antonia Abbey (1982) studied female and male perceptions of sexual interest. In this study, opposite-sex dyads conversed for five minutes while hidden male and female subjects observed the interaction. Results indicated that, in comparison to female observers, male observers more often perceived female friendliness as seduction, made more judgments that female interactants were promiscuous, and frequently reported being sexually attracted to female interactants. Male observers also rated male interactants' behavior as sexual in nature, whereas female observers did not perceive as much sexuality in male subjects' behavior. From these results, Abbey concluded that "men are more likely to perceive the world in sexual terms and to make sexual judgments than women are" (p. 830). Mongeau, Yeazell, & Hale (1994) conducted similar research on motivational attributions in first and second dates. Men tended to perceive heterosexual interaction in more intimate and sexual ways than females. Men appear to be more likely to perceive sexual interest when, in fact, it may not be there. For our male readers, it may be worth checking out your perceptions before you assume them to be true—it could forestall some inappropriate behavior.

> *I never watched anybody make love, so how do you know if you're doing it right?*
>
> *Kevin Costner,*
> *actor & director*

In her review of the literature about men and women in love, Peplau (1994) examined the cultural stereotype that suggests men initiate increasing sexual intimacy and women set the limits and control the progress toward intercourse. She wondered if this stereotype had changed since it was first researched in the 1950s. She concluded it had not: "Despite the sexual permissiveness of many couples, a traditional pattern of male initiation and female limit-setting was apparent . . . the traditional pattern provides a familiar and well-rehearsed script that enables the partners to interact comfortably" (p. 28). Hendrick and Hendrick (1992) suggest this tendency may be based in biology. The male of many species maximized their reproductive strategies by maximizing the number of offspring they have, while females maximize success by having the offspring grow to adulthood. This leads females to be more choosy, with the net result that males compete for sexual access to females and females are the guardians of that access. We are not suggesting this pattern *should* change, but a couple shouldn't assume the stereotype will hold for them or be shocked if the roles become reversed. It is possible for the woman to be the initiator and the man to be the one setting the limits.

In a study sponsored by the Medical Research Institute of San Francisco, Barbara Critchlow Leigh (1989) explored sex-role stereotypes that suggest people differ in their reasons for engaging in sexual activity. A random sample of 844 individuals, 76 percent of whom described themselves as heterosexual, and 24 percent as homosexual or bisexual, were asked to rate the importance of a variety of reasons for having and avoiding sexual activity. Differences emerged between female and male subjects, as well as between sexual orientations. Among reasons to have sex, male subjects placed more importance on pleasure, pleasing one's partner, and relieving tension than female subjects. Women in the study rated the expression of emotional closeness as a more important reason or motivation for having sex than male subjects. Male-female differences emerging in Leigh's study were consistent across sexual orientations. Gay male subjects reported similar reasons for engaging in sexual activity as heterosexual men, while lesbians connected sexual activity as closely to love and emotional involvement as did heterosexual women. Among reasons to avoid sexual activity, female subjects gave high ratings to fear of pregnancy, lack of interest in the partner, and a general lack of enjoyment in sexual acts. Male subjects rated the fear of AIDS and a fear of rejection more highly than female subjects. These findings led Leigh to conclude the following:

> Men attached more importance than women to sexual pleasure, conquest, and the relief of sexual tension as reasons for sex, while women saw emotional closeness as more important than did men. These sex differences appeared in both heterosexuals and homosexuals, lending credence to the notion that men's and women's motivations for sex are different, no matter what the sex of their partners. (p. 205)

Other research has produced consistent findings regarding sexual orientation and motives for engaging in sexual activity (Basow, 1992; Bell & Weinberg, 1978; Peplau, 1981; Peplau & Gordon, 1983).

In a similar survey about college students' motives and sexual activity, researchers posed the question, "For you, is an emotional involvement a prerequisite for participating in sexual intercourse?" (Carroll, Volk, & Hyde, 1985, p. 135). Results indicated that 85 percent of female subjects in the study, as compared to 40 percent of the male subjects, responded "always" or "most of the time"; 15 percent of the women responded either "sometimes" or "never," as compared to 60 percent of the men. The most frequent response from women in this study to the question, "What would be your primary reason for refusing to have sexual intercourse with someone?" was "not enough love/commitment" (p. 135). The most frequent answer provided by men was "never neglect an opportunity," meaning that they would never refuse to have intercourse (p. 135).

Corroborating findings emerged from a study by gender psychologist Bernard Whitley (1988). He asked college students, "What was your most important reason for having sexual intercourse on the most recent occasion?" (p. 623) In his study, 45 percent of the female subjects compared to 21 percent of the male subjects indicated that love and emotional fulfillment were their primary reasons for engaging in sexual activities. In contrast, 38 percent of the men compared to only 10 percent of the women indicated lust or pleasure as their reasons. Furthermore, the biological sex of Whitley's subjects was a better predictor of reasons for engaging in sexual activity than psychological gender. In other words, a subject who was androgynous tended to have similar reasons for having sexual intercourse as persons of his or her same sex. The results of these studies and others (DeLamater, 1987; DeLamater & MacCorquodale, 1979; DeLucia, 1987; Hatfield, 1983; Hite, 1976) are epitomized in Leigh's (1989) comment that research findings are "consistent with the notion that the expression of love is a more important motivator of sexual activity in women than in men" (p. 200).

These contemporary research findings suggest male-female differences in both the perception of sexual interest and the motivations for having and avoiding sexual activity. What can be made of these results? Do the researchers' findings match your experience or the experiences of your friends? Is it your perception that men tend to read more sexuality into things, while women attribute other causes or motivations for what they see? Or do you think that the difference is more a stereotype than a reality? One thing seems obvious to us: Stereotypes or not, given findings that reveal potential differences in women's and men's approaches to sexual activity in their relationships, it seems to be even more critical for relational partners to communicate openly and honestly about sex.

When Women and Men Talk about Sex

Talking about sexual activity represents a proactive approach to what can be a critical turning point in a relationship, although some may see it as taking the romance out of the act or the situation. Some research suggests that, traditionally, the woman's role in sexual game playing has been to hint, to convey subtly or nonverbally, whether or not she is sexually interested. Then the man is supposed to catch the clue and either abstain from or initiate sexual involvement (Anderson, Schultz, & Staley, 1987; Grauerholz & Serpe, 1985; McCormick & Jesser, 1983; Perper & Weis, 1987). Could it be that this hinting and guessing game in the name of preserving romance causes more problems than it's worth?

> *It seems that talking about sex requires more intimacy than actually doing it.*
>
> *Jane Fonda, actor & political activist*

Talking about Sex

A survey by sociologists Knox and Wilson (1981) of the dating and sexual behaviors of over 300 college students asked, "What do university men and women do to encourage their partners to become more sexually intimate?" (p. 257). One-third of the female and one-fourth of the male subjects responded that they preferred to "be open about sexual desires and expectations" (p. 257). Other less direct methods of expressing sexual expectations included "creating an atmosphere" for sexual intimacy, "expressing love," "moving closer to" a partner, and "hinting" (p. 257). Additional research has shown that couples who can talk about sex have higher levels of sexual satisfaction, and that the inability to talk about sex leads to sexuality-related problems (Baus & Allen, 1996; Wheeless & Parsons, 1995). These findings suggest that direct, open discussion of sexual activity isn't a first option for many people, but it's becoming a viable option as opposed to the guessing games that can cause misunderstanding. Honest communication appears to be preferable to trying to read each others' minds (and nonverbal cues), or expecting sexual activity to be like it is portrayed on television or in the movies, or taking the plunge only to discover that one's haste was a real mistake—one that may cost a relationship.

Just how do you approach the topic of sex with someone you're involved with or dating? When we say approach the topic of sex, we mean having a conversation about sexual activity in a relationship—no matter your views on whether sexual activity outside of marriage is wrong in general, inadvisable for you and a partner, or something that might occur in your relationship. This also involves discussing topics related to sexual activity, such as birth control, monogamy versus multiple partners, and views about protection from sexually transmitted diseases, especially AIDS (Edgar & Fitzpatrick, 1988). Communication researcher Sheer (1995) analyzed appeals for condom use in the initiation of a sexual relationship. Even though awareness of the need to use a condom has vastly increased, it remains a difficult point in relationships. She found, not too surprisingly, that persuasion appeals implying caring, responsibility, and pleasure are recommended.

Even if you believe that this kind of discussion is important, it doesn't necessarily make actually talking over sexual issues any easier. Many of us were raised with the belief that honest discussion about sexual acts was somehow improper, particularly in mixed company. Communication researchers Anderson, Schultz, and Staley (1987) explored some of the issues involved when a woman must become assertive in a sexual situation. Women are not usually taught or encouraged to talk about sex or to use sexual words in normal conversation; thus, their societal conditioning may work against them when they confront the need to be assertive. But Anderson, Schultz, and Staley contend that initiating a conversation about sexual activity with one's partner isn't a role one sex is expected to take, rather than the other. It is equally appropriate for the female or the male partner to initiate a discussion of this kind.

Sex and Language

Another problem is that our language doesn't provide much help; in fact it often works against honest, serious discussion (Potorti, 1992). What language can you use in a frank discussion with your partner about sex?

I had pretty much always been promiscuous, but right after I started doing Cheers, well, I was going on three dates a day. As a guy, you're raised to get as much as you can. Sex, sex, sex, that's what you're after. But after a while, I realized what I was doing was foolhardy. Still, it took some time to travel from the brain... groinward.

Woody Harrelson, actor

RECAP

---

promiscuity, monogamy, abstinence, celibacy, sexual activity, sexually transmitted diseases (STDs), sexual standards

---

Your options are (1) to use clinical, scientific terms, such as to say, "You believe that sexual intercourse and oral sex should be postponed until marriage, but heavy petting of clothed genitalia is okay?"; (2) to use euphemisms that may sound immature or condescending, such as "When I get close to you, my 'thing' reacts"; or (3) to use "gutter" terms for sexual acts and body parts, examples of which you're probably well aware. Many of us are uncomfortable using clinical terms, as though we'll come off sounding like we're quoting the latest anatomy textbook. Euphemisms can bring about such embarrassment or laughter that the discussion goes off-track. "Gutter" terms don't represent an option that many of us are comfortable with either; they can make sexual activity sound crude and unappealing, rather than the way one partner wants it to sound to another. There's no perfect way to talk to a partner about sex and, for now at least, it appears there's no way around the language problems. We encourage you to acknowledge the language limitations with your partner, maybe even to have a good laugh about the situation, and then to make the best of it as you work your way through an honest discussion about sexual activity. Defects in the language don't have to become an excuse for avoiding a discussion about sex.

Love, romance, and sex sometimes lead to a more long-term arrangement for the relationship—marriage—and we consider that next.

Marriage

The Marriage Tradition

Will you get married? An informal class survey might indicate your classmates' intentions. Ask the ones who say "no" to getting married how they feel about making that opinion public. Do they feel shy about expressing it? A little defensive? As if they aren't doing the right thing? There is a very strong cultural push to marry and raise a family. As we describe below, that pressure seems to be increasing. Some statistics say that in spite of the alternatives to marriage (living together, remaining single, communal living, etc.) approximately 95 percent of all Americans will get married (Information Please, 1998).

This societal pressure led writer Gerri Hirshey (1989) to describe what she calls the "tyranny of the couple." Not only is marriage still in, it is hip, it's the thing to do. She calls it "commitment obsession" (p. 49). Couples argue that they are doing what comes naturally, two by two. Writer Barbara Yost (1996) made the point quite strongly: "Single Americans are as welcome as pot-smoking hippies at a Bob Dole party" (p. H1). This attitude, she says, is hard on singles. Couples become so self-involved that they just leave single friends out. Married women see single women as potential threats. Single men who dress well and keep their houses neat may find their sexual orientation questioned (Yost, 1996) (remember the movie *In and Out?*). Hirshey jokes about the situation: "Question: How does a single woman get rid of roaches in her apartment? Answer: She asks them for a commitment" (p. 49). After a period in the 1970s when alternate lifestyles became acceptable alternatives to marriage, the culture now seems to be struggling back to the traditional model. "Lifestyle apologists defend retro tendencies under the rubric of 'The New Traditionalism,'" Yost explains (p. 53). Divorce rates have leveled off and even dropped in some areas. Yost sees a return to the idea that "People are expected to grow up, get married, and stay married—or risk the wrath of politicians who brandish spouse and children like banners of morality" (p. H1). It's all wrapped up in the question, "So how come you're still single?"

In spite of tremendous gains in many areas of life, work, recreation, education, and even politics, tradition seems to hold fast within most marriages. The pull of traditional role expectations has a powerful influence on many marriages. People who consider themselves highly liberated often undergo a metamorphosis once they marry, when they may be met head-on by a large dose of old-fashioned reality. The philosopher Goethe expressed it quite aptly when he said, "Love is an ideal thing; marriage is a real thing." And with that reality comes all the excess baggage of your first family, your marriage and family role models. As Tom, a young married man, said at one point, "I understand that things are supposed to be different in today's relationships, but still I can't help feeling that husbands are supposed to do some things and wives something else. Maybe I was born a hundred years too late."

Was he? Or were he and his partner, Beth, responding more to a complicated series of conflicting messages: Be liberated, look out for number 1, put your spouse's needs first, you can have it all, be a man. These and many similar contradictory messages make it very difficult to know what to do. What is a marriage supposed to be? How are the changes in gender roles to be handled? You may find yourself in a marriage or family and notice that you're acting just like your parents—doing some of those things you swore you would never do.

No single relationship is likely to be more important than the one with your spouse. Yet so many people enter marriage with little more than romantic dreams and good intentions. They feel that if and when they find the right person, they will live happily ever after. Listen to what Carl Rogers (as quoted in Buscaglia, 1986) had to say about today's marriages:

> Though modern marriage is a tremendous laboratory its members are often utterly without preparation for the partnership function. How much agony and remorse and failure could have been avoided if there had been at least some rudimentary learning before they entered the partnership (p. 28).

So are things that bad? Should you even consider getting married? Even the most skeptical among us admit that marriage seems to be good for people.

Single men and women report more stress, use more drugs, and contemplate suicide more often than married people of either sex. Both married women and men are happier and more secure than single people, have higher rates of financial satisfaction, and enjoy better mental and physical health (Marks, 1996; Stack & Ross, 1998). Marks points out a small gender difference however: Single women fare better overall than single men, and in some areas fare better than married people. There are obvious advantages to the partnership of marriage.

Given that you will probably enter a long-term relationship, what does it take to succeed? How can you increase your chances of reaping the benefits and avoiding the pitfalls? We don't have all the answers, but we would like to explore and share some of the research we have gathered and the experiences we have personally participated in that may contribute to success in both marriage and family relationships. Of the many communication and gender variables that can be considered, we have chosen to focus on three and apply each to marriage: *communication patterns, power and empowerment,* and *intimacy.* We explore these three points to provide a focus for discussing gender in marriage, a springboard for learning about improving marital communication, and a means of developing a wider repertoire of communication behaviors for both sexes that lead to greater personal effectiveness.

Communication Patterns

First of all, just what are *patterns?* Pearson (1989) defines patterns as "predictable and manageable sets of behaviors that are unique to the family and are distinctive from any one family member's own actions" (p. 34). Every relationship develops its own patterns. Most of the time, these patterns seem to develop on their own, formed by general societal rules and norms, or by the individual's needs and desires. For the most part, people in relationships don't sit down together and say, "Let's work out our pattern of communication." You will have noticed, however, that we have advocated exactly that in more than one chapter. We believe talking about it makes it better, that couples need to hold periodic conversations about the quality of their relationship, and that these conversations will help develop effective patterns of communication. Various marriage researchers and therapists (Bodermann, 1997; Hickmon, Protinsky, & Singh, 1997; Worthington, McCullough, Shortz, & Mindes, 1995) researched the value of this type of conversation in marriage enrichment groups and found significant increases in marital satisfaction for couples who talked openly about their communication patterns. The sooner in the relationship this is done, the more likely it is that patterns will be formed purposefully rather than by accident.

Patterns are a way to reduce uncertainty in a relationship. As discussed in Chapter 6, individuals who feel uncertain about their relationships will do what they can to reduce that uncertainty. One clear way to reduce uncertainty is to develop rituals and routines in communication. These patterns help lend predictability to a situation, and the predictability breeds security

(Bruess & Pearson, 1997). Perhaps this explains, to an extent, why some people are working hard to go back to the more traditional view of marriage—it is more predictable.

Security through predictability, however, can be achieved through means other than jumping on the traditional marriage bandwagon. It involves, as you might guess, developing patterns for your own relationship that support the kind of communication and relationship you want to achieve and maintain. We're reminded of a couple, Ken and Diane, who are nearing their golden anniversary. From their honeymoon, into their children's diapers, and through the children's teen years, Ken and Diane have had a weekly date. Sometimes it is simply a cup of tea late at night after chores are done and kids are in bed; other times it involves planning and working together on a household project; and other dates might actually be a weekend getaway for just the two of them. What is important is that these weekly dates are as regular as clockwork. Ken and Diane prioritize their relationship. Sometimes the discussions are heated, and sometimes they are tender. But they always happen. These weekly dates have become a predicable pattern for both Ken and Diane, one that has created a strong sense of security while reducing a large degree of uncertainty in this long-standing marriage.

The Relationship of Patterns to Reported Satisfaction

Assuming you are convinced of the need to talk about and develop your own communication patterns with your marriage partner, what kind of patterns does the research say you might try to develop? Communication researchers Dainton, Stafford, and McNeilis (1992) looked at the question of what type of routine patterns of behavior were related to satisfaction. They found that sharing tasks (such as housework), keeping everyday interactions pleasant and positive, a high level of mutual self-disclosure, assurances of worth and love, and sharing time together were identified as important to satisfaction and to relationship maintenance. In similar research, Yogev and Brett (1985) found that both husbands and wives report greater marital satisfaction when they equally share home and child-rearing responsibilities. These research results do not fit the traditional model of marriages. The results suggest a higher level of involvement of men in the relationship through a pattern of increased disclosure, sharing of responsibilities, and positive relationship comments.

In other research, happily married couples appear to be more flexible in their communication patterns with each other than distressed couples. Their patterns with each other are more relaxed, open, friendly, dramatic, and attentive (Honeycutt, Wilson, & Parker, 1982). They listen more; they talk less. Research shows satisfied couples also score high in mutual trust and supportive communication; nonreciprocated trust together with a lack of support are often good indicators of a failing marriage (Cutrona & Suhr, 1994; Honeycutt, Wilson, & Parker, 1982). Often trust is taken for granted, especially during the early stages of a relationship. With starry eyes, and usually little experience in causing each other pain, trust tends to be automatic. It is rarely even talked about. But as the honeymoon ends, and days turn into years, something happens, especially if the subject of trust is just taken for granted and never talked about. Little by little trust is broken, it is not reciprocated or nurtured, and soon the security of a once-strong relationship becomes a failed marriage statistic. Satisfied couples, on the other hand, work to reciprocate trust and support.

Problems in Patterns

Some potential problems are associated with the conscious development of communication patterns. Many times the patterns can remain unexamined over a period of time. Johnson (1991) suggests that people who say their relationship is good usually will not look at it carefully, will not see all the major and minor frustrations. Johnson writes, "the longer they have been together, the more built-up pressure there is, the more terrified they are of breakup, and therefore the more resistance they have to seeing themselves truthfully" (p. 74). Sometimes it takes a degree of courage to sit down and carefully examine the patterns of your relationship, especially if the patterns are ineffective. Researchers have identified a number of negative patterns, including the demand-withdraw pattern in which one partner makes a request or demand for a change, and the other partner reacts by withdrawing (Julien, Arellano, & Turgeon, 1997; Klinetob & Smith, 1996). Klinetob and Smith point out that "the spouse with the most to gain by maintaining the status quo is likely to withdraw, and the discontented spouse demands change. Insofar as the status quo in marriage generally tends to favor men, men will appear most frequently as withdrawers" (p. 954). They state that breaking out of such a negative pattern is quite difficult, especially if the status quo works well for the dominant person.

There is no magic answer for this dilemma, but perhaps a little technique called "I'm listening" will assist you in this endeavor. This is a useful technique, though men may not be able to use this technique easily if they approach listening in a stereotypic, got-to-solve-your-problem fashion. The technique proceeds like this: The partner who feels a need to bring up an uncomfortable topic can ask his or her partner to simply listen. The partner's only response throughout can be "I'm listening," with little physical response other than nodding the head. As the partner pauses in talking, the listening partner can say, "I'm listening," in an encouraging tone. When the partner initiating the encounter feels that he or she is through talking, they switch places. This technique can help both people openly share while reducing fear, anger, and frustration so a more level-headed, caring conversation can take place.

Carol Gilligan (1981) spoke of misunderstandings internal to the relationship as a factor that interferes with effective communication patterns:

> What a man will see as care and respect, a woman may experience as neglect. What she sees as care and concern, he may see as interference with his autonomy. A woman who sees herself as loving may discover that her man views her as manipulative, castrating, and out of control. Women consider failure to respond as a serious moral problem. A man who sees himself as caring may be surprised to find that his woman finds him cold and unresponsive (p. 64).

As this quote suggests, it is highly important to develop a shared perception of communication patterns and to realize that significant sex differences exist in these perceptions.

At times, the patterns change due to circumstances outside the couple's relationship. The arrival of a child, change in employment, a move to a new city, and other changes will have a clear (and sometimes negative) impact on the communication patterns in the marriage (Sinclair & McCluskey, 1996).

Communication patterns in marriage are important, and the longer they are in existence, the harder they are to change. That is why it is critical to establish the patterns early and evaluate them regularly. In spite of your best efforts, problems may occur. At times establishing, evaluating, and changing patterns within a relationship can be painful, but the effort can be worth it.

Power and Empowerment

No matter how effectively you establish the patterns, one fact of any marriage is the reality of differences. Yet many people believe these differences will not lead to conflict or problems. In Chapter 7, we referred to the dysfunctional relationship beliefs described by Epstein and his colleagues (Eidelson & Epstein, 1982). Two that apply here are that disagreement is destructive, and that partners cannot change. The first of these two is sometimes manifested in the belief that, "We'll never fight, we love each other too much." Then the first fight does come, the relationship fails, and it's home to mom. The second is evidenced when one (or both) partners say to themselves "He/She won't change, what's the use? I'm out of here." In either case, the relationship is in jeopardy. Communication researchers Metts and Cupach (1990) investigated the correlation between these dysfunctional beliefs and destructive problem-solving responses in couples. Their research showed a positive correlation between these dysfunctional beliefs and ineffective problem-solving behaviors such as exiting and neglect.

While not all relationship problems can be solved by communication, many can. We advocate developing a

> *I hate pants. This is something I have inherited from my father. He despised pants, and my mother was never allowed to wear them at home. I still feel this way, and neither my mother nor Maria is allowed to go out with me in pants.*
>
> *Arnold Schwarzenegger,*
> *actor*

pattern in which relationship issues concerning change and control can be worked out. One book about this topic published in the 1970s was *Intimate Enemy: How to Fight Fair in Love and Marriage* (Bach & Wyden, 1968). Some students have difficulty with the idea of "fighting fair" in a relationship because they think that learning how to fight will just cause more fights to occur. That's not our experience. Since disagreements are going to happen, it makes sense to develop communication patterns that support the chances for a mutually satisfying resolution to the issue. For instance, one pattern that one of your authors, Phil, and his partner have developed when involved in a heated disagreement is to disallow "carpetbagging," or raising unrelated issues during an argument. In the early stages of their marriage they mutually agreed (established a pattern) to discuss only the matter at hand when in the throes of an argument. If the topic of discussion is money, neither partner is allowed to bring up unrelated frustrations about each other that happen to come to mind at the time. This pattern, for them, has been an effective one for encouraging fair fighting. When the one topic is resolved or exhausted, they mutually agree to get on with their lives or to discuss another issue.

Another type of pattern that appears to be central to long-term relationship effectiveness is the pattern of control. In keeping with the values we described in Chapter 1, we believe a pattern of equality of control in a marriage is the most effective for both people. In virtually all instances, it seems shared decision making is a benefit. Research in this area is beginning to support the value of equitable, shared decision making. Research has shown a positive correlation between equality of decision making and decision-making satisfaction (Ting-Toomey, 1984). In other research, both husbands and wives report greater marital satisfaction when they equally share home and child-rearing responsibilities in addition to decision making (Rosenbluth, Steil, & Whitcomb, 1998). Conversely, a lack of equitable decision making is related to low satisfaction. Wives, more than husbands, feel distress when the relationship is inequitable (Ragolin & Hansen, 1985). Changing the balance of decision making toward more equitability can initially mean greater costs to men and greater benefits to women (Rosenbluth, Steil, & Whitcomb, 1998), but the costs and benefits even out over time. This research suggests that equality of control can lead to greater satisfaction and can help overall decision making. Perhaps this is an idea whose time has come.

Equality of control is a related issue. Shared control in a marriage is more likely to occur when the norms (the patterns) are egalitarian and when the wife and the husband perceive their competence levels to be the same (Nye, 1982). Developing this equality seems to involve three dimensions: integrity (respecting each other), reciprocity (what is good for one is good for the other), and flexibility (both are able to adapt to shifts in conditions) (Bate and Memmott, 1984). Equality will not happen, according to psychologist Carol Gilligan (1981), until both the man and the woman move from the traditional roles. Women, according to Gilligan, must understand their own needs as well as those of others: "until a woman, in any relationship, can give up saying that she has no needs and desires or that they are not important and that all she wants to do is what the other person wants, she is bound to be resentful and there are bound to be problems in a relationship" (p. 64). The corollary for men appears to be to take some of the focus off personal needs and turn attention to balancing the needs of both people. Balance in a relationship may be acquired as well as given. It seems that as the traditional man moves away from attempting to exert control, and the traditional woman moves away from acquiescence or indirect methods of control, both people might discover greater satisfaction and effectiveness.

Dominance

Dominance has long been part of the marital relationship, and tradition dictates that men usually hold the dominant role. Like so many other parts of marriage, that appears to be changing as well—with good reason: Research has consistently shown that imbalances in power and dominance lead to ineffective problem solving. Note the distinction between dominance and being domineering. Being domineering means being willing to assert one's own wishes (Rogers & Millar, 1979), whereas dominance in a marriage means one partner asserts a controlling power over the other person. Dominance can also be described by one person's "one-up statement" being followed by the other person's "one-down statement." If Cec says "Let's go to lunch," and Eric responds "OK," Cec is in the dominating position. However, if Eric would have responded with, "OK, but first I want to finish watching this video," he would have been exhibiting domineeringness. The interesting part of the research that relates to our value of equality of power is that statements of domineeringness decrease the other person's dominance. However, research shows that high domineeringness in both sexes is inversely related to marital satisfaction, though scores were lower for men (Rogers & Millar, 1979). It would appear that domineeringness is related to assertiveness. The judicious use of domineeringness may help keep one person or the other from being too dominant.

Ownership

Johnson (1991) discusses a source of conflict in a relationship related to control: ownership. She contends that married people attempt to own one another in body, time, attention, talents, energy, and loyalty. According to Johnson, the concept of ownership underlies all (or most of) the interactions, puzzles, and muddles of relationships. She gives an example that may sound familiar to many of you. Couples generally need to negotiate to allow adequate time both for each other and for themselves. In Johnson's case, she and her partner worked at home (both were writers), so they had 24 hours per day to negotiate. How much of your partner's time do you own? How much is theirs? How much of their time do you give them permission to use?

Conflict

We have talked of the reality of conflict in marriage. Communication researchers Duck and Wood (1995) state: "In the process of everyday living, even close partners encounter challenges and travails, hit flat spots, have relational 'bad hair days,' and generally mix the rough with the smooth in ways wisely foreseen by the writers of traditional wedding vows" (pp. 1–2). Are there sex differences in approaches to conflict? Taylor and Miller (1994) believe sex differences in conflict resolution begin with socialization: "Girls are socialized to value relationships and maintain harmony while boys are socialized to value status and seek victory . . . This is thought to translate into women taking a cooperative stance in conflict situations, whereas men are more competitive" (p. 155). Communication researchers Burggraf and Sillars (1987) reported that sex differences were barely apparent in marital conflict. Similarly, Fitzpatrick (1988) reported that conflict style was more related to marital type than sex. Fitzpatrick identified three types of marriage and corresponding conflict styles: (1) *traditionals,* who have a high level of interdependence, a willingness to engage in conflict, and espouse conventional ideas of marriage; (2) *independents,* who emphasize autonomy and sharing, engage in conflict, and reject traditional ideas of marriage; and (3) *separates,* who express a need for autonomy and their own space, plus little willingness to engage in conflict.

Keashly (1994) summarized research on gender differences in couples, finding few gender differences in preferred conflict management styles. She found that both women and men preferred to handle conflict through the following strategies, in descending order: accommodation, avoidance, compromise, collaboration, and least of all, competition. However, in practice, women portrayed themselves, as did their partners, as more emotional and critical of the man's insensitivity. In turn, men portrayed themselves, as did their partners, as logical and unemotional, showing open anger, and providing reasons for delay. Women tended to be more direct in managing their conflicts than men. In research predicting marriage outcomes, marriage researcher Gottman and his associates (Gottman, Coan, Carrere, & Swanson, 1998) found that the possibility of divorce could be predicted by negative conflict initiation by the wife, a couple's inability to break out of a negative conflict pattern, and the refusal of the husband to accept influence by the wife.

Communication researchers Harward and Cavanaugh (1997) describe a pattern similar to the demand-withdraw pattern we discussed earlier in this chapter. They cite research (Christensen & Shenk, 1991; Weiss & Dehle, 1994) showing that men are more likely to avoid conflict and women more likely to approach it. Women tend to confront conflict because they perceive confrontation as problem solving and as an opportunity to get closer to their partner, whereas men tend to view their wives' behavior as nagging and unproductive. Harward and Cavanaugh (1997) reported few gender differences in conflict issues, but they did note "there were no accounts of couples having their first big fight because the male wanted more time and attention from his partner" (p. 12). An interesting note.

In other research related to conflict, interpersonal communication researcher Ritter (1989) concluded that husbands often argue to win, wives argue to get approval from the other. Similarly, communication researcher Krueger

(1986) found that women see control over process and the agenda as important as men's control over content. Eells and O'Flaherty (1996) point out that most conflicts come from perceptual differences. Couples who encode and decode messages in a similar manner, who see the issues and the methods of handling those issues in the same way, do not have severe relational problems. The message from research indicates that since women and men view the conflict process somewhat differently, talking about the differences overtly and determining shared relational meanings are critical to resolving relational conflict. It is clear from the research that the ability to discover negative conflict patterns in a relationship and to change them toward more positive patterns is critical to long-term relationship success (Gottman, Coan, Carrere, & Swanson, 1998).

Duck and Wood (1995) make the point that conflict and happiness are not necessarily opposites, but intertwined. "Relationships are complex experiences in which grief and joy, pleasure and pain, enjoyment and irritation, ease and discomfort, satisfaction and frustration are recurrent and paired elements" (p. 6). Issues of power and control in personal and relationship change will continue to be difficult challenges for both men and women. Acquiring the ability to share power and implementing strategies to empower others constitute a significant shift in communication patterns for many people. Unresolved, these issues can become barriers to a common relationship goal, the achievement of intimacy and satisfaction.

Intimacy and Satisfaction

Everyone wants to live happily ever after, and most people want to enter into relationships they find intimate and satisfying. If developing a satisfying relationship is the goal, then it is probably useful to examine what research and what married people report about the strategies that help reach this goal.

Intimacy

Realizing that the term *intimacy* can mean different things to different people, psychological researchers Waring, Tillman, Frelick, Russell, and Weisz (1980) asked a wide variety of individuals the question, "What does intimacy mean to you?" They organized the answers around four themes: (1) sharing private thoughts, dreams, and beliefs; (2) sexuality, with an emphasis on affection and commitment; (3) having a personal sense of identity; and (4) absence of anger, resentment, and criticism. In similar research, Feldman (1979) found that intimacy involved the characteristics of a close, personal, and usually affectionate relationship; detailed and deep knowledge of the other; and sexual relations. Arliss (1993) describes the contemporary expectation that couples create a union with emotional connectedness at its core. She says spouses are supposed to be best friends as well as serve a variety of pragmatic roles (e. g., maintaining a household). While different definitions of intimacy do exist, it is important that husbands and wives share a definition of intimacy. Psychologists Heller and Wood (1998) found couples who were less accurate in predicting partner responses to a relationship intimacy questionnaire experienced lower intimacy and experienced intimacy in different ways. Couples who could accurately predict partner responses reported much greater satisfaction with the relationship's level of intimacy.

Sex differences in approaches to intimacy are clearly present in marriages. Feldman (1982) suggests that sex role conditioning has a negative impact on marital intimacy, encouraging male inexpressiveness and even nagging by women. In a similar point of view, Fitzpatrick and Induik (1982) report:

> The husbands in our sample perceived themselves as rarely nurturant, passive, or dependent, always dominant and task-oriented, and generally incapable of discussing or expressing their feelings. Consequently, it falls to the wives in these relationships to maintain some level of expressivity . . . when wives cannot or refuse to be expressive, the relationship suffers. Wives may be said to bear the burden of expressivity in their marital relationships. (p. 696)

More recent research supports these findings. Psychologists Heller and Wood (1998) found that women reported higher levels of intimacy than did their partners and were better than men in predicting their partner's feelings. Men were less attuned to intimacy. These sex differences, and one sex's lack of awareness of the other sex's tendencies, lead to diminished intimacy. A wide range of other research supports this conclusion. Among the differences identified, wives are more likely to use a range of affective responses and greater emotional expressiveness than husbands (Notarius & Johnson, 1982) and are more expressive and affectionate (Thompson & Walker, 1989). Men are sometimes confused and mystified by these differences in what women want in intimacy (McGoldrick, 1989). Yet there is a lack of direct conversation about these differences (Rubin, 1984), especially among men—women were more likely to talk about these issues and to value related disclosure (Shimanoff, 1985). Some differences in intimacy can be traced to different perceptions of disclosure. Rubin (1984) found that women may fail to recognize their husband's comments as self-disclosure, and men may feel that just being in physical proximity with their wives is intimacy. Physical closeness, however, may not replace clarity of information. Purnine and Carey (1997) found that men's understanding of their wives' sexual preferences contributed to overall satisfaction with the relationship.

We've given you a considerable list of research to point out the strength of the traditional model. This model identifies a role for both men and women—men as inexpressive, women as emotional. Our question to you is this: Will you be bound by these traditions? Does this research reflect the way it has to be? In Chapter 6 we covered gender differences related to disclosure in some detail, and we suggested that each sex broaden its range of behaviors regarding disclosure. This becomes more critical in a marriage. Levels of intimacy and satisfaction are linked to effective disclosure.

To achieve an increased level of satisfaction, balanced definitions of intimacy are critical. Gottman, Katz, and Hooven (1997) describe the value of conversations about "meta-emotion" in developing a shared perception of the emotional quality of the relationship and the factors that contribute to its positive development. The couple can express the balanced definitions they arrive at through what Galvin and Brommel (1991) call "relational currencies": agreed-upon ways of conveying affection, information, caring, and other relational variables. The key is the mutual definition of the currency. It is through this mutual definition that couples are able to be more empathetic with each other, leading to greater clarity in the relationship (Ickes & Simpson, 1997), thus leading to greater reciprocity in emotional behavior (Gaines, 1996). For example, if a man thinks he is expressing affection through an activity like tuning up his wife's car, but she doesn't see that act as affectionate, then these two have not yet achieved a mutual agreement on defining the currency of affection.

Developing definitions of relational currency and recognizing the role of open expression of thoughts and feelings is an important part of the perception of satisfaction. Montgomery (1981) found that satisfying communication in marriage requires four things: openness through mutual self-disclosure, confirmation and acceptance, transactional management, and situational adaptability. Pearson and Spitzberg (1990) support this view; they found four stages in developing an effective relationship: (1) sharing self, (2) affirming the other, (3), becoming one, and (4) transcending one. Cartensen, Graff, Levenson, and Gottman (1996) present another argument for the importance of emotional depth and investment in a relationship: Couples with a heavier positive emotional investment have better mental and physical health in addition to having a more satisfying relationship, they say.

Increasing the amount of information sharing can do more than increase understanding and intimacy. It can also have a significant impact on the level of commitment to the relationship. Family researcher Mary Lund (1985) defines commitment as "an attitude about continuing a relationship that is strengthened by a person's own acts of investing time, effort, and resources in the relationship" (p. 4). The more a person has invested in the relationship, the less likely she or he is to leave it. The investment itself continues and becomes a barrier to reducing commitment in the relationship. In some ways, commitment is related more to investment than to rewards. Lund says that commitment can be predicted from a combination of satisfaction, investments in a relationship, and poor prospects for alternate relationships. If men and women follow the traditional roles we have described, then men are less likely to invest, and thus less likely to commit.

These variables, then, appear to be intertwined. Sharing information and disclosing feelings not only increase understanding, but also lead to the development of a greater commitment to the relationship and increased feelings of satisfaction. However, we can't say that more is always better when it comes to sharing information. For example, communication researchers Sillars, Folwell, Hill, Maki, Hurst, and Casano (1992) investigated the extent to which communication produced greater understanding in a relationship. Sometimes a couple's best efforts to communicate only reinforce the misunderstandings. Discussions about the patterns of intimacy, about the currency of the relationship, and the limitations of sex roles can help avoid the misunderstandings these researchers identified.

Satisfaction

What are the keys to a good marriage? A recent newspaper article (Maugh, 1998) claims, "If you want your marriage to last for a long time, the newest advice from psychologists is quite simple: Just do what your wife says. Go ahead, give in to her" (p. 14A). While we believe this message to be an exaggeration, it is a good example of what the popular press sees as the key to relational satisfaction and success.

Most people, however, would say that love is the basis for satisfaction—despite the difficulty in defining love, as we discussed in the previous chapter. Communication researchers Marston, Hecht, and Robers (1986) investigated the subjective experience of romantic love and discovered six different levels of love:

1. Collaborative love, characterized by feelings of increased energy, intensified emotional response, and reciprocal support.
2. Active love, characterized by feelings of strength and doing things together.
3. Secure love, manifested in a strong feeling of security and discussion of intimate topics.
4. Intuitive love, experienced, though not expressed verbally.
5. Committed love, being together and planning the future.
6. Traditional romantic love.

When members of a couple experience different kinds of love, they may have trouble attaining the satisfaction they desire. Even if members of a couple experience the same type of love, research in marital satisfaction shows that both love and satisfaction decline in the first two years of marriage (Huston, McHale, & Crouter, 1986). It is not easy maintaining a level of satisfaction.

Certainly, many ingredients are important for satisfaction in marriage. According to Lauer and Lauer (1985), 350 couples who claimed satisfaction with their marriages tended to find mutual satisfaction in such things as, "my spouse is my best friend," "I like my spouse as a person," "marriage is a long-term commitment," " marriage is sacred," "we agree on aims and goals," "my spouse has grown more interesting," and "I want the relationship to succeed" (p. 5). While statements like this are usually thought to be the statements of the female partner, it is clear that both partners, particularly the man, need to state them. It's not an exaggeration to say that without healthy patterns that include some kind of regular discussion about themselves and their relationship this kind of mutual satisfaction would simply not exist.

For many couples, mutual satisfaction doesn't exist. Communication writer Mary Anne Fitzpatrick (1988) observed that researchers have consistently found low correlations between husbands' and wives' judgments of marital satisfaction. Perhaps the two people in the marriage experience it differently

(Bernard, 1972). Satisfaction, like a successful marriage, is never guaranteed. However, statements like those above can lead to increased clarity of feelings of satisfaction. Achieving satisfaction in a relationship is an ongoing process. In most relationships, each partner has her or his own agenda regarding satisfaction. For instance, at least for some women, satisfaction is related to their ability to meet and exceed the role expectations their spouses express (Petronio, 1982). It would probably be safe to say there are at least an equal number of women who would find little if any satisfaction with this kind of marriage pattern. As we have described elsewhere, sexes tend to report more satisfaction in marriages where equality is the pattern. Communicating about the factors that bring you satisfaction with your partner can be helpful in producing satisfaction, for few of us are mind readers. The ability to bring up important issues, talk them over, and adapt messages to your partner's individual beliefs and needs not only fits with the important value of treating the other person as an individual, but also leads to greater reported marital satisfaction (deTurck & Miller, 1986: Wilkie, Ferree, & Ratcliff, 1998).

Vangelisti and Huston (1992) investigated the relationship between satisfaction and love by correlating eight factors (assessment of leisure time, division of household labor, communication with partner, influence in making decisions, sexual relationship, time spent with partner, contact with friends, and the couple's financial situation). While not conclusive, the findings are very interesting. During the first year of marriage, wives' satisfaction focused on the amount of time they had to do things as a couple and the amount of time they spent with friends. In the second year, however, wives' focus changed. In that year, wives who were satisfied with the quality of communication and the nature of the sexual relationship were more satisfied overall. In the third year, wives' emphasis again moved to quality of communication, to division of household labor, and influence in decision making. For husbands, none of the eight indicators listed by Vangelisti and Huston were associated with satisfaction in the first year of marriage. In the second year, satisfaction with relational influence and quality of communication were associated with overall satisfaction.

These researchers also compared these factors to expressions of love. For women, none of the eight were significantly associated with feelings of love in the first year of marriage. During the second year, wives who were more satisfied with the way they had been spending their free time were significantly more in love with their husbands. In the third year, wives who were more satisfied with their sexual relationship tended to report stronger feelings of love. Those husbands in the first year of marriage who were satisfied with the sexual relationship were significantly more in love with their wives. None of the eight factors correlated in the second year. In the third year, husbands' satisfaction with finances was negatively associated with love (the more I like the money, the less I like you), and the quality of sexual relations was marginally associated with their love.

Satisfaction is also related to relationship dimensions less romantic than love. In the article, "Time, Dirt, and Money," sociologists Baker, Kiger, and Riley (1996) argued that economic, time, and household-task arrangements are critical aspects of a couple's satisfaction with day-to-day life. Not surprisingly, these researchers found that men are more satisfied, overall, with household-task arrangements than are women and that satisfaction is also related to the amount of communication. While the relationship is complex, it may be safe to say highly satisfied couples engage in significantly more communication than do less satisfied couples (Burleson & Denton, 1997; Richmond, 1995; Teichner & Farnden-Lyster, 1997).

Sillars, Sheen, Macintosh, and Pomegranate (1997) went one step further to analyze aspects of communication patterns and found those satisfied with marriage were distinguished by a focus on joint versus individual identity as reflected in pronoun use (we versus I and you), cross-referencing of language, (checking with each other for understanding), and confirming statements. Burleson and Denton (1997) examined differences between distressed couples and satisfied couples. The primary differences were that distressed couples spent significantly more time communicating negative messages; wives reported greater satisfaction when husbands could accurately perceive their feelings; and husbands reported greater satisfaction with spouses who had strong communication skills and were more cognitively complex. Satisfaction may also come from having a shared, effective public identity. Couples able to participate effectively in communal life tend to be more attracted to each other and to have a more satisfying relationship (Sanders, 1997). Satisfaction is a complex issue. The factors of satisfaction identified above suggest gender differences related to satisfaction and indicate at least a few ways that couples can move toward greater satisfaction.

We have covered only a small part of the available information about communication in marriage. Our focus has been on creating effective communication patterns and developing those patterns into communication behaviors that increase both the equality of power within the relationship and the opportunities for intimacy.

CONCLUSION

Gender communication in love, sex, romance, and marriage is complicated by a wide range of sociological, biological, linguistic, and relational factors. Success in these relationships is never guaranteed, but the chances for success can be increased by broadening the range of communication behaviors that you bring to these contexts.

Romance, sex, love, acceptance, autonomy, change, monogamy, commitment, respect—these are just some of the integral issues within a romantic relationship. Although the tensions in romance aren't particularly easy to write or talk about, they're easier to talk about than to negotiate in an actual relationship. Your own experience, the experiences of your friends, and what we've described in this chapter should reemphasize the considerable complexities inherent in romantic relationships.

We are particularly interested in the patterns of communication within intimate relationships because effective patterns lead to success and feelings of satisfaction whereas ineffective patterns lead to any number of destructive possibilities. It may sound simple, for example, to read about negotiating a balance between your sense of independence apart from the relationship and the time spent together. However, when you actually confront that first discussion and witness the hurt as a result of one partner's assertion of independence, you find that it's a much harder and more complex issue to manage. It's easy to give lip service to the sentiment, "I love you for what you are; I'll never want to change you," but what happens when you really, honestly think your way is better? Even understanding the complexity involved in these kinds of relationships, however, isn't enough to scare us away from romance and marriage. When it's going well, when it's right, there's hardly anything comparable.

As we have advocated in other chapters in this text, we continue to suggest that communicating is preferable to *not* communicating. Most of us function better with information than when we feel we've been cut out of the loop, and romantic partners need information. It's fairly safe to say that an expanded communication repertoire and a willingness to openly communicate with one's partner in a way that's not stereotyped by sex is a more successful way to approach romantic relationships than the reverse. This approach doesn't mean you'll be successful every time—you know there are no guarantees, especially in the romantic context. But, given the chances that your relationship success ratio could improve, it's probably well worth it to attempt to expand the range of your gender communication in this unique context.

Key Terms

romantic relationship
relational partner
significant other
tensions
autonomy
connection
acceptance
change
commitment
commitmentphobia
promiscuity
monogamy

abstinence
celibacy
sexual activity
sexually transmitted
    diseases (STDs)
sexual standards
traditional model
marriage
communication patterns
control
dominance
ownership

conflict
relational currency
satisfaction
expression of love
power
empowerment
pulse of the relationship
routine communication
    agendas
reciprocal trust

Discussion Starters

1. Consider the language used to refer to special people in our lives. How did you refer to the person in your first romantic relationship, like the first boy or girl you really liked in a different way from the rest? How did those references change as you grew up and experienced different types of relationships? Does the term *relational partner* work for you, or can you suggest a better term?

2. Think of an example—in your own life or the life of someone close to you—that epitomizes the tension of autonomy versus connection. If you are married, was it difficult when you and your spouse experienced that first rift of independence? Did it happen while you were dating, or after you got married? Have you seen this issue arise in other married couples? How did they handle it? How did you and your spouse handle it? Do you think this issue is more easily negotiated between marital partners as compared to persons who are only steadily dating?

3. Review the information in this chapter on "commitmentphobia." Did this information change your views regarding commitment and the sexes? Is it your current opinion that men are generally more fearful of commitment in a romantic relationship than women, or the reverse, or neither? Could it be that commitmentphobia has more to do with personality variables and family background, for instance, than with sex or gender?

4. Think of a time when someone tested you or your relationship. Was the test a major event or crisis, such as unfaithfulness or dishonesty? Or was it more of a secret test, the more subtle way of finding out how your partner feels about you, like we described in this chapter? How did you respond to the test?

5. Let's do a "best-worst" kind of exercise. Imagine that you are currently in a romantic relationship. (If you *are* in one, then the imagining won't be necessary; just use your own relationship for the example.) The relationship has the usual ups and downs, but generally things are going fairly well. Now imagine that your relational partner is breaking up with you—it's terrible, we know, but it might be wise to think about this. How would you prefer that your partner terminate the relationship? Do you prefer an impersonal phone call or letter, so that you don't have the embarrassment of losing face or getting upset? Would you prefer a rational, open face-to-face discussion about the break-up? Or a shouting match, so that each person could express his or her views and emotions without restraint? How do you respond to the old "I still want to be friends" line? What's the best way for your partner to communicate bad news to you?

6. Do you think that negotiating the sexual waters with a relational partner is a difficult communication challenge? If so, why is it that women and men may have difficulty openly discussing sexual activity in their relationship? What are the barriers to a successful discussion of this kind? If you don't think that this sort of communication is problematic, how have you avoided the difficulty?

7. Do you find that college-age people are moving to embrace the traditional model of relationships? Or do you find that these students are continuing to seek alternate relationship styles?
8. What is the best pattern of communication you have seen in a marriage? What made it effective? Did the two people involved develop this consciously or did the pattern tend to evolve out of trial and error? How should decisions be made in a marriage or similar relationship? Should each decision be a 50–50 proposition? Should different partners take the lead on different things? How are these to be negotiated?
9. How can feelings of intimacy be maintained over a long period of time? Is it even possible? Should a relationship expect to go through periods of time of less intimacy? What are the patterns of communication within a marriage that promote feelings of intimacy?

References

ABBEY, A. (1982). Sex Differences in attributions for friendly behavior: Do males misperceive females' friendliness? *Journal of Personality and Social Psychology, 42,* 830–838.

ANDERSON, J., SCHULTZ, B., & STALEY, C. C. (1987). Training in argumentativeness: New hope for nonassertive women. *Women's Studies in Communication, 10,* 58–66.

ARLISS, L. P. (1993). When myths endure and realities change: Communication in romantic relationships. In L. P. Arliss & D. J. Borisoff (Eds.), *Women and men communicating: Challenges and changes* (pp. 71–85). Fort Worth, TX: Harcourt Brace Jovanovich.

AVERY, C. S. (1989, May). How do you build intimacy? *Psychology Today,* 27–31.

BABER, K. M., & MONAGHAN, P. (1988). College women's career and motherhood expectations. New options, old dilemmas. *Sex Roles, 19,* 189–203.

BACH, G. R. & WYDEN, P. (1968) *The intimate enemy: How to fight fair in love and marriage.* New York: Avon Books.

BAKER, R., KIGER, G., & RILEY, P. J. (1996). Time, dirt, and money: The effects of gender, gender ideology, and type of earner marriage on time, household-task, and economic satisfaction among couples with children. *Journal of Social Behavior & Personality, 11,* 161–177.

BALL, F. L. J., COWAN, P., & COWAN, C. P. (1995). Who's got the power? Gender differences in partners' perceptions of influence during marital problem-solving discussions. *Family Process, 34,* 303–321.

BANKS, S., ALTENDORF, D., GREENE, J., & CODY, M. (1987). An examination of relationship disengagement: Perceptions, breakup strategies and outcomes. *Western Journal of Speech Communication, 51,* 19–41.

BASOW, S. A. (1992). *Gender: Stereotypes and roles* (3rd ed.). Pacific Grove, CA: Brooks/Cole.

BATE, B., & MEMMOTT, J. (1984, March). *Three principles for dual career marriages.* Paper presented at Northern Illinois University, DeKalb, Il.

BAUS, R. D., & ALLEN, J. L. (1996). Solidarity and sexual communication as selective filters: A report on intimate relationship development. *Communication Research Reports, 13,* 1–7.

BAXTER, L. A. (1982). Strategies for ending relationships: Two studies. *Western Journal of Speech Communication, 46,* 223–241.

BAXTER, L. A. (1988). A dialectical perspective on communication strategies in relationship development. In S. Duck (Ed.), *Handbook of personal relationships: Theory, research and interventions* (pp. 257–273). New York: Wiley.

BAXTER, L. A., & WILMOT, W. W. (1984). "Secret tests": Social strategies for acquiring information about the state of the relationship. *Human Communication Research, 11,* 171–201.

BELL, A. P., & WEINBERG, M. S. (1978). *Homosexualities: A study of diversity among men and women.* New York: Simon & Schuster.

BELL, R. A., & BUERKEL-ROTHFUSS, N. L. (1990). S(he) loves me, s(he) loves me not: Predictors of relational information-seeking in courtship and beyond. *Communication Quarterly, 38,* 64–82.

BERNARD, J. (1972). *The future of marriage.* New York: World.

BODERMANN, G. (1997). Can divorce be prevented by enhancing the coping skills of couples? *Journal of Divorce & Remarriage, 27,* 177–194.

BRUESS, C. J. S., & PEARSON, J. C. (1997). Interpersonal rituals in marriage and adult friendship. *Communication Monographs, 64,* 25–46.

BUHRKE, R. A., & FUQUA, D. R. (1987). Sex differences in same-and cross-sex supportive relationships. *Sex Roles, 17,* 339–351.

BULLIS, C., CLARK, C., and SLIVE, R. (1993). From passion to commitment: Turning points in romantic relationships. In P. J. Kalbfleisch (Ed.), *Interpersonal communication: Evolving interpersonal relationships* (pp. 213–236). Hillsdale, NJ: Lawrence Erlbaum.

BURGGRAF, C., & SILLARS, A. L. (1987). A critical examination of sex differences in marital communication. *Communication Monographs, 54,* 276–94.

BURLESON, B. R., & DENTON, W. H. (1997). The relationship between communication skill and marital satisfaction: Some moderating effects. *Journal of Marriage & the Family, 59,* 884–902.

BUSCALGIA, L. F. (1986). *Loving each other: The challenge of human relationships.* New York: Fawcett/Combine.

BUSS, D. M., & MALAMUTH, N. M. (Eds.) (1996). *Sex, power, conflict: Evolutionary and feminist perspectives.* New York: Oxford University Press.

CARROLL, J. L., VOLK, K. D., & HYDE, J. S. (1985). Differences between males and females in motives for engaging in sexual intercourse. *Archives of Sexual Behavior, 14,* 131–139.

CARTENSEN, L. L., GRAFF, J., LEVENSON, R. W., & GOTTMAN, J. M. (1996). Affect in intimate relationships: The developmental course of marriage. In C. Magai, & S. H. McFadden (Eds.), *Handbook of emotion, adult development, and aging* (pp. 227–247). San Diego, CA: Academic Press.

CHRISTENSEN, A., & SHENK, J. L. (1991). Communication, conflict, and psychological distance in the demand/withdraw pattern of marital conflict. *Journal of Personality and Social Psychology, 59,* 458–463.

CLINE, R. J., & MUSOLF, K. E. (1985). Disclosure as social exchange: Anticipated length of relationship, sex roles, and disclosure intimacy. *Western Journal of Speech Communication, 49,* 43–56.

CODY, M. (1982). A typology of disengagement strategies and an examination of the role intimacy, reactions to inequity and relational problems play in strategy selection. *Communication Monographs, 49,* 148–170.

CUTRONA, C. E. (1996). Social support as a determinant of marital quality: The interplay of negative and supportive behaviors. In G. R. Pierce, B. R. Sarason, & I. G. Sarason (Eds.), *Handbook of social support and the family* (pp. 173–194). New York: Plenum Press.

CUTRONA, C. E., & SUHR, J. A. (1994). Social support communication in the context of marriage: An analysis of couples' supportive interactions. In B. R. Burleson, T. L. Albrecht, & I. G. Sarason (Eds.), *Communication of social support: Messages, interactions, relationships, and community* (pp. 113–135). Thousand Oaks, CA: Sage.

DAINTON, M., STAFFORD, L., & CANARY, D. (1994). Maintenance strategies and physical affection as predictors of love, liking, and satisfaction in marriage, *Communication Reports, 7,* 88–98.

DAINTON, M., STAFFORD, L. & MCNEILIS, K. S. (1992, November). *The maintenance of relationships through the use of routine behaviors.* Paper presented at the annual meeting of the Speech Communication Association, Chicago.

DELAMATER, J. (1989). Gender differences in sexual scenarios. In K. Kelly (Ed.), *Females, males, and sexuality.* Albany, NY: SUNY Press.

DELAMATER, J., & MACCORQUODALE, P. (1979). *Premarital sexuality: Attitudes, relationships, behaviors.* Madison: University of Wisconsin Press.

DELUCIA, J. L. (1987). Gender role identity and dating behavior: What is the relationship? *Sex Roles, 17,* 153–161.

DESROCHERS, S. (1995). What types of men are most attractive and most repulsive to women? *Sex Roles, 32,* 375–391.

DE TURCK, M. & MILLER, G. (1986) The effects of husband's and wive's social cognition on their marital adjustment, conjugal power, and self-esteem. *Journal of Marriage and the Family, 48,* 714–724.

DICKSON, F. C. (1995). Understudied relationships: Off the beaten track. In J. T. Wood & S. Duck (Eds.), *Understudied relationships: Off the beaten track* (pp. 22–50). Thousand Oaks, CA: Sage.

DORMEN, L. (1990, October). Healthy love: How nineties couples create it. *Glamour,* 270–271, 310–311.

DUCK, S. (1988). *Relating to others.* Chicago: Dorsey.

DUCK, S., & WOOD, J. T. (1995). For better, for worse, for richer, for poorer: The rough and the smooth of relationships. In S. Duck & J. T. Wood (Eds.), *Confronting relationship challenges* (pp. 1–21). Thousand Oaks, CA: Sage.

EDGAR, T., & FITZPATRICK, M. A. (1988). Compliance-gaining in relational interaction: When your life depends on it. *Southern Speech Communication Journal, 53,* 385–405.

EELLS, L. W., & O'FLAHERTY, K. (1996). Gender perceptual differences in relation to marital problems. *Journal of Divorce & Remarriage, 25,* 95–116.

EIDELSON, S., & EPSTIEN, D. (1982). Development of a measure of dysfunctional relationship beliefs. *Journal of Consulting and Clinical Psychology, 50,* 715–720.

FEENEY, J. A. (1994). Attachment style, communication patterns and satisfaction across the life cycle of marriage. *Personal Relationships, 1,* 333–348.

FELDMAN, L. B. (1979). Marital conflict and marital intimacy: An integrative psychodynamic-behavioral systematic model. *Family Process, 18,* 69–78.

FELDMAN, L. B. (1982). Sex roles and family dynamics. In F. Walsh (Ed.), *Normal family processes* (pp. 345–382). New York: Guilford Press.

FITZPATRICK, M. A. (1988). *Between husbands and wives: Communication in marriage.* Newbury Park, CA: Sage.

GAINES, S. O. (1996). Impact of interpersonal traits and gender-role compliance on interpersonal resource exchange among dating and engaged/married couples. *Journal of Social & Personal Relationships, 13,* 241–261.

GALVIN, K. (1993). First marriage families: Gender and communication. In L. P. Arliss & D. J. Borisoff (Eds.), *Women and men communicating: Challenges and changes* (pp. 86–101). Fort Worth, TX: Harcourt Brace Jovanovich.

GALVIN, K. M., & BROMMEL, B. J. (1991). *Family communication: Cohesion and change* (3rd ed.). New York: Harper Collins.

GILLIGAN, C. (1981, December). Are women more moral than men? *Ms.,* 63–65.

GOLDSMITH, D. (1990). A dialectic perspective on the expression of autonomy and connection in romantic relationships. *Western Journal of Speech Communication, 54,* 537–556.

GOODMAN, E. (1979, May 20). *Utica Observer Dispatch,* p. 10A.

GOTTMAN, J. M., COAN, J., CARRERE, S., & SWANSON, C. (1998). Predicting marital happiness and stability from newlywed interactions. *Journal of Marriage and the Family, 60,* 5–22.

GOTTMAN, J. M. K., KATZ, L. F., & HOOVEN, C. (1997). *Meta-emotion: How families communicate emotionally.* Mahwah, NJ: Lawrence Erlbaum.

GRAUERHOLZ, E., & SERPE, R. T. (1985). Initiation and response: The dynamics of sexual interaction. *Sex Roles, 12,* 1041–1059.

GREEN, S. K., & SANDOS, P. (1983). Perceptions of male and female initiators of relationships. *Sex Roles, 9,* 619–638.

HARWARD, H. L., & CAVANAUGH, D. (1997, November). *Men, women, and interpersonal relationships: A qualitative analysis of the first big fight.* Paper presented at the meeting of the National Communication Association, Chicago, IL.

HATFIELD, E. (1983). What do women and men want from love and sex? In E. R. Allgeier & N. B. McCormick (Eds.), *Changing boundaries: Gender roles and sexual behavior.* Palo Alto, CA: Mayfield.

HATFIELD, E., & RAPSON, R. L. (1996). *Love and sex: Cross-cultural perspectives.* Boston : Allyn & Bacon.

HELLER, P. E., & WOOD, B. (1998). The process of intimacy: Similarity, understanding and gender. *Journal of Marriage & Family Counseling, 24,* 273–288.

HENDRICK, S. S., & HENDRICK, C. (1992). *Romantic love.* Newbury Park, CA: Sage.

HICKMON, W. A., JR., PROTINSKY, H. O., & SINGH, K. (1997). Increasing marital intimacy: Lessons from marital enrichment. *Contemporary Family Therapy: An International Journal, 19,* 581–589.

HIRSHEY, G. (1989, March/April). Coupledom uber alles: Tyranny of the couples. *Utne Reader,* 48–55.

HITE, S. (1976). *The Hite report.* New York: MacMillan.

HONEYCUTT, J. M., CANTRILL, J. G., & GREENE, R. W. (1989). Memory structure for relational escalation: A cognitive test of sequencing of relational actions and stages. *Human Communication Research, 16,* 62–90.

HONEYCUTT, J. M., WILSON C., & PARKER, C. (1982). Effects of sex and degrees of happiness on perceived styles of communicating in and out of the marital relationship. *Journal of Marriage and Family Counseling, 44,* 395–496.

HUSTON, T. L., MCHALE, S., & CROUTER, A. (1986) When the honeymoon's over: Changes in the marriage relationship over the first year. In R. Gilmour & S. Duck (Eds.), *The emerging field of personal relationships* (pp. 109–132), Hillsdale, NJ: Lawrence Erlbaum.

ICKES, W. J., & SIMPSON, J. A. (1997). Managing empathic accuracy in close relationships. In W. J. Ickes (Ed.), *Empathic accuracy,* (218–250). New York: Guilford Press.

IFERT, D. E., & ROLOFF, M. E. (1996). Responding to refusals of requests: The role of requester sex on persistence. *Communication Reports, 9,* 119–126.

Information please almanac. (1998). Boston : Information Please.

JOHNSON, S. (1991). *The ship that sailed into the living room: Sex and intimacy reconsidered.* Estancia, NM: Wildfire Books.

JULIEN, D., ARELLANO, C., & TURGEON, L. (1997). Gender issues in heterosexual, gay and lesbian couples. In Halford, W. K. Halford, H. J. Markman, & H. J. K. Halford, (Eds.), *Clinical handbook of marriage and couples' interventions* (pp. 107–127). Chichester, England: John Wiley & Sons, Inc.

KEASHLY, L. (1994). Gender and conflict: What does psychological research tell us? In A. Taylor, & J. B. Miller (Eds.). *Conflict and gender* (pp. 168–190). Cresskill, NJ: Hampton Press.

KLINETOB, N. A., & SMITH, D. A. (1996). Demand-withdraw communication in marital interaction: Tests of interpersonal contingency and gender role hypotheses. *Journal of Marriage & the Family, 58,* 945–957.

KELLERMAN, K., REYNOLDS, R., & CHEN, J. B. (1991). Strategies of conversational retreat: When parting is not sweet sorrow. *Communication Monographs, 58,* 362–383.

KENRICK, D. T., SADALLA, E. K., GROTH, G., & TROST, M. R. (1990). Courtship: Qualifying the parental investment model. *Journal of Personality, 58,* 97–115.

KNOX, D., & WILSON, K. (1981). Dating behaviors of university students. *Family Relations, 30,* 255–258.

KROKOFF, L. J. (1990). Hidden agendas in marriage: Affective and longitudinal dimensions, *Communication Research, 17,* 83–99.

KRUEGER, D. L. (1986). Communications strategies and patterns in dual career couples. *Southern Speech Communication Journal, 15,* 164–173.

LARSON, J. H., ANDERSON, S. M., HOLMAN, T. B., & NIEMANN, B. K. (1998). A longitudinal study of the effects of premarital communication, relationship stability, and self-esteem on sexual satisfaction in the first year of marriage. *Journal of Sex & Marital Therapy, 24,* 193–206.

LAUER, J., & LAUER, R. (1985, June). Marriages made to last. *Psychology Today,* 22–26.

LEIGH, B. C. (1989). Reasons for having and avoiding sex: Gender, sexual orientation, and relationship to sexual behavior. *Journal of Sex Research, 26,* 199–209.

LUND, M. (1985). The development of investment and commitment scales for predicting continuity of personal relationships. *Journal of Social and Personal Relationships, 2,* 3–23.

MARKS, N. F. (1996). Flying solo at midlife: Gender, marital status, and psychological well-being. *Journal of Marriage & the Family, 58,* 917–932.

MARSTON, P. J., HECHT, M. L., & ROBERS, T. (1986, February). *What is this thing called love? The subjective experience and communication of romantic love.* Paper presented at the meeting of the Western Speech Communication Association, Tuscon, AZ.

MAUGH, T. H. (1998, February 21). Key to a good marriage: Husband gives in. *Yakima Herald Republic,* p. 14A.

McCORMICK, N. B., & JESSER, J. C. (1983). The courtship game: Power in the sexual encounter. In E. R. Allgeier & N. B. McCormick (Eds.), *Changing boundaries: Gender roles and sexual behavior* (pp. 64–86). Palo Alto, CA: Mayfield.

McGOLDRICK, M. (1989). The joining of families through marriage: The new couple. In G. Carter & M. McGoldrick (Eds.), *The changing family life cycle* (2nd ed.) (pp. 200–226). Boston: Allyn & Bacon.

McKINNEY, K. (1987). Age and gender differences in college students' attitudes toward women: A replication and extension. *Sex Roles, 17,* 353–358.

MEERLOO, J. A. (1952). *Conversation and communication.* New York: International Universities Press.

MEHTA, P., & CLARK, M. S. (1994). Toward understanding emotions in intimate relationships. In A. L. Weber & J. H. Harvey (Eds.), *Perspectives on close relationships* (pp. 88–109). Boston: Allyn & Bacon.

METTS, S., & CUPACH, W. R. (1990). The influence of relationship beliefs and problem solving responses on satisfaction in romantic relationships. *Human Communication Research, 17,* 170–185.

MINTON, L. (1997, October, 12). Fresh voices. *Parade Magazine,* 18.

MONGEAU, P. A., YEAZELL, M., & HALE, J. (1994). Sex differences in relational message interpretations on male- and female-initiated first dates. *Journal of Social Behavior and Personality, 9,* 731–742.

MONTGOMERY, B. M. (1981). The form and function of quality communication in marriage. *Family Relations, 20,* 21–29.

NOTARIUS, C. I. (1996). Marriage: Will I be happy or will I be sad? In N. Vanzetti, & S. Duck, (Eds.), *A lifetime of relationships.* (pp. 265–289) Pacific Grove, CA: Brooks/Cole Publishing Co.

NOTARIUS, C., & JOHNSON, J. (1982). Emotional expression in husbands and wives. *Journal of Marriage and the Family, 44,* 483–490.

NOZICK, R. (1993). Love's bond. In A. Minas (Ed.), *Gender basics: Feminist perspectives on women and men* (pp. 152–159). Belmont, CA: Wadsworth.

NYE, F. I. (1982). *Family relationships: Rewards and costs.* Beverly Hills, CA: Sage.

OWEN, W. F. (1987). The verbal expression of love by women and men as a critical communication event in personal relationships. *Women's Studies in Communication, 10,* 15–24.

PEARSON, J. C. (1989). *Communication in the family.* New York: Harper/Collins.

PEARSON, J. C., & SPITZBERG, B. H. (1990). *Interpersonal communication: Concepts, components, and contexts* (2nd ed.). Dubuque, IA: Wm. C. Brown.

PEPLAU, L. A. (1981). What homosexuals want in relationships. *Psychology Today, 15,* 28–37.

PEPLAU, L. A. (1983). Roles and gender. In H. H. Kelley (Ed.), *Close relationships.* San Francisco: W. H. Freeman.

PEPLAU, L. A. (1994). Men and women in love. In D. L. Sollie & L. A. Leslie (Eds.), *Gender, families, and close relationships* (pp. 19–49). Newbury Park, CA: Sage.

PEPLAU, L. A., & GORDON, S. L. (1983). The intimate relationships of lesbians and gay men. In E. R. Allgeier & N. B. McCormick (Eds.), *Changing boundaries: Gender roles and sexual behavior.* Palo Alto, CA: Mayfield.

PERPER, T., & WEIS, D. L. (1987). Proceptive and rejective strategies of U.S. and Canadian college women. *Journal of Sex Research, 23,* 455–480.

PETRONIO, S. S. (1982). The effect of interpersonal communication on women's family role satisfaction. *Western Journal of Speech Communication, 46,* 208–222.

POTORTI, P. (1992). Personal communication, October.

PURNINE, D. M., & CAREY, M. P. (1997). Interpersonal communication and sexual adjustment: The roles of understanding and agreement. *Journal of Consulting & Clinical Psychology, 65,* 1017–1025.

RAGOLIN, V. C., & HANSEN, J. C. (1985). The impact of equity or egalitarianism on dual-career couples. *Family Therapy, 2,* 151–162.

RAWLINS, W. (1982). Negotiating close friendship: The dialectic of conjunctive freedom. *Human Communication Research, 9,* 255–266.

RICHMOND, V. P. (1995). Amount of communication in marital dyads as a function of dyad and individual marital satisfaction. *Communication Research Reports, 12,* 152–159.

RITTER, M. (1989, September 17). She was a woman, he was a man—and they fought. *The Milwaukee Journal*, p. 6G.

ROGERS, C. (1970). *On becoming a person.* Boston: Houghton Mifflin.

ROGERS, L. E., & MILLAR, F. E. (1979) Domineeringness and dominance: A transactional view. *Human Communication Research, 5,* 238–246.

ROLOFF, M. E. (1981). *Interpersonal communication: The exchange approach.* Beverly Hills: Sage.

ROSENBLUTH, S. C., STEIL, J. M., & WHITCOMB, J. H. (1998). Marital equality: What does it mean? *Journal of Family Issues, 19,* 227–244.

RUBIN, L. B. (1984). *Intimate strangers: Men and women together.* New York: Harper and Row.

RUBIN, A., PEPLAU, L. A., & HILL, C. T. (1981). Loving and leaving: Sex differences in romantic attachments. *Sex Roles, 7,* 821–835.

RUBLE, T. A., & SCHNEER, J. A. (1994). Gender differences in conflict-handling styles: Less than meets the eye? In A. Taylor & J. B. Miller (Eds.), *Conflict and gender* (pp. 155–166). Cresskill, NJ: Hampton Press.

SABOURIN, T. C. (1996). The role of communication in verbal abuse between spouses. In D. D. Cahn, & S. A. Lloyd, (Eds.), *Family violence from a communication perspective* (pp. 199–217). Thousand Oaks, CA: Sage.

SANDERS, R. E. (1997). Find your partner and do-si-do: The formation of personal relationships between social beings. *Journal of Social & Personal Relationships, 14,* 387–415.

SCHNALL, M. (1981, May). Commitmentphobia. *Savvy,* 37–41.

SHEER, V. C. (1995). Sensation seeking predispositions and susceptibility to a sexual partner's appeals for condom use. *Journal of Applied Communication Research, 23,* 212–229.

SHIMANOFF, S. B. (1985). Rules governing the verbal expression of emotions between married couples. *Western Journal of Speech Communication, 49,* 85–100.

SILLARS, A. L., FOLWELL, A. L., HILL, K. C., & MAKI, B. K. (1994). Marital communication and the persistence of misunderstanding. *Journal of Social & Personal Relationships, 11,* 611–617.

SILLARS, A. L., FOLWELL, A. L., HILL, K. L., MAKI, B. K., HURST, A. P., & CASANO, R. A. (1992, November). *Levels of understanding in martial relationships.* Paper presented at the meeting of the Speech Communication Association, Chicago, IL.

SILLARS, A., SHELLEN, W., MCINTOSH, A., & POMEGRANATE, M. (1997). Relational characteristics of language: Elaboration and differentiation in marital conversations. *Western Journal of Communication, 61,* 403–422.

SINCLAIR, I., & MCCLUSKEY, U. (1996). Invasive partners: An exploration of attachment, communication and family patterns. *Journal of Family Therapy, 18,* 61–78.

SOLLIE, D. L., & LESLIE, L. A. (Eds.). *Gender, families, and close relationships* (pp. 19–49). Newbury Park, CA: Sage.

STACK, S., & ROSS, E. J. (1998). Marital status and happiness: A 17-nation study. *Journal of Marriage and the Family, 60,* 527–536.

STEIL, J. M. (1997). *Marital equality: Its relationship to the well-being of husbands and wives.* Thousand Oaks, CA: Sage.

TAYLOR, A., & MILLER, J. B. (Eds.) (1994). *Conflict and gender.* Cresskill, NJ: Hampton Press.

TEICHNER, G., & FARNDEN-LYSTER, R. (1997). Recently married couples' length of relationship marital communication, relational style, and marital satisfaction. *Psychological Reports, 80,* 490.

THOMPSON, L., & WALKER, H. (1989). Gender in families: Women and men in marriage, work, and parenthood. *Journal of Marriage and the Family, 51,* 845–871.

TING-TOOMEY, S. (1984). Perceived decision-making power and marital adjustment. *Communication Research Reports, 1,* 15–20.

UNGER, R., & CRAWFORD, M. (1996). *Women and gender: A feminist psychology* (2nd ed.). New York: McGraw-Hill.

VANGELISTA, A. L., & HUSTON, T. L. (1992, November). *Maintaining marital satisfaction and love.* Paper presented at the meeting of the Speech Communication Association, Chicago, IL.

WARING, E., TILLMAN, M., FRELICK, L., RUSSELL, L., & WEISZ, G. (1980). Concepts of intimacy in the general population. *Journal of Nervous and Mental Disease, 168,* 471–474.

WEISS, R. L., & DEHLE, C. (1994). Cognitive behavioral perspectives on marital conflict. In D. D. Cahn (Ed.), *Conflict in personal relationships* (pp. 95–115). Hillsdale, NJ: Lawerence Erlbaum.

WHEELESS, L. R., & PARSONS, L. A. (1995). What you feel is what you might get: Exploring communication apprehension and sexual communication satisfaction. *Communication Research Reports, 12,* 39–45.

WHITLEY, B. E. JR. (1988). The relation of gender-role orientation to sexual experience among college students. *Sex Roles, 19,* 619–638.

WILKIE, J. R., FERREE, M. M., & RATCLIFF, K. S. (1998). Gender and fairness: Marital satisfaction in two-earner couples. *Journal of Marriage and the Family, 60,* 577–594.

WORTHINGTON, E. L., McCULLOUGH, M. E., SHORTZ, J. L., MINDES, E. J. (1995). Can couples' assessment and feedback improve relationships? Assessment as a brief relationship enrichment procedure. *Journal of Counseling Psychology, 42,* 466–475.

YOGEV, S., & BRETT, J. M. (1985). Patterns of work and family involvement among single and dual earner couples. *Journal of Applied Psychology, 70,* 754–768.

YOST, B. (1996, November 17). Alone in a world of couples: Society's aversion to singlehood remains strongly rooted in tradition. *Corpus Christi Caller Times,* pp. H1, H5.

CHAPTER NINE

POWER ABUSES IN HUMAN RELATIONSHIPS

A NON-CASE STUDY

The information in this chapter is difficult to write about, and it's going to be difficult to read. Certainly it isn't the first time you've read or heard about sexual harassment, sexual assault and rape, and partner violence. But it may be the most concentrated presentation of these topics you've been assigned in college. This chapter focuses on power abuses in human relationships, the downside of interacting with others, and how communication creates options for those situations.

It doesn't seem appropriate to start this chapter the way we start the others—with a case study to engage your thinking and energize you for the pages to come. Many cases could be included because many people suffer abuses in relationships. But we prefer to tell some of those stories in context, along with the information on each topic. Here's why: It's very hard to focus on how people abuse one another; it takes us out of our comfort zones to think or talk about it. Even when we do decide to think or talk about it, we still tend to distance ourselves from it—to view it as a social problem, a bunch of statistics, or something that happens to someone else. These are understandable ways to protect ourselves from having to confront the tough issues. But you don't really understand a problem until you put a face on it. That's what the cases in the chapter are designed to do—to make these issues real by putting human faces on them. You may be able to put the face of a relative, friend, or co-worker into the situations we describe. While that's painful, we encourage you to do just that, because it will enable you to more fully understand these problems and what can be done about them.

We also realize that some of you reading this material *are* those human faces—your case could be substituted for one here. The abuses we discuss don't just happen to someone else; they happen to *us*. We hope that none of you has experienced what we examine in this chapter, but it's very likely that some of you have. If you've lived through power abuses in the past, reading this chapter will no doubt bring up unpleasant reminders for you. But perhaps you will gain a deeper understanding of what you went through or a comparison for how you coped with your situation. If you're currently in an abusive situation, our sincere hope is that this information will help you realize that you do not deserve or cause the abuse, and that you have options.

Not-So-Hot Topics

- The role of *power* and *communication* in abusive situations
- Statistics and types of *sexual harassment* at work and school
- A *receiver-oriented* view of sexual harassment
- *Strategies* for how to respond to and report sexual harassment, including legal updates
- Forms of *rape* and the language of *survivors*
- The prevalence of *date rape* and *date rape drugs* in American society
- *Myths* about rape and *sexual aggression*
- *Rape prevention programs* and the status of rape laws
- The language of *partner violence*
- Statistics and types of partner violence, including *gay and lesbian partner abuse*
- *Myths* about battering, including the *blame-the-victim* stance
- *Battered woman's syndrome*, one explanation of why victims stay with abusers
- Laws and *women's shelters* that provide hope

AT THE CENTER OF ABUSIVE SITUATIONS: COMMUNICATING POWER

What do sexual harassment, sexual assault, and partner (domestic) violence have in common? None of these is really about sex, but instead about power (Berryman-Fink, 1993). The abusive behavior stems from an attempt to control, influence, and dominate another person. Harassers, rapists, and batterers all have varying degrees of anger and needs for power that they inflict on their victims in the worst way, by preying on their sexuality or physicality. It's important to keep the emphasis on power when talking about these issues because thinking they're about something else muddies the waters and makes it harder to understand the complexity.

Another common thread throughout these issues is that they all involve communication. Sexual harassment is accomplished through verbal and nonverbal communication. Acquaintance sexual assault or rape and partner violence usually involve a context of communication that precedes the assault, and a context of communication usually follows the battering situation. Most important, full recovery from these abuses must involve communication. Not talking about sexual harassment doesn't make the harassment go away or allow the victim to get past it. One of the worst things a victim can do, but something that happens frequently is to hide in shame and guilt and not tell anyone what happened. Communication makes an experience real, which is frightening but necessary for recovery. So these abuses are things that communication people—especially people with an interest in gender communication—should study.

A final element before we address the first topic of this chapter: We are aware, from having written the first edition of this text, from talking to instructors who use the text across the country, and from teaching the gender communication course many times, that students have concerns about male-bashing. Men and women alike have difficulty with material that seems to critique men and favor women or that addresses men as the oppressors and women as the oppressed. Bergman and Surrey (1993), researchers at Wellesley College who conduct relationship workshops, address this issue:

> More women are beginning to speak out about rape, harassment, and abuse. But some still feel that it is risky to speak out—and with good reason. Men, too, are placed in a difficult position. They are confused and annoyed about this issue: on the one hand, they feel accused, and on the other, they feel that it is difficult to take a moral stand against the problem without dissociating from their gender: "Yeah, some men do that stuff, but not *me*." (p. 17)

We have made constant attempts in this book and in our teaching to be balanced and fair in our representation of research and discussions of trends. Much of the work that has been done to bring these issues and problems to the forefront has been done by women because it is generally the case that members of a historically oppressed group are the ones to raise issues in an attempt to change their plight and create more options for themselves. The same holds true for women's liberation and feminism, movements that are primarily made up of women seriously concerned with upgrading women's status and increasing their opportunities. But whether someone's claims of male-bashing are legitimate is not the issue, because feeling bashed isn't ever a good feeling.

For our male readers, you may indeed feel bashed when reading this chapter. For our female readers, you may feel protective or defensive toward men you perceive are being bashed. But, for this chapter, could we possibly suspend the male-bashing reaction for the greater good of truly understanding these difficult societal problems? Gentlemen, could you avoid taking the statistics and research findings about male harassers, rapists, and batterers personally, as though the information was an indictment of you and your entire sex? Could we all just view these problems as *human* problems and look them squarely in the face? As you'll see, the fact is that 95 percent of reported sexual harassment in businesses and academic institutions *is* perpetrated by males against females. The fact is that most rapists of women and of other men *are men*. The fact is that far more partner abuse is committed by men against women than the reverse. In this chapter we want to talk about both "the rule" and, when appropriate, "exceptions to the rule." Instead of feeling bashed, we hope that men *and* women feel deeply concerned about these problems, appalled by what is happening, and challenged to do something about it.

ATTENTION? COMPLIMENTING? FLIRTING? SEXUAL HARASSMENT?

Some of you may have to jog your memories to recall the dramatic events that were played out on national television in the fall of 1991. For others of you, the image of Anita Hill claiming she was sexually harassed by now Supreme Court Justice Clarence Thomas, who called his Senate Judicial hearing a "high-tech lynching," is permanently etched into your memory. No matter which party you believed, no matter what your reaction to this event, the Hill-Thomas hearing had at least one profoundly positive effect: It opened a floodgate of discussion on sexual harassment. The Equal Employment Opportunity Commission (EEOC) experienced a 23 percent increase in the number of sexual harassment complaints and a 150 percent increase in inquiries within weeks after Hill-Thomas (Baker, 1992). Communication scholars and business leaders had been researching sexual harassment for at least two decades prior to this event, but Hill-Thomas generated a flurry of discussion, debate, and research unparalleled in previous years.

Do We Still Have a Problem after Hill-Thomas?

Many people like to think that sexual harassment has gone away or that we've solved the problem since the nation's collective conscience was jolted by Hill-Thomas. Instead we may be witnessing fatigue over the issue or a backlash of sorts. A 1998 Time/CNN poll found that 52 percent of American women and 57 percent of men believe "we have gone too far in making common interactions between employees into cases of sexual harassment" (as in Steinem, 1998, p. 62). The poll also found that only 26 percent of those surveyed viewed sexual harassment as "a big problem," compared to 37 percent in 1991 (Cloud, 1998).

But here are some statistics that show we're not past the problem of sexual harassment, much as we'd like to be. Since 1991, over 500 verdicts supporting complaints of sexual harassment have been granted by juries. Over 15,000 new sexual harassment cases are filed yearly, compared to around 7,000 cases in 1991 (Cloud, 1998). Stanford law professor Deborah Rhode (1997) discusses the current status of workplace sexual harassment in her article "Harassment Is Alive and Well and Living at the Water Cooler." Rhode contends that the denial that serious workplace harassment still occurs, and frequently is a "variation on the traditional view that it didn't happen at all" (p. 28).

On the education front, a 1993 national scientific survey from the American Association of University Women examined sexual harassment in public schools. Out of 1,700 students in grades 8 through 11 across 79 schools, 85 percent of girls and 76 percent of boys reported experiencing sexual harassment.

Copyright, 1991, Boston Globe. Distributed by Los Angeles Times Syndicate. Reprinted with permission.

Studies of university students and faculty show a persistent, alarming campus problem (Cochran, Frazier, & Olson, 1997; Geist & Townsley, 1997; Gelfand, Fitzgerald, & Drasgow, 1995; Krolokke, 1998; Sandler, 1997; Seals, 1997). Read the case study below and think about whether this is classic sexual harassment or just going too far.

Olivia's Great New Job

Olivia landed a great job right after college graduation as a manager at a medium-sized company. She was hired by Bernie, her supervisor, and in her first year on the job, she'd come to trust Bernie's advice, to value the mentoring relationship they'd developed, and to appreciate the opportunities he'd given her to excel on the job. Then things took a downturn.

At the end of a meeting on sales strategy, Bernie steered the conversation to more personal topics. He asked Olivia if she was dating or sexually involved with anyone at the time, if she thought her work went more smoothly when her sex life was running smoothly, if she found older men sexy, and so forth. Bernie and Olivia always maintained a friendly, informal working relationship, so at first Olivia laughed off Bernie's questions—until they became too personal and made her feel uncomfortable. When Bernie pushed for sexual information, Olivia masked her discomfort by saying "Well, now that this conversation is going downhill, I think we should end our meeting because customers are waiting, sales are out there to be made, ha, ha, ha . . ." Olivia made her way back to her office, knowing that something very wrong had just happened. But she couldn't make sense out of it or out of what she was feeling. She felt like she'd been punched in the stomach.

Over the next few weeks, Olivia tried to operate in a "business as usual" manner, but Bernie continued to show romantic interest. He got close to Olivia when talking to her; occasionally he would touch her arm or try to hug her while praising the good job she was doing. Once in a meeting with several other managers Bernie leaned over to Olivia, put his arm around her shoulders, and whispered to her about a colleague's ideas. By this time, Olivia was really bothered by Bernie's unprofessional behavior. She'd always thought Bernie a somewhat attractive man, but he was at least 20 years her senior and he was married—happily, so she thought.

Finally, over lunch one day Olivia told a co-worker about her problem with Bernie. She explained that it was the first time a boss had said anything personal or sexual to her; it bothered her to think that maybe Bernie had been looking at her all along in a sexual way, rather than as a professional colleague. She wondered if this was sexual harassment. Olivia's co-worker didn't exactly offer what you'd call a textbook empathic response. She teased Olivia about her boss having a crush on her, saying she ought to be complimented that someone in the company of such status as Bernie had shown her special attention. But Olivia didn't feel complimented.

What's your reaction to this story? Was Bernie's attention nothing more than complimentary? Was he merely being friendly or flirtatious—nothing serious enough to warrant the stigmatizing label of sexual harassment? Or was this classic sexual harassment on the job? Is your opinion affected by the fact that Bernie is married?

Sexual harassment on the job is not a problem for virtuous women.

Phyllis Schlafly, anti-feminist activist

The Basics of Sexual Harassment

In his introduction to a collection of articles on sexual harassment, Gary Kreps (1993) states: "Communication is the primary medium through which sexual harassment is expressed; it is the means by which those who are harassed respond to harassment, and it is also the primary means by which policies for eliminating sexual harassment in the workplace can be implemented" (p. 1). Olivia and Bernie's case illustrates several key elements related to sexual harassment. Before we explore them, let's make sure we're all on the same page in how we talk about and define sexual harassment.

The Power of Naming

Just exactly what *is* sexual harassment? Gloria Steinem (1983) answered that question like this: "A few years ago this was just called life" (p. 149). There actually was no term for this age-old problem until feminists in the 1970s coined the term *sexual harassment* (Wise & Stanley, 1987). There's power in naming— just ask medical people who get to assign their names to discoveries or diseases. Naming something makes it real, gives it significance, and brings it from silence to voice (Spender, 1984). As gender scholar Julia Wood (1992) explains, "Like victims of date rape, those who were sexually harassed had no legitimated way to label what occurred, much less to enlist others' help with this 'problem that had no name.' There was no common language to describe the feelings such incidents evoked, and there were no words to depict sexualized interactions that transpired . . . " (pp. 352–353).

An inspection of the language surrounding sexual harassment justifies the struggle of many people to bring this problem into the open. Harassing behavior used to be described (and probably still is) in romantic language, such as "seduction," "overtures," "advances," "going too far," or "passes." But as Wood (1993) suggests, "Using terminology associated with amorous contexts obscures the ugliness, unwantedness, violation, repugnance, and sheer darkness of sexual harassment" (p. 14).

Other ways to excuse sexual harassment besides a "boys will be boys" attitude include viewing unwanted attention as merely complimenting the target. If the victim didn't view it as such, she or he wasn't being "gracious" and accepting the compliment. A prime way to blame a target of harassment and direct attention away from a harasser's behavior is the "just kidding" suggestion. If you couch communication as kidding, joking, or teasing, then when it's interpreted as harassment, a harasser can blame the victim for "not getting the joke" or "not having a sense of humor." A prime example of this blame-shifting technique is telling a victim to "lighten up."

The language of sexual harassment has changed since the 1980s, so that we now have "targets" or "victims" instead of "objects of attention," "whistle-blowers," "prudes," "complainers," and "whiners." "Pushy" or "forward" people are now named "harassers" and in some cases, "defendants." What once was an "advance" is now a "violation of individual rights" (Wood, 1992; 1993). But we've also seen a resurgence of euphemisms for sexual harassment, such as "inappropriate behavior," "disrespect," "personal misconduct," and "poor decision making," stemming from various scandals involving such politicians as former Senator Bob Packwood and President Bill Clinton (Ivy, 1999).

First the Name, Then the Legal Definition

The definition of sexual harassment is fairly straightforward; however, the interpretation as to what behaviors constitute sexual harassment is much more complicated. Let's track back in time a bit, before a definition was available. The fight against sexual harassment in the workplace was led by women of color and working-class women. The first victory came in the form of Title VII of the Civil Rights Act of 1964, which protected citizens from discrimination based on a variety of factors, one of which was sex. In essence, this law made sexual harassment illegal. Under Title VII, Congress gave the EEOC formal authority to investigate claims of workplace sexual harassment (Peach, 1998). Later, with the passage of Title IX in 1972, educational institutions were mandated by law to avoid sex discrimination (Wood, 1992). Title IX defined sexual harassment as "the use of authority to emphasize the sexuality or sexual identity of students" (Peach, 1998, p. 291). But, as you can well imagine, sexual harassment continued despite the legislation.

Law professor and champion of women's rights Catherine MacKinnon (1979) was one of the first to label and define sexual harassment. She termed it "the imposition of unwanted sexually related behaviors within the context of an unequal power relationship" (p. 1). In 1980 the EEOC produced the following set of guidelines on sexual harassment:

> Unwelcome sexual advances, requests for sexual favors, and other verbal or physical conduct of a sexual nature constitute sexual harassment when (1) submission to such conduct is made either explicitly or implicitly a term or condition of an individual's employment, (2) submission to or rejection of such conduct by an individual is used as the basis for employment decisions affecting such individual, or (3) such conduct has the intention or effect of unreasonably interfering with an individual's work performance or of creating an intimidating, hostile, or offensive working environment. (EEOC, 1980)

Up to this time, most documented cases of sexual harassment were *quid pro quo*, the "Have sex with me or lose your job" type of harassment. In 1986 the U.S. Supreme Court acted upon the third clause in the EEOC guidelines, the *hostile climate* clause, extending and legitimizing complaints of sexual harassment beyond quid pro quo (*Meritor Savings Bank* v. *Vinson*, as in Paetzold & O'Leary-Kelly, 1993). Hostile climate harassment is far more prevalent than quid pro quo, but it's difficult for organizations and institutions to address. It often involves sexist structures, policies, and practices long ignored, overlooked, or even accepted as a part of the organizational culture (Carroll, 1993). Quite often behavior is sexual power play designed to put someone in a one-down position or to emphasize the harasser's status or power over another person. If this behavior falls short of actually threatening something tangible (like one's job, promotion, or raise), it may be termed hostile climate harassment. The EEOC recognized this as sexual harassment because it pervades the victim's working or learning environment enough to create a hostile situation.

Sexual Harassment Is Power Play

Professor and author Susan Bordo (1998) describes sexual harassment as "the actions of gender bullies, trying to bring uppity women down to size, to restore a balance of power in which they were on top" (p. B6). Communication scholar Kay Payne (1993) offers this insight into sexual harassment as power play:

> The power myths about men and women suggest that a sort of contest occurs during sexual harassment. Contests involve play, and play suggests that all those participating have a clear appreciation that play is occurring. If more than one participant is involved, then all must be freely willing to play. Everyone must understand the rules of play and have the power to refuse an invitation to play or to terminate the play once it has begun. In the case of sexual harassment, men appear to be playing a game in which women feel confused, feel unclear about the rules, and feel threatened by the more dominant participant. In an unmatched contest, knowing when to quit remains the responsibility of the stronger player. (pp. 134–135)

Sexual harassment can occur between individuals who function within clearly structured hierarchies; these relationships are termed *status-differentiated* (such as boss-employee, teacher-student, doctor-patient). A status-differentiated relationship may be distant and impersonal, so that harassment introduced into such a relationship is bewildering. But other such relationships may be well-established and trusting, like a mentor relationship in which the lower-status person looks up to, believes, and confides in the higher status person (Taylor & Conrad, 1992). Harassment in these relationships is devastating. Some receivers of harassment, most often called *targets* or *victims*, describe a grooming process in which the harasser (who desires a sexual connection) slowly develops a friendly relationship with the target, winning her or his trust and admiration before attempting to extend the relationship into a sexual arena. This type of power abuse is devastating to a target's self-esteem and professional development.

Peer sexual harassment, harassment occurring between persons of equal status, occurs on the job as well. In academic settings—from elementary schools to universities—it is much more prevalent than teacher-to-student harassment (Ivy & Hamlet, 1996; Loredo, Reid, & Deaux, 1995; Zirkel, 1995). Yet another form has been termed *contrapower harassment*, which involves a person of lower rank or status sexually harassing someone of higher rank or status (Benson, 1984). Sexual harassment has gone "high tech" as well, meaning that *electronic* or *virtual harassment* has become a problem (Brail, 1996; Salaimo, 1997). A survey of 700 female computer scientists and programmers found that 19 percent reported experiencing some form of sexual harassment on-line, through the use of e-mail, computer bulletin boards or conferences, and chat rooms (King, 1993).

Most reported and researched sexual harassment involves heterosexuals, with a male-harasser, female-target profile (Ivy & Hamlet, 1996; McKinney & Maroules, 1991). Female sexual harassment of men does occur, but it is reported and pursued in the courts with far less frequency than male-to-female

---

RECAP

---

male-bashing, sexual harassment, Equal Employment Opportunity Commission (EEOC), quid pro quo sexual harassment, hostile climate sexual harassment, status-differentiated relationships, targets, victims, grooming process, peer sexual harassment, contrapower sexual harassment, electronic or virtual sexual harassment

---

harassment and has historically been neglected by research (Clair, 1998). Incidences of same-sex or homosexual harassment occur also. In fact, two federal district court rulings supported male employees' claims of sexual harassment by their male supervisors (Texas Employment Commission, 1995).

A Receiver-Oriented View

We trust that you know the principles of the *receiver orientation to communication* backwards and forwards by now. In a nutshell, a receiver view of communication places more importance on a listener's interpretation of a message than it does on a sender's intentions or what a sender meant to convey. Sexually harassing communication exemplifies the receiver orientation so well that we used a harassment example to illustrate it in Chapter 1. But did you know that the law takes a receiver view also?

A Target Orientation to Sexual Harassment

Sexual harassment is different from other kinds of offenses in that the laws and courts tend to take a receiver approach, meaning that when someone believes communication directed to her or him is sexually harassing, that receiver's perception carries more weight than the sender's intentions. The sender may have meant his or her comments as a joke, a mere compliment, or simple teasing among friendly co-workers or classmates. Or the sender may have been trying to "get a rise" out of the target or "put out a feeler," just to see what the response would be. Certainly courts take into account the context of the situation, the history of the relationship between the parties, and any past behavior by the accused that might indicate a pattern of harassment rather than an isolated incident. But the laws are primarily designed to favor a target's perception of harassment.

Consider our example of Olivia and Bernie. From a sender's perspective, one could argue that Bernie was not sexually harassing Olivia. His questions about her sexual life were simply ways to get to know her better, meant to create closeness between a boss and an employee. His nonverbal actions of coming close and touching Olivia were merely expressions of a mentor's affection, ways of communicating his positive regard for a valued employee. If you knew Bernie, if you'd seen him around other employees, then you might think "He's like that with lots of people; he didn't single her out for special attention. "She's going too far if she thinks that's harassment."

On the receiver's side, Olivia didn't interpret Bernie's verbal and nonverbal communication in a benign way. On the contrary, she deemed his questions unwelcome, unwarranted intrusions into her personal life. His actions were designed to make him look powerful and make her feel uncomfortable and powerless. Such behavior puts a target in a classic double bind—a damned if you do, damned if you don't situation. How could Olivia have reacted to Bernie? If she answered his questions, she would have fallen into the trap of revealing personal information when she really didn't want to. And that conversation would likely have opened the door for more questions. If she refused to answer, she could have been accused of being rude and disrespectful to her boss who, after all, was simply trying to get to know her better.

Two Sides to Every Story

You could say that Bernie and Olivia's situation was a simple case of *"he said, she said."* But describing it this way is unproductive; it clouds the issue because *most* harassment is "he said, she said." It most often occurs in private, without any witnesses. Research also consistently shows that women view harassment much more seriously than men (Alberts, 1992; Haunani Solomon & Miller Williams, 1997; Ivy & Hamlet, 1996; Mongeau & Blalock, 1994). So minimizing or dismissing harassment by calling it "he said, she said" perpetuates a power imbalance, especially for women who are more frequently targets of sexual harassment.

Making Sure People "Get It"

The Olivia-Bernie example illustrates one of the main problems surrounding sexual harassment: What is deemed sexual harassment by one person may not be viewed as harassment by another. One person's flirtation is another person's sexual harassment. We cannot stress this enough because it seems that many people "just don't get it"—men and women alike. But in talking with students, they really *want* to get it, especially before they land career-type jobs.

Even the most off-the-top-of-your-head comment can be taken differently than you intended. For example, if what you meant as a simple, one-time compliment designed to make a co-worker feel good was taken by that co-worker as too personal and an unwelcome entrance of sexuality into a professional setting, then your co-worker has a right to claim sexual harassment. Proving it or obtaining legal recourse may be a challenge, but the person has grounds. You can believe that the employee is paranoid and insecure, is out to get you, is an oddball, or hates your sex. But given the tense climate surrounding this issue, some action toward you, such as a reprimand from a superior, could result.

Concerns over sexual harassment have led to a sense that we're "walking on eggshells" and "nothing's funny anymore" at work. Instead of viewing this climate as inhibiting freedom, however, we could look at it as an opportunity for everyone on the job to "clean up their act" and learn some sensitive communication. A reporter for *M Magazine* described men's reactions after the

Hill-Thomas situation hit the airwaves: "All the men I talked to told me they had reexamined their conduct in the office, some to avoid future litigation, some to reassure themselves that they were politically correct. Many were appalled at the things they remembered saying and doing. One company executive said that . . . the Clarence Thomas hearings marked 'one of those pivotal moments, and the office will never be the same'" (Baker, 1992, p. 70). If the threat of being deemed "Neanderthal" or being sued for sexual harassment causes us to think about the effects of our words and actions on others, then perhaps that's the impetus we need to learn to communicate in a more professional, respectful, and equity-based manner.

Initial Reactions to Sexual Harassment

Reactions to sexual harassment are as numerous as the persons who have experienced it, but let's review some of the more common reactions found in studies.

Taking Its Toll

Research documents the serious toll sexual harassment takes on its victims—emotionally, physically, academically, professionally, and economically. The emotional harm leaves victims angry, afraid, alternatively passive and aggressive, anxious, nervous, depressed, and with extremely low self-esteem (Cochran, Frazier, & Olson, 1997). They are more likely to abuse substances and to become dysfunctional in relationships (Taylor & Conrad, 1992). They may develop serious health problems such as severe weight loss, stomach problems, and sleeplessness (Clair, 1998). There are even documented diagnoses of *posttraumatic stress disorder,* characterized by nightmares, muscle tremors, cold sweats, hallucinations, and flashbacks (Castaneda, 1992). Any victim can exhibit these symptoms, but statistics are highest among military women who suffer frequent sexual harassment and abuse (Egan, 1996).

Academically speaking, victims tend to miss classes and their grades suffer (AAUW, 1993). Harassment may also affect their future course choices; damage to achievement over the long haul hurts their future career and economic potential (Gill, 1993). Professional impairment includes missing work, being less productive on the job, and feeling isolated and ostracized by coworkers (Hickson, Grierson, & Linder, 1991). Economic costs are mostly associated with changes in or the loss of employment. If a grievance or lawsuit is filed, the obvious legal costs are exacerbated in many cases by the fact that the victim may be out of work or on leave (many times without pay) until the situation is resolved. In general, frivolous claims of sexual harassment are few because, as you can see, the economic hardships are real.

Calling It What It Is

It's important to know when to call something sexual harassment, which sounds simpler than it really is. Research indicates that one of the more common reactions to sexual harassment is a reluctance to call it harassment

(Cochran, Frazier, & Olson, 1997; Ivy & Hamlet, 1996). This is particularly true of women who report becoming numb to harassing behavior because they grew up with it. They adopt a "boys will be boys" attitude because they see so much harassment around them or they learn that women fare better if they don't rock the boat.

Targets of sexual harassment may doubt or deny the event occurred as they remember it. Since sexual harassment is power play, a harasser intends to cause the target doubt, discomfort, and "loss of face." When a target becomes befuddled or embarrassed over a comment or touch, for example, then the harasser's power play has had its intended effect. If you're a victim of sexual harassment, realize that questioning the reality of the situation and your feelings of embarrassment or shame are common, understandable reactions. Also realize that you have an empowering right to label the behavior "sexual harassment." You're not exaggerating, stirring up trouble, or making something out of nothing.

Blaming Oneself

Another quite common, understandable reaction is for the receiver of sexual harassment to blame herself or himself for the situation (Hughes & Sandler, 1986). Targets report such negative self-messages as, "If I'd only seen it coming," "I should have let him know that I wouldn't go for that sort of talk," and "Did I do something wrong? Did I encourage this person, or somehow give off clues that it was okay to talk to me like that?" It's not uncommon for a target to replay the event later, wondering in hindsight if another response would have been better (the old "I should have said . . ." dilemma). The thing to remember is that sexual harassment, by its very definition, involves *unwarranted, unwelcome* behavior. If the target deserved or welcomed the behavior, if the target brought about the behavior, it wouldn't be considered harassment.

However—and this is a *big* however—there are certain behaviors that increase the possibility that someone will become a target of sexual harassment (Jacobs, 1993). For example, the odds go up that a female employee will be seen as a sex object when she wears unprofessionally short skirts, extremely high heels, overdone makeup and hair, and flashy jewelry to work. A man who tolerates sexual teasing from female co-workers or who engages in sexual banter as a way to be accepted or to deflect attention may be tacitly condoning and contributing to that kind of atmosphere. Understand that this is not a *blame the victim* stance; we're not saying that people who dress provocatively or join in sexual joking deserve to be harassed. We're saying that people who present themselves in an unprofessional, sexual manner in the workplace or classroom are "playing with fire." They don't deserve unprofessional treatment, but their behavior increases the likelihood that they'll be taken any way but seriously.

After the Deed's Been Done: Responding to Harassment

Research provides some guidance about personal, professional, and legal responses to harassment. But keep in mind that, particularly for female victims, the prime motivation or goal is to get a harasser to leave her alone (Bingham, 1991; Payne, 1993). When counseled, most victims say, "I just want it to stop."

A Range of Responses

Sociologist James Gruber (1989) adapted conflict resolution strategies to develop a range of responses to sexual harassment. Ranging from least assertive to most assertive, these responses include *avoidance, defusion, negotiation,* and *confrontation*. There is no "best" response to sexual harassment. Being assertive is not necessarily wiser than avoiding or ignoring a harasser; a judgment of a best response is up to the target because there are pros and cons to each.

Given targets' discomfort and feelings of powerlessness, along with perceptions of potential threats by harassers, it's understandable that the most common response is to *avoid* or ignore harassment. Most targets of harassment try to get out of the situation as quickly and gracefully as they can, putting as much distance between themselves and the harasser as possible. Unfortunately, some people feel forced to go to great lengths to get this distance, including transferring units within a company (or the military), quitting a job, dropping a class in which they've been harassed by a teacher or classmate, transferring schools, and even moving to another residence or city. But the problem is that when victims passively try to "let it go," they usually suffer great personal loss of self-esteem, confidence, and comfort at work or in school. As Payne (1993) suggests, "Ignoring the situation will not make it go away" (p. 145). On the contrary, it increases the likelihood that it will happen again to the same victim, someone else, or both.

A second common strategy, one step away from avoidance, is to attempt to *defuse* or "take the sting out" of a situation by joking about it or trivializing it with one's peers (Clair, McGoun, & Spirek, 1993; Cochran, Frazier, & Olson, 1997). Many times female targets simply "laugh off a comment," "act as though I don't understand what was said," or "stumble out a 'thank you' to a compliment I don't really appreciate." However, these actions may simply delay the process of confronting the problem (if not the harasser). Defusion responses often leave victims feeling dissatisfied, anxious about the future, and concerned about themselves (Maypole, 1986). Downplaying an event may reduce emotional stress and create a perception that there's no longer a need for negotiation or confrontation with the harasser. But then the harassment and the harasser aren't labeled as such publicly, so the behavior is likely perpetuated.

Some targets *negotiate* with a harasser, typically in the form of directly requesting that the behavior stop. A negotiating response might be, "I think that kind of talk is inappropriate and it makes me uncomfortable, so I'd appreciate it if you would stop talking to me like that." Organizational communication scholar Shereen Bingham (1991) suggests that "More frequent and effective use of interpersonal communication for dealing with sexual harassment may improve relationships between men and women at work and reduce costs to organizations . . ." (p. 110). However, for many victims, saying anything at all directly to a harasser is a tall order. Remember that harassment is, by design, a show of power. The person in the less powerful position is often unable to summon enough will to comment directly to a harasser. If the harasser is a supervisor or professor—someone who can hold one's professional, economic, or academic future as a type of ransom—the wisest thing in the victim's estimation may be to do nothing.

The final level of response is to *confront* the harasser by issuing an ultimatum such as "Keep your distance and stop asking me personal questions or else I'll have to talk to the boss about it." Assertive tactics like negotiation and confrontation are more likely to be used in closer relationships that have a longer history, one in which trust was set up and then violated, than when the harasser is an acquaintance. Confrontation is the least often reported response, but what's confusing is that this is the advice victims often get from people. People say, "Stand up for yourself. Just tell him to back off, that you're not going to put up with that crap." Those of us who have experienced sexual harassment know just how difficult it is to take that advice. Most of the time, harassment is so surprising, disgusting, and upsetting that a victim has a hard time saying *anything.* Perhaps after some time passes a victim might feel empowered enough to directly confront or negotiate with a harasser, but that's an individual choice. Our hope is that more and better information about sexual harassment will cause victims to feel more empowered, to believe that they can use assertive responses to stop a harasser's behavior without serious jeopardy to themselves. But we should all be careful about being quick or cavalier in our advice to victims of harassment.

The Downside of Secrecy

Keeping harassment bottled up is an immediate, understandable reaction. In fact, research documents a characteristic time-lag for responding to harassment, due to the victim's feelings of helplessness and shame and because it takes many victims time to realize that sexual harassment has actually occurred (Clair, 1998; Taylor & Conrad, 1992). People who have researched and experienced sexual harassment understand why, for example, Anita Hill waited 10 years before going public with her claims of sexual harassment (whether they believe her allegations or not) (Foss & Rogers, 1992). In Hill's case, she did not actually file a sexual harassment complaint against Clarence Thomas; she would not have gone public were it not that the press was about to expose her story.

But we suggest that if you are a victim of sexual harassment—if you even just *think* that you may have been harassed—*tell someone.* We're not talking about reporting the harassment here, but making it real by saying it out loud. It's critical to tell a friend, family member, clergy member, classmate, or co-worker what happened, what you interpreted from the incident, how it made you feel, how you currently feel about yourself and your job (or class, if it happened at school), and so forth. Communication allows a victim to gain back confidence and get useful perspectives from others (Witteman, 1993). It also creates documentation that can be used for possible professional and legal action in the future (Booth-Butterfield, 1986; Payne, 1993).

One caution from experience and research regarding confiding in some-one about harassment: *Be careful about the person you select to talk to.* Remem-ber our previous discussion about sex differences in listening and respond-ing—how men tend to react to women's communication by problem solving, rather than responding empathically to what women feel? If you're a female victim of sexual harassment—at work, school, wherever—think long and hard before deciding that the first person you'll tell is your hus-band, boyfriend, or father. We're not suggesting that you *shouldn't* tell one of these persons, but it's wise to apply the principles of the receiver orienta-tion here. Consider what a man's reaction might be to your sexual harass-ment experience. If you do decide to confide in him, think about *how* you will tell him. You may have heard stories like those we've heard of men who took on women's problems by confronting the harasser (often vio-lently) or by going to the woman's or the harasser's boss—actions that often made the situation worse. It's more empowering to fight your own harass-ment battle, with as many sources of support as possible *behind* you. This strategy will do more to repair your self-esteem and enhance your re-spectability in others' eyes.

If you're the person a victim speaks to about a sexually harassing experi-ence, your knowledge of sexual harassment will be a great comfort to that vic-tim. Apply the principles of the receiver orientation and your understanding of gender communication to help you respond in a helpful way, keeping in mind that the problem belongs to the victim and it is her or his decision about what to do. The best thing you can do for someone who confides in you is to listen—with your eyes as well as your ears, watching for nonverbal cues about what the victim is feeling and needs.

Going a Step Further: Reporting Sexual Harassment

After you've told someone about the incident, think about how you want to deal with it. For example, if the harasser is one of your professors, how will you handle being in his or her class the rest of the semester? Will you drop the class, become passive and withdrawn so as to endure the class, confront the professor and possibly risk your grade, report the harassment to the profes-sor's department chair, or file an official grievance? If the harasser is a co-worker, will you report the harassment? Ask for a transfer? Quit your job?

We don't mean to lay guilt trips here by saying that victims must report their harassment. Reporting is an individual decision because there are always costs involved. In fact, research shows that less than 5 percent of victims ever report the harassment to an authority; fewer still bring state or federal charges against harassers or their organizations (Fitzgerald, 1993). But a victim also has to weigh the costs of *not* reporting harassment. Unreported harassment leaves the harasser free from responsibility for her or his behavior, and free to harass again. As Payne (1993) contends, "The failure to report suggests that nothing is wrong and extends the power imbalance" (p. 142).

Preparing to Claim Sexual Harassment

Remembering our old friends Olivia and Bernie, let's say that Olivia decides to make a claim of sexual harassment. Many targets initiate an *internal grievance*, rather than using less familiar, higher profile measures such as filing a complaint with the EEOC or launching a lawsuit. Whether Olivia decides to use an internal route involving her company in the problem or an external process, the first thing she should do is ask herself this question: "What do I want to happen?" Knowing one's expectations or goals before starting the grievance process is critical; it can save some emotional toll down the road.

Once she is clear on her goals, Olivia should inventory the whole episode. Did she make any notes on the harassment, meaning what Bernie said and did and what Olivia said and did, if she responded? Creating a paper trail is a good idea, even if you don't expect harassment to recur and don't anticipate filing a grievance. But many victims are so taken aback by the behavior and reluctant to view it as sexual harassment that requiring written documentation is unrealistic. It's not necessary to have a paper trail, but it no doubt strengthens a case. If Olivia doesn't have any notes, she should write an account of harassing events, recalling specific dates, what was said and done, and other details with as much accuracy and information as possible.

Were there any witnesses to the conversations and events Olivia considers harassing? Did she ever tell Bernie directly that his behavior was unwelcome, and did anyone else witness or know about her telling him such? Notifying a harasser that the behavior is unwelcome is a key element courts look for; it's not a requirement, but again, it strengthens one's claims. Did Olivia tell anyone about the experiences, at the time they happened or later? If so, could those people be relied upon to verify Olivia's claims?

The Hunt for the Handbook

Olivia's next action might logically be to consult an employee handbook for a policy on sexual harassment and procedures for filing a grievance. Some company and university policies have time limits for filing grievances (which we disagree with); often employees and students are unaware of this constraint (Geist & Townsley, 1997). However, Olivia might have the rude awakening that her company doesn't have such a document, hasn't developed a policy, or has guidelines that are so vague or outdated that they make her situation more difficult to pursue (Cloud, 1998). A target's options will either be more limited because of ignorance among the organization's leaders or enhanced because the organization was caught unprepared to handle this situation. In some instances, organizations' ignorance on this issue has cost them dearly.

If there is a sexual harassment policy (and even if there isn't), it probably advises employees to report the problem to an immediate supervisor. Since Bernie *is* Olivia's supervisor, she will go further up the chain of command to Bernie's supervisor. Another option is to report harassment to human resources personnel or an EEO office, if the company or institution has these departments. Many targets only request that their complaint be taken seriously and that the supervisor take action to stop the behavior from recurring. However, in some instances the target asks that the harasser be fired, removed, or suspended. Our sincere hope is that the victim's complaint will be taken seriously and the policy (if there is one) will be followed carefully and fairly, for the sake of all parties involved. If not, Olivia can take her complaint to the courts.

Of Laws and Lawsuits

Legal recourse for victims of sexual harassment action is costly and time consuming, and it offers no guarantee of a desired outcome. But as this issue continues to come "out of the closet," more charges are filed, harassment is taken more seriously, laws and policies are strengthened, and more victims are compensated. Compare again the 1991 statistic showing that about 7,000 sexual harassment cases were filed with the statistic of over 15,000 cases per year toward the end of the decade (Cloud, 1998). Today's organizations are taking more seriously the prospect of sexual harassment litigation by reviewing or creating policies and grievance procedures and by conducting training sessions. A 1992 *Working Woman* survey showed that among Fortune 500 companies, 81 percent reported having training programs dealing with sexual harassment. That figure compares to only 60 percent from a similar survey in 1988 (Sandroff, 1992).

Case law continues to change the way sexual harassment is viewed and victims are compensated, although some rulings are contradictory, just to make things more confusing. The 1991 Civil Rights Act makes it possible for sexually harassed individuals to sue for both punitive and compensatory damages (Clair, 1992; Wood, 1992). Prior to 1991, victims could only sue for compensation, such as lost wages and benefits, but now they can receive remuneration for the personal, psychological, and physical effects of harassment.

Another area of concern is legal liability, meaning who is responsible and who must compensate for harassment. Several rulings indicate that managers and companies can be held legally liable for harassment among their employees. In the late 1990s, two U.S. Supreme Court rulings expanded the scope of employer liability. In *Ellerth* v. *Burlington Industries,* the court held that even if an employee did not suffer financial, job-related harm as a result of a supervisor's sexual harassment, the employer was still liable for other forms of injury to the victim. Findings in *Faragher* v. *The City of Boca Raton* made the previous ruling more specific, stating that employers are not liable for supervisory harassment if (1) they exercise reasonable care to prevent and correct the behavior, and (2) they can show that the victim of harassment failed to take advantage of an available remedy for the situation, such as a company policy or training program (Casey, Desai, & Ulrich, 1998).

Does the law hold schools legally liable for sexual harassment, as well as the teachers and classmates who harass? The answer is murky. Schools, school districts, and universities have been held legally liable for harassment within status-differentiated, peer, and contra-relationships, whether or not officials knew the harassment was occurring (Hughes & Sandler, 1988). However, there were inconsistent rulings on institutional liability during the 1990s (Carroll, 1993; Sherer, 1992). Previous rulings held schools liable, but in 1998 the U.S. Supreme Court ruled that schools and school districts were not legally liable for a teacher's sexual harassment of a student unless they knew about it and purposefully looked the other way (*Gebser* v. *Lago Vista Independent School District,* Casey, Desai, & Ulrich, 1998).

So if Olivia pursues an internal grievance but isn't pleased with the outcome, she can file a civil suit against the company. She should do so only after weighing the risks and getting legal advice about the current status of the law and her chances of winning a case, however. Some people go as far as they can with their claims; others never report harassment. Let's remember that as outsiders to a situation, we aren't really in a position to judge a victim's decision to take action after the fact. So many factors depend on circumstances that advising a specific response is inappropriate and unhelpful. The best advice is for victims to get as much information as possible in order to make the best decision possible. Having options, and knowing what they are, is critical.

Parting Considerations about Sexual Harassment

When students ask how to avoid sexual harassment, here's our answer: Communicate professionally—not personally or sexually—with bosses, co-workers, professors, and classmates. Including classmates in that list may seem harsh, but at least start out on this track until you're very sure (and we mean *very, very* sure) that personal communication is appropriate. This is not a suggestion that you "walk on eggshells," but that you exercise personally effective communication. You now know what your options are and how you can respond if you're in the unfortunate circumstance of being sexually harassed. Put your knowledge of gender communication to work to minimize the likelihood of being accused of harassment. If someone reacts nonverbally with embarrassment or discomfort, or says that she or he doesn't appreciate what you've said or done, try not to get defensive. Be responsible for your own behavior and try to rectify the situation, not by explaining what you meant or trying to justify your behavior, but by apologizing and offering to make amends. If the person won't accept your apology, then *leave her or him alone.* Accept the person's interpretation of the event, rather than asserting your will into the situation. Chalk up that experience and learn some lessons from it; perhaps you'll get a chance to start anew if the person is ready at some future point.

One final suggestion is to communicate equally and consistently, meaning in the same professional manner with members of the same and opposite sex. For example, it's unwise for women to communicate professionally with female co-workers but flirtatiously with male co-workers. It's unwise to communicate with deference to a male professor, but talk to a female professor as though she were "just one of us girls." For the men, would you tell a joke with equal comfort in "mixed company"? Do you speak to male colleagues with respect, but treat female co-workers like girls, rather than professionals? Do you compliment

---

RECAP

receiver orientation to communication, target orientation to sexual harassment, "he said, she said", posttraumatic stress disorder, "blame the victim", avoidance, defusion, negotiation, confrontation, internal grievance, punitive damages, compensatory damages, legal liability

---

a male colleague's suit just as often as you compliment a female colleague's dress? These are just a few important things that will help you initiate and maintain more respectful, successful relationships at school and on the job.

Personal Rights and Sexuality

For much of our history, male supremacy has reigned in sexual matters. Scholars Hatfield and Rapson (1996) give a startling view of history and current worldwide practices that relegate women to second-class status at best, to the role of victim of violence at worst. Although significant strides have been made in recent years toward gender equity in sexual matters, the goal is not yet reached. As teachers, we see vestiges of these attitudes in some students who express in overt or subtle ways an expectation that men have a right to assert their sexual needs. Recall our discussion in Chapter 2 about biology becoming a cop-out from focusing on sociocultural factors to explain gender differences in communication. The belief that some men commit sexual assault because their physical urges overtake their reason, the thinking that "men just have to have it," is a similar cop-out. This is blaming it on biology taken to its most ridiculous extent.

Power at the Core, Again

We've said that the abuses explored in this chapter are about power, not about sex. Power is obvious in stranger rape, because a stranger must render a victim powerless in order to assault. Here's how power emerges when the assaulter is someone the victim knows: When sexual expectations and interests in a romantic or social situation differ, when one person's sexual intentions or desires don't match another's, then the sexual motive becomes a power motive, a case of someone getting his or her way no matter the cost or the wishes of the other person. One person engages in sexual conduct against the will of another person; someone's personal rights are violated in the terrible form of rape.

Changing Language As We Learn More

The law recognizes different types of rape, some of which, unfortunately, are hard to prove. *Forcible rape,* as defined by the Federal Bureau of Investigation, is "the carnal knowledge of a female forcibly and against her will" (FBI, 1989). However, the FBI's outdated and conservative view of rape has been roundly criticized because it narrowly defines rape as vaginal intercourse without consent. Their definition does not mention male victims of rape or include forced oral sex, anal sex, and penetration with an object, which are included in many researchers' definitions when studying this problem (Crichton, 1993).

In contrast with *stranger rape, date rape* (also termed *acquaintance rape*) occurs in the context of persons who know one another, even if they have just met. Researchers Jean O'Gorman Hughes and Bernice Sandler (1987) define date rape as "forced, unwanted intercourse with a person you know. It is a violation of your body and your trust" (p. 1). They also offer another important distinction—the difference between *seduction* and rape: "Seduction occurs when a woman is manipulated or cajoled into agreeing to have sex; the key word is 'agreeing.' Acquaintance rape often occurs when seduction fails and the man goes ahead and has sex with the woman anyway, despite any protests and without her agreement" (p. 2).

After years of being ignored, attention is now being paid to the very serious societal problem of acquaintance rape. We spend a good deal of time in this chapter on this form, because it's the most common sexual offense college students experience. While on the surface date rape appears to be about sexual motivations, the need to overcome someone's resistance is all about power. Hughes and Sandler (1987) explain, "Acquaintance rape is not simply a crime of passion, or merely a result of miscommunication. It is, instead, often an attempt to assert power and anger" (p. 2). While cases of homosexual date rape continue to be documented, few victims of date rape are male; the vast majority of victims are female. Some claim, in fact, that "the possibility of being raped is certainly one of the defining characteristics of being a woman in our culture" (Peach, 1998). Thus, most of the literature refers to the rapist as "he" and the person raped as "she." We will be consistent with this language, given your understanding that rape victims can be male and rape can be homosexual as well as heterosexual.

Other terminology and definitional issues need to be addressed before going further with this discussion. The word *rape* is the historical term for this crime, but that word can be a *trigger word* for people who've experienced it. By *trigger word,* we mean that simply hearing the term can remind victims of the trauma they went through, sometimes making them feel victimized again. This is one of the primary reasons you hear the term *sexual assault* instead of *rape.* We are concerned about the impact of trigger words for those of you who have survived rape. But we also know that part of the healing process is being able to call the act what it is rather than using a more comfortable euphemism that can dilute or trivialize the experience. Another factor in word choice is that in some information on this topic, sexual assault refers to a category of behavior that includes forced kissing or petting, but stops short of intercourse (Unger & Crawford, 1996). In other usages, *sexual assault* is the term for a broader category, a range of offenses that includes rape (defined as vaginal intercourse) as well as other forms of sexual invasion, such as forced sodomy (oral sex) and anal penetration. We realize this is confusing and difficult language on an uncomfortable topic, but it's important to be clear on terms so that we can accurately and honestly discuss this life-altering experience.

The preferred term for persons who've experienced rape and sexual assault and lived through the ordeal is *survivors,* not *victims* or *targets* as we've used until this point. This is a great term because it signals respect and hope, so for the rest of this section we will be consistent with this language. Rape also occurs among marital partners (together or separated) and between persons who used to be married; at long last, all 50 states have laws on the books prosecuting this form of rape. Other terms for this offense include *marital rape, spousal rape,* and *wife rape,* defined as "sexual acts committed without a person's consent and/or against a person's will, when the perpetrator (attacker) is the woman's husband or ex-husband" (*The Wife Rape Information Page,* 1998, p. 1). We prefer the term *partner rape,* because homosexual partners and people who are cohabiting can be raped just as persons who are legally married, separated, or divorced can.

Other forms of rape include *gang rape,* which involves multiple rapists and a single victim (although there are accounts of gang rapes of multiple victims). In most gang rapes, the perpetrators are acquaintances of the victim (Ehrhart & Sandler, 1985; O'Sullivan, 1991). *Statutory rape* is the rape of a minor, someone who has not yet attained the age of consent (Eaves, 1992). Finally, a form of rape even exists on the Internet, although it involves only psychological, not physical, assault and is not legally recognized or prosecuted. In a provocative yet disturbing article in *Ms.* magazine, Debra Michals (1997) describes entering an on-line chat room in which a gang rape was taking place. As Michals explains, *cyber-rape* or *virtual rape* "is not the same as the rape a woman experiences in the physical world. But something as yet unnameable is going on in chat rooms where an erotic scenario can shift to a gang bang with a few keystrokes" (p. 69). Now that we've defined the terms, how bad is the problem?

Underestimates of an Underreported Problem

Although we start with a few numbers to illustrate the extent of the problem, realize that numbers do not tell even half of the story when it comes to rape and sexual assault. Upon first glance at FBI crime statistics for 1995 and 1996, you'd be pleased to find that rates of violent crimes (murders, robberies, and rapes) dropped nationwide. Murders dropped 11 percent and rapes dropped 3 percent, but remember: Rape rates reflect *reported* cases. Annette Fuentes (1997) concludes, "By all accounts, rape remains the most underreported violent crime. The U.S. Department of Justice, using FBI data, says only 36 percent of rapes are reported. Because the FBI's Reporting Program reflects only crimes reported to police, its rape numbers may be off by almost two thirds" (p. 20). Underreporting is particularly the case for partner rape because many women do not consider sexual assaults by their husbands to be rape (*The Wife Rape Information*

Page, 1998). Research estimates that one in every seven married women will be sexually assaulted by her husband (Koss & Harvey, 1991).

Another national survey summarized in *Rape in America: A Report to the Nation* estimated that only about 16 percent of rapes were reported to authorities (Kilpatrick, Edmunds, Seymour, & Boyle, 1992). FBI figures for 1990 showed about 102,000 rapes of women over the age of 18, and the National Crime Survey poll estimated 130,000 such rapes. But the more accurate, comprehensive methods used by *Rape in America* researchers produced "a mind-blowing" number: 683,000 rapes in one year (as in Fuentes, 1997, p. 21). Criticism over ways the feds estimated violence against women caused a change in 1995. After using their "new and improved" survey, Bureau of Justice statistics estimated 500,000 sexual assaults on women occurring annually, including 170,000 rapes and 140,000 attempted rapes (Sniffen, 1995). Other studies reveal that 62 percent of all forcible rapes occur to girls younger than 18, with 29 percent occurring before age 11, primarily committed by persons known to these girls (Fuentes, 1997). So the 683,000 number cited earlier really represents less than half the total, if you were to include females under the age of 18. The numbers are staggering.

Statistics on Date Rape

It's a devastating fact that most women are raped by persons they know; only one in five rapes are committed by strangers (FBI, 1995). The effects on young women are enormous, especially in the damage done to their ability to trust or form intimate relationships. Late in 1998, NBC's *Dateline* reported the story of a 12-year-old girl who was sexually assaulted by four boys on a school bus. The bus driver was dismissed, criminal charges were pending, and the family intended to sue the school district, but the emotional scars on the young girl were immeasurable. Mary Pipher, author of *Reviving Ophelia: Saving the Selves of Adolescent Girls* (1994), explains, "Young women who are raped are more fearful. Their invisible shield of invulnerability has been shattered" (p. 230). Pipher provides some statistics on the aftermath of rape: 41 percent of survivors expect to be raped again; 30 percent consider suicide; 31 percent seek therapy; 22 percent enroll in self-defense courses; 82 percent say they are permanently changed by the experience.

One name that repeatedly surfaces in research on this topic is Mary Koss, author of multiple studies on rape and currently a principal investigator for the Arizona Rape and Sexual Assault Surveillance Project. In an effort to get a more accurate picture of rape rates, Koss compared the number of rapes reported to police to the number of calls to rape crisis centers in Arizona's major cities. In 1994–95,

> *It's not like she was tortured or chopped up.*
>
> Jerome Marks, Manhattan Supreme Court justice, on giving a light sentence to a rapist

Koss found over six times as many hotline calls reporting rapes than the number of rapes reported to police; in 1995–96, the hotline received eight times the number of calls as reported cases (as in Fuentes, 1997).

In an earlier study, Koss and colleagues surveyed 7,000 students across 32 American college campuses and found the following:

1. One out of every 12 men responding to the survey said they had tried or actually succeeded in forcing a woman to have sexual intercourse.
2. None of the men who admitted such behavior called themselves rapists.
3. One in eight women responding to the survey revealed that they were survivors of rape.
4. Only a little over half of these rape survivors actually called their experiences rape; the others had a hard time viewing their experience as rape.
5. Five percent of the women who reported surviving rape had been raped by multiple offenders (gang raped).
6. The rate of college student victimization is about three times the rate for the general population (Koss, Gidyhcz, & Wisniewski, 1987).

This gives you further indication of the magnitude of the problem.

Slip 'Em a Mickey

Some of you are too young to know what "slipping a Mickey" means, but it's a reference to a Mickey Finn, meaning the use of substances to involuntarily sedate someone for the purpose of assaulting or taking advantage of her or him. The old phrase "get her drunk and take advantage of her" has a 21st-century incarnation in the form of date rape drugs.

You may have heard or read about this, but the practice of placing sedatives in people's drinks without their knowledge is increasing at an alarming rate. According to the Washington DC Rape Crisis Center web site (1998), the mostly commonly used, easily obtained substances are as follows (street names included): Rohypnol (Roofies, Roachies, La Rocha, The Forget Pill); Gamma Hydroxybutyrate or GHB (Grievous Bodily Harm, Easy Lay); and Ketamine (Special K). The most well-known of these, Rohypnol, is a medication prescribed internationally for people with severe and debilitating sleep disorders. It's illegal in the U.S., but it's being smuggled in and sold as a street drug. The Swiss-based company that manufactures Rohypnol has reformulated the drug so that it releases a blue dye when dissolved in a liquid. While this is a step in the right direction, the problem is that the blue dye is difficult to detect in dark drinks and dark settings, such as bars and clubs.

When this tasteless, odorless drug is slipped into a person's drink, within 20 to 30 minutes the person will show symptoms of being sedated. Limited motion and voice production are two common effects; drugged rape survivors report feeling in a daze, as though they are too heavy to move or call out. But perhaps the most devastating effect of the drug is its memory-impairment. The DC Rape Crisis Center describes it this way: "Because survivors will have been heavily sedated, they may not have complete recall of the assault. It is likely that they will be uncertain about exactly what happened and who was involved. The unknowns may create tremendous anxiety as survivors are left to fill in the gaps with their imagination" (pp. 4-5). Some persons who've been drugged have no memory of the incident; they wake up, sometimes in a hospital, to learn that they've been raped, but can't remember how it happened or who raped them.

If you or a friend suspect you've been drugged because you feel dizzy or confused after drinking something, try to get to a hospital. If you believe you've been raped (and there are reported cases of men being drugged with Rohypnol and raped), crisis centers recommend that you get to a safe place and call a crisis center or 911. If you decide to report the assault to the police, be sure not to shower, bathe, douche, change clothes, or straighten up the area where you suspect the rape took place, until medical and legal evidence is collected. Then go to a hospital or other facility where you can receive treatment for injuries, tests for pregnancy and sexually transmitted diseases, a urine test, and counseling. The urine test is important because Rohypnol can be found in urine up to 72 hours after ingestion, depending on someone's metabolism and the dose of the drug. The Drug-Induced Rape Prevention and Punishment Act, passed in October 1996, punishes persons who commit rape by administering a controlled substance without the victim's knowledge.

Who Are the Rapists?

The normal, gentle, nice-looking guy sitting next to you in class could be a rapist. Does that sound paranoid or absurd? The point we're trying to make is that persons capable of committing date or partner rape look just like all of us. Their profiles cross racial and ethnic, class, age, and religious lines. Research has isolated a number of characteristics more common among date rapists, such as the use or abuse of alcohol, athletic affiliation, fraternity affiliation, a history of family violence, and early and varied sexual experience (Unger & Crawford, 1996). But a date rapist *could be anybody.* We don't want to make you overly suspicious, so you see criminals everywhere you look, but we do want you to realize that the "crazed man jumping out of the bushes" to rape is much more the exception than the rule. Most rapists are people you know: family members, friends of the family, classmates, boyfriends, teachers, co-workers, bosses, doctors, lawyers, ministers. As a reporter for the *San Antonio Express-News* asserted, in an article educating the community about rape, "In 80% of sexual assaults, the victim is acquainted with the rapist in some way. Most rapists don't break into homes to terrorize their victims. More often than not, they are welcomed at the front door or they already live there" (Aaron, 1997).

Contributing Effects of Gender-Role Socialization

Many cultures socialize men to be aggressive and competitive and women to be submissive and not "rock the boat." While we are making progress and changing some of that *gender-role socialization,* change in the sexual arena hasn't kept pace. For example, we continue to become more aware of serious health risks associated with sexual activity, but our culture still reinforces men for expressing and exploring their sexuality. Such was the case with the Spur Posse in California, a group in the news in the mid-1990s whose story shocked the country. In this case, a group of about 25 high school boys competed for points based on "scoring" (having intercourse) with high school girls. When seven girls, ages 11 to 17, complained of sexual molestation and rape, some of the boys were arrested. The California community was split between those who called the girls "trash" and claimed their poor self-esteem led to their accusations, versus those who were appalled at the "boys will be boys" attitude (Sadker & Sadker, 1994; Smolowe, 1993).

Women hear a variety of mixed messages about sexuality. On the one hand, they are encouraged to take responsibility for sex, for example, by carrying condoms rather than expecting a sexual partner to have them. They may be told that they can be sexual creatures and that they need to learn to express their sexual desires and openly discuss the limits they want to place on sexual activity (topics often discussed at campus workshops, for instance). Yet on the other hand, they also see people become squeamish and prudish when such subjects as female anatomy, masturbation, and orgasm come up. They see rape laws that encourage male sexuality and question women's. They see constant attempts in rape trials to determine if a woman behaved in a sexual manner that brought about her own rape. This approach is related to the antiquated belief that women tease men and lead them on unfairly, only to deny them something they have a right to deserve and expect. There is still much more openness and acceptance of male sexuality in our society than female sexuality, which adds to the power imbalance.

Psychologists Unger and Crawford (1996) believe that a patriarchal society such as ours offers a double-edged sword to women. They assert:

> Dominance and aggression are rewarded in men while submission and humbleness are rewarded in women. This submission, however, makes women more vulnerable to male violence. Our culture teaches men to protect women and women to look to others for safety and security. Ironically, in a chivalrous society, men are both those who commit violence and those who protect. Chivalry promotes the man as the protector and the woman as the protected, the man as the aggressor and the woman as the victim. (p. 551)

Along with these differences in socialization, other structures readily embraced in society reinforce the woman-as-victim role. For example, few women are taught to protect and defend themselves, women are encouraged to limit developing their bodies and increasing their strength (although women can be strong, they are told it's unfeminine to be stronger than a man), and women are blatantly encouraged to wear tight clothing and shoes that inhibit their movement and prevent easy escape. Then there's the age-old message that women need men for economic support (Unger & Crawford, 1996).

Common Myths about Rape

Important research from 1980 documents the existence of a set of rape myths, beliefs about rape that aren't based in fact (Burt, 1980). While these myths emerged 20 years ago, many people still adhere to them. They include the following:

1. Women say "no" when they mean "yes" to avoid being seen as promiscuous (discussed further below).
2. Men must overcome women if they resist.
3. Some women deserve to be raped.
4. Some women actually enjoy rape, because it fulfills one of their sexual fantasies.
5. Some men just can't help themselves when they are aroused; they *have* to have sexual intercourse, even if they have to be aggressive to get it.
6. "Good girls" don't get raped, a myth related to prior sexual activity. A man may believe that if a woman has been sexually active, she will willingly have sex with anyone, including him. The "only virgins can be raped" myth suggests that sexually active women cannot be raped.

A related myth is the belief that if a woman has had sex with a man but refuses to have sex with him again, it's not rape if he forces her (Shotland & Goldstein, 1992). This couldn't be farther from the truth. Unwanted, nonconsensual sex is rape, no matter if there have been instances of prior consent.

From this research, Burt developed a Rape Myth Acceptance Scale, an instrument that asks subjects questions about their experiences with sexual violence and determines to what level an individual accepts or believes certain myths about rape. Subsequent studies on rape myth acceptance consistently found that men who scored high in traditional masculinity traits on scales (such as the Bem Sex-Role Inventory, discussed in Chapter 2) and who held traditional attitudes about sex roles were much more likely to believe in rape myths and describe past or future aggression toward females than less traditionally masculine males (Abbey & Harnish, 1995; Good, Heppner, Hillenbrand-Gunn, & Wang, 1995; Malamuth, Sockloskie, Koss, & Tanaka, 1991; Truman, Tokar, & Fischer, 1996). Other research determined a connection between exposure to pornography, sexually violent media, and mainstream media depictions of women acting aroused during rape and a reinforced belief in rape myths (Malamuth, 1984; Mullin, 1995; Zillman & Bryant, 1982).

A Web page for the Washington DC Rape Crisis Center (1998) lists a few more myths about rape that have recently emerged:

1. Rape is not a big deal; it is only sex.
2. Most rapes are interracial; most rapes are committed by black men against white women or white men against black women. (The reality is that about 90 percent of all rapes occur between members of the same race.)
3. Most rapists are psychotic men. (Actually, most rapists are not mentally ill.)

Changing sexual standards may lead some college-aged men to expect sex from women, almost as a given or a reward for having dated someone a few times. Some men believe that they are entitled to sex when they have spent money on a date, that somehow sex and money are an even exchange.

RECAP

---

forcible rape; stranger rape; date or acquaintance rape; seduction; trigger words; sexual assault; survivors; marital, spousal, or wife rape, partner rape; gang rape; statutory rape; cyber- or virtual rape; Rohypnol and date rape drugs; gender-role socialization; rape myths; sexual aggression

---

Sexually Aggressive Tendencies

Studies have attempted to predict some of the characteristics of men who are likely to be sexual aggressors. Keep in mind that the term *sexual aggression* describes a continuum of behaviors, with consensual sexual activity on one end (meaning that consensual sex can involve aggressive behavior) and violent rape on the other (Unger & Crawford, 1996). Prominent sexual assault researcher Neil Malamuth and colleagues found that sexually aggressive men were incompetent in decoding women's negative emotions and had more suspicious interpretations of women's verbal communication (as in doubting that a woman's "no" really meant "no"). They failed to distinguish between assertiveness and hostility, and between friendliness and seduction in women's communication (Malamuth & Brown, 1994). Sexually aggressive men also tend to be more domineering in casual conversation, using one-up messages, bragging, criticizing others, and attempting to dominate conversation by controlling the topic and interrupting others. The researchers suggest that a sexually aggressive man might be domineering in conversation as a way to assess the vulnerability of a female target (Malamuth & Thornhill, 1994).

Other studies found that physically aggressive men who held traditional views of sex roles were more likely to have sexually aggressive tendencies toward women (Cachie & deMan, 1997; Muehlenhard & Falcon, 1990) and that men who accepted rape myths and had poor argumentation skills resorted to verbal aggression, which had the potential to lead to physical aggression, sexual aggression, or both (Andonian & Droge, 1993).

An Evening Out with Annie and Kris

Besides being a professor of communication, the female co-author of this text (whom we'll just refer to as "the professor") is the Director of the Women's Center at her university. In that capacity, she makes presentations and conducts workshops on gender-related topics on campus and in the community. One recent campus event is particularly memorable; it illustrates our discussion of socialization and sexuality.

The professor was recently asked by a resident assistant (RA), a former student, to speak to a group of her residents about gender communication. The event drew about 20 or so students on a week night, with more women than men in attendance. The discussion started generally, but as usual in addressing gender communication in an informal setting, it fairly quickly turned to topics of sex. At one point, the RA said that a friend of hers (whom we'll call Annie) was studying and couldn't attend the gathering, but had an important question she was going to phone in.

Annie's question was about men and claims of "blue balls" (pardon the bluntness and use of this crude term). She said that at the end of a date, she'd been making out with her boyfriend (whom we'll call Kris) in his car and the activity went a bit further than usual, at which point she resisted. She told Kris "You know that I'm not into that; I'm not ready to go all the way with you." He got flustered, as she said was typical of him, but this time became angry as well. Kris said Annie was responsible for him having a "permanent case of blue balls" and that she had to have sex with him or it would hurt his health. His claim was that being sexually aroused but ungratified caused an uncomfortable and unhealthy condition for men. He said Annie owed it to him not to tease him, and he knew she really wanted sex as much as he did.

As best she could, not being a physician (or a man), the professor explained the condition Annie's boyfriend described. A state of pressure, swelling, and discomfort can develop in men as a result of arousal that doesn't consummate in ejaculation, but it isn't permanent as Kris claimed. The condition goes away shortly, as the build-up of fluid due to arousal retreats, is absorbed, or is ejaculated via masturbation. But here's the main point the professor tried to get across to Annie: The physical state termed "blue balls" is in no way a justification for sexual coercion or aggression. Kris had no right to make Annie feel guilty for arousing him by kissing and then not giving in to his insistence on sex because of the threat of some debilitating condition. On hearing this, Annie started to cry over the phone.

There was more to the story. Annie said she felt bad about making Kris angry, she cared about him, and she didn't want to do something that would hurt him physically because she really didn't know anything about the "blue balls" condition. She'd had sex before in a prior relationship, but wasn't ready to have sex with Kris. It turned out that Annie had intercourse with Kris that night in the car. In Annie's perception, she didn't really say yes; she didn't say no—she just didn't resist when Kris started in again. But she kept saying no all the time in her head. She didn't enjoy the experience because she wasn't ready to go that far with Kris and she was worried someone would see them in the car. It wasn't until later that she started to question his justification for having sex.

Was this a case of consensual sex or date rape? Answers to that question reveal the complexity of the issue. One could argue that this was a classic case of date rape because Annie felt coerced into sex, and although she complied with Kris's desires, she didn't really consent because she kept saying no in her head. He should have stopped when she first said she didn't want to have sex.

But what is Kris's story likely to be? What if he thought he was just being honest with Annie by telling her that he was frustrated and needed to have sex? Kris may have thought that he was just fulfilling his male role, that it's up to the guy to make the first move and that women are expected to resist. Then when the man keeps pressing, they give in and get what they really wanted all along. Does this sound familiar? Does it sound reasonable? Whose interpretation is the right one? Is there a right one?

The answer is that it's complicated, although we have to say that we agree with Annie's interpretation and believe that this was, indeed, date rape. But we can all probably imagine what would happen if Annie attempted to claim rape and take Kris to court. The issue of consent is murky, both in the law and in Annie's story as she recounted it. While she resisted at first, she ultimately did have sex; Kris had no way of knowing Annie was saying no in her head the whole time. She said no at first, but said nothing at all later, so they had sex. Kris believed that he'd successfully persuaded Annie to have sex, something he assumed she'd enjoy if she'd just let him do it. You can bet that Kris didn't view his actions as rape.

One lesson among many emerges from this story: A sexual situation like this involves power, but that power isn't always easy to detect or counter. In this situation, Kris used the power of persuasion by talking about a male condition he knew Annie probably wouldn't understand and by making it sound like a dire situation if she didn't comply. This is a classic "men have to have it" example in which one person controls events by declaring a "need," then claiming that the other person is at fault if she doesn't give him what he needs. The result is that someone felt she had to do something she really didn't want to do. Annie had a hard time calling it rape; she couldn't fathom charging Kris with rape, but she stopped dating him right after this experience. It was clear that the event would stay with Annie a long time.

Communication and the Abuse of Power in Sexual Assault

Of special interest to our study of gender communication is the miscommunication that occurs in situations that end up as sexual assault and date rape. Just to be clear, we aren't labeling date rape a simple situation of miscommunication. That's as bad as calling sexual harassment misbehavior, as we discussed earlier in this chapter. But some communication elements common to abusive episodes are worth talking about.

When Women Say "Yes" *and* "No"

Research indicates that men tend to interpret sexual messages from flirtatious behavior, while women tend to distinguish between behavior that is flirtatious or playful versus sexual (Abbey, 1982; Metts & Cupach, 1989). Therefore, being clear with verbal and nonverbal communication becomes even more important. Women and men alike are learning how critical it is to be as clear as possible with their sexual intentions and desires—even though this kind of communication is tough for many women.

We don't want to insinuate that women who are date raped are at fault for poor communication that somehow confused men. But as writer Stephen

Schulhofer (1998) suggests, "Beneath the surface, in the messy, emotionally ambiguous real world of dating, petting, and sexual exploration, 'no' doesn't always mean no" (p. 59). Some women do give mixed messages about sexual activity, like saying "no" when their actions say "yes" or feigning resistance to sexual overtures in an effort to tease a man they want to have sex with. Some men think that a woman's "no" really doesn't mean no, but means "maybe," "try harder," or "try again."

Research at different universities from the late 1980s through the mid 1990s found evidence of mixed messages. Surveys of university students in Hawaii, Pennsylvania, Texas, and the Midwest found that upwards of 39 percent of women surveyed revealed "token resistance," meaning that they first said "no" to a man they had every intention of having sex with. These women reported that they wanted their initial "no" to be respected and their dates to wait for sex, and that they wanted to be "talked into" sex. If this is the case, then the mantra "no means no" that feminists and rape prevention activist groups have worked to get across is meaningless, or at least greatly undermined (Schulhofer, 1998).

Sometimes women send mixed signals for fear that, if they agree to sex too easily or quickly, they'll be seen as slutty. They may even avoid discussing sex for the same reason, worried that a frank conversation will make them appear nerdy or too overt about sex, as though they have "been around." But as all the research on this topic advocates, the best approach for women is to say "no" when they mean no and "yes" when they mean yes, avoiding game playing and pretense in romantic or sexual situations. Even if women think that sexual teasing and sending mixed signals heightens their own and the man's arousal, they should definitely avoid teasing because such behavior contributes to a greater problem. Will the next woman to be with a man someone has teased handle it differently? If her "no" really means no, will the guy still expect her to behave like the first woman?

When a Man Hears "No"

On the flip side, in some situations women say "no" and mean no, but the man chooses to reject that "no." In sexual encounters, these men may try to turn a woman's no into a yes, by continuing to physically arouse their partner or by displaying anger or frustration with the intent of making the woman feel nervous, uncomfortable, or guilty enough to give in. However, some men work to unlearn these responses and to interpret a woman's no as actually meaning no. Researchers' advice is to take a woman's no at face value, assuming that no really does mean no—no questions asked nor disagreement voiced. Any actions beyond the woman's no are sexual violations, and sexual activity without agreement or consent is rape.

This may seem like an overstatement to you, but everything you've learned about gender communication and personal effectiveness from this text applies with even more urgency to this situation of negotiating sexual waters with a relational partner. The principles behind the receiver orientation to communication and the value of expanding one's repertoire of communication to provide alternatives for confronting different situations are highly applicable and useful in sexual contexts.

Date Rape Prevention Programs

Many colleges and universities have implemented programs to prevent date rape. Research describes both the content and results of some of these programs designed to raise awareness of women and men about the definition of date rape and ways to avoid it (Baker & Meadows, 1997; Becky & Farren, 1997; Earle, 1996; Holcomb & Seehafer, 1996; Kier, 1996). One consistent tendency that emerged in these programs was that many students, both men and women, were unaware of the fact that some dating incidents were actually rape.

Before discussing these programs further we have to say this: One of the things we resent most about this whole topic of rape and sexual assault is the focus on women in educational programs and literature, as though women are to blame for rape. Rapists are to blame for rape. The constant suggestion that women should learn how to prevent rape, as though they are responsible for whether or not a date ends in rape, contributes to the belief that rape is just a women's issue. Granted, women *should* become educated in preventing date rape; they *should* be clear and consistent with their communication with men. But date rape is another area, like sexual harassment, in which blame-the-victim attitudes are rampant. Most of the educational programs, films, and materials on date and stranger rape are aimed at teaching women how to walk defiantly, talk clearly, dress appropriately, and not do "stupid" things, like walking alone to their cars at night after class. This places the burden on women to prevent men from

> *Once in cabinet we had to deal with the fact that there had been an outbreak of assaults on women at night. One minister suggested a curfew: women should stay home after dark. I said, "But it's the men who are attacking the women. If there's to be a curfew, let the men stay home, not the women."*
>
> Golda Meir,
> *former Israeli prime minister*

raping. As Ron Aaron (1997) wrote (in his article about rape in San Antonio, referenced earlier):

> The extraordinary focus on what women should do to prevent rape reinforces one of the most troubling myths about rape, that victims not perpetrators are responsible for sexual assault. That's simply not true. Failing to lock doors and windows or going out alone at night doesn't cause rape. Indeed, it's not her responsibility to prevent rape. It's his obligation to stop doing it.

So we ask: Where are the programs that teach men not to rape?

Unger and Crawford (1996) describe a few innovative programs on college campuses that target all-male groups, such as fraternities and athletic teams, as well as community-based, male-led campaigns to stop sexual assault. But materials and programs geared for men on the topic of date rape are seriously lacking, and men need good information about this problem. So we start this section with advice to men, drawn from the limited available information from this point of view; we then move to advice for women.

Attention: Men

An excellent Web site, simply entitled *Sexual Assault and Rape: Advice for Men,* offers this current, helpful information.

1. Think about whether you really want to have sex with someone who doesn't want to have sex with you; how will you feel afterwards if your partner tells you she or he didn't want to have sex?
2. If you are getting a double message from a woman, speak up and clarify what she wants. If you find yourself in a situation with a woman who is unsure about having sex or is saying "no," back off. Suggest talking about it.
3. Be sensitive to women who are unsure whether they want to have sex. If you put pressure on them, you might be forcing them.
4. Do not assume you both want the same degree of intimacy. She might be interested in some sexual contact other than intercourse. There may be several kinds of sexual activity you might mutually agree to share.
5. Stay in touch with your sexual desires. Ask yourself if you are really hearing what she wants. Do not let your desires control your actions.
6. Communicate your sexual desires honestly and as early as possible.
7. Do not assume her desire for affection is the same as a desire for sex.
8. A woman who turns you down for sex is not necessarily rejecting you as a person; she is expressing her decision not to participate in a single act at that time.
9. No one asks to be raped. No matter how a woman behaves, she does not deserve to have her body used in ways she does not want.
10. The fact that you were intoxicated [or high] is not legal defense to rape. You are responsible for your actions, whether you are drunk or sober.
11. Be aware that a man's size and physical presence can be intimidating to a woman. Many victims report that the fear they felt based on the man's size and presence was the reason they did not fight back or struggle. (p. 1)

Attention: Women

Hughes and Sandler (1987) offered useful guidelines that are still applicable today to help minimize the potential for date rape. While this advice is aimed at women, men need to understand these points and be aware that acting on this advice may not come easily for some women. Hughes and Sandler suggest the following:

1. Examine your feelings about sex.
2. Set sexual limits for yourself and your partner or date.
3. Decide early if you would like to have sex, and communicate your decision clearly and firmly.
4. Do not give mixed messages; be alert to other unconscious messages you may be giving.
5. Be forceful and firm; don't worry about being "polite."
6. Be independent and aware—you can have input on dates about where you'd like to go, what you think is appropriate, and so on.
7. Do not do anything you do not want to just to avoid a scene or unpleasantness.
8. Be aware of specific situations in which you do not feel relaxed or in charge.
9. If things start to get out of hand, protest loudly, leave, or go for help.
10. Realize that drugs and alcohol are often present in date rape situations. (p. 3)

A Word about Rape Laws

The laws governing the prosecution of various forms of rape are very complex and beyond the parameters of this chapter. As a whole, they are also archaic; our frustration with the status of rape laws also leads us to abbreviate a discussion of them. Rape laws seem to be at least two decades behind sexual harassment laws in terms of understanding the problem, placing blame where it appropriately belongs, and vindicating the abused. These laws are sender based, as opposed to the receiver-based laws for sexual harassment. Rape laws focus on a rapist's intentions, meaning what was in the mind of the accused during the "incident."

Stephen Schulhofer (1998) outlines the many problems with the current law, mainly conceptualizations of force and consent. He explains, "Standards remain extraordinarily murky, especially for determining when a man's behavior amounts to prohibited force or when a woman's conduct signals her consent" (p. 56). The problem is an archaic view of force, meaning that jurors don't view a woman's unwillingness as enough to prove rape. Even if she objects, "intercourse is still not considered rape or any other form of felonious assault unless the assailant used physical force or threatened bodily injury" (p. 56). Such actions as coerced penetration or pinning a victim down aren't considered force, in and of themselves. The force must be "something beyond the acts involved in intercourse—something that physically 'compels' the woman to submit" (p. 56). So if a rapist doesn't exert any force beyond subduing and penetrating a woman, the victim's only recourse, if she's going to successfully prosecute her attacker, is to fight back. And fighting back can sometimes cost someone her life.

Even if a rapist uses the "right" kind of force (in a court's view), many prosecutors won't go near rape cases because they are so difficult to win. The least frequent form of rape—stranger rape—has the best chance of being successfully prosecuted (Buzawa, 1995). Date rape prosecutions are prone to the same kind of "he said-she said" problem we discussed regarding sexual harassment. Except for situations of gang rape, most rapes occur in private. As law professor and rape survivor Susan Estrich (1993) explains, the "he said-she said" aspect that emerges in many rape trials has led to the so-called *nuts and sluts defense* of the accused rapist. According to Estrich, "Today, if you're trying to destroy a woman's credibility, you argue that she's sexually permissive (so she consented) and unstable (so she lied about it)" (p. 64).

Schulhofer (1998) reports that rape law reformers are working to extend the legal definition of force from physical violence to other types of coercion. But rape survivors face uphill battles trying to prove rape, punish rapists, and receive justice. We encourage rape survivors to seek justice in the courts and prosecutors to find the guts and determination to prosecute offenders, rather than instantly deciding a case doesn't have a chance. Rape laws in this country do little to deter rape, so we must work to try to reform them. Outdated rape laws are overturned or rewritten when survivors and prosecutors bring cases forward and persevere through the court system.

Parting Considerations about Sexual Assault and Rape

It's obvious that members of both sexes need to become more aware of the different forms of sexual assault, how prevalent rape is in our culture, what elements embedded in our society actually condone and reinforce the problem, how devastating rape is (particularly date rape), and what all of us can do to help combat this crime. It should be obvious to you that rape laws are in serious need of reform. But let us not be deterred by lousy laws; there are things that all of us can do on our campuses.

See if your campus has literature and educational programs on date rape, such as a "Take Back the Night" march. These marches exist on many campuses, typically as part of a celebration of Women's History Month. They honor survivors of rape and generate awareness of the problem. If there are no such programs on your campus, start one. Educate yourself about the best procedure to follow in the unfortunate chance you or a friend are assaulted on campus. For example, certain hospitals might have agreements with your campus to examine students and provide rape counseling. If you drive a friend or a friend drives you somewhere to get help, you need to know where to go. And what will be your response if you learn that someone is a date rapist? What are the legal responsibilities and implications of such knowledge?

As Hughes and Sandler (1987) explain, "Rape is violence. It strikes at the heart of the personal relationship between a man and a woman, how they treat each other, and how they respect each other's wishes" (p. 2). We can't bury our heads in the sand about this problem, pretending it doesn't happen. Look around your classrooms; there are rape survivors sitting there. Maybe you're one of them, but we hope not. Like sexual harassment, sexual assault isn't a woman's or a man's problem; it's a human problem that we all must work to overcome.

PARTNER VIOLENCE

What do the three areas we discuss in this chapter have in common? Certainly, the primary commonality is that sexual harassment, sexual assault and rape, and partner violence are all extreme abuses of power. They all involve one person's attempt to control, dominate, and render powerless another person. Another commonality is privacy, meaning that most abusive episodes occur behind closed doors, not in front of witnesses. Partner violence is a bit different from harassment and rape, in that it may occur within earshot or eyeshot of children. But there is a closed-doors quality to this too, in that violence in the home may be kept within the family and rarely spoken about outside the home. As we'll see in the next few pages, this closed-doors quality is one of the main problems in situations of domestic violence (as it is with harassment and rape as well).

Another common element across the three abuses is the tendency to blame the victim. We described this tendency in sexual harassment and assault contexts, but it is very typical of partner abuse as well. Most harassment, rape, and battering is done by men upon women. But remember, as we said in the opening pages of this chapter, it's important to try to keep any feelings of male-bashing to a minimum (if you have them at all), realizing that this material does not indict all *man*kind. Remember, because statistics show that the overwhelming majority of harassers, rapists, and batterers are male, we choose to talk about the problem in those terms. But we don't want to send the message that *all* men are abusive or that women *cannot be* abusive; we want men and women alike to become more outraged about these problems so that we can all do something about them. The final commonality across the three areas is that the laws for each are complex and in a constant state of flux as society continues to learn about and unmask these crimes.

Effects of Headlines on Issues of Abuse

Some say that what the Anita Hill–Clarence Thomas hearings did for sexual harassment, the O. J. Simpson trials did for domestic violence (LaMorte, 1998). It's hard to think of these traumatic national events as making positive contributions, but the Simpson debacle did raise society's collective consciousness about partner violence in a way it had not been raised before.

You'll be relieved to know that we're not going to talk extensively about the O. J. trial, but here is an important point: Beating one's spouse or partner or date is *not* an action based on love. You'll remember that, a few years before the murders, Simpson pleaded "no contest" when he was arrested for battering his then-wife Nicole. In an *Esquire* magazine interview Celia Farber conducted with Simpson after he was held liable in a civil case for the murders of Nicole Brown and Ronald Goldman, Simpson said the following: "Let's say I committed this crime. Even if I did do this, it would have to have been because I loved her very much, right?" (Salter, 1998, p. A10). Here's journalist Stephanie Salter's response:

> The truth is: If he hits her, it isn't love. If he threatens to kill her, it isn't love. If he rapes her in their marital bed, it isn't love. If he rips the phone cord out of the wall because she "talks too much" to her friends or her mother, it isn't love. If he screams at her that she's ugly, fat, a lousy housekeeper, a bad mother, stupid, dirt, a whore or frigid, it isn't love. If he humiliates her in front of their families, friends or children, it isn't love. If he comes home in the middle of the day to check up on her, accuses her of having affairs (or of wanting to) with every man who looks at her, it isn't love. If he refuses to let her take a job or a walk alone or to use the car or the checking account, it isn't love. If he gets drunk, shoves and bruises her, then, the next morning, cries, apologizes and promises—again—that he'll never hurt her because he loves her more than anything in the world, he's a liar. It isn't love. (p. A10)

Love complicates the picture of domestic violence, but love is never a motivation for violence. Let's first work on our language, then look at how pervasive the problem of domestic violence is in our culture.

The Language of Violence

Before we explore the many different terms for this kind of abuse, we want to ask you to join us in ridding the language of the phrase *rule of thumb*. You may not know the historical derivation of that phrase. It refers to an old English law that made it legal for a husband to beat or whip his wife, as long as he used a stick or switch no larger than the width of his thumb (Hirshman, 1994). A statement like "A good rule of thumb is to . . ." can easily be rephrased to say "A good guideline to follow is to . . .".

Family violence is probably the widest-ranging term because it encompasses child, spousal, and elderly abuse. Family violence is defined as "an act carried out by one family member against another family member that causes or is intended to cause physical or emotional pain or injury to that person" (Heffernan, Shuttlesworth, & Ambrosino, 1997, p. 364). However, our focus is on abuse between adults, so terms such as *domestic violence, marital abuse, spousal abuse, battering,* and the most blatant term, *wife beating,* are more descriptive. But there are problems with these terms, too.

It's Not about Political Correctness

We're not trying to find the most politically correct term for this problem; we're just trying to use language that allows people to accurately, honestly communicate about the problem. Domestic violence has been defined as "a crime of power and control committed mainly by men against women, a crime in which the perpetrator does not consult the victim's wishes and from which he will not let her escape" (Jones, 1994, p. 126). But one problem is that the term *domestic* tends to obscure or undermine the seriousness of the abuse. *Battering* is a term you hear often and one that we will use in this discussion, but it typically implies only physical abuse rather than other forms. Ann Jones (1994), author of *Next Time She'll Be Dead: Battering and How to Stop It*, describes problems with these two terms: "It makes the violence sound domesticated, like a special category of violence that is somehow different from other kinds—less serious. The more difficult term is 'battered woman,' because it suggests a woman who is more or less permanently black and blue and helpless. And of course most women who are abused and controlled by men don't think of themselves as battered women" (as in Jacobs, 1994, p. 56).

> *I didn't say a word. I went over and hit her. I certainly must have knocked a lot of teeth out of her. She ended up in a corner all in a heap.*
>
> Frank Capra, director
> (It's a Wonderful Life),
> on his first wife

Wife beating leaves out husbands and other male partners, as well as persons in homosexual relationships who are abused. While the overwhelming majority of victims of abuse are female, a small percentage involves female abusers and male victims. Marital or spousal abuse isn't as inclusive a term as *partner violence* because persons in both heterosexual and homosexual nonmarital relationships (those who cohabitate, date, or are separated or divorced) also suffer abuse. Abusers are referred to as *batterers, wife beaters*, or, as we found at one interesting Web site, *intimate enemies* (Women Killed, 1998).

Yet another form of abuse is *courtship violence*, also known as *dating violence* or *premarital violence*. This abuse involves "acts of aggression occurring between young unmarried women and men" (Unger & Crawford, 1996, pp. 527–528). Because the predominance of this abuse is carried out by young men on young women, it's also been termed *boyfriend violence*. A study conducted by the Family Research Laboratory at the University of New Hampshire showed that up to 28 percent of teenagers suffer dating violence, from verbal abuse to slaps in the face to battering and rape (Harris, 1996). In another national survey, over one-third of college women and men reported being physically aggressive toward a date and receiving physical aggression from a date (White & Koss, 1991). Because the previous section of the chapter focused mostly on date rape, we're going to emphasize partner abuse in this last section. Much of the patterns and problems inherent in partner abuse apply to courtship violence as well.

Two Ways to Hurt Your Lover

Partner abuse is usually discussed in two forms: physical and psychological. Physical abuse ranges from a push or slap to a beating to the use of a weapon. Psychological abuse is a broad category that subsumes emotional and verbal abuse. Communication researchers have become interested in ways in which women and men exhibit verbal aggression and in the potential for verbal aggression to escalate into physical violence (Chandler Sabourin, 1995). It typically involves such things as severe criticism, intimidation, threats, humiliation (private and public), isolation, and degradation (Marshall, 1994). Research suggests that psychological abuse is more harmful and long-lasting than physical abuse, although in most instances, the two go hand in hand. Psychological abuse destroys self-esteem and leaves devastating emotional scars; physical abuse often leaves more than emotional scars (Unger & Crawford, 1996).

The Extent of the Problem

How long has it taken you to read this far in this chapter? Twenty or thirty minutes? Forty-five minutes? Statistics indicate that a woman is battered in the United States every 15 seconds (Women's Action Coalition, 1993). Let's say you've worked through this material in 30 minutes. We'll do the math for you; in the time it's taken you to read this far in the chapter, 120 women have been beaten in this country. Do you know when the rate of battering is at its highest? Women's shelters report that they are at their busiest with calls and women arriving in need of protection on Sunday evenings in the fall, after televised professional football games are over.

An "Epidemic"

That's what the American Medical Association called partner violence in 1992 (Peach, 1998). FBI statistics (1995) show that in an average year, about 600,000 violent victimizations of women at the hands of intimates occur, compared to about 49,000 such victimizations against men. This rate of violence is consistent across racial and ethnic groups. Women are more likely to suffer violence from people they know than from strangers, whereas for men, it is the opposite (FBI, 1995). Ninety-five percent of partner abuse is perpetrated by men on women and 60 percent of beaten women are pregnant at the time of the abuse (Davis, 1995; WAC, 1993). Research has estimated that over half of all women, either in a marriage or a long-term relationship, will be hit at least once by their partners. In various studies, 25 to 35 percent of women visiting hospital emergency rooms and clinics had injuries resulting from partner violence (Davis, 1995; Hamberger, Saunders, & Hovey, 1992).

From Abuse to Death

Many victims of partner abuse die at the hands of their abusers or as a result of severe injuries. Bureau of Justice statistics reveal that four women each day die as a result of domestic violence (Bureau of Justice, 1994). Over twice as many women are murdered by their boyfriends or husbands as are killed by strangers (Kellerman, 1992). During the 1990s, estimates of women who were killed by their husbands, ex-husbands, or boyfriends constituted 28 percent of the total number of homicides of women in a given year at the low end (over 1,400 women) and 55 percent at the high end (Colburn, 1994; FBI, 1995). This compares to a low estimate of 3 percent (over 600 men) and a high of 20 percent of homicides in which men were killed by their wives, ex-wives, or girlfriends. Other statistics show that over half of the total murders of women are committed by former or current partners (Browne & Williams, 1993). One study found that half of the homicides of female partners were committed by abusive men from whom these women were separated (*General Facts*, 1998).

Abuse during Separation or Divorce

From a survey of middle-class marriages, 22 percent of divorced couples cited violence as the number one reason for their divorce (*General Facts*, 1998). But being separated or divorced doesn't exempt or protect a person from abuse. About 75 percent of calls to police for assistance and intervention with domestic violence occur after separation from a batterer (*General Facts*, 1998). (If you followed the Simpson criminal trial, you'll remember that Nicole Brown placed a 911 call for assistance after O. J. kicked down her door and threatened her; they were separated at the time.) Women who are separated suffer twice as much violence from their partners as divorced women, six times as much as married women, and 12 times as much as never-married women (*Sex Differences*, 1997).

Common Myths about Battering

Statistics for partner violence, like those for sexual assault and rape, are much lower than the reality because so much goes unreported. A high degree of shame and guilt is associated with partner violence, on both the part of the batterer and the battered. But a primary reason for underreporting this crime relates to myths or outdated beliefs about male-female relationships.

Everybody Does It

You'll be surprised at how many people still believe that wife beating is a normal part of marriage (Browne, 1993). Men used to joke with one another (and we fear some still do) about needing to "give the old lady a pop" or "a good thrashing," and keeping a woman in line by "smacking her around a bit." Only recently has society begun to treat partner violence as a crime and to decry those who batter their partners. Some of you are old enough to remember the greatly loved television series, *The Honeymooners*. While no physical domestic violence was portrayed on that show, Jackie Gleason's character, Ralph Cramden, used to pump his fist near his wife's face and yell "To the moon, Alice!" Lots of us thought that bit was hilarious, but would it be hilarious now?

Blaming the Victim, Again

Another myth about partner abuse is that the person being abused deserves it or is to blame for the abuse. This parallels blame-the-victim attitudes in both sexual harassment and sexual assault, but it is probably most often heard in relation to battering. As sociologists Heffernan, Shuttlesworth, and Ambrosino (1997) explain, "It is much easier for the general public to become concerned about abused children than abused women. Many individuals still subscribe to the myth that women who are beaten somehow deserve it, or that they must enjoy it or they would not put up with it" (p. 365). One study found that a significant number of ministers who counseled women in abusive marriages tended to hold traditional attitudes about marital roles and actually blamed battered victims for causing marital strife (Wood & McHugh, 1994).

A few studies have interviewed male batterers to get their accounts of how domestic violence occurred in their homes. In one study, male abusers interviewed by researchers blamed the victim as well (Stamp & Chandler Sabourin, 1995). They described their wives (or partners) as the abusers and attempted to justify, excuse, minimize, or deny their own abusive behavior. These findings parallel other studies. For example, Sirles, Lipchik, and Kowalski (1993) found that only a third of male abusers in their study held themselves accountable for physical violence while 40 percent asserted that the violence was mutually provoked and 27 percent blamed their wives and denied any responsibility for their brutality. Dobash, Dobash, Cavanagh, and Lewis (1998) found that male abusers underestimated both their use of particular forms of violence and the frequency of that use.

One factor that leads some people to blame victims or to suggest that they make their plight worse relates to victims' communication. Communication researchers Rudd and Burant (1995) found that battered women used two main strategies during arguments that escalated into violence: submissive strategies in an attempt to smooth over a conflict and aggressive strategies to escalate the conflict. These aggressive strategies fuel the perception that women are to blame for the battering they receive, but they are actually not inappropriate strategies. As Rudd and Burant explain, "Perhaps battered women's use of aggressive strategies are a means for them to escalate the inevitable violence so that the conflict will end. Abused women have often reported that the fear of not knowing when the violence is going to occur is as frightening as the violent act itself" (p. 141).

Only the Poor Are Abusive

Some people believe that partner abuse only occurs in low-income and minority families. While more abuse does occur among lower-income families in which one or both spouses are unemployed, partner abuse extends across all social classes, races, and ethnicities (FBI, 1995; Gelles & Straus, 1988). Again, the

Simpson case reminds us that partner violence can occur within the wealthiest of households and among marriages of persons from different racial groups.

Gay and Lesbian Partner Abuse

Many of us adhere to the myth that partner abuse occurs only within heterosexual relationships, yet another disturbing aspect of this problem is its existence among gay and lesbian couples (Peach, 1998). Studies show that upwards of 37 percent of lesbians report having been in abusive relationships (Lie & Gentlewarrior, 1991; Lie, Schilit, Bush, Montagne, & Reyes, 1991). According to one study, gay men experience less frequent abuse than lesbians, but the violence inherent in their abuse is more severe (Waterman, Dawson, & Bologna, 1989). In one study, the brutality lesbian subjects reported involved pushing; shoving; hitting with fists or open hands; scratching or hitting the face, breasts, or genitals; and throwing things (Renzetti, 1989). These subjects reported psychological abuse as well as physical, primarily in the form of verbal threats.

Researchers Morrow and Hawxhurst (1989) provide four myths about women, in general, and lesbian relationships, in specific, that lead to secrecy surrounding lesbian abuse. First is the myth that because women are socialized to be less aggressive than men, they are incapable of brutalizing other women. While women tend to exhibit less aggression than men as a rule, they are certainly capable of being physically aggressive as a means of exerting power and control over another person. A second myth is that battering only occurs because of substance abuse or in clubs or bars. Third, because feminist lesbians are committed to equality in relationships, they do not batter. Finally, since lesbians are women, they are incapable of inflicting serious physical harm. Some say that, compared to opposite-sex violence, the brutality that members of the same sex can inflict on each other is worse because they know best how to hurt each other.

The violence within gay male relationships also tends to be shrouded in secrecy. But many gay men report being in more than one relationship in which they experienced physical violence. That violence typically includes punching with fists, beating the head against a wall or floor, and brutal rape. One victim even recounted that his partner tried to run him down with his car. One of the reasons gay men batter relates to something we talked about back in Chapter 1, in our discussion of homophobia. The third definition we gave of homophobia was an in-group use of the term to mean gays' own hatred toward homosexuals and toward themselves for being homosexual. One of the causes of battering is rage that is an outgrowth of homophobia and self-hatred. Also, because gays are often ostracized or isolated in a society that's predominantly straight and because many are made to feel they must keep their sexual orientation a secret, they may turn their resulting rage onto one another.

Unlike for lesbian victims of violence, there are few, if any, men's shelters, or societally sanctioned places where gay men can get counseling or safe haven from an abusive partner. But as a society, we are becoming more aware of this unspoken problem, as interesting books on the subject of gay and lesbian partner violence such as David Island and Patrick Letellier's (1991) *Men Who Beat the*

RECAP

rule of thumb; family violence; domestic violence; marital or spousal abuse; battering; wife beating; partner violence; intimate enemies; courtship, dating, premarital, or boyfriend violence; physical abuse; psychological abuse; battering myths

---

Men Who Love Them: Battered Gay Men and Domestic Violence and Kerry Lobel's (1986) *Naming the Violence: Speaking Out About Lesbian Battering,* show.

One thing to keep in mind is that, just like in heterosexual partner violence, one partner tends to be the dominant member of the relationship and does most, if not all, of the battering. You might think that in a same-sex abusive relationship both partners batter, but the reality is otherwise. In Renzetti's (1989) study, 78 percent of the subjects said that they did try at some point in the relationship to defend themselves against their batterers, but that most often these attempts were unsuccessful or only temporarily successful in stopping the abuse. A final, sad note to this topic is this: Because of homophobia and lack of training in same-sex abuse, abused gays and lesbians report that institutional sources of support, such as police officers, attorneys, and physicians, prove to be very unhelpful (Renzetti, 1992). Abused lesbians report that they receive the most help from women's shelters and community groups that support gay and lesbian causes (Morrow & Hawxhurst, 1989; Renzetti, 1992).

Abused Partners: How Do They Stand It? Why Do They Stay?

Explanations of the dynamic between an abuser and a victim vary. One body of literature suggests that women stay with abusers because their self-esteem is so low, their powerlessness so pervasive, that they blame themselves for their victimization. Another line of thought suggests that abused women don't blame themselves; they blame external factors or their abusers, which causes them to stay in abusive relationships as well. Let's explore both of these explanations.

Blaming Oneself

It's very hard for those who haven't experienced battering to understand the dynamic between abuser and abused. One group of authors explain it this way:

> Battering relationships are extreme versions of the traditional marriage relationship characterized by male dominance and female subordination. The subordinate wife in a battering relationship feels helpless and consequently develops unrealistically low self-esteem plus anxiety and depression. The dominant husband develops unrealistically inflated self-esteem and is dependent on the subordinate to maintain the feelings of power and self-aggrandizement. Each partner comes to require the other to satisfy needs developed as a consequence of the power imbalance. (Graham, Rawlings, & Rimini, 1988, pp. 220–221)

Important contributions in this area have been made by Lenore Walker, whose research coined the terms *learned helplessness* and *battered woman's syndrome*. Walker (1979, 1984, 1993) describes battered woman's syndrome as including a feeling of helplessness when battered women realize they cannot change their partners or their relationships with them. When a violent episode is followed by the batterer's guilt and begging for forgiveness, followed by acts of kindness, followed again by more brutality, battered women feel they have no way of protecting themselves or escaping. Many also fear that their partners will kill them (and possibly their children) if they leave, have their partners arrested, or attempt to get a restraining order. This is a very real fear, because many abusive husbands threaten to kill their wives if they leave. For many women, economic pressures and commitments to children heighten the perception that they cannot leave the abusive relationship. This cycle creates a learned helplessness, which is so overpowering that some battered women see no solution but to kill their abusers.

Battered woman's syndrome helps us understand why women remain in abusive relationships. Abused women often believe they are so worthless, so unlovable, that they deserve the anger and violent displays their partners perpetrate on them. They tear themselves down psychologically, saying things to themselves like, "If I was just prettier (thinner, sexier, younger), he wouldn't be so disgusted with me" and "If I just say and do the right things, if I become a better housekeeper and cook and mother, he won't treat me this way." Lest you are thinking, "How pathetic that someone could let themselves get so low," think again. Even persons with the strongest of self-concepts and most optimistic of dispositions are susceptible to power abuses from ones they love.

In abusive episodes, victims tend not to panic or fly into an uncontrolled rage, but to exhibit what's been termed "frozen fright," a hysterical, emotional state of numbness or paralysis (Graham, Rawlings, & Rimini, 1988, p. 220). The most important thing is survival. When victims realize that their abuser holds power over their very lives, and when abusers allow victims to live, the victims' response is often a strange sort of gratitude. The shell-shock type of reaction after an abusive episode affects the psyche, causing the victim to realize that she or he may be physically free for the moment, but still not psychologically free. The chronic physical and psychological trauma battered women experience may lead to *posttraumatic stress disorder* (as we discussed with sexual harassment), not unlike victims of catastrophe, hostage crises, or other forms of violence report.

Studies conducted with women in shelters have taught us a good deal about the kind of communication that occurs before, during, and after a violent encounter. One of the main things we've learned backs up Walker's observations: Battered women can recall almost every detail of every violent incident, including what blows landed where, how he looked when he started the beating, the terrible things he said, and how he acted afterward (Rudd, Dobos, Vogl-Bauer, & Beatty, 1997).

Blaming the Abuser, Not the Abused

Another view about responses to abuse, one that differs from responses to both sexual harassment and assault, is that battered partners tend *not* to blame themselves for the violence they receive. Research from this perspective shows that abused wives are much more likely to blame external factors (such as their husband being unemployed or having a bad day at work) or their abuser's personality or behaviors (his feeling guilty about being a poor provider, his drinking, or his bad temper, which cause him to turn violent) (Cantos, Neidig, & O'Leary, 1993). While these are interesting responses that seem better than blaming the self, don't adopt a rosy interpretation too quickly. Those same external factors or character flaws often give women reasons to stay with their abusers. If the battered partner perceives the cause as external or about the abuser rather than about the victim, the partner thinks that these things can change. Thinking like "once he gets a job, this will stop" or "if he'd stop drinking we'd be happier" causes women to persevere in dangerous, dead-end (often literally) relationships.

Living Happily Ever After

Leah (not her real name) was an attractive woman, probably about in her mid-30s, who came back to school to get her degree after her divorce. She (wisely) chose communication as her major and (wisely) enrolled in a gender communication course. On the day when the class focused on issues of violence and abuse, the instructor encouraged some of the students who had not yet entered the discussion to speak up if they had something to say or ask. At that point the instructor made eye contact with Leah, and she started to tell her story. This was clearly one of those instances where you could put a face to a problem.

Leah told us of her "picture perfect" courtship with her now ex-husband (whom we'll call Matt), how he seemed like the perfect man, or near perfect anyway. The couple was the envy of all their friends and they certainly made their parents proud when they married. But less than a year into the marriage, when their first child was six weeks old, Leah's husband erupted during an argument. She really didn't see it coming; she had no hints that he was capable of being so brutal. In all the time they'd dated and been engaged he'd never raised a hand to her. But it happened with her infant son just down the hall in their home.

Matt's anger was exacerbated by his drinking. The episodes became more frequent, as many days he would leave work early and head to a bar, drink for the rest of the afternoon, and arrive home that night in an abusive rage. A typical evening involved Matt slapping and punching Leah, yelling and calling her obscene names, and threatening to "really teach her a lesson" if she left him. She learned quickly how to cover bruises with makeup. A day or two later, Matt would show the typical batterer's remorse for "losing his temper" and Leah would try to convince herself that the "incident" wouldn't happen again. But it did happen again; she never knew what would trigger a violent episode.

Her self-esteem plummeted; she constantly questioned herself about what she was doing wrong and what she could do better to stave off Matt's anger. She tiptoed through her life, but it seemed that nothing she tried worked.

Finally, Leah contacted Matt's parents and told them what was going on. At first they denied that their precious son could be capable of such horrible behavior. Then they downplayed it, calling it a "misunderstanding," "a show of temper," and "having a bad day." On several occasions they blamed Leah, saying that she must have done something to make Matt act this way. After Leah made repeated calls to Matt's parents to report yet another beating, they finally offered to help, but this is how: When Matt went out drinking or came home drunk, Leah would call his parents; they would pick him up, take him to their house, and keep him there until the next day when he sobered up. That way they could keep him from "misbehaving" or "throwing a fit."

Knowing that Leah was divorced, the instructor in the class asked how Leah finally managed to pull herself out of the relationship and get a divorce. She said, "Well, after about 10 years of this, I decided . . . ." The instructor had to interrupt because she, and no doubt the other students in the class, were thinking, "TEN years?" Leah said, "Yes, I put up with it for 10 years, all the while thinking it would stop." It took her another year to untangle from the relationship. She still has tremendous emotional scars from the experience, not only from Matt but from his parents as well for their role in protecting the abuser and leaving their daughter-in-law and grandchild in a life-threatening situation.

Leah experienced much of what Walker described as battered woman's syndrome—feelings of helplessness, terror, dependency, and rage, mixed with strange feelings of love and commitment. Those mixed emotions allowed her to tolerate for 10 years what seems to us—those of us who haven't experienced battering—to be an intolerable situation. She received a divorce and custody of their son and began putting herself and her life back together. She told everyone in class that she'd often heard the phrase "never say never," but she wanted to reject that and say that she would never, NEVER again tolerate a man who tried to control her. If she stayed single the rest of her life, if she never had another romantic relationship with a man, that was fine. She hoped she might meet someone wonderful and was open to the possibility, but she didn't feel less of a woman because she wasn't in a relationship or marriage. She knew that she'd never put up with an abuser again.

A Word about Partner Violence Laws

Statistics show that police are more likely to respond within five minutes if an offender is a stranger than a person known to a female victim (Bureau of Justice Statistics, 1994). One study found that a majority of battered women actively attempt to secure help and protection from an abuser by contacting police, lawyers, shelters, counselors, and ministers (Hutchison & Hirschel, 1998). But approximately 90 percent of all family violence defendants are never prosecuted (*Response from the Criminal Justice System*, 1993).

Feminist attorneys are working to reform partner violence laws, the primary impetus being that many battered women who suffer repeated physical and psychological abuse and fear their children will be the next victims resort to killing their abusive partners. According to one source, women serving prison sentences for homicide convictions are twice as likely to have killed an abusive partner than a relative, friend, or stranger (Snell, 1991). Many attorneys consider battered woman's syndrome to be a mitigating circumstance that should cause judges and juries to view these homicides differently. However, as author Martha Mahoney (1998) explains, "litigation and judicial decision-making in cases of severe violence reflect implicit or explicit assumptions that domestic violence is rare or exceptional" (p. 324).

A significant legal development was the passage in the mid 1990s of the *Violence Against Women Act (VAWA)*, which made it a criminal offense to cross state lines to inflict violence upon one's spouse and enforced protection orders from state to state (Hirshman, 1994). A civil rights component of the VAWA allows women to sue their attackers in federal court for both punitive and compensatory damages. The civil nature of this component increases the chances of victims successfully prosecuting batterers because the standards of proof in civil actions are less stringent than in criminal actions. Law professor Linda Hirshman (1994) asserts, "The VAWA marks the first time in history that the violence women face in their own homes will be taken seriously by the government whose mandate it is to protect them" (p. 47).

Shelters Give Support and Hope

Women's shelters are safe havens for victims of partner violence and their children. Besides providing temporary room and board, as well as counseling for abused women (and in some locations for abused men as well), most offer 24-hour crisis hotlines so that victims can call and receive support and advice. In 1964, a group of women in San Gabriel Valley, California, opened the first refuge for battered women in the United States, called Haven House. In the early 1970s, the first hotline for battered women was created in St. Paul, Minnesota (Gillespie, 1994a). In the mid 1990s, one successful shelter-sponsored program was the Clothesline Project, in which battered women designed T-shirts to depict their experiences with abuse. Many locations in the country displayed clotheslines of these T-shirts on hangers as a means of creating awareness of the problem (Garza, 1996).

Not all cities have women's shelters. Here's a revealing statistic: There are three times as many animal shelters in the United States as there are battered women's shelters (Majority Staff of the Senate Judiciary Committee, 1992). As Ann Jones explains, "Unfortunately we need a lot more shelters, because the problem is so great that they're turning away many women. They do save a great many lives. But what they've really done is save the lives of *men*. The rate of women killing men has gone down, and its decline began with the advent of battered women's shelters" (as in Jacobs, 1994, p. 59).

Parting Considerations about Partner Violence

As you now realize, partner violence is an enormous problem that crosses boundaries of sex, sexual orientation, race, class, educational level, age, and nationality. It's becoming less and less a silent destroyer of families and lives as survivors emerge, tell their stories, and give other abused persons hope. From outsiders' perspectives, none of us can truly know the depth of despair this kind of victimization causes. We'll have to take the word of people who have experienced it—and there are far more of them than we'd like to think. Let's all give our attention to this issue and decide what we can do about it. If you're in an abusive relationship, perhaps the information in this chapter will give you options and maybe some hope. If you know someone who is being abused by a partner, perhaps you now know more about the problem, what to do, and how to help. We'll end this section with the eloquent words of Marcia Ann Gillespie, editor of *Ms.*, as she wrote for a special edition of the magazine, devoted to the problem of partner violence:

> For the sake of all the women in this world who've been killed—whose names we will never know—for all the women who are beaten, who have been beaten and brutalized, for my sake, and yours, and for our daughters, and their daughters, and yes, for the sake of men's souls, let us mobilize as never before to ensure that women are protected, abusers are truly held accountable for their actions, our communities are held responsible for putting an end to the violence, and our nations acknowledge that men's violence against women is a human rights violation. Society is responsible for allowing domestic violence to flourish—and for making it stop. (1994b, p. 1)

CONCLUSION

You're probably glad you made it through this chapter; we realize it's a drain to consider all the terrible things people do to one another. It was a drain to research these topics and write about them, but we're sure you'll agree they're extremely important. We provided statistics and research findings in an effort to bring you the most relevant information possible, but we also put a face on each of these problems. Many of you were probably able to substitute a more familiar face for the people in our stories—Olivia and Bernie, Annie and Kris, Leah and Matt. The faces of the people who have suffered abuse are more real, more meaningful than all the statistics and research in the world.

We have to think about ways people use and abuse power in our society and across the world. Burying our heads in the sand, not wanting to believe that our fellow human beings commit such atrocities, not wanting to do anything to stop it, makes us part of the problem, not the solution. One of the coauthors of this text often uses this adapted phrase, "Pick ye rebellions where ye may." Perhaps one of your own personal rebellions against injustice may be to see that sexual harassment, sexual assault and rape, or partner violence never happen to you and the ones you love.

KEY TERMS

male-bashing
sexual harassment
Equal Employment
   Opportunity
   Commission (EEOC)
quid pro quo sexual
   harassment
hostile climate sexual
   harassment
status-differentiated
   relationships
targets
victims
grooming process
peer sexual harassment
contrapower sexual
   harassment
electronic or virtual
   sexual harassment
receiver orientation to
   communication
he said-she said defense
posttraumatic stress
   syndrome
blame-the-victim stance
avoidance

defusion
negotiation
confrontation
sexual harassment
   inventory
legal liability
punitive damages
compensatory damages
forcible rape
stranger rape
date rape
acquaintance rape
seduction
trigger words
sexual assault
survivors
marital rape
spousal rape
wife rape
partner rape
gang rape
statutory rape
cyber-rape
virtual rape
Rohypnol
gender-role socialization

rape myths
sexual aggression
nuts and sluts defense
rule of thumb
family violence
domestic violence
marital abuse
spousal abuse
battering
wife beating
partner violence
intimate enemies
courtship violence
dating violence
premarital violence
boyfriend violence
physical abuse
psychological abuse
battering myths
learned helplessness
battered woman's
   syndrome
Violence Against Women
   Act (VAWA)
women's shelters

Discussion Starters

1. From the fairly extensive discussion of *sexual harassment* in this chapter, think of something you learned, something you did not know before reading this chapter. For example, did you know that sexual harassment was about power, not sex? Did you disagree with any points raised in the sexual harassment section?

2. Imagine that you were an attorney representing either Olivia or Bernie from our sexual harassment case study in this chapter. Knowing what you now know about harassment, how would you prosecute or defend Bernie and the company in a harassment suit? What would be the weaknesses or gray areas you might point out?

3. Whether you are female or male, think about how you would react if you were sexually harassed on the job. (Perhaps some of you have experienced it. If so, how did you react?) Do you imagine you'd respond by *avoiding* or *defusing* the situation or would you attempt to *negotiate* or *confront* the harasser? What would be some possible risks of confronting the harasser, if he or she is your boss rather than a co-worker?

4. Imagine that you (and an organization you belong to on campus) were asked to present a *date rape* awareness and prevention program on campus. Knowing what you now know about this serious problem, what would you choose to highlight in such a program? Would you spend equal amounts of time teaching men not to rape as you might teaching women how to prevent their own victimization?

5. Think about the complexity of communication in sexual contexts. What's your view of the difference between flirtation and teasing, versus leading someone on? How can people enjoy sexual tension, but not base that tension on a struggle of wills between the two people in the intimate situation?

6. Why do you think people continue to adhere to *myths* about *rape* and *battering*? Are these forms of abuse just too terrible to face so we manufacture false ideas about them? Knowing that these myths exist because somebody believes them, how can you expose and debunk them?

7. If it were in your power to change the existing laws or write new ones for *sexual harassment, sexual assault* and *rape*, or *partner violence* (or all of these problems), what laws would you write? What gaps exist in current law that need to be covered?

References

AARON, R. (1997, February 25). Don't blame victim of sexual violence. *San Antonio Express-News.* [On-line]. Feminista! Available: http://www.feminista.com

ABBEY, A. (1982). Sex differences in attributions for friendly behavior: Do males misperceive females' friendliness? *Journal of Personality and Social Psychology, 42,* 830–838.

ABBEY, A., & HARNISH, R. J. (1995). Perception of sexual intent: The role of gender, alcohol consumption, and rape supportive attitudes. *Sex Roles, 32,* 297–314.

ALBERTS, J. K. (1992). Teasing and sexual harassment: Double-bind communication in the workplace. In L. A. M. Perry, L. H. Turner, & H. M. Sterk (Eds.), *Constructing and reconstructing gender: The links among communication, language, and gender* (pp. 185–196). Albany: State University of New York Press.

AMERICAN ASSOCIATION OF UNIVERSITY WOMEN. (1993). *Hostile hallways: The AAUW survey on sexual harassment in America's schools.* Washington, DC: AAUW Educational Foundation.

ANDONIAN, K. K., & DROGE, D. (1993, February). *Verbal aggressiveness and sexual violence in dating relationships: An exploratory study of antecedents of date rape.* Paper presented at the meeting of the Western States Communication Association, Albuquerque, NM.

BAKER, B. J., & MEADOWS, M. (1997). Two year college students and date rape: An empowerment model. (ERIC Document Reproduction Service No. ED 409 067)

BAKER, M. (1992, February). Sexual shock and the emergence of the new man. *M Magazine,* 69–75.

BECKY, D., & FARREN, P. M. (1997). Teaching students how to understand and avoid abusive relationships. *School Counselor, 44,* 303–308.

BENSON, K. (1984). Comment on Crocker's "An analysis of university definitions of sexual harassment." *Signs, 9,* 516–519.

BERGMAN, S. J., & SURREY, J. (1993). Relationships on campus: Impasses and possibilities. *Educational Record, Winter,* 13–20.

BERRYMAN-FINK, C. (1993). Preventing sexual harassment through male-female communication training. In G. L. Kreps (Ed.), *Sexual harassment: Communication implications* (pp. 267–280). Cresskill, NJ: Hampton.

BINGHAM, S. G. (1991). Communication strategies for managing sexual harassment in organizations: Understanding message options and their effects. *Journal of Applied Communication, 19,* 88–115.

BOOTH-BUTTERFIELD, M. (1986). Recognizing and communicating in harassment-prone organizational climates. *Women's Studies in Communication, 9,* 42–51.

BORDO, S. (1998, May 1). Sexual harassment is about bullying, not sex. *The Chronicle of Higher Education,* p. B6.

BRAIL, S. (1996). The price of admission: Harassment and free speech in the wild, wild west. In L. Cherny & E. R. Weise (Eds.), *Wired women: Gender and new realities in cyberspace* (pp. 141–157). Seattle: Seal.

BROWNE, A. (1993). Violence against women by male partners: Prevalence, outcomes, and policy implications. *American Psychologist, 48,* 1077–1087.

BROWNE, A., & WILLIAMS, K. R. (1993). Gender, intimacy, and lethal violence: Trends from 1976 to 1987. *Gender & Society, 7,* 78–98.

BUREAU OF JUSTICE STATISTICS. (1994). *Violence against women: A national crime victimization survey report.* [On-line]. Available: http://www.ojp.usdoj.gov

BURT, M. R. (1980). Cultural myths and supports for rape. *Journal of Personality and Social Psychology, 38,* 217–230.

BUZAWA, E. (1995). Responding to crimes of violence against women: Gender differences versus organization imperatives. *Crime and Delinquency, 41,* 443–466.

CACHIE, L., & DEMAN, A. F. (1997). Correlates of sexual aggression among male university students. *Sex Roles, 37,* 451–457.

CANTOS, A. L., NEIDIG, P. H., & O'LEARY, K. D. (1993). Men's and women's attributions of blame for domestic violence. *Journal of Family Violence, 8,* 289–302.

CARROLL, C. M. (1993). Sexual harassment on campus: Enhancing awareness and promoting change. *Educational Record, Winter,* 21–26.

CASEY, T., DESAI, S., & ULRICH, J. (1998, Fall). Supreme Court unpredictable on harassment and sex. *National NOW Times,* pp. 6, 15.

CASTANEDA, C. J. (1992, August 3). Tailhook investigation "no help." *USA Today,* p. 3A.

CHANDLER SABOURIN, T. (1995). The role of negative reciprocity in spouse abuse: A relational control analysis. *Journal of Applied Communication Research, 23,* 271–283.

CLAIR, R. P. (1992, November). *A critique of institutional discourse employed by the "Big Ten" universities to address sexual harassment.* Paper presented at the meeting of the Speech Communication Association, Chicago, IL.

CLAIR, R. P. (1998). *Organizing silence.* Albany: State University of New York Press.

CLAIR, R. P., McGOUN, M. J., & SPIREK, M. M. (1993). Sexual harassment responses of working women: An assessment of current communication-oriented typologies and perceived effectiveness of the response. In G. L. Kreps (Ed.), *Sexual harassment: Communication implications* (pp. 209–233). Cresskill, NJ: Hampton.

CLOUD, J. (1998, March 23). Sex and the law. *Time,* 48–54.

COCHRAN, C. C., FRAZIER, P. A., & OLSON, A. M. (1997). Predictors of responses to unwanted sexual attention. *Psychology of Women Quarterly, 21,* 207–226.

COLBURN, D. (1994, March 15). When violence begins at home: AMA conference addresses "problem of shocking dimension." *Washington Post.*

CRICHTON, S. (1993, October 25). Sexual correctness: Has it gone too far? *Newsweek,* 52–56.

DAVIS, L. (1995). Domestic violence. In *Encyclopedia of social work* (Vol. 1, pp. 780–789). Washington, DC: National Association of Social Work (NASW).

DOBASH, R. P., DOBASH, R. E., CAVANAGH, K., & LEWIS, R. (1998). Separate and intersecting realities: A comparison of men's and women's accounts of violence against women. *Violence Against Women, 4,* 382–414.

EARLE, J. P. (1996). Acquaintance rape workshops: Their effectiveness in changing the attitudes of first year college students. *NASPA Journal, 34,* 2–18.

EAVES, M. H. (1992, November). *A male-dominated legal system: A feminist response to statutory rape.* Paper presented at the meeting of the Speech Communication Association, Chicago, IL.

EGAN, T. (1996, November 17). Army faces gender conflicts: Sexual harassment is common problem. *Corpus Christi Caller Times,* pp. A17, A23.

EHRHART, J. K., & SANDLER, B. R. (1985). *Campus gang rape: Party games.* Washington, DC: Project on the Status and Education of Women, Association of American Colleges.

ESTRICH, S. (1993, October 25). Balancing act. *Newsweek, 64.*

FEDERAL BUREAU OF INVESTIGATION. (1989). *Crime in the United States: Uniform crime reports.* Washington, DC: U.S. Department of Justice.

FEDERAL BUREAU OF INVESTIGATION. (1995). *Violence against women: Estimates from the redesigned survey, August 1995.* [On-line]. Available: http://www.ojp.usdoj.gov

FITZGERALD, L. F. (1993). Sexual harassment: A research analysis and agenda for the 1990s. *Journal of Vocational Behavior, 42,* 5–27.

FOSS, K. A., & ROGERS, R. A. (1992, February). *Observations on the Clarence Thomas-Anita Hill hearings: Through the lens of gender.* Paper presented at the meeting of the Western States Communication Association, Boise, ID.

FUENTES, A. (1997, November-December). Crime rates are down . . . but what about rape? *Ms.,* 19–22.

GARZA, T. Z. (1996, April 30). Women's Shelter gives students a dose of reality. *Island Waves,* p. 9.

GEIST, P., & TOWNSLEY, N. (1997, November). *"Swept under the rug" and other disappearing acts: Legitimate concerns for university's sexual harassment policy and procedures.* Paper presented at the meeting of the National Communication Association, Chicago, IL.

GELFAND, M. J., FITZGERALD, L. F., & DRASGOW, F. (1995). The structure of sexual harassment: A confirmatory analysis across cultures and settings. *Journal of Vocational Behavior, 47,* 164–177.

GELLES, R. J., & STRAUS, M. A. (1988). *Intimate violence.* New York: Simon & Schuster.

General facts about domestic violence. (1998). [On-line]. Available: http://www.new countrycanada.com

GILL, M. M. (1993). Academic sexual harassment: Perceptions of behaviors. In G. L. Kreps (Ed.), *Sexual harassment: Communication implications* (pp. 149–169). Cresskill, NJ: Hampton.

GILLESPIE, M. A. (1994a, September-October). Domestic violence. *Ms.,* 33.

GILLESPIE, M. A. (1994b, September-October). Memories to keep. *Ms.,* 1.

GOOD, G. E., HEPPNER, M. J., HILLENBRAND-GUNN, T. L., & WANG, L. (1995). Sexual and psychological violence: An exploratory study of predictors in college men. *Journal of Men's Studies, 4,* 59–71.

GRAHAM, D. L. R., RAWLINGS, E., & RIMINI, N. (1988). Survivors of terror. In K. Yllo & M. Bograd (Eds.), *Feminist perspectives on wife abuse* (pp. 217–233). Newbury Park, CA: Sage.

GRUBER, J. E. (1989). How women handle sexual harassment: A literature review. *Sociology and Social Research, 74,* 3–7.

HAMBERGER, L. K., SAUNDERS, D. G., & HOVEY, M. (1992). The prevalence of domestic violence in community practice and rate of physician inquiry. *Family Medicine, 24,* 283–287.

HARRIS, L. (1996, September 22). The hidden world of dating violence. *Parade Magazine,* 4–6.

HATFIELD, E., & RAPSON, R. L. (1996). *Love and sex: Cross-cultural perspectives.* Boston: Allyn & Bacon.

HAUNANI SOLOMON, D., & MILLER WILLIAMS, M. L. (1997). Perceptions of social-sexual communication at work: The effects of message, situation, and observer characteristics on judgments of sexual harassment. *Journal of Applied Communication Research, 25,* 196–216.

HEFFERNAN, J., SHUTTLESWORTH, G., & AMBROSINO, R. (1997). *Social work and social welfare* (3rd ed.). New York: West.

HICKSON, M. III., GRIERSON, R. D., & LINDER, B. C. (1991). A communication perspective on sexual harassment: Affiliative nonverbal behaviors in asynchronous relationships. *Communication Quarterly, 39,* 111–118.

HIRSHMAN, L. (1994, September-October). Making safety a civil right. *Ms.,* 44–47.

HOLCOMB, D. R., & SEEHAFER, R. W. (1996). Enhancing dating attitudes through peer education as a date rape prevention strategy. *Peer Facilitator Quarterly, 12,* 16–20.

HUGHES, J. O., & SANDLER, B. R. (1986). *In case of sexual harassment: A guide for women students.* Washington, DC: Project on the Status and Education of Women, Association of American Colleges.

HUGHES, J. O., & SANDLER, B. R. (1987). *"Friends" raping friends: Could it happen to you?* Washington, DC: Project on the Status and Education of Women, Association of American Colleges.

HUGHES, J. O., & SANDLER, B. R. (1988). *Peer harassment: Hassles for women on campus.* Washington, DC: Project on the Status and Education of Women, Association of American Colleges.

HUTCHISON, I. W., & HIRSCHEL, J. D. (1998). Abused women. *Violence Against Women, 4,* 436–456.

ISLAND, D., & LETELLIER, P. (1991). *Men who beat the men who love them: Battered gay men and domestic violence.* Binghamton, NY: Haworth.

IVY, D. K. (1999). *"Monica madness": A feminist look at language in the Clinton sex scandal.* Unpublished manuscript.

IVY, D. K., & HAMLET, S. (1996). College students and sexual dynamics: Two studies of peer sexual harassment. *Communication Education, 45,* 149–166.

JACOBS, C. (1993, February). *Giving students a corporate picture: Sexual harassment in the workplace.* Paper presented at the meeting of the Western States Communication Association, Albuquerque, NM.

JACOBS, G. (1994, September-October). Where do we go from here? An interview with Ann Jones. *Ms.,* 56–63.

JONES, A. (1994). *Next time she'll be dead.* Boston: Beacon.

KELLERMAN, A. (1992). Men, women, and murder. *Journal of Trauma,* 1–5.

KIER, F. J. (1996, January). *Acquaintance rape on college campuses: A review of the literature.* Paper presented at the meeting of the Southwest Education Research Association, New Orleans, LA.

KILPATRICK, D. G., EDMUNDS, C. N., SEYMOUR, A., & BOYLE, J. (1992). *Rape in America: A report to the nation.* Charleston, SC: Crime Victims Research and Treatment Center.

KING, J. (1993, September-October). Harassment on-line. *New Age Journal,* 20.

KOSS, M. P., GIDYCZ, C. A., & WISNIEWSKI, N. (1987). The scope of rape: Incidence and prevalence of sexual aggression and victimization in a national sample of higher education students. *Journal of Consulting and Clinical Psychology, 55,* 162–170.

KOSS, M. P., & HARVEY, M. R. (1991). *The rape victim.* New York: Sage.

KREPS, G. L. (1993). Introduction: Sexual harassment and communication. In G. L. Kreps (Ed.), *Sexual harassment: Communication implications* (pp. 1–5). Cresskill, NJ: Hampton.

KROLOKKE, C. (1998). Women professors' assertive-empathic and non-assertive communication in sexual harassment situations. *Women's Studies in Communication, 21,* 91–103.

LAMORTE, D. (1998, September 13). Poll: 95% of Texans think domestic abuse is a serious problem. *Corpus Christi Caller Times,* p. A9.

LIE, G-Y., & GENTLEWARRIOR, S. (1991). Intimate violence in lesbian relationships: Discussion of survey findings and practical implications. *Journal of Social Service Research, 15,* 41–59.

LIE, G-Y., SCHILIT, R., BUSH, J., MONTAGNE, M., & REYES, L. (1991). Lesbians in currently aggressive relationships: How frequently do they report aggressive past relationships? *Violence and Victims, 6,* 121–135.

LOBEL, K. (Ed.). (1986). *Naming the violence: Speaking out about lesbian battering.* Seattle: Seal.

LOREDO, C., REID, A., & DEAUX, K. (1995). Judgments and definitions of sexual harassment by high school students. *Sex Roles, 32,* 29–45.

MACKINNON, C. A. (1979). *Sexual harassment of working women: A case of sex discrimination.* New Haven, CT: Yale University Press.

MAHONEY, M. R. (1998). Legal images of battered women (excerpt). In L. J. Peach (Ed.), *Women in culture: A women's studies anthology* (pp. 323–338). Malden, MA: Blackwell.

MAJORITY STAFF OF THE SENATE JUDICIARY COMMITTEE. (1992). *Violence against women: A week in the life of America.* Washington, DC: Congressional Printing Office.

MALAMUTH, N. M. (1984). Aggression against women: Cultural and individual causes. In B. Malamuth & E. Donnerstein (Ed.), *Pornography and sexual aggression* (pp. 19–52). Orlando, FL: Harcourt Brace Jovanovich.

MALAMUTH, N. M., & BROWN, L. (1994). Sexually aggressive men's perceptions of women's communication: Testing three explanations. *Journal of Personality and Social Psychology, 47,* 699–712.

MALAMUTH, N. M., SOCKLOSKIE, R. M., KOSS, M. P., & TANAKA, J. S. (1991). Characteristics of aggressors against women: Testing a model using a national sample of college students. *Journal of Consulting and Clinical Psychology, 59,* 670–681.

MALAMUTH, N. M., & THORNHILL, N. W. (1994). Hostile masculinity, sexual aggression, and gender-biased domineeringness in conversations. *Aggressive Behavior, 20,* 185–194.

MARSHALL, L. L. (1994). Physical and psychological abuse. In W. R. Cupach & B. H. Spitzberg (Eds.), *The dark side of interpersonal communication* (pp. 281–311). Hillsdale, NJ: Lawrence Erlbaum.

MAYPOLE, D. E. (1986). Sexual harassment of social workers at work: Injustice within? *Social Work,* January-February, 29–34.

McKinney, K., & Maroules, N. (1991). Sexual harassment. In E. Grauerholz & M. A. Koralewski (Eds.), *Sexual coercion* (pp. 29–44). Lexington, MA: Lexington Books.

Metts, S., & Cupach, W. R. (1989). The role of communication in human sexuality. In K. McKinney & S. Sprecher (Eds.), *Human sexuality: The societal and interpersonal context* (pp. 139–161). Norwood, NJ: Ablex.

Michals, D. (1997, March-April). Cyber-rape: How virtual is it? *Ms.,* 68–73.

Mongeau, P. A., & Blalock, J. (1994). Student evaluations of instructor immediacy and sexually harassing behaviors: An experimental investigation. *Journal of Applied Communication Research, 22,* 256–272.

Morrow, S. L., & Hawxhurst, D. M. (1989). Lesbian partner abuse: Implications for therapists. *Journal of Counseling and Development, 68,* 58–62.

Muehlenhard, C. L., & Falcon, P. L. (1990). Men's heterosexual skill and attitudes toward women as predictors of verbal sexual coercion and forceful rape. *Sex Roles, 23,* 241–259.

Mullin, C. R. (1995). Desensitization and resensitization to violence against women: Effects of exposure to sexually violent films on judgments of domestic violence victims. *Journal of Personality & Social Psychology, 69,* 449–459.

O'Sullivan, C. S. (1991). Acquaintance gang rape on campus. In A. Parrot & L. Bechhofer (Eds.), *Acquaintance rape: The hidden crime* (pp. 140–156). New York: Wiley.

Paetzold, R. L., & O'Leary-Kelly, A. M. (1993). Organizational communication and the legal dimensions of hostile work environment sexual harassment. In G. L. Kreps (Ed.), *Sexual harassment: Communication implications* (pp. 63–77). Cresskill, NJ: Hampton.

Payne, K. E. (1993). The power game: Sexual harassment on the college campus. In G. L. Kreps (Ed.), *Sexual harassment: Communication implications* (pp. 133–148). Cresskill, NJ: Hampton.

Peach, L. J. (1998). Sex, sexism, sexual harassment, and sexual abuse: Introduction. In L. J. Peach (Ed.), *Women in culture: A women's studies anthology* (pp. 283–301). Malden, MA: Blackwell.

Pipher, M. (1994). *Reviving Ophelia: Saving the selves of adolescent girls.* New York: Ballantine.

Renzetti, C. M. (1989). Building a second closet: Third party responses to victims of lesbian partner abuse. *Family Relations, 38,* 157–163.

Renzetti, C. M. (1992). *Violent betrayal: Partner abuse in lesbian relationships.* Newbury Park, CA: Sage.

Response from the criminal justice system. (1993). [On-line]. Available: http://www.newcountrycanada.com

Rhode, D. L. (1997, November-December). Harassment is alive and well and living at the water cooler. *Ms.,* 28–29.

Rudd, J. E., & Burant, P. A. (1995). A study of women's compliance-gaining behaviors in violent and non-violent relationships. *Communication Research Reports, 12,* 134–144.

Rudd, J. E., Dobos, J. A., Vogl-Bauer, S., & Beatty, M. J. (1997). Women's narrative accounts of recent abusive episodes. *Women's Studies in Communication, 20,* 45–58.

Sadker, M., & Sadker, D. (1994). *Failing at fairness: How America's schools cheat girls.* New York: Charles Scribner's Sons.

Salaimo, D. M. (1997). Electronic sexual harassment. In B. R. Sandler & R. J. Shoop (Eds.), *Sexual harassment on campus: A guide for administrators, faculty, and students* (pp. 85–103). Boston: Allyn & Bacon.

Salter, S. (1998, January 18). O. J. Simpson and twisted definitions of love. *Corpus Christi Caller Times,* p. A10.

Sandler, B. R. (1997). Student-to-student sexual harassment. In B. R. Sandler & R. J. Shoop (Eds.), *Sexual harassment on campus: A guide for administrators, faculty, and students* (pp. 50–65). Boston: Allyn & Bacon.

Sandroff, R. (1992, June). Sexual harassment: The inside story. *Working Woman,* 47–51, 78.

Schulhofer, S. (1998, October). Unwanted sex. *The Atlantic Monthly,* 55–66.

Seals, B. (1997). Faculty-to-faculty sexual harassment. In B. R. Sandler & R. J. Shoop (Eds.), *Sexual harassment on campus: A guide for administrators, faculty, and students* (pp. 66–84). Boston: Allyn & Bacon.

Sex differences in violent victimization, 1994. (1997, September). Washington, DC: U.S. Department of Justice Office of Justice Programs and Bureau of Justice Statistics.

Sexual assault and rape: Advice for men. (1998). [On-line]. Available: http://www.ncf.carleton.ca/freenet

SHERER, M. L. (1992). School liability under Title IX for peer sexual harassment. *Pennsylvania Law Review, 141,* 2119–2175.

SHOTLAND, R. L., & GOLDSTEIN, L. (1992). Sexual precedence reduces the perceived legitimacy of sexual refusal: An examination of attributions concerning date rape and consensual sex. *Personality and Social Psychology Bulletin, 18,* 756–764.

SIRLES, E. A., LIPCHIK, E., & KOWALSKI, K. (1993). A consumer's perspective on domestic violence intervention. *Journal of Family Violence, 8,* 267–276.

SMOLOWE, J. (1993, April 5). Sex with a scorecard. *Time,* 41.

SNELL, T. (1991). *Bureau of Justice statistics special report: Women in prison.* Washington, DC: U.S. Department of Justice.

SNIFFEN, M. J. (1995, August 17). New questions turn up more evidence of rape. *Corpus Christi Caller Times,* p. A5.

SPENDER, D. (1984). Defining reality: A powerful tool. In C. Kramarae, M. Schultz, & W. O'Barr (Eds.), *Language and power* (pp. 9–22). Beverly Hills: Sage.

STAMP, G. H., & CHANDLER SABOURIN, T. (1995). Accounting for violence: An analysis of male spousal abuse narratives. *Journal of Applied Communication Research, 23,* 284–307.

STEINEM, G. (1983). *Outrageous acts and everyday rebellions.* New York: Holt, Rinehart, & Winston.

STEINEM, G. (1998, May-June). Yes means yes, no means no: Why sex scandals don't mean harassment. *Ms.,* 62–64.

TAYLOR, B., & CONRAD, C. (1992). Narratives of sexual harassment: Organizational dimensions. *Journal of Applied Communication, 20,* 401–418.

TEXAS EMPLOYMENT COMMISSION. (1995, Summer-Autumn). *Equal opportunity notes.* Austin, TX: Author.

TRUMAN, D. M., TOKAR, D. M., & FISCHER, A. R. (1996). Dimensions of masculinity: Relations to date rape supportive attitudes and sexual aggression in dating situations. *Journal of Counseling & Development, 74,* 555–562.

UNGER, R., & CRAWFORD, M. (1996). *Women and gender: A feminist psychology* (2nd ed.). New York: McGraw-Hill.

WALKER, L. (1979). *The battered woman.* New York: Harper Colophon.

WALKER, L. (1984). *The battered woman syndrome.* New York: Springer.

WALKER, L. (1993). The battered woman syndrome is a psychological consequence of abuse. In R. J. Gelles & D. R. Loseke (Eds.), *Current controversies on family violence* (pp. 133–153). Newbury Park, CA: Sage.

WASHINGTON DC RAPE CRISIS CENTER. (1998). *Myths about rape.* [On-line]. Available: http://www.dcrcc.org

WATERMAN, C., DAWSON, L., & BOLOGNA, M. (1989). Sexual coercion in gay and lesbian relationships: Predictors and implications for support services. *Journal of Sex Research, 26,* 118–124.

WHITE, J. W., & KOSS, M. P. (1991). Courtship violence: Incidence in a national sample of higher education students. *Violence and Victims, 6,* 247–256.

The wife rape information page. (1998). [On-line]. Available: http://www.unh.edu

WISE, S., & STANLEY, L. (1987). *Georgie porgie: Sexual harassment in everyday life.* New York: Pandora.

WITTEMAN, H. (1993). The interface between sexual harassment and organizational romance. In G. L. Kreps (Ed.), *Sexual harassment: Communication implications* (pp. 27–62). Cresskill, NJ: Hampton.

Women killed by partner/spouse. (1998). [On-line]. Available: http://www.newcountrycanada.com

WOMEN'S ACTION COALITION. (1993). *WAC stats: The facts about women.* New York: The New Press.

WOOD, A. D., & McHUGH, M. C. (1994). Woman battering: The response of the clergy. *Pastoral Psychology, 42,* 185–196.

WOOD, J. T. (1992). Telling our stories: Narratives as a basis for theorizing sexual harassment. *Journal of Applied Communication, 20,* 349–362.

WOOD, J. T. (1993). Naming and interpreting sexual harassment: A conceptual framework for scholarship. In G. L. Kreps (Ed.), *Sexual harassment: Communication implications* (pp. 9–26). Cresskill, NJ: Hampton.

ZILLMAN, D., & BRYANT, J. (1982). Pornography, sexual callousness, and the trivialization of rape. *Journal of Communication, 32,* 10–21.

ZIRKEL, P. A. (1995). Student-to-student sexual harassment. *Phi Delta Kappan, 76,* 648–650.

CHAPTER TEN

WOMEN AND MEN
IN THE WORKPLACE

The Challenges of Talking Shop

CASE STUDY: DECISIONS
ABOUT CAREERS AND FAMILIES

When Chris took the baby to the park, they got a great deal of attention from mothers and nannies. Was it because the baby was so new and small? Exceptionally beautiful or advanced for its age? Why did the other childcare-givers stop their conversations when Chris approached them to sit down? Why did they seem uncomfortable continuing what they were talking about when Chris walked up? Did Chris just have this effect on people in general?

The effects we describe are due to the fact that Chris is the baby's *father*, not its mother. Granted, you probably know several fathers who take their children to the park; we do too. But how many fathers do you know who take their children to the park on weekday mornings or weekday afternoons? How many families do you know in which the father is the primary childcare-giver, while the mother pursues her career? It's safe to say that if you know any families like this, that's more than you knew even a few short years ago. This new profile of family life has been emerging and gaining prevalence for several years, but it is still far—very far—from the norm.

We explored gender-related family roles in Chapters 2 and 3 when we discussed hunter-gatherer cultures and the roots of male and female sex roles within American society. We also mentioned one of the only nontraditional family arrangements we knew of to date—the family in which the father tends full-time to the two children while the mother continues her highly successful career as an attorney. Just like Chris in this example, our friend told us that he attracted an enormous amount of attention at first from mothers and nannies, mainly because the presence of a man in the midst of female caregivers was so unusual. After the novelty wore off, everyone treated him normally and included him in helpful conversations about such topics as the advantages of certain baby products or the current wisdom on feeding and sleep cycles.

How does this example apply to communication at work? Think about Chris's or our friend's life before children. What makes men who are successfully pursuing careers or who are in jobs they enjoy decide to step out of that role and stay home to raise children? What happens to women who become pregnant, take maternity leaves at their jobs, and then return and resume their careers? Do you think these individuals are ridiculed and ostracized, or praised and supported for their choices? These choices and how they affect workplace relationships is just one of the topics in the fascinating area of workplace communication explored in this chapter.

Hot Topics

- How *gender* and *sex-based stereotypes* can impede the likelihood of getting hired
- The debate over *Affirmative Action* and its effects on the workplace
- How *relational and content approaches to communication* emerge in job interviewing
- *Verbal* and *nonverbal* indications of *sex bias* in job interviews
- Detecting and responding to *unethical job interview questions*
- Men's and women's *advancement* on the job
- The status of the *glass ceiling* for female professionals
- *Managerial communication* styles of women and men
- An update on the problem of *sexual harassment* in the workplace

WOMEN AND MEN WORKING TOGETHER: WALKING ON EGGSHELLS?

This chapter turns our attention to how gender communication occurs within occupational or workplace settings. Some of you may have quit a full-time job and entered college to finish your degree or to begin one. For others, work experience may consist of summer jobs or jobs during the year to supplement your income while you're in school. Still others of you who are putting yourselves through college may be juggling full-time school and a full-time job. If you fit this last description, you know that "personal life" is virtually a thing of the past.

For many of us, our work is our livelihood, our most time-consuming activity. In fact, Americans are working longer hours, spending 10 percent more time on the job than in 1969 (Cloud, 1998). Work can be a rewarding experience or a real downer for self-esteem. At times how we feel about our jobs or our work productivity is how we feel about ourselves. There's a fairly healthy list of things that make a job worthwhile and rewarding, like the satisfaction of getting an important sale, making a client happy, receiving a raise or a promotion, watching a student learn a new idea, or healing someone's mental, physical, or spiritual pain. However, when asked what makes their jobs enjoyable, most working persons—men and women alike—say that their relationships with people they work with make the most difference between job satisfaction and dissatisfaction.

At the same time that people feel co-worker relationships are important, they also reveal a sense that co-worker communication—especially between female and male co-workers—is complicated. Because some of the rules, roles, and boundaries continue to shift in the world of work, people often feel that they're "walking on eggshells" so as to not say the wrong thing and get themselves or someone else into trouble. Effective communication on the job is possible and many professional people learn to do it quite well. As we've said throughout this text, the key is to tap your expanded repertoire of communication in order to avoid a rigid style of communication that ignores the context of the situation.

Just how complicated is communication between male and female co-workers? Before addressing that question, think about your own work experience—whether that experience involved a full-time position of rank within a corporate giant or occasional baby-sitting for the neighbors' kids. Think about the people you worked with and ask how your communication differed with these people, compared to communication with people outside of work such as friends, dates, a spouse, or family members. Think of the most memorable person you worked with at that job and what made her or him memorable. Was that person your boss, a co-worker on the same level as you, or a subordinate? Was that person the same sex as you or opposite? Now think of the most dramatic or memorable instance in which poor communication occurred during this job; think about who was involved and how the situation was resolved (if it was resolved). What variable was most responsible for how the miscommunication arose—a status difference, a simple misunderstanding, a power struggle, something to do with sex or gender?

We're not suggesting that a gender or sex element is in the center of every ineffective communication situation at work; in fact, stressful workplace communication is quite often related to things other than a male-female dynamic. However, a good number of problems in the workplace that appear to be power- or status-based are really problems between the sexes. What's the likelihood that you will be working with members of both sexes in your next job? Granted, it depends on the job. But, generally speaking, if you're a woman, your chances of working with male bosses and co-workers are very good. If you're a man, your chances of having female bosses and co-workers are better than they used to be. Your chances of having female subordinates are as good as they've always been, according to statistics.

In 1998, labor statistics revealed that the civilian workforce was 52 percent female and 48 percent male. It is projected that by the year 2000, women will account for 63 percent of all employees (Neher, 1997). Also in 1998, of all men aged 16 and over, 75 percent were in the civilian labor force, as compared to 60 percent of women aged 16 and older. Just to put those figures in perspective, in 1980 the percentages were 77 percent for men and 52 percent for women; in 1960, they were 83 percent for men and 38 percent for women

(Dunn, 1997; U.S. Bureau of Labor Statistics, 1998). As more women continue to enter the labor force with each passing decade, their presence at managerial levels roughly parallels the growth rate. For example, in 1990, 57 percent of managers were male and 43 percent were female, compared to 70 percent male and 30 percent female in 1980 (St. George, 1995).

However, the growth trend for women is not reflected among the highest levels of employment. Recent surveys of Fortune 1500 companies reveal that, during the 1990s, 95 to 97 percent of senior managers, meaning vice presidents and above, were men. In 1994, only two women were CEOs of Fortune 1000 companies (Federal Glass Ceiling Commission, 1997). Women—particularly minority women—are greatly underrepresented in higher-ranking, higher-paying occupations.

> *The truth is that women's income, on average, will always be a fraction of men's, so long as America remains free.*
>
> *Patrick Buchanan, television show host & former presidential candidate*

What about where it hits home the most—in the pocket or pocketbook? Recent U.S. labor statistics show that the average woman working full-time makes about 76 cents for every dollar a man makes. You may have heard statistics like that before, but consider that the gap costs that woman $420,000 in salary over her lifetime, compared to a man. The discrepancy is also affected by race and ethnicity. Statistics show that Hispanic women earn 56 cents, black women 63 cents, and white women 80 cents to men's dollars, so minority women suffer the greatest pay discrimination (U.S. Bureau of Labor Statistics, 1994; Wage Gap, 1996).

It is beyond the parameters of our discussion in this chapter to interpret trends in workforce statistics, nor do we want to attempt to assess the impact of working women on American society. We do want to explore some possible explanations for the fact that in recent years only a minuscule increase has been achieved among the ranks of female senior management. We also examine how the increased presence of women in the workplace is affecting professional communication and the dynamics between the sexes, particularly at the management level. However, before tackling these on-the-job issues, it's a good idea to understand how one's sex may affect getting a job in the first place.

GETTING THAT ALL-IMPORTANT JOB

Gender and sex bias may impede you from getting a chance at a job. Often you don't know that this has happened; you just never get a response from an organization to your resume. If and when you do get job interviews, sex bias may be operating as well.

The Affirmative Action Debate: Equal Opportunity or Reverse Discrimination?

The topic of the role such factors as sex, age, and race play in creating opportunities for individuals has been hotly debated in recent years. It is not our intent in this section of the chapter to provide an exhaustive account of the evolution of Affirmative Action, but to highlight some important factors that may be operating in job searches and professional schools.

History and Definitions, in Brief

The 1964 Civil Rights Act, which created the Equal Employment Opportunities Commission, was the catalyst for Affirmative Action. Between 1961 and 1973, Presidents Kennedy, Johnson, and Nixon issued executive orders designed to eliminate discrimination. President Johnson was the one to actually attach the term *Affirmative Action* to his contribution (Daniels, Spiker, & Papa, 1997). These orders were originally applied to federal contractors or firms who conducted business with the government, but they were rapidly expanded to affect recruitment, hiring, training, and promoting practices in business, as well as a range of policies pertaining to higher education. Affirmative Action has been described as a "means of modifying employment practices to insure that minorities and women have equal job access with white men" (Reskin & Padavic, 1994, p. 70), as an effort to force organizations to engage in "vigorous efforts to bring people of color into jobs from which they had previously been excluded" (American Civil Liberties Union, 1995, p. 1), and as a "series of laws intended to overcome such barriers that seemed to exclude minorities and women in a systematic way" (Neher, 1997, p. 67).

Pros and Cons of Affirmative Action

The American Civil Liberties Union (ACLU) points out four major misconceptions about Affirmative Action. First, the ACLU contends that Affirmative Action is not the same as quota systems, which are illegal. Companies that assume Affirmative Action forces them into hiring certain numbers of women and representatives from minority groups are interpreting the goals of Affirmative Action in a superficial, inaccurate, and harmful way. A second misconception is that Affirmative Action actually enhances preferential treatment, rather than equalizing opportunity. This perception is echoed in many persons' views that Affirmative Action creates preferences rather than equality. A third misconception the ACLU discusses regards qualifications, meaning the notion that unqualified women or persons of color are hired over more qualified white men. Daniels, Spiker, and Papa (1997) argue that "Affirmative Action has never been about hiring people *solely* because of their color or sex without concern for their abilities" (p. 240). Finally, the ACLU rejects the notion that Affirmative Action

> *When a man gets up to speak, people listen, then look. When a woman gets up, people look; then, if they like what they see, they listen.*
>
> Pauline Frederick,
> *news correspondent*

is reverse discrimination against white males, rather than a "helping hand" to previously disadvantaged or underutilized groups.

In our public speaking classes, students often explore the pros and cons of Affirmative Action in their speeches. Male students in particular generate heated discussions about how unfair and unnecessary they believe Affirmative Action to be. One student recently argued, "Affirmative Action keeps the best people from getting a job. The person who has the toughest time getting a job these days is the white male." Some immediate responses he heard across the classroom expressed the sentiment, "Well, it's about time," meaning that white males have had employment privilege for so long, that it's only fair they feel the isolation and discrimination others have felt for a long time. As an article in *The Chronicle of Higher Education* explained,

> Arguments for and against Affirmative Action have been summarized like this:
>   Affirmative Action fueled the growth of the black middle class, but it has barely touched the problems of the ghetto. It has created workplaces and student bodies that "look like America," but it may have helped slow the country's economic growth. It rectifies past injustices to women and members of minority groups, but it stigmatizes talented people who could get ahead on their own. Equal opportunity. Reverse discrimination. (Analyzing Affirmative Action, 1995, p. A6)

The ACLU's listing of common misconceptions provides insight into the pro-Affirmative Action stance. However, on the con side, many Americans have come to believe that Affirmative Action is no longer necessary, that we have outgrown the need for guilt-induced, federally mandated standards to protect against workplace and university discrimination (Franklin, 1997). In fact, Presidents Reagan and Bush communicated open opposition to Affirmative Action (Reskin & Padavic, 1994). Former House Speaker Newt Gingrich urged the elimination of Affirmative Action programs, while President Clinton called for a "national conversation on Affirmative Action" and ordered a review of current Affirmative Action policies (Nacoste, 1995, p. A48). One criticism of particular interest is that Affirmative Action has helped one group far more than others: white women. Labor statistics show that white women have benefited the most from Affirmative Action over the 30 years since its creation, at least among entry and lower-level management positions (Blum, 1997; St. George, 1995).

Things Are Still Changing

Perhaps you are aware of the recent court rulings and state referenda on the topic. Among them, three developments are especially important. In June of 1995, the U.S. Supreme Court reinstated a reverse discrimination decision in favor of a white-owned construction company that lost a project to a minority-owned company. The effect of this ruling was to significantly limit the federal government's authority to implement programs that favor racial minorities. Justice Clarence Thomas, outspokenly anti-Affirmative Action, called racial preferences "poisonous and pernicious" and a form of "racial paternalism" (Texas Employment Commission, 1995, p. 3).

In 1996, the state of California passed the Civil Rights Initiative, a constitutional amendment barring state colleges and universities from using racial or gender preferences in admissions, hiring, and contracting (Schmidt, 1996). The initiative's purpose was to bring about "a color-blind legal code" (Mercer, 1994, p. A25). Also in 1996, the U.S. Fifth Circuit Court of Appeals handed down what is referred to informally as the Hopwood Decision. The decision barred the University of Texas law school from including race as a factor in its admissions, stating that universities could only use racial considerations to compensate for past racial discrimination (Greve, 1996). The court ruled that "Diversifying the student body—the objective that colleges most often cite to justify their Affirmative Action policies—is not a legitimate rationale for those programs" (Lederman, 1996, p. A40). Look for more court rulings and legislation on Affirmative Action—both upholding its practices and signaling its doom—because it is still being debated across the country.

You will no doubt want to know how professional schools (like law schools or medical schools) and potential employers view Affirmative Action and if they have programs in place that enhance the diversification of their student bodies and workforces. Some employers and admissions boards have discovered that an Affirmative Action policy or plan is to their benefit because it helps recruit talented employees and students (Reskin & Padavic, 1994). Then you will have to weigh that information with your own stance on the issue. One thing to consider is this: If one type of person dominates employment opportunities to the exclusion of other persons, the system protects itself from change. How can a qualified person who happens to not fit the profile ever get a chance? On the other hand, we sympathize with the frustration qualified persons feel when they believe they are denied employment simply because they are the wrong sex, color, nationality, sexual orientation, ethnicity, and the like.

Sex and Gender Issues and the Job Interview

Once you've landed an interview, your insight into gender communication will assist you in the process. Use your knowledge of why and how women and men communicate and your expanded repertoire of communication skills—your communicative "bag of tricks"—to help you adapt successfully to any interview situation and land the job you want.

Approaches to Talk: Insight into the Interview

To begin, what application to the job interview can you make of the information in Chapter 5 about *relational and content approaches to communication*? First, a caution: Don't take the relational-content instruction too far by assuming that a person's sex delineates his or her preferred approach to communication. Research suggests a *tendency* for men to view conversation as functioning to impart content or information and women to view it as relationship maintenance or a means of connecting with others. Use this knowledge to better understand yourself and your own approach to communication, and maybe to help you read "clues" from an interviewer.

For example, an appropriate goal for a job interview may be to simply communicate who you are and establish some sense of relationship between yourself and the interviewer so as to enhance your chances of being hired. But that may just as well be an inappropriate goal, depending on the situation. What if the interviewer is very informative and factual in approach, terse in tone, and rushed for time? What if that behavior comes from a woman, someone you expected to take a very different approach to the interview? Conversely, have you ever been to a job interview where all the interviewer wanted to do was just chit-chat and get to know you, as opposed to discussing the particulars of the job? If you went in expecting lots of information, you may be frustrated with what you aren't told or what you have to pry out of the interviewer.

As suggested before, a well-developed communication repertoire, good listening skills, an alertness to nonverbal cues, and a flexible communication style will increase the likelihood of success in the interview context (as well as most other contexts for communication). It's wise to survey yourself to understand your goals for an interview and your own preferences regarding approaches to talk. Then, without expecting a sex-typed approach from the interviewer, you will be able to detect when relational or content approaches are in use and align your behavior with that of the interviewer.

Being Taken Seriously

Unfortunately, this issue still applies more to female than male candidates for jobs. Women in the workforce are nothing new, but their presence is noted in a different way than a man's. The old expectation still exists that men work out of necessity—they're the breadwinners and *that's just what men do.* Although the corresponding stereotype for women is diminishing, some still believe that women work outside the home for distraction, for a secondary supplemental income, or as an interim activity before they settle down and have families. Alternative explanations given for why women work are far more numerous than the simple possibility that they work for the same reasons as men.

Nonverbal Indications of Sex Bias

Nonverbal communication is critical in a job interview; the nonverbal often carries more of the true message than the verbal communication (Knapp & Hall, 1997). But just how are sex-role expectations revealed nonverbally during a job interview? A dead give-away (or at least a fairly reliable nonverbal signal that a sex stereotype is in operation) comes in the opening greeting, especially the handshake. Often men and women alike appear awkward when shaking hands with a woman. This situation is improving, but women still get the "cup the fingers, half handshake" (the one that translates into "You sweet, frail thing; I couldn't possibly grasp your whole hand because it'd fall right off"). A potential employer likely has no intention of conveying negative impressions regarding a female applicant's credibility; the person just has a lousy handshake or has never learned the importance of a firm one. Nonetheless, it should raise the eyebrows of a female applicant when the handshake extended to her is less firm or confidence inducing than one extended to a male applicant or colleague. This can be a subtle indication of a sex-based value system that is tolerated and perpetuated within the organization.

Besides the handshake in an interview, sex bias may be subtly communicated by nonverbal indications of general disinterest such as a lack of eye contact, which communicates that you're just not being taken seriously for the position. If the interviewer seems unprepared, if she or he rushes through the interview or shows impatience by interrupting or overlapping your answers to questions, or if he or she accepts multiple interruptions from associates or phone calls, these actions can send direct signals that the candidate is not a serious contender for the job. Granted, you can't always tell whether the behavior has to do with your sex, your qualifications, some idiosyncratic reaction on the part of the interviewer, or some other variable totally unrelated to you and your interview. But it's important to take in as many nonverbal cues as possible and apply caution when interpreting what the cues mean.

Verbal Indications of Sex Bias

Another way that sex-role stereotypes are evidenced in job interviews has to do with the interviewer questioning process. If a potential employer holds some doubt as to whether a person of your sex is serious about a job or is capable of handling the job, the interviewer might reveal these doubts by asking leading questions. Leading questions are designed to trap the interviewee into a forced response or a no-win situation. They often take the form of a posed hypothetical situation followed by a question as to what the applicant would do. For example, when men apply for jobs in a currently female-dominated field such as nursing, they may receive leading questions that translate into doubts about their nurturing abilities. Or a woman applying for a position in a male-dominated office might get a leading question such as, "What would you do if a male colleague disagreed with one of your ideas and started to argue with you in front of your co-workers? Would you be able to handle that?"

One of the more overt means of communicating sex bias in a job interview is the use of unethical and illegal questions to applicants. It is illegal for a potential employer to ask an applicant about his or her marital status, parental status, or sexual orientation, among other things. Most employers know this, so most of them avoid these areas. But if they want to know this information before making a hiring decision, they have to use covert means or be indirect in how they approach these subjects during a job interview. By covert means, we refer to checking out a person's background, learning information in roundabout ways from former employers, and similar tactics. Here's an example to clarify these indirect approaches.

The female co-author of your textbook experienced an awkward situation some years back. During a segment of a job interview with a high-ranking member of an organization, the subject of transition was raised. The interviewer talked about how moving from one job and one state to another was stressful, even more so if one had a spouse and children who were uprooted in the process. After making this statement, he stopped talking, made direct eye contact, and waited for her response. Even though she knew what information he was after, she wanted the job, so her reply revealed her current marital and parental status.

Another example involves a woman who was put in an awkward position not as much by her interviewers, as occurred in the first example, but by a man who joined them for lunch. The woman was interviewing for a prestigious position within the organization, so you can imagine her surprise and dismay when the lunch guest, a relative of one of the interviewers, began quizzing her about her private life. He asked whether she was married, whether she had ever been married, whether she had any plans to be married, whether she had or wanted to have children, and so forth. What was quite unfortunate, and what almost caused the woman to turn down the job offer, was that the hiring body made no attempt to stop the guest's unethical behavior. It was as though they knew they weren't liable or at fault since the questions weren't coming from them, so they let a secondary source elicit the information. The woman stammered, hesitated, and somehow managed to avoid answering the guest's intrusive, unethical questions.

The first example is fairly typical of the way an employer might attempt to learn information that cannot be asked directly. This strategy throws off an applicant who knows that such aspects of private life should not be discussed, but who wants to communicate smoothly, wants the job, and doesn't want to insinuate that any interviewer impropriety has occurred. In this example, hindsight caused the applicant to think, "I wish I hadn't fallen into that trap; I could have simply agreed with him by saying 'Yes, transition can be quite stressful.'" In the second example, the woman defused the situation, choosing not to respond to the unethical questions. There are nonconfrontational ways to communicate effectively to an employer that you know what's going on and you're not going to play along. One option is to respond to the question with a question, as though you didn't understand what the interviewer was getting at. You may decide to use more confrontational, educative responses, but you have to weigh the risks of such tactics (such as not getting the job). The main thing to think about is whether or not you want to work for a company whose interviewers would use strategies like these, as the woman in the second example had to do. When verbal and nonverbal indications of sex bias surface in a job interview, it increases the likelihood that sex-biased behavior and attitudes will be in evidence on the job.

When Working Women Walk, Talk, and Look Like Working Men

Most everyone knows the basic message behind the "dress for success" slogan, meaning that you need to dress well and exude confidence in an interview, to appear attractive (physically and in your personality), and to dress in a manner consistent with (or a bit more formal than) the employees who work where you are interviewing. For male job candidates, the "dress for success" advice generally works well, but it's not so straightforward for women.

Communication researchers Borisoff and Merrill (1998) describe what women experience when they must strike some acceptable balance between femininity and masculinity in order to be taken seriously. They explain, "The double bind faced by women applying for professional positions lies in finding how to communicate their 'in-group' status without dressing in a manner regarded as 'too masculine,' which could result in negative hiring decisions . . . On the other hand, 'too feminine' apparel would be considered too frivolous for the workplace" (pp. 93–94). If a woman is also highly physically attractive her looks may be a deterrent to her getting a job because of the stereotype that female beauty is accompanied by a lack of intelligence. Another suspicion that accompanies high physical attractiveness is that the woman will cause more problems on the job than she is worth by "being a distraction" or inciting male interest. With increased concerns about sexual harassment, these concerns are real. If you think these statements are ridiculous, imagine them in the reverse. Would a male job applicant be likely to lose credibility or be deemed not right for the job because he was perceived as too masculine in an interview? Would a handsome man be denied a job because he might be unintelligent or too distracting to his female co-workers?

> *I'm so excited to be around other women who do what I do—I don't even care what it stands for. Can you, as a man, imagine working in an entirely female workplace, from the boss down? You'd be, like, "Periods—whatever!"*
>
> *Liz Phair,*
> *singer/songwriter*

cathy®   **by Cathy Guisewite**

Women have reacted in some interesting ways to the realization of this double bind. During the 1970s when American society witnessed a significant increase in women working outside the home, female applicants who wished to be accepted into the male-dominated workforce dressed like little versions of men (as the advice books advocated) (Watkins, 1996). They wore dark, pin-striped suits with skirts instead of pants and bows or scarves at the neck instead of ties. They wore wing-tipped pumps and carried leather briefcases, because heaven help a woman who showed up in a professional setting carrying a purse! They kept their jewelry, perfume, and makeup to a minimum, generally in attempts to play down the fact that they were women vying for the same positions as men. They did everything they could to be taken seriously. What happened?

In some instances women gained some ground, but, in large part, emulating men didn't work. What women have learned since then is that when they attempt to imitate powerful men—their dress, their verbal displays of aggressiveness and competitiveness, even their joking behaviors or co-worker banter—they aren't received in the same favorable manner. This approach can also cause a woman to lose her own identity as a professional (Borisoff & Merrill, 1998). Thus, since the 1970s, women have continued to find ways of creating their own paths and making their own voices heard within the world of work. For example, now it is quite common to see working women in dress that combines traditional, conservative lines with softer materials and wider-ranging colors. While the area of professional dress has broadened women's choices and provided some relief to the double bind, other areas haven't kept pace. Sex-role stereotypes are still alive and the double bind is still active for women who attempt to enter the workforce.

The best guideline for students regarding job interviewing should sound quite familiar to you by now: Develop your communicative repertoire as fully as possible, employing masculine and feminine behaviors that can be effectively used given the demands of the interview situation and the particulars of the job and the company. For female readers, realize that society continues to

---

RECAP

equal employment opportunity; Affirmative Action; relational and content approaches to communication; nonverbal and verbal indications of sex bias; leading, hypothetical, and unethical questions; double binds

---

change regarding what is appropriate female professional demeanor. In some settings, communicating confidently and assertively in a job interview will be perceived positively. In other settings and with other interviewers, sex-role stereotypes may be operating; an interviewer may view some behavior as masculine and, therefore, inappropriate coming from a female applicant (Borisoff & Merrill, 1998). For male readers, think about the possibility that the interviewer may highly value some of the behaviors stereotypically labeled feminine—like verbal and nonverbal affiliative, supportive behaviors—so it will be to your advantage to work these behaviors into how you present yourself in an interview.

ON THE JOB AND MOVING UP

Congratulations! You got the job. You're on the job. So what sex- or gender-related variables might emerge at your job? How will you respond?

Moving Up: Advancement within an Organization

Refer back to the statistics cited early in this chapter—you might conclude that the workforce is becoming more equitable since the numbers indicate that women are steadily increasing their presence in the work arena. But a more careful inspection will reveal a problem that has gained a great deal of attention: While more women are being hired than in times past, greater numbers of men than women achieve the higher, more responsible and more rewarding ranks. Even though *Fortune* magazine could produce its first "Fifty Most Powerful Women" list in October 1998 and other indications of gains at higher levels can be cited, significant inequity still exists (Sellers, 1998). For example, statistics show that women represent 43 percent of graduating classes at American law schools, a figure that is up from a mere 7 percent in 1972. These women have achieved in all aspects of the practice of law except for one: positions of power. Women are still greatly underrepresented in partnerships and the management of law firms (Sege, 1996). What factors are connected to the continuing trends regarding advancement?

Difficult Choices: Family, Career, or Both?

One of the most obvious factors that complicates women's professional advancement is a basic biological function (one we explored in Chapter 2)—the fact that

J have yet to hear a man ask for advice on how to combine marriage and a career.

Gloria Steinem,
author & political activist

women give birth to babies. As a culture we have moved forward on this front, creating more choices for families. Efforts in the '70s and '80s helped to break the constricted thinking that women would automatically choose home and family over careers. In the 1990s, women who could afford to give up their paychecks to stay home and raise young children have felt more free to do so without feeling that they'd violated some basic tenet of women's liberation. We've witnessed political progress through such laws as Title VII of the Civil Rights Act (1964), the Pregnancy Disability Act (1978), the EEOC's guidelines on sexual harassment (1980), and the Family and Medical Leave Act (1996) (McDorman, 1998).

Another positive workplace change is the increasing number of on-site childcare facilities and company-sponsored programs that increase employees' access to childcare. Changing workplace language indicates changing attitudes toward work and family. In the 1980s, women were described as "superwomen" who were "doing it all" and "having it all" because they raised children while maintaining their careers (Friedan, 1981). Then the term *second shift* was coined to describe the work of employed married women who returned home from their jobs to hours of cleaning, cooking, and childcare (Hochschild, 1989, as in Saltzman Chafetz, 1997). The 1990s brought about the "Mommy track" (a variation of "fast track"), which applied to women who sought advancement in the workplace at the same time as they had serious childcare responsibilities. One study found that 51 percent of mothers with children at home work full time and another 18 percent work part time, suggesting that the majority of mothers have to or choose to work outside the home (Booher, 1997). Articles and books, such as Elizabeth Perle McKenna's (1997) *When Work Doesn't Work Anymore* and Joan K. Peters' (1997) *When Mothers Work: Loving Our Children Without Sacrificing Ourselves,* offer advice on juggling and balancing family and job that are reality for many professional people.

But with all of this awareness and these important innovations, a nagging perception still exists in the minds of many: Women in the workforce just can't be counted on over the long haul. They are likely to want to have children at some point in their careers and that means maternity leaves, a greater potential for absenteeism, and the likelihood that they will vacate their positions in favor of staying home and raising their children (all of which costs organizations money). This is a stereotype—a painful one to write and read. Our experience and that of many students has been that, no matter how equality based many organizations (including universities) like to believe they are, some persons in authority still retain this stereotype about female employees. They may never say it, but it still crosses many people's minds and causes them to think twice about hiring or promoting women into positions of authority.

Management researcher Kathleen Reardon (1997), writing about dysfunctional communication patterns in the workplace, describes how the popular trend of downsizing has exacerbated the impact of pregnancy on the workforce. She quotes a corporate program director as saying, "I know I'm not supposed to say this, but pregnant women are getting to be a real problem for us. Each time one of them gets pregnant, the whole program is upset" (p. 175). The communication climate for pregnant workers or new mothers often changes. Reardon cites examples of patronizing communication such as, "you're glowing," assumptions that one's abilities are compromised, and being passed over for plum job assignments because they involve travel, something it is assumed a pregnant woman or new mother would want to avoid.

Another complicating factor is the reality of the tension many women feel between their careers and obligations to bear and raise children (Gerson, 1997). We grant that the stereotype that women contribute significantly to organizational turnover because of pregnancy and childrearing duties has some basis in reality. Women do struggle with multiple demands on their time and energies, particularly if they don't have a spouse or don't receive much help from one. A recent example bears out the difficult decisions many professional women face. One of the few women in the country to achieve a top corporate position, Brenda Barnes, Chief Executive Officer of Pepsico, quit her job in 1997, saying, "I suppose a lot of chief executives can find a way to balance work and family, but I couldn't figure out how to do it" (as in Stead, 1997, p. D3). Barnes missed her children after years of putting in long hours, but she warned: "I hope it doesn't tell people that women can't stay in a big job because they have kids" (p. D3). Like Brenda Barnes, many mothers feel significant guilt if they choose to continue their careers rather than to discard the professional strides they have made in favor of staying home with young children (Jones, 1998). Society magnifies that guilt by repeated insinuations that a working mother isn't a good mother. There are constant attempts to blame women who work outside the home for the decay of the American family. Career women may also face negative after-effects of maternity leaves, including learning that

> *At work, you think of the children you have left at home. At home, you think of the work you've left unfinished. Such a struggle is unleashed within yourself. Your heart is rent.*
>
> *Golda Meir,*
> *former Israeli prime minister*

their careers have plateaued, their jobs have been rerouted into less attractive trajectories, or their ability to influence has been lost or diminished (Miller, Casey, Lamphear-Van Horn, & Ethington, 1993).

You also have to think more broadly about this problem: The decision between home and family must be placed in the context of the persistent fact that few working men experience the same tension as women when children come into the picture (Kelly, 1997; Reardon, 1997). You don't see very many men struggle with the career versus family decision. Why? Could it be because society hasn't evolved to the point where men are equal partners in the childrearing process? Could it be because most people still operate on the hunter-gatherer model, the male-as-breadwinner and female-as-childcare-giver model we described in Chapter 2? Just to illustrate what we mean, go back a page and change the sex throughout the discussion to male, as in the "Daddy track" and "Men in the workforce can't be counted on because they are likely to want to have children . . .". Seems ludicrous, right? But it points to some of the problems and the hypocrisy perpetuated in our "modern" workplace.

The reality is that many two-parent families simply cannot afford the luxury of having only one income while the other parent is the primary childcare giver; for single-parent families, there are few if any choices between work and family. So, when trying to understand how basic biology factors into women's advancement (or lack thereof) in the workforce, there are many complicated factors to consider.

Is the Ceiling Still Made of Glass?

We expect you've heard the *glass ceiling* term before. It stems from a larger metaphor for working women who operate in "glass houses," whose behavior is not only scrutinized by individuals on every level of the organization, but whose success or failure might affect the status of working women everywhere. Professional women who look higher, see the possibilities, yet are unable to reach them because of a transparent barrier have encountered the glass ceiling (Kanter, 1977; Reskin & Padavic, 1994). In the mid-1980s, a group of researchers at the Center for Creative Leadership began a three-year study, the Executive Women Project (Morrison, White, & Van Velsor, 1987). This group coined the term *glass ceiling,* which they described as follows: "Many women have paid their dues, even a premium, for a chance at a top position, only to find a glass ceiling be-

> *If women can sleep their way to the top, how come they aren't there? There must be an epidemic of insomnia out there.*
>
> Ellen Goodman,
> columnist

tween them and their goal. The glass ceiling is not simply a barrier for an individual, based on the person's inability to handle a higher-level job. Rather the glass ceiling applies to women as a group who are kept from advancing higher *because they are women*" (p. 13). Out of their extensive investigation of executives in the top 100 companies of the Fortune 500, these researchers placed the barrier for women at "just short of the general manager position" (p. 13).

In 1991 the Federal Glass Ceiling Commission was formed, headed by then Secretary of Labor Lynn Martin. This group's Glass Ceiling Initiative studied nine Fortune 500 companies in order to understand the barriers to advancement for women and minorities and to assist corporations in determining strategies for eliminating the barriers. As a result of this study, Martin issued the following challenge: "The glass ceiling, where it exists, hinders not only individuals but society as a whole. It effectively cuts our pool of potential corporate leaders by eliminating over one-half of our population. If our end game is to compete successfully in today's global market, then we have to unleash the full potential of the American work force. The time has come to tear down, to dismantle the 'Glass Ceiling'" (p. 2). Some factors contributing to the barrier for female and minority advancement include the following:

1. Corporate lack of attention to equal opportunity principles, such as monitoring the progress and development, as well as compensation patterns, for all employees.
2. Discriminatory placement patterns.
3. Inadequate recordkeeping.
4. Internal recruitment practices that maintain white male-dominated networks.
5. A lack of EEO (Equal Employment Opportunity) involvement in the hiring processes for mid- and upper-level management positions.

In 1995, the Federal Glass Ceiling Commission synthesized research findings and reported that women were occupying less than 5 percent of senior managerial and executive positions in large American corporations.

The Authority Gap

Researchers Reskin and Padavic (1994) offer three explanations for what they term an "authority gap" in the American workplace. The first is the "human-capital inequities" explanation, which suggests that women are still acquiring the education and experience that will enable them to rise to positions of authority. Reskin and Padavic counter this explanation with statistics that show that "Women have not advanced into authority-conferring jobs in proportion to their presence in the lower ranks. Women were 15 percent of all managers in 1968, so they should be 15 percent of senior managers today. Instead, in 1990 they were only 3 percent of senior managers . . . If women's rate of progress proceeds at the present pace, women will not achieve equitable representation and pay at all management levels for another 75 to 100 years" (pp. 95–96).

The second explanation is related to workplace segregation, the fact that the most frequently held managerial positions for women are in personnel and public relations—areas that typically involve little authority and power within organizations. Their third explanation for the authority gap stems from cultural bias. Reskin and Padavic contend that many employers still "adhere to an informal segregation code that keeps women from supervising men and that reserves the training slots leading to higher-level jobs for men" (p. 96). Probably most of you reading this text have had some job experience; nontraditional students have likely had extensive work experience (outside the home). Think about all the supervisors and bosses you've had—how many of them were women? Do you remember when you first worked for a female boss? Did you have any different expectations of or reactions to that female supervisor?

Other explanations for the discrepant advancement of female and male professionals have been suggested. Researchers like Deborah Tannen (1994) and Dianne Horgan (1990) contend that, beyond external barriers to advancement, women often face internal barriers; that is, they communicate and behave in ways that hold themselves back from advancement. Some of these behaviors include avoiding even moderate boasting about successes, de-emphasizing and trivializing successes by attributing them to luck or circumstance rather than to ability, emphasizing failures rather than promoting successes, being quick to pleasantly take blame even when not at fault, and accepting and perpetuating sex-typed language that widens the sexes' credibility gap.

But as gender communication researchers Nadler and Nadler (1987) point out, "The condemnation of women for their communication patterns seems inappropriate, as it would be like blaming the victim for being abused" (p. 130). While some internal factors may play a role in convincing women that they aren't "management material," the external factors are more devastating and actually reinforce the internal doubts that many women hold. As organizational communication researchers Stewart and Clarke-Kudless (1993) explain, "Women have not reached the top of the corporate hierarchy in part because of the sex-role stereotype held by many corporate decision makers that women do not have the personality characteristics necessary for top leadership roles" (p. 150). This points to the stereotypical judgment that because women are naturally affiliative and nurturing, they cannot make tough decisions that might disappoint others—they opt not to make decisions out of a fear of rocking the boat. Whether one locates the problem internally, externally, or both, the glass ceiling for women still remains intact.

Nadler and Nadler (1987) suggest a dual approach to combating the problem. The first isn't immediately gratifying because it calls for societal change. These authors contend that organizations must actively ensure that male and female employees' careers are developed with equal attention. They also encourage teachers, parents, and academic advisors and mentors to work with children at early ages to eliminate negative sex-role stereotypes *where they begin*. The second approach to change lies within the woman's own behavior. Nadler and Nadler suggest that women rely on those skills stereotypically related to their sex, but that are generally perceived positively in work settings. These skills include active and empathic listening, open communication styles, well-honed verbal and writing abilities, and nonverbal sensitivity. A final suggestion to women is to plan their careers well in advance and to proactively seek the advancement of their careers, rather than waiting for a superior to notice and reward their accomplishments. When women do advance within organizations, they may again face perceptions that their behavior is nontraditional or not the norm, distinctions that pose special challenges.

Women and Men in Leadership Positions

Communication researchers, organizational behavior experts, and gender scholars alike have focused attention for decades on how the sexes approach leadership, management, conflict resolution, and decision making. They have attempted to separate myth from fact in the perception that members of one sex versus the other make better managers.

How Are Male and Female Managers Perceived?

Research on this topic has produced varying results, in part because there are so many on-the-job factors that influence one's perception of manager or leader effectiveness. For example, in one study employees who perceived their boss as having considerable power within the organization held highly favorable views of the boss, regardless of the boss's sex (Ragins, 1992). But as the researcher points out, since women still tend to hold lower power positions within organizations, power and a person's sex are intertwined. Another study found that interpersonal communication skills were perceived as more valuable than other managerial attributes (Fine, Johnson, & Foss, 1991).

This information is inconsistent with the long-held attitude that, as communication scholars Berryman-Fink and Eman Wheeless (1987) point out, men "possess such stereotypically masculine characteristics as aggressiveness and competitiveness, are more capable, more acceptable, and preferred for management positions" (p. 85). Berryman-Fink and Eman Wheeless examined whether male and female employees held different attitudes regarding women in general, women as managers, and the communication competencies of women versus men in management. Female employees in the study held women in higher regard than male employees, viewed female managers in a more positive light, and believed that female managers were communicatively competent. However, male employees evaluated the communication and management of female managers negatively in this study. This finding raises a concern about the mediating effects of sex when a manager is being evaluated.

This study also exposed problems with traditional, male-oriented management approaches based on military and team-sports models that emphasize competitiveness, aggressiveness, risk taking, strategizing, and adhering to the chain of command. In organizations dominated by male management styles, female management styles will be deemed "deficient" (Berryman-Fink & Eman Wheeless, 1987, p. 91). The most interesting point raised by the Berryman-Fink and Eman Wheeless study was that female employees' perceptions about female managers were positive—females see females as competent communicators. The authors conclude: "Thus, as more women enter management spheres, the male-oriented management model is likely to give way to a flexible style that integrates traditional female behaviors and skills with traditional male behaviors. Management trends already are evolving to combine task-oriented skills (traditionally masculine) with people-oriented skills (traditionally feminine) to meet the demands of a changing work force and competitive marketplace" (p. 91). Did you catch the reference to "flexible style" in that quotation? That sounds like something we've been talking about throughout this book—using an expanded, flexible repertoire of communication behaviors in a personally effective manner appropriate to the situation.

How Do They Communicate as Managers?

Attempts to corroborate perception-based findings have produced mixed results. Researchers Wilkins and Andersen (1991) reviewed many studies on this subject and found "no meaningful difference in the behavior of male and female managers" (p. 27). In contrast, studies by organizational communication scholars and a survey of female and male managers conducted by the International Women's Forum found that female managers, with both female and male employees, were more likely to use an interactive style of leadership. They tended to resolve problems within the organization through collaboration with peers and subordinates, open discussion of diverse viewpoints, and supportive communication. Male managers were more likely to be competitive and nonaccommodating and to use power strategies and organizational protocol to resolve disputes, such as invoking a company policy as a means of solving a problem (Burrell, Buzzanell, & McMillan, 1992; Roesner, 1993).

Author Sally Helgesen (1990) contends that sex differences are readily detectable among leaders, differences that she believes constitute a female advantage. Generally speaking, a feminine management style involves supportive, facilitative leadership that is effective in participatory, democratic work settings. In contrast, Helgesen characterizes a masculine management style as one involving control or power over employees and a competitive tone that strives to create winners and losers. Findings from a survey conducted by Korn/Ferry International, an international executive-search firm, support the emergence of a new profile of a nonautocratic leader that sounds similar to the feminine style. They suggest that "the all-powerful, controlling boss—or 'controllasaurus'—would be extinct within a decade" (Nelton, 1997, p. 19).

In a similar vein, communication scholar Steven May (1997) describes a changing workplace and a changing worker as contributing factors to the "feminization of management" (p. 3). May contends:

> No longer told to "check your brains at the door," workers in high-wage manufacturing and service economies are asked to abandon the idea that their jobs are static and, instead, work more independently, contribute to problem-solving and cost-reduction, be more customer-oriented and vendor-minded, and do what is needed rather than what the job description prescribes. Thus, as workers become self-managing, managers are told to reorient themselves toward a new role of coordinating, facilitating, coaching, supporting, and nurturing their employees. (p. 4)

May identifies three themes in current managerial literature, themes that reveal a "thread of feminization" (p. 9). The first is advice to managers to replace the notion of control with shared responsibility. Instead of commanding, directing, and deciding, "the new ideal is a manager who relinquishes control and shares responsibility, authority, and the limelight" (p. 10). The second theme is one of helping and developing employees, as opposed to regulating and supervising them. This theme underlies the team-building approach that is popular among modern American organizations. The final theme stresses the importance of building meaningful networks of relationships, both internal and external to the organization.

While May found these themes consistent with feminine traits identified in our culture, none of the literature he surveyed used the term "feminine style of management." In fact, authors struggled to find another name or metaphor for the style. May contends that a recommended management style based on feminine qualities such as nurturance, along with an unwillingness to label that style feminine, bears witness to continued bias in the workplace. He concludes that "the culture is deeply ambivalent about elevating the status of the female and femininity; doing so would call into question the entire system of gender relations that underpins most organization and management theory" (pp. 22–23).

Can Effective Managers Have It Both Ways?

Research and popular literature on the subject of sex and gender and management describe a blended style, one that draws upon both masculine and feminine strengths in communication and leadership (Berryman-Fink & Eman Wheeless, 1987; Hayes Andrews, Herschel, & Baird, 1996). This represents a move away from the traditional, male-oriented management style, corresponding to the change to less traditional, less hierarchically based, flatter, and more decentralized organizations that face global competition. As Tom Peters, co-author of the best-selling management treatise, *In Search of Excellence,* explains, "Gone are the days of women succeeding by learning to play men's games. Instead the time has come for men on the move to learn to play women's games" (as in Fierman, 1990, p. 115).

One of the strongest and earliest proponents of the blended management approach was Alice Sargent, author of *The Androgynous Manager* (1981). Androgynous management involves blending linear, systematic problem solving with intuitive approaches, balancing competition and collaboration, and dealing with power as well as emotion. Sargent argues that men and women alike have suffered the consequences of a masculine management style, citing stress and related health problems as negative consequences.

However, there are some cautions to consider regarding an androgynous management style. This may surprise you, since we are such advocates of androgyny and gender blending throughout this text. In most other contexts, an androgynous approach stemming from a well-developed communication repertoire seems to elicit the most positive responses from others. The problem is that, in some organizational settings, exhibiting behaviors stereotypically associated with the opposite sex can actually backfire (Lamude & Daniels, 1990).

RECAP

second shift, Mommy track, glass ceiling, authority gap, workplace segregation, management styles, feminization of management, androgynous management style

---

For example, a male manager who reacts emotionally to bad news at work may be labeled the "corporate wimp," rather than be valued for his honest reaction. A female manager who aggressively communicates her views to colleagues may be labeled the "corporate bitch." When women attempt to emulate the management behaviors of their male counterparts, they perpetuate the male-oriented system and are often devalued for this behavior. Sometimes, when a female manager uses stereotypically feminine behaviors, she receives negative reactions as well (Daniels, Spiker, & Papa, 1997). Things are changing and female managers are still finding their way in a male-dominated arena, so the decision to adopt an androgynous management style, or any management style, depends upon the context within which you work.

No matter what jobs men and women hold—from assembly workers to school teachers to directors of nonprofit agencies to corporate CEOs—they will most likely face some complications related to sex and gender. Right now, members of both sexes are trying to work together productively, trying to decide what kind of woman or man they want to be on the job, and trying to communicate effectively and be received positively. All this "trying" represents the current struggle in the workplace, but this struggle is manifested most dramatically by the problem of sexual harassment—the subject of the final section of this chapter.

THE PROBLEM OF SEXUAL HARASSMENT IN THE WORKPLACE

Just reading this heading may make you want to put the book down. As difficult as sexual harassment is to think about, it's important to examine this topic because many of you are nearing graduation and will be launching careers. We hope you don't encounter sexual harassment at work, but whether or not you experience it firsthand, you need to be current and knowledgeable on the topic if you want to function successfully on the job. Sexual harassment is such a critical problem in our culture that we've discussed it in multiple places in this text. The most thorough discussion is in Chapter 9; we briefly discuss how it occurs and is dealt with in educational settings in Chapter 11. Here we summarize current information particularly pertinent to the workplace.

The Pervasiveness of the Problem

Sexual harassment in the workplace continues to be talked about and researched. Since 1991, juries have granted over 500 verdicts supporting complaints of sexual harassment. Over 15,000 new sexual harassment cases are filed yearly, compared to around 7,000 cases in 1991 (Cloud, 1998). Sale of corporate insurance policies covering sexual harassment settlements doubled between 1996 and 1998, from $100 million to over $200 million (Jacobs & Bonavoglia, 1998). Six million dollars a year is the estimated cost of sexual harassment for Fortune 500 companies (Rhode, 1997). But don't get the idea that sexual harassment is only a recent phenomenon, one that only gained attention in the 1990s because of Anita Hill's sexual harassment claims during the Clarence Thomas Supreme Court confirmation hearings or because of the Navy's Tailhook scandal (Violanti, 1996). In the late 1970s, feminists coined the label *sexual harassment,* but one can imagine that as long as men and women have worked together in many diverse settings, sexual harassment has occurred. Many organizations have had sexual harassment policies in place for years, while others without policies or with vague, outdated policies are working on them now (or they could be in serious jeopardy).

In her article "Harassment Is Alive and Well and Living at the Water Cooler," Stanford law professor Deborah Rhode (1997) discusses the current status of workplace sexual harassment. Rhode explores why, after the Hill-Thomas incident and highly publicized court cases, and "after two decades of enforcing prohibitions on harassment, are we still seeing so many egregious examples of it?" (p. 28) The popular media refers to how the public is tired of hearing about harassment, leading to the perception that the problem isn't occurring in today's "modern" and "highly informed" society, at least not nearly with the frequency it occurred prior to Hill and Thomas. Rhode contends that this denial that serious workplace harassment still occurs, and frequently occurs, is a "variation on the traditional view that it didn't happen at all" (p. 28). By citing recent cases of overt and dramatic harassment that were not decided in favor of the complainant, Rhode makes us aware of the popular, but wrongheaded thinking that sexual harassment has disappeared from the American workplace. Frivolous claims, particularly lurid, headline-grabbing cases (especially those involving men claiming harassment by female co-workers, as in the movie *Disclosure*) tend to deflect or camouflage the problem. Rhode suggests, "for every one of these aberrant but endlessly cited cases, there are countless less-publicized illustrations of the converse problem" (p. 28).

Most workplace sexual harassment that is reported and researched involves heterosexuals, with a male-harasser, female-target profile (Leonard et al., 1993; McKinney & Maroules, 1991; Reilly, Lott, Caldwell, & DeLuca, 1992; Rubin & Borgers, 1990). Female sexual harassment of men does occur, but it is reported and pursued in the courts with far less frequency than male-to-female harassment. Incidences of same-sex or homosexual harassment occur also. In fact, two federal district court rulings supported male employees' claims of sexual harassment by their male supervisors (Texas Employment Commission, 1995). Many instances of sexual harassment occur between individuals who function within clearly drawn power lines, such as in relationships of boss-employer, teacher-student, doctor-patient, lawyer-client. However, research shows that peer harassment—sexually harassing communication between co-workers of equal or similar rank and power—occurs frequently within organizations (Ivy, 1993; Ivy & Hamlet, 1996; Paetzold & O'Leary-Kelly, 1993).

In Chapter 9, we define sexual harassment in some depth. For the purpose of quick review, here is the 1980 Equal Employment Opportunity Commission's (EEOC) definition of sexual harassment:

> Unwelcome sexual advances, requests for sexual favors, and other verbal or physical conduct of a sexual nature constitute sexual harassment when (1) submission to such conduct is made either explicitly or implicitly a term or condition of an individual's employment, (2) submission to or rejection of such conduct by an individual is used as the basis for employment decisions affecting such individual, or (3) such conduct has the intention or effect of unreasonably interfering with an individual's work performance or of creating an intimidating, hostile, or offensive working environment. (EEOC Guidelines, 1980)

The first two forms reflect "quid pro quo" harassment, which means "this for that" or "something for something." This is the more traditional or historical view of harassment, involving a threat by superiors that unless subordinates engage in some form of sexual behavior, they will lose their jobs, be overlooked for promotions and raises, be transferred to less desirable units or locations, and so forth. The more overt, tangible nature of quid pro quo harassment is more easily recognizable by the courts as a form of illegal sex discrimination than the second form of harassment, hostile climate (Paetzold & O'Leary-Kelly, 1993).

Working in a Hostile Environment

Hostile climate or work environment sexual harassment only began to be viewed as illegal sex discrimination by the U.S. Supreme Court in 1986. To date this form of harassment has generated the largest number of court cases, while also producing the most amount of confusion surrounding what actions could or could not be regarded as sexual harassment (Berryman-Fink & Vanover Riley, 1997; Jacobs & Bonavoglia, 1998). Research provides some examples from the workplace that can substantiate claims of hostile climate harassment: posters, flyers, calendars, and other "decorative" materials that contain nudity or sexual representations; lewd or insulting graffiti in workplace areas; pornographic or sexually explicit materials; vandalism of one's personal belongings or work space; and behaviors such as making repeated phone calls; leaving e-mail or voice mail messages; placing intimidating or sexist materials in an employee's mailbox; staring, following, or stalking someone; and performing office pranks (Paetzold & O'Leary-Kelly, 1993).

One element that makes this so difficult and makes people feel they are walking on eggshells is the fine line between flirting and harassment. Since the average American spends much more time at work than in decades past, more of us are likely to look to the workplace for friendship and romantic liaisons. While an office romance can make you look more forward to getting out of bed and going to work each day, it can also create huge problems. One person's friendly, teasing, or flirtatious behavior is another person's sexual harassment (Alberts, 1992; Haunani Solomon & Miller Williams, 1997; Keyton, 1993). While some organizations believe workplace romances are private and not causes for concern, worries about romantic workplace relationships and potential liability have led some organizations to create policies that out and out ban office romance (Buzzanell, 1992; Eisenberg & Goodall, 1993; Witteman, 1993). Other organizations may rely on informal channels, such as the employee grapevine, to communicate management's position on office romance. We don't want to suggest what adults should or should not do on this issue, but we do want to offer one caution: Be very careful about office romances—they are unpredictable, they involve a strange mix of the personal and the professional (which sometimes causes added conflict within the relationship), and, if they end (and end badly), they increase the potential for a claim of sexual harassment due to hostile work environment.

Authors Gloria Jacobs and Angela Bonavoglia (1998) address the question, "When does harmless workplace behavior morph into a potentially hostile environment?" (p. 51). They provide the following examples, asking readers to decide what is and is not hostile climate harassment: a guy accidentally e-mailing everyone in his organization (instead of his closest buddies) "The 50 Worst Things About Women"; a man using various communication channels (e.g., e-mail, voice mail, fax) to repeatedly ask a female co-worker on a date; a male manager whispering compliments and invading the space of a female co-worker; guys in a mail room exchanging the latest raunchy joke within earshot of a female worker; a male professor who uses a copy of *Hustler* magazine to teach female anatomy; and a female administrator, whose office contains male-bashing posters and cartoons, who is assigned a male office mate. Jacobs and Bonavoglia conclude that all of these situations could involve sexual harassment, with the exception of the first one—the accidental e-mail. They contend that if this was indeed a one-time, unintended mistake, a claim of sexual harassment would be a stretch. But we challenge these authors to think again—does the name Paula Jones ring a bell?

Obviously, an e-mail mistake is very different from an allegation of a superior exposing his genitals to a subordinate and asking for oral sex. But here is the point: With the hostile climate element of sexual harassment law, one relatively benign incident can become the next highly publicized sexual harassment suit. Also remember the consistent research findings that women react more strongly to inappropriate behavior and view more behaviors as potential sexual harassment than men (Berryman-Fink & Vanover Riley, 1997; Ivy & Hamlet, 1996; Mongeau & Blalock, 1994). The one-time e-mail would probably not be considered pervasive enough of an action to constitute hostile climate sexual harassment, just as the one-time encounter described by Paula Jones resulted in her suit being thrown out of court. But, as Gwendolyn Mink wrote in a *New York Times* article, "there is no numerical threshold for harassment" (1998, p. A20). After President Clinton's admission of an "inappropriate relationship" with Monica Lewinsky, more people began to believe Paula Jones's claims and her suit gained momentum as the date for her appeal neared. With these developments and impending impeachment hearings, the Clinton camp decided the best course of action was to thwart the appeal by reaching a monetary settlement with Paula Jones. We draw the comparison between the two examples not to make some political statement or to encourage the "walking-on-eggshells" approach to the workplace, but to illustrate just how complex the hostile climate aspect of sexual harassment can be.

A Proactive Approach to Workplace Sexual Harassment

So how can an organization educate its employees, create respectful, harassment-free working climates, and protect the rights of its workers if and when harassment occurs? Everything we have experienced and read about sexual harassment calls for a proactive approach, meaning that organizations and workers shouldn't bury their heads in the sand as if sexual harassment didn't exist or couldn't happen to them or their businesses, or as if they were exempt or insulated from harassment litigation. Ignoring the problem is very risky because employers are legally liable for sexual harassment in their workplaces whether or not they knew the harassment was occurring. In fact, two U.S. Supreme Court rulings in 1998 further expanded the scope of employer liability (Casey, Desai, & Ulrich, 1998). The proactive approach we recommend for organizations involves a four-part strategy, including the development of a sexual harassment policy, the institution of a training program, use of mediation services, and the establishment and maintenance of a supportive, open communication climate.

Getting Something on Paper

While one survey shows that 9 out of 10 American companies have policies on sexual harassment, many of those policies are brief, vague, incomplete, out of date, and weak, according to Ellen Bravo, co-director of the National Association of Working Women (as in Cloud, 1998). Lax or outdated policies can greatly imperil an organization, both in terms of worker productivity and satisfaction and in potential costs of employee turnover, litigation, and settlements.

Organizations must develop clear and comprehensive policies on sexual harassment. Along with a statement of the organization's philosophical stance on workplace equality and freedom from discrimination, the policy should detail procedures for both reporting and responding to claims of sexual harassment. A thorough explanation of the range of behaviors that could constitute sexual harassment in the workplace should be provided since the policy will educate workers about sexual harassment in general and outline the organization's procedures in specific.

Management researchers Paetzold and O'Leary-Kelly (1993) suggest two other important additions to a policy: (1) a description of the variety of ways an employee can indicate that a harasser's conduct is unwelcome and offensive, and (2) a clear statement of the consequences for harassers, enumerating steps the organization will take once a claim of harassment is made or a person's behavior is called into question. Since harassment court rulings and laws continue to change, organizations should outline a procedure for a periodic review and updating of the policy.

Providing Meaningful, Useful Training

We put these adjectives in the heading because we've been to some training programs that seemed to be conducted for appearances' sake. They were offered as token attempts at dealing with a problem that they didn't really believe was a problem, but that someone else (in a higher or influential position) *said* was a problem. Have you been to sessions like this? One of the first things that reveals the seriousness of a training session is who is involved, meaning who puts on the training and who is expected (or required) to attend. For example, internal trainers may be more trusted and familiar, thereby increasing the potential for meaningful discussion of a difficult subject. However, external consultants may be viewed as more credible, with their fees signaling how seriously the organization views the subject. Probably the best situation is a mixed-sex team of trainers, so as to diminish perceptions and stereotypes linked to sex.

A mandated training program sends a different message than a voluntary program; voluntary programs sometimes suffer from low attendance because of employees' fears that they'll be perceived as either victims of harassment or as harassers who were "advised" to attend. A training program that targets lower-level employees while exempting upper levels will certainly send the wrong message. And it won't help an organization much, since research indicates that sexual harassment occurs at all levels within organizations, regardless of the salary, status, or power of an employee. Training human resources personnel and supervisors, for example, is commendable but incomplete. In an insightful chapter on effective training, communication scholar Cynthia Berryman-Fink (1993) offers this suggestion: "In addition to teaching supervisors how to recognize, detect, and deal with sexual harassment, organizations need to educate employees about professional behavior that is neither sexually intimidating nor sexually inviting" (p. 268). Training programs that include everyone in an organization will produce the best results; this includes temporary workers, who, as research documents, are especially vulnerable to workplace sexual harassment (Rogers & Henson, 1997). Finally, plans need to be instituted for repeating training sessions as an organization experiences turnover, with provisions for including sexual harassment information in new employee orientation sessions or personnel interviews.

One approach to training that has received recognition is DuPont's "A Matter of Respect" program. Role playing, videos, and groups discussions are used with employees at all levels within the company to help them understand workplace safety risks, such as sexual harassment and rape. DuPont is considered a leader in its attempts to "create policies that rely on judgment and communication rather than specific rules" (Jacobs & Bonavoglia, 1998, p. 55). The company also established a 24-hour hotline where counselors provide callers with advice and information on personal security and sexual harassment (Hayes Andrews, Herschel, & Baird, 1996). One factor that makes training programs like this a success is active participation from employees instead of delivering information in a lecture format. Since research shows that sex-based and individual differences exist in setting standards that define sexual harassment, employees need to have forums where they can comfortably discuss their perspectives (Haunani Solomon & Miller Williams, 1997).

Mediation and Communication

Organizations might want to consider the wisdom of developing in-house mediation services. Mediation is a middle step between a complaint and litigation that agencies, courts, and organizations may require. It calls for complaining parties to have a conversation—a highly structured conversation controlled (mediated) by an impartial third party. Many times situations can be rectified and compromises reached before they escalate into expensive and time-consuming lawsuits. Of course, in-house mediation services are more feasible for larger organizations than small because of the costs involved and the potential frequency of usage. But mediation services are springing up in many communities, small and large, typically offering services at no or low cost.

Finally, but probably most importantly, organizations must develop communication climates in which employees feel safe and comfortable bringing their concerns to the attention of employers. This is neither easily nor quickly accomplished in an organization. But as Paetzold and O'Leary-Kelly (1993) appropriately suggest, "Employers bear the responsibility of communicating a desexualized and degendered culture to their employees" (p. 70). Organizational leaders must continually work with managers and employees at all levels to create and foster open lines of communication so that an organizational climate is established and maintained in which concerns can be communicated. Sexual harassment is a difficult problem to discuss; for victims it is deeply personal and emotional, and often embarrassing, which makes it even harder to talk about with anyone. An organizational climate of openness—one in which female employees, in particular, know that their problems will be taken seriously—will contribute more to successful employee relations than extensive policies, great training programs, and the presence of mediators.

Whether we want to believe it or not, sexual harassment is a reality in the workplace—not in all workplaces, but in more than you'd imagine. Sometimes it arises out of ignorance, sometimes out of sincere intentions to get acquainted or to compliment, and many times out of a desire to embarrass and outpower another individual. Most of the time it comes from men and is aimed at women, but it does happen in the reverse and between same-sex individuals. The best advice research gives on this point is to communicate professionally, not personally and certainly not sexually, with all co-workers—subordinates, peers, and superiors. Sexual innuendo, the dissemination of sexual material, sexist language and jokes, excessive compliments about appearance rather than professional performance, questions about private life, requests for social contact, invasive and unwelcome nonverbal behaviors—anything of this sort basically *has no place at work*. Consultants advise, "If what you're thinking even vaguely involves sex, keep it to yourself" (Cloud, 1998, p. 52). It's best to avoid this kind of communication unless, and *only* unless, you have negotiated these "dangerous waters" with persons at work and you all feel *completely* comfortable with this kind of communication. But, as a caution, there are very few of us who feel completely comfortable with this kind of communication with all of our co-workers, across all situations, at all times. You can never really know what is in someone's mind or how someone will react.

CONCLUSION

This chapter has presented some of the more predominant issues that challenge today's working women and men. We've explored this particular context with students in mind, considering situations and concerns that may arise when students launch, restart, or redirect their careers. We've examined the current status of Affirmative Action, as well as what research says about job interviewing, on-the-job communication, advancement opportunities and barriers, and management styles. The complicated topic of sexual harassment has also been explored for its effects on work relationships and the work environment. Are you now magically equipped with a solution for every problem and a strategy for overcoming every obstacle you encounter at work? Will you be able to confront sex bias and gender-related communication perplexities with skill and ease? The answers are "probably not" to the first question, and "we hope so" to the second one.

Again, when it comes to gender communication, to the unique and complex dynamics of communication between women and men, there are no magical formulas, no sure-fire remedies, no easy answers. But by ridding your professional communication of stereotypes and personal or sexual forms of communication that are inappropriate in the workplace and by assuming a flexible, communicative style with colleagues, bosses, and clients that is not sex specific, you will have gone a long way to project a professional, successful image at work.

Key Terms

equal employment
  opportunity
Affirmative Action
relational approach
  to communication
content approach
  to communication
nonverbal bias
verbal bias
leading questions
hypothetical questions
unethical questions

double binds
second shift
Mommy track
glass ceiling
authority gap
workplace segregation
management styles
feminization of
  management
androgynous
  management style
sexual harassment

Equal Employment
  Opportunity
  Commission
quid pro quo sexual
  harassment
hostile environment
  sexual harassment
workplace romance
mediation

Discussion Starters

1. Have you formed an opinion about whether *Affirmative Action* is still necessary today or if its time has passed? Think about your own profile, considering sex, gender, race, religion, and sexual orientation. Are you a person who has benefited or will benefit from Affirmative Action? How will the job market be affected if Affirmative Action no longer exists in your state?

2. Think of a time you interviewed for a job you really wanted. It could be any kind of job—paper route, baby-sitter, part-time waiter, and so on. Now imagine yourself in that interview, but as a member of the opposite sex. Would the person who interviewed you treat you any differently? If so, how so? Do you think your sex had anything to do with getting or not getting that job?

3. In this chapter, we discussed a *double bind* for professional women—how they are "damned if they do" and "damned if they don't" act like men. Do you think this double bind is real for working women? Have you ever experienced it or do you know of a woman who has faced this kind of challenge in her job? Is there a corresponding double bind for male managers? Are there any options out of a double bind?

4. Think of a person who holds a position of power and authority in her or his job. This person might be one of your parents, your doctor, someone you've worked for, and so on. What is the sex of that person? If that person is male, do you think he'd have as much power and respect in his job if he were female? Would he have to change his communication style or the way he deals with co-workers, subordinates, and clients if he were female? If the person is female, what kinds of barriers or challenges has she faced as she achieved that position of respectability? Do you see evidence of an *authority gap* among professional people?

5. People are much more educated these days about *sexual harassment*, but do you think we've heard so much about it that we've become saturated and tend to tune out this topic? In other words, do you think the research and emphasis on sexual harassment have generated a backlash effect? If so, what should be done?

6. Think about the difference between *quid pro quo* and *hostile climate sexual harassment*. Have you ever known anyone who experienced quid pro quo harassment? Think about jobs you've had; was there anything in your workplace that someone could have interpreted as contributing to a hostile sexual environment?

7. Some people claim that sexual dynamics between women and men impede successful working relationships, meaning that sexual tension taints the workplace and undermines professional relationships. Others believe that *workplace romances* are inevitable and may lead to greater productivity on the job. What's your opinion? Do you know someone in a workplace romance whose ability to work was positively or negatively affected?

References

ALBERTS, J. K. (1992). Teasing and sexual harassment: Double-bind communication in the workplace. In L. A. M. Perry, L. H. Turner, & H. M. Sterk (Eds.), *Constructing and reconstructing gender: The links among communication, language, and gender* (pp. 185–196). Albany: State University of New York Press.

AMERICAN CIVIL LIBERTIES UNION. (1995). *Affirmative Action: Still effective, still needed in the pursuit of equal opportunity in the '90s.* New York: American Civil Liberties Union Press.

Analyzing Affirmative Action. (1995, November 17). *The Chronicle of Higher Education*, p. A6.

BERRYMAN-FINK, C. (1993). Preventing sexual harassment through male-female communication training. In G. L. Kreps (Ed.), *Sexual harassment: Communication implications* (pp. 267–280). Cresskill, NJ: Hampton.

BERRYMAN-FINK, C., & EMAN WHEELESS, V. (1987). Male and female perceptions of women as managers. In L. P. Stewart & S. Ting-Toomey (Eds.), *Communication, gender, and sex roles in diverse interaction contexts* (pp. 85–95). Norwood, NJ: Ablex.

BERRYMAN-FINK, C., & VANOVER RILEY, K. (1997). The effect of sex and feminist orientation on perceptions in sexually harassing communication. *Women's Studies in Communication, 20*, 25–44.

BLUM, L. M. (1997). Possibilities and limits of the comparable worth movement. In D. Dunn (Ed.), *Workplace/women's place: An anthology* (pp. 88–99). Los Angeles: Roxbury.

BOOHER, D. (1997). *10 smart moves for women who want to succeed in love and life.* New York: Trade Life Books.

BORISOFF, D., & MERRILL, L. (1998). *The power to communicate: Gender differences as barriers* (3rd ed.). Prospect Heights, IL: Waveland.

BURRELL, N. A., BUZZANELL, P. M., & McMILLAN, J. J. (1992). Feminine tensions in conflict situations as revealed by metaphoric analyses. *Management Communication Quarterly, 6*, 115–149.

BUZZANELL, P. M. (1992). Sex, romance, and organizational taboos. In L. A. M. Perry, L. H. Turner, & H. M. Sterk (Eds.), *Constructing and reconstructing gender: The links among communication, language, and gender* (pp. 175–184). Albany: State University of New York Press.

CASEY, T., DESAI, S., & ULRICH, J. (1998, Fall). Supreme Court unpredictable on harassment and sex. *National NOW Times*, pp. 6, 15.

CLOUD, J. (1998, March 23). Sex and the law. *Time*, 48–54.

DANIELS, T. D., SPIKER, B. K., & PAPA, M. J. (1997). *Perspectives on organizational communication* (4th ed.). Dubuque, IA: Brown & Benchmark.

DUNN, D. (1997). Introduction to the study of women and work. In D. Dunn (Ed.), *Workplace/women's place: An anthology* (pp. 1–13). Los Angeles: Roxbury.

EISENBERG, E. M., & GOODALL, H. L. JR. (1993). *Organizational communication: Balancing creativity and constraint.* New York: St. Martin's.

FEDERAL GLASS CEILING COMMISSION. (1995). *A solid investment: Making full use of the nation's human capital.* Washington, DC: U. S. Government Printing Office.

FEDERAL GLASS CEILING COMMISSION. (1997). The glass ceiling. In D. Dunn (Ed.), *Workplace/women's place: An anthology* (pp. 226–233). Los Angeles: Roxbury.

FIERMAN, J. (1990, December 17). Do women manage differently? *Fortune*, 115–117.

FINE, M. G., JOHNSON, F. L., & FOSS, K. A. (1991). Student perceptions of gender in managerial communication. *Women's Studies in Communication, 14*, 24–48.

FRANKLIN, S. (1997, March 30). The angry white male strikes back. *Corpus Christi Caller Times*, p. D4.

FRIEDAN, B. (1981). *The second stage*. New York: Summit.

GERSON, K. (1997). Combining work and motherhood. In D. Dunn (Ed.), *Workplace/women's place: An anthology* (pp. 132–149). Los Angeles: Roxbury.

GREVE, M. S. (1996, March 29). Ruling out race: A bold step to make colleges colorblind. *The Chronicle of Higher Education*, p. B2.

HAUNANI SOLOMON, D., & MILLER WILLIAMS, M. L. (1997). Perceptions of social-sexual communication at work: The effects of message, situation, and observer characteristics on judgments of sexual harassment. *Journal of Applied Communication Research, 25*, 196–216.

HAYES ANDREWS, P., HERSCHEL, R. T., & BAIRD, J. E. JR. (1996). *Organizational communication: Empowerment in a technological society*. Boston: Houghton-Mifflin.

HELGESEN, S. (1990). *The female advantage: Women's ways of leadership*. New York: Doubleday.

HORGAN, D. (1990, November-December). Why women sometimes talk themselves out of success and how managers can help. *Performance & Instruction*, 20–22.

IVY, D. K. (1993, February). *When the power lines aren't clearly drawn: A survey of peer sexual harassment*. Paper presented at the meeting of the Western States Communication Association, Albuquerque, NM.

IVY, D. K., & HAMLET, S. (1996). College students and sexual dynamics: Two studies of peer sexual harassment. *Communication Education, 45*, 149–166.

JACOBS, G., & BONAVOGLIA, A. (1998, May-June). Confused by the rules. *Ms.*, 48–55.

JONES, D. (1998, July-August). Memo to mothers at work: Stop feeling guilty! *Ms.*, 40–43.

KANTER, R. M. (1977). *Men and women of the corporation*. New York: Basic Books.

KELLY, R. M. (1997). Sex-role spillover: Personal, familial, and organizational roles. In D. Dunn (Ed.), *Workplace/women's place: An anthology* (pp. 150–160). Los Angeles: Roxbury.

KEYTON, J. (1993, November). *Examining flirting in context: Are there implications for harassment?* Paper presented at the meeting of the Speech Communication Association, Miami, FL.

KNAPP, M. L., & HALL, J. A. (1997). *Nonverbal communication in human interaction* (4th ed.). Fort Worth, TX: Harcourt Brace.

LAMUDE, K. G., & DANIELS, T. D. (1990). Mutual evaluations of communication competence in superior-subordinate relationships. *Women's Studies in Communication, 13*, 39–56.

LEDERMAN, D. (1996, April 19). Georgia's attorney general urges colleges to curb Affirmative Action. *The Chronicle of Higher Education*, p. A40.

LEONARD, R., CARROLL LING, L., HANKINS, G. A., MAIDON, C. H., POTORTI, P. F., & ROGERS, J. M. (1993). Sexual harassment at North Carolina State University. In G. L. Kreps (Ed.), *Sexual harassment: Communication implications* (pp. 170–194). Cresskill, NJ: Hampton.

MARTIN, L. (1991). *A report on the Glass Ceiling Initiative*. Washington, DC: U. S. Department of Labor.

MAY, S. K. (1997, November). *Silencing the feminine in managerial discourse*. Paper presented at the meeting of the National Communication Association, Chicago, IL.

MCDORMAN, T. F. (1998). Uniting legal doctrine and discourse to rethink women's workplace rights. *Women's Studies in Communication, 21*, 27–54.

MCKINNEY, K., & MAROULES, N. (1991). Sexual harassment. In E. Grauerholz & M. A. Koralewski (Eds.), *Sexual coercion* (pp. 29–44). Lexington, MA: Lexington Books.

MERCER, J. (1994, March 16). Assault on Affirmative Action. *The Chronicle of Higher Education*, pp. A25, A30.

MILLER, V., CASEY, M. K., LAMPHEAR-VAN HORN, M. J., & ETHINGTON, C. (1993, November). *The maternity leave as a role negotiation process: A conceptual framework*. Paper presented at the meeting of the Speech Communication Association, Miami, FL.

MINK, G. (1998, March 30). Misreading sexual harassment law. *New York Times*, p. A20.

MONGEAU, P. A., & BLALOCK, J. (1994). Student evaluations of instructor immediacy and sexually harassing behaviors: An experimental investigation. *Journal of Applied Communication Research, 22,* 256–272.

MORRISON, A. M., WHITE, R. P., & VAN VELSOR, E. (1987). *Breaking the glass ceiling: Can women reach the top of America's largest corporations?* Reading, MA: Addison-Wesley.

NACOSTE, R. W. (1995, April 7). The truth about Affirmative Action. *The Chronicle of Higher Education,* A48.

NADLER, J. K., & NADLER, L. B. (1987). Communication, gender and intraorganizational negotiation ability. In L. P. Stewart & S. Ting-Toomey (Eds.), *Communication, gender, and sex roles in diverse interaction contexts* (pp. 119–134). Norwood, NJ: Ablex.

NEHER, W. W. (1997). *Organizational communication: Challenges of change, diversity, and continuity.* Boston: Allyn & Bacon.

NELTON, S. (1997, May). Leadership for the new age. *Nation's Business,* 18–27.

PAETZOLD, R. L., & O'LEARY-KELLY, A. M. (1993). Organizational communication and the legal dimensions of hostile work environment sexual harassment. In G. L. Kreps (Ed.), *Sexual harassment: Communication implications* (pp. 63–77). Cresskill, NJ: Hampton.

PERLE MCKENNA, E. (1997). *When work doesn't work anymore: Women, work, and identity.* New York: Delacorte.

PETERS, J. K. (1997). *When mothers work: Loving our children without sacrificing ourselves.* Reading, MA: Addison-Wesley.

RAGINS, B. R. (1992). Power and subordinate evaluations of male and female leaders. In L. A. M. Perry, L. H. Turner, & H. M. Sterk (Eds.), *Constructing and reconstructing gender: The links among communication, language, and gender* (pp. 163–174). Albany: State University of New York Press.

REARDON, K. K. (1997). Dysfunctional communication patterns in the workplace: Closing the gap. In D. Dunn (Ed.), *Workplace/women's place: An anthology* (pp. 165–180). Los Angeles: Roxbury.

REILLY, M. E., LOTT, B., CALDWELL, D., & DELUCA, L. (1992). Tolerance for sexual harassment related to self-reported sexual victimization. *Gender & Society, 6,* 122–138.

RESKIN, B., & PADAVIC, I. (1994). *Women and men at work.* Thousand Oaks, CA: Pine Forge Press.

RHODE, D. L. (1997, November/December). Harassment is alive and well and living at the water cooler. *Ms.,* 28–29.

ROESNER, J. R. (1993, August 15). Ways women lead. *New York Times,* p. F6.

ROGERS, J. K., & HENSON, K. D. (1997). "Hey, why don't you wear a shorter skirt?" Structural vulnerability and the organization of sexual harassment in temporary clerical employment. *Gender & Society, 11,* 215–237.

RUBIN, L. J., & BORGERS, S. B. (1990). Sexual harassment in universities during the 1980s. *Sex Roles, 23,* 397–411.

SALTZMAN CHAFETZ, J. (1997). "I need a (traditional) wife!" Employment-family conflicts. In D. Dunn (Ed.), *Workplace/women's place: An anthology* (pp. 116–124). Los Angeles: Roxbury.

SARGENT, A. G. (1981). *The androgynous manager.* New York: AMACOM.

SCHMIDT, P. (1996, March 1). Californians likely to vote this fall on ending racial preferences. *The Chronicle of Higher Education,* p. A34.

SEGE, I. (1996, May 30). Sisters in law. *Corpus Christi Caller Times,* pp. C1, C2.

SELLERS, P. (1998, October 12). The 50 most powerful women in American business. *Fortune,* 76–130.

STEAD, D. (1997, October 26). Working women face familiar balancing act. *Corpus Christi Caller Times,* p. D3.

STEWART, L. P., & CLARKE-KUDLESS, D. (1993). Communication in corporate settings. In L. P. Arliss & D. J. Borisoff (Eds.), *Women and men communicating: Challenges and changes* (pp. 142–152). Fort Worth, TX: Harcourt Brace Jovanovich.

ST. GEORGE, D. (1995, March 19). Analysts: Affirmative Action helps white women. *Corpus Christi Caller Times,* p. A8.

TANNEN, D. (1994). *Talking from 9 to 5: How women's and men's conversational styles affect who gets heard, who gets credit, and what gets done at work.* New York: William Morrow.

TEXAS EMPLOYMENT COMMISSION. (1995, Summer-Autumn). *Equal opportunity notes.* Austin, TX: Author.

U. S. BUREAU OF LABOR STATISTICS. (1994). Washington, DC: Government Printing Office.

U. S. BUREAU OF LABOR STATISTICS. (1998). The employment situation news release. [On-line]. Available: http://stats.bls.gov

VIOLANTI, M. T. (1996). Hooked on expectations: An analysis of influence and relationships in the Tailhook reports. *Journal of Applied Communication Research, 24,* 67–82.

The wage gap. (1996, March-April). *Ms.,* 36–37.

WATKINS, P. G. (1996). Women in the work force in non-traditional jobs. In P. Lester (Ed.), *Images that injure* (pp. 69–74). Westport, CT: Praeger.

WILKINS, B. M., & ANDERSEN, P. A. (1991). Gender differences and similarities in management communication: A meta-analysis. *Management Communication Quarterly, 5,* 6–35.

WITTEMAN, H. (1993). The interface between sexual harassment and organizational romance. In L. A. M. Perry, L. H. Turner, & H. M. Sterk (Eds.), *Constructing and reconstructing gender: The links among communication, language, and gender* (pp. 27–62). Albany: State University of New York Press.

CHAPTER ELEVEN

A "CLASS ACT"

Gender Communication in Educational Settings

CASE STUDY

Stacy just transferred to a private university that was much smaller than the state school she'd attended her first year in college. She didn't really know what to expect, other than smaller classes. What she really didn't expect was how quickly she relaxed into the class, how comfortable she felt introducing herself when the professor went around the room. She actually asked the professor a question about the syllabus—on the *first* day. As the semester progressed, Stacy continued to enjoy her classes because they seemed less competitive and pressured than ones she'd had in the past. She felt like she wasn't on display, that her comments or questions didn't seem stupid to her classmates, that what she wore to class didn't matter to anyone, and that nobody cared (or particularly noticed) when she didn't wear makeup or had a "bad hair day." She actually looked forward to going to class. Stacy was learning, thriving in higher education, and her grades soared.

Javier knew college wouldn't be anything like high school, and he looked forward to the discipline of life in a military academy. That may sound strange, but Javier knew the structure and competition would be good for him. He'd been bored and a bit of a slacker in high school, but made good enough grades and scored well enough on the SAT to get admitted to a good college. It took a few weeks, but Javier adapted to the strict environment and was accepted into the corps of cadets, quite an achievement for an entering freshman. He felt less conspicuous in classes, like he didn't have to show off, be macho, or act the class clown to get attention from girls. There was competition among his classmates because everyone wanted to be right or to have the best answer for the professor, but Javier expected this. He viewed it as a challenge, one that would make him smarter and stronger. He found his subjects interesting (well, *most* of them anyway), and earned a decent grade point average in his first semester.

What's going on in these two scenarios? Does this only happen in professors' dreams? No; what you've read are accounts of students attending single-sex institutions of higher learning. This is a topic of considerable controversy, heightened by headline-grabbing cases in the mid-1990s involving two military colleges, the Citadel and the Virginia Military Institute (VMI). Because these institutions accepted public funds to operate, their all-male student status came under fire (Jaschik, 1995; Lederman, 1996).

Texas Woman's University—the country's largest university primarily for women—is concerned about the rising tide against single-sex education. (TWU is a public university that does admit men, but, historically and currently, its student body and faculty are predominantly female.) The concern was prompted (this time) by a report from the American Association of University Women (AAUW, 1998a), a national organization that conducts research on trends in education. The AAUW concluded that single-sex education was not necessarily better for girls in grades K–12 than coeducation, although they detected trends in single-sex programs that included "a heightened regard by girls for mathematics and science; an increase in girls' risk-taking; and a gain in girls' confidence from academic competence" (*Gender Mindbender,* 1998, p. 1). The controversy will no doubt continue, as opposition to single-sex education emerges from odd places such as the National Organization for Women, which believes that segregated education is discriminatory and a step in the wrong direction toward achieving gender equality (Burk, 1998).

Back to the opening scenarios for a moment: did you find yourself thinking about what it would be like to be in an all-female or all-male college classroom? Perhaps some of you are taking this course at a single-sex or predominantly one-sex, so what we describe isn't a stretch for you. But most of you attend coeducational institutions, so as this chapter explores communication and gender in mixed-sex educational settings, keep a couple of questions in mind: What if my classmates and professors were only of my same sex? How would my education be affected?

Hot Topics

- Children's fairy tales and nursery rhymes, as agents of early *gender-role socialization*
- Textbooks and other educational literature that contribute to children's ideas about sex and gender
- How sex and gender *expectations* form to affect classroom interaction and student learning
- How textbooks and communication styles affect college *classroom interaction*
- Factors that contribute to a *chilly classroom climate* for women in higher education
- Teacher and student classroom behaviors that are sex- and gender-linked
- The problem of *peer sexual harassment* in educational settings

THE SOCIALIZING EFFECTS OF SCHOOL

As you began to grow and develop, your ideas about your own sex and gender began to form. Many influences or agents of socialization shaped your ideas, the primary ones being your parents and other family members, friends, and the media. Educational institutions also provide formal lessons, as well as some important informal lessons about what being female or male means, differences and similarities between women and men, and how the sexes communicate with one another.

Do you view educational institutions as havens of equality, as places where such aspects of human diversity as gender and race are left outside the ivy-covered walls? While some of us who have made education our careers like to believe that academic institutions may be more sensitive to diversity issues than other types of organizations, no institution is exempt from discrimination. In this chapter, we examine a few forms of sexism lurking in the halls of education. Sexism—subtle and not-so-subtle—in such an influential socializing agent as school has to have an effect on the individual. As you read the information in this chapter, weigh it against your own experience in educational settings—from preschool to junior high to your college career. Consider the contributions of your education and your educators to your attitudes and communication with women and men.

CHILDREN'S LITERATURE AND GENDER-ROLE SOCIALIZATION

When we think back to childhood, many experiences come to mind—some good, maybe some not so good. Do your fonder memories include the stories a parent read you before you went to sleep or stories you read with a teacher and classmates as part of your early education? Can you remember imagining yourself as one of the characters of a particular story? Did you ever want to be Gretel, who saves her brother by pushing the witch into the oven, or the prince who kisses Snow White and awakens her from her poison-induced sleep? Maybe it seems silly to think about these things now, but it's possible that who you are as an adult—your view of self, others, relationships, and communication within those relationships—has been affected in some way by the early lessons you received from children's literature at home and at school. Those early lessons are part of *gender-role socialization*, meaning the way messages about what it means to be female or male affect your attitudes, self-concept, and development throughout your life.

Fairy Tales, Nursery Rhymes, and Gender Roles

We know what you're thinking: "Hey, don't go getting all analytical with my favorite kids' stories." We ask you to try to suspend any doubts or disbelief for just a moment to consider the potential effects of reading or hearing a number of stories with the same basic plot. The young, beautiful, helpless, or abandoned girl encounters a series of obstacles (events or people) that place her in jeopardy. Enter the young, handsome, usually wealthy prince or king who rescues and marries the girl. With minor deviations, this basic theme serves as the plot for such fairy tales as *Cinderella, Snow White and the Seven Dwarfs, Sleeping Beauty, Goldilocks and the Three Bears, Little Red Riding Hood,* and *Rapunzel,* to name only a few of the more well-known tales in American folk culture. The attributes of female leading characters in such tales include beauty, innocence, passivity, patience (since they often have to wait a long time for the prince to come), dependence, powerlessness, and self-sacrifice (Bottigheimer, 1986). Male characters as rescuers have to be handsome, independent, brave, strong, action oriented, successful, romantic, and kind-hearted (for the most part). Does this characterization seem overdrawn to you? Do the characters' descriptors reflect stereotypical male-female traits? What's the potential effect of these depictions?

Once Upon a Time: Fairy Tale Stereotypes

Researchers continue to examine the effects of stereotypical, sexist portrayals in fairy tales, especially Disney tales that are alternatively criticized for their biased depictions of female roles and praised for their occasional themes of feminine empowerment (Addison, 1995; Sells, 1995; Trites, 1991; Zipes, 1995). With specific regard for effects on girls, gender scholar Sharon Downey (1996) suggests: "The fairy tale's popularity in children's literature is unsurpassed. Their joint universalizing and culture-specific themes contribute to the process of 'civilizing' society's young because fairy tales encourage conformity to culturally-sanctioned roles. The 'truths' validated through folktales, however, often reinforce disparaging images of females" (p. 185). Researcher Marcia Lieberman (1986) contends that "Millions of women must surely have formed their psycho-sexual self-concepts, and their ideas of what they could or could not accomplish, what sort of behavior would be rewarded, and of the nature of reward itself, in part from their favorite fairy tales. These stories have been made the repositories of the dreams, hopes, and fantasies of generations of girls" (p. 187).

Author Karen Rowe (1986) discusses the relationship between fantasy and reality in storybook characters and relationships that may become a standard of how life is "supposed to be." She explains, "Subconsciously, women may transfer from fairy tales into real life cultural norms which exalt passivity, dependency, and self-sacrifice as a female's cardinal virtues. In short, fairy tales perpetuate the patriarchal status quo by making female subordination seem a romantically desirable, indeed an inescapable fate" (p. 209). Although not the focus of these scholars' analyses, male consumers of such fiction may form standards for their own behavior, as well as for the behavior of women in relationships, based on idealized characterizations.

To make these scholars' claims more concrete, consider the story of Cinderella, the beautiful girl who was terrorized and subjugated by her evil stepmother and two stepsisters after her father's death. She lives virtually as a slave until a benevolent fairy godmother hears her crying, transforms her, and

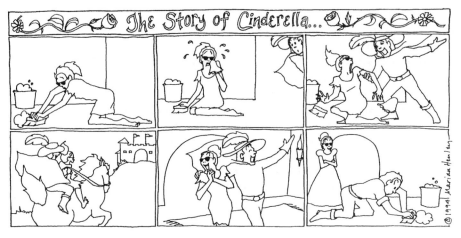

Maxine! Comix by Marian Henley. Reprinted by permission of the artist.

sends her to the prince's ball. Everyone in the land knows that the handsome prince is searching for a wife, so all the eligible women are decked out and positioned at the ball in order to win the prince's favor. You know how the story turns out: Cinderella steals the show and loses her slipper as she exits the ball, causing the prince to search for her. He is reunited with Cinderella because of her tiny, feminine shoe size, after which he punishes her stepfamily and triumphantly marries Cinderella.

Both Rowe and Lieberman draw some themes from this tale and others. First, the main characters must be physically attractive to be worthy of romance. Does this tell young children that only beautiful people deserve to find love and romance? The second theme is one of competition; that is, the primary female character must often compete with other women for the attention and affection of the hero. This message runs counter to the female tendency to cooperate rather than compete to accomplish goals. And third, rewards for stereotypically sex-linked behavior include romance, marriage, often wealth, and a happy-ever-after life. This may reinforce a message to girls that the ultimate goal in life is to marry a wonderful man who will protect them and make their lives completely happy. There's nothing necessarily wrong with this goal, but is it the *only* appropriate goal? Could it communicate too much importance on having a relationship, especially on getting married, rather than exploring a range of options for fulfillment? Since many women (even the most postmodern of modern women) describe the pressure they feel to be in a relationship and to partner, it's important to examine where those thoughts originated.

Living Happily Ever After: Effects on Relationships

Before you conclude that this examination of traditional fairy tales is gender paranoia or an affront to American folk history, consider some adult variations on the themes. Why do you think so many people worldwide tuned in to the marriage ceremony of Prince Charles and Lady Diana? Many viewers were caught up in the romantic events—the beautiful, innocent girl swept off her feet by a modern-day prince; the stately, elegant ceremony; the romantic exit in a horse-drawn carriage. The princess and prince roles seemed fairly clear at that time, but then the world watched the fairy tale fracture as the couple's royal relationship disintegrated, the princess and the prince divorced, and, with Diana's untimely death, this fairy tale ended for all time.

For another example, why do romance novels constitute such a huge and profitable industry? Could it be that romance novels are mere extensions of the romantic themes we learned first as children reading fairy tales? Even though life isn't often like the fairy tales, do we still want to believe that relationships can be like that? Do we hold these idealized images of women, men, and romantic love as some sort of standard for how relationships really ought to be? What happens to people when the ideal and the reality don't intersect? Rowe's (1986) perspective on this issue is illuminating:

> Precisely this close relationship between fantasy and reality, art and life, explains why romantic tales have in the past and continue in the present to influence so significantly female expectations of their role in patriarchal cultures. Even in the "liberated" twentieth century, many women internalize romantic patterns from ancient tales. Although conscious that all men are not princes and some are unconvertible beasts and that she isn't a princess, even in disguise, still the female dreams of that "fabulous man." But as long as modern women continue to tailor their aspirations and capabilities to conform with romantic paradigms, they will live with deceptions, disillusionments, and/or ambivalences. (p. 222)

So you're wondering: "What's this have to do with me?" Maybe you're actually one of the lucky few, one of those people whose relational life has turned out like a fairy tale. (We don't know any people or relationships like this, but we acknowledge the possibility.) But have you ever thought that maybe these early, idealized images of what men and women were supposed to be for one another generated some unattainable standards for your adult life? Maybe they didn't create exaggerated expectations, but the gap between the ideal and the real may cause you disappointment and disillusionment because life and relationships just didn't turn out the way you thought they were supposed to.

For example, think about a man who grew up believing that his role as provider and protector and his superior strength and independence were characteristics that would "win" women for him, characteristics that would allow him to "rescue" the fairer sex. What happens when he confronts a liberated, independent, self-sufficient woman? She may not need rescuing or protecting; she may be stronger and more independent than he is or than he expected. His efforts at rescuing may turn her off. Or she may feel in need of rescuing when they first meet, only to lose interest in him later. So what happens to his version of "ideal"? Consider the outcome for a woman who believes that some dashing, princelike figure on a white steed will come charging up to rescue her from life's more unpleasant circumstances. What happens when women expect princelike qualities, when they form expectations of men that are too high and all-encompassing for virtually any man to fulfill? What happens if the "prince" turns into a "beast"? One of the few things you get to see in fairy tales is what happens *after* the marriage ceremony; you only get the "happily ever after" closing line.

Obviously, many people cope with incongruencies of life and fantasy. Most people don't live their lives in complete frustration because relationships don't mirror the movies or romance novels or childhood fairy tales. We learn—sometimes the hard way—that perfect people and perfect relationships are neither possible, nor particularly interesting for that matter. We come to learn that the imperfections and the struggles are more worth our interest and energy than something we could call "ideal." But should we have to work to dismiss the early images? Could the early stories we're exposed to as children better prepare us for the realities we will soon encounter? Could the female and male characters represent more positive, balanced, realistic images of persons we'll likely deal with as we age and mature?

Contemporary Attempts at Unbiased Children's Literature

Some writers of children's literature are attempting to counter the stereotypical images found in traditional fairy tales and nursery rhymes. Consider the following examples:

Jack and Jill Be Nimble
Jack be nimble, Jack be quick,
Jack jump over the candlestick!
Jill be nimble, jump it too,
If Jack can do it, so can you! (*Father Gander,* Larche, 1985)

The Old Couple Who Lived in a Shoe
There was an old couple who lived in a shoe,
They had so many children they didn't know what to do.
So they gave them some broth and some good whole wheat bread,
And kissed them all sweetly and sent them to bed.
There's only one issue I don't understand
If they didn't want so many why didn't they plan? (*Father Gander,* Larche, 1985)

Have you ever heard these versions of two well-known nursery rhymes? They represent one author's attempts to "ungenderize" traditional children's nursery rhymes. Doug Larche (aka, Father Gander) published a book of rewritten, unbiased nursery rhymes in an attempt to alter the adherence to sex-stereotypical portrayals of male and female characters. *Father Gander* has been extremely successful among parents who are concerned about perpetuating limited, discriminatory stereotypes of men and women. Another author, Jack Zipes (1986), produced a volume of fairy tales written from feminist perspectives that don't perpetuate sex stereotypes. Sources exist to help parents and teachers locate stories with more realistic, bias-free characterizations and story lines. One such source is *Let's Hear It for the Girls,* a guidebook to 375 books featuring girls in strong, problem-solving, adventurous, and brave roles (as in Spratling, 1997).

One school is using fairy tale literature as an opportunity to teach students to think critically. Teachers at the Longfellow School in Teaneck, New Jersey, indulge students by reading *Cinderella* in class, but the reading is followed by questions designed to elicit students' insights into the characterizations and plot. Such questions as "Will Cinderella be happy after she and the prince are married?" and "Wouldn't it be better if Cinderella had wanted other things to make her happy?" are posed to get students thinking beyond the "happily ever after" ending (Sunstein Hymowitz, 1991).

Do these efforts seem like a stretch to you, as if people are trying to find harm in the most innocent of places? Students sometimes balk at the notion that children's literature contributes to sex-role stereotyping and gender bias. Have you ever thought that the early stories and nursery rhymes you were exposed to had an effect on your expectations and communication behavior, especially with members of the opposite sex? If you have children, what kinds of literature do you read with them? If you don't yet have children but would like to some day, think about how fairy tales, nursery rhymes, and other forms of literature might affect them. What decisions will you make when you get to that point?

Gender Depiction in Textbooks and Educational Literature for Children

Gender bias in children's textbooks and supplemental educational literature emerges in several ways, primarily in the numbers of depictions of and references to men versus women and in stereotypical role portrayals of characters (Cooper, 1993; Tetenbaum & Pearson, 1989).

Depictions Speak Louder than Words

In her groundbreaking book, *Reviving Ophelia: Saving the Selves of Adolescent Girls,* Mary Pipher (1994) reports that only one-seventh of all illustrations in children's textbooks are of girls. And, according to Pipher, "Girls are exposed to almost three times as many boy-centered stories as girl-centered stories. Boys tend to be portrayed as clever, brave, creative and resourceful, while girls are depicted as kind, dependent and docile. Girls read six times as many biographies of males as of females. Even in animal stories, the animals are twice as likely to be males" (p. 62).

Education researcher Melissa Steineger (1993) contends, "Bias in classroom materials, from literature to math books, is pervasive despite almost 20 years of efforts to balance curriculum materials. The consequences of bias in literature and textbooks can be a limitation of aspirations for girls" (p. E1). Steineger lists six common forms of sex bias in instructional materials: exclusion of women and girls, stereotyping of members of both sexes, degradation and subordination of girls and women, isolation of materials on women, superficial attention paid to contemporary social problems, and cultural inaccuracies. According to instructional communication scholar Pamela Cooper

(1993), male characters, figures, and pictures, and references to male authors still greatly outnumber those of females in current public school textbooks.

Dick and Jane: Slow to Change

In a study of award-winning children's books, Cooper (1991b) found that between the years of 1967 and 1987, a mere 14 of 97 books depicted female characters who worked outside the home. According to research, the old "Dick and Jane" breadwinner-homemaker images and sex-typed behaviors are alive and well in children's literature (Cooper, 1987; Heintz, 1987; Peterson & Lach, 1990; White, 1986). Cooper cites various examples from textbooks for such content areas as science, economics, mathematics, and history. She describes a speech communication text that offers such hypothetical applications of communication skills as a woman making an announcement in a PTA meeting while a man argues a case in court. These images reinforce the roles that many children see operating in their own worlds. But they may also offer false, stereotypical images that are inconsistent with reality. Think of the impact of what a child reads in school, how that reading material can shape a child's vision of what is "right," acceptable, or "normal" in life. What if, for example, a child grows up in a single-parent household in which the parent must hold down multiple jobs just to make ends meet? How can this child compare "Dick and Jane" portrayals to her or his own existence? How "normal" does life look in comparison to what that child reads?

Some alternative reading materials are being produced to widen the range of experience for schoolchildren; however, wading through the bureaucracy to gain acceptance in the school systems can be a time-consuming task. Peggy Orenstein (1997), author of *SchoolGirls: Young Women, Self-Esteem, and the Confidence Gap,* describes one California school system's use of gender-inclusive and ethnically diverse history texts. These students' required English writing includes an essay about abortion, and they read *Streams to the River, River to the Sea,* a historical novel in which Sacagawea is presented as a courageous hero. Another popular alternative to male-dominated textbooks is *My Daddy is a Nurse,* a supplemental reader for elementary grades that depicts nontraditional career paths and roles for men and women. Other titles include *Dear America,* a series of diary readings portraying women's historical contributions; *Mothers Can Do Anything,* a book by Joe Lasker that describes mothers in traditional and nontraditional jobs; *Winning Kicker,* Thomas Dygard's story of a girl who joins a boys' football team; and Bette Greene's *Philip Hall Likes Me, I Reckon Maybe,* a story about an enduring friendship between a girl and a boy (Steineger, 1993; Vinnedge, 1996).

In some cases, however, schools disapprove of books with modern depictions of alternative lifestyles. One such book is entitled *Daddy's Roommate* by Michael Willhoite. This book has stirred up a great deal of controversy across the country, since it is about a young boy whose parents divorce because the father is gay. Its intention is to teach young children how to cope with having

---

RECAP

---

single-sex education, co-education, gender-role socialization, fairy tales, nursery rhymes, stereotypical roles, textbooks, educational literature

---

a homosexual parent or parents. One passage from the book explains, "Mommy says Daddy and Frank are gay. At first I didn't know what that meant. So she explained it. Being gay is just one more kind of love. And love is the best kind of happiness. Daddy and his roommate are very happy together. And I'm happy too!" (Willhoite, as in Seese, 1992, p. 1B) Children's books such as this one that depict or attempt to explain adult situations are often deemed too controversial for adoption by a school district. What's your opinion? Should the decision to expose children to such reading material and enlighten them on forms of diversity in American culture best be made by schools or left to parents' discretion?

Can you imagine what your reaction would have been to some of these contemporary books when you were in grade school? What would have been your mother's or father's reaction? Some of you may have already dealt with such controversies while raising your own children. How do you or have you used reading material to educate your children about the roles of the sexes in society? For students yet to raise children, how do you think you will approach this issue when you have kids? It's important to consider the kinds of subtle messages you may pass on to future generations, either by what you allow your children to read or how you react to what they read in school. We're not insinuating that there's a "correct" message, but it's important to be aware that children get some kind of message from books and stories, just as they do from the programs they watch on television.

EDUCATIONAL EXPECTATIONS AND GENDER BIAS IN THE CLASSROOM

Teachers and students come to the educational setting with their own sets of beliefs, values, opinions, and experiences, some of which relate to sex and gender. Here we use both terms *sex* and *gender* because attitudes generally go beyond mere biology, or sex. Attitudes apply to such things as one's view of appropriate roles for women and men in society, what is deemed masculine and feminine behavior, and how sexual orientation affects the picture. These are components of gender, as we have used the term throughout this text. So no one begins an education with a clean slate; we all approach educational situations and contexts with imprints of our experiences. However, when we allow these imprints to lead us to rigid expectations about the aptitude and appropriate behavior of the sexes, bias may be the result.

Expectations about Academic Achievement: The Early Years

In Chapter 2 we discussed some of the brain studies that suggest differences between the sexes. However, studies do not indicate that girls and boys have differing learning potential. Gender scholars Borisoff and Merrill (1998) contend: "Although girls' and boys' potential for academic learning is equal, several studies suggest that expectations for academic achievement exert a potent influence on the extent to which a child's potential is fulfilled" (p. 83). With effective instruction, equal opportunities to acquire quality education, unbiased expectations from teachers and parents, and coaching and encouragement free from sex-based stereotypes, boys and girls both can achieve extraordinary things.

Sex and Gender as Parts of the Picture

Research in the 1980s and early 1990s consistently showed that the elements necessary for equal achievement by boys and girls were not in place (Brophy, 1983; Cooper & Good, 1983; Dusek & Joseph, 1983). In one study, teachers of grades 1 through 12 read descriptions of male and female students, high-achieving female and male students, and low-achieving male and female students. They then assigned each description a masculine, feminine, androgynous, or undifferentiated label, based on scores from the Bem Sex Role Inventory (explained in Chapter 2). Results showed that, across female and male teachers and across grade levels, teachers more often expected high-achieving students to be masculine or androgynous and low-achieving students to be feminine or undifferentiated, regardless of student sex. The researchers concluded that "If teachers expect girls to be feminine and boys to be masculine, the results clearly show what playing the roles can mean in terms of academic behavior" (Benz, Pfeiffer, & Newman, 1981, p. 298).

Sex differences in schoolchildren's levels of self-esteem are consistently documented, with girls suffering more self-esteem loss than boys. A survey of 3,000 schoolchildren showed that self-esteem decreases between elementary grades and high school, evidenced in students' responses to such items as "I am happy the way I am," "I like most things about myself," and "I wish I were

> *Instead of being presented with stereotypes by age, sex, color, class, or religion, children must have the opportunity to learn that within each range, some people are loathsome and some are delightful.*
>
> *Margaret Mead, anthropologist*

somebody else" (American Association of University Women, 1991). Myra and David Sadker, authors of the excellent book, *Failing At Fairness: How America's Schools Cheat Girls* (1994), describe boys' self-esteem as a "self-esteem slide," but girls' self-esteem as a "free-fall" (p. 77). This self-esteem loss often stays with a student throughout college (and beyond), and profoundly affects achievement, curriculum choices, and, ultimately, career decisions.

Sadker and Sadker (1994) explain the sex difference in self-esteem levels by pointing to such factors as boys feeling better able to do things than girls. Girls' beliefs in their own abilities declines steadily over the course of their education. Another factor is the differential reinforcement boys receive from athletics, which helps them cope with changes in their bodies better than girls. (This is changing as more and more school systems, as well as colleges and universities, recognize the impact of athletic accomplishment on students' self-esteem.) Other factors relate to girls' concerns about being popular and liked by boys, compounded by mediated images of "perfect" girls and women, which encourage young girls to focus on appearance rather than intelligence. A huge factor is the different treatment the sexes receive in classrooms, as we examine later in the chapter.

Problems in the "Hard" Sciences

Studies continue to examine achievement differences among school girls and boys in such areas as math, science, and computer literacy. Most of this research shows that male students are more likely to achieve in math, science, engineering, and other areas that rely on problem-solving ability, while female students typically shy away from these areas (Lakes Matyas, 1997; Sadker & Sadker, 1994). This aversion to math and science begins early on in a girl's education. Researcher Catherine Paglin (1993) summarizes results of studies on this problem as follows:

- Boys receive more encouragement from adults to take math and science
- Boys have more out-of-school experiences related to math and science
- Girls do not find role models in classes or texts
- In laboratory situations, boys tend to do the experiments while girls fall into the role of recorder
- Teachers give less attention to girls
- Girls lack self-confidence in math and science, perceiving it as too difficult, unfeminine, and not relevant (p. E6).

Here's an example that illustrates the problem. The Mattel Corporation produced Teen Talk Barbie in 1992; one the first lines they put in the doll's mouth was "Math class is tough." The *Washington Post* quickly dubbed the doll "Foot-in-Mouth Barbie" and the AAUW, along with math teachers across the country, registered their disgust (Unger & Crawford, 1996).

Since adults create such products, it is clear that some adults (parents and teachers) also carry the attitude that "math is too hard for girls" or "math and science are unfeminine." In turn, they subtly and not-so-subtly communicate these attitudes to female and male students in the schools. The detrimental effects on young female students are obvious, in that girls may believe that they cannot and should not achieve in math and science. The effects may also be negative on boys, in that they often feel pressured by the expectation that they are supposed to excel in math and science. What if they're just not very good at math or science, or they *just don't like these subjects*? Should girls feel less feminine and boys feel less masculine, just because of some manufactured expectation of what they should achieve?

Closing a Few Gender Gaps

But with all this bad news, there is also some good news. A report by the American Association of University Women (1998b) shows that girls have finally closed the gap with boys in math and science achievement. This finding, first, suggests that information about differential expectations, gender-stereotypical treatment, and resulting achievement has permeated schools throughout the country. Teachers, counselors, and parents are realizing the disservice done to girls and boys when sex- and gender-typed expectations are imposed on scholastic achievement. We credit such significant works as Sadker and Sadker's *Failing At Fairness* (1985), Mary Pipher's book, *Reviving Ophelia* (1994), and the ongoing work of the AAUW for advancing American culture and education on these fronts. Second, the finding is an affirmation of the many teachers and parents who embody feminist ideals (whether or not they call themselves feminists) and have communicated balanced messages and instilled values of equality in children.

The AAUW (1998b) report does show, however, that girls still lag behind boys in interest and competence in computer science. Janice Weinman, Executive Director of the AAUW, explained: "Girls have narrowed some significant gender gaps, but technology is now the new 'boy's club' in our nation's public schools. While boys program and problem solve with computers, girls use computers for word processing, the 1990s version of typing" (AAUW, 1998c, p. 1). Computers were supposed to be gender-neutral and to level the academic playing field. However, research reveals that three-fourths of children enrolled in computer camps in the 1980s were males; three times as many male students as female students entered school with prior, at-home computer instruction; and the primary figures in educational and recreational computer games are male (Borisoff & Merrill, 1998; Nelson & Watson, 1991; Sadker & Sadker, 1994).

As a result of these trends, efforts have been made to encourage girls' achievement in computer skills, including girls' computer institutes and programs and projects for math and science teachers, like the Computer Equity Expert Project funded by the National Science Foundation (Paglin, 1993). Some researchers indicate that it is not a question of aptitude that causes girls to achieve less than boys in computer science; rather, it is a question of interest. Paglin (1993) explains how bias in computer software, in such forms as "shoot 'em up themes" and explosions as rewards for correct answers, turns off girls. She cites a math teacher who attended the National Science

Foundation's project as saying, "Girls are more attracted to software that shows relevance to the real world and stresses cooperation to achieve goals" (p. E6). Our hopes are that, given the efforts to gender-neutralize computers, we can report a different trend early in the new millennium.

Expectations about Academic Achievement: The College Years

The expectations communicated to us as schoolchildren have profound effects—so profound that they tend to follow us into our college years. It's hard to "un-learn" an early message that "poetry is for girls" and "math is for boys." But, just like most things in life, those early expectations become more complex and have more serious implications as one ages.

What Does This Professor Expect from Me?

Did you ever sit in a classroom and feel like the teacher had formed an expectation about you before you even had a chance to open your mouth? Did you sense in high school, for example, that a teacher had labeled you a "jock," "bad girl," or "nerd" and then acted toward you based on that label? Did you ever feel that a teacher thought you were a C student in a class and that no matter how hard you tried or what you said or did, you were going to get a C in that class? These things point to the impact of expectations on achievement and enjoyment in a classroom setting, but how do sex and gender fit into the expectations picture?

One study examined whether sex was a factor in the evaluation of students' writing. Readers critiqued two students' essays—one with an unidentified writer and one that identified the sex of the writer. Reflecting a bias and stereotype that women are better at language skills, readers inflated grades when they knew they were reading a female-authored essay, compared to essays in which the author's sex was unknown. Similarly, readers who knew they were reading a male-authored essay gave lower evaluations than when they did not know the sex of the writer (Haswell & Haswell, 1995). This is one example of the kind of sex bias that can endanger someone's academic success.

If you're a male reader, have you ever experienced treatment from a female college professor that conveyed to you a specific expectation, merely because you were male? You might have picked up an attitude like, "You're a man, so you'll think like a man and probably be a chauvinist or a potential harasser. You probably won't respond to this material as well as the women." Maybe you sensed an attitude that communicated that you were more highly valued than female students in a class, simply because you were male. Or what about with teachers of your same sex? Did you ever feel like a male professor expected you to agree or comply with his terms, simply because of some expectation of male camaraderie ? Did you ever feel like a male professor was harder on you than he was on your female counterparts?

For the female readers, did you ever feel like a male professor held expectations of how women were going to approach his course content and how they were going to achieve in the class, in comparison to male students? Think about a more obvious example—the lone female student in an engineering class full of male students and taught by a male professor. Gender or sex bias might not necessarily exist in that classroom, but then again, it might. Conversely, did you ever feel that a female professor expected you to agree with her information and views, just because of some standard of sisterhood? What happened when you voiced a dissenting opinion or interpretation? These are just a few hypothetical examples of how teacher expectations can affect your involvement, appreciation, and achievement in a class.

What Does This Student Expect from Me?

Student expectations also play a role in this process. The female co-author of your text works hard to "ungenderize" herself, meaning that she has encountered some students in gender and interpersonal communication courses who diminish or write off her information as unimportant, thinking it stems from a "woman's agenda." Many feminist instructors around the country describe similar problems: When they teach a controversial course like gender communication, they are viewed as women with a feminist agenda, rather than professors who present cutting-edge information to make their students think. Female instructors also occasionally feel that students hold them up to more scrutiny in the classroom than male colleagues, as if to say "Show me what you know." Some female teachers envy what they perceive to be male teachers' "instant credibility." However, the male co-author of your text has also sensed that female and male students alike entered his communication classes with a "show me" attitude because he is male and communication is considered more of a women's field than a man's. In gender communication classes, in particular, he occasionally senses an attitude from students that translates into, "So what would *you* know about sex discrimination? You're a man in a man's world."

Communication researchers Lawrence Nadler and Marjorie Keeshan Nadler (1990) focused on college students' perceptions of their own and their instructors' classroom behavior as a means of examining how expectations are translated into behaviors. Their results indicated that students brought expectations regarding the behaviors of female and male instructors into class with them. Specifically, "male instructors were depicted as more dominant . . . while female instructors were viewed as more supportive than their male counterparts" (p. 60).

However, expectations of teacher behavior did not vary according to the sex of the student. The Nadlers report that "students did not believe they were treated differently by instructors based on sex and reported few differences in their own class-related communication behavior" (p. 60). They conclude, "Clearly, perceptions of sex-related differences in patterns of classroom communication in the college setting exist. Awareness of the nature and impact of the sex-related communication patterns is a necessary condition for beneficially altering these practices in the college classroom" (p. 3). Knowing that gender-biased expectations may possibly emerge in a classroom is useful

---

RECAP

sex bias, gender bias, learning potential, expectations, stereotypes

---

information, but just what are these "practices" to which research refers? Just how do instructors and students communicate a sense of sex and gender bias via their classroom behavior?

GENDER COMMUNICATION AND THE COLLEGE CLASSROOM

The history of higher education in America reveals a predominantly male domain. For an interesting account of the struggle women faced when they "invaded" male-dominated higher education, we refer you to Chapter 2 of Sadker and Sadker's excellent book, *Failing At Fairness: How America's Schools Cheat Girls* (1994). Even only a few years ago, it was clear that the ideal of equality for men and women was not achieved in the average college classroom. Through the 1950s, '60s, and into the '70s, men and women had very different educational opportunities. For example, one of your authors overheard a male professor in 1973 say, "Women are not capable of teaching at the college level and should not be admitted to doctoral programs." Certain fields (for example, engineering and accounting) were completely male domains. Women were guided to elementary school teaching, nursing, and home economics. A standard joke of that time period (and you still hear it some today) was that, "Women come to college to get their MRS. degree."

How much has changed in the past few decades? While some advances have been made, there is still significant evidence of gender bias in universities. As researchers Wellhousen and Yin (1997) describe, "Gender bias is so prevalent in American society and classrooms that it often goes undetected" (p. 35). For example, how many contributions by women in history are you likely to study in the typical American History course, in comparison to men's contributions? Is this because of sheer numbers, as in the assumption that simply because there were more key men in history than women, it's appropriate for men to be studied more than women? Were there *really* more key male figures in history than female? Perhaps it's all in how you define the term *key*. Many times students aren't aware of women's contributions until they take a women's history course, which to many seems a token gesture that assumes all other history courses are men's history courses.

How close are we to the ideal of equality in education? As a student, do you believe that women and men have equal opportunities to communicate in the average college classroom? That they receive similar treatment from professors? That they have equal access to careers? Research reviewed below suggests that men and women do not have the same experiences in the classroom, which has a profound impact on their education. What occurs at colleges and universities that contributes to this situation?

Sex Bias in Textbooks

A significant contributing factor to sex bias in education is the reading material used in courses. Textbooks are prime examples of subtle, but pervasive sex bias and sex-role stereotyping. Studies in the 1980s, for example, revealed that science texts included approximately three times as many pictures of men than women and that adult women were almost never presented in scientific roles (Nilsen, 1987). Education researcher Balzer (1989) remarked, "If women do not see women in science, if their teachers are 95 percent men, and if textbooks are predominantly male, they won't go into science unless they're specifically out to break down those barriers" (p. 33). In these texts, men controlled the action and women watched the action; boys performed experiments, girls cleaned up. Sadker and Sadker (1980) found that the predominance of teacher education textbooks available at the time devoted less than 1 percent of book space to issues of gender equity. They concluded, "Using these college texts, tomorrow's teachers would actually learn to be more sexist" (as in Sadker & Sadker, 1994, p. 174).

Has the problem continued into the 1990s? Cooper (1993) concludes that "despite the adoption of nonsexist guidelines during the past decade, textbook publishers have made relatively few changes to increase the viability of females and decrease the stereotyping of males and females . . . 'Nonbiased' material is sometimes added to the center or end of a text, without any attempt to integrate it into the overall format of the rest of the book" (p. 125). Sadker and Sadker (1994) describe token attempts to inject women and their accomplishments into college textbooks. They cite English literature texts of "great works" that devote only 15 percent of their content to women writers (and there have been great women writers throughout history). Other texts include devices that "give a nod" to women's issues and experiences, such as sections or boxes within chapters called "Female Authors," "Famous Women Scientists," and "American Diversity: Founding Mothers" (p. 176).

Many texts from such disciplines as psychology, economics, sociology, and art rarely mention names of female contributors to these fields. But it's not just whether women are depicted in textbook illustrations or discussed in the content; the use of masculine language as generics to stand for all people reveals sexism as well. Communication textbooks are not immune to sex-stereotyped behavior, although improvements have been made, particularly in the use of nonsexist language. Since such key groups as the American Psychological Association and the National Council of Teachers of English established guidelines for nonsexist language usage (in 1977 and 1975, respectively), textbooks have begun to equalize their language. Back in 1975, communication scholar Jo Sprague (1975) reported that most public speaking texts only featured speeches by men. While still far from creating an equal picture, most current public speaking texts provide examples of female speakers' accomplishments, such as Barbara Jordan's and Ann Richards's keynote speeches at Democratic Party conventions, Elizabeth Dole's and Susan Molinari's speeches at the 1996 Republican Party convention, and various presentations by Hillary Rodham Clinton.

As you move through your college career, it might be interesting to examine your textbooks for evidence of sex or gender bias. Which sex is represented more in examples and illustrations within a text? Does a text treat both sexes equally in discussing applications of the material or careers? Does it offer other ways of thinking than what might be considered the traditional male pattern? Does it use nonsexist language, meaning that *she* and *he* both appear as personal pronouns? Reading textbooks with these questions in mind may help point out examples where the ideal we allude to is still not being met.

The "Chill" in Higher Education: Students' Classroom Communication

In the ideal college classroom, students of both sexes participate with about the same frequency, ask similar amounts and types of questions, and actively engage in their own learning. However, research over three decades indicates this has not been the case; student participation continues to be far from ideal, in terms of sex-based behavior.

"Ice Age" Research

Research in the 1970s found that men more often dominated class discussions, while women were less verbally aggressive (Karp & Yoels, 1977; Rich, 1979; Sternglanz & Lyberger-Ficek, 1977; Thorne, 1979). Interest in these kinds of differences accelerated throughout the 1980s. Research found that most classrooms tended to favor a traditionally male approach to learning and devalued or disconfirmed a traditionally female approach (Belenky, Clinchy, Goldberger, & Tarule, 1986; Gilligan, 1982; Treichler & Kramarae, 1983). Studies showed that male students initiated more interactions of greater length with teachers than female students; interrupted professors and other students significantly more often than women, particularly in female-taught classes; and were more likely to control such nonverbal aspects as physical space in a classroom (Brooks, 1982; Brophy, 1985; Krupnick, 1985; Sandler & Hall, 1986). These behaviors have a silencing effect on female students.

Differences in female and male students' communication in college classrooms and the way professors communicated with these students were so pronounced that they gave rise to the term *chilly climate* as a descriptor for academic settings (Hall & Sandler, 1982, 1984; Sandler & Hall, 1986). Educational researchers Roberta Hall and Bernice Sandler described the difficulties women faced in the average college classroom in the 1980s—difficulties most men did not face. Research they reviewed on classroom interaction determined the following:

1. Men talked more than women.
2. Men talked for longer periods and took more turns at speaking.
3. Men exerted more control over the topic of conversation.
4. Men interrupted women much more frequently than women interrupted men.
5. Men's interruptions of women more often introduced trivial or inappropriately personal comments that brought the women's discussion to an end or changed its focus.

Hall and Sandler concluded that women were not given the same opportunity as men to express themselves, verbally and nonverbally, in the average college classroom.

Little Evidence of a Thaw

A 1996 report from the National Association for Women in Education reaffirmed the presence of the chilly climate on college campuses. One of the report's authors, Bernice Sandler, asserts, "The classroom is still quite chilly, but we have more ideas about how to warm it up" (as in Gose, 1996, p. A38). For example, the report describes how male students tend to blurt out answers to teachers' questions, while female students take time to gather their thoughts before raising their hands to be recognized by a teacher. You could interpret these behaviors as male enthusiasm on the one hand or dominance on the other; as female passivity and powerlessness, or thoughtfulness and depth. No matter the interpretation, the report recommends that professors wait a few seconds before taking responses from students or that they pose questions directly to female students in order to balance male contributions.

Instructional scholars believe that higher education is still strongly influenced by this tradition of male dominance (Bowker & Regan Dunkin, 1992; Wood & Lenze, 1991). Cooper (1993) contends that "an enormous amount of differential treatment, with regard to both the academic and social climate for women still exists in some form at all institutions" (p. 123). She describes the conventional model of classroom interaction as emphasizing "objectivity, separateness, competitiveness, and hierarchical structure," which are more indicative of male characteristics than female (p. 122). Communication researchers Wood and Lenze (1991) summarize research results on this issue as follows:

> In most classrooms, asserting self is more rewarded than waiting one's turn, individual achievement is valued more highly than collaborative efforts, talking is encouraged more than listening, presenting new ideas is emphasized whereas responding to and synthesizing classmates' ideas is not, competition is stressed more than cooperation, and advancing firm conclusions is more highly regarded than holding tentative ones. (p. 17)

Recent research on *communication apprehension,* defined back in the 1980s as "an individual's level of fear or anxiety associated with either real or anticipated communication," explored the relationship between student sex and level of apprehension (McCroskey, 1982, p. 127). Scholar Marjorie Jaasma (1997) found that, in general, female students suffered more *classroom communication apprehension* than male students. Younger or traditionally-aged students in this study were more apprehensive than older students, and students from minority groups were more apprehensive than white students. Jaasma concludes: "It appears that females view the forum of the college classroom as one in which they are conspicuous and are judged by peers and instructors" (p. 224).

Based on all this research, most classrooms appear to follow a male pattern of communication. Does this match your experience in college classes? We have noticed, in our teaching, that many female students use stereotypical feminine linguistic patterns (detailed in Chapter 5) in classrooms, such as disclaimers, hesitations, tag questions, and generally deferential patterns of speech that decrease their dominance. Regarding female use of disclaimers, Sadker and Sadker (1994) reveal, "These female preambles of self-deprecation are a predictable part of the college classroom" (p. 171).

We also continue to notice—no matter the ratio of males to females in a particular class, no matter the subject of discussion—that male students speak up first and frequently in classroom discussions. For example, one day in a recent gender communication class of about 17 women and 10 men, the female co-author of your textbook introduced the topic of images in advertising that contribute to women's low self-esteem and the effects on women's health of pressurizing messages about thinness and beauty. When she opened up the discussion, several male students' hands went up first and one just started talking. She interrupted, "Whoa—what's happening here? We're focusing on images of women and you guys want to do the talking?" The same thing happens with such topics as PMS, breast cancer and other women's health topics, and sexual assault and rape. This isn't to say men don't have valuable contributions to make on these and other topics; we just find it fascinating that the male-dominant communication pattern documented by decades of research seems to be alive and well in contemporary college classrooms. In fact, in a 1998 study, a majority of college faculty agreed that male students interrupt more frequently, assume leadership roles more frequently, are less likely to seek outside help, and are less open to constructive criticism than female students (Condravy, Skirboll, & Taylor, 1998). Do you communicate in classrooms in accord with the research findings on members of your sex? Do you find that members of the opposite sex communicate as the research describes?

The "Chill" in Higher Education: Teachers' Classroom Communication

Beyond students' communication patterns in classrooms, research has also identified differential communication behavior some faculty accord male and female students (AAUW, 1992). Learning in the classroom is mediated through the communication process and if communication is biased, then the educational opportunities students receive may be biased as well (Cooper, 1991a). Research on classroom interaction, comparing single-sex and co-ed classrooms, has led to the "demand that teachers frame pedagogy specifically in terms of achieving gender equity. Awareness of gender as it plays out in the learning process must inform our teaching" (Allen, Cantor, Grady, & Hill, 1997, p. 46).

Chillin' with Your Professors

In her analysis of classroom communication patterns, Cooper (1993) found that teachers tend to use sexist language, call on male students more often, and ask male students more complex questions than female students. Other research indicates that male students are perceived as being more fun to teach than female students and that male students are given more opportunities to interact with the teacher (Sadker & Sadker, 1985), more time to talk (Keegan, 1989), and longer explanations about class assignments and procedures (Cooper, 1993). Coinciding with the higher incidence of male participation in classrooms, male students generally receive more attention from teachers, in the form of both praise and discipline (Brophy, 1985; Sadker & Sadker, 1994).

> *Don't shut yourself up in a bandbox because you are a woman, but understand what is going on, and educate yourself to take part in the world's work for it all affects you and yours.*
>
> *Louisa May Alcott, author*

In their analysis of the chilly climate for women in university settings, Hall and Sandler (1982) described a number of areas of differential behavior. Their findings began with the fact that most faculty were men and faculty tended to affirm students of their own sex more than students of the other sex. This simple difference may lead to different levels of confirmation and support. Hall and Sandler identified the following behaviors that represent differential treatment of men and women in the classroom:

1. Ignoring female students while recognizing male students
2. Calling directly on male students but not on female students
3. Calling male students by name more often than female students
4. Addressing the class as if no women were present (e.g., "When you were a boy . . .")
5. Working toward a fuller answer to a question by probing or coaching male students for additional information
6. Waiting longer for men than for women to answer a question

7. Interrupting female students and allowing them to be interrupted by class-mates
8. Asking women lower-order, more simplistic questions
9. Responding more extensively to men's comments than to women's
10. Making seemingly helpful comments that imply women are not as competent as men
11. Phrasing classroom examples in a way that reinforces stereotypical, negative views of women's psychological traits
12. Using classroom examples that reflect stereotyped ideas about men's and women's social and professional roles
13. Using the generic *he* to represent both men and women
14. Reacting to comments or questions articulated in a "feminine style" as inherently of less value than those stated in a "masculine style"
15. Making eye contact more often with men than with women
16. Nodding and gesturing more often in response to men's questions and comments than women's
17. Changing vocal tone to indicate a more serious treatment of men's comments
18. Assuming a posture of attentiveness when men speak and the opposite when women make comments
19. Habitually choosing locations within classrooms that are near men students
20. Excluding women from course-related activities
21. Grouping students according to sex
22. Allowing women to be physically "squeezed out" from viewing laboratory assignments
23. Favoring men as student assistants (pp. 7–9)

This is quite an extensive list. Sad but true, the research shows that many students experience at least some of the differential treatment described here.

Professor Variables Down Cold

Research spanning multiple decades suggests that a professor's sex may make a difference in how students perceive teachers and in students' classroom interaction patterns (Ryan, 1989). Important studies in the 1970s found that male students in male-taught classes were much more likely than female students to be directly questioned by the professor and to respond. In female-taught classes, however, professors were equally likely to directly question male and female students, and participation by students of both sexes was more equal (Karp & Yoels, 1977; Sternglanz & Lyberger-Ficek, 1977). Research in the 1980s determined that classes taught by women incorporated more student input, more teacher and student questions, more feedback, more overall student interaction, and less direct reprimands and confrontation (Macke, Richardson, & Cook, 1980; Richardson, Cook, & Macke, 1981).

   In the 1990s, findings aren't so clear-cut. For example, communication researchers Pearson and West (1991) found that male instructors received more student questions than female instructors and that male students asked more questions than female students in the classes of male instructors. However, Nadler and Nadler (1990), in exploring sex differences in students' perceptions of instructors' classroom communication, found that male students did not report receiving more supportive behaviors and female students did not report receiving more dominant behaviors from instructors of the opposite sex. In this study, students did not believe they were treated differently by instructors of different sexes; they reported few differences in their own classroom communication behavior. Jaasma's (1997) study of classroom communication apprehension revealed that while female students were more apprehensive than male students in general, that trend was unaffected by whether the teacher was male or female.

Students' judgments are also related to perceptions of a teacher as being nonsexist or *egalitarian*, defined as the belief that one's sex does not determine or limit one's abilities or opportunities. Students who perceive that their teachers are sexists generally dislike those teachers and describe their classes as less supportive and innovative than those taught by nonsexist teachers (Cooper, 1993; Rosenfeld & Jarrard, 1986). Students of egalitarian teachers tend to develop more positive attitudes about the class and its subject matter (Petersen, Kearney, Plax, & Waldeck, 1997). Even though research findings reveal different trends, it appears that a professor's sex and her or his attitudes toward the sexes may have at least some influence in a classroom. Again, if you are enrolled in courses taught by both sexes, compare the research findings to your class experiences. What patterns can you observe in your classes?

Effects of Educational Sexism on Students

Sex bias also affects students' curriculum decisions and occupational choices (AAUW, 1998b; Bem, 1993; Cooper, 1993; Hernandez, 1993; Jamieson, 1995). Educational researchers Leonard and Sigall (1989) found that women's grades, career goals, and self-esteem decline over the four-year span of college more so than men's. Here are some effects of sex bias in education, according to Hall and Sandler (1982):

1. Dropping or avoiding certain classes
2. Minimizing one's relationship with faculty
3. Diminished career aspirations related to certain fields of study
4. A general undermining of self-confidence because of suggestions that certain areas within college curricula are too difficult or are inappropriate for members of one's sex

Curriculum decisions and resulting occupational choices are related to self-confidence, as well as to how students are advised and reinforced, but not to ability (Borisoff & Merrill, 1998; Paglin, 1993; Unger & Crawford, 1996). Hall and Sandler (1984) report that "Counselors and academic advisors alike may overtly or subtly discourage many women by counseling students in accord with stereotypical ideas of 'male' and 'female' majors and careers" (p. 7). Educational personnel only contribute part of the problem; parents have a huge effect. As education researcher Lakes Matyas (1997) asserts, "It will require the combined effort of teachers, parents, and counselors to break this pattern and to offer female students the chance to excel in science, mathematics, and engineering" (p. 60).

Changing the Educational Climate for Women and Men

Gender scholars Bate and Bowker (1997) describe college as the most masculine of learning environments. But they also discuss the changing mix of the average college classroom and note that more and more nontraditional students (particularly women) who have high income potential in business and in technical areas are returning to college. These changes are evidenced by a greater balance in the numbers of women and men in traditionally male-dominated college majors. As the demographics of the typical university begin to reflect the demographics of the society at large, more changes are expected.

How do we change the system? The male-as-norm conception of educational purposes, of students, of teachers, of curricula, of pedagogy, indeed of the profession of education, must be closely examined (Leach & Davies, 1990). Cooper (1993) suggests gathering more information about the diversity of the female experience, reconceptualizing curricula, and infusing alternative approaches into the curriculum. She also describes the value of a perspective in education that focuses on personal knowledge, empowerment, diversity, and change.

However, gender communication scholar Eric Peterson (1991) found that when a department consciously tried to incorporate gender-balance in the curriculum, student response was mixed. Efforts to affect the climate for women and men included revising courses to include material on sex and gender diversity; incorporating into course content some significant works of female scholars, rather than relying totally or primarily on male contributions; and acknowledging alternative ways of knowing and conducting educational inquiry. Some students found these changes interesting and valuable, while others found them too oriented toward women or were confused about how they applied to their lives. How would you respond if your department undertook a conscious effort to become more sex and gender sensitive?

The most applicable suggestions for students focus on classroom dynamics. The following suggestions were adapted from lists written primarily for faculty members to help them bring their classes to the ideal we described earlier in the chapter. Perhaps you might find yourself in a position to enlighten your teachers and to help ensure that these behaviors occur more frequently.

1. Engage in interaction patterns during the first few weeks of classes that draw women into discussions.
2. Design and enforce course policy statements that make it clear that biased comments and behavior are inappropriate in the classroom.
3. Incorporate the institution's policy on classroom climate and sex bias into one's teaching.

4. Make a specific effort to call directly on female as well as on male students.
5. Use terminology that includes both women and men.
6. Respond to male and female students in similar ways when they make comparable contributions in class.
7. Intervene when communication patterns develop among students that may shut out women.
8. Give male and female students an equal amount of time to respond after asking a question.
9. Give female and male students the same opportunity to ask for and receive detailed instructions about the requirements for an assignment.
10. When talking about occupations or professions in class discussion, use language that does not reinforce limited views of male and female role and career choices.
11. Avoid placing professional women in a special category, such as "female doctor."
12. Use the same tone of voice when responding to both male and female students.
13. Eliminate sexist materials from course readings and information.
14. Include items about classroom climate and sex bias on student evaluations.

While this list is lengthy, it serves as an effective way to analyze and guide potential areas for change. But the list does not exhaust the possible suggestions. Wood and Lenze (1991) describe the gender sensitive classroom as one that includes "balanced content that highlights the strengths of traditionally masculine and feminine . . . inclinations," texts that "acknowledge and value both women's and men's concerns about interpersonal communication," and an educational climate "that equally values the interaction style women tend to learn . . . , but also advances important social goals such as cooperation, effective listening, and being open minded" (pp. 16–17). They then provide strategies for creating or enhancing gender sensitivity in the classroom. As a student, you might note the presence or absence of these strategies in courses you take. Examples include content that overemphasizes, neglects, devalues, or misrepresents the concerns generally associated with one sex; an emphasis on traditional productivity and power approaches to leadership, approaches that are typically associated with masculinity; and the neglect of such issues as relationships and empowerment that are typically associated with femininity.

Integrating different communication styles and reducing the chilly climate in education will not be easy. Different students see different dimensions of the problem; some see no problem at all. If an individual class or an entire university undertakes a discussion of classroom climate and sex bias, it's probably necessary for everyone to realize that "just because it didn't happen to you doesn't mean it didn't happen." Male and female students, as well as faculty and administration, need to be sensitive to sex and gender differences that may exist within the hallowed halls of the university.

RECAP

---

sex bias, chilly climate, campus, classroom interaction, communication apprehension, classroom communication apprehension, feminine linguistic patterns,
disclaimers, hesitations, tag questions, egalitarianism, curriculum decisions, occupational choices

---

PEER SEXUAL HARASSMENT: CLASSMATES WILL BE CLASSMATES?

In Chapter 9, we discussed sexual harassment in some detail. In Chapter 10, we
explored the problem of sexual harassment in the workplace, in particular the
most complicated aspect of the EEOC's guidelines, the *hostile climate* clause.
Many academic institutions have expanded the EEOC definition to reflect their
unique concerns, as in the phrase *hostile learning climate.* In this chapter we examine a specific form of harassment that has a pervasive effect on students'
lives. As you know from previous reading, the pattern of sexual harassment
most often documented in research involves a male harasser and a female target in a *status-differentiated relationship,* such as boss-employee or doctor-patient.
But you probably did not know that harassment is far more prevalent among
peers than in status-differentiated relationships (Loredo, Reid, & Deaux, 1995;
Zirkel, 1995). The treatment you receive from your classmates directly contributes to the creation of a hostile or nonhostile learning climate.

Research shows that sexual harassment, just like sexual assault, has much
more to do with power than with sex (Berryman-Fink, 1993). However, it appears that we may need to expand our view of power. As educational researcher Katherine McKinney (1990a) contends, "Most researchers in the area of
sexual harassment have assumed that harassment occurs only when the offender has more formal or position power than the harasser. Recently, it has
been recognized that other types of power can be used by the offender . . ."
(p. 435). Sexual harassment between persons of equal status, such as co-workers,
classmates, and social acquaintances, has been termed *peer sexual harassment.*
Harassment directed from someone of lower status to someone of higher status
is called *contrapower sexual harassment* (Benson, 1984).

What people are realizing is that the learning environment is greatly affected by relationships with peers, possibly even more so than relationships
with teachers. Yet more attention is paid, in research and discussions about
harassment, to situations involving a clearly defined, even institutionalized
status or power differential. What about power abuses within relationships in
which no clear power lines exist? What about power plays between classmates? Before discussing the current status of this problem, let's think about
how the problem got to be a problem.

Back to Basics

Think back to when you were in grade school, when you were on the playground and a boy ran up to some girl and kissed her, to the screams of her friends and the whoops and laughter of his. Maybe this never happened at your school, but it's a common occurrence when kids test the boundaries of acceptable behavior and attempt to engage the opposite sex. If the little boy's kiss was unwelcome, should his behavior be deemed sexual harassment or is this merely an example of "boys being boys?" You may think we've lost our collective marbles here, but just such an incident occurred in an elementary school in 1997. A six-year-old boy was suspended from school for a few days for kissing a girl—an action that she (and her parents) viewed as unwarranted and unwelcome. When the boy's mother sued the school district over the suspension, the media picked up the story (of course). News talk shows were full of discussions of "feminism gone overboard" and outrage that a child could be accused of inappropriate "sexual" conduct. We put that term in quotes because it was a central part of the argument—that a child who was not capable of sexual activity could be accused of mischief, but certainly not sexual harassment.

Now back to your experience. For the female readers, you or a schoolmate in junior high or middle school may have received unwanted attention from boys because of your developing body (and their developing hormones). How did you respond—with embarrassment, anger, flirtation? Do you remember how such attention made you feel, in a positive or negative way (or both)? Did you tell anyone about it? Would it be a stretch for you to call such attention from boys peer sexual harassment? Hold off answering that question for a moment.

For the male readers, do you remember the same time period, when a wide variety of surprising things brought about a certain sexual reaction? This is when boys first learned the art of carrying their schoolbooks and papers in front of them, instead of on their hips like girls did. (Now everything's in book bags, so modern boys have no doubt found modern methods of coping with this age-old dilemma.) When you think about this time period, did you ever get teased by a girl because she detected some kind of sexual arousal in you? Did a girl—maybe a girl older than you—come on to you or show you her "new developments"? Would you have called these girls' behavior peer sexual harassment? Here's a tougher question: Could some of your behavior toward girls in your younger years have been deemed sexual harassment?

What we're getting at is this: Sexual harassment doesn't just all of a sudden become a behavior of choice for some people. It doesn't just mysteriously become a problem only adults have to deal with. It starts somewhere. Maybe it should be called something else, something without the sexual implications of the term *sexual harassment*. The term implies that sexual harassment is about sex, when it is really about power. As Orenstein (1994) explains:

> Overwhelmingly boys harass and girls (or other boys) are harassed, indicating that the behavior is less a statement about sexuality than an assertion of dominance. The prevalence of sexual harassment reminds us that boys learn at a very young age to see girls as less capable and less worthy of respect. Middle-class and affluent girls in particular tend to accept sexual harassment as inevitable. And why not? The sexual teasing, stalking, and grabbing merely reinforces other, more subtle lessons: it reminds them that they are defined by their bodies; it underscores their lack of entitlement in the classroom (in fact, the harassment frequently *happens* in the classroom); it confirms their belief that boys' sexuality is uncontrollable while their own must remain in check. (pp. 116–117)

In our own research and others', women report "becoming numb" to behavior that could be viewed as sexual harassment by today's standards. The phrase, "boys will be boys," may be at the heart of this problem. Teasing and disrespecting members of the opposite sex do not have to be a rite of passage. We're not necessarily advocating the suspension of elementary schoolchildren, but we do think there's something to be learned from that situation and others like it. Turning our heads and adopting a tolerant stance of "they're just being kids" could perpetuate the problem. And the problem does worsen in middle and high school.

The "Hostile Hallways" of Middle and High School

An article in the *Dallas Morning News* reads:

> The four teenagers rattle off examples of lewd acts they've become accustomed to seeing at their Dallas middle school. A boy bit a girl on her breast in a classroom. A girl grabbed a boy's genitals in the hallway. A boy lifted a girl's dress and sent her screaming to the principal's office. In schools around the nation as well as in Texas, children and adolescents are facing sexual harassment and abuse from one another. Girls are usually the victims, but boys sometimes are accosted. Same-sex incidents happen too. (Everbach & Saul, 1998, p. 37A)

According to a school district official interviewed for the story, "It's happening a lot more than people think it is. A lot of young boys don't realize the line is much nearer than they think it is. What some boys think is a friendly touch can be construed as harassment" (p. 37A).

The AAUW report of 1993, *Hostile Hallways*, was the first national scientific survey of sexual harassment in public schools. From about 1,700 students in grades 8–11 across 79 schools, 85 percent of girls and 76 percent of boys reported experiencing sexual harassment. These figures do not reflect the harassment students indicated they had received from school employees; the AAUW report stated that harassment from employees "was dwarfed by student reports of peer-to-peer harassment" (p. 11). These are alarming figures, the high rate for boys being particularly surprising. While boys and girls are both affected, the research showed a sex difference in terms of frequency of harassment, with girls reporting many more instances of harassment than boys. The sexual harassment also takes a greater toll on girls than boys, according to the study. Harassed girls reported being more afraid in school and feeling less confident about themselves than boys.

Besides the loss of self-esteem and the fear associated with sexual harassment, the most common outcome of the experience is not wanting to attend school. Harassment leads to absenteeism and truancy, which contribute to the drop-out rate. A second outcome of harassment is a silencing effect, meaning that victims don't want to talk as much in class. This is prime example of our discussion earlier of a chill in the educational environment. Thirty-two percent of girls, compared to 13 percent of boys, reported this effect, which helps explain research findings of male dominance in classroom interaction. The report states, "Sexual harassment is clearly and measurably taking a toll on a significant percentage of students' educational, emotional, and behavioral lives. And although girls are experiencing more harassment—and suffering graver consequences—in the end, sexual harassment is everyone's problem. For when children's self-esteem and development are hampered, the repercussions echo throughout our society" (p. 21).

So what can be done about this problem? The AAUW found that 57 percent of students didn't know if their school had a policy on sexual harassment. In those schools with sexual harassment policies, most deal only with teacher-to-student harassment, not peer harassment. Having no policy or an incomplete one leaves school districts vulnerable to legal liability and victims without a clear mechanism for responding to the harassment. This increases the likelihood that they will not respond, but rather internalize the harassment and blame themselves. The harasser's behavior is then tolerated and a terrible cycle is reinforced.

The first step for schools is to realize that there is a problem rather than burying their heads in the sand, assuming that their students are not capable of such behavior. They must approach the problem realistically and involve a cross-section of the school and community in the development of a comprehensive sexual harassment policy. We emphasize the cross-section aspect, because research also shows that administrators do not always offer helpful responses to reports of peer harassment. As Bate and Bowker (1997) suggest, "Explaining the harassing behavior to a person who, from the student's point of view, may or may not understand the vocabulary and nuances of the student's generation adds complicating factors that students may choose to avoid" (p. 253). It's wise for administrators, teachers, counselors, and other school personnel to join parents and students in the development of a policy and procedure for dealing with harassment.

Another proactive approach is to conduct educational programs on the topic. While some schools do hold such sessions, they tend to be provided for school personnel only. Few of these programs involve parents and students, and fewer still educate students about peer harassment—the most prevalent form of sexual harassment they are likely to experience. A comprehensive training program—honest, current, conducted in language that engages students, and repeated over time—can help curb the peer sexual harassment trend before it tracks through college and into the workforce.

Peer Sexual Harassment: Another "Chilling" Effect in College

One of the first discussions of the problem of peer sexual harassment on college campuses was co-authored by Hughes and Sandler (1988) of the Association of American Colleges. At that time, only a few colleges and universities had examined the problem. A Cornell University survey indicated that 78 percent of female students had received sexist comments and 68 percent had received unwelcome sexual attention from their male peers. At MIT, 92 percent of women and 57 percent of men reported having been targets of at least one form of sexual harassment. Hughes and Sandler asserted, "There is a darker side to campus life, often unnoticed. If acknowledged, it is too often brushed off as 'normal' behavior. This darker side is peer harassment, particularly the harassment of female students by male students" (p. 1). The range of behaviors Hughes and Sandler included in their description of peer harassment started at "teasing, sexual innuendoes, and bullying of a sexist nature, both physical and verbal" and ended with "sexual aggression" (p. 1).

Studies among students and faculty colleagues continue to reveal a persistent, alarming problem on college campuses (Geist & Townsley, 1997; Gelfand, Fitzgerald, & Drasgow, 1995; Krolokke, 1998; Sandler, 1997; Seals, 1997). The rates of reported peer sexual harassment are dramatically high, but that's just the *reported* cases. The *actual* rate of occurrence is likely to be significantly higher (Gill, 1993). Psychologists Cochran, Frazier, and Olson (1997) surveyed over 1,500 undergraduates and 500 graduate students at a large university and found the following:

1. Women reporting harassment were almost always harassed by men.
2. Men reported being harassed 56 percent of the time by women and 37 percent of the time by men.
3. Of the harassment reported by undergrads, 76 percent came from peers while 14 percent came from faculty members.

They concluded that "researchers must look not only at power associated with one's position in an organization but also at power associated with one's status in society" (p. 222).

Profile of a Peer Harasser

In a fascinating study, communication researchers examined the attitudes and communication tendencies that characterize harassers. Bingham and Burleson (1996) proposed, "Because most sexual harassment is perpetrated by men, research that is designed to identify the characteristics that may differentiate men who are and are not likely to engage in particular forms of sexual harassment may suggest important strategies for combating the problem" (p. 309). In their study, 145 male undergraduates completed a questionnaire asking them to imagine themselves as a manager at a large organization who has just hired an "outgoing and friendly" female employee. In the scenario, the manager thought the female employee was attractive, so he asked her out several times but was always turned down. Following the scenario the researchers listed "strategies men said they might use in this situation." Students were to indicate how likely they would be to use each strategy after being turned down over and over again for a date. In actuality, the behaviors in the list were included because, by law, they were highly likely to be considered sexual harassment in a work environment.

Two general categories of strategies emerged: (1) *quid pro quo harassment* (e.g., threatening to fire the employee if she didn't go out), and (2) *intrusive harassment* (e.g., commenting on the employee's appearance and asking questions about her personal life). The results of the study showed that 7 percent of the male subjects reported that they were likely to use some quid pro quo strategies in order to obtain a date with the female employee. Of this finding, Bingham and Burleson stated, "Although this percentage is small in an absolute sense, any number of respondents who report even a slight likelihood of engaging in such blatant sexual harassment is disturbing. Since the males who participated in this study can be expected to move from the university into full-time employment within the next few years, the finding also suggests the need for strong educational and enforcement efforts by organizations" (pp. 321–322).

The researchers found responses in the intrusive harassment category disturbing as well (as did we) because 70 percent of the men in the study indicated "some likelihood" of engaging in behavior later categorized as intrusive harassment. Another 29 percent said that they would be "more likely than not" to use the strategies listed. Bingham and Burleson relate these findings to the likelihood that men in this study did not view the behaviors they said they would use to actually be sexual harassment. The tendency for women to view certain actions as severe and harassing, when men do not, consistently emerges in research (Cochran, Frazier, & Olson, 1997; Ivy & Hamlet, 1996; McKinney, 1990b; Mongeau & Blalock, 1994).

A "Close to Home" Campus Project on Peer Sexual Harassment

To better understand how peer sexual harassment affects college students' lives, the female co-author of your textbook conducted two studies at a large university (Ivy & Hamlet, 1996). Results indicate that students are becoming educated about the problem of peer sexual harassment; however, from students' accounts, it appears that peer sexual harassment really is a problem on college campuses.

Study 1: Experiences with Peer Sexual Harassment

A sample of 824 undergraduates, evenly divided by sex, completed a survey about experiences with peer sexual harassment. Almost half of the students reported being victims of peer sexual harassment, with 68 percent of the women reporting multiple instances of verbal and nonverbal harassment from male peers. Twenty-five percent of the men had experienced peer harassment primarily from women, but with more incidences of homosexual harassment than reported by women. While we expected some general sex differences in victimization, we didn't expect the experiential gulf. Beyond the number of victims, women's harassing episodes occurred much more often than men's. These gaps illustrate how far apart women's and men's experiences appear to be on this issue. However, when asked if they perceived peer sexual harassment to be a problem on college campuses, 81 percent of the women and 64 percent of the men said yes. Again, more women than men recognized the problem, but these figures show that there may be less of an attitudinal gap than an experiential gap.

Figures like the ones we found are extremely disturbing, but more disturbing still were students' descriptions of their harassment. The main verbal type of harassment aimed at women was sexual innuendo or "lewd" comments from classmates, like "guys know what it takes for girls to get an 'A' in this class," remarks about body parts or physical appearance, and one male student's declaration in front of an entire class that he wanted to have oral sex with a female classmate. Other verbal harassment involved sexual jokes, sexual notes or drawings left on desktops, repeated invitations for dates or sex (after having said no), being asked intimate details about personal or sexual life, and descriptions of dreams or fantasies harassers had about targets. Verbal harassment of men also involved repeatedly being asked out and comments about physical appearance and body parts, as well as descriptions of desired sexual activity and offers of sexual favors in exchange for help on assignments or exams. One repeated comment from the men, but not the women, related to female classmates talking in sexual ways about their own body parts, which the men said made them uncomfortable.

Nonverbal harassment mainly involved unwanted and repeated touching. Other common forms included invading one's personal space and continual staring from a classmate, especially "staring up and down," the kind that makes someone feel unclothed. Some women reported situations where harassment turned uglier, such as stalking in the parking lot and a dramatic, tragic account of a beating and date rape in a male student's dorm room. In multiple instances, sexual harassment escalated into date rape.

Many students in our study were unwilling to label their experiences sexual harassment, a tendency described by one female student as "becoming numb to it." This involves becoming so used to bad behavior—being whistled at; hearing rude, often disgusting, comments about appearance and sexuality from male onlookers; being the "butt" of sexual jokes; expecting men's sexual urges to get mildly out of hand—that you're reluctant to call it something as strong as sexual harassment. Research supports this tendency of victims being reluctant to label their abuse sexual harassment (Brooks & Perot, 1991; Cochran, Frazier, & Olson, 1997; Fitzgerald & Ormerod, 1991). But what we're finding out is that assigning the label to the behavior is extremely empowering. It vindicates the victim in some ways to know that what happened has a name, with all the legitimacy that comes with naming. It's empowering to know that the behavior is illegal, other people have experienced it, and, in almost all instances, it's not the victim's fault.

Study 2: Seriousness of Harassment

The second study grew out of the first, in that many students felt a major problem was the lack of agreement over which actions were likely to be seen as harassing and which ones were not. Certain behaviors might be taken by one person as sexually harassing, but as harmless teasing, flirtation, or simple complimenting by another person. Male students in particular expressed a need for a clear-cut, concrete definition, but the problem, of course, is that it's just not that simple. Verbal and nonverbal communication is complex, individually based, and culturally rooted; there's no clear-cut way to know the effect of your words and behavior so that harassment can always be avoided. But these students' concerns raised this question: While *we* knew what behaviors research deemed harassing, did *students* view those behaviors as sexual harassment? Were there levels, degrees, or distinctions between certain behaviors, in terms of how seriously harassing or inappropriate they were? Did female and male students agree about what constituted sexual harassment and the seriousness of it?

To address these issues, we developed a questionnaire to assess students' perceptions of whether 15 behaviors were peer sexual harassment and the severity attached to each. Students were asked to assume that the behaviors were committed toward themselves by an opposite-sex casual acquaintance whom they considered a peer. The results showed that only one of the 15 behaviors (humor and jokes about sex or about women or men) was *not* perceived as sexual harassment by the majority of subjects. Twelve behaviors received high agreement, meaning most students considered those behaviors sexual harassment. For two items on the questionnaire—implied or overt sexual threats and attempted or actual kissing—women assigned much higher levels of severity than men. For 9 of the 15 behaviors, women assigned somewhat higher levels of severity. This finding was consistent with previous research showing that women take a harsher view of harassment than men (Gill, 1993; McKinney, 1990b; Mongeau & Blalock, 1994).

The Law and Peer Sexual Harassment

Managers and companies can be held legally liable for harassment among their employees, but might instructors and institutions be held accountable for peer harassment in their classrooms? Hughes and Sandler (1988) warn, "Just as courts have held under Title IX that co-workers and peers can cause an employer to be liable for sexual harassment through the creation of an offensive environment, so, too, it is expected that schools would be held liable under Title IX for sexual harassment of students by students, including the creation of an offensive environment that interferes with a student's learning and well-being" (p. 8).

Court cases in the 1990s examined public schools' liability (with findings that affect colleges and universities as well), but their rulings are far from consistent (Carroll, 1993; Paludi, 1990; Sherer, 1992). One federal appeals court found that a school district could be held liable for peer sexual harassment if it knowingly failed to take action to remedy a hostile environment because that would be a violation of a student's rights (*Davis* v. *Monroe County Board of Education,* 1996). But another federal appeals court decided just the opposite, relieving school districts of liability and stating, "Unwanted sexual advances of fellow students do not carry the same coercive effect or abuse of power as those made by a teacher, employer, or co-worker" (*Rowinsky* v. *Bryan Independent School District,* 1997). While not specifically dealing with peer harassment, a U.S. Supreme Court ruling in 1998 held that school officials are not legally liable for a teacher's sexual harassment of a student unless they knew about it and purposefully looked the other way (*Gebser* v. *Lago Vista Independent School District*). So for the time being, school and university personnel will not be held legally liable unless they intentionally ignore sexual harassment. This is quite a different standard than that for employers who can be held accountable for sexual harassment, whether or not they know it's occurring.

It's Happening, but What Can We Do?

Classrooms are not exempt locales when it comes to peer sexual harassment. There are no simple solutions, except maybe for one: Treat classmates and co-workers—your peers—as individuals worthy of respect. Keep personal and sexual verbal and nonverbal communication out of your interaction until you're *completely* sure that your actions or words will be received in a positive manner (and even then it's risky). Beyond the advice to the individual, the same suggestions as those made earlier for public schools apply to universities. First, naiveté or denial of the problem, reflected in statements such as "This doesn't happen in my classes," makes students and teachers part of the problem. Even the most well-organized, professionally run, and academically scintillating class contains students who have grown up in a society that socializes them in some negative ways. Many students simply do not know what harassment is and that their behavior might be construed as harassing. Results from our campus survey and other research indicate that students are ready to learn.

Colleges and universities, for the most part, have become much more aware of the detrimental effect and legal liability associated with sexual harassment. They've instituted policies and procedures for reporting and responding to claims of sexual harassment, and many conduct educational programs for faculty and other campus personnel. Programs sponsored by such campus organizations as women's centers and offices of student activities, and classes like first-year seminars (the "how to survive college" type of classes) are working to educate students about sexual harassment. But, a word of caution is appropriate: Just like public schools, many, if not most, university policies and programs are more attuned to harassment in status-differentiated relationships than among peers. It's important to develop programs that take a comprehensive approach to the problem (Paetzold & O'Leary-Kelly, 1993).

After reading this material, you may want to do your own "campus inventory." First, note whether your professors include a sexual harassment policy statement in their course syllabi. Do they create and foster a classroom climate of mutual respect, one that allows for safe reporting of harassment should it occur? Next, it might be worthwhile to locate and read your institution's sexual harassment policy. Does it contain any provisions for peer harassment? If a student is harassed by another student, who can she or he talk to for comfort and advice? Are campus counselors available and knowledgeable on this issue so they can help someone suffering the very real pains of sexual harassment? If your campus has student housing and resident advisors, are those RAs trained on this topic? They may have received some training on sexual harassment, but did it cover peer harassment? Where does a victim take a complaint? If you find that your campus is lacking in awareness of the peer sexual harassment issue, that may signal it's time for you to get involved and find an avenue for volunteering your considerable knowledge on this topic.

CONCLUSION

This wraps up this final part of the text on gender communication in specific kinds of relationships and certain contexts. Intuitively, you know that the exact same thing said among family members will be taken differently by a friend, a romantic partner, a classmate, or a co-worker. But intuition or what some people like to call common sense isn't common to everyone, as Benjamin Franklin once said. Some people don't realize the power of a context to affect a message. We expect that, after reading these chapters, you won't be among these people. We expect that the last several pages of this text have reinforced the importance of context in gender communication.

Learning all you can about communication in educational settings, as well as about how gender communication operates in other contexts and in various types of relationships, will take you a long way toward personal effectiveness as a communicator. Practicing what you've learned, talking with women and men about what you know, making mistakes but being wise enough to stare down those mistakes, learn from them, and avoid repeating them all put you even closer to the personal effectiveness goal. Becoming an effective communicator in a world complicated by gender, for starters, is an incredible challenge. We think you're up to it.

Key Terms

single-sex education
coeducation
gender-role socialization
fairy tales
nursery rhymes
stereotypical roles
textbooks
educational literature
sex bias
gender bias
learning potential
expectations
stereotypes

sex bias
chilly campus climate
classroom interaction
communication
  apprehension
classroom communication
  apprehension
feminine linguistic
  patterns
disclaimers
hesitations
tag questions
egalitarianism

curriculum decisions
occupational choices
hostile climate
hostile learning climate
status-differentiated
  relationships
peer sexual harassment
contrapower sexual
  harassment
power plays
quid pro quo harassment
intrusive harassment
legal liability

Discussion Starters

1. Think about your favorite children's fairy tale, maybe a Disney story or a favorite story a parent read to you when you were young. Analyze the main characters. Is the female main character the center of the story? How would you describe her character, both physically and in personality? Does her character represent a feminine stereotype? How would you describe the main male character in the story? Is he stereotypically drawn? What interpretations did you make of the story as a child? Do you have different interpretations now, as an adult?

2. If you believe that women and men should have equal opportunities and be treated equally in our society, but you see *gender bias* around you, then how will you communicate a nonbiased attitude to your future children? If you already have children, how have you confronted this issue with them? Have you thought about the nursery rhymes, fairy tales, and stories you will expose your children to? Have you thought about how you might discuss gender roles with a child?

3. This chapter discussed some of the effects of teacher *expectations* on students' learning and academic achievement. Can you think of a time, either in school or college, when you became acutely aware that one of your teachers held certain expectations of you? Were the expectations positive or negative, such as an instructor expecting you to excel or to fail? Were the expectations in any way related to your sex? How did the realization that those expectations were operating make you feel and affect your learning?

4. Take some of the specific "chilly" behaviors mentioned in this chapter and see if you detect them in your college classes. As examples, when your instructor raises a question, see if male hands go up first and if more men than women are called on to speak. Do any of your teachers seem to direct more complex questions to male students and then coach them through the answers, in a different way than they do female students?

5. We realize that considering the teasing young boys and girls engage in to be sexual harassment may be a stretch for you. But have you ever thought about the roots of *peer sexual harassment*? Where do harassers first learn this behavior? How can we change school systems so that students learn to respect each other rather than engage in "power play"?
6. Think about the problem of peer sexual harassment on your home campus. Have you encountered any harassing experiences in college classrooms or at social events? Do you know people who believe they've been sexually harassed by a peer? Have friends told you of experiences with sexual harassment, but been reluctant to attach the label to the behavior? Knowing what you now know about the problem, will you respond to peer sexual harassment—either directed at you or at a friend—any differently?

References

ADDISON, E. (1995). Saving other women from other men: Disney's *Aladdin. Camera Obscura, 31,* 5–19.

ALLEN, S., CANTOR, A., GRADY, H., & HILL, P. (1997). Classroom talk: Coed classes that work for girls. *Women & Language, 20,* 41–46.

AMERICAN ASSOCIATION OF UNIVERSITY WOMEN. (1991). *Shortchanging girls, shortchanging America.* Washington, DC: AAUW Educational Foundation.

AMERICAN ASSOCIATION OF UNIVERSITY WOMEN. (1992). *The AAUW report: How schools shortchange girls.* Washington, DC: AAUW Educational Foundation and the National Educational Association.

AMERICAN ASSOCIATION OF UNIVERSITY WOMEN. (1993). *Hostile hallways: The AAUW survey on sexual harassment in America's schools.* Washington, DC: AAUW Educational Foundation.

AMERICAN ASSOCIATION OF UNIVERSITY WOMEN. (1998a). *Separated by sex: A critical look at single-sex education for girls.* Washington, DC: AAUW Educational Foundation.

AMERICAN ASSOCIATION OF UNIVERSITY WOMEN. (1998b). *Gender gaps: Where schools still fail our children.* Washington, DC: AAUW Educational Foundation.

AMERICAN ASSOCIATION OF UNIVERSITY WOMEN. (1998c). *News release: Technology gender gap develops while gaps in math and science narrow, AAUW Foundation report shows.* [On-line]. Available: http://www.aauw.org

AMERICAN PSYCHOLOGICAL ASSOCIATION. (1994). Guidelines to reduce bias in language. In *Publication manual of the American Psychological Association* (4th ed.). Washington, DC: Author.

BALZER, J. (1989, November). Chem text photos discourage women. *NEA Today, 33.*

BATE, B., & BOWKER, J. (1997). *Communication and the sexes* (2nd ed.). Prospect Heights, IL: Waveland.

BELENKY, M., CLINCHY, B., GOLDBERGER, N., & TARULE, J. (1986). *Women's ways of knowing.* New York: Basic Books.

BEM, S. L. (1993). *The lenses of gender: Transforming the debate on sexual inequality.* New Haven, CT: Yale University Press.

BENSON, K. (1984). Comment on Crocker's "An analysis of university definitions of sexual harassment." *Signs, 9,* 516–519.

BENZ, C., PFEIFFER, I., & NEWMAN, I. (1981). Sex role expectations of classroom teachers, grades 1–12. *American Educational Research Journal, 18,* 289–302.

BERRYMAN-FINK, C. (1993). Preventing sexual harassment through male-female communication training. In G. L. Kreps (Ed.), *Sexual harassment: Communication implications.* (pp. 267–280) Cresskill, NJ: Hampton.

BINGHAM, S. G., & BURLESON, B. R. (1996). The development of a Sexual Harassment Proclivity Scale: Construct validation and relationship to communication competence. *Communication Quarterly, 44,* 308–325.

BORISOFF, D., & MERRILL, L. (1998). *The power to communicate: Gender differences as barriers* (3rd ed.). Prospect Heights, IL: Waveland.

BOTTIGHEIMER, R. B. (1986). Silenced women in the Grimms' tales: The "fit" between fairy tales and society in their historical context. In R. B. Bottigheimer (Ed.), *Fairy tales and society: Illusion, allusion, and paradigm* (pp. 115–132). Philadelphia: University of Pennsylvania Press.

BOWKER, J. K., & REGAN DUNKIN, P. (1992). Enacting feminism in the teaching of communication. In L. A. M. Perry, L. H. Turner, & H. M. Sterk (Eds.), *Constructing and reconstructing gender: The links among communication, language, and gender* (pp. 261–268). Albany: State University of New York Press.

BROOKS, L., & PEROT, A. (1991). Reporting sexual harassment: Exploring a predictive model. *Psychology of Women Quarterly, 15,* 31–47.

BROOKS, V. (1982). Sex differences in student dominance behavior in female and male professors' classrooms. *Sex Roles, 8,* 683–690.

BROPHY, J. E. (1983). Research on the self-fulfilling prophecy and teacher expectations. *Journal of Educational Psychology, 75,* 631–661.

BROPHY, J. E. (1985). Interactions of male and female students with male and female teachers. In L. C. Wilkinson & C. B. Marrett (Eds.), *Gender influence in classroom interaction* (pp. 115–142). Orlando, FL: Academic Press.

BURK, M. (1998, July/August). NOW invokes Title IX to fight an all-girls school. *Ms.,* 24–25.

CARROLL, C. M. (1993). Sexual harassment on campus: Enhancing awareness and promoting change. *Educational Record, Winter,* 21–26.

COCHRAN, C. C., FRAZIER, P. A., & OLSON, A. M. (1997). Predictors of responses to unwanted sexual attention. *Psychology of Women Quarterly, 21,* 207–226.

CONDRAVY, J., SKIRBOLL, E., & TAYLOR, R. (1998). Faculty perceptions of classroom gender dynamics. *Women & Language, 21,* 18–27.

COOPER, P. J. (1987). Sex role stereotypes of stepparents in children's literature. In L. P. Stewart & S. Ting-Toomey (Eds.), *Communication, gender, and sex roles in diverse interaction contexts* (pp. 61–82). Norwood, NJ: Ablex.

COOPER, P. J. (1991a). *Speech communication for the classroom teacher* (4th ed.). Scottsdale, AZ: Gorsuch-Scarisbrick.

COOPER, P. J. (1991b). *Women and power in the Caldecott and Newbery Winners.* Paper presented at the meeting of the Central States Communication Association, Chicago, IL.

COOPER, P. J. (1993). Communication and gender in the classroom. In L. P. Arliss & D. J. Borisoff (Eds.), *Women and men communicating: Challenges and changes* (pp. 122–141). Fort Worth, TX: Harcourt Brace Jovanovich.

COOPER, H., & GOOD, T. (1983). *Pygmalion grows up: Studies in the expectation communication process.* New York: Longman.

DOWNEY, S. D. (1996). Feminine empowerment in Disney's *Beauty and the Beast. Women's Studies in Communication, 19,* 185–212.

DUSEK, J. B., & JOSEPH, G. (1983). The bases of teacher expectancies: A meta-analysis. *Journal of Educational Psychology, 75,* 327–346.

EVERBACH, T., & SAUL, M. (1998, May 23). Confronting peer pressure: Students facing more frequent sexual harassment, abuse from classmates. *Dallas Morning News,* pp. 37A, 41A.

FITZGERALD, L. F., & ORMEROD, A. L. (1991). Perceptions of sexual harassment: The influence of gender and academic context. *Psychology of Women Quarterly, 15,* 281–294.

GEIST, P., & TOWNSLEY, N. (1997, November). *"Swept under the rug" and other disappearing acts: Legitimate concerns for university's sexual harassment policy and procedures.* Paper presented at the meeting of the National Communication Association, Chicago, IL.

GELFAND, M. J., FITZGERALD, L. F., & DRASGOW, F. (1995). The structure of sexual harassment: A confirmatory analysis across cultures and settings. *Journal of Vocational Behavior, 47,* 164–177.

Gender mindbender: Should single sex education remain an option? (1998, Summer). *Texas Woman's University Times,* pp. 1, 8.

GILL, M. M. (1993). Academic sexual harassment: Perceptions of behaviors. In G. L. Kreps (Ed.), *Sexual harassment: Communication implications* (pp. 149–169). Cresskill, NJ: Hampton.

GILLIGAN, C. (1982). *In a different voice.* Cambridge: Harvard University Press.

GOSE, B. (1996, March 1). Classroom climate found still "chilly" for women. *The Chronicle of Higher Education,* p. A38.

HALL, R., & SANDLER, B. (1982). *The classroom climate: A chilly one for women?* Washington, DC: Project on the Status and Education of Women, Association of American Colleges.

HALL, R. M., & SANDLER, B. R. (1984). *Out of the classroom: A chilly campus climate for women?* Washington, DC: Project on the Status and Education of Women, Association of American Colleges.

HASWELL, J., & HASWELL, R. H. (1995). Gendership and the miswriting of students. *College Composition and Communication, 46,* 223–254.

HEINTZ, K. E. (1987). An examination of sex and occupational-role presentations of female characters in children's picture books. *Women's Studies in Communication, 11,* 67–78.

HERNANDEZ, B. (1993). Career choices unlimited. *Northwest report: The challenge of sex equity.* Portland, OR: Northwest Regional Educational Laboratory.

HUGHES, J. O., & SANDLER, B. R. (1988). *Peer harassment: Hassles for women on campus.* Washington, DC: Project on the Status and Education of Women, Association of American Colleges.

IVY, D. K., & HAMLET, S. (1996). College students and sexual dynamics: Two studies of peer sexual harassment. *Communication Education, 45,* 149–166.

JAASMA, M. (1997). Classroom communication apprehension: Does being male or female make a difference? *Communication Reports, 10,* 219–228.

JAMIESON, K. H. (1995). *Beyond the double bind: Women and leadership.* New York: Oxford University Press.

JASCHIK, S. (1995, April 21). Court orders Citadel to admit woman, but provides escape clause. *The Chronicle of Higher Education,* p. A37.

KARP, D. A., & YOELS, W. C. (1977). The college classroom: Some observations on the meanings of student participation. *Sociology and Social Research, 60,* 421–439.

KEEGAN, P. (1989, August 6). Playing favorites. *New York Times,* p. 26A.

KROLOKKE, C. (1998). Women professors' assertive-empathic and non-assertive communication in sexual harassment situations. *Women's Studies in Communication, 21,* 91–103.

KRUPNICK, C. (1985). Women and men in the classroom: Inequality and its remedies. *Teaching and Learning: Journal of the Harvard Danforth Center, 1,* 18–25.

LAKES MATYAS, M. (1997). Factors affecting female achievement and interest in science and scientific careers. In D. Dunn (Ed.), *Workplace/women's place* (pp. 53–63). Los Angeles: Roxbury.

LARCHE, D. (1985). *Father Gander.* New York: Methuen.

LEACH, M., & DAVIES, B. (1990). Crossing the boundaries: Educational thought and gender equity. *Educational Theory, 40,* 321–332.

LEDERMAN, D. (1996, January 26). Supreme Court hears arguments on VMI admissions policy. *The Chronicle of Higher Education,* p. A28.

LEONARD, M. M., & SIGALL, B. A. (1989). Empowering women student leaders: A leadership development model. In C. S. Pearson, D. L. Shavlik, & J. B. Touchton (Eds.), *Educating the majority: Women challenge tradition in higher education* (pp. 230–249). New York: ACE/Macmillan.

LIEBERMAN, M. K. (1986). "Some day my prince will come": Female acculturation through the fairy tale. In J. Zipes (Ed.), *Don't bet on the prince: Contemporary feminist fairy tales in North America and England* (pp. 185–200). New York: Methuen.

LOREDO, C., REID, A., & DEAUX, K. (1995). Judgments and definitions of sexual harassment by high school students. *Sex Roles, 32,* 29–45.

MACKE, A. S., RICHARDSON, L. W., & COOK, J. (1980). *Sex-typed teaching styles of university professors and student reactions.* Columbus: Ohio State University Research Foundation.

McCROSKEY, J. C. (1982). Oral communication apprehension: A reconceptualization. In M. Burgoon (Ed.), *Communication yearbook 6* (pp. 136–170). Beverly Hills: Sage.

McKINNEY, K. (1990a). Sexual harassment of university faculty by colleagues and students. *Sex Roles, 23,* 421–438.

McKINNEY, K. (1990b). Attitudes toward sexual harassment and perceptions of blame: Views of male and female graduate students. *Free Inquiry in Creative Sociology, 18,* 73–76.

MONGEAU, P. A., & BLALOCK, J. (1994). Student evaluations of instructor immediacy and sexually harassing behaviors: An experimental investigation. *Journal of Applied Communication Research, 22,* 256–272.

NADLER, L. B., & NADLER, M. K. (1990). Perceptions of sex differences in classroom communication. *Women's Studies in Communication, 13,* 46–65.

NATIONAL COUNCIL OF TEACHERS OF ENGLISH. (1975). *Guidelines for nonsexist use of language in NCTE publications.* Urbana, IL: Author.

NELSON, C., & WATSON, J. A. (1991). The computer gender gap: Children's attitudes, performance, and socialization. *Journal of Educational Technology Systems, 9,* 345–353.

NILSEN, A. P. (1987). Three decades of sexism in school science materials. *School Library Journal, 33,* 117–122.

ORENSTEIN, P. (1994). *Schoolgirls: Young women, self-esteem, and the confidence gap.* New York: Doubleday.

ORENSTEIN, P. (1997). Shortchanging girls: Gender socialization in schools. In D. Dunn (Ed.), *Workplace/women's place* (pp. 43–52). Los Angeles: Roxbury.

PAETZOLD, R. L., & O'LEARY-KELLY, A. M. (1993). Organizational communication and the legal dimension of hostile work environment sexual harassment. In G. L. Kreps (Ed.), *Sexual harassment: Communication implications* (pp. 63–77). Cresskill, NJ: Hampton.

PAGLIN, C. (1993). Girls face barriers in science and mathematics. *Northwest report: The challenge of sex equity.* Portland, OR: Northwest Regional Educational Laboratory.

PALUDI, M. A. (Ed.) (1990). *Ivory power: Sexual harassment on campus.* Albany: State University of New York Press.

PEARSON, J. C., & WEST, R. (1991). An initial investigation of the effects of gender on student questions in the classroom: Developing a descriptive base. *Communication Education, 40,* 22–32.

PETERSEN, T. M., KEARNEY, P., PLAX, T. G., & WALDECK, J. H. (1997). Students' affective evaluations of the professor and course: To what extent is teacher sexism relevant? *Women's Studies in Communication, 20,* 151–165.

PETERSON, E. E. (1991). Moving toward a gender balanced curriculum in basic speech communication courses. *Communication Education, 40,* 60–72.

PETERSON, S., & LACH, M. (1990). Gender stereotypes in children's books: Their prevalence and influence on cognitive and affective development. *Gender and Education, 2,* 185–197.

PIPHER, M. (1994). *Reviving Ophelia: Saving the selves of adolescent girls.* New York: Ballantine.

RICH, A. (1979). *On lies, secrets, and silence: Selected prose 1966–1978.* New York: W. W. Norton.

RICHARDSON, L. W., COOK, J., & MACKE, A. S. (1981). Classroom management strategies of male and female university professors. In L. Richardson & V. Taylor (Eds.), *Issues in sex, gender, and society.* Lexington, MA: D. C. Heath.

ROSENFELD, L. B., & JARRARD, M. W. (1986). Student coping mechanisms in sexist and nonsexist professors' classes. *Communication Education, 35,* 157–162.

ROWE, K. E. (1986). Feminism and fairy tales. In J. Zipes (Ed.), *Don't bet on the prince: Contemporary feminist fairy tales in North America and England* (pp. 209–226). New York: Methuen.

RYAN, M. (1989). Classroom and contexts: The challenge of feminist pedagogy. *Feminist Teacher, 4,* 39–42.

SADKER, M., & SADKER, D. (1980). *Beyond pictures and pronouns: Sexism in teacher education textbooks.* Washington, DC: Office of Education.

SADKER, M., & SADKER, D. (1985, March). Sexism in the schoolroom of the '80's. *Psychology Today,* 54–57.

SADKER, M., & SADKER, D. (1994). *Failing at fairness: How America's schools cheat girls.* New York: Charles Scribner's Sons.

SANDLER, B. R. (1997). Student-to-student sexual harassment. In B. R. Sandler & R. J. Shoop (Eds.), *Sexual harassment on campus: A guide for administrators, faculty, and students* (pp. 50–65). Boston: Allyn & Bacon.

SANDLER, B. R., & HALL, R. M. (1986). *The campus climate revisited: Chilly for women faculty, administrators, and graduate students.* Washington, DC: Project on the Status and Education of Women, Association of American Colleges.

SEALS, B. (1997). Faculty-to-faculty sexual harassment. In B. R. Sandler & R. J. Shoop (Eds.), *Sexual harassment on campus: A guide for administrators, faculty, and students* (pp. 66–84). Boston: Allyn & Bacon.

SEESE, D. (1992, July 24). Kids' book about gay father sets town abuzz. *Raleigh News and Observer,* pp. 1B, 5B.

SELLS, L. (1995). Where do the mermaids stand? Voice and body in *The Little Mermaid*. In E. Bell, L. Haas, & L. Sells (Eds.), *From mouse to mermaid: The politics of film, gender, and culture* (pp. 175–192). Bloomington: Indiana University Press.

SHERER, M. L. (1992). School liability under Title IX for peer sexual harassment. *Pennsylvania Law Review, 141,* 2119–2175.

SPRAGUE, J. (1975). The reduction of sexism in speech communication education. *Speech Teacher, 24,* 37–45.

SPRATLING, C. (1997, April 17). Brave, clever girls grace new volumes: Heroines in new girls' books don't sit around waiting on the prince. *Corpus Christi Caller Times,* pp. B1, B7.

STEINEGER, M. (1993, September). Gender bias persists in texts and literature. *Northwest report: The challenge of sex equity.* Portland, OR: Northwest Regional Educational Laboratory.

STERNGLANZ, S. H., & LYBERGER-FICEK, S. (1977). Sex differences in student-teacher interactions in the college classroom. *Sex Roles, 3,* 345–352.

SUNSTEIN HYMOWITZ, K. (1991, August 19 & 26). Babar the racist. *The New Republic,* 12–13.

TETENBAUM, T. J., & PEARSON, J. (1989). The voices in children's literature: The impact of gender on the moral decisions of storybook characters. *Sex Roles, 20,* 381–395.

THORNE, B. (1979). *Claiming verbal space: Women, speech, and language in college classrooms.* Paper presented at the Conference on Educational Environments and the Undergraduate Woman, Wellesley College, Wellesley, MA.

TREICHLER, P. A., & KRAMARAE, C. (1983). Women's talk in the ivory tower. *Communication Quarterly, 31,* 118–132.

TRITES, R. (1991). Disney's sub/version of Andersen's *The Little Mermaid. Journal of Popular Film and Television, 18,* 145–152.

UNGER, R., & CRAWFORD, M. (1996). *Women and gender: A feminist psychology* (2nd ed.). New York: McGraw-Hill.

VINNEDGE, M. (1996, December 29). Historical novel series aimed at girl readers. *Corpus Christi Caller Times,* p. G13.

WELLHOUSEN, K., & YIN, Z. (1997). "Peter Pan isn't a girls' part": An investigation of gender bias in a kindergarten classroom. *Women & Language, 20,* 35–39.

WHITE, H. (1986). Damsels in distress: Dependency themes in fiction for children and adolescents. *Adolescence, 21,* 251–256.

WOOD, J. T., & LENZE, L. F. (1991). Strategies to enhance gender sensitivity in communication education. *Communication Education, 40,* 16–21.

ZIPES, J. (1986). *Don't bet on the prince: Contemporary feminist fairy tales in North America and England.* New York: Methuen.

ZIPES, J. (1995). Breaking the Disney spell. In E. Bell, L. Haas, & L. Sells (Eds.), *From mouse to mermaid: The politics of film, gender, and culture* (pp. 21–42). Bloomington: Indiana University Press.

ZIRKEL, P. A. (1995). Student-to-student sexual harassment. *Phi Delta Kappan, 76,* 648–650.

THE IMPACT OF SOCIAL MOVEMENTS ON GENDER COMMUNICATION

You Must Know Where You've Been to Know Where You're Going

As you now approach the end of the semester, we suspect that you've written papers, given presentations, and been tested over some of the information in this textbook. Imagine for a moment that, because of effective teaching and students' hard work, on each test you've taken in this class everyone has received a score of 100 percent. Yet when you receive a listing of the grades in the class, something is amiss. The men's scores reflect 100 percent, but each woman receives a grade of 75 percent. The teacher records As for the male students and Cs for the female students. How can this be? We use this scenario to exemplify the point that in 1995 women still received approximately 75 cents to each dollar of pay men received (Neft & Levine, 1997).

So where do we go from here? Previous chapters afforded the opportunity to examine contemporary gender communication, but it is also important to recognize some of the historical and cultural events that have shaped where we are today. In the pages that follow we survey history, both women's movements and men's movements, and take a look at some of the individuals who have contributed to social, economic, and political changes that have affected and will continue to affect gender communication. But it is beyond the scope of this epilogue to focus on each and every social movement that has had an impact. If we fail to mention individuals or movements you deem significant, we hope you will use the omission as a beginning point for class discussions.

*This epilogue benefited from the significant contributions of a guest author, Nada Frazier Cano.

LEARNING "HERSTORY"

Regardless of whether you personally embrace feminism, much of what you do and enjoy today is the result of actions and advocacies of feminists. Some of you no doubt have grown up taking equality for granted; fortunately, it may be all you have ever known. But it is because of dedicated feminists that many of you are sitting in this classroom today.

It's impossible to detail every significant feminist in American history. The truth is we simply don't know or don't have information about each significant women's rights and civil rights advocate. Those we do know about are not representative of all who fought to get us where we are today. It's important to remember, especially with respect to women and members of minority groups, that most were considered the property of privileged men. They were not always afforded educational opportunities and often were denied a voice. Those we discuss here somehow made their way into the annals of history, but they are by no means the only ones who made valuable contributions. While history books today are much more inclusive than they've ever been, many would argue they are still "his story," as opposed to "her story." Let's begin by focusing on developments in the realm of education.

Men, Education, and Women—in That Order

When you enter class today look around you. Notice the number of university students who once were barred from the education you are receiving today. Who's responsible for education expanding and becoming accessible to everyone? How did it happen? Have you ever wondered what it was that motivated women and minorities to openly challenge their social status and work so passionately for basic human rights? It is in details such as the ones that follow where we see those moments in history that led to where we sit today.

In Colonial times American women, under the guidance of men, focused on their "helpmeet" role, which centered on economically essential household production (Theriot, 1996, p. 17). In 1778 a Quaker grammar school opened to educate rural mothers responsible for teaching their children (Bernikow, 1997). Emma Hart Willard is often considered the first important female educator in America (Weatherford, 1994). In 1818 Willard appealed to the New York state legislature to allocate taxes for the education of young women, an outlandish concept at the time. Her requests were denied. Most legislators were shocked that Willard proposed to teach anatomy; they believed her curriculum contrary to God's will for women. She later founded the Troy Female Seminary in New York state, which incorporated an unprecedented mathematics and science curriculum that sought to provide women with a comparable education to men's (Lunardini, 1994; Weatherford, 1994).

The first public high school for girls opened in 1824 in Worcester, Massachusetts. Connecticut Quaker Prudence Crandall was arrested and convicted of defying Connecticut's "black law" (Weatherford, 1994, p. 93) when she dared to educate "negro girls" in her boarding school (Bernikow, 1997, p. 127). All shops and meeting houses in the town were closed to her and her pupils. Doctors would not treat them, the well on her property was filled with manure, and rotten eggs and stones were hurled at her home. In 1834 Crandall's school was set ablaze and burned to the ground.

In 1837 Mary Lyon founded Mount Holyoke Female Seminary in South Hadley, Massachusetts, which was the first to educate women who were not from the upper class. In 1837 Oberlin College began to admit women students, as did Antioch College in 1853 and Vassar College in 1865 (Bernikow, 1997). However, these progressive steps were still far from ensuring women's equality in education.

Dr. Edward Clarke, a prestigious Harvard Medical School professor, was vehemently opposed to the formal education of women, claiming higher education harmed not only women but their offspring as well. Doctors who followed Clarke's teachings included S. Weir Mitchell, a then-famous neurologist, who treated Charlotte Perkins Gilman, a commercial artist and writer, and instructed her to "Live as domestic a life as possible. Have but two hours of intellectual life a day. And never touch pen, brush, or pencil as long as you live" (Bernikow, 1997, pp. 153, 154). Gilman defiantly recovered from Mitchell's "cure" and wrote about it in her 1890 short story *The Yellow Wallpaper*, which fictionalized her mental breakdown and contained a radically feminist thesis for the time.

In 1908 New York City teachers, struggling for equal pay for equal work, were forced to resign when they married. School authorities were even known to search the schools for pregnant teachers. Henrietta Rodman, a high school English teacher, quarreled that teachers should be fired for misconduct, but that "marriage is not misconduct." She was suspended when she wrote a letter to the *New York Tribune* protesting the Board of Education's "mother-baiting," and in 1916 went on to form the Teacher's League, later to become the American Federation of Teachers (Bernikow, 1997, p. 148).

The First Wave of Feminism

England's Mary Wollstonecraft is regarded as one of the first feminists. Her book *A Vindication of the Rights of Woman*, which called for women's equality with men, is still widely studied today. Abigail Smith Adams, wife of the second U.S. President John Adams and mother of the sixth president, John Quincy Adams, is considered an early feminist as well. She is credited with writing letters in 1776 to her husband while he was at the Continental Congress, prodding him to "remember the ladies" (Lunardini, 1994, p. 16). However, the Constitution originally barred women, African-Americans, American Indians, and many poor people from participation. For years after the Constitution was adopted women were legally subjugated to their husbands. According to the laws in most states, a married woman "literally did not own the clothes on her back"; her husband legally possessed her and

Women are systematically degraded by receiving the trivial attentions which men think it manly to pay to the sex, when, in fact, men are insultingly supporting their own superiority.

Mary Wollstonecraft, British feminist

everything she earned (Weatherford, 1994, p. 222). Married women could not sign contracts or obtain credit. The first middle-class women employed by the federal government in the Patent Office received paychecks made out to their husbands (Weatherford, 1994).

Suffragists: The Early Equality Seekers

Imagine that as you leave class today you go to vote in the student government elections, only to find that men are allowed to vote but the women on campus are being turned away or are arrested and imprisoned for voting. This was what America was like less than 100 years ago. The origins of feminism can be found in antislavery (abolitionist) and temperance campaigns (Humm, 1992). One of the initial launching grounds for women's organized efforts was in 1837 at the first national antislavery convention in New York. Celebrated female abolitionists at the time included Lucy Stone, Angelina Grimke, Sarah Grimke, Lucretia Mott, Elizabeth Cady Stanton, and Susan B. Anthony. Mott was a delegate at the World Antislavery Convention in London where American women were excluded from participation and forced to sit in the balcony behind a curtain (Greenspan, 1994). After this event Mott's and Stanton's activism for women's equality, particularly their efforts to win women's right to vote, intensified.

On July 19, 1848, the first Women's Rights Convention was held in Seneca Falls, New York, with some 300 women and men attending. (Feminists worldwide celebrated the 150th anniversary of this historic convention in 1998 with another convention on women's rights at Seneca Falls.) Mott and Stanton, along with other early feminists Jane Hunt, Mary McClintock, and Martha Wright, advocated for social policy changes including equality between husbands and wives and women's suffrage. Stanton wrote the "Declaration of Sentiments," modeled after the Declaration of Independence, which stated, "We hold these truths to be self evident, that all men *and women* are created equal" (Ruth, 1990, p. 460). It further listed 18 legal grievances and called for major reform in suffrage, marriage, and inheritance laws (Greenspan, 1994).

Reprinted with special permission of King Features Syndicate.

As is the case today with feminists, varying opinions on issues emerged that led to the establishment of two distinct suffrage organizations, the National Woman Suffrage Association (NWSA) founded by Susan B. Anthony and Elizabeth Cady Stanton, and the American Woman Suffrage Association (AWSA) founded by Lucy Stone. (Stone graduated first in her class in 1847 at Oberlin College, but was forced to sit in the audience while a male student read her valedictory speech.) Lucy Stone is also known for retaining her birth name and not taking her husband's name when she married. Women who followed her lead became known as "Lucy Stoners" (Bernikow, 1997, p. 287). NWSA argued that as long as women were denied their rights, all other issues had to be secondary. The AWSA disagreed with a "radical" nationwide suffrage movement and instead focused on enacting change to individual state constitutions (Lunardini, 1994).

Feminist discontent intensified in 1870 when the 15th Amendment to the Constitution ensured former male slaves the right to vote, but did not extend that right to women (Lunardini, 1994). As a result, the national election of 1872 was fraught with controversy, even by today's standards. Although she didn't have the legal right to vote, activist Victoria Woodhull, called "Mrs. Satan" by her many opponents, ran for President of the United States (Bernikow, 1997, p. 7). Woodhull's bid for the presidency ended when she was arrested by moral crusader Anthony Comstock for disseminating "obscene" material through the mail, although she was eventually acquitted under First Amendment protections (Lunardini, 1994, p. 92). The material Comstock found obscene was Woodhull's writings that advocated free love, shorter skirts for women, and legalized prostitution.

Also during the 1872 election Susan B. Anthony and hundreds of women attempted to vote, knowing that it was against the law (Lunardini, 1994). Anthony was arrested for daring to cast a vote, tried in a U.S. District Court, convicted, and ordered to pay a $100 fine (Weatherford, 1994). Anthony was not allowed to speak at her trial as the law deemed her incompetent to testify because she was a woman. There were other "subversive" attempts to vote: Dr. Mary Walker dressed in men's clothes and tried to vote in Oswego, New York, and Sojourner Truth tried to vote in Battle Creek, Michigan, but to no avail for both (Bernikow, 1997).

> *It pisses me off when women, for whatever reason, don't use the word "feminist" when they are all benefiting from the great feminists who struggled and suffered and worked to give us everything women now enjoy—including the right to vote, to bring a lawsuit, the right to custody in a divorce—everything. I feel it is my responsibility to use that word because of all the sacrifices women have made.*
>
> *Cybill Shepherd, actor*

Women continued to fight for the right to vote, but success would not come easily. Suffragists organized massive rallies and demonstrations, staged boycotts and hunger strikes, destroyed property, chained themselves to public buildings, and carried out other acts of civil disobedience (Neft & Levine, 1997). Thousands continued to march; they picketed the White House six days a week, and over a period of two militant years, 500 women were arrested (Bernikow, 1997).

Other notable early feminists were Harriett Tubman and Sojourner Truth. Escaped slave Tubman is best known for running the Underground Railroad, but she was also a feminist, nurse, and Civil War spy for the North (Ventura, 1998). Tubman is credited with leading an 1863 raid that freed 750 slaves, and she became the first American woman to lead troops into battle in the Civil War (Greenspan, 1994). At the 1851 Women's Rights Convention, Sojourner Truth made one of her marks in history. Truth was the only woman of color in attendance and amidst the jeers of hostile men she delivered her famous "Ain't I a Woman" speech (Greenspan, 1994, p. 237). Truth, a preacher, suffragist, and abolitionist, was born a slave, sold away from her parents, and traded numerous times. As an adult, her children were sold away from her (Ventura, 1998). Truth dedicated her life to activism against slavery and for segregation and women's rights.

After decades of activism, finally in 1920 the 19th Amendment granting women the right to vote was ratified into law. Many of you probably were unaware of the fact that white women and women of color did not have the right to vote in this country until 50 years after black men (former slaves) were granted their right to vote. Once women obtained the right to vote the public's interest in women's rights waned and, collectively, feminism lay dormant for years, until World War II changed everything.

Enter "Rosie the Riveter"

World War II sent men off to war and motivated women to enter the work-force to fill industry jobs. More than 6 million women went to work outside the home for the first time, with the majority employed in factory or clerical jobs in war-related industries (Neft & Levine, 1997). "Rosie the Riveter" be-came a national symbol for women's contributions to the war effort (Colman, 1995). Some employers still refused to hire women, causing the War Depart-ment in 1943 to distribute the booklet *You're Going to Employ Women*. The pub-lication advised employers as follows: "In some respects women workers are superior to men. Properly hired, properly trained, properly handled, new women employees are splendidly efficient workers. The desire of a new worker to help win the war—to shorten it even by a minute—gives her an en-thusiasm that more than offsets industrial experience" (Colman, 1995, p. 73). Women became employed as welders, electricians, mechanics, police officers, lawyers, statisticians, journalists, and boilermakers. They operated streetcars, taxis, cranes, buses, tractors, and planes.

Job opportunities for women dried up in 1945 when the war ended. Women were terminated in order to ensure jobs for men returning home from the war. Propaganda from government and industry tried to sell women on the idea that it was their patriotic duty to return home and take care of their husbands and children. Those women who attempted to keep their war-time jobs were still laid off or forced into lower-paying jobs. Women who wanted or needed employment were encouraged to find tradi-tional women's work as teachers, nurses, or clerical workers. The obvious message to women was that it was their role or duty to focus on husband, children, and home. And for many, home they went and home they stayed (Colman, 1995).

The Civil Rights Movement

Life in Montgomery, Alabama, in 1955 was much different than it is today. Racism was rampant; racist and segregationist rules and practices were the norm. African Americans riding city buses had to enter the front of a bus to pay a fare, and then get off and enter the bus again from the rear door. They were also required to give up their seats if white people were standing (Lunar-dini, 1994). Rosa Parks, a mild-mannered African American seamstress in her mid-forties, was seated in the first row of the blacks only section when the white section filled up, leaving a white man without a seat (Ventura, 1998). Parks was arrested for failing to follow the bus driver's instructions to surren-der her bus seat to the white man (Lunardini, 1994; Ventura, 1998). Parks was found guilty of the offense but refused to pay her fine and appealed the deci-sion. Both Parks and her husband lost their jobs and received threats to their lives (Ventura, 1998). Within three days of Park's arrest, Alabama African Americans began a massive bus boycott that continued for a year until Al-abama's state and city bus segregation policies were found unconstitutional (Lunardini, 1994).

From this point on, Martin Luther King, Jr., and other civil rights leaders began to vehemently demand overdue civil rights reforms. Women and men fought for racial progress by joining organizations such as the Students' Non-violent Coordinating Committee (SNCC) and Students for a Democratic Society (SDS). Soon Martin Luther King, Jr., Malcolm X, John F. Kennedy, and Robert Kennedy would all be assassinated. Young men would head off to fight the Vietnam War while others would protest it by proclaiming we should "make love, not war." For many, the 1960s were about change and challenging "the establishment." For some, it was a time of sexual revolution—a revolution with profound impact on relationships and communication between women and men.

The Sexual Revolution

We've spent time in previous chapters discussing gender communication in intimate relationships. Again, relevant historical events provide glimpses of some of the roads we traveled to get where we are today. Some women have practiced birth control in one form or another throughout history, just not always legally. Margaret Sanger was among the first to make the connection between reproductive rights and women's economic and social equality. She felt that birth control was the key to women's equality (Ventura, 1998). In 1914 Sanger began publishing a journal entitled *Woman Rebel*. Even though it contained no specific contraceptive information, it violated laws of the time and led to Sanger's arrest and indictment by an all-male grand jury. In 1916 she opened a Brooklyn clinic where, in the 10 days before police shut it down and arrested Sanger, 500 women were given diaphragms smuggled in from Europe (Weatherford, 1994). While upholding the laws of the day, courts did allow physicians to prescribe contraceptives for women and condoms for men to prevent venereal disease (Lunardini, 1994). By 1938 federal courts altered obscenity laws. Sanger and associates opened a network of 300 birth control clinics nationwide and in 1942 they established the Birth Control League, which later would become the Planned Parenthood Association (Lunardini, 1994).

In 1960 the Food and Drug Administration approved the manufacture and sale of "the pill" as a new form of contraception, which quickly became the keystone of the so-called sexual revolution (Lunardini, 1994, p. 297). Many people believe that this one innovation in the form of a simple pill helped make the ideas of women's liberation more practical and acceptable to a wider range of American women. In 1965 the Supreme Court ruled that states could not ban the distribution of contraceptives to married people; in 1972 rights were extended to purchase contraceptives without regard to marital status (Weatherford, 1994). For many, the sexual revolution marked the first time that women could freely explore their sexuality without serious concern of becoming pregnant.

The sexual revolution accompanied the escalation of a "singles" culture, including the hippie movement's advocacy of "free sex" and the 1970s "swinging" lifestyle, which led to a higher rate of cohabitation and sexual partner switching (Lunardini, 1994, pp. 297–298). Since the 1960s, the number of American heterosexual couples living together has increased by approximately 600 percent (Neft & Levine, 1997). Approximately half a million couples cohabited in 1960; by 1994 that figure had grown to 3.6 million. The gay rights movement emerged as well during this period, which opened discussions on sexuality and the oppression of homosexuals in society. In 1973 the American Psychiatric Association officially declassified homosexuality as a psychiatric disorder (Bernikow, 1997). Yes, the times, they were a changing, as goes the Bob Dylan song.

The Second Wave of Feminism

In 1953 French writer and philosopher Simone de Beauvoir published *The Second Sex,* which "argued that women—like all human beings—were in essence free but that they had almost always been trapped by particularly inflexible and limiting conditions. Only by means of courageous action and self-assertive creativity could a woman become a completely free person and escape the role of the inferior 'other' that men had constructed for her gender" (McKay, Hill, & Buckler, 1995, p. 1055).

The Second-Class Status of Women

In 1961 President John F. Kennedy appointed Eleanor Roosevelt to chair the Commission on the Status of Women (Weatherford, 1994). Author of several books on women's history, Louise Bernikow (1997) describes the status of U.S. women before 1965:

> Married women could not establish credit in their own names, which meant no credit cards or mortgages or other financial transactions were possible without a husband's agreement. Newspapers carried sex-segregated help-wanted ads. Employers routinely assigned certain jobs to women, others to men, with the women's jobs paying far less. There were few women in law or medical school and few visibly prominent in those professions. Under most state laws, women were routinely not allowed to be administrators of estates. Working women who became pregnant could be fired. An employer who insisted that in order to keep her job, a female employee have sex with him or submit to fondling was not breaking the law. (pp. 43–44)

The report from the Commission on the Status of Women documented discriminatory practices in government, education, and employment and included recommendations for reform. Many states followed suit and identified state discriminations. Hundreds of daily situations exemplified the second-class status of women in our society.

Here's an example. We have it on good authority that some (and we emphasize the word *some*) students (over the age of 21, of course) have been known to frequent an occasional bar or dance club. Today most would not consider that unusual. However, in the 19th and much of the 20th century, women who frequented bars were generally assumed to be prostitutes. Businesses wanting a respectable reputation either banned women or provided a separate ladies' lounge. During World War II millions of women entered bars for the first time to join men in smoking and drinking. In 1948 an unsuccessful lawsuit was filed attempting to overturn legislation that prohibited women from working as bartenders unless their husbands or fathers owned the bar. Some states even maintained legislation into the 1970s that prohibited women from sitting at a bar, rather than at a table (Weatherford, 1994).

At the recommendation of the president's Commission on the Status of Women, Congress passed the Equal Pay Act of 1963, which was the first national legislation for women's employment since the Progressive era. However, it has proved rather difficult to enforce (Lunardini, 1994). The Civil Rights Act of 1964 prohibited private employers from discriminating on the basis of race, color, religion, national origin, or sex.

The Problem That Has No Name

In 1963 American author Betty Friedan, a Smith College graduate who shortly after graduation married and began raising her family, helped awaken the feminist movement with the publication of her book, *The Feminine Mystique*. Friedan wrote of the "problem that has no name," which she described as a vague feeling of discontent and aimlessness (p. 15). Friedan's book helped break the silence on issues such as unequal salaries, limited opportunities, and women's powerlessness in family and society (Lunardini, 1994). Friedan argued that editors of women's magazines, advertising experts, Freudian psychologists, social scientists, and educators "contributed to a romanticization of domesticity she termed 'the feminine mystique'" (Kerber & De Hart, 1991, p. 505). She further asserted that women should help themselves out of their malaise and take positive steps to reassert their identities (Lunardini, 1994). Quickly Friedan became a celebrity with a mission.

For those of you who often fly on airplanes, think about the diversity you now see among flight attendants. Did you know that up until the late 1960s, flight attendants (called "stewardesses" at the time) were forced to resign when they reached their early 30s, gained too much weight, or married? When hired, they were expected to be the "American image of the wholesome 'girl-next-door,' which meant white and attractive in a feminine, youthful sense" (Tobias, 1997, p. 88). In 1966 Betty Friedan testified against the airlines' inherent sex discrimination policies and further disclosed the bottom line: Airlines saved substantial amounts of money by firing women before they had time to accumulate pay increases, vacation time, and pension rights (Friedan, 1963).

Getting Their Acts Together

In 1966 Friedan and 27 other women attending the Washington, D.C., Third National Conference of the Commission on the Status of Women founded the National Organization for Women, commonly referred to as NOW (NOW, 1998). NOW committed to "take action to bring women into full participation in the mainstream of American society . . . " (Friedan, 1963, p. 384). The organization clearly communicated that women were ready for action *now*. In NOW's first five years, it grew from 28 members to 15,000 (Lunardini, 1994). In 1998 NOW included 250,000 members with more than 550 chapters in the 50 states and the District of Columbia (NOW, 1998). NOW incorporates both traditional and nontraditional ways to advance social change, including extensive lobbying, filing of lawsuits, mass marches, rallies, picketing, and nonviolent civil disobedience. NOW's official priorities include winning economic equality and securing it with a Constitutional amendment guaranteeing equal rights for women; championing abortion rights, reproductive freedom, and other women's health issues; and opposing racism, fighting bigotry against lesbians and gays, and ending violence against women.

Other organizations such as the Women's Equity Action League (WEAL) formed to further women's issues. In 1987 the Feminist Majority was founded to promote "equality for women and men, non-violence, social justice and economic development and to enhance feminist participation in public policy" with a mission to "empower feminists to win equality for women at the decision-making tables of the state, nation, and the world" (Feminist Majority, 1998, p. 1).

Ms. Gloria Steinem

"Gloria Steinem's name is synonymous with feminism" (Ventura, 1998, p. 160). Steinem is certainly one of the most renowned feminists. She is often remembered for her journalistic undercover assignment in 1963 as a Playboy Bunny, which she subsequently wrote about. Steinem, a leading activist in the early days of NOW, joined Bella Abzug and Shirley Chisholm in 1971 to found the National Women's Political Caucus (Weatherford, 1994). This group encourages women to become involved as officeholders, volunteers, political appointees, convention delegates, judges, and committee members (Lunardini, 1994). Steinem then created *Ms.* magazine, which became the first mainstream feminist magazine in American history (Ventura, 1997). In 1971 the preview issue of *Ms.* hit the stands, and the initial 300,000 copies were sold out within 10 days (Thom, 1997). The *Ms.* Foundation for Women, organized in 1972, further supports the efforts of women and girls to govern their own lives and influence the world around them (*Ms.* Foundation for Women, 1998).

Feminist activists made numerous other groundbreaking accomplishments in a short period of time. In 1969 San Diego State University established the first women's studies baccalaureate degree program (Lunardini, 1994). In 1970 the first congressional hearings on sex discrimination in education were held. In 1972 Title IX of the Education Omnibus Act passed, penalizing educational institutions for sex discrimination in schools. In 1973 the *Roe* v. *Wade* Supreme Court decision legalized abortion. In 1975 the Equal Credit Opportunity Act made credit more available to women. In 1975 the Rhodes Scholarship Foundation, which funded undergraduate study at Oxford University, no longer excluded women from consideration as Rhodes Scholars (Bernikow, 1997). In 1981 Sandra Day O'Connor was appointed the first female justice on the U.S.

Supreme Court. In 1983 Sally Ride became the first female astronaut. In 1984 Geraldine Ferraro became the first female vice presidential candidate, as running mate in Walter Mondale's bid for the presidency. Granted, there were lots of changes, but women still did not have the same, full equal rights as men.

The Equal Rights Amendment (ERA)

Much like gaining the right to vote brought first wave feminists together to focus on a common goal, ratification of the Equal Rights Amendment (ERA) united many second wave feminists. You may not realize that the ERA was first introduced to Congress in 1923 (Andersen, 1997). For almost 50 years it lay dormant. The 1972 version of the ERA states, "Equality of rights under the law shall not be denied or abridged by the United States or by any State on account of sex" (Kerber & De Hart, 1991, p. 547). By an overwhelming majority, both houses of Congress passed the ERA in 1972. Shortly thereafter, 28 of the needed 38 states had ratified the ERA (Lunardini, 1994). Phyllis Schlafly, a staunchly conservative voice of the time, rallied in opposition to the ERA, predicting the destruction of the family, among other things. A campaign known as STOP-ERA spread fear that women would be drafted and might have to serve in combat if the ERA passed (Andersen, 1997; Lunardini, 1994). In 1982 the ERA failed, just 3 states shy of the 38 needed for ratification. In 1983 the amendment was reintroduced to Congress, but its passage is still pending (Kerber & De Hart, 1991).

> *[The fight for the Equal Rights Amendment] is about a socialist, anti-family political movement that encourages women to leave their husbands, kill their children, practice witchcraft, destroy capitalism, and become lesbians.*
>
> *Pat Robertson, televangelist & former presidential candidate*

No Such Thing as "THE" Feminists

One way to reduce or contain the power of something is to disassemble it. In our history we've seen whole treaties devoted to dismantling nuclear weaponry, for example. One way to reduce the perceived power of a movement, such as civil rights or feminism, is to suggest that members of the movement should be one cohesive group, all in agreement, all using the same rhetoric, and all dedicated to the same causes. When it is inevitably discovered that disagreement or diversity exists within the ranks, then the movement can be criticized and the causes ignored, because "they can't even agree among themselves." The perceived threat to the status quo is thereby reduced, the people in power protected.

Feminism has always been diverse; the belief in the value of diverse approaches and voices is one of feminism's strengths, not its weakness. But people continue to criticize the movement because of a perceived lack of cohesiveness. This was quite evident during the Clinton sex scandal of 1998, when feminists were roundly chastised for not speaking out "with one voice" in defense of women who were hurt by Clinton's actions. Remember hearing the pundits and politicians ask "Where are *the* feminists on this issue?"

During the first wave of feminism, philosophies about women's rights diverged and followers splintered off into separate groups. But women still achieved the goal of getting the right to vote, among other goals. In the second wave of feminism, even more viewpoints developed. Some believe that we're still in the second wave; however, some assert that that wave ended with the failure to ratify the ERA. As we discussed back in Chapter 1, there are those who celebrate the "death of feminism," suggesting that it's no longer needed because women today have just as many options and privileges as men. These persons believe we live in a postfeminist time. Still others argue that we are experiencing a third wave of feminism (discussed in more detail below), one that younger generations have taken up and that is very much alive in working to improve the status of women in our culture.

To attempt to place each and every feminist in a tidy, clearly discernible philosophical box is limiting at best and inaccurate at worst. Feminism is not definitive. Feminism, by its very nature, resists definition and embraces diversity and choice. Yet, there are certain ideologies within different subsets of feminism that can be described. In the following paragraphs, we explore various types of feminism we've researched, but we ask you to realize that this list is not exhaustive and that some descriptions may rely on generalities.

Diverse Ideologies within the Women's Movement

In the late 1960s and early 1970s, there were various movements within the women's movement. Sociologist Margaret Andersen (1997) proposes that the feminist movement evolved into basically two major ideologies: the women's rights branch and the women's liberation branch. The primary objective of the women's rights group was to work for equal rights, particularly through legal reform and antidiscrimination policies. Leaders of the women's rights branch tended to be older, to have had work experiences or professional training, and to have been more likely to form or join organized feminist groups (Kerber & DeHart, 1991). The women's liberation branch sought further evolution through transformation in women's status, requiring not just legal and political reform but also radical transformation of such basic social institutions as the family, sexuality, religion, and education (Andersen, 1997). Women's liberationists tended to be younger and less highly educated, and their political style was often shaped by the dissent and violence of the 1960s (Kerber & DeHart, 1991).

Popular writings and media sound bites communicate a plethora of feminist messages, including ecofeminism, which combines interests in women's and environmental issues (Eve Online, 1998), Christian feminism, and womanism (a label that now applies specifically to the feminism of African Americans) (Humm, 1992, pp. 404, 409), power feminism, academic feminism (Wolf, 1994, pp. 3, 53), gender feminism, equity feminism (Hoff Sommers, 1994, pp. 16, 18), pod feminism, postideological feminism (Faludi, 1995, pp. 2, 6), dissident feminism (Paglia, as in Madigan, 1995, p. 9), "do me feminism," and "who me?" feminism (Pollit, 1994, p. 369). According to Karen Lehrman (1992), writing in the *New Republic*, "'Multicultural feminism' has spawned so many divisions and subsets—Native American feminists, gay feminists, Jewish feminists, biracial feminists—that the whole concept of 'sisterhood' is fast dissolving" (p. 11). Certain strands of feminism have faded into history while others have prominently emerged. It is not uncommon, however, for feminist philosophies or viewpoints to blend or overlap at times and for various strands to share members, because, as we've stated, no one guiding perspective can be identified as *the* feminist perspective. Generally, however, three feminist theories are predominant: liberal, socialist, and radical feminism (Andersen, 1997).

Liberal Feminism. Women's studies scholar Maggie Humm (1992) defines *liberal feminism* as "the theory of individual freedom for women. Liberal feminism is one of the main streams of feminist political and social theory and has the most long-term history" (p. 407). The focus of this feminism is on social and legal reform through policies designed to create equal opportunities for women. Liberal reforms center around reproductive rights, equity in employment, and increased public consciousness of women's rights.

Socialist Feminism. "Socialist feminism believes that women are second-class citizens in patriarchal capitalism which depends for its survival on the exploitation of working people, and on the special exploitation of women" (Humm, 1992, p. 409). Socialist feminists believe that patriarchy and capitalism interact to create women's oppression, to further define women as the property of men, and to exploit them for the purposes of profit (Andersen, 1997).

Radical Feminism. According to Humm (1992), radical feminism "argues that women's oppression comes from being categorized as an inferior class on the basis of gender. Radical feminism aims to destroy this sex class system. What makes this feminism radical is that it focuses on the roots of male domination and claims that all forms of oppression are extensions of male supremacy" (p. 408). Radical feminism is predominantly based in Marxist doctrine; it focuses on patriarchy as the significant cause of women's oppression (Andersen, 1997). This movement embraces a separatist philosophy of radical lesbian feminism, which promotes a woman-centered world that excludes men.

With the diversity of feminism and the blurring of feminist camp lines, some women felt (and still feel) alienated by the movement. Women who worked inside the home and enjoyed more traditional family styles often felt that they had little in common with feminists. Some feminists perpetuated the mistrust by not validating those women who truly wanted to be traditional housewives and mothers (Lunardini, 1994). While feminists vehemently pushed to further their causes and gain choice, they violated the feminist golden rule—they often devalued the choices of women who followed more traditional paths.

The Third Wave of Feminism

Some media in the 1990s enjoyed publicizing the notion that feminism died a slow and painful death, resulting in postfeminism (Hoff Sommers, 1994). However, Pulitzer Prize–winning journalist Susan Faludi, author of *Backlash: The Undeclared War Against American Women* (1991), proposes that each time women move towards equality, a backlash occurs to restrain them, as was the case for both the first and second waves of feminism. A backlash, according to Faludi, is not an organized conspiracy, but a subtle, yet persuasive, campaign against feminist objectives which emerges in attempts to rescind many of the gains previously made by the women's movement. It is a deceptive force that permeates American culture via national and local politics and the mass media, and it prompts women to question whether equality is what they really want. A backlash will identify feminism as the devil incarnate and feminists as miserable, lonely, childless, and emotionally unstable.

But look out now for "the third wave," a feminist movement for the 21st century (briefly mentioned in Chapter 1). In her book *Faces of Feminism: An Activist's Reflections on the Women's Movement*, Sheila Tobias (1997) describes this new strain of feminism that women in their 20s and 30s who are proud to call themselves "the third wave" developed in the 1990s (p. 252). These young feminists have not only increased their individual commitments to feminism, but also have shown a growing willingness to take collective action to effect change. Third wave feminists focus on such issues as parental consent laws; AIDS education and awareness; reproductive rights; freedom from sexual abuse, violence, and rape;

> *I'm proud to be a lifelong one [feminist]. It's as natural as breathing, feeling, and thinking. Never go back, never apologize, and never forget we're half the human race.*
>
> *Bella Abzug,*
> *political activist*

anorexia and bulimia; poverty; and homelessness among youth (Renzetti & Curran, 1995; Tobias, 1997).

Third wavers Rebecca Walker, daughter of feminist author Alice Walker, and Barbara Findlen, an associate editor for *Ms.*, claim to have registered 25,000 new inner-city voters in one year (Tobias, 1997). Other third wavers have formed such groups as the National Women's Student Coalition and the Third Wave Direct Action Corporation, which are said to be loosely organized and nonhierarchical, often employing radical tactics to effect social and political change. Most third wave feminist groups focus on inclusion, have a multicultural emphasis, and strive to address problems stemming from sexism, racism, social class inequality, and homophobia (Renzetti & Curran, 1995).

Like we said earlier in this epilogue, no matter whether you call yourself a feminist or embrace feminist ideals, you are now likely to be more aware of the opportunities and freedoms you enjoy that are a direct result of feminists' hard work, determination, and dedication to equality. None of us arrived where we are today without the help and work of others. In the next and final section of this chapter, we explore the development of men's movements to see how their contributions continue to affect relationships and communication between women and men.

So What about "His Story?"

As women's movements have progressed, men's lives have also changed significantly, often as a result of that progress. We've discussed the fact that many men enjoy privilege based on their biological sex. Privilege, however, varies from man to man, depending on ethnicity, race, social class, age, physical ability, and sexual orientation (Renzetti & Curran, 1995). Men's movements, like women's movements, are not made up of one central group united around a common cause; they reflect a rich diversity of issues and followers. Some movements aren't really considered movements at all, especially if you believe that movements result from people coming together to fight injustice. We'll call them movements in this chapter, but some groups we identify and discuss view themselves more as efforts to improve the human condition through societal, political, and personal change. As we did for women's movements, we also look at men's movements from a historical standpoint since they have affected and will continue to affect gender communication.

Early Male Supporters of Women's Rights

Historically in the United States men have benefited from a patriarchally constructed society. There have always been exceptional men who fought societal trends and supported women and their causes. Frederick Douglass, James Mott, and Henry Blackwell openly advocated women's suffrage when it certainly wasn't stylish to do so (Bernikow, 1997). After his passionate speech at the Seneca Falls Convention, antislavery leader Frederick Douglass was maligned in Syracuse newspapers, which first called him a "wimp," then referred to him as an "Aunt Nancy" (Kimmel, 1997, p. 58). James Mott, a Quaker businessperson, co-chaired the women's rights meeting at Seneca Falls with his suffragist wife, Lucretia Mott. Persistent women's rights advocate Henry Blackwell helped his wife, Lucy Stone, and daughter, Alice Stone Blackwell, publish *The Woman's Journal* (Bernikow, 1997). In 1910 Columbia philosophy instructor Max Eastman co-founded the Men's League for Woman Suffrage (Kimmel, 1997). While they weren't chaining themselves to fences for women's suffrage, the public support from these men was exceptional for the time.

Effects of the Sexual Revolution on Men

Over time male sex and gender roles have evolved, if not as dramatically or visibly as women's. Noted author James Doyle (1995) identifies three developments that challenged traditional views of the male gender role: technological advances, distrust of established institutions, and the women's movement. As the Industrial Revolution changed our society from an agrarian basis to a technological, service-oriented one, men's role as providers (or "hunters," as they once were in hunter-gatherer cultures) diminished.

In the 1960s and 1970s social conflicts such as the Vietnam War, college campus antiwar protests, the beating of demonstrators at the 1968 Democratic National Convention in Chicago, and the killing of four students at Kent State University turned many against the government (Doyle, 1995). The 1960s saw a convergence of the civil rights movement, the women's movement, the antiwar movement, and the new left movement (Astrachan, 1986). When respect for the traditionally masculine role of soldier declined with America's increasing disillusionment with the military and the government, men experienced a significant shift in role. Along with the women's movement, this shift made it a confusing time to decide just what it meant to be a man. However, some believe that the process of reconsidering sex roles and opening up new avenues of communication between men and women was a very necessary, healthy development. Professor and Vietnam veteran Terry Anderson (1995) contends, "Feminists confronted sexism, provoked men to reconsider their views, and along the way brought about men's liberation. Men have the freedom to choose whether to be the provider, the decision-maker, to stay at home with the children, or to remain single" (p. 419).

Men Raised Consciousness Too

We most often think of consciousness raising as an activity of the women's liberation movement. However, the men's movement (actually more a trend than a movement per se) in the 1970s involved consciousness raising groups, most often focusing on individual growth as well. These groups "triggered changes in the lives of a few participants, but none excited people to the collective action that affected the whole society, as many women's gatherings did" (Astrachan, 1986, pp. 290–291). Up to the mid-1980s, most men actively participating in men's groups held a single guiding ideology: the elimination of the belief that one sex is superior to the other, or the eradication of sexism (Doyle, 1995). Men considered to be profeminist agreed generally with the feminist critique of patriarchy and organized themselves collectively to change men's behavior and attitudes (Mechling & Mechling, 1994). In 1975 the First National Conference on Men and Masculinity was held in Knoxville, Tennessee. Associations such as the National Organization for Men Against Sexism (originally called the National Organization for Changing Men) were founded during this time (Astrachan, 1986).

Profeminist men (many of whom simply call themselves feminists) are still active today—your male textbook co-author is one of them. Groups of profeminists may well be active on your campus. University profeminist men often organize Take Back the Night marches, which are programs that honor survivors of rape and sexual assault; present programs on sexual assault to fraternities, dorms, and athletic teams; and teach and take courses on masculinity (Kimmel, 1997). They also initiate and join campus groups such as Men Acting for Change (MAC), Men Opposed to Sexist Tradition (MOST), Men Against Sexual Harassment (MASH), Men Against Sexual Assault (MASA), and Men Against Rape and Sexism (MARS) (Kimmel, 1997). Hobart College in Geneva, New York, started a men's studies academic program in 1997, but it has been criticized for offering "fluff" and "touchy-feely" courses that are more like therapy than legitimate content courses. That is the same criticism that has been leveled at women's studies programs for decades.

A Movement of Fathers

Another movement of men in the 1960s and 1970s involved fathers' rights in divorce and child custody cases. In Colonial times fathers retained domestic control and defined and supervised their children's development; wives were expected to defer to their husbands (Furstenberg, 1988, as in Skolnick & Skolnick, 1997). Until the middle of the 19th century, if "marital disruption" occurred the father was typically awarded custody because fathers "were assumed to maintain control over marital property (of which the children were a part)" (Furstenberg, 1988, p. 224). During this time period women often died in childbirth, leaving their widowed husbands responsible for their children. The children were most often turned over to another woman in the family to raise. With the Industrial Revolution, public and private spheres became more separate—men worked in the outside world and women worked in the home attending to the needs of the children (Doyle, 1995).

By the end of the century women predominantly were awarded custody of their children because women were believed to possess superior parenting skills (Furstenberg, 1988). The courts subsequently adopted a "tender years presumption," meaning that during a child's younger years she or he needed a mother more than a father (Renzetti & Curran, 1995, p. 217). This dramatically shifted custody decisions in favor of mothers and against fathers, a practice that many believe still continues in today's courts. This trend has led many men around the country to challenge the courts and move for equal custody and parenting rights. Attorney and activist Andrew Kimbrell (1995) asserts that as men promote a national fatherhood policy, it is just as important to change our culture's view of men and fatherhood as it is to change laws and public policy. Support groups and activist organizations have been formed, such as Fathers United for Equal Rights, U.S. Divorce Reform, the Coalition Organized for Parental Equality (COPE), Divorced American Men Unite (DAMU), and the National Congress for Men (NCM) (Astrachan, 1986).

There Are Some "Wild Men" Out There

Another often-discussed contemporary social movement is most often referred to simply as the men's movement, but its more elaborate name is the mythopoetic movement. The most noteworthy spokesperson for the mythopoetic movement is author and poet Robert Bly. Bly's 1990 best-selling book *Iron John* utilizes mythology and Grimm's fairy tales to help men find the "community inside the psyche" (p. 227). This means that men are encouraged to seek out different parts or roles within themselves, including the King, the Warrior, the Lover, the Trickster, the Mythologist, the Cook, the Grief

> *Shaq is not the man. He's the man because the NBA wants him to be the man, but before you can be the man, you've got to be the man.*
>
> *Dennis Rodman, basketball player, on Shaquille O'Neal*

Man, and the Wild Man (Bly, 1990). According to Bly (1990), complicated interchanges occur with interior beings and "a whole community of beings is what is called a grown man" (p. 227).

Bly and other mythopoetics promote men's self-discovery and masculinity through nature and tribal rituals. At retreats, often called "Wildman gatherings," men beat drums, tearfully hug one another, dance in ritualistic circles, smear one another's bodies with mud, and huddle around a campfire howling (Kimbrell, 1995, p. 133; Natharius, 1992). To ensure that every man gets his opportunity to bare his soul, some groups use a talking stick, a ceremonial object that guarantees the holder will be heard without interruption (Adler, 1991). Often another goal of such gatherings is to encourage men to explore the complicated relationships most have with their fathers, engaging the psychological and emotional wounds left over from childhood. In turn, the hope is that these men will become better fathers to their own children. Kimbrell (1995) describes these gatherings as follows:

> Clearly the Wildman gatherings and other similar events were not designed to undermine American working men, nor to begin the process of the genocide of women or children. Rather these gatherings are one of the few places in our society where men can come together in numbers to break the masculine mystique and to recapture, however briefly, a relationship to the earth, to the male community, and to their own masculine identity. (p. 136)

The Million Man March

On October 16, 1995, an estimated 400,000 men attended the Million Man March on the Federal Mall in Washington, D.C. (*USA Today*, 1996). Organized by the controversial head of the Nation of Islam, Louis Farrakhan, the march was to rally the black community and strengthen black families by emphasizing the role of fathers. Farrakhan (1998) described the event as "A Holy Day of Atonement and Reconciliation"; he called for "one million disciplined, committed, and dedicated Black men, from all walks of life in America, to march in Washington, D.C. . . . " (p. 1). Emphasizing the need for fathers to bolster black family life, Farrakhan asserted that "as men, we must recognize and unconditionally atone for the absence, in too many cases, of the Black male as the head of the household, positive role model and building block of our community. We believe that we must atone for, and establish positive solutions to, the abuse and misuse of our women and girls" (p. 1). Farrakhan (1998) also challenged the approximately 8 million eligible African Americans in the United States to register to vote. Since that time, similar marches among African American women and, more recently, a rally for black youth in Harlem, have occurred to strengthen young African Americans' self-esteem and pride and to build community .

Keeping Those Promises

Most of you probably have heard of the Promise Keepers, a movement based on fundamental Christian traditions and beliefs; perhaps some of you belong to or support the movement. Bill McCartney, successful University of Colorado head football coach, and his friend, Dave Wardell, conceived of the organization in 1990 as they were driving to a Fellowship of Christian Athletes dinner (McCartney, 1995). The two discussed the idea of filling a stadium with Christian men coming together for the purpose of Christian discipleship. McCartney (1995) believes "we've sat idle too long in this country as men abdicated the role of leadership to their wives. Men have drifted away from God and their wives. And they've turned a deaf ear when their children needed them" (p. 289). The first Promise Keepers conference was attended by 4,200 men in July 1991. Since that time, more than 2 million men have attended approximately 50 Promise Keepers stadium conferences (Promise Keepers, 1998).

In its mission statement, the Promise Keepers organization is described as a "Christ-centered ministry dedicated to uniting men through vital relationships to become Godly influences in their world" (Promise Keepers, 1998, p. 1). A Promise Keeper subscribes to seven basic values: honoring Jesus Christ, pursuing vital relationships with other men, practicing personal integrity, building strong marriages and families, supporting his pastor and church, demonstrating biblical unity, and influencing his world. The promises these men make are intended to guide them toward Christ and to transform them as people so they will work for transformation in their homes, among their friends, in their churches, and in the nation (Dobson, et al., 1994). Small discussion groups within the movement are intended to draw men into a closer relationship with Christ, while stadium events are meant as a catalyst to motivate men to pursue spiritual growth, with the ultimate goal being to help men keep their promises (Promise Keepers, 1998).

The demographics of Promise Keepers reflect that 60 percent of attendees hold a bachelor's or higher degree, 81 percent are married, and 57 percent have spouses working outside the home. On the average, they have two children living at home, are approximately 40 years of age, and make a median household income of $48,000 (Promise Keepers, 1998). The organization has attempted to incorporate diversity into its membership; about half of the rally speakers are members of minority groups, while the Promise Keepers' group symbol or logo shows white, brown, and black arms raising a flag (Shapiro, 1995).

The Promise Keepers movement is not without controversy. Promise Keepers' stance on homosexuality is that the Bible "clearly teaches that homosexuality violates God's creative design for a husband and wife and that it is a sin" (Promise Keepers, 1998, p. 1). Although the organization declares that it is not politically motivated in any way, others disagree. Conason, Ross, and Cokorinos (1996), writing in *The Nation*, assert that "Promise Keepers appears to be one of the most sophisticated creations of the religious right" (p. 19), which includes such highly conservative factions as the Christian Coalition, a group with a definite political agenda. According to *Promise Keepers Watch* , a publication and service provided by the Center for Democracy Studies (1998):

> Promise Keepers is one of the most important new organizations on the right. Deceptive and carefully conceived, Promise Keepers attempts to mainstream its image by using a seductive vocabulary of male-only self-improvement, opposition to religious "denominationalism," and an alleged commitment to radical "reconciliation," to advance the strategic political agenda of the Christian right. (p. 1)

The National Organization for Women organized a Promise Keepers Mobilization Project in order to monitor the activities of the group. NOW President Patricia Ireland said of the organization, "Promise Keepers is the hottest religious right marketing tool since televangelism. Their message of submission of women is extremely political and anti-woman" (NOW, 1997, p. 1).

NOW's interpretation is that Promise Keepers' messages encourage the domination of women by suggesting that men have a God-given right to lead their families and to expect their wives to submit to husbands' decisions and will.

Popular Promise Keeper speaker and team chaplain for the Dallas Mavericks, Tony Evans, is one of the most controversial Promise Keepers. In his chapter in the book *Seven Promises of a Promise Keeper* (Dobson, et al., 1994), Evans encourages "spiritual purity" and warns of a national crisis involving the "feminization of the American male." He contends that "sissified" men have abdicated their role as spiritually pure leaders, forcing women to pick up the slack (p. 73). In one section entitled "Reclaiming Your Manhood," Evans gives this advice to Promise Keepers:

> The first thing you do is sit down with your wife and say something like this: "Honey, I've made a terrible mistake. I've given you my role. I gave up leading this family, and I forced you to take my place. Now I must reclaim that role." Don't misunderstand what I'm saying here. I'm not suggesting that you ask for your role back, I'm urging you to *take it back* . . . Your wife's concerns may be justified. Unfortunately, however, there can be no compromise here. If you're going to lead, you must lead. Be sensitive. Listen. Treat the lady gently and lovingly. But *lead!* (Dobson, et al., 1994, p. 80)

Evans further directs women to give back leadership to their husbands for the sake of "your family and the survival of our culture" (Dobson, et al., 1994, p. 80).

We contend that the survival of our culture hinges on other social developments than those proposed by Tony Evans. Naturally, feminists (not just NOW) are seriously concerned about such groups as Promise Keepers because of the possibility that exhortations to men to reclaim some "rightful" place as family and societal leaders will turn back the clocks on advances in women's rights and equality. An added dimension is the "divine right" aspect particular to the Promise Keepers' rhetoric. If a man asserts his right to be head of the household and make decisions for his wife and children out of some belief that it is his God-given or ordained right to do so, no matter the preference of other family members, that is a frightening arrangement in the mind of many people. It conjures up images of power and domination, not leadership.

However, Promise Keepers describe the husband-wife relationship as one of partnership, as in McCartney's and others' continual rhetoric to the effect that "the man doesn't dominate his wife, but he comes up along beside her, and the two of them together make decisions to strengthen their family." But when really pushed to give a definitive answer on the question of who makes the final decision in the event a couple cannot agree, as McCartney was in the late 1990s during an interview with Ted Koppell on ABC's *Nightline,* the response was revealing. After four or so deflections, McCartney finally admitted that he believed it to be God's plan that the husband must make the final decision, that the buck absolutely stopped with the husband, after all attempts at negotiation and joint decision making between husband and wife had failed.

Christian feminists are of two minds (at least) about Promise Keepers. On the one hand, an effort that causes men to reassess their lives and their commitments to God, their wives, and their children isn't necessarily a bad thing. Many women applaud the work of the Promise Keepers, believing that it truly has transformed their family relationships. However, others share the concerns mentioned above for the tendency of some men to turn the partnership or shared leadership idea into a power play and an opportunity to dominate women.

It will be interesting to track the progress of the several men's movements, including the Promise Keepers (who in 1998 experienced severe financial trouble and decreased attendance at stadium rallies), into the next century. Will the mythopoetic wild men still be around? Will we see growth in men's studies programs on college campuses? Will fathers win more custody suits and change the trend in the courts? Will there be more marches on the capitol in the name of one sex or the other? We suspect that women's and men's movements will continue, but it might be interesting to see if a "human" movement emerges in the new millennium.

GENDER COMMUNICATION AND THE SURVIVAL OF OUR CULTURE

Why have we included so much information on women's and men's movements in this epilogue? Relevant historical events that shape gender communication are either skimmed over or not taught at most secondary school levels. In some school districts, parents strongly affirm traditional sex roles and believe that controversial topics such as women's movements, homosexuality, and the Vietnam War are to be avoided (Loewen, 1995). Even in colleges and universities today, often only students enrolled in specialized courses in women's history are exposed to this important material.

It's important to understand how our current state of gender communication came to be, to realize that there is a historical context for why women and men relate to one another as they do. A grasp of history and social movements adds new dimensions to understanding communication. When you hear feminists demand passage of the Equal Rights Amendment or men argue for fathers' rights, knowing some of the historical details that preceded the status quo facilitates more effective gender communication. When you embrace racial diversity, it's important to comprehend what people of color have historically encountered. When you participate in intimate relationships and grapple with reproductive issues, it completes your perspective to understand the history of birth control and controversies surrounding reproductive rights. When you hear a statistic cited that less than 40 percent of eligible voters in the United States actually vote these days, perhaps it will make you wonder if suffragists are rolling over in their graves.

When you think back over the theories and effective tools of gender communication we've explored in this text, we hope that looking at our past has helped you plan your future. And as for that class where men received a

100 percent grade and women a lower score, those of you who received the unfair marks can just be thankful you didn't take this class in 1982—your score would have been 62 percent and you would have failed.

References

ADLER, J. (1991, June 24). Drums, sweat and tears. *Newsweek*, 46–51.

ANDERSEN, M. (1997). *Thinking about women: Sociological perspectives on sex and gender* (4th ed.). Boston: Allyn & Bacon.

ANDERSON, T. (1995). *The movement and the sixties: Protest in America from Greensboro to Wounded Knee*. New York: Oxford University Press.

ASTRACHAN, A. (1986). *How men feel: Their response to women's demands for equality and power*. Garden City, NY: Anchor Press/Doubleday.

BERNIKOW, L. (1997). *The American women's almanac: An inspiring and irreverent women's history*. New York: Berkley Books.

BLY, R. (1990). *Iron John: A book about men*. Reading, MA: Addison-Wesley.

CENTER FOR DEMOCRACY STUDIES. (1998, October 14). Promise Keepers watch. *Center for Democracy Studies*. [On-line]. Available: http://www.cdresearch.org/promise_keepers_watch.html

COLMAN, P. (1995). *Rosie the riveter*. New York: Crown.

CONASON, J., ROSS, A., & COKORINOS, L. (1996, October 7). The Promise Keepers are coming: The third wave of the religious right. *The Nation*, 11–19.

DOBSON, J., BRIGHT, B., COLE, E., EVANS, T., McCARTNEY, B., PALAU, L., PHILLIPS, R., & SMALLEY, G. (1994). *Seven promises of a Promise Keeper*. Colorado Springs: Focus on the Family.

DOYLE, J. (1995). *The male experience* (3rd ed.). Madison, WI: Brown & Benchmark.

EVE ONLINE. (1998, November 14). What is ecofeminism anyway? *Ecofeminist Visions Emerging*. [On-line]. Available: http://www.enviroweb.org/eve/what.html

FALUDI, S. (1991). *Backlash: The undeclared war against American women*. New York: Crown.

FALUDI, S. (1995, March). "I'm not a feminist but I play one on TV." *Ms.*, 30–39.

FARRAKHAN, L. (1998, November 16). Second opinion. *Minister Louis Farrakhan on the Million Man March*. [On-line]. Available: http://users.aol.com/camikem/eyeview/millionman.html

FEMINIST MAJORITY. (1998, November 18). The Feminist Majority. *Feminist Majority Foundation Home Page*. [On-line]. Available: http://www.feminist.org/welcome/fm_1987-88.html

FRIEDAN, B. (1963). *The feminine mystique*. New York: Laurel.

FURSTENBERG, F. F. JR. (1988). Good dads—bad dads: Two faces of fatherhood. In A. Cherlin (Ed.), *The changing American family*. New York: Urban Institute Press.

GREENSPAN, K. (1994). *The timetables of women's history: A chronology of the most important people and events in women's history*. New York: Simon & Schuster.

HOFF SOMMERS, C. (1994). *Who stole feminism? How women have betrayed women*. New York: Simon & Schuster.

HUMM, M. (Ed.). (1992). *Modern feminisms: Political, literary, cultural*. New York: Columbia University Press.

KERBER, L., & DE HART, J. (1991). *Women's America: Refocusing the past* (3rd ed.). New York: Oxford University Press.

KIMBRELL, A. (1995). *The masculine mystique: The politics of masculinity*. New York: Ballantine Books.

KIMMEL, M. (1997, November-December). Real men join the movement. *Ms.*, 52–59.

LEHRMAN, K. (1992, March 16). The feminist mystique—*Backlash: The undeclared war against American women* by Susan Faludi/*Revolution from within: A book of self-esteem* by Gloria Steinem. *The New Republic*, 30–34.

LOEWEN, J. (1995). *Lies my teacher told me: Everything your American history textbook got wrong*. New York: Touchstone.

LUNARDINI, C. (1994). *What every American should know about women's history*. Holbrook, MA: Bob Adams.

MADIGAN, T. J. (1995, Spring). Camille Paglia on free thought, feminism, and iconoclasm. *Free Inquiry*, 5–8.

McCARTNEY, B., & DILES, D. (1995). *From ashes to glory.* Nashville: Thomas Nelson.

McKAY, J., HILL, B., & BUCKER, J. (1995). *A history of western society, volume II: From absolutism to the present* (5th ed.) Boston: Houghton Mifflin.

MECHLING, E., & MECHLING, J. (1994). The Jung and the restless: The mythopoetic men's movement. *Southern Communication Journal, 59,* 97–111.

MILLION MAN MARCH. (1995, October 16). Million Man March fact sheet. [On-line]. Available: http://www.igc.apc.org/africanam/hot/facts.html

Ms. Foundation for Women. (1998). What does the *Ms.* Foundation for Women do? [On-line]. Available: http://www.ms.foundation./org/ms/msdo97.html

NATHARIUS, D. (1992, October). *From The hazards of being male to Fire in the belly: Are men finally getting it and, if so, what are they getting?* Paper presented at the meeting of the Speech Communication Association, Chicago, IL.

NATIONAL ORGANIZATION FOR WOMEN. (1997, October). NOW promises "no surrender" to right-wing Promise Keepers. *NOW National Times,* p. 1.

NATIONAL ORGANIZATION FOR WOMEN. (1998, November 18). The history of the National Organization for Women. *National Organization for Women (NOW) Home Page.* [On-line]. Available: http://www.now.org/history/history.html

NEFT, N., & LEVINE, A. (1997). *Where women stand: An international report on the status of women in 140 countries, 1997–1998.* New York: Random House.

POLLIT, K. (1994, March 21). Subject to debate. *The Nation, 369.*

PROMISE KEEPERS. (1996). *A man of his word, New Testament.* Colorado Springs: International Bible Society.

PROMISE KEEPERS. (1998, October 14). Mission statement. *Official Promise Keepers Site* [On-line]. Available: http://www.promisekeepers.org.html

RENZETTI, C., & CURRAN, D. (1995). *Women, men and society* (3rd ed.). Boston: Allyn & Bacon.

RUTH, S. (1990). *Issues in feminism: An introduction to women's studies.* Mountain View, CA: Mayfield.

SHAPIRO, J. (1995, October 2). Heavenly promises. *U.S. News & World Report,* 68–70.

SKOLNICK, A., & SKOLNICK, J. (1997). *Family in transition* (9th ed.). New York: Longman.

THERIOT, N. (1996). *Mothers and daughters in nineteenth-century America: The biosocial construction of femininity.* Lexington: University of Kentucky Press.

THOM, M. (1997). *Inside Ms.: 25 years of the magazine and the feminist movement.* New York: Henry Holt.

TOBIAS, S. (1997). *Faces of feminism: An activist's reflections on the women's movement.* Boulder, CO: Westview.

USA TODAY. (1996, February 16). Washington's great gatherings. *USA Today.* [On-line]. Available: http://www.usatoday.com/news/index/nman006.html

VENTURA, V. (1998). *Sheroes: Bold, brash, and absolutely unabashed superwomen.* Berkeley, CA: Conari.

WEATHERFORD, D. (1994). *American women's history: An A to Z of people, organizations, issues, and events.* New York: Prentice-Hall.

WOLF, N. (1994). *Fire with fire: The new female power and how to use it.* New York: Fawcett Columbine.

Author Index

Subject Index

507